Learn Beginner and Intermediate French for Adults

Speak French In 30 Days!

5 Books in 1

Explore to Win

THIS COLLECTION INCLUDES THE FOLLOWING BOOKS:

Complete French Workbook for Adult Beginners:
Your Proven Guide to Speaking French in 30 Days!

Learn French Handbook for Adult Beginners:
Essential French Words And Phrases You Must Know!

Learn French with Short Stories for Adult Beginners:
Engaging Stories To Shortcut Your French Fluency! (Fun & Easy Reads)

Learn Intermediate French for Adults Workbook:
Go from French Beginner to Intermediate in 30 Days!

Learn French with Short Stories for Adult Intermediates:
Engaging Stories To Shortcut Your French Fluency! (Fun & Easy Reads)

© Copyright - All rights reserved.

The content contained within this book may not be reproduced, duplicated, or transmitted without direct written permission from the author or the publisher.

Under no circumstances will any blame or legal responsibility be held against the publisher, or author, for any damages, reparation, or monetary loss due to the information contained within this book, either directly or indirectly.

Legal Notice:

This book is copyright protected. It is only for personal use. You cannot amend, distribute, sell, use, quote, or paraphrase any part, or the content within this book, without the consent of the author or publisher.

Disclaimer Notice:

Please note the information contained within this document is for educational and entertainment purposes only. All effort has been executed to present accurate, up to date, reliable and complete information. No warranties of any kind are declared or implied. Readers acknowledge that the author is not engaging in the rendering of legal, financial, medical, or professional advice. The content within this book has been derived from various sources. Please consult a licensed professional before attempting any techniques outlined in this book.

By reading this document, the reader agrees that under no circumstances is the author responsible for any losses, direct or indirect, that are incurred as a result of the use of the information contained within this document, including, but not limited to, errors, omissions, or inaccuracies.

Table of Contents

Complete French Workbook for Adult Beginners   9

  Book 1 Description   1

  Introduction   2

  Abbreviations   5

  Pronunciation Guide   6

  Chapter 1: It all starts with Bonjour   10

  Chapter 2: All about you   22

  Chapter 3: I speak a little French   32

  Chapter 4: This is not a pipe   42

  Chapter 5: How may I help you?   49

  Chapter 6: One big happy family   56

  Chapter 7: A city dweller   63

  Chapter 8: The ball's in your court!   71

  Chapter 9: Beyond baguettes   79

  Chapter 10: No rain check allowed   87

  Chapter 11: The hands of time   93

  Chapter 12: An ordinary day   101

  Chapter 13: How about a drink?   108

  Chapter 14: The art of French dining   118

  Chapter 15: At the crossroads   125

  Chapter 16: Ready for an adventure   133

  Chapter 17: A thing of the past   140

  Chapter 18: The adventure continues   149

  Vocabulary Lists by Theme   155

  Verb Conjugations   172

  Grammar Topic Index   176

Learn French Handbook for Adult Beginners   179

  Book 2 Description   180

  Introduction   182

  Chapter 1: French Pronunciation and Alphabet   187

  Chapter 2: Basic French Grammar   196

  Chapter 3: Basic Vocabulary   209

  Chapter 4: Greetings and Civilities   215

Chapter 5: Meeting People ... 222
Chapter 6: Time ... 230
Chapter 7: Weather ... 236
Chapter 8: Traveling ... 239
Chapter 9: Accomodation ... 246
Chapter 10: Culture and Entertainment ... 249
Chapter 11: Transportation ... 253
Chapter 12: Food and Drink ... 262
Chapter 13: Shopping ... 270
Chapter 14: Bank / Exchange Office / Post Office ... 277
Chapter 15: Business ... 280
Chapter 16: Health and Wellbeing ... 284
Chapter 17: Telephone and Internet ... 292
Chapter 18: Emergencies ... 296
Conclusion ... 299

Learn French with Short Stories for Adult Beginners   303

Book 3 description ... 304
Introduction ... 306
Chapter 1: Habits and Present Tense ... 309
Chapter 2: Describing people ... 319
Chapter 3: Expressing Quantity and Cooking ... 330
Chapter 4: My family ... 338
Chapter 5: Traveling and Weather ... 347
Chapter 6: Shopping ... 357
Chapter 7: Telling someone about a dream ... 366
Chapter 8: Finding a job ... 375
Chapter 9: Traveling ... 383
Chapter 10: Expressing opinions ... 391
Chapter 11: Apartment Renovation ... 398
Answers ... 405
Conclusion ... 409

Learn Intermediate French for Adults Workbook: 411

Book 4 description ... 412
Introduction ... 413
Abbreviations ... 416

Pronunciation Guide	417
Chapter 1: Lights, Camera, Action!	421
Chapter 2: All manner of people	432
Chapter 3: Fits like a glove	439
Chapter 4: Feeling under the weather	450
Chapter 5: Bearer of news	457
Chapter 6: You're hired	464
Chapter 7: Go above and beyond	474
Chapter 8: Call me back	481
Chapter 9: To whom it may concern	489
Chapter 10: Welcome home	496
Chapter 11: It's a bargain!	505
Chapter 12: Accident prone	513
Chapter 13: Blow a fuse?	522
Chapter 14: Time for a change	530
Chapter 15: Food for thought	540
Chapter 16: Making headlines	550
Vocabulary Lists by Theme	559
Verb Conjugations	569
Grammar Topic Index	575

Learn French with Short Stories for Adult Intermediates — 578

Book 5 description	579
Introduction	581
Chapter 1: City Sightseeing	584
Chapter 2: Telling stories	593
Chapter 3: Bad Experience	602
Chapter 4: Talking with Friends	611
Chapter 5: In the Museum	619
Chapter 6: At the Flea Market	626
Chapter 7: About my Friend	634
Chapter 8: In a Bar	641
Chapter 9: Our planet	649
Chapter 10: Anniversary	657
Chapter 11: At the Doctor's	663
Conclusion	677

~~$39~~ FREE BONUSES

Learn French Fundamentals Audiobook

+ Printable "French Verb Conjugations" Practice Worksheets Download

Scan QR code above to claim your free bonuses

―――― OR ――――

exploretowin.com/frenchaudio10

Ready To Start Speaking French?

Inside this Learn French Fundamentals Audiobook + printable practice worksheets combo you'll discover:

✓ **Pronunciation guides:** English to French pronunciation translations so you can sound right the first time which means you'll sound like a natural easily.

✓ **How to avoid awkward fumbling:** explore core French grammar principles to avoid situations where you're left blank, not knowing what to say.

✓ **Improved recall:** Confidently express yourself in French by learning high-frequency verbs conjugations - taught through fun practice sheets!

Scan QR code above to claim your free bonuses

―――― OR ――――

exploretowin.com/frenchaudio10

BOOK 1

Complete French Workbook for Adult Beginners

Your Proven Guide to Speaking French in 30 Days!

Explore to Win

Book 1 Description

Do you want to learn French but don't know where to begin? Are you tired of memorizing grammar rules you don't understand or repeating vocabulary lists you don't seem to retain? Are you done with simply dreaming of becoming a fluent French speaker? Are you ready to take action today?

If you have answered yes to any one of the questions above, then this book is for you. Problem, meet solution: **Complete French Workbook for Adult Beginners: Your Proven Guide to Speaking French in 30 Days!**

You read that right. With this book, you will be able to achieve a beginner's fluency in French within 30 days. In fact, you are expected to speak the language right from Day 1! Written by French linguists whose life's mission is to make learning French easier, fun and more efficient, this book is based on a communicative approach. While most learning resources simply list vocabularies or give you grammar pointers without context, this book teaches you French through meaningful scenarios. Take it from their years of experience and training: this is the right way to learn. By studying French in context, you'll remember new words with little effort, use them the way the natives do, and understand how the language's grammar logic works. Learn to be conversational from dialogues, instead of staring at a list of isolated words you are expected to magically memorize!

With **Complete French Workbook for Adult Beginners: Your Proven Guide to Speaking French in 30 Days!**, you'll discover:

- sample dialogues and texts that will contextualize what you learn and help you store knowledge in your long-term memory bank
- vocabularies that are frequently and *actually* used in real-life French conversations
- effective techniques to understand and absorb grammar structures
- ways to avoid common mistakes English speakers make when learning French
- a pronunciation guide, a vocabulary list by theme, verb conjugation references, exercises with answer key after each chapter (this book is as complete as they get!)
- and overall: the secrets to communicating like a French native in situations most common to daily life

Taking the first step is always the toughest part. But once you've gained momentum, there is nothing that you can't achieve. Even if you have never learned a foreign language in your life, you will be able to follow this book with ease and take a step towards your goal of learning French.

Introduction

There are some 100 million people currently learning French. Many have been so charmed by its elegance and melodious sounds, they named it the language of romance. It is a sensual language where simple phrases like asking for a glass of wine — *Je voudrais un verre de vin* — sounds like a verse from a Baudelaire poem. It is also a very rich language, where you can choose from a wealth of words to describe precisely how a scenery makes you feel: it could be *impressionnant, bucolique, sublime, idyllique, paradisiaque, saisissant, époustouflant*, the list goes on! For others yet, French represents a language of discovery. It is not just a means to communicate with the almost 300 million people who speak it, it is also a gateway to a new world of opportunities and a window to a fascinating culture.

That said, the French language is sometimes thought of as difficult. How do you roll those R's? Or produce those nasal O's without pinching your nose? How do you memorize the gender of nouns? What is the subjunctive and why should you care? Who even had the idea of creating so many rules with just as many exceptions? The task might seem daunting, but let us comfort you right away. Quite the contrary, certain institutes believe that French is in fact one of the easiest languages to learn for English speakers. If you're not convinced, rely on the statistics: 45 percent of English words are actually of French origin! The fear of the unknown can be paralyzing, and as they say, starting is always the hardest part. But guess what? By opening this book, you have overcome your first hurdle. This is where your adventure begins, and it is going to be rewarding.

About this book

Complete French Workbook for Adult Beginners: Your Proven Guide to Speaking French in 30 Days! is designed to help you achieve a beginner's level of French. This means that by the end of this 30-day course, you will be able to:

- communicate in subjects of most immediate relevance to you.
- talk about yourself, your family, your city and your routines.
- handle daily situations like describing the weather, shopping, eating out or socializing with friends.
- use the language while traveling, for reserving a room or asking for directions.
- relate present, past and future events.

The goal of this book is to have you speaking everyday French within 30 days. Since English and French have the same kind of sentence structure, the early stages of your learning will be surprisingly quick. You will notice that even after the very first chapter, you will already be able to hold a simple conversation. With this book, you will achieve a good understanding of the basics of French well within a month.

In each chapter, you will find **the lesson proper** that revolves around a specific communicative function and features related grammatical concepts and vocabulary. Every lesson in this book is taught <u>in context</u> and <u>with a purpose</u>. Some lessons will also feature short texts or dialogues to help you see how phrases are used in actual conversation.

The chapters end with a **Key Takeaways** section which summarizes the main points learned. These are particularly useful for quick future references. Then, there are **Exercises** with **Answer Keys** to help you practice what you've learned. Finally, we've added some **Culture Tips** that offer pointers on French etiquette and customs.

To make reviewing easier, we also included in the final pages of the book: **Vocabulary Lists by Themes, Verb Conjugations** and a **Grammar Topic Index**.

Our approach to learning

This book was prepared by French linguists who have considerable experience in teaching French as a foreign language. They are passionate — some might say obsessed — with the science of language acquisition and the art of accompanying language learners.

In writing this book, they implement a **communicative framework**. This means that you will learn concepts in context, and that the ultimate goal is to allow you to communicate in real-life situations. Gone are the days when grammar rules were simply memorized. Here, you will understand the grammar logic and put them to use. You are expected to speak the language even from the very first lesson.

To take the most out of this book, the authors advise you to follow the progression as intended, without skipping chapters. They favored a **spiral approach**, meaning you will study concepts in increments, starting from its most basic elements and building up with more and more details. Why is this effective? First, because instead of providing one overwhelming chunk of topic, you get to confirm your understanding before moving on to the next stage. Second, because spaced retrieval is not a myth. By revisiting the same words, for example, you absorb them in your long-term memory bank with little to no effort.

How to use this book

You can use this book as your **stand-alone resource for self-study**. Studying a language on your own can be challenging. But with this book, you no longer have to wonder where to begin learning or how. All you need to do is study to your heart's content and have fun.

This of course does not mean that you have no autonomy in your learning. The beauty of self-studying is just that, you can study at your own pace and practice using methods most effective to you. Take the time to learn everything you can from a chapter. You can even go back to a previous one if you need to. If writing down vocabulary items helps you memorize better — and we do recommend this — then keep a pen and a notebook at reach while studying. Auditory learners will find the audio supplement of this book a welcome addition.

You can also use this book as **a complement to a French beginners' course** you are taking. In the classroom, we sometimes don't have the luxury to ask for a more elaborate explanation of a concept. In this case, you'll find the index helpful for searching a topic and learning more about it through our explanations.

Some final tips

- **Read the chapters actively.** Repeat aloud the phrases and words you will encounter. Allow your mouth and tongue to get used to producing these sounds. Take some notes. Make lists or tables. You can even draw illustrations to help you remember new words!
- **Start small.** For the first few days, you might spend 30 minutes a day learning from this book. As you progress, you can slowly increase your study time.
- **Practice as much as possible.** You don't have to be sitting down in front of a desk to study. While you're cooking, think about how to say each ingredient in French. While jogging in the morning, look at your surroundings, how can you describe them in French? Or how about a French film during the weekend for some passive learning session?
- **Enjoy the ride.** They say language learning is a marathon, not a sprint. But we'd like to think of it more as a road trip. The journey might be long, but along the way, you'll see the most amazing things. A few miles may lead you to incredible sightseeing spots. You'd even get the chance to make new friends. It's the same with language learning. Rewards await you at each milestone, celebrate them. By learning French, you've become part of a community who are undertaking the same adventure, remember that.

Can you hear the open road calling your name? Without further ado or *sans plus tarder* as the French say, let's get to it! Your journey starts with *Bonjour*.

Abbreviations

lit.	literal translation
for.	formal
inf.	informal
m.	masculine
f.	feminine
sing.	singular
plur.	plural
n.	noun
v.	verb
adj.	adjective
adv.	adverb
prep.	preposition

Pronunciation Guide

English speakers might find French pronunciation a bit challenging at first. Some sounds will initially be unfamiliar to you. With practice and effort, however, you will be able to master them in no time.

Consonants

Letters	Examples	Pronunciation Guide
b	**b**lanc	Pronounced the same as in English.
d	**d**eux	
f	**f**ilm	
k	**k**ilo	
l	**l**it	
m	**m**ain	
n	**n**on	
p	**p**ère	
s	**s**ol	
t	**t**erre	
v	**v**oix	
z	**z**ut	
c	**c**arte /kart/ **c**ôte /koht/ **c**ette /seht/ i**c**i /ee-see/	C is pronounced as /k/ before A, O, and U. C is pronounced as /s/ Before E, I and Y. Ç with cedilla is pronounced like an /s/ as well.
ç	le**ç**on /leu-sohñ/	
ch	**ch**apeau /shah-po/	CH is pronounced like /sh/ as though you are producing a shushing sound.
q	**q**uiz /kweez/ cin**q** /sank/	QU and Q as final letters are both pronounced as /k/.
g	**g**olf /golf/	Before the vowels A, O, and U, the letter G is pronounced like the English G in *great*. GU before the vowels E, I and Y are pronounced the same way.

	guitare /gee-tar/ man**g**er /mahn-zheh/	G is pronounced as /zh/ before the letters E, I and Y. This sound is the same as the *S* in the word *leisure*.
gn	ma**gn**ifique /mah-nyee-feek/	GN is pronounced as /ny/, like the *ni* in the word *opinion*.
h	**h**ôpital /oh-pee-tahl/	H is generally mute in French.
j	**j**ouer /zhoo-weh/	J is pronounced like /zh/, again like the *S* in the English word *leisure*.
r	**r**ue /rew/	To pronounce the French *R*, place the tip of your tongue at the bottom of your mouth, against your front teeth.
s	**s**ol /sohl/ mai**s**on /meh-zohñ/	S is pronounced the same in English unless it is sandwiched by two vowels. In this case, it is pronounced like a /z/.
th	**th**on /ton/	TH is pronounced like an English /t/.
x	e**x**cellent /eksch-lahñ/ e**x**emples /egzohm-pleuh/ si**x** /sees/	X is pronounced as /ks/ when followed by a consonant. When followed by a vowel, it is pronounced as /gs/. Pronounce X as /s/ when it is the final letter.

Vowels

Letters	Examples	Pronunciation Guide
a	m**a**l /mahl/	Pronounced as /ah/
à	voil**à** /vwa-lah/	
â	p**â**te /paht/	
ai	m**ai** /meh/	Pronounced as /eh/
au	f**au**x /fo/	Pronounced as /o/
eau	p**eau** /po/	

e	le /leu/	E is pronounced as /eu/ in one syllable words, or when followed by a consonant in long words.
	premier /preu-myeh/	
é	thé /tay/	Pronounced as /ay/
ez	nez /nay/	
è	mère /mehr/	Pronounced as /eh/
ê	tête /teht/	
et	mets /meh/	
ei	seize /sehz/	
i	livre /leev-reu/	Pronounced as /ee/
î	île /eel/	
o	océan /o-seh-yahñ/	Pronounced as /o/
ô	hôte /ot/	
ou	pour /poohr/	Pronounced as /ooh/
u	tu /tchew/	Pronounced as /ew/

Semi-vowels

Letters	Examples	Pronunciation Guide
y	yaourt /yah-oort/	Pronounced as /yuh/
yer	payer /peh-yeh/	
ille	fille /fiy/	
ouill	mouillé /mou-yeh/	
eil	bouteille /boo-tey/	
ail	ail /ahy/	
euille	feuille /feuy/	
ui	lui /loo-wee/	Pronounced as /wuh/
ué(e)	ruée /rew-weh/	
uin	juin /zhoo-wañ/	
ueu	sueur /sew-weur/	
oi	moi /mwah/	Pronounced as /wah/
oy	employé /ahm̃-plwah-yeh/	
oui	Louis /loo-weeh/	Pronounced as /weeh/
oue	ouest /ou-west/	

Nasal vowels

Nasal sounds are produced by letting air pass through the nose. In this book, we use the tilde symbol (~) to indicate a nasal sound.

Letters	Examples	Pronunciation Guide
an	enfant /ahñ-fahñt/	Pronounced as /ahñ/ or /ahm̃/, like the preposition *on* in English, but without stressing the letter *n*.
am	chambre /shahm̃b-reu/	
en	en /ahñ/	
em	embarrass /ahm̃-bah-rah/	
in	matin /mah-tañ/	Pronounced as /añ/ or /am̃/, like the article *an* in English, but without stressing the letter *n*.
im	impoli /am̃-po-lee/	
ain	pain /pañ/	
aim	faim /fam̃/	
ien	bien /byañ/	Pronounced as /yañ/
on	son /sohñ/	Pronounced as /ohñ/ or /ohm̃/
om	nom /nohm̃/	
un	un /uhñ/	Pronounced as /uhñ/

Pronunciation and spelling tips

- The French language has five letter accents: the acute (é); the grave (à, è, ù); the circumflex which resembles a roof (â, ê, î, ô, û); the cedilla (ç) and the dieresis (ë, ï).
- The final consonant of a word is generally not pronounced, except for the letters C, R, F and L. For example, in the word *bas* /bah/ (below), the –s is mute. But in the word *truc* /trewk/ (thing), the final –c is pronounced. The exception is for verbs, where the final R is not pronounced. For example, *manger* (to eat) is pronounced as /mahñ-zheh/.
- If you wish to sound native, one of the most important things to learn is the *liaison*. Liaison means pronouncing the final consonant of a word with the first vowel of the next word. For example, in the sentence:

*Vou**s** êtes français.*

We link the final –s of the word *vous*, with the ê- of *êtes*. We thus pronounce it as such: /Voo zeht frahN-seh/.

Chapter 1: It all starts with Bonjour

Bonjour, bonsoir, merci, sont trois règles de la vie.

Good day, good evening, thank you, are the three rules of life.

- a Breton proverb

Bonjour (Hello, Good day) is one of those words you will hear a lot when you go to France. It is an essential word to start a conversation, both formal and informal. When asking for directions, for example, you might start with a polite *Bonjour*. When entering a store, the post office, an elevator, or a restaurant, there's nothing more native-like than greeting with this expression. There is thus no better way to start your journey than by learning this word.

In the first part of this chapter, you will learn commonly used expressions to greet someone and say goodbye. And then, we will teach you how to introduce yourself or ask how someone is. *On y va !* Let's go!

Greetings

The French language distinguishes between formal and informal situations. As the name suggests, a formal situation demands the use of more polite expressions. Formal situations include talking to a stranger and addressing people in professional or commercial situations (for example, speaking to your boss or to a shop owner). On the other hand, informal situations include talking to your friends and family, to close colleagues and classmates, or to children.

One must keep in mind the difference between these two situations when greeting someone. Another consideration to make is the time of the day. For instance, there are four ways one can say "hello" depending on the social context and time:

Bonjour	Means "hello" or "good day".
	Used in both formal and informal situations.
	Used all day until around 6 p.m.
Bonsoir	Means "good evening".
	Used in both formal and informal situations.
	Used from 6 p.m. onwards.
Salut	Means "hello" and "bye".
	Used uniquely in informal situations.
	Used any time of the day.
Coucou	Means "hi".

Very informal and playful.

Used any time of the day.

Let us put this in context. Say, you are entering a bakery, you would say *Bonjour*. You meet a group of friends in a coffee shop, you might say *Salut*. You text a very close friend, you write *Coucou*. You dine at a restaurant in the evening, you will greet the waiters with *Bonsoir*.

CULTURE TIP

To kiss or not to kiss?

Cheek-kissing is an important part of French culture. It is called *faire la bise* (v. give a kiss on the cheek) and is done when saying hello or bidding someone goodbye. It might be difficult to grasp the etiquette in the beginning. Here are some reminders to avoid a greeting faux pas:

- It is common for friends and family to *faire la bise*.
- It is common to *faire la bise* among young adults when introduced to a friend of a friend.
- It is common between two women or between a man and a woman.
- Between two men, unless family or very close friends, it is less common.
- Kissing two cheeks (each side) is most typical.
- In Southern France, it is common to do three *bises* (left, right then left again for example).
- A few regions do up to *five bises*!

A good rule of thumb – and this is true for every cultural aspect of the language – is of course to let the French native lead. If the person inclines his or her head towards you, you'd know that you are about to *faire la bise*.

Saying goodbye

Like greetings, parting expressions also vary according to the social setting. Some can be used at any time of the day:

Au revoir	Means "goodbye".
	Used in both formal and informal situations.
Salut	Means "bye".
	Used in informal situations.

Others may be used whatever the social setting, but at a specific time of the day:

Bonne journée	Have a good day
Bon après-midi	Have a good afternoon
Bonne fin de journée	Have a good day's end (used mostly when the day is about to end)
Bonne soirée	Have a good evening
Bonne nuit	Good night

Or, if you are expecting to see somebody again, you can also say:

À tout de suite	See you in a moment
À tout à l'heure	See you in a bit
À bientôt	See you soon
À plus (inf.) ***À plus tard***	See you later
À demain	See you tomorrow
À la prochaine	Until next time

You might be familiar with the expression *Adieu*, which also means goodbye. Note, however, that this is rarely used and is a form of grim farewell. *Adieu* means you will never see the person again. In fact, it is so final it literally translates to "To God"! It is thus best to avoid using this expression unless you are definitively cutting ties with someone.

First meetings

Let's look at this short dialogue between Pierre and Hélène who are meeting each other for the first time.

Pierre : *Bonjour.*	Hello.
Hélène : *Bonjour.*	Hello.
Pierre : *Comment vous appelez-vous ?*	What is your name?
Hélène : *Je m'appelle Hélène, et vous ?*	My name is Hélène, and you?
Pierre : *Je m'appelle Pierre. Enchanté.*	My name is Pierre. Nice to meet you.
Hélène : *Enchantée, Pierre.*	Nice to meet you, Pierre.

Asking one's name

To ask someone's name, you can say *Comment vous appelez-vous ?* like Pierre did. Or, you can also use the variation *Vous vous appelez comment ?* Both of these phrases are for formal situations. In casual situations you can say *Comment tu t'appelles ?* or *Tu t'appelles comment ?*

We know, that looks like a bunch of alien words with some odd repetitions. So let's break this down. *Comment vous appelez-vous ?* literally translates to "How do you call yourself?":

Comment | vous | appelez-vous ?
How (do) | you | call yourself?

The variation is in fact just a simple inversion:

Vous | vous appelez | comment ?
You | call yourself | how?

Vous refers to the pronoun "you". It is used in formal situations or when addressing two or more people. For example, when you want to ask the names of two people, even in informal situations, you would use *vous*.

As for the informal way of asking one's name, we use *tu* instead of *vous*.

Comment | tu | t'appelles ?
How (do) | you | call yourself?

Again, we can invert this phrase:

Tu | t'appelles | comment ?
You | call yourself | how?

Use *tu* when asking the name of someone your age or someone who is much younger. Also, if you are introduced to a friend of a friend, it is very natural to use the pronoun *tu*.

Introducing yourself

Now, to introduce yourself, you say *Je m'appelle...* (lit. "I call myself..."), followed by your first name. In the dialogue above, we saw the use of this phrase:

- **Je m'appelle** Hélène.
- **Je m'appelle** Pierre.

An alternative, more informal way of introducing yourself is by using the expression *Moi, c'est...* (lit. "Me, it's..."), followed again by your first name.

- **Moi, c'est** Hélène.
- **Moi, c'est** Pierre.

Finally, once names are exchanged, one usually says "Nice to meet you" or *Enchanté(e)* in French. For male speakers, it is written simply as *Enchanté*. For female speakers, it is written with an extra –e, as in *Enchantée*. Both are pronounced the same way.

Introducing someone else

To introduce someone else, we use the verb *s'appeler* as well. Note that *il* refers to the pronoun "he", and *elle* to the pronoun "she".

***Il s'appelle** Marc.*
His name is Marc. (lit. He calls himself Marc.)

***Elle s'appelle** Lucile.*
Her name is Lucile.

When introducing two or more people, we use the pronoun "they". In French, there are two words for "they", *ils* and *elles*. As you might have guessed, it has to do with the gender of the subject referred to. *Ils* refers to a masculine "they", while *elles* refers to a feminine "they".

***Ils s'appellent** Marc et Jean.*
Their names are Marc and Jean. (lit. They call themselves Marc and Jean.)

***Elles s'appellent** Lucile et Véronique.*
Their names are Lucile and Véronique.

If referring to a group of people with both male and female subjects, we use *ils* as the neutral pronoun. And so, for instance:

***Ils s'appellent** Clara et Arthur.*
Their names are Clara and Arthur.

You can also indicate your relationship to the person you are introducing, using the word *voici*. For example:

***Voici mon ami,** Arthur.*
This is my friend, Arthur.

***Voici ma collègue,** Clara*
This is my colleague, Clara.

***Voici mes amis,** Jules et Sophie.*
These are my friends, Jules and Sophie.

GRAMMAR TIP

The verb *s'appeler*

By now, you must be familiar with the verb *s'appeler*, used especially in indicating or asking one's name. Like in many languages, French verbs are conjugated. This means that they change according to the subject. We've seen all of these combinations previously, except for *nous* which refers to the pronoun "we".

	s'appeler
Je	m'appelle
Tu	t'appelles
Il/Elle	s'appelle
Nous	nous appelons
Vous	vous appelez
Ils/Elles	s'appellent

You've probably noticed that the verb is composed of two parts, both of which change during conjugation. We will learn more about this kind of verb later on.

Here's a bonus tip for pronunciation: the words *appelle, appelles, appellent* are actually pronounced the exact same way: /ah-pehl/

Exchanging niceties

Pierre and Hélène meet each other for a second time. Let's look at how their conversation would go.

Pierre : *Bonjour Hélène.*	Hello Hélène.
Hélène : *Bonjour Pierre.*	Hello Pierre.
Pierre : *Comment allez-vous ?*	How are you?
Hélène : *Je vais bien, merci, et vous ?*	I'm fine, thank you, and you?
Pierre : *Très bien, merci.*	Very well, thank you.

Asking how someone is

There are a number of ways to ask "How are you?" in French. Like Pierre, you can say *Comment allez-vous ?*, which is a formal variation. Others include:

- *Vous allez bien ?*
- *Tu vas bien ?*
- *Comment ça va ?*
- *Ça va ?*

The last three are used in informal situations. Remember, as we discussed above, that *tu* is the informal "you". We use *vous* in formal situations or when addressing two or more people.

Indicating how you are

To respond, you can use these expressions:

Comment allez-vous ? *Vous allez bien ?* *Tu vas bien ?*	**Je vais bien.** (I'm fine, I'm doing well.) **Je vais très bien.** (I'm doing very well.)
Comment ça va ? *Ça va ?*	**Oui, ça va.** (Yes, I'm fine.) **Ça va.** (I'm fine.) **Ça va bien.** (I'm fine.)

Don't forget that you can also ask back the question by saying, "And you?", which is *Et vous ?* in formal, and *Et toi ?* in informal settings.

Other basic expressions

Here are other basic expressions used in everyday situations that you must keep in mind.

Oui	Yes
Non	No
S'il vous plaît	Please ex. *Je voudrais une baguette, **s'il vous plaît**.* (I would like a baguette, please.)

Pardon	Pardon me; Excuse me ex. ***Pardon ? Pouvez-vous répéter s'il vous plaît ?*** (Pardon me? Can you repeat that please?) When you bump into someone by accident, you can also use *pardon* to apologize. If you go to Paris, you'll hear this word a lot in crowded subway stations!
Excusez-moi	Excuse me ex. ***Excusez-moi, où est la gare ?*** (Excuse me, where is the train station?)
Merci (beaucoup)	Thank you (very much)

Key Takeaways

Let's see what we learned today before moving on to the practice exercises.

- The social setting will indicate the proper greeting to use, as well as the appropriate pronoun "you" (*tu* or *vous*). We learned the difference between formal and informal situations.

Formal Situations	**Informal Situations**
Talking to a stranger	Talking to family and friends
Addressing people in professional situations (for example, employee to boss or student to teacher)	Talking to close colleagues and classmates
Addressing people in commercial situations (at a shop, bank, restaurant, etc.)	Talking to a child

- The most common ways to say "hello" are *bonjour*, *bonsoir*, *salut* and *coucou*.
- The most common ways to say "goodbye" are *au revoir*, *bonne journée*, *bonne soirée*, and *salut*.
- To ask one's name, introduce oneself, or introduce someone else, we use the verb *s'appeler*.

Asking one's name
Comment vous appelez-vous ? / Vous vous appelez comment ?
Comment tu t'appelles ? / Tu t'appelles comment ?
Introducing oneself
Je m'appelle...
Moi, c'est...

Introducing someone else
Il s'appelle… / Elle s'appelle…
Ils s'appellent… / Elles s'appellent…
Voici mon ami / mes amis…

- French verbs are conjugated according to the pronouns. The subject pronouns are *je*, *tu*, *il*, *elle*, *nous*, *vous*, *ils* and *elles*.
- We learned how to conjugate the verb *s'appeler: je m'appelle, tu t'appelles, il/elle s'appelle, nous nous appelons, vous vous appelez, ils/elles s'appellent*.
- *Tu* and *vous* both refer to the pronoun "you". *Tu* is used when talking to family, friends, or children. *Vous* is for formal situations. It is also used when referring to two or more people.
- To ask how someone is, you can say *Comment allez-vous ?* or *Vous allez bien ?* in formal situations. In casual settings, say *Tu vas bien ?* or *Ça va ?* To respond, we use the following expressions accordingly, *Je vais bien* or *Ça va (bien)*.

In the next chapter, we will learn more about introducing oneself, like indicating one's profession and age. We will also talk about two very important verbs, *être* (to be) and *avoir* (to have).

Exercises

How about putting to use what we've learned so far? Complete the exercises below to test your understanding of this chapter.

1. Categorize the following greetings. Which ones are used to greet somebody? Which ones are used to say goodbye?

    *Bonsoir • Coucou • Salut • Bonne journée •
    Bonjour • Bonne fin de journée • À plus*

Greetings	Parting Expressions

2. Choose the appropriate response to the following sentence: *Comment allez-vous ?*

    a. Je m'appelle Fabienne.
    b. Oui, ça va.
    c. Très bien, et vous ?

3. Choose the appropriate response: *Comment tu t'appelles ?*

    a. Bien, merci.
    b. Moi, c'est Sophie.
    c. Ils s'appellent Adrien et Olivier.

4. You enter a shop in the evening. How would you greet the vendors?

    a. Bonsoir.
    b. Ça va ?
    c. Bon après-midi.

5. Complete with the correct form of *s'appeler*: Tu _____ comment?

6. Choose the appropriate response: *Comment ça va ?*

    a. À tout à l'heure.
    b. Ça va bien.
    c. Adieu.

7. Complete with the correct form of *s'appeler*: Elle _____ Zoé.

8. Complete the dialogue with the appropriate word or phrase:

    - Bonjour ! _____ ?
    - Je m'appelle Jules, et _____ ?
    - Moi, _____ Nathan.
    - Enchanté.

9. Associate the following expressions to the correct translation:

Excusez-moi	See you soon
Bonne nuit	Goodbye
Au revoir	See you tomorrow
À demain	Excuse me
À bientôt	Good night

10. Write 2 to 3 sentences, introducing yourself and a friend.

_____

_____

_____

Answer Key

1.

Greetings	Parting Expressions
Bonsoir	Salut
Coucou	Bonne journée
Salut	Bonne fin de journée
Bonjour	*À plus*

2. c

3. b

4. a

5. t'appelles

6. b

7. s'appelle

8. - Bonjour ! <u>Comment vous appelez-vous / Vous vous appelez comment</u> ?
    - Je m'appelle Jules, et <u>vous</u> ?
    - Moi, <u>c'est</u> Nathan.
    - Enchanté.

9.
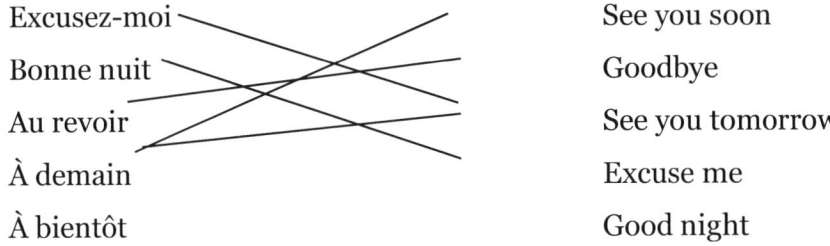

Excusez-moi — See you soon
Bonne nuit — Goodbye
Au revoir — See you tomorrow
À demain — Excuse me
À bientôt — Good night

10. Sample response: *Bonjour ! Je m'appelle Marie. Voici mon ami, Lucas.*

Chapter 2: All about you

Je pense, donc je suis.

I think, therefore I am.

- René Descartes

You now know how to greet someone, introduce yourself and ask how someone is. After meeting someone a few times, you would perhaps want to know more about him or her: his or her profession, age, country of origin, and so on. This goes both ways, as you too might be encouraged to talk a bit more about yourself.

In this lesson, you will learn how to indicate and ask one's profession and age. You will also encounter *avoir* and *être*, two very important verbs at the heart of the French language. *C'est parti !* Here we go!

Professions

Let's look at this dialogue between Pierre and Hélène.

Pierre : *Qu'est-ce que vous faites dans la vie ?*   What do you do for a living?

Hélène : *Je suis infirmière à l'Hôpital Paris Saint-Joseph. Et vous ? Quel est votre métier ?*

I am a nurse in the Paris Saint-Joseph hospital. And you? What is your job?

Pierre : *Je suis enseignant de français à l'Université.*

I am a French teacher in the University.

Asking one's profession

As we learned in the previous chapter, the French language differentiates between formal and informal social settings. *Tu* is an informal "you", while *vous* is the formal variation. Keep this in mind when asking for someone's profession. In informal settings, we might ask:

Qu'est-ce que tu fais dans la vie ?
Tu fais quoi dans la vie ?

What do you do for a living? (lit. What do you do in life?)

That potentially alarming jumble of words *Qu'est-ce que* simply refers to the interrogative pronoun "what". The pronunciation is not complicated: /kehs-keuh/. Now, both the sentences above translate to "What do you do for a living?" *Vie* means "life", as in the famous Edith Piaf song *La vie en rose* (Life in pink).

Otherwise, you can also use the following expressions:

Qu'est-ce que tu fais comme métier ?
Qu'est-ce que tu fais comme travail ?

Both mean, "What do you do as a job?". The words *métier* and *travail* are synonymous, and refer to the noun "job" or "work".

In formal situations, you guessed it, we use the pronoun *vous*.

Qu'est-ce que vous faites dans la vie ?
Qu'est-ce que vous faites comme métier ?
Qu'est-ce que vous faites comme travail ?

In even more formal settings, like an interview for a visa application for example, you might hear the expressions below:

Quel est votre métier ?
Quelle est votre profession ?

CULTURE TIP

How NOT to start a French conversation

Money, religion and politics – these are three topics you really don't want to talk about with someone you are just meeting for the first time. Don't ask how much someone makes or what is one's religion. These can be seen as intrusive questions. Asking for one's political preferences is just as risky a terrain.

Some things that in other cultures are natural can be seen as impolite in France. For example, asking someone's profession when you just met is not a common thing. This is because it has something to do with one of the taboo topics above: money. Asking about someone's civil status, whether one is married or has kids, can also be considered rude.

So what exactly can you talk about? Well, first-meeting conversations can revolve around culture. You can chat about French gastronomy, art or music, without worrying about causing someone discomfort!

Indicating one's profession

To indicate one's profession in English, we use the verb "to be". For example, "I **am** a teacher." It's the same in French, where we use the verb *être*, the equivalent of "to be". Remember that French verbs are conjugated according to the subject. Here's how we conjugate the verb *être* in the present tense:

être

Je	suis	/swee/
Tu	es	/eh/
Il/Elle	est	/eh/
Nous	sommes	/sohm/
Vous	êtes	/eht/
Ils/Elles	sont	/sohN/

Are all verb conjugations so complicated? The verb *être* is actually an irregular verb, so don't panic. Verb conjugations are generally simpler, as we will show you later on.

Now, to indicate one's profession, we follow the same structure in English:

SUBJECT + VERB + NOUN / ADJECTIVE

For example:

Je suis enseignant.
I am a teacher.

So, we start with the subject *Je* (I), then add the correct conjugation of the verb *être* (am) and finally, the profession *enseignant* (teacher). Notice that in English, you would say "**a** teacher", with the indefinite article "a". In French, we omit the article, and simply say "I am teacher". Why is that? To put it simply, French professions are adjectives in this specific sentence structure. So in the example above, *enseignant* is considered an adjective, unlike in English where it is a noun.

Let's look at some other examples:

Je suis étudiant.
I am a student.

Je suis médecin.
I am a doctor.

Je suis ingénieur.
I am an engineer.

Since you already know all the subject pronouns and conjugated forms of *être*, you can also indicate someone else's profession or even ask a specific question. For instance:

Elle est dentiste.
She is a dentist.

Ils sont boulangers.
They are bakers.

Nous sommes acteurs.
We are actors.

Vous êtes avocat ?
Are you a lawyer? (lit. You are a lawyer?)

As we mentioned earlier, the professions in these sentence structures are adjectives. In French, adjectives change according to the gender and number of the noun. As such, professions too differ in spelling according to the subject. Look at these two examples:

*Nathan est **avocat**.*
Nathan is a lawyer.

*Clara est **avocate**.*
Clara is a lawyer.

Notice how the adjective *avocat* (lawyer) changes according to the subject noun. For the masculine subject, we say *avocat*, while for the feminine subject, we add an extra –e, as in *avocate*. Let's look at some more examples.

*Paul est **enseignant**.*
Paul is a teacher.

*Camille est **enseignante**.*
Camille is a teacher.

Like the word *avocat*, we add an extra –e to *enseignant* for feminine subjects.

How about plural subjects? In this case, we add an extra –s while taking into consideration the gender of the nouns. So, for instance:

*Paul et Clara sont **enseignants**.*
Paul and Clara are teachers.

*Clara et Sarah sont **enseignantes**.*
Clara and Sarah are teachers.

Professions vocabulary

Masculine form	Feminine form	Translation
acteur	*actrice*	actor
boulanger	*boulangère*	baker
charpentier	*charpentière*	carpenter
chef		cook
dentiste		dentist
employé	*employée*	employee
enseignant	*enseignante*	teacher
fonctionnaire		civil servant
infirmier	*infirmière*	nurse
ingénieur	*ingénieure*	engineer
médecin		doctor
policier	*policière*	police officer

serveur	*serveuse*	waiter

GRAMMAR TIP
Noun-adjective agreement for professions

Noun-adjective agreement simply means that French adjectives change according to the gender and number of the noun they are describing. For most adjectives, we follow two general rules:

- To form the feminine, we add an –e to the end of the masculine adjective.
- To form the plural, we add an –s.

And so, *avocat* (lawyer) would be *avocate* in feminine form. In plural form, depending on the gender of the nouns, the adjective can be *avocats* or *avocates*.

Are there exceptions? Yes, there are. There are certain adjectives that generally call for different endings or that require no change at all.

Professions ending in		**The feminine form is...**
-ien	→	*-ienne*
-er	→	*-ère*
-eur	→	*-euse*
-teur	→	*-trice*
-iste	→	*-iste*
-e	→	*-e*

And so, *opticien* (optician) becomes *opticienne* in feminine form. *Boulanger* becomes *boulangère*; *serveur* becomes *serveuse*; *acteur* becomes *actrice*. *Pharmacien* (pharmacist) does not change in form. It is the same for adjectives already ending in –e. For example, *dentiste* is used for both masculine and feminine forms.

Age and numbers

The conversation between Pierre and Hélène continues:

Pierre : *Vous avez quel âge ?*		How old are you?
Hélène : *J'ai vingt-neuf ans. Et vous ?*		I'm twenty-nine years old. And you?
Pierre : *J'ai trente-trois ans.*		I'm thirty-three years old.

Asking one's age

To ask one's age in formal situations, we can say:

Vous avez quel âge ?
How old are you? (lit. You have what age?)

Quel âge avez-vous ?
How old are you? (lit. What age do you have?)

For informal settings, use the following expression:

Tu as quel âge ?
How old are you? (lit. You have what age?)

In the French language, age is indicated with the verb "to have". In English for instance, one would say "How old are you?" or "I am 20 years old", using the verb "to be" (are). In French however, the literal translation of these expressions are "What age do you have?" and "I have 20 years".

The verb *avoir* means "to have". It is used to indicate possession like its English counterpart. For example, you can say, *J'ai un sac* (I have a bag). *Avoir* is also used in special cases like in indicating one's age. To conjugate:

	avoir	
J'	ai	/ay/
Tu	as	/ah/
Il/Elle	a	/ah/
Nous	avons	/ah-vohñ/
Vous	avez	/ah-vay/
Ils/Elles	ont	/ohñ/

Notice that we contract the pronoun *Je* before a vowel, so *Je ai* becomes *J'ai* (I have). This is not the universe's way to make your French learner's life more complicated. Quite the contrary, we contract *Je* to simplify the pronunciation. Isn't it much easier to say *J'ai* than *Je ai*?

Indicating one's age

To say your age in French, we use the following structure:

SUBJECT + *AVOIR* + NUMBER + the word *ANS* (years).

Here are some examples:

- *J'ai 10 ans.*
- *Elle a 47 ans.*
- *Vous avez 30 ans ?*
- *Hugo a 25 ans.*

The word *ans* translates to "years". And so, the last sentence literally means "Hugo has 25 years". Of course, in order to say your age, you'd have to know how to count!

Numbers 1 to 50

Take the time to memorize numbers 1 to 50 before moving forward.

0	zéro				
1	un	21	vingt et un	41	quarante et un
2	deux	22	vingt-deux	42	quarante-deux
3	trois	23	vingt-trois	43	quarante-trois
4	quatre	24	vingt-quatre	44	quarante-quatre
5	cinq	25	vingt-cinq	45	quarante-cinq
6	six	26	vingt-six	46	quarante-six
7	sept	27	vingt-sept	47	quarante-sept
8	huit	28	vingt-huit	48	quarante-huit
9	neuf	29	vingt-neuf	49	quarante-neuf
10	dix	30	trente	50	cinquante
11	onze	31	trente et un		
12	douze	32	trente-deux		
13	treize	33	trente-trois		
14	quatorze	34	trente-quatre		
15	quinze	35	trente-cinq		
16	seize	36	trente-six		
17	dix-sept	37	trente-sept		
18	dix-huit	38	trente-huit		
19	dix-neuf	39	trente-neuf		
20	vingt	40	quarante		

From twenty onwards, you simply need to add numbers 1 to 9 to the tens (*vingt, trente, quarante...*) to form the numbers. This makes them easier to remember.

How do I memorize all this, you say? Practice is key. Try saying your telephone number aloud to practice. Or better yet, read all the phone numbers in your contacts list. Another great idea would be to use number flashcards. Want an extra challenge? Opt for addition or multiplication flashcards!

Key Takeaways

- To ask one's profession and age, we use the following expressions:

Asking one's profession
Qu'est-ce que tu fais dans la vie ?
Tu fais quoi dans la vie ?
Qu'est-ce que vous faites dans la vie ?
Qu'est-ce que vous faites comme métier ?
Qu'est-ce que vous faites comme travail ?
Quel est votre métier ?
Quelle est votre profession ?
Asking one's age
Tu as quel âge ?
Vous avez quel âge ?
Quel âge avez-vous ?

- To indicate one's profession, we use the verb *être: je suis, tu es, il/elle est, nous sommes, vous êtes, ils/elles sont.*
- To indicate one's age, we use the verb *avoir: j'ai, tu as, il/elle a, nous avons, vous avez, ils/elles ont.*
- French adjectives agree in gender and number with the noun they describe. Generally, we form the feminine by adding an –e to the adjective, and the plural by adding an –s.

In the next chapter, you will learn how to indicate the languages you speak, as well as your country of origin. We will also have a look at what we call –ER verbs. These are regular verbs that are much easier to conjugate than *avoir* and *être*, we promise!

Exercises

1. Choose the appropriate response to the following sentence: *Qu'est-ce que vous faites comme métier ?*

    a. Je m'appelle Arthur.
    b. Je suis actrice.
    c. Vous êtes dentiste.
    d. J'ai 22 ans.

2. Choose the appropriate response: *Tu as quel âge ?*

    a. Il a 33 ans.
    b. J'ai 22 ans.
    c. Vous avez 41 ans.
    d. Je vais bien.

3. Choose the appropriate response: *Lucas a quel âge ?*

    a. Elle a 12 ans.
    b. Ils ont 22 ans.
    c. Il a 17 ans.

4. Choose the appropriate response: *Vous êtes enseignants ?*

    a. Oui, je suis infirmière.
    b. J'ai 12 ans.
    c. Non, nous sommes étudiants.

5 – 7. Read the following text and indicate whether the statements below are true or false.

> *Jules et Marie sont mariés. Jules a cinquante ans. Il est enseignant de mathématiques. Marie a quarante-neuf ans. Elle est médecin.*

   5. Marie is a doctor.
   6. Jules is younger than Marie.
   7. Jules teaches French.

8 – 10. Answer the following mathematical problems. Write down the answers in words, not in figures.

   8. $10 \times 3 =$ _____

   9. $50 - 23 =$ _____

   10. $8 + 3 =$ _____

Answer Key

1. b
2. b
3. c
4. c
5. True.
6. False. Jules is 50 years old while Marie is 49.
7. False. Jules teaches Mathematics.
8. trente
9. vingt-sept
10. onze

Chapter 3: I speak a little French

Avoir une autre langue, c'est posséder une deuxième âme.

To have another language is to possess a second soul.

- Charlemagne

Wouldn't it be nice to be able to say "I speak French"? Or at least, "I speak a little French"? Well, by the end of this chapter, you'll be able to say it so proudly! If you meet French natives while traveling in France, you might find yourself being asked where you're from or what other languages you speak. This chapter will also prepare you for such instances.

In this lesson, you will learn how to indicate and ask one's language, nationality and country of origin. You will also learn how to conjugate your first regular verbs and produce basic subject-predicate sentences.

Nationalities

Asking and indicating one's nationality

To ask one's nationality, you can say:

Vous êtes de quelle nationalité ?
What is your nationality? (lit. You are of what nationality?)

Vous venez d'où ?
Where do you come from? (lit. You come from where?)

Can you tell which verb is used in the first sentence? Yes, it's the verb *être* (to be) that we learned in the previous chapter. In more formal scenarios, you might also be asked:

Quelle est votre nationalité ?
What is your nationality?

Now, to answer these two questions, you use the same structure as you would in English:

SUBJECT + VERB + ADJECTIVE.

And so, for instance, you might say "I am American". In French, using the verb *être*, that would be:

Je suis américain.

Je suis américaine.

Like we've seen earlier, adjectives change according to the gender of the noun it refers to. Masculine subjects would thus say *américain*; and feminine subjects, *américaine* with an added –e. Let's look at other examples.

Harry est anglais. Amelia est anglaise.
Harry is English. Amelia is English.

Mario et Alessandro sont italiens.
Mario and Alessandro are Italian.

Mei et Yui sont japonaises.
Mei and Yui are Japanese.

Mon amie Sofia est espagnole.
My friend Sofia is Spanish.

Nous sommes vietnamiens.
We are Vietnamese.

In the next section, you will find a list of some nationalities, in both masculine and feminine forms.

Nationalities vocabulary

Masculine form	Feminine form	Translation
allemand	allemande	German
américain	américaine	American
anglais	anglaise	English
autrichien	autrichienne	Austrian
belge	belge	Belgian
canadien	canadienne	Canadian
chinois	chinoise	Chinese
coréen	coréenne	Korean
espagnol	espagnole	Spanish
français	française	French
grec	grecque	Greek
japonais	japonaise	Japanese
marocain	marocaine	Moroccan
mexicain	mexicaine	Mexican
portugais	portugaise	Portuguese
russe	russe	Russian
suédois	suédoise	Swede
vietnamien	vietnamienne	Vietnamese

Remember that as a general rule, we add an –e to adjectives to form the feminine, and an –s to form the plural. Notice however, that this is not the case for certain adjectives of nationality. To make it simpler, we've summarized the common rules below. We've also included pronunciation notes. The pronunciation of the feminine form may sometimes differ from the masculine form.

Nationalities ending in...	Add...	Examples
-ais -ois -ain -and -ol	-e	*français* → *français**e*** /frahñ-seh/ → /frahñ-seh**z**/
		chinois → *chinois**e*** /shee-nwah/ → /shee-nwah**z**/
		américain → *américain**e*** /ah-meh-ree-kahñ/ → /ah-meh-ree-**kehn**/
		allemand → *allemand**e*** /ah-leh-mahñ/ → /ah-leh-mahñ**D**/
		espagnol → *espagnol**e*** /ehs-pah-nyol/ (no change in pronunciation)
-ien -éen	-ne	*canadien* → *canadien**ne*** /kah-nah-dyahñ/ → /kah-nah-dy**ehn**/
		coréen → *coréen**ne*** /ko-re-yahñ/ → /ko-re-y**ehn**/
-e	none	*russe* /rews/ (no change in pronunciation)

The word for "Greek" is an irregular case. For masculine subjects, we say *grec* and for feminine, *grecque*. Both are pronounced the same way, as /grek/.

Languages

Asking and indicating one's language

If you want to ask which languages one speaks, you can say:

Vous parlez quelles langues ?
You speak which languages?

Quelles langues parlez-vous ?
Which languages do you speak?

The second expression is used in more formal scenarios. As you know by now, in informal situations, we use the pronoun *tu*.

Tu parles quelles langues ?

You speak which languages?

To indicate which languages you speak, we also use the verb *parler* (to speak). In English, one might say "I speak English". In French, that would be:

Je parle anglais.
I speak English.

A quick writing tip: the first letter of languages and nationalities are not capitalized in French. Let's look at some other examples:

Mathis parle français.
Mathis speaks French.

Elle parle mandarin et arabe.
She speaks Mandarin and Arabic.

Nous parlons un peu espagnol.
We speak a little Spanish.

Je parle couramment italien.
I speak Italian fluently.

As in the last two sentences, you can use *un peu* (a little) and *couramment* (fluently) to specify your fluency in the language.

GRAMMAR TIP

-ER verbs in French

There are three types of French regular verbs, categorized according to their endings. –ER verbs are those whose unconjugated forms end in –er. –IR verbs end in –ir while –RE verbs end in –re. And so, for example, *parler* is an –ER verb; *venir* (to come) is an –IR verb and *descendre* (to go down) is an –RE verb.

Now what's this all about, you might ask? These categorizations actually make learning verb conjugations much easier. Simply because, all verbs under the same category are usually conjugated the exact same way!

To conjugate –ER verbs in the present tense, we simply remove the –er of the infinitive form and replace them with a set of fixed endings. And so, for example, we remove the –er in the verb *parler* and then we add the appropriate endings:

parler	→ *parl*		
Je	+e	parl**e**	I speak
Tu	+es	parl**es**	You speak (inf.)
Il/Elle	+e	parl**e**	He/She speaks
Nous	+ons	parl**ons**	We speak
Vous	+ez	parl**ez**	You speak (for.)
Ils/Elles	+ent	parl**ent**	They speak

Thus, in order to conjugate a verb within a category, all you have to do is keep in mind the endings for each pronoun.

Languages vocabulary

You'll notice that in French, most of the languages are in fact the word for the nationalities in masculine form. And so, English would be *anglais*, French would be *français* and Russian would be *russe*. Of course, there are some languages that don't share the term with the words for nationality. For example, *mandarin* for Mandarin, *pendjabi* for Punjabi or *swahili* for Swahili.

Cities and Countries

Asking and indicating where you live

To ask where someone lives, use the verb *habiter*:

Vous habitez où ?
Where do you live?

To indicate where you live, you might specify your city and country by saying:

J'habite à New York, aux États-Unis.
I live in New York, in the US.

The verb *habiter* (to live) is an –ER verb because it ends with –er. It is thus in the same category as the verb *parler* and is conjugated the same way:

habiter	→ *habit*	
J'	+e	habit**e**
Tu	+es	habit**es**
Il/Elle	+e	habit**e**
Nous	+ons	habit**ons**
Vous	+ez	habit**ez**
Ils/Elles	+ent	habit**ent**

Since the h is silent, we contract the pronoun *je* before the verb. It's just like what we saw with the verb *avoir*. And so, we say *j'habite* /jah-beet/, and not *je habite*.

Now that you understand the conjugation of the verb *habiter*, let's focus our attention on the prepositions.

Before cities, we always use the preposition *à*, which is an equivalent of "in" in English. So you might say, *à Paris, à Tokyo, à Rome, à Jakarta*, etc. For countries, the preposition changes according to gender and number.

Gender again? Yes, but we promise you'll soon get used to it. As you're probably realizing by now, gender is an important part of the French language. In French, every noun has a gender, including countries.

Let's look at how the preposition *à* (in) changes according to the gender and number of the country:

For countries that...	Preposition *à*	Examples
are feminine	*en*	**en** France, **en** Grèce
start with a vowel		**en** Iran, **en** Italie
are masculine	*au*	**au** Canada, **au** Japon
are plural	*aux*	**aux** États-unis, **aux** Philippines

Of course, the million-dollar question is, how do you know the gender of the countries? Those ending in –e are feminine (ex. *France, Italie, Pologne, Corée*). The rest is masculine. The good news is there are only four exceptions to this rule: *Cambodge, Mexique, Zimbabwe* and *Mozambique* are masculine nouns.

It is simpler to know which countries are plural. More often than not, if they are plural in English, it's the same in French. For example, the United States (*les États-unis*), the United Arab Emirates (*les Émirats arabes unis*), or the Netherlands (*les Pays-Bas*).

Countries vocabulary

Masculine		Feminine	
le Canada	Canada	*la Chine*	China
le Danemark	Denmark	*la Grèce*	Greece
le Japon	Japan	*la France*	France
le Portugal	Portugal	*la Pologne*	Poland
le Royaume-Uni	the United Kingdom	*la Russie*	Russia
Plural			
les États-unis		the United States	
les Émirats arabes unis		the United Arab Emirates	
les Pays-Bas		the Netherlands	

CULTURE TIP

The World of Francophonie

La Francophonie refers to the community of francophones or French speakers. There are currently 29 countries that speak French as a national or official language: Belgium, Benin, Burkina Faso, Burundi, Cameroon, Canada, Chad, the Ivory Coast, the Democratic Republic of the Congo, Djibouti, Equatorial Guinea, France, Haiti, Luxembourg, Madagascar, Mali, Monaco, Niger, Rwanda, Senegal, Seychelles, Switzerland, Togo and Vanuatu.

Key Takeaways

- To ask and indicate one's nationality, we use the following expressions:

Ask one's nationality
Vous êtes de quelle nationalité ?
Vous venez d'où ?
Quelle est votre nationalité ?
Indicate one's nationality
Subject pronoun + *être* + nationality adjective

- Adjectives of nationality agree in gender and number with the noun it refers to. Generally, for nationalities ending in –ais, –ois, –ain, –and, –ol, we simply add an –e to form the feminine. For those ending in –ien or –éen, we add –ne. Nationalities that already end in –e in masculine form does not change in the feminine form. To form the plural, we add an –s.
- To ask and indicate one's language, we use the following expressions:

Ask one's language
Vous parlez quelles langues ?
Quelles langues parlez-vous ?
Tu parles quelles langues ?
Indicate one's language
Subject pronoun + *parler* + (*un peu/couramment*) + language

- To conjugate –ER verbs, we remove the –er ending and add the following: *-e, -es, -e, -ons, -ez, -ent*
- To ask and indicate where one lives, we use the following expressions:

Ask where one lives
Vous habitez où ?
Indicate one's city and country
Subject pronoun + *habiter* + *à* + place

- The preposition *à* changes according to the gender and number of the country. Most countries ending in –e are feminine, and those in –s, plural.
- When referring to cities, the preposition *à* does not change.

In the next chapter, you will learn how to present and describe common objects using the expressions *c'est* and *ce sont*. We will also look at some basic French adjectives.

Exercises

1. Answer the question using the expressions learned: *Vous êtes de quelle nationalité ?*

2. Answer the question using the expressions learned: *Vous parlez quelles langues ?*

3 – 7. What is the feminine form of the following nationalities?

       3. français → _____
       4. coréen → _____
       5. italien → _____
       6. grec → _____
       7. russe → _____

8-10. Complete the text with the correct form of the preposition *à*.

Bonjour ! Je m'appelle Sandrine. Je suis française, mais j'habite actuellement 8.____ Tokyo, 9.____ Japon. Voici mon amie Mei. Elle est chinoise. Elle parle couramment anglais. Elle habite à Beijing, 10.____ Chine.

Answer Key

1. Sample answer: Je suis américain.
2. Sample answer: Je parle anglais, espagnol et un peu français.
3. française
4. coréenne
5. italienne
6. grecque
7. russe
8. à
9. au
10. en

Chapter 4: This is not a pipe

Ceci n'est pas une pipe.

This is not a pipe.

- René Magritte

Do you know Belgian surrealist painter René Magritte? Our title comes from his painting called *La Trahison des Images* (The Treachery of Images). It is a painting of a pipe with the inscription *Ceci n'est pas une pipe* (This is not a pipe). It simply means that the pipe in the painting is not a pipe, but the painting of a pipe! Phew!

In this lesson, we will learn how to present and describe something. We won't use *ceci* like Magritte, for this is actually a formal term for the pronoun "this". Instead, we'll focus on more natural sounding expressions like *c'est* and *ce sont*. Alongside, we will also learn about articles and adjectives in this chapter.

Presenting something

C'est and ce sont

To present something or someone, we use the expressions *c'est* and *ce sont*. *Ce* or the contracted *C'* is the equivalent of the demonstrative pronouns "this" and "these". As you can see, they are combined with the verb *être*. *C'est* means "this is" or "it is". *Ce sont* translates to "these are" or "they are". You can combine these expressions with a noun, a pronoun, an adjective or an adverb. Let's look at some examples:

C'est un livre.
It's a book. / This is a book.

Ce sont des livres.
These are books.

C'est moi.
It's me.

C'est facile.
It's easy.
C'est bientôt.
It's soon.

For now, let us focus on the first two sentences above. Notice how we use *C'est* for singular nouns (*un livre*), and *Ce sont* for plural nouns (*des livres*). Observe these other examples:

C'est un sac. Ce sont des sacs.
This is a bag. These are bags.

C'est une photo. Ce sont des photos.
This is a photo. These are photos.

Remember that you will choose between these two expressions according to the number of the noun referred to.

GRAMMAR TIP

Definite and indefinite articles

There are two types of articles in French: definite and indefinite. Definite articles refer to the word "the" in English, while indefinite articles are the equivalent of "a" and "an". For example:

*C'est **un** livre.* (It's a book.)

*C'est **le** livre que j'adore.* (It's the book I love.)

Like in English, you use definite articles to point to a specific noun, and indefinite articles to an unspecific noun.

Now, in French, the articles change according to the gender and number of the noun. In English, there is only one "the", in French there are four. In English, we have "a" and "an", while in French we have three equivalents. In the table below, you'll find which article to use in which case. We also added some examples:

	Indefinite articles	Definite articles
masculine	**un** *stylo* (a pen)	*le livre* (the book)
feminine	**une** *banane* (a banana)	*la femme* (the woman)
plural	**des** *cahiers* (notebooks)	*les plantes* (the plants)
before a vowel or *h*		*l'étudiant* (the student)
		l'homme (the man)

Here we go again with gender! How do you know the gender of nouns? We'll give you the abridged version of the general rule for now: Words ending in –e or –ion are often feminine, except those ending in –age, –ege, –é, or –isme, which are often masculine.

This is not a foolproof rule. In fact, we recommend that instead of memorizing the common endings, you should instead just memorize the gender of words progressively. How? Every time you come across a new word, memorize it with the article. For example, don't just memorize *livre* for book, but *un livre*, with the article indicating it is masculine.

Common Objects Vocabulary

	Translation
un cahier	a notebook
un crayon	a pencil
un livre	a book
un ordinateur	a computer
un ordinateur portable	a laptop
un (téléphone) portable	a mobile phone
un sac	a bag
un sac à dos	a backpack
un stylo	a pen
un tableau blanc	a whiteboard
une chaise	a chair
une règle	a ruler
une table	a table

CULTURE TIP

20 for God

French schools and universities use a 20-point grading system with 20 being the highest. But there is a common saying that goes: "20 is for God, 19 is for the King and 18 is for the President." And so, the highest score students would often get is a 17. In reality, a grade of 14 is already considered good!

If you study in France, you will receive your diploma with the specification of your *mention* or honors. A grade of 14 to 16 yields a *mention bien* (good), 16 to 18 a *mention très bien* (very good) and 18 above a *mention excellent* (outstanding).

Describing something

Using the expressions *c'est* and *ce sont*, you can also describe something:

*C'est **délicieux**!*
It's delicious. / This is delicious.

*C'est **difficile**.*
It's difficult.

Or you can also use it with a noun and adjective combination:

*C'est un stylo **noir**.*
It's a black pen.

*C'est une femme **gentille**.*
It's a kind woman.

*C'est une **petite** maison.*
It's a small house.

Common Adjectives Vocabulary

Adjectives	Translation
beau (m.) / belle (f.)	beautiful
blanc (m.) / blanche (f.)	white
bon marché (m./f.)	cheap
cher (m.) / chère (f.)	expensive
court (m.) / courte (f.)	short
difficile (m./f.)	difficult
facile (m./f.)	easy
faible (m./f.)	weak
fort (m.) / forte (f.)	strong
gentil (m.) / gentille (f.)	kind
grand (m.) / grande (f.)	big
heureux (m.) / heureuse (f.)	happy
laid (m.) / laide (f.)	ugly
léger (m.) / légère (f.)	light
long (m.) / longue (f.)	long
lourd (m.) / lourde (f.)	heavy
petit (m.) / petite (f.)	small
triste (m./f.)	sad

| méchant (m.) / méchante (f.) | mean |
| noir (m.) / noire (f.) | black |

Placing adjectives

In French, adjectives are generally placed after the noun. Adjectives of color always come after the noun. For example:

*C'est un test **difficile**.*
It's a difficult test.

*C'est une chemise **blanche**.*
It's a white blouse.

Exceptions include shorter adjectives like *beau, bon, long, petit*, which are placed before the noun.

*C'est une **petite** maison.*
It's a small house.

*C'est un **long** chemin.*
It's a long road.

We will learn later on as well that certain adjectives change meaning according to their position. But let's not get ahead of ourselves! For now, remember these two rules.

Key Takeaways

- To present or describe something, we use the expressions *C'est* (It is / This is) and *Ce sont* (They are / These are). These two can be followed by a noun, pronoun, an adjective or an adverb.
- The definite articles in French are: *le* (m.), *la* (f.), *les* (plur.) and *l'* (before a vowel). All of these translate to "the" in English.
- The indefinite articles in French are: *un* (m.), *une* (f.) and *des* (pl.). All of these translate to "a" or "an" in English.
- Nouns ending in –e or –ion are often feminine, except those ending in –age, –ege, –é, or –isme, which are often masculine.
- Adjectives in French are usually placed after the noun. Certain shorter adjectives such as *beau, bon, long, petit* are placed before the noun.

In the next chapter, you will learn how to ask for information politely. You will also learn how to say numbers above 50 and how to read telephone numbers in French.

Exercises

1-5. Present the following objects using *c'est* or *ce sont*:

   1. A book
   2. A pen
   3. Some photos
   4. A black notebook
   5. Some heavy bags

6. Complete with the correct <u>indefinite</u> article: *Ce sont _____ ordinateurs.*

7. Complete with the correct <u>definite</u> article: *C'est _____ chaise blanche.*

8. Complete with the correct <u>indefinite</u> article: *C'est _____ homme méchant.*

9. Add the correct form of the adjective "kind": *C'est une femme.*

10. Add the correct form of the adjective "small": *C'est une table.*

Answer Key

1. C'est un livre.
2. C'est un stylo.
3. Ce sont des photos.
4. C'est un cahier noir.
5. Ce sont des sacs lourds.
6. des
7. la
8. un
9. C'est une femme <u>gentille</u>.
10. C'est une <u>petite</u> table.

Chapter 5: How may I help you?

Un peu d'aide nous fait grand bien.

A little help does us a lot of good.

- Jean Frain du Tremblay

If traveling or moving to France, it is essential to know how to ask and gather information. By learning how to formulate questions, you will be able to get by in various instances, as in asking for help at the train station, post office or bank.

In this lesson, you will learn how to obtain information using the interrogative pronoun *quel* and the conditional expression *je voudrais*. We will also study the rest of the numbers in French.

Asking for information

Isabella goes to Paris to learn French. To complete her immersion experience, she decides to enroll in a language course. She asks for information at the reception:

Receptionist: *Bonjour, comment puis-je vous aider ?*
Isabella: *Bonjour Madame. C'est pour une inscription. Je voudrais des informations s'il vous plaît.*
Receptionist: *Bien sûr. C'est pour quelle langue ?*
Isabella: *Le français pour débutants.*
Receptionist: *D'accord. Vous complétez un formulaire et vous présentez une pièce d'identité...*
Isabella: *Et combien ça coûte ?*
Receptionist: *Ça coûte 400 euros pour 36 heures de cours.*

Let us focus on the expression pairs we see in the dialogue:

Comment puis-je vous aider ? (for.)
How may I help you?

To ask for information, we reply with:

Je voudrais des informations s'il vous plaît.
I would like some information please.

The polite expression *je voudrais* translates to "I would like" and is used not only when you seek information, but also when ordering in a restaurant. Note that you can specify what kind of information you are looking for with the expression *c'est*. For example: *C'est pour une inscription* (It's for an enrollment).

Asking for price

To ask for the price, we can say:

Combien ça coûte ?
How much does it cost?

And to indicate the price:

Ça coûte...
It costs...

Interrogative pronoun quel

The receptionist helps Isabella fill in the enrollment form. With our previous lessons, you will be able to understand most of the dialogue below:

Receptionist: *Quel est votre nom ?*
Isabella: *Bianchi.*
Receptionist: *Quel est votre prénom ?*
Isabella: *Isabella.*
Receptionist: *Quelle est votre nationalité ?*
Isabella : *Je suis italienne.*
Receptionist: *Quelle est votre adresse ?*
Isabella : *J'habite 8 avenue Émile-Zola, dans le 15ème.*
Receptionist: *Et quel est votre numéro de téléphone ?*
Isabella : *C'est le 07 64 82 30 10.*

One of the ways we can formulate a question in French is by using the interrogative pronoun *quel*. *Quel* may be roughly translated to "what" or "which". It changes according to the gender and number of the noun it refers to. For example:

Quel (m.) *est votre* **nom (m.)** *?*
What is your surname?

Quelle (f.) *est votre* **nationalité (f.)** *?*
What is your nationality?

Since *nom* is a masculine noun, we use *quel*; *nationalité* is a feminine noun, so we use *quelle*. The table below summarizes the variations of *quel*. All of them are pronounced the same way as /kel/.

Gender / Number	Quel	Examples
masculine	quel	**Quel** *est votre nom ?* **Quel** *est votre prénom ?*
feminine	quelle	**Quelle** *est votre nationalité ?*

		Quelle est votre adresse ?
plural masculine	*quels*	*Quels* sont vos noms ?
plural feminine	*quelles*	*Quelles* sont vos coordonnées ?

A few notes regarding the vocabulary here: *un nom* is used to refer to both surname and complete name while *un prénom* refers to one's first name. *Les coordonnées* (f. plur.) translates to "contact details". If asked for your *coordonnées*, you are thus expected to specify your address and phone number.

GRAMMAR TIP

The possessive pronoun "your"

French possessive pronouns are used much like their English counterparts. They are placed before a noun to indicate possession, for example **mon** sac (**my** bag). The only difference is that pronouns in French change according to the gender and number of the noun, not the possessor. For now, let's learn the equivalent of the pronoun *your*:

	your (for.)
masculine	***votre*** nom
feminine	***votre*** adresse
plural	***vos*** amis

Note that this is the formal "your". Later on, we will learn the informal variation.

Numbers 60 to 100

In Chapter 2, we learned numbers 1 to 50. Don't hesitate to review this chapter if needed. When you're ready, complete your vocabulary by memorizing the numbers below:

50	cinquante	70	soixante-dix	90	quatre-vingt-dix
51	cinquante et un	71	soixante-et-onze	91	quatre-vingt-onze
52	cinquante-deux	72	soixante-douze	92	quatre-vingt-douze
53	cinquante-trois	73	soixante-treize	93	quatre-vingt-treize
54	cinquante-quatre	74	soixante-quatorze	94	quatre-vingt-quatorze
55	cinquante-cinq	75	soixante-quinze	95	quatre-vingt-quinze
56	cinquante-six	76	soixante-seize	96	quatre-vingt-seize

57	cinquante-sept	**77**	soixante-dix-sept	**97**	quatre-vingt-dix-sept
58	cinquante-huit	**78**	soixante-dix-huit	**98**	quatre-vingt-dix-huit
59	cinquante-neuf	**79**	soixante-dix-neuf	**99**	quatre-vingt-dix-neuf
60	soixante	**80**	quatre-vingts	**100**	cent
61	soixante et un	**81**	quatre-vingt-un		
62	soixante-deux	**82**	quatre-vingt-deux		
63	soixante-trois	**83**	quatre-vingt-trois		
64	soixante-quatre	**84**	quatre-vingt-quatre		
65	soixante-cinq	**85**	quatre-vingt-cinq		
66	soixante-six	**86**	quatre-vingt-six		
67	soixante-sept	**87**	quatre-vingt-sept		
68	soixante-huit	**88**	quatre-vingt-huit		
69	soixante-neuf	**89**	quatre-vingt-neuf		

CULTURE TIP

What's your number?

French numbers are recited and written in tens. For instance, to read this mobile number:

06 89 41 22 30

zéro six, quatre-vingt-neuf, quarante et un, vingt-deux, trente

To give your mobile number, you will use *C'est* with the definite article *le*. This is a fixed expression, so *le* never changes.

C'est le 06 89 41 22 30.

How about practicing by reciting your own number aloud?

Key Takeaways

- We learned the following expressions:

Help or ask for information
Comment puis-je vous aider ?
Je voudrais des informations s'il vous plaît.
Indicate or ask for price
Combien ça coûte ?
Ça coûte...

- To formulate questions in French, we can use the interrogative pronoun *quel*, which changes according to the gender and number of the noun it refers to: *quel* (m.), *quelle* (f.), *quels* (m.plur.), *quelles* (f.plur.).
- The possessive pronoun "your" changes according to the number of the antecedent as well: *votre* (sing.) and *vos* (pl.).
- To indicate a mobile or fixed phone number, we use the expression *C'est le*.

In the next chapter, you will learn how to present your family. We will review the verb *avoir* and learn more about possessive adjectives.

Exercises

1-2. Complete the dialogue with the appropriate missing words:

- Bonjour Madame, comment 1._____ vous aider ?
- Bonjour. C'est pour une inscription. Je 2._____ des informations s'il vous plaît.

3-4. Complete the dialogue with the appropriate missing words:

- 3. _____ coûte l'inscription ?
- Ça 4._____ 200 euros.

5. Complete with the correct form of *quel*: _____ est votre prénom ?

6. Complete with the correct form of *quel*: _____ sont vos coordonnées ?

7. Complete with the correct form of *quel*: _____ est votre adresse ?

8. Complete with the correct form of "your": *Quelle est _____ nationalité ?*

9. Complete with the correct form of "your": *Quels sont _____ noms ?*

10. Write the following mobile number in letters, then read aloud: 07 12 99 56 87.

Answer Key

1. puis-je
2. voudrais
3. Combien
4. coûte
5. Quel
6. Quelles
7. Quelle
8. votre
9. vos
10. zéro sept, douze, quatre-vingt-dix-neuf, cinquante-six, quatre-vingt-sept

Chapter 6: One big happy family

La famille sera toujours la base des sociétés.

The family will always be the basis of societies.

- Honoré de Balzac

To have a beginners' fluency in French means to be able to talk about what is most intimate to you. And what topic is more intimate than family or *la famille*. In this lesson, you will learn how to present your family using possessive adjectives. We will revisit the verb *avoir* (to have) and look at vocabulary related to family.

Talking about one's family

Family vocabulary

We included below some terms used for informal direct address. In English, it's odd to directly address your mother as "mother". Instead, we opt for terms like "mom" or "mama". It's the same in French. One would call his or her mom, *maman* and not *mère*.

	Translation
des frères et sœurs	siblings
un cousin	a male cousin
un enfant	a child
un fils	a son
un frère	a brother
un grand-père	a grandfather (*papi* or *papy* for informal direct address)
un mari	a husband
un oncle	an uncle
un parent	a relative, a parent
un père	a father (*papa* for informal direct address)
un petit-fils	a grandson
une cousine	a female cousin
une famille	a family
une femme	a wife

une fille	a daughter
une grand-mère	a grandmother (*mamie* for informal direct address)
une mère	a mother (*maman* for informal direct address)
une petite-fille	a granddaughter
une sœur	a sister
une tante	a aunt
une nièce	a niece
un neveu	a nephew

Can you guess the plural forms of the nouns above? Yes, we simply add the letter –s as ending! So *un père* would be *des pères*, *une cousine* becomes *des cousines*, etc. The only exceptions here are *un fils* whose plural form is also *des fils* and *un neveu*, whose plural form is *des neveux*.

Presenting one's family

We learned in Chapter 1 how to formally present someone with the word *voici*:

Voici *mes parents Sarah et Théo.*
These are my parents, Sarah and Théo.

You can also use other formal phrases to present a family member:

Je vous présente *mon mari, Jacques.*
I present to you my husband, Jacques.

It sounds like you're presenting royalty, right? Use this expression in formal events or when talking to elders or those in positions of authority. In less formal situations, you might say:

Je te présente *ma femme, Louise.*
I present to you my wife, Louise.

Among friends, you'd want to use the expression *c'est* or *ce sont*:

C'est *mon cousin, Yanis.*
This is my cousin, Yanis.

Ce sont *mes parents, Emma et Jules.*
These are my parents, Emma and Jules.

At some point, conversing in French, you might also be asked how many siblings you have. Note that in French, there is no one word for siblings. Instead we use the term *des frères et sœurs* (lit. brothers and sisters):

Vous avez combien de frères et sœurs ? (for.)
Tu as combien de frères et sœurs ? (inf.)
How many siblings do you have?

Does the word *combien* look familiar? A gold star for you if you remember that we learned it in the last chapter! *Combien ça coûte* means "how much does it cost". The word *combien* is a quantity interrogative pronoun that can be roughly translated to "how much" or "how many". Let's look at other examples:

__Tu as combien de cousins ?__
How many cousins do you have?

__Vous avez combien d'enfants ?__
How many children do you have?

Note that after *combien*, the preposition *de* is never plural. However, it contracts before a vowel and becomes *d'*. This might seem like an anomaly because in English there is no preposition used after "how many". In French though, *combien* always comes with *de* when followed by a noun. In a sense, it means, "how many of something". Look at the difference between the two sentences below:

__Combien coûte__ le billet ?
How much does the ticket cost?

Tu as __combien de voitures__ ?
How many cars do you have?

In the first example, *combien* is followed by the verb *coûter* (to cost). In the second, it is followed by the noun *voitures*, hence we add the preposition *de*.

To specify the number of family members one has, we use the verb *avoir*. Here are some examples:

- *J'ai deux frères et trois sœurs.*
- *J'ai un enfant.*
- *Nous avons quatre enfants.*
- *Anne a douze cousins !*

Possessive adjectives

We learned the equivalent of "your" in the previous chapter, *votre* and *vos*. It is important to remember that in French, possessive adjectives agree with the gender and number of the <u>noun referred to</u> and not the possessor. In English, one might say:

This is **his** car.

We choose "his", because we are referring to the male owner of the car. If the owner is female, we'll say:

This is **her** car.

In French, we would say:

*C'est **sa** voiture.*

The possessive adjective *sa* here can both mean "his" or "her". It has nothing to do with the gender of the possessor. But it has everything to do with the gender and number of the object possessed, *la voiture* which is a singular feminine noun.

*Ce sont **ses** voitures.*

This means "These are his/her cars". We use *ses* because this time, the object is plural.

Try translating this sentence: "This is her bag."

Remember that bag is a masculine noun in French, *un sac*. Again, we would disregard the gender of the possessor. So it would be: *C'est son sac.*

Below is a list of all the possessive adjectives in French:

Masc. singular	Fem. singular	Plural	Translation
mon	*ma* *mon* (before a vowel)	*mes*	my
ton	*ta* *ton* (before a vowel)	*tes*	your (inf.)
son	*sa* *son* (before a vowel)	*ses*	his / her / its
notre	*notre*	*nos*	our
votre	*votre*	*vos*	your (for.)
leur	*leur*	*leurs*	their

Note that if a feminine noun starts with a vowel, we will use the adjectives *mon*, *ton*, and *son*. Why? To make pronunciation easier. For example, "my address" would be *mon adresse*, even though *adresse* is feminine, simply because it's difficult to say *ma adresse*!

CULTURE TIP

Yes, I do.

In France, there are two main forms of union that can legally bind a couple. There is of course, the traditional marriage or *le mariage*. In 1999, the government created the *PACS* or *le Pacte Civil de Solidarité* (Civil Solidarity Pact), originally as a form of union for same-sex couples. Nowadays, many straight couples choose to get *PACSÉ* instead of getting married. While it does not provide the same legal rights as a marriage, it is much easier to dissolve. Couples do not have to go through a divorce, but simply have to send a letter to the court.

The law also recognizes *le concubinage*, and no, this does not mean having a concubine! It simply means that a couple is living together but is not bound by the same obligations as a marriage or a *PACS*.

To indicate your marital status, you use the verb *être*. For example, you can say:

- ***Je suis célibataire.*** I am single.
- ***Je suis marié(e).*** I am married.

- ***Je suis divorcé(e).*** I am divorced.
- ***Je suis pacsé(e).*** I am in a civil union.

Key Takeaways

- To present your family, you can use the following expressions: *Voici, Je vous présente, Je te présente, C'est* and *Ce sont.*
- To ask how many family members one has, we can use the expression *combien de,* which means "how many". The interrogative pronoun *combien* is combined with *de* only when followed by a noun.
- The possessive adjectives in the first person *je* are: *mon, ma* and *mes.*
- In the second person *tu* and *vous*: *ton, ta* and *tes; votre* and *vos.*
- In the first person *nous*: *notre* and *nos.*
- In the third person *il* and *elle*: *son, sa* and *ses.*
- Finally, in the third person plural *ils* and *elles*: *leur* and *leurs.*
- Possessive pronouns change in gender and number according to the noun it refers to and not according to that of the possessor.

In the next chapter, you will learn how to talk about your home and city. We will also study the prepositions of place.

Exercises

1. Complete the dialogue with the appropriate missing words:

    - Vous avez _____ enfants ?
    - J'ai trois enfants : deux filles et un fils.

2. Complete the dialogue with the appropriate missing words:

    - Bonjour, je vous _____ ma femme : Elle s'appelle Camille.
    - Enchanté Camille.

3-6. Read the following text. Are the statements that follow true or false?

   Jacques et Camille sont mariés. Ils ont quatre enfants : Sarah, Arthur, Hugo et Nathan. Sarah, Arthur et Hugo sont célibataires. Nathan est pacsé. Il a une fille. Elle s'appelle Nathalie.

   3. Camille est la femme de Jacques.
   4. Arthur est le frère de Sarah.
   5. Nathan a deux enfants.
   6. Jacques est le père de Nathalie.

7-10. Complete the following sentences with the correct possessive adjective, by looking at the indicated subject in the first sentence.

   7. Arthur a une voiture. C'est _____ voiture.
   8. Tom et Inès ont des livres. Ce sont _____ livres.
   9. Vous avez un enfant. C'est _____ enfant.
   10. J'ai une amie. C'est _____ amie.

Answer Key

1. combien d'
2. présente
3. True.
4. True.
5. False. Nathan has only one daughter.
6. False. Nathan is the father of Nathalie.
7. sa
8. leurs
9. votre
10. mon

Chapter 7: A city dweller

Comme une mère, une ville natale ne se remplace pas.

Like a mother, a hometown cannot be replaced.

- Albert Memmi

Knowing the names of places in a city is not only useful for when you travel to France. It also comes in handy when you want to talk about where you come from, your hometown, what you love (or don't particularly love?) about living there.

In this lesson, you will learn how to describe your home and your city. You will also learn how to indicate the location of a place using commonly used prepositions. Are you ready to talk about *chez toi*, your home? Let's get to it!

Talking about one's hometown

Birthplace

In Chapter 3, we learned the expression *Vous habitez où ?*, to ask where one comes from. To this, we can reply with the phrase *J'habite à*, followed by one's city and country.

An alternative way to ask about someone's hometown is by using the verb *naître* (to be born). For example,

Vous êtes né(e) où ?
Where were you born?

To reply, we might say,

Je suis né(e) à Tokyo.
I was born in Tokyo.

Note that when the person referred to is female, *né* is spelled with an extra –e. But both *né* and *née* are pronounced the same way, as /nay/. *Né* is the past participle of the verb *naître*. We will learn about the past tense later on. For now, memorize this fixed expression. Take note as well of the prepositions used with countries. We learned them in Chapter 3 (*en, au, aux*).

Places in the city vocabulary

	Translation
en ville	in the city
le centre-ville	downtown
un appartement	an apartment
un bâtiment	a building
un bureau de poste	a post office (colloquially, one would simply say *la poste*)
un café	a coffee shop
un centre commercial	a shopping mall
un cinéma	a cinema
un hôpital	a hospital
un hôtel	a hotel
un marché	a market
un musée	a museum
un parc	a park
un parking	a parking
un restaurant	a restaurant
un supermarché	a supermarket
un théâtre	a theater
une banque	a bank
une bibliothèque	a library
une école	a school
une gare	a train station
une mairie	a city hall or town hall
une station de métro	a subway station
une université	a university

Let's look at the text below. Pierre is describing his city, Paris:

> *J'habite dans un appartement à Paris. Dans ma ville, il y a un cinéma, un centre commercial, des musées, des théâtres, des restaurants... Il y a tout ! Mon appartement est à côté du restaurant Chez Jean et près de la station de métro. C'est loin de l'Université où je travaille, mais le loyer n'est pas cher.*

> I live in an apartment in Paris. In my city, there is a cinema, a mall, museums, theaters, restaurants... There is everything! My apartment is beside the Chez Jean restaurant and near the subway station. It is far from the University where I work, but the rent is not expensive.

To indicate places in your city, you can use *il y a*, which means "there is" or "there are". Note that *il y a* does not change according to the number of the noun that follows. Let's look at some examples:

*Dans ma ville, **il y a** une bibliothèque.*
In my city, there is a library.
*À Paris, **il y a** des hôtels et des restaurants partout !*
In Paris, there are hotels and restaurants everywhere!

*Dans ma ville, **il n'y a pas de** parcs.*
In my city, there are no parks.

Notice how we use *il n'y a pas de* to mean "There is no" or "there are no". Again, this is a fixed phrase that does not change according to the number of the noun.

Prepositions of place

To specify the location of a place, we use the following prepositions:

	Translation
dans	in, inside
près de	near
loin de	far from
devant	in front of
derrière	behind
en face de	across
à côté de	beside
sur	on, on top of
sous	under
à gauche de	to the left of
à droite de	to the right of

Using these prepositions may be a bit challenging because they often differ from their English counterparts in terms of structure. Let's break them down, starting with the simplest ones:

*Il y a un café **dans** le musée.*
There is a coffee shop in the museum.

*Il y a un café **devant** le musée.*
There is a coffee shop in front of the museum.

*Il y a un café **derrière** le musée.*
There is a coffee shop behind the museum.

In example 1, the coffee shop is found quite literally inside the museum, *dans le musée*. Note in example 2, that *devant* is not followed by a preposition unlike the English "in front of". All of the prepositions above are simply followed by an article, in this case *le*.

On the other hand, some require the preposition *de*:

Le restaurant est **près de** *l'université.*
The restaurant is near the university.

L'école est **loin des** *parcs.*
The school is far from the parks.

L'hôtel est **en face de la** *gare.*
The hotel is across the train station.

L'hôpital est **à côté du** *parc.*
The hospital is beside the park.

Le centre commercial est **à gauche de la** *mairie.*
The mall is to the left of the city hall.

Le cinéma est **à droite de la** *poste.*
The cinema is to the right of the post office.

The preposition *de* changes according to the gender and number of the noun. Here is a table that summarizes the four variations of *de*:

For nouns that...	Preposition *de*	Examples
start with a vowel	*de l'*	***de l'*** *école*
are masculine	*du*	***du*** *musée*
are feminine	*de la*	***de la*** *mairie*
are plural	*des*	***des*** *écoles,* ***des*** *musées*

Talking about one's home

In French slang, it is common to refer to one's home as *chez moi* (my place). To talk about the rooms in a house or an apartment, we use the expression *il y a*. For example:

Dans notre appartement, **il y a** *un salon, deux chambres, un bureau...*
In our apartment, there is a living room, two bedrooms, an office...

Try describing where you live. *Il y a combien de pièces ?* How many rooms are there? To help you out, we listed some common parts of the house below.

Parts of the house vocabulary

	Translation
un balcon	a balcony
un bureau	an office
un escalier	a staircase
un garage	a garage

un salon	a living room
un sous-sol	a basement
des w.c. (m.plur.)	toilets (w.c. is pronounced as /vay-say/)
des toilettes (f.plur.)	
une chambre	a bedroom
une cuisine	a kitchen
une maison	a house
une pièce	a room
une salle de bain	a bathroom
une terrasse	a patio

CULTURE TIP

Which floor again?

You rented an apartment in France. Everything is great. The landlord tells you it is located on the second floor. You go up the stairs, but your apartment is not there! Let's imagine another situation. Imagine a building that has 3 levels. Someone who lives in America will say that the building has three floors. A French native, however, would say there are two! Are the French counting differently? You start to wonder.

Yes, they are. In France, the first floor is not the first but the zero floor. Imagine the building with three levels again. In France, the first level is called the *rez-de-chaussée* (ground floor). The second level would be the first floor (*premier étage*) and the third level would be the (*deuxième étage*). Don't get confused ever again!

Speaking of levels, to form the ordinal numbers in French, we add –ième to the number. The only exception is the word for "first", *premier* or *première*. So that would be *premier/première, deuxième, troisième... dixième, onzième*, and so on.

Key Takeaways

- To ask where one is born, we say: *Vous êtes né(e) où ?*
- To indicate where one is born, we say: *Je suis né(e)* + preposition *à* + place.
- To indicate the existence of something, we use the expression *il y a* (there is / there are).
- The negated form of *il y a* is *il n'y a pas de* (there is no / there are no).
- The prepositions of place *dans, devant, derrière, sur* and *sous*, are always followed by an indefinite or a definite article.

- The prepositions *près de, loin de, en face de, à côté de, à gauche de* and *à droite de*, always require *de*.
- The preposition *de* changes according to the gender and number of the noun, or its first letter: *de l'* (before a vowel), *du* (m.), *de la* (f.), *des* (plur.).
- French ordinal numbers are formed by adding –ième to the number. The word "first", *premier* (m.) or *première* (f.), is an exception.

In the next chapter, you will learn how to talk about your hobbies. We will also look at tonic pronouns and two verbs, *faire* (to do) and *jouer* (to play).

Exercises

1. Answer the following question using the expressions learned: *Vous êtes né(e) où ?*

2-5. Read the following text. Are the statements that follow true or false?

> **Pierre**: *Dans ma ville, il y a un cinéma, un centre commercial, un restaurant... mais il n'y a pas de bibliothèques. Mon appartement est à côté du bureau de poste et près de la banque. C'est très pratique.*

    2. In Pierre's city, there are no libraries.
    3. Pierre's apartment is far from the bank.
    4. There is a shopping mall in Pierre's city.
    5. Pierre's apartment is behind the post office.

6-8. Complete the sentences with the correct form of the preposition *de*.

    6. La gare est loin _____ université.
    7. Le cinéma est à gauche _____ café.
    8. Le parking est en face _____ restaurants.

9-10. Read the description and indicate the corresponding room in French.

    9. It is the room where one sleeps.
    10. It is the room where one welcomes guests.

Answer Key

1. Sample answer: Je suis né(e) aux États-Unis OR Je suis né(e) à New York.
2. True.
3. False. It is near the bank.
4. True.
5. False. It is beside the post office.
6. de l'
7. du
8. des
9. Une chambre OR la chambre.
10. Un salon OR le salon.

Chapter 8: The ball's in your court!

Le loisir, voilà la plus grande joie et la plus belle conquête de l'homme.

Leisure, this is the greatest joy and the most beautiful conquest of man.

- Rémy de Gourmont

Friendships are often formed on the basis of a shared pastime. What better way to make friends with French speakers than to share your hobbies or your likes and dislikes?

In this lesson, we will learn how to talk about leisure activities, such as music or sports. To be able to do so, you will need to study two verbs, *faire* (to do) and *jouer* (to play). We will also look at verb negation and tonic pronouns.

Talking about one's likes and dislikes

To ask about someone's hobbies, you can say:

Quels sont vos loisirs ?
What are your hobbies?

To talk about your likes and dislikes, you can use the following expressions:

***J'aime** la cuisine.*
I like cooking.

***J'adore** les animaux.*
I love animals.

***Je n'aime pas** le sport.*
I don't like sports.

***Je déteste** la lecture.*
I hate reading.

As you might have noticed, these expressions are followed by a noun, preceded by a definite article. This is an important rule to remember: when talking about something in general, for example, sports (*le sport*) or animals (*les animaux*), we always use definite articles.

The expressions above can also be followed by a verb. For example:

*J'aime **cuisiner**.*
I like cooking.

*J'adore **lire**.*
I love reading.

*Je n'aime pas **chanter**.*
I don't like singing.

*Je déteste **danser**.*
I hate dancing.

Note that the second verbs are in the infinitive, meaning they are not conjugated. For example in the sentence *Je n'aime pas chanter*, the verb *chanter* is in the infinitive form. When combining two verbs in French, it is only the first verb that is conjugated.

GRAMMAR TIP

Negation

To negate a verb, we simply add the words *ne* or *n'* and *pas*. Use *n'* if the verb starts with a vowel or a silent h. These two elements "sandwich" the main verb. For example:

- ***Je chante.*** I sing.
- ***Je ne chante pas.*** I don't sing.

We put *ne* before the verb and *pas* after it. Remember to contract the *ne* before a vowel:

- ***J'aime le sport.*** I like sports.
- ***Je n'aime pas le sport.*** I don't like sports.

Hobbies vocabulary

	Translation
la cuisine	cooking
la danse	dancing
la lecture	reading
la mode	fashion
la musique	music
la peinture	painting
le chant	singing
le jardinage	gardening
le sport	sports
le voyage	traveling
les jeux vidéo	video games

Which of the following activities above do you like doing? Try saying them aloud using the expressions we learned: *j'aime, j'adore, je n'aime pas* or *je déteste*.

Tonic pronouns

Tonic pronouns are used to emphasize the subject of a sentence. For example, we can say:

Moi, *j'aime la cuisine.* **Lui,** *il déteste la cuisine.*
Me, I like cooking. Him, he hates cooking.

Here are the corresponding tonic pronouns according to the subject:

Subject	Tonic pronoun
je	*moi*
tu	*toi*
il	*lui*
elle	*elle*
nous	*nous*
vous	*vous*
ils	*eux*
elles	*elles*

Let's look at some more examples:

***Eux**, ils adorent le sport.*
Them, they love sports.

***Elle**, elle n'aime pas la lecture.*
Her, she hates reading.

Talking about one's hobbies

To talk about one's hobbies, we use the verbs *faire* (to do) and *jouer* (to play). These two verbs are not interchangeable. Each one is used with a specific area of activity.

Sports

The verb *jouer* is generally used to talk about doing sports or playing a musical instrument. When talking about sports, it is followed by the preposition *à*. This preposition, as always, changes according to the gender and number of the noun:

Je joue au foot.
I play football.

Nous jouons au tennis.
We play tennis.

Elle aime jouer au volley.
I like playing volleyball.

Tu joues aux échecs ?
Do you play chess?

The preposition *à* changes accordingly:

For nouns that...	Preposition *à*
are feminine	*à la*
start with a vowel	*à l'*
are masculine	*au*
are plural	*aux*

In Chapter 3, we learned that the preposition *à* changes to *en*, *au* and *aux* before countries. This is only the case with <u>countries</u>. With general nouns, we follow the forms summarized in the table above.

We also use the verb *faire* with sports, usually when it is a sport done alone or when it does not involve the use of tools like ball, bat, etc.

Nous faisons de la boxe.
We box.

Je fais de la natation.
I swim.

Louise fait du jogging tous les jours.
Louise jogs every day.

Music

When talking about music, we also use the verb *jouer*, but with the preposition *de*:

Il joue du piano.
He plays the piano.

Martin joue de la guitare.
Martin plays the guitar.

As we learned in the previous chapter, *de* changes according to the gender and number of the noun:

For nouns that...	Preposition *de*
are feminine	*de la*
start with a vowel	*de l'*
are masculine	*du*
are plural	*des*

GRAMMAR TIP

The verb *faire*

The verb faire translates to "to do" or "to make". It is an irregular verb that is conjugated as follows:

	faire
Je	fais
Tu	fais
Il/Elle	fait
Nous	faisons
Vous	faites
Ils/Elles	font

Sports and music vocabulary

In the vocabulary list below, we included the verbal phrase that goes with each activity. This way, you will best remember whether to use *faire* or *jouer*.

	Translation
faire de l'équitation	to go horseback riding
faire de la boxe	to box
faire de la natation	to swim
faire de la randonnée	to go mountain climbing
faire du ski	to ski
faire du vélo	to bike
jouer au basket	to play basketball
jouer au foot	to play football
jouer au tennis	to play tennis
jouer au volley	to play volleyball
jouer aux cartes	to play cards
jouer de la batterie	to play drums
jouer de la guitare	to play the guitar
jouer du piano	to play the piano
jouer du violon	to play the violin

> **CULTURE TIP**
>
> *Fans of pétanque*
>
> *La pétanque* is a popular French sport played outdoors. There are usually two teams that compete. Each takes turns to throw *une boule*, a metallic ball about the size of an apple, towards a smaller ball called *le cochonnet*. The one who gets it closest to the *cochonnet* gains points.

Key Takeaways

- To ask or indicate one's hobbies, we use the following expressions:

Ask one's hobbies	
Quels sont vos loisirs ?	
Indicate one's hobbies	
J'aime...	+ definite article and noun
J'adore...	
Je n'aime pas...	OR
Je déteste...	+ verb

- To negate a verb, we simply place it in between *ne* or *n'* and *pas*.
- Tonic pronouns are used to emphasize the subject of a sentence: *moi, toi, lui, elle, nous, vous, eux* and *elles*.
- The verb *jouer* is generally used to talk about sports and music. Before sports-related nouns, we use the preposition *à* (*à l'*, *au*, *à la*, *aux*). Before music-related nouns, we use *de* (*de la*, *de l'*, *du*, *des*).
- The verb *faire* is used to talk about sports done alone. It is followed by the preposition *de*.
- We conjugate the verb *faire* as follows: *je fais, tu fais, il/elle fait, nous faisons, vous faites, ils/elles font*.

In the next chapter, we move to the realm of food. You will learn how to buy at the market, ask for prices and indicate quantities. We will also study how to say numbers above 100 in French.

Exercises

1-5. *Faire de, jouer de* or *jouer à*? Complete the sentences with the appropriate verbal phrase. Don't forget to conjugate the verbs and change the prepositions according to the gender and number of the noun.

    1. Sarah _____ ski.
    2. Je _____ guitare.
    3. Elle aime _____ basket.
    4. Tu _____ cartes ?
    5. Louise et Nathan _____ natation.

6-8. Read the text below and indicate whether the statements are true or false.

> *Pierre aime la musique et le sport. Il joue du piano et de la guitare. Le week-end, il joue au foot dans le parc avec ses amis. Parfois, il fait aussi de la natation. Sa femme, Camille, adore aussi la musique. Elle, elle joue du violon.*

    6. Both Pierre and his wife can play musical instruments.
    7. Camille plays football during weekends.
    8. Pierre knows how to swim.

9. Negate the following sentence: *J'aime la peinture.*

10. Negate the following sentence: *Adrien aime la danse.*

Answer Key

1. fait du
2. joue de la
3. jouer au
4. joues aux
5. font de la
6. True.
7. False. It is Pierre who does.
8. True.
9. Je n'aime pas la peinture.
10. Adrien n'aime pas la danse.

Chapter 9: Beyond baguettes

Faute de pain, on mange de la galette.

For lack of bread, we eat pancakes.

- Quebec proverb

France, a paradise for food-lovers! When one thinks of France, food – bread and cheese in particular – comes to mind. If traveling to France, it would be a foodie's mistake not to try the famous *baguettes* and *croissants* fresh from the oven of a traditional bakery. Those who love fruits would want to visit the *marché* (market) for some fresh produce.

In this lesson, you will learn how to communicate in food-related, buy-and-sell situations. You will learn how to ask for prices and indicate quantities. Finally, we will also study how to read numbers above 100.

At the bakery

It's 8 a.m. and Pierre goes to a bakery to buy some breakfast:

Pierre: *Bonjour Madame.* ***Je voudrais*** *une baguette, quatre pains au chocolat et une tarte aux fraises.*
Vendor: *Bien sûr...* ***et avec ceci ?***
Pierre: ***Je vais aussi prendre*** *une baguette.*
Vendor: *D'accord.* ***Ce sera tout ?***
Pierre: *Oui. C'est combien s'il vous plaît ?*
Vendor: ***Ça vous fait*** *9 euros.*

We already learned how to use the expression *je voudrais* (I would like) to ask for something in French. Like Pierre, you can also say *je vais aussi prendre* (I will also take) to ask for something else.

It is useful to remember the phrases a vendor might say, so you can reply!

Et avec ceci ?
What else would you like? (lit. And with that?)

Ce sera tout ?
Would that be all?

Baked goods vocabulary

	Translation
un croissant	a croissant
un gâteau	a cake
un gâteau au chocolat	a chocolate cake
une baguette	a baguette
une tarte	a pie
une tarte aux fraises	a strawberry pie
une tarte au citron	a lemon pie
un pain au chocolat	a chocolate bread
un chausson aux pommes	an apple turnover
un pain complet	a whole-wheat bread
un pain de mie	a sandwich loaf

Pro tip: flavors in French are generally preceded by the preposition *à*. For example, a lemon pie would be *une tarte **au** citron*, while strawberry ice cream would be *une glace **à la** fraise*.

Asking or indicating price

Remember that we previously learned *Combien ça coûte ?* to ask for the price of something. You can also say *C'est combien ?* Or at the counter, you can ask for the total price by saying *Ça fait combien ?* Vendors would often indicate the price using the same expression: *Ça fait ... euros*.

At the fruit stand

Hélène goes to the market to buy some fruits:

Hélène: *Bonjour Monsieur, je voudrais 500 grammes de fraises, deux melons et un kilo de pommes.*
Vendor: *Voilà Madame. Ce sera tout ?*
Hélène: *Oui, merci. Ça fait combien ?*
Vendor: *Ça vous fait 17 euros. **Vous payez par carte ou en espèces ?***
Hélène: *Je vais payer par carte.*

Indicating mode of payment

A vendor might ask you how you wish to pay:

Vous payez par carte ou en espèces ?
Do you pay by card or with cash?

To which, you can reply:

Je vais payer par carte.
I will pay by card.

Je vais payer en espèces.
I will pay with cash.

Indicating quantity

To indicate quantity, we can use the following measure words: *un kilo* (a kilo), *un litre* (a liter), *une douzaine* (a dozen). The term *un demi-kilo* is rarely used to mean "half a kilo", instead we say *500 grammes* (500 grams).

All of these measure words are followed by the preposition *de*. This time, *de* does not change according to the gender and number. It does however contract before a vowel. So for example, *un kilo **de** fraises*, *un kilo **d'**abricots*.

Here are other useful measure words:

	Translation
un peu de	a little bit of
	ex. **un peu de** *persil* (a little bit of parsley)
beaucoup de	a lot of, many
	ex. **beaucoup de** *fruits* (a lot of fruits)
une tranche de	a slice of
	ex. **une tranche de** *jambon* (a slice of ham)
un morceau de	a piece of, a slice of
	ex. **un morceau de** *fromage* (a slice of cheese)
une bouteille de	a bottle of
	ex. **une bouteille d'***huile* (a bottle of oil)

CULTURE TIP

The many meanings of baguette

Did you know that the word *baguette* in French does not only refer to the famous bread? We also call the following *une baguette*:

- A magician's wand
- A musical conductor's baton

- A musical drumstick
- Chopsticks

Like the bread, all of these objects have the same elongated shape! Note that chopsticks are always in plural form, *des baguettes*.

Fruits and vegetables vocabulary

Fruits	Translation
des cerises	cherries
du raisin	grapes
un abricot	an apricot
un ananas	a pineapple
un citron	a lemon
une banane	a banana
une fraise	a strawberry
une orange	an orange
une pêche	a peach
une poire	a pear
une pomme	an apple
Vegetables	**Translation**
de l'ail	garlic
des haricots verts	green beans
un brocoli	a broccoli
un chou	a cabbage
un oignon	an onion
une aubergine	an eggplant
une carotte	a carrot
une pomme de terre	a potato
une salade	a lettuce
une tomate	a tomato

Numbers 100 above

To count from 100 up, we use the following words:

cent 100, hundred
mille 1000, thousand
million 1 000 000, million
milliard 1 000 000 000, billion

Surely no baguette would cost a billion. Still, it is useful to memorize them. To form numbers 100 and above, we follow the same structure in English. Assemble the numbers from biggest to smallest. For example: hundred + tens + units.

100 *cent*
200 *deux-cents*
235 *deux-cent-trente-cinq*
500 *cinq-cents*
555 *cinq-cent-cinquante-cinq*

Notice that the –s in *cents* disappears when followed by other numerals. Let's look at higher numbers:

1 000 *mille*
2 379 *deux-mille-trois-cent-soixante-dix-neuf*

Or even higher:

2 000 000 *deux-millions*
2 900 110 *deux-millions-neuf-cent-mille-cent-dix*

When indicating a price, the French distinguish cents by placing it after the euros. For example: 10,50€ is read as *dix euros cinquante centimes* or simply, *dix euros cinquante*. In written French, the cent unit is separated with a comma not a period.

Key Takeaways

- Here are the expressions you must know when buying at the bakery or at the market:

Je voudrais…
Je vais aussi prendre…
Ask for price
C'est combien ?
Ça fait combien ?
Combien ça coûte ?
Indicate price
Ça fait … euros.
Ask or indicate mode of payment

Vous payez par carte ou en espèces ?
Je vais payer par carte.
Je vais payer en espèces.

- To indicate quantity, we use measure words like *un kilo, un litre, une douzaine, 500 grammes, un peu de, beaucoup de, une tranche de, un morceau de* and *une bouteille de*. The preposition *de* contracts to *d'* before a vowel but does not change otherwise.
- To count from 100 up, we use the following words: *cent, mille, million, milliard.*
- We form numbers starting with the biggest unit to the smallest.
- To distinguish cents in prices, we say *euros* before the cents.

In the next chapter, we head to the skies. You will learn how to describe the weather and talk about seasons. We will also study some French weather idioms to help you sound like a real native!

Exercises

1-5. Complete the dialogue with the appropriate missing words:

aussi – payer – ceci - voudrais – combien

- Bonjour Monsieur. Je 1._____ une baguette s'il vous plaît.
- Et avec 2._____ ?
- Je vais 3._____ prendre deux croissants.
- Ce sera tout ?
- Oui, ça fait 4._____ ?
- Cinq euros trente.
- Je vais 5._____ en espèces.

6-10. Write the following numbers in words:

6. 800
7. 420
8. 1930
9. 30,75€
10. 40 800

Answer Key

1. voudrais
2. ceci
3. aussi
4. combien
5. payer
6. huit-cents
7. quatre-cent-vingt
8. mille-neuf-cent-trente
9. trente euros soixante-quinze (centimes)
10. quarante-mille-huit-cents

Chapter 10: No rain check allowed

Les raisons d'aimer et de vivre, varient comme font les saisons.

The reasons for loving and living, vary like the seasons.

- Louis Aragon

One of the most common topics when making small talk is the weather. In fact, in French, there is an expression that directly links small talk to weather: *parler de la pluie et du beau temps*, which means "to make small talk" (the literal translation is "to talk about the rain and the good weather").

In this lesson, you will learn how to ask about and describe the weather. We will also learn the words for seasons in French.

Weather

Asking about the weather

To refer to the weather, we can use the words *le temps* or *la météo*. *Le temps* refers to the climate while *la météo* refers to the weather or weather forecast. Note that *le temps* is also the general word for "time".

To ask what the weather's like, we say:

> ***Quel temps fait-il ?*** (for.)
> ***Il fait quel temps ?*** (inf.)
> What's the weather like?

To ask about the temperature, we say:

> ***Quelle température fait-il ?*** (for.)
> ***Il fait quelle température ?*** (inf.)
> What is the temperature?

In France, the Celsius is used. You don't have to specify it though when indicating the temperature.

Describing the weather

There are three ways to describe the weather. First, using the fixed expression *il fait*:

- ***Il fait beau.*** The weather is nice.
- ***Il fait mauvais.*** The weather is bad.
- ***Il ne fait pas beau.*** The weather is not nice.
- ***Il fait chaud.*** It's hot.
- ***Il fait froid.*** It's cold.

- **Il fait 30 degrés**. It's 30 degrees (Celsius).

Don't be tempted to use the verb *être* to describe the weather. While in English, one might say "It is hot", in French, it is incorrect to say *Il est chaud* when referring to the climate. We have to use the expression *il fait*, as in *il fait chaud*.

The second way to describe the weather involves using specific verbs:

- **Il pleut**. It's raining.
- **Il neige**. It's snowing.

Finally, you can use the expression *il y a* with the preposition *de*:

- **Il y a du brouillard**. It's foggy. (lit. There is fog.)
- **Il y a du vent**. It's windy. (lit. There is wind.)
- **Il y a de l'orage**. There's a storm.
- **Il y a des nuages**. It's cloudy. (lit. There are clouds.)
- **Il y a du soleil**. It's sunny. (lit. There is sun.)

By now, you probably know that the preposition *de* changes in form to correspond to the gender and number of the noun it follows.

Weather vocabulary

Here are other useful vocabularies related to weather:

	Translation
la lune	the moon
la grêle	the hail
la neige	the snow
la pluie	the rain
le soleil	the sun
le tonnerre	the thunder
un arc-en-ciel	a rainbow
un éclair	a lightning
une étoile	a star
un thermomètre	a thermometer
une tempête	a storm

CULTURE TIP
Some weather idioms

Learning some weather idioms is a great way to sound like a native. We list below three expressions that are used in colloquial French:

- ***Il fait un soleil de plomb !***

    The sun is blazing hot.
- ***Il pleut des cordes.***

    It's raining heavily. (lit. It's raining ropes)
- ***Il fait un froid de canard.***

    It's freezing. (lit. It's duck-like cold)

Seasons

Let us now talk about *les saisons* (seasons). Read the text below. Can you tell how the four seasons are called in French?

> ***Au printemps, de mars à juin, il fait beau. Après le printemps, c'est l'été. En été, de juin à septembre, il fait chaud. En automne, de septembre à décembre, les feuilles tombent. En hiver, de décembre à mars, il fait froid.***

> In the spring, from March to June, the weather is nice. After spring, it's summer. In summer, from June to September, it is hot. In fall, from September to December, the leaves fall. In winter, from December to March, it is cold.

Did you guess right? The four seasons are:

- ***Le printemps*** spring
- ***L'été*** summer
- ***L'automne*** fall
- ***L'hiver*** winter

Take note that we use the preposition *en* with the *été, automne* and *hiver*. For *printemps*, the preposition *au* is used:

- ***au printemps*** in spring
- ***en été*** in summer
- ***en automne*** in fall
- ***en hiver*** in winter

Key Takeaways

- There are three ways to describe the weather: (1) with *il fait*, (2) with specific verbs and (3) with *il y a*:

Ask about the weather	
Quel temps fait-il ? (for.)	
Il fait quel temps ? (inf.)	
Quelle température fait-il ? (for.)	
Il fait quelle température ? (inf.)	
Describe the weather	
Il fait	*beau.*
	mauvais.
	chaud.
	froid.
	... degrés.
Il pleut.	
Il neige.	
Il y a	*du brouillard.*
	du vent.
	de l'orage.
	des nuages.
	du soleil.

- The four seasons are: *le printemps, l'été, l'automne* and *l'hiver*. We use the preposition *au* with *printemps*, and *en* with the other three.

In the next chapter, we will talk about time. You will finally be able to use those numbers you memorized from the previous chapters! We will also study the days of the week in French.

Exercises

1-5. Translate the following sentences:

    1. It is sunny.
    2. It is hot.
    3. The weather is nice.
    4. There's a storm.
    5. What's the weather like?

6-8. Specify the season being described.

    6. The season when people go to the beach.
    7. The season when people wear heavy coats.
    8. The season when leaves fall.

9. Complete the dialogue with the missing word:

    - *Il fait quelle _____ ?*
    - *Il fait 23 degrés.*

10. Complete the idiomatic expression: *Il fait un _____ de canard!*

Answer Key

1. Il y a du soleil.
2. Il fait chaud.
3. Il fait beau.
4. Il y a de l'orage.
5. Quel temps fait-il ? OR Il fait quel temps ?
6. En été.
7. En hiver.
8. En automne.
9. température
10. froid

Chapter 11: The hands of time

Le temps adoucit tout.

Time softens everything.

- Voltaire

Time structures our everyday lives. We plan our days by the hour, sometimes even by the minute. We wake up at a certain time, go to work or school at this time, come home at this time; meet up with friends at this time, and so on. Being able to tell the time is thus an important skill to have when learning not just French, but any language.

In this chapter, you will learn how to tell time. We will also study how to indicate dates. Telling time in French is not particularly difficult. Quite often, what intimidates learners is the mastery of numbers required to naturally and speedily read time. Feel free to review the numbers in Chapters 2, 5 and 9 or consult the annex for the complete list.

Time

We learned in the previous chapter that *le temps* can mean both weather (as in the phrase *il fait quel temps ?*) or time, in the general sense. For instance, to say "I spend my time watching films", you can say *Je passe mon temps à regarder des films*. Or, if someone invites you out but you're busy, you might say *Désolé(e), je n'ai pas le temps* (Sorry, I don't have time.) Le temps is also used in fixed expressions:

- ***de temps en temps*** from time to time
- ***la plupart du temps*** most of the time
- ***pendant ce temps*** during this time.

Now, when we are referring to time as in <u>clock</u> time, we use the term *l'heure* (f.). For example, to ask and tell the time, you use *l'heure* and not *le temps*.

L'heure (f.) literally translates to "hour". Minutes in French is *minutes* (f.), while seconds is *secondes* (f.). The C in *secondes* is pronounced like a hard g, like the g in the English word *guitar*.

Asking the time

To ask what time it is, you can say:

Quelle heure est-il ? (for.)
Il est quelle heure ? (inf.)
What time is it?

This is a fixed expression. The pronoun *il* never changes. You can also say:

Vous avez l'heure ? (for.)
Tu as l'heure ? (inf.)

Do you have the time?

Telling the time

To tell the time, you use the expression *Il est*:

Il est 12h00.
It is 12 o'clock.

Il est 9h30.
It is 9:30 a.m.

There are a few things to keep in mind:
- French time uses the 24-hour clock military time. So for example, 1 p.m. would be *treize heures* or 13h.
- Note that when written down, French hours are not separated from the minutes with a colon. Instead, the letter h for *heure* is used. For example, 10:30 would be written as *10h30*.
- There are words for a.m. (*du matin*) and p.m. (*de l'après-midi* for until 6 p.m. and *du soir* for later) but they are rarely used. Since we refer to a 24-hour clock, it is clear that when we say *14h* for example, we mean 2 in the afternoon.

To tell the time, we say *il est* + numbers 1 to 24 + *heures* + number of minutes. While in English, you can omit the "o'clock" and say for instance, "It's 8". In French, you cannot omit the word *heure*. Let's look at some examples:

Il est neuf heures.	It is 9 a.m.
Il est six heures dix.	It is 6:10 a.m.
Il est quatorze heures.	It is 2 p.m.
Il est quinze heures vingt-cinq.	It is 3:25 p.m.
Il est vingt-deux heures.	It is 10 p.m.

We say *midi* for noon and *minuit* for midnight:

Il est midi.	It is noon.
Il est minuit.	It is midnight.

Now, to say "half past", we use the term *demi* or *demie*. "Quarter past" would be *et quart* and "quarter to" would be *moins le quart*. Look at the examples below:

Il est six heures et demie.	It is 6:30 a.m.
Il est dix heures et demie.	It is 10:30 a.m.
Il est midi et demi.	It is 12:30 p.m.
Il est minuit et demi.	It is 00:30 a.m.
Il est huit heures et quart.	It is 8:15 a.m.
Il est sept heures moins le quart.	It is 6:45 a.m.

Except for *midi* and *minuit*, we always write *demie* with an –e. Note that *demi(e)* can only be used from 1 to 12. Past twelve, we use the word thirty or *trente*:

Il est quatorze heures trente.	It is 2:30 p.m.
Il est vingt-trois heures trente.	It is 11:30 p.m.

For 31 to 59 minutes past the hour, we can use the word *moins* (less) the number of minutes. For example:

Il est dix heures moins vingt.	It is 9:40 a.m. (lit. It is 10 hrs. minus 20.)
Il est onze heures moins dix.	It is 10:50 a.m. (lit. It is 11 hrs. minus 10.)

When referring to time in general sentences, we use the preposition *à*. For example:
- *Je finis le travail à 18h.* I finish work at 6 p.m.
- *Les enfants rentrent à 15h.* The kids come home at 3 p.m.

GRAMMAR TIP
-IR verbs

To conjugate regular –IR verbs in the present tense, we simply remove the –ir of the infinitive form and replace them with a set of fixed endings. And so, for example, we remove the –ir in the verb *finir* (to finish) and then we add the appropriate endings:

finir → *fin*		
Je	+is	fin**is**
Tu	+is	fin**is**
Il/Elle/On	+it	fin**it**
Nous	+issons	fin**issons**
Vous	+issez	fin**issez**
Ils/Elles	+issent	fin**issent**

Date

Asking and indicating the day

The word for a day in French is *un jour*. You can ask the day of the week using the following expressions:

Quel jour sommes-nous aujourd'hui ? (for.)
Nous sommes quel jour aujourd'hui ? (for.)
On est quel jour aujourd'hui ? (inf.)
What day is it today?

To indicate the day, we say: *Nous sommes* (for.) or *On est* (inf.) + the day.

Nous sommes lundi.
It's Monday (lit. We are Monday.)

On est mardi.
It's Tuesday (lit. We are Tuesday.)

Days of the week vocabulary

	Translation
lundi	Monday
mardi	Tuesday
mercredi	Wednesday
jeudi	Thursday
vendredi	Friday
samedi	Saturday
dimanche	Sunday

Asking and indicating the date

The word for the date in French is *la date*. You can ask the date using the following expressions:

Quelle date sommes-nous aujourd'hui ? (for.)
On est quelle date aujourd'hui ? (inf.)
What date is it today?

To indicate the day, we say: *Nous sommes* (for.) or *On est* (inf.) + the day.

Nous sommes le 6 octobre.
It's October 6th.

On est le 3 janvier.
It's January 3rd.

For the first day of the month, use the ordinal number *premier*:

On est le premier mars.
It's March 1st.

Note that the dates in French are written starting with the day and not the month. They are always preceded by the article *le*. To say your birthdate for example:

Je suis né(e) le 2 août 1989.
I was born on August 2nd, 1989.

Months vocabulary

The word for a month in French is *un mois*. A year is *une année*.

	Translation
janvier	January
février	February
mars	March
avril	April
mai	May
juin	June
juillet	July
août	August
septembre	September
octobre	October
novembre	November
décembre	December

In French, the months are not capitalized. When indicating a month (<u>without</u> the day), we use the preposition *en*. For example, "in January" would be *en janvier*, "in March", *en mars*, and so on.

Key Takeaways

- *Le temps* refers to time in general while *l'heure* refers to clock time.
- To ask or indicate the time and date, we use the following expressions:

Ask and tell time	
Quelle heure est-il ? (for.) *Il est quelle heure ? (inf.)* *Vous avez l'heure ? (for.)* *Tu as l'heure ? (inf.)*	*Il est... heures.*
Ask and tell dates	

Quel jour sommes-nous aujourd'hui ? (for.) *Nous sommes quel jour aujourd'hui ? (for.)* *On est quel jour aujourd'hui ? (inf.)*	*Nous sommes* *On est* + day
Quelle date sommes-nous aujourd'hui ? (for.) *On est quelle date aujourd'hui ? (inf.)*	*Nous sommes le* *On est le* + date

- We can also indicate time using the fixed expressions: *demi(e), et quart, moins le quart* and *moins*.
- The days in French are: *lundi, mardi, mercredi, jeudi, vendredi, samedi* and *dimanche*.
- The months in French are: *janvier, février, mars, avril, mai, juin, juillet, août, septembre, octobre, novembre* and *décembre*. We use the preposition *en* with months.
- To conjugate -IR verbs, we replace the ending with the following: *-is, -is, -it, -issons, -issez* and *-issent*.

In the next chapter, you will learn how to talk about your daily routine. You will also learn expressions of time and frequency, alongside pronominal verbs.

Exercises

1-5. Complete the short dialogues with the missing words:

1. - *On est quel _____ aujourd'hui ?*
   - *On est samedi.*
2. - *Quelle _____ est-il ?*
   - *Il est midi.*
3. - *Nous sommes _____ date aujourd'hui ?*
   - *Nous sommes le 20 mai.*
4. - *Tu as l'heure ?*
   - *Oui, _____ est 13 heures.*
5. - *Nous sommes quel jour aujourd'hui ?*
   - *Nous _____ mercredi.*

6-10. Write the following times in words:

6. It's 3 p.m.
7. It's 4:45 a.m.
8. It's noon.
9. It's 7:30 a.m.
10. It's 6:30 p.m.

Answer Key

1. jour
2. heure
3. quelle
4. il
5. sommes
6. Il est quinze heures.
7. Il est cinq heures moins le quart. OR Il est quatre heures quarante-cinq.
8. Il est midi.
9. Il est sept heures et demie.
10. Il est dix-huit heures trente.

Chapter 12: An ordinary day

L'habitude est une seconde nature.

Habit is second nature.

- Augustin D'Hippone

If time structures our lives, habits are the ones that constitute them. For most people, the order of the day is clear. They wake up, eat breakfast, brush their teeth, take a shower then go to work or school, then come back home. Routines, schedules and habits are what organize our days.

In this lesson, you will learn how to talk about your daily routine. In order to do so, you would need to master pronominal verbs and expressions of frequency.

Talking about daily habits

In the text below, Pierre describes his daily routine:

> **Je me réveille** tous les jours à 8h. Ensuite, **je me lève**… **Je me prépare** pour aller au travail : **je me douche**, **je me rase** et **je m'habille**. Je prends mon petit-déjeuner, puis **je me brosse** les dents. Je vais au travail à 9h. Je rentre vers 18h. Le soir, **je me repose** devant un film. Je dîne. Puis, à 22h, **je me couche**.

> I wake up every day at 8 a.m. Then I get up… I get ready to go to work: I shower, I shave and I get dressed. I eat my breakfast, then I brush my teeth. I go to work at 9 a.m. I come back at around 6 p.m. In the evening, I rest in front of a movie. I eat dinner. Then, at 10 p.m., I go to bed.

The verbs in bold are what we call "pronominal verbs". You already encountered one in the first chapter, the verb *s'appeler*.

There are a lot of pronominal verbs used when talking about daily routines. To start, what are they?

Pronominal verbs

In English, there are no pronominal verbs. In French, these are verbs combined with pronouns, hence the appellation *pronominal*. These verbs are always composed of two parts, a pronoun and a verb. They are reflexive, meaning the action or verb is done to the subject of the sentence. Look at these two sentences:

Je me douche. I take a shower.
Je douche… I shower…

The first one has the pronominal verb *me doucher* which literally means, "to shower myself". So, *je me douche* means, "I take a shower". The second one means: I shower… probably someone else! Without the reflexive pronoun *me*, you will be saying that you're giving someone else a bath!

Remember that not all verbs in French are pronominal. Let's look at other verbs within this category:

	Translation
s'endormir	to fall asleep
s'habiller	to get dressed
se coucher	to go to bed
se déshabiller	to undress
se doucher	to take a shower
se lever	to get up
se maquiller	to put makeup on
se préparer	to get ready
se raser	to shave oneself
se reposer	to rest
se réveiller	to wake up

How then do we conjugate pronominal verbs? Just like *s'appeler*, the reflexive pronoun changes according to the subject. The verb is then conjugated according to its ending. For example:

se réveiller

Je	me réveille
Tu	te réveilles
Il/Elle	se réveille
Nous	nous réveillons
Vous	vous réveillez
Ils/Elles	se réveillent

Daily activities vocabulary

Here are other daily activities you should remember:

	Translation
aller à l'école	to go to school
aller à l'université	to go to the university
aller à la fac	to go to the university (slang)
aller au travail	to go to work
boire du café	to drink coffee
déjeuner	to eat lunch
dîner	to eat dinner

lire le journal	to read the newspaper
manger	to eat
prendre le petit-déjeuner	to eat breakfast
regarder la télé	to watch TV
rentrer	to go home

GRAMMAR TIP

The verb *aller*

The verb *aller* means "to go". It is an irregular verb that is conjugated as follows:

	aller
Je	vais
Tu	vas
Il/Elle	va
Nous	allons
Vous	allez
Ils/Elles	vont

Let's look at this verb in context:

- ***Je vais au travail à 8h.*** I go to work at 8 a.m.
- ***Vous allez au cinéma ?*** Are you going to the cinema?
- ***Nous allons au parc.*** We are going to the park.

Indicating frequency

When talking about habits, it is essential to know expressions of time and adverbs of frequency.

Expressions of time

To indicate the moments of the day, we can say:
- *le matin* in the morning
- *l'après-midi* in the afternoon
- *le soir* in the evening

Other common expressions include:
- *tôt* early
- *tard* late
- *maintenant* right now
- *plus tard* later
- *aujourd'hui* today
- *hier* yesterday
- *demain* tomorrow

Adverbs of frequency

	Translation
de temps en temps	from time to time
d'habitude	usually
fréquemment	frequently, often
en général	generally
généralement	
parfois	sometimes
rarement	rarely, seldom
toujours	always
tous les jours	everyday
tous les lundis	every Monday
tous les mois	every month
toutes les semaines	every week
une fois par semaine	once a week
deux fois par semaine	twice a week

In general, adverbs in French are placed after the verb. For example, we can say:

*Je me maquille **rarement**.*
I rarely put makeup on.

*Lucile lit **toujours** le journal.*
Lucile always reads the newspaper.

However, certain adverbs like *d'habitude, généralement, en général* and *parfois* are placed at the beginning of the sentence.

D'habitude, *je prends mon petit-déjeuner à 7h.*
Usually, I have breakfast at 7 a.m.

Parfois, *elle se réveille tard.*
Sometimes, she wakes up late.

CULTURE TIP
Such a chore!

While pretty much no one likes doing chores, our daily life is filled with them. Let's look at some common expressions related to housekeeping:

- ***faire la lessive*** to do laundry
- ***faire la vaisselle*** to do the dishes
- ***faire les courses*** to go grocery shopping
- ***passer l'aspirateur*** to vacuum
- ***ranger*** to clean up, to organize
- ***sortir la poubelle*** to take out the garbage

Key Takeaways

- Pronominal verbs are often used when describing one's daily routine. They are composed of two elements, a pronoun and a verb. To conjugate, the pronouns *me, te, se, nous, vous* and *se* are added to the verb.
- The verb *aller* is conjugated as follows: *je vais, tu vas, il/elle va, nous allons, vous allez, ils/elles vont*.
- The moments of the day are: *le matin, l'après-midi* and *le soir*.
- Other time expressions include: *tôt, tard, maintenant, plus tard, aujourd'hui, hier* and *demain*.
- Adverbs of frequency are placed after the verb, except for *d'habitude, généralement, en général* and *parfois*.

Are you a social butterfly? In the next chapter, we will talk about inviting someone out and accepting or refusing invitations. We will also study modal verbs and the imperative mood.

Exercises

1-5. Conjugate the indicated pronominal verbs:

1. *Je (**se doucher**) _____ tous les jours.*
2. *Anne, tu (**se brosser**) _____ les dents maintenant !*
3. *Nous (**se préparer**) _____ tôt le matin.*
4. *Véronique (**se maquiller**) _____ souvent.*
5. *Ils (**se raser**) _____ toutes les semaines.*

6-10. Translate the following sentences.

6. I go to work every day at 7 a.m.
7. Usually, she wakes up early.
8. The children brush their teeth every day.
9. I do the laundry every week.
10. Do you go to bed late?

Answer Key

1. me douche
2. te brosses
3. nous préparons
4. se maquille
5. se rasent
6. Je vais au travail tous les jours à 7h.
7. D'habitude, elle se réveille tôt.
8. Les enfants se brossent les dents tous les jours.
9. Je fais la lessive toutes les semaines.
10. Tu te couches tard ? OR Vous vous couchez tard ?

Chapter 13: How about a drink?

Il n'y a pas d'ami, il n'y a que des moments d'amitié.

There are no friends, there are only moments of friendship.

- Jules Renard

We learn a language not simply to communicate, but to connect with people. From the previous chapters, you now know how to talk about yourself, your city and your family, discuss hobbies or find common interests with someone. You can now handle first-meeting conversations with ease. But in order to cultivate the new relationships you make, you'd need to spend more time with your new *ami(e)* (friend), perhaps, invite them for a drink or to a party.

In this lesson, you will learn how to invite someone out and how to accept or refuse invitations. We will study how to formulate questions in French using interrogative pronouns. We will also have a look at the three modal verbs: *vouloir* (to want), *pouvoir* (to be able to) and *devoir* (to have to).

Asking someone out

Let's begin with a dialogue. Mathis calls Lucile and invites her for a drink with friends:

>**Mathis** : *Qu'est-ce que tu fais ce week-end ? Tu veux sortir samedi ?*
>**Lucile** : *Samedi soir ? Je ne peux pas. Je dois travailler.*
>**Mathis** : *Et vendredi ? Tu es dispo ?*
>**Lucile** : *Oui, vendredi ça me va ! On va où ?*
>**Mathis** : *On peut aller dans un bar avec mes amis, prendre un verre ?*
>**Lucile** : *Ça marche ! On se retrouve où ?*
>**Mathis** : *On se retrouve à 19h devant le métro Place d'Italie ?*
>**Lucile** : *OK, 19h ce vendredi !*

Let's look at the questions posed by Mathis. To ask someone out, we can say:

>***Qu'est-ce que tu fais ce week-end ?***
>What are you doing this weekend?

Remember that we previously learned the interrogative expression *qu'est-ce que* (what). This pronoun can be used in both formal and informal situations. Note that the *que* contracts to *qu'* before a vowel. For example, *qu'est-ce **qu'**elle fait* (what is she doing).

In <u>very</u> informal situations, you can also say:

>***Tu fais quoi ce week-end ?***
>What are you doing this weekend?

Alternatively, you can also ask if someone is free using the following expressions:

> *Est-ce que tu es disponible ce soir ?*
> *Tu es disponible ce soir ?*
> *Tu es dispo ce soir ?*
> Are you free tonight ?

All the three questions above mean the same. What is the difference? The first with the expression *est-ce que*, is slightly informal. The second is informal and the last is <u>very</u> informal (the slang for *disponible* is *dispo*).

Finally, we can also ask somebody out using the verb vouloir:

> *Tu veux sortir ce samedi ?*
> Do you want to go out this Saturday?

> *Tu veux aller boire un verre ?*
> Do you want to go have a drink (with me)?

The verb vouloir

The verb *vouloir* means to want to. We have actually seen this verb in its conditional mood before, in the expression *je voudrais*. *Vouloir* is an irregular verb that is conjugated in the present tense as follows:

	vouloir
Je	veux
Tu	veux
Il/Elle	veut
Nous	voulons
Vous	voulez
Ils/Elles	veulent

Remember that when two verbs are used, only the first verb is conjugated. Let's look at some examples:

- ***Je veux sortir avec mes amis.*** I want to go out with my friends.
- ***Lucas et Sophie veulent regarder un film.*** Lucas and Sophie want to watch a film.
- ***Tu veux aller en boîte ?*** Do you want to go clubbing?

Social activities vocabulary

	Translation
aller au restaurant	go to the restaurant
aller en boîte	to go clubbing
assister à un match de foot	to attend a football match
assister à un concert	to attend a concert

assister à une fête	to attend a party
boire un verre	to have a drink
dîner	to dine
prendre un verre	to have a drink
sortir	to go out
un bar	a bar, a pub
une boîte (de nuit)	a club
une fête	a party
une pendaison de crémaillère	a housewarming party
une sortie	an outing
visiter un musée	to visit a museum
voir un film	to watch a movie
voir une pièce de théâtre	to see a play

GRAMMAR TIP

The pronoun *on*

In the dialogue above, we see Lucile say: *On se retrouve où ?* for "Where do we meet?" We learned that the pronoun "we" in French is *nous*, so what is this *on* doing here?

On is a subject pronoun that may refer to one of these:

1. The informal variation of "we".
2. "somebody" or "someone".
3. "people in general".

Let's look at some examples:

1. **On va au restaurant.** We are going to the restaurant (inf.).

2. **On vous appelle.** Someone is calling you.

3. **En France, on aime boire du vin.** In France, people like drinking wine.

> Take note that *on* is conjugated the same way as *il* and *elle*.

Accepting or refusing invitations

To accept invitations, we can simply say:

Oui, je suis disponible.
Yes, I am available.

Oui, ça me va.
Yes, that works for me. (inf.)

You can also use informal expressions of agreement like *OK*, *d'accord* (Okay) or *ça marche* (that works). Note that *ça marche* is slang, and very informal.

In the dialogue above, Lucile says she can't go out Saturday night. Let's review that part:

Samedi soir ? Je ne peux pas. Je dois travailler.
Saturday night? I can't. I have to work.

To refuse an invitation, you can say:

Je ne peux pas.
I can't.

Je ne suis pas disponible.
Je ne suis pas dispo. (inf.)
I'm not available.

You can give an excuse (or make up one!) using the verb *devoir* which means "to have to":

Je dois rencontrer un ami.
I have to meet a friend.

Je dois rester chez moi.
I have to stay at home.

The verb pouvoir

The verb *pouvoir* means to be able to. It is conjugated in the present tense as such:

	pouvoir
Je	peux
Tu	peux
Il/Elle	peut
Nous	pouvons
Vous	pouvez

Ils/Elles	peuvent

Let's look at some examples:

- ***Je peux t'aider si tu veux.*** I can help you if you want.
- ***Tu peux me réveiller dans une heure ?*** Can you wake me up in an hour?
- ***On peut se retrouver devant le café.*** We can meet up in front of the coffee shop.

Note that the verb *pouvoir* is not used with skills, unlike in English. You can say for example "I can swim" in English, but in French, you need to use the verb "to know", which is *savoir*: *Je sais nager* (I can swim).

The verb devoir

The verb *devoir* means to have to. To conjugate in the present tense:

	devoir
Je	dois
Tu	dois
Il/Elle	doit
Nous	devons
Vous	devez
Ils/Elles	doivent

Let's look at some examples:

- ***Je dois partir.*** I have to leave.
- ***Anne doit étudier.*** Anne has to study.
- ***On doit manger.*** We have to eat.

Formulating questions

We have seen two ways to form questions, using *est-ce que* and *qu'est-ce que*. In learning question-formulation in French, it is important to understand the difference between closed and open questions.

Closed questions are questions we can answer with "yes" or "no". All the rest are open questions:

- ***Tu es français ?*** Are you French? (closed)
- ***Vous allez au parc ?*** Are you going to the park? (closed)
- ***Qu'est-ce que tu fais ?*** What are you doing? (open)
- ***Nous partons quand ?*** When are we leaving? (open)
- ***Pourquoi apprenez-vous le français ?*** Why are you learning French? (open)

Closed questions

There are three ways to formulate closed questions. We list them here from the informal to the most formal way:

1. Add a question mark to the end of a declarative sentence and pronounce it with a rising intonation.
2. Start the question with *est-ce que*.
3. Invert the subject and verb and place a hyphen in between.

For example, you want to ask someone, "Are you free tomorrow?". You can thus say it three ways:

1. *Vous êtes disponible ?*
2. ***Est-ce que*** *vous êtes disponible ?*
3. ***Êtes-vous*** *disponible ?*

Let's look at another example. This time, you want to ask "Does she ski?":

1. *Elle fait du ski ?*
2. ***Est-ce qu'****elle fait du ski ?*
3. ***Fait-elle*** *du ski ?*

Est-ce que has no specific translation in English. Think of it as an expression that signals to the listener that you are posing a question and not a declarative sentence. It's quite similar to the word "do", as in "Do you work?" *Est-ce que tu travailles?* Note that before a vowel *est-ce que* contracts to *est-ce qu'*.

Open questions

When you're asking what, when, why, how, etc., you are posing an open question. Just like in English, we use question words in French for open questions. Again, there are three ways we can formulate these questions, from the informal to the most formal way:

1. Add a question word to the declarative sentence.
2. Question word + *est-ce que* + declarative sentence.
3. Question word + subject-verb inversion.

Let's examine how these questions would look like. We take as an example the question "Where are you going?":

1. *Vous allez où ?*
2. *Où est-ce que vous allez ?*
3. *Où allez-vous ?*

The question word here is *où* (where). Let's look at another example, this time with *quand* (when). All of the sentences below translate to "When does she leave?":

1. *Elle part quand ?*
2. *Quand est-ce qu'elle part ?*
3. *Quand part-elle ?*

Question words

Below is a list of question words. In formal grammar, we call them interrogative adjectives:

	Translation
combien	how much, how many
comment	how
d'où	from where
où	where
pourquoi	why
quand	when

CULTURE TIP

My love, my cabbage

How do you feel about calling your partner a cabbage? A bit odd, right? Well, in France, it's just another common term of endearment. Let's look at some other terms French speakers use to call their special someone:

- **mon amour** my love
- **mon chéri / ma chérie** my darling
- **mon chou** my cabbage
- **mon ange** my angel

Key Takeaways

- To ask someone out, accept or refuse invitations, we use the following expressions:

Ask someone out
Qu'est-ce que tu fais ce week-end ?
(Est-ce que) tu es disponible ce soir ?
Tu veux sortir ce + day ?
Tu veux + activity ?
Accept invitation
Oui, je suis disponible.
Oui, ça me va.

OK.
D'accord.
Ça marche !
Refuse invitation
Je ne suis pas disponible.
Je ne peux pas.
Je dois + verb

- The verb *vouloir* is conjugated as follows: *je veux, tu veux, il/elle/on veut, nous voulons, vous voulez, ils/elles veulent.*
- The verb *pouvoir*: *je peux, tu peux, il/elle/on peut, nous pouvons, vous pouvez, ils/elles peuvent.*
- The verb *devoir*: *je dois, tu dois, il/elle/on doit, nous devons, vous devez, ils/elles doivent.*
- The pronoun *on* can mean: an informal "we", "someone" or "somebody", or "people" in general.
- To formulate closed questions we can: put a question mark at the end of a declarative sentence, add *est-ce que* at the beginning, or invert the subject and verb.
- To formulate open questions we can: add a question word to a declarative sentence, add question word and *est-ce que*, or invert the subject and verb.
- The question words are: *combien, comment, d'où, où, pourquoi* and *quand*.

In the next chapter, we will talk about eating out. You will learn how to order in a restaurant. We will also study the pronoun *en*.

Exercises

1-5. Complete the sentence with the correct conjugation of the indicated modal verb.

1. *Tu (**vouloir**) _____ sortir demain ?*
2. *On (**devoir**) _____ faire la lessive.*
3. *Nous (**pouvoir**) _____ payer en ligne ?*
4. *Véronique et Jules (**devoir**) _____ partir bientôt.*
5. *Ils (**vouloir**) _____ voir une pièce de théâtre.*

6-8. Translate this question the three ways we learned: *Vous êtes disponibles ce soir ?*

6. _____
7. _____
8. _____

9. Complete the sentence with the missing word: *Qu'est-ce ____ tu fais mardi soir?*

10. Transform the sentence to informal using the pronoun *on*: *Nous aimons le sport !*

Answer Key

1. veux
2. doit
3. pouvons
4. doivent
5. veulent
6 - 8. Vous êtes disponibles ce soir ? / Est-ce que vous êtes disponibles ce soir / Êtes-vous disponibles ce soir ?
9. que
10. On aime le sport !

Chapter 14: The art of French dining

L'appétit vient en mangeant, la soif s'en va en buvant.

Appetite comes by eating, thirst leaves by drinking.

- Rabelais

If our discussion about buying food in Chapter 9 left you hungry for more (pun fully intended), look no further – for in this lesson, we go back to the world of gastronomy. After learning how to invite someone out in the previous chapter, you've decided to call up a French friend to hang out. Said friend invites you to dine at a restaurant. You panic because you don't know yet how to order in French. Until of course, you open this chapter.

In this lesson, you will learn how to politely order in a restaurant and how to get the check. We will also study the pronoun *en*.

At the restaurant

Ordering

If you have a reservation, you can specify this by saying:

J'ai une réservation au nom de + your surname or full name.
I have a reservation under the name...

You will be given the menu, called *la carte* in French. The waiter will usually come back after some time to take your order, using any of the expressions below:

- **Vous avez choisi ?** Have you chosen (from the menu)?
- **Qu'est-ce que vous désirez ?** What would you like ?
- **Vous désirez ?** What would you like?

To order in a restaurant, you can use the expressions we previously learned: *je voudrais* and *je vais prendre*. To specify *la cuisson* (lit. cooking) of your steak, you use the following terms: *bleu* (very rare), *saignant* (rare), *à point* (medium-rare) or *bien cuit* (well done).

Meat vocabulary

	Translation
de la viande	meat
du boeuf	beef
un steak	a steak
de l'agneau (m.)	lamb
du porc	pork
du poulet	chicken
de la dinde	turkey
du canard	duck
du saumon	salmon
du thon	tuna
des fruits de mer (m.)	seafood
des moules (f.)	mussels

Pro tip: In French, food in unspecified quantity is preceded by the partitive article *de*: *de l'* (before vowel or h), *du* (m.) *de la* (f.) and *des* (pl.) .

CULTURE TIP

French meals take forever

A meal is called *un repas*. In a French household, you'd hear one call out *À table !* just before meal time. This expression means "it is time to eat" or "the meal is ready". Its literal translation is "to the table". Before eating, one would usually say *Bon appétit* (enjoy your meal).

If invited to eat at a French home, you'd find that the meals are exceptionally long and can last for hours! That is because meals are considered small social gatherings – a time to chat and dine. A dinner might start with *un apéro* (aperitif or pre-dinner drink). Drinks will be served as well as appetizers like chips, *saucissons* (dried sausage), or olives. You'll be tempted to munch a lot, but don't! The real meal is yet to start. Traditionally an *apéro* will be followed by a first course like salad, the main course and the dessert. To finish the meal, the French also often take a cup of coffee.

Dining vocabulary

	Translation
choisir	to choose
commander	to order
l'addition (f.)	the check, the bill
l'eau (f.)	water
la carte	the menu
le plat du jour	the dish of the day
payer	to pay
réserver	to reserve
un dessert	a dessert
un menu	a special, a set meal
un plat	a dish
un plat principal	a main dish, a main course
une boisson	a drink
une carafe	a carafe, a jug
une entrée	an appetizer
une formule	a set meal

Paying

After finishing a meal, you'd want to pay of course! To ask for the bill, you can say:

Je voudrais l'addition s'il vous plaît.
I would like the check please.

Or simply:

L'addition s'il vous plaît.
The check please.

Do you remember how to ask or indicate the preferred mode of payment? You might be asked *Vous payez par carte ou en espèces ?* To which you can reply, *Je vais payer par carte* or *Je vais payer en espèces*.

GRAMMAR TIP

The pronoun en

In Chapter 1, we studied the preposition *en* and how it precedes feminine countries (*en France, en Italie*). Not to be confused with this preposition, the word *en* is also a pronoun in French. Let's recall some definitions here: if a preposition precedes a noun or a pronoun to express relation with an element, a pronoun replaces a noun. Pronouns are used mainly to avoid repetitions.

The pronoun *en* is used to replace a noun preceded by the preposition *de*. Let's look at some examples:

1. *Tu veux du café ?* → ***J'en veux.***

Do you want some coffee? Yes, I would like some (of it).

2. *Vous prenez combien de pommes ?* → ***J'en prends deux.***

How many apples do you take? I take two (of them).

3. *Pierre a des enfants ?* → ***Oui, il en a quatre.***

(Does) Pierre have kids ? Yes, he has four (of them).

In example 1, one asks *tu veux du café*, and instead of repeating the noun by replying *je veux du café*, we replace *du café* with the pronoun *en*. You can think of *en* as "some of something". Remember that *en* is always placed before the verb.

En is also used to indicate the quantity. We place the number after the verb, as in examples 2 and 3. Here's another example:

4. *Jean prend trois pommes.* → ***Jean en prend trois.***

Notice how *pommes* (apples) is replaced by the pronoun *en*. The quantity *trois* (three) is placed after the verb.

Key Takeaways

- To communicate in a restaurant, we use the following expressions:

Entering and ordering
J'ai une réservation au nom de + your surname or full name.
Vous avez choisi ?
Qu'est-ce que vous désirez ?
Vous désirez ?
Je voudrais...
Je vais prendre...
Paying
Je voudrais l'addition s'il vous plaît.
L'addition s'il vous plaît.

- The pronoun *en* is used to replace a noun preceded by the preposition *de*. It is placed before the verb.
- We can also specify the quantity with *en*, by placing the number after the verb.

In the next chapter, we will talk about giving and asking directions. We will also study the imperative mood to give commands.

Exercises

1-2. Complete the dialogue with the appropriate missing words:

- Bonjour Madame, vous avez 1._____ ?
- Oui, je vais 2._____ deux plats du jour.

3. Complete the dialogue with the appropriate missing words:

- 3. Quelle _____ pour votre steak ?
- Saignant, s'il vous plaît.

4-8. Replace the underlined noun with *en*, following the example.

ex. *Je veux du café.* → _J'en veux_ .

4. Claire prend des bananes. _____.
5. Nous avons trois enfants. _____.
6. Tu prends des tomates ? _____.
7. Sophie et Éric ont dix stylos. _____.
8. On a deux kilos d'abricots. _____.

9. How would you ask for the bill in French?

10. How would you say you have a reservation at a restaurant?

Answer Key

1. choisi
2. prendre
3. cuisson
4. Claire en prend.
5. Nous en avons trois.
6. Tu en prends ?
7. Sophie et Éric en ont dix.
8. On en a deux kilos.
9. Je voudrais l'addition s'il vous plaît. OR L'addition s'il vous plaît.
10. Sample answer: J'ai une réservation au nom de (Monique) Dupont.

Chapter 15: At the crossroads

Qui s'effraie d'un nuage ne fait pas long voyage.

He who is frightened by a cloud does not travel long.

- French proverb

If you are big on traveling, odds are you've already found yourself lost in the middle of nowhere once or twice. You got too caught up on the beauty of everything that you've walked too far from where your tour group is supposed to meet up. For the first 5 minutes you panic. And then for about 10 minutes you convince yourself it's all part of the adventure. But after one hour of fatigue and thirst, you start to wish you can just magically acquire the linguistic capacity to, quite simply, ask for directions.

In this lesson, you will learn how to ask directions and understand them. We'll have a look at the imperative mood as well as the conjugation of -RE verbs.

Asking for directions

You would want to start with a polite *Excusez-moi* or *Pardon*. For example:

> ***Excusez-moi, Madame. Je cherche la station de métro Olympiades ?***
> Excuse me, madam. I'm looking for the subway station Olympiades?

> ***Pardon, Madame. Je pense que je suis perdu(e). Pourriez-vous m'aider?***
> Pardon me, madam. I think I'm lost. Could you please help me?

Alternatively, you can pose direct questions:

> ***Pardon, Monsieur. Où est la station de métro Olympiades ?***
> Pardon me, sir. Where is the subway station Olympiades?

> ***Excusez-moi, Madame. Pourriez-vous m'indiquer la rue Emile Zola ?***
> Excuse me, madam. Could you point me to the Emile Zola street?

Giving directions

Just as important as knowing how to ask for directions is understanding them when they are given!

Imagine that someone gives you directions to the Olympiades subway station:

> ***Vous n'êtes pas dans la bonne direction. Prenez la deuxième rue à droite, traversez le pont, puis continuez tout droit. Descendez vers la cathédrale Saint-Pierre. Tournez à gauche. Montez l'avenue Montaigne. Au carrefour, vous allez voir la station de métro, juste à côté du restaurant Chez Jean.***

You are not in the right direction. Take the second street to the right, cross the bridge, then go straight. Go down to the Saint-Pierre Cathedral. Turn left. Go up the Montaigne Avenue. At the intersection, you are going to see the subway station, just beside the Chez Jean restaurant.

Let us break down some of these expressions. To say go straight, we can say:

- ***Allez tout droit.***
- ***Continuez tout droit.***

To indicate a turn, we can say:

- ***Tournez à gauche.***
- ***Tournez à droite.***
- ***Prenez à gauche.***
- ***Prenez à droite.***

À gauche means to the left and *à droite*, to the right.

One may also indicate the street to take by saying:

- ***Prenez la rue Emile Zola.***
- ***Prenez la première rue à gauche.***
- ***Prenez la deuxième rue à droite.***

Like in English, the ordinal numbers are used here, as in "first street to the left", or "second street to the right".

If the road is uphill or downhill, we can also use the verbs *monter* (to go up) and *descendre* (to go down).

- ***Montez la rue Emile Zola.***
- ***Descendez l'avenue Montaigne.***

If it's not accessible by walking, you might also be advised to take public transport. Take note of the following expressions:

- ***aller à pied*** go by foot
- ***aller en bus / en train / en métro*** go by bus / by train / by subway
- ***prendre le train / le bus / le métro*** take the train / bus / subway

The verbs used to give directions are usually in the imperative mood. This is why the subject is omitted. We'll learn this in a while. Take note however that sometimes, the present tense form can be used to give directions. So instead of saying *Continuez tout droit*, one can also say *Vous continuez tout droit* or *Tu continues tout droit*.

GRAMMAR TIP

-RE verbs in French

To conjugate –RE verbs in the present tense, we simply remove the –re of the infinitive form and replace them with a set of fixed endings. And so, for example, we remove the –re in the verb *descendre* (to go down) and then we add the appropriate endings:

descendre → *descend*		
Je	+s	descend**s**
Tu	+s	descend**s**
Il/Elle/On	(none)	descend
Nous	+ons	descend**ons**
Vous	+ez	descend**ez**
Ils/Elles	+ent	descend**ent**

Note that irregular verbs do not follow this rule. An example is the verb *prendre* (to take):

prendre	
Je	prends
Tu	prends
Il/Elle/On	prend
Nous	prenons
Vous	prenez
Ils/Elles	prennent

For a list of basic verb conjugations, don't forget to consult the annex of this book.

Directions vocabulary

Here are other useful expressions to remember:

Verbs	Translation
se trouver	to be located at
aller à	to go to
aller jusqu'à	to go until
tourner	to turn (left or right)

prendre	to take, to turn (left or right)
traverser	to cross
revenir	to come back
retourner	to return
monter	to go up
descendre	to go down

Position	Translation
sur votre gauche	to your left
sur votre droite	to your right
au bout de (la rue)	at the end of (the street)
avant	before
après	after
au carrefour	at the intersection
dans la rue	in the street
sur le boulevard	on the boulevard
sur l'avenue	on the avenue
au feu	at the stoplight

Giving orders

To give orders, we conjugate verbs in what we call the imperative mood. This mood is not only used when giving directions. The imperative in French is similar to English, in that it is used to give a command, an advice, or even a warning. Let's look at some examples:

- (command) **Fais tes devoirs!** Do your homework!
- (advice) **Sois content de ce que tu as.** Be happy with what you have.
- (warning) **Ne fumez pas ici.** Don't smoke here.

The imperative mood has three forms which correspond to the subject pronouns *tu*, *vous* and *nous*. The conjugation is simple: we just take the present tense conjugations of these pronouns and remove the subject. The only exception is for -ER verbs. When conjugated in the *tu* form, we remove the -s.

Say, you want to order someone to close the door. In formal settings, you will use the *vous*-form of the imperative. So, we just take the usual present conjugation of that verb and omit the subject:

Fermez la porte.
Close the door.

A quick warning though, you might want to add a *s'il vous plait* at the end of this sentence unless you want to sound mean!

Here's another example, this time with the verb *faire*. We learned that to conjugate *faire* in the second person present tense, we say *fais*. So, if we want to say "do the dishes" informally, we would again follow this conjugation:

Fais la vaisselle.
Do the dishes.

Now, for -ER verbs, we remove the -s in the imperative form. Do you remember how to conjugate *parler* (to speak) with *tu*?

A+ for you if you answered *parles*! In the imperative mood, we need to remove the -s:

Parle plus fort !
Speak louder!

Finally, we have the *nous* form. This is the equivalent of the English "let's". Again, we just take the present tense conjugation of the verb. So if you want to say "let's go to the park":

Allons au parc !
Let's go to the park!

Key Takeaways

- To ask for directions, we say *Excusez-moi / Pardon + Madame / Monsieur* and the following expressions:

Ask for directions
Je cherche la station de métro Olympiades ?
Je pense que je suis perdu(e). Pourriez-vous m'aider ?
Où est la station de métro Olympiades ?
Pourriez-vous m'indiquer la rue Emile Zola ?

- To give directions, we use the following expressions:

Go straight
Allez tout droit
Continuez tout droit
Take a turn
Tournez à gauche / à droite.
Prenez à gauche / à droite.
Take a street / avenue/ boulevard
Prenez la rue Emile Zola.
Prenez la première rue à gauche.
Montez la rue Emile Zola.
Descendez l'avenue Montaigne.

- To conjugate -RE verbs, we remove the -re ending and add the following: *-s, -s,* (none), *-ons, -ez, ent.*
- Certain -RE verbs are irregular, like *prendre: je prends, tu prends, il/elle/on prend, nous prenons, vous prenez, ils/elles prennent.*
- To form the imperative, we use the present tense conjugation of verbs in the pronouns *tu, vous* and *nous*. For -ER verbs, we form the imperative mood in the second person *tu* by removing the -s.

Exercises

1-2. Complete the dialogue with the appropriate missing words:

- Bonjour Madame, où est la gare s'il vous plaît ?
- Continuez tout 1._____ et prenez la première 2._____ à droite.

3-4. Complete the dialogue with the appropriate missing words:

- Excusez-moi Monsieur, je 3._____ l'hôpital ?
- 4._____ à gauche, l'hôpital est en face du Café des Deux Moulins.

5-6. Conjugate the indicated verb in the present tense.

5. Je (descendre) _____ la rue Michelet.
6. Sophie et Lucas (prendre) _____ le train pour aller au travail.

7-10. Transform the following declarative sentences into commands, using the imperative mood.

7. *Tu tournes à gauche.* _____.
8. *Tu fais la lessive.* _____.
9. *Nous prenons le train.* _____.
10. *Vous montez la rue Louis Blanc.* _____.

Answer Key

1. droit
2. rue
3. cherche
4. Tournez OR Prenez
5. descends
6. prennent
7. Tourne à gauche.
8. Fais la lessive.
9. Prenons le train.
10. Montez la rue Louis Blanc.

Chapter 16: Ready for an adventure

Le plus beau voyage, c'est celui qu'on n'a pas encore fait.

The most beautiful journey is the one we have yet to take.

- Loïck Peyron

Even the most spontaneous travelers take some time to plan for a trip. This means looking for accommodation and choosing which touristic activities to do and which spots to visit. If you wish to spend holidays in a French-speaking country then this chapter will prepare you for these essential tasks.

In this lesson, you will learn how to reserve a hotel room. We will also study how to describe the places you see.

Reserving a room

To call for a reservation, we can use the following expressions:

- ***Je voudrais faire une réservation.*** I would like to make a reservation.
- ***C'est pour une réservation.*** It's for a reservation.
- ***Je voudrais réserver une chambre.*** I would like to reserve a room.

To indicate the date, duration and number of guests, you can say:

Est-ce que vous avez de la place ce soir / lundi prochain / le 8 janvier ?
Do you have a room tonight / next Monday / January 8.

Je voudrais réserver une chambre pour une nuit / trois nuits / une semaine.
I would like to reserve a room for one night / three nights / a week.

C'est pour deux personnes.
It's for two people.

Nous sommes trois.
We are three (guests).

You can also ask for additional information using the following expressions:

Est-ce qu'il y a une télévision dans la chambre ?
Is there a TV in the room?

Est-ce qu'il y a du wifi dans la chambre ?
Is there wifi in the room?

Est-ce qu'il y a une piscine dans l'hôtel ?

Is there a swimming pool in the hotel?

Est-ce que le petit déjeuner est compris ?
Is breakfast included ?

À quelle heure est le petit déjeuner ?
At what time is breakfast (served)?

À quelle heure peut-on s'enregistrer dans la chambre ?
At what time can we check in the room?

À quelle heure doit-on libérer la chambre ?
At what time is the check out? (lit. At what time must one free the room?)

Hotel reservation vocabulary

	Translation
avec vue sur	with a view on
connexion (f.) wifi	wifi connection
des serviettes (f.)	towels
l'ascenseur (m.)	the elevator
la clé	the key
la réception	the reception
le numéro de la chambre	the room number
un lit double	a double bed
un lit simple	a single bed
un plan	a map
une chambre à deux lits	a twin bedroom
une chambre double	a double bedroom
une chambre simple	a single bedroom

If you find yourself reserving a room *en ligne* (online) or *sur place* (on-site), these phrases will surely help:

J'ai fait une réservation en ligne au nom de...
I made a reservation online under the name...

Je n'ai pas de réservation. Avez-vous une chambre disponible ?
I don't have a reservation. Do you have a room available?

Touring the city

Below, we list some common vocabulary related to tourism:

Tourism vocabulary

	Translation
une location de voiture	a car rental
un dépliant	a leaflet
un guide touristique	a tour guide
un itinéraire	an itinerary
un logement	a lodging, an accommodation
un monument	a monument
un plan	a map
un vol	a flight
une agence de voyages	a travel agency
une brochure	a brochure
une carte	a map
une croisière	a cruise

GRAMMAR TIP

The pronoun y

Let's study an excerpt of a brochure:

> **Cette place est la plus grande place de la ville. On y trouve la Statue du Petit Prince.** (This square is the biggest square in the city. One finds there the Statue of the Petit Prince.)

Notice how instead of repeating *cette place*, we replace it instead with the word *y*:

On trouve **sur cette place** → On **y** trouve la Statue du Petit Prince.

The pronoun *y*, as you may observe here, is used to replace a place. It can be roughly translated to the English "here" or "there". To specify, *y* replaces:

- places preceded by the prepositions *à*, *chez*, *dans*, *en* or *sur*.

- places that are implied though not specified.

Let's look at some examples:

- *Mathis joue **au parc**.* → *Mathis **y** joue.*
- *Je vais **chez un ami**.* → *J'**y** vais.*
- *On se retrouve **au café** ?* → *On s'**y** retrouve ?*
- *On **y** va?* ("Let's go?" – the destination here is implied).

Like the pronoun *en*, *y* is generally placed before the verb.

Touristic activities

We list below some common touristic activities:

	Translation
faire du shopping	to go shopping
faire du tourisme	to go sightseeing
marcher	to walk
partir en vacances	to go on vacation
se baigner	to go swimming
se promener	to go for a walk, to take a walk
visiter le centre-ville	to visit downtown
visiter un musée	to visit a museum

Describing tourist spots

Demonstrative pronouns

There are many ways to describe a tourist spot. In Chapter 4, we learned how to use basic adjectives in French. Remember that they are generally placed after the noun. For example:

Cette plage se trouve en Grèce.
This beach is located in Greece.

When pointing to a specific noun, we use demonstrative pronouns. In English, for instance, we use "this" or "these" when referring to something near the speaker. In French, the demonstrative pronouns change according to gender and number. Let's look at some examples:

- **Ce château est magnifique !** This castle is magnificent!

- ***Cet endroit est extraordinaire.*** This place is extraordinary.
- ***Cette ville est pittoresque.*** This city is picturesque.
- ***Ce quartier est très calme.*** This neighborhood is very calm.

Study the table below:

	Demonstrative Pronoun	
masculine, starts with a consonant	**ce**	**ce** *parc*, **ce** *café*
masculine, starts with a vowel or *h*	**cet**	**cet** *endroit*, **cet** *hôtel*
feminine	**cette**	**cette** *église*, **cette** *école*
plural	**ces**	**ces** *parcs*, **ces** *écoles*

Note that before masculine nouns starting with a vowel, we use the variation *cet*, and not *ce*.

Key Takeaways

- To make a hotel reservation, we use the following expressions:

Introduction
Je voudrais faire une réservation.
C'est pour une réservation.
Giving details
Est-ce que vous avez de la place ce soir / lundi prochain / le 8 janvier ?
Je voudrais réserver une chambre pour une nuit / trois nuits.
C'est pour deux personnes.
Nous sommes trois.
Asking about amenities
Est-ce qu'il y a une télévision / du wifi dans la chambre ?
Est-ce qu'il y a une piscine dans l'hôtel ?
Est-ce que le petit déjeuner est compris ?
À quelle heure est le petit déjeuner ?
À quelle heure peut-on s'enregistrer dans la chambre ?
À quelle heure doit-on libérer la chambre ?

- The pronoun *y* replaces places that are preceded by the prepositions *à*, *chez*, *dans*, *en* or *sur*. It also replaces places that are implied in the context.
- The demonstrative pronouns "this" and "these" in French are: *ce*, *cet*, *cette* and *ces*.

Up until now, we've only looked at verbs conjugated in the present tense form. In the next chapter, you will learn how to conjugate them in the composed past tense, to talk about past events. We will also study vocabulary related to holidays and traditions.

Exercises

1-2. Complete the dialogue with the appropriate missing words:

- Bonjour Monsieur, est-ce que vous avez de la 1._____ ce soir ?
- C'est pour combien de personnes ?
- Nous sommes deux.
- D'accord... Nous avons une 2._____ à deux lits disponible.

3. Complete the dialogue with the appropriate missing words:

- 3._____ le petit déjeuner est compris ?
- Oui Monsieur, le petit déjeuner est inclus dans le prix.

4-7. Replace the underlined noun with *y*, following the example.

ex. *Je vais <u>au parc</u>.* → _J'y vais_ .

    4. Éric est <u>à la plage</u>. _____.
    5. Vous allez <u>en France</u> demain? _____.
    6. Nous dînons <u>chez Jean</u>. _____.
    7. On achète des stylos <u>dans ce magasin</u>. _____.

8-10. Complete the sentences with the appropriate demonstrative pronoun.

    8. J'adore _____ musée !
    9. _____ étudiant ne fait pas ses devoirs.
    10. _____ belles plages se trouvent en Thaïlande.

Answer Key

1. place
2. chambre
3. Est-ce que
4. Éric y va.
5. Vous y allez demain ?
6. Nous y dînons.
7. On y achète des stylos.
8. ce
9. Cet
10. Ces

Chapter 17: A thing of the past

> *Le passé, c'est la lampe qui éclaire l'avenir.*
>
> The past, it's the lamp that lights the future.
>
> - Jean-Louis-Auguste Commerson

The holidays just ended. Your friends ask you what you did or how it was. And so, you tell them what meal you had or what gifts you received. And for some laughs, you even add a few funny anecdotes. You had a fun time. You realize this as you relive the past by describing what happened.

In order to relate events that have already taken place, you would need to master the past tenses (yes, plural). In French language learning circles, the past tenses have gained quite a reputation as a difficult subject. Of particular notoriety is choosing which kind of past tense to use in specific contexts. Don't fret, for by the time you finish this lesson, you will be able to talk about the past using the correct grammatical tense. We will also learn how to talk about holidays and traditions.

Talking about the holidays

Camille describes how she spent Christmas:

> *Noël dernier, **je suis allée** chez ma grand-mère. **Il neigeait** fort le matin, donc **nous ne sommes pas sortis** de la maison. L'après-midi, **j'ai fait** un bonhomme de neige avec les enfants. Ma grand-mère **a préparé** beaucoup de plats : foie gras fait maison, canard à l'orange, noix de Saint-Jacques sautées à l'ail... **Elle a** aussi **fait** un gâteau, **c'était** délicieux ! Après le repas, **nous avons ouvert** les cadeaux. **J'ai reçu** des chaussures !*

Last Christmas, I spent Christmas at my grandmother's place. It was snowing heavily in the morning, so we didn't leave the house. In the afternoon, I made a snowman with the kids. My grandmother prepared a lot of dishes: homemade foie gras, duck à l'orange, sautéed scallops with garlic... She also made a cake, it was delicious! After the meal, we opened the presents. I got shoes!

Observe the highlighted phrases above. These are all in the past tense. In French, there are two grammatical tenses used to express the past: *le passé composé* (the composed past tense) and *l'imparfait* (the imperfect tense).

Composed past tense

The composed past is used to relate:

- successive actions or events.
- actions or events that happened at a specific point of time.
- actions or events that happened suddenly.

We'll delve deeper into the uses of the composed past in a while, when we compare it to the imperfect tense.

For now, let's look at how the composed past is formed. The formula is:

AVOIR or *ÊTRE* IN PRESENT TENSE + PAST PARTICIPLE OF THE VERB

For example, in the sentence above — *Elle a fait un gâteau* (She made a cake) — we have the auxiliary verb *avoir* conjugated in the present tense (*a*), and the past participle of the verb *faire* (*fait*). Let's look at other examples:

- ***J'ai dansé toute la nuit.*** *I danced all night.*
- ***Nous avons regardé un film.*** *We watched a film.*
- ***Vous êtes allés à la bibliothèque*** ? *Did you go to the library?*

How do we know whether to use *avoir* or *être*? For most verbs, we use *avoir*. *Être* is used only with the following verbs:

- *aller* — to go
- *arriver* — to arrive
- *descendre* — to go down
- *devenir* — to become
- *entrer* — to go in
- *monter* — to go up
- *mourir* — to die
- *naître* — to be born
- *partir* — to leave, to go
- *rentrer* — to go back, to come home
- *rester* — to stay
- *retourner* — to go back, to return
- *sortir* — to go out
- *tomber* — to fall
- *venir* — to come

Now that you know whether to choose *avoir* or *être*, all that's left is to add the past participle. To form the past participle, here are the rules to follow.

- For -ER verbs, change the ending to é. (ex. *manger* → *mangé*).
- For - IR verbs, change the ending to i. (ex. *partir* → *parti*).
- For -RE verbs, change the ending to u. (ex. *descendre* → *descendu*).

Remember that these are general rules. And as we've painfully learned by now, there are some exceptions. For now, start with these basic rules and move forward after mastering them.

Here is one last thing to remember when forming the composed past. When the auxiliary verb used is *être*, the past participle agrees in gender and number with the subject. For feminine subjects, we add an -e. For plural subjects, we add an -s. Remember that this is not the case when we use *avoir*. And so, for example:

- ***Hélène est partie tôt.*** Hélène left early.
- ***Hélène a mangé le sandwich.*** Hélène ate the sandwich.

Notice that we change *parti* to *partie* because the subject is feminine. But, in the second sentence, since we're using *avoir*, the past participle does not change at all. Here are other examples:

- ***Elle est déjà arrivée.*** She already arrived.
- ***Nous sommes allés au parc.*** We went to the park.
- ***Léa et Claire sont rentrées tard.*** Léa and Claire came home late.

The imperfect tense

The imperfect tense is used to relate:

- past descriptions (weather, time, feelings, etc.).
- events with no definite ending.
- actions or events that are repeated.
- simultaneous actions.

To form the imperfect tense, we take the present tense of the verb conjugated in *nous* form, and add specific endings. For example, let's look at the imperfect tense of *aimer* (to like). So, first we take the present tense conjugation of *aimer* in *nous*, which is *nous aimons*. And then, we remove -ons and replace them with these endings.

(nous) aim~~ons~~ → *aim-*		
Je	+ais	aim**ais**
Tu	+ais	aim**ais**
Il/Elle/On	+ait	aim**ait**
Nous	+ions	aim**ions**
Vous	+iez	aim**iez**
Ils/Elles	+aient	aim**aient**

Let's look at another example. How about the verb *partir*? In present tense *nous*, we conjugate it as *nous partons*, and so:

(nous) part~~ons~~ → *part-*		
Je	+ais	part**ais**
Tu	+ais	part**ais**
Il/Elle/On	+ait	part**ait**
Nous	+ions	part**ions**
Vous	+iez	part**iez**

| Ils/Elles | +aient | part**aient** |

Avoir and *être* have irregular conjugation. We follow the endings above, but the root is different. For *avoir*, it is av- :

	avoir
J'	avais
Tu	avais
Il/Elle/On	avait
Nous	avions
Vous	aviez
Ils/Elles	avaient

For *être*, it's ét- :

	être
J'	étais
Tu	étais
Il/Elle/On	était
Nous	étions
Vous	étiez
Ils/Elles	étaient

Composed past vs. imperfect

Now that you know how to form these two tenses, you need to learn when to use them. Above, we've listed the uses of each. Let's look at them again, but this time with examples:

Composed past tense	Imperfect tense
• successive actions or events ***J'ai fait les courses, j'ai cuisiné, puis j'ai mangé.*** (I did the grocery, I cooked, then I ate.)	• past descriptions ***Il faisait beau. J'étais content.*** (The weather was nice. I was glad.)
• actions or events that happened at a specific point of time ***La semaine dernière, je suis allé à Bordeaux.*** (Last week, I went to Bordeaux.)	• events with no definite ending ***Je passais la journée devant la télé.*** (I was spending the day in front of the TV.)
• actions or events that happened suddenly ***J'ai reçu un appel.*** (I received a call).	• actions or events that are repeated ***Tous les jours, je faisais du jogging.*** (Everyday, I went jogging.)
	• simultaneous actions ***Je faisais la lessive pendant qu'il cuisinait.*** (I was doing the laundry while he was cooking.)

An alternative way of thinking about the difference between these two is imagining a theatrical play. What happens in the background would be in the imperfect tense, while the main action would be the composed past.

CULTURE TIP

Holidays in France

A celebration in French is called *une fête*. Here are some of the traditional celebrations in France:

- *le 1er janvier, le jour de l'An* (New Year's)
- *le 14 février, la Saint-Valentin* (Valentine's Day)
- *le 22 mars – 25 avril, Pâques* (Easter)
- *le 1er mai, la fête du Travail* (Labor Day)
- *le 21 juin, la fête de la Musique* (Music Festival)
- *le 14 juillet, la fête nationale* (National Day)
- *le 1er novembre, la Toussaint* (All Saints' Day)
- *le 25 décembre, Noël* (Christmas)

A holiday, meaning those celebrations where we don't need to go to work (yippee!), is called *un jour férié*. Not all of the celebrations listed above are officially recognized as *férié*.

Celebrations vocabulary

	Translation
Bonne année !	Happy new year!
des feux d'artifice (m.)	fireworks
fêter	to celebrate
Joyeux Noël !	Merry Christmas !
un bouquet de fleurs	a bouquet of flowers
un cadeau	a gift
un sapin de Noël	a Christmas tree
une carte de vœux	a greeting card
une fête	a party, a celebration

Key Takeaways

- To express the past in French, we use the composed past tense and the imperfect tense. The composed past is used to relate actions or events that are successive, that happened at a specific point of time, or that happened suddenly. The imperfect tense is used to relate past descriptions, events with no definite ending, or repeated and simultaneous actions.

- To form the composed past, we follow the formula: *avoir* or *être* in present tense + past participle of the verb.
- We use *avoir* for most verbs. We use *être* for the following verbs: *aller, arriver, descendre, devenir, entrer, monter, mourir, naître, partir, rentrer, rester, retourner, sortir, tomber* and *venir*.
- To form the past participle, we change the endings: ER becomes *é*, IR becomes *i* and RE becomes *u*.
- To form the imperfect tense, we take the present tense conjugation of the verb in *nous*, then replace the endings with: *-ais, -ais, -ait, -ions, -iez, -aient*.
- The verbs *avoir* and *être* have irregular conjugations in the imperfect tense. For *avoir*, the base is *av-* and for *être*, *ét-*.

In the final chapter of this book, we head to the future. You will learn how to talk about your future plans and your dreams.

Exercises

1-3. Transform the indicated verbs into the composed past tense.

    1. Les enfants (manger) _____ des bonbons.
    2. Le 1er janvier, la famille (aller) _____ chez une amie.
    3. Nous (partir) _____ en Suisse pour la Saint-Valentin.

4-6. Transform the indicated verbs into the imperfect tense.

    4. Quand on est arrivé, il (faire) _____ mauvais.
    5. Jacques (chanter) _____.
    6. Je (avoir) _____ un problème.

7-10. Composed past or imperfect tense? Conjugate the indicated verbs using the appropriate past tense.

Ce jour-là, il faisait beau. Nathan et ses enfants (aller) _____ dans le parc. Ils (jouer) _____ au foot. Les enfants (être) _____ très heureux.

Answer Key

1. ont mangé
2. est allée (because *la famille* is a singular, feminine noun.)
3. sommes partis
4. faisait
5. chantait
6. J'avais
7. faisait
8. sont allés
9. ont joué
10. étaient

Chapter 18: The adventure continues

> *L'avenir est une porte, le passé en est la clé.*
>
> The future is the door, the past is its key.
>
> - Victor Hugo

What better way to conclude your journey in learning beginner's French than to dream of a hopeful future? Being able to talk about the future is an important language skill to acquire. And we're not only talking about the big picture here, as in your career plans or projects. The future also plays a role in our daily lives.

We have mastered quite a lot of verb tenses since we started, some a bit more complicated than others. The great news is that the future tense is in fact one of the simplest conjugations you'll learn. In this chapter, we'll teach you how to describe your plans and how to express predictions.

Plans and projects

There are two future tenses in French. "Not again!", we can hear you grumbling. But not to worry, the conjugation of these tenses is much more straight-forward than the past ones. The two future tenses are called *le futur proche* (near future) *and le futur simple* (simple future).

Near future

The near future tense, called *le futur proche* in French, is used to talk about things that will certainly happen. It is also the more common, more informal of the two types of future tenses.

To form this tense, we simply add the verb *aller* (to go) in the present tense to the infinitive form of the verb. It's quite literally like the English verbal phrase "going to do something". For example, if you want to say, "I am going to eat with my friends", in French that would be:

*Je **vais manger** avec mes amis.*

So you have the present tense of *aller* (*vais*) which is added to the infinitive form of the main verb (*manger*).

Let's look at other examples:

- ***La famille va partir en vacances la semaine prochaine.*** The family will go on holidays next week.
- ***Vous allez fêter son anniversaire où ?*** You will celebrate his birthday where?
- ***Mes parents vont rentrer tard.*** My parents will come home late.

Quite simple right? Here's an added surprise: there are no exceptions to the rule. Finally!

GRAMMAR TIP
The present as future

Take note that the present tense can also be used to talk about the future, especially when the event will happen soon. It's the same in English: you can say "The family <u>is going</u> on holidays next week." instead of "The family <u>will go</u> on holidays next week".

Similarly, in French, you can either use the present *La famille part en vacances*. Or the future, *La famille va partir en vacances*.

Predictions and hypothesis

The next type of future tense is called *le futur simple*. This tense is mostly used to express plans in the distant future. It is more formal than the near future. Note as well that this tense is <u>not</u> as frequently used in conversations.

Simple future

The simple future is used for predictions, like with the weather for example:

Il y aura des nuages demain.
It will be cloudy tomorrow (lit. There will be clouds tomorrow).

It is also used for hypothetical statements, especially with the relative pronouns *si* (if) and *quand* (when):

S'il fait beau demain, j'irai au parc.
If the weather is nice tomorrow, I will go to the park.

Si tu t'entraines, tu seras plus fort.
If you train, you will be stronger.

Quand j'aurai le temps, j'apprendrai le français.
When I have time, I will learn French.

Quand je serai grand, je serai pilote.
When I grow up, I will be a pilot.

To form the simple future, it's simple! We add the endings *ai, as, a, ons, ez* and *ont* to the infinitive form. Look at the table below:

donner (to give)		
Je	+ai	donner**ai**
Tu	+as	donner**as**
Il/Elle/On	+a	donner**a**

Nous	+ons	donner**ons**
Vous	+ez	donner**ez**
Ils/Elles	+ont	donner**ont**

This is the rule for regular verbs, whatever their ending may be, -ER, -IR, or -RE.

There are some irregular verbs, like *avoir*, *être* and *aller*. For *avoir*, the base form is *aur-*, *ser-* for *être*, *fer-* for *faire*, and *ir-* for *aller*.

avoir	*être*	*faire*	*aller*
*j'*aurai	*je* serai	*je* ferai	*j'*irai
tu auras	*tu* seras	*tu* feras	*tu* iras
il/elle/on aura	*il/elle/on* sera	*il/elle/on* fera	*il/elle/on* ira
nous aurons	*nous* serons	*nous* ferons	*nous* irons
vous aurez	*vous* serez	*vous* ferez	*vous* irez
ils/elles auront	*ils/elles* seront	*ils/elles* feront	*ils/elles* iront

CULTURE TIP
Expressions with venir

We learned that the verb *venir* means to come. In French, the future is called *avenir*, which originally means *à venir* (to come, to happen). Here are some other expressions that use this verb:

- *dans les mois à venir* in the months to come
- *dans les années à venir* in the years to come
- *ça va venir* it will come, it will happen

Key Takeaways
- There are two future tenses in French. The near future is used to talk about events that will certainly happen in the near future. The simple future is used to express predictions and hypotheses in the distant future. Of the two, the near future is less formal and used more often.
- The present tense can also be used to indicate future events.
- To form the near future, we add the present tense of the verb *aller* to the infinitive form of the main verb.

- To form the simple future, we add the following endings to the infinitive form of the verb : *-ai, -as, -a, -ons, -ez* and *-ont*.
- The verb *avoir* is irregular, its base form (to which we will add the endings) is *aur-*.
- For *être*, the base form is *ser-*.
- For *aller*, the base form is *ir-*.

Bien joué ! Well done for getting this far! This may be the final chapter of this book, but it's not yet the end! Don't forget to review what you've learned by checking the vocabulary lists and verb conjugations in the annex.

What's next

As this chapter's title says, the adventure continues! And not to worry, for we are right there with you. If you want to take your French further, you'll find it ideal to follow through with the next book in our series: **Learn Intermediate French for Adults Workbook**. With this book, you will be able to build on what you learned here and achieve an intermediate level of fluency in French. We will look at longer conversations, more complex topics and more nuanced vocabularies, all with the same simplicity and clarity that this present book offers. *À bientôt l'aventurier*, see you soon adventurer!

Exercises

1-5. Transform the indicated verbs into the near future tense.

    1. Je (acheter) _____ cette chemise.
    2. Martin et ses amis (regarder) _____ le match de foot ce week-end.
    3. On (partir) _____ de la maison à 9h.
    4. Vous (prendre) _____ l'ascenseur ?
    5. Mes collègues (organiser) _____ une fête de départ.

6-10. Transform the indicated verbs into the simple future tense.

    6. Plus tard, je (avoir) _____ une grande maison.
    7. Dans dix mois, Christelle (quitter) _____ ce travail.
    8. Il (faire) _____ beau la semaine prochaine.
    9-10. Quand je (être) _____ en France, je (passer) _____ mes journées dans les musées.

Answer Key

1. vais acheter
2. vont regarder
3. va partir
4. allez prendre
5. vont organiser
6. j'aurai
7. quittera
8. fera
9. serai, passerai

Vocabulary Lists by Theme

Greetings and basic expressions

Bye	*Salut*
Excuse me	*Excusez-moi*
Good evening	*Bonsoir*
Good night	*Bonne nuit*
Goodbye	*Au revoir*
Have a good afternoon	*Bon après-midi*
Have a good day	*Bonne journée*
Have a good day's end	*Bonne fin de journée*
Have a good evening	*Bonne soirée*
Hello, Bye	*Salut*
Hello, Good day	*Bonjour*
Hi	*Coucou*
No	*Non*
Pardon me, Excuse me	*Pardon*
Please	*S'il vous plaît*
See you in a bit	*À tout à l'heure*
See you in a moment	*À tout de suite*
See you later	*À plus (inf.), À plus tard*
See you soon	*À bientôt*
See you tomorrow	*À demain*
Thank you (very much)	*Merci (beaucoup)*
Until next time	*À la prochaine*
Yes	*Oui*

Professions

an actor	*un acteur / une actrice*
a baker	*un boulanger / une boulangère*
a carpenter	*un charpentier / une charpentière*
a civil servant	*un/une fonctionnaire*
a cook	*un chef / une cheffe*
a dentist	*un/une dentiste*

a doctor	*un/une médecin*
an employee	*un/une employé(e)*
an engineer	*un/une ingénieur(e)*
a nurse	*un infirmier / une infirmière*
a police officer	*un policier / une policière*
a teacher	*un/une enseignant(e)*
a waiter	*un serveur / une serveuse*

Nationalities

American	*américain(e)*
Austrian	*autrichien(ne)*
Belgian	*belge*
Canadian	*canadien(ne)*
Chinese	*chinois(e)*
English	*anglais(e)*
French	*français(e)*
German	*allemand(e)*
Greek	*grec(que)*
Japanese	*japonais(e)*
Korean	*coréen(ne)*
Mexican	*mexicain(e)*
Moroccan	*marocain(e)*
Portuguese	*portugais(e)*
Russian	*russe*
Spanish	*espagnol(e)*
Swede	*suédois(e)*
Vietnamese	*vietnamien(ne)*

Countries

Algeria	*l'Algérie (f.)*
Australia	*l'Australie (f.)*
Austria	*l'Autriche (f.)*
Belgium	*la Belgique*
Brazil	*le Brésil*

Brunei	*le Brunéi*
Bulgaria	*la Bulgarie*
Cambodia	*le Cambodge*
Cameroon	*le Cameroun*
Canada	*le Canada*
Colombia	*la Colombie*
Congo	*le Congo*
Czech Republic	*la République tchèque*
Denmark	*le Danemark*
Egypt	*l'Égypte (f.)*
England	*l'Angleterre (f.)*
Finland	*la Finlande*
France	*la France*
Gabon	*le Gabon*
Gambia	*la Gambie*
Germany	*l'Allemagne (f.)*
Greece	*la Grèce*
Haiti	*Haïti*
Hungary	*la Hongrie*
Iceland	*l'Islande (f.)*
India	*l'Inde (f.)*
Indonesia	*l'Indonésie (f.)*
Iran	*l'Iran (f.)*
Iraq	*l'Irak (f.)*
Ireland	*l'Irlande (f.)*
Israel	*Israël (m.)*
Italy	*l'Italie (f.)*
Japan	*le Japon*
Malaysia	*la Malaisie*
Mexico	*le Mexique*
Morocco	*le Maroc*
Netherlands	*les Pays-Bas*
New Zealand	*la Nouvelle-Zélande*
Norway	*la Norvège*

Poland	*la Pologne*
Portugal	*le Portugal*
Russia	*la Russie*
Saudi Arabia	*l'Arabie saoudite (f.)*
Scotland	*l'Écosse (f.)*
Slovakia	*la Slovaquie*
Slovenia	*la Slovénie*
South Africa	*l'Afrique du Sud (f.)*
South Korea	*la Corée du Sud*
Spain	*l'Espagne (f.)*
Sri Lanka	*le Sri Lanka*
Switzerland	*la Suisse*
Thailand	*la Thaïlande*
United Arab Emirates	*les Émirats arabes unis (m.)*
United Kingdom	*le Royaume-Uni*
United States	*les États-Unis (m.)*
Vietnam	*le Viêt Nam*

School objects

a backpack	*un sac à dos*
a bag	*un sac*
a book	*un livre*
a chair	*une chaise*
a computer	*un ordinateur*
a laptop	*un ordinateur portable*
a mobile phone	*un (téléphone) portable*
a notebook	*un cahier*
a pen	*un stylo*
a pencil	*un crayon*
a ruler	*une règle*
a table	*une table*
a whiteboard	*un tableau blanc*

Basic adjectives

beautiful	*beau/belle*
big	*grand/grande*
black	*noir/noire*
cheap	*bon marché*
difficult	*difficile*
easy	*facile*
expensive	*cher/chère*
happy	*heureux/heureuse*
heavy	*lourd/lourde*
kind	*gentil/gentille*
light	*léger/légère*
long	*long/longue*
mean	*méchant/méchante*
sad	*triste*
short	*court/courte*
small	*petit/petite*
strong	*fort/forte*
ugly	*laid/laide*
weak	*faible*
white	*blanc/blanche*

Numbers

0	*zéro*	40	*quarante*	80	*quatre-vingts*
1	*un*	41	*quarante et un*	81	*quatre-vingt-un*
2	*deux*	42	*quarante-deux*	82	*quatre-vingt-deux*
3	*trois*	43	*quarante-trois*	83	*quatre-vingt-trois*
4	*quatre*	44	*quarante-quatre*	84	*quatre-vingt-quatre*
5	*cinq*	45	*quarante-cinq*	85	*quatre-vingt-cinq*
6	*six*	46	*quarante-six*	86	*quatre-vingt-six*
7	*sept*	47	*quarante-sept*	87	*quatre-vingt-sept*
8	*huit*	48	*quarante-huit*	88	*quatre-vingt-huit*
9	*neuf*	49	*quarante-neuf*	89	*quatre-vingt-neuf*
10	*dix*	50	*cinquante*	90	*quatre-vingt-dix*

11	onze	51	cinquante et un	91	quatre-vingt-onze
12	douze	52	cinquante-deux	92	quatre-vingt-douze
13	treize	53	cinquante-trois	93	quatre-vingt-treize
14	quatorze	54	cinquante-quatre	94	quatre-vingt-quatorze
15	quinze	55	cinquante-cinq	95	quatre-vingt-quinze
16	seize	56	cinquante-six	96	quatre-vingt-seize
17	dix-sept	57	cinquante-sept	97	quatre-vingt-dix-sept
18	dix-huit	58	cinquante-huit	98	quatre-vingt-dix-huit
19	dix-neuf	59	cinquante-neuf	99	quatre-vingt-dix-neuf
20	vingt	60	soixante	100	cent
21	vingt et un	61	soixante et un	1 000	mille
22	vingt-deux	62	soixante-deux	million	million
23	vingt-trois	63	soixante-trois	billion	milliard
24	vingt-quatre	64	soixante-quatre		
25	vingt-cinq	65	soixante-cinq		
26	vingt-six	66	soixante-six		
27	vingt-sept	67	soixante-sept		
28	vingt-huit	68	soixante-huit		
29	vingt-neuf	69	soixante-neuf		
30	trente	70	soixante-dix		
31	trente et un	71	soixante-et-onze		
32	trente-deux	72	soixante-douze		
33	trente-trois	73	soixante-treize		
34	trente-quatre	74	soixante-quatorze		
35	trente-cinq	75	soixante-quinze		
36	trente-six	76	soixante-seize		
37	trente-sept	77	soixante-dix-sept		
38	trente-huit	78	soixante-dix-huit		
39	trente-neuf	79	soixante-dix-neuf		

Family

an aunt	une tante
a brother	un frère
a child	un enfant

a daughter	*une fille*
a family	*une famille*
a father	*un père (papa)*
a female cousin	*une cousine*
a granddaughter	*une petite-fille*
a grandfather	*un grand-père (papy, papi)*
a grandmother	*une grand-mère (mamie)*
a grandson	*un petit-fils*
a husband	*un mari*
a male cousin	*un cousin*
a mother	*une mère (maman)*
a nephew	*un neveu*
a niece	*une nièce*
a relative, a parent	*un parent*
siblings	*des frères et sœurs*
a sister	*une sœur*
a son	*un fils*
an uncle	*un oncle*
a wife	*une femme*

Places in the city

an apartment	*un appartement*
a bank	*une banque*
a building	*un bâtiment*
a cinema	*un cinéma*
a city hall	*une mairie*
a coffee shop	*un café*
downtown	*le centre-ville*
a hospital	*un hôpital*
a hotel	*un hôtel*
in the city	*en ville*
a library	*une bibliothèque*
a shopping mall	*un centre commercial*
a market	*un marché*

a museum	*un musée*
a park	*un parc*
a parking	*un parking*
a post office	*un bureau de poste*
a restaurant	*un restaurant*
a school	*une école*
a subway station	*une station de métro*
a supermarket	*un supermarché*
a theater	*un théâtre*
a train station	*une gare*
a university	*une université*

Parts of the house

a balcony	*un balcon*
a basement	*un sous-sol*
a bathroom	*une salle de bains*
a bedroom	*une chambre*
a garage	*un garage*
a house	*une maison*
a kitchen	*une cuisine*
a living room	*un salon*
an office	*un bureau*
a patio	*une terrasse*
a room	*une pièce*
a staircase	*un escalier*
toilets	*des w.c. (m.plur.), des toilettes (f.plur.)*

Hobbies

cooking	*la cuisine*
dancing	*la danse*
fashion	*la mode*
gardening	*le jardinage*
music	*la musique*
painting	*la peinture*

reading	*la lecture*
singing	*le chant*
sports	*le sport*
traveling	*le voyage*
video games	*les jeux vidéo*

Sports and music

to bike	*faire du vélo*
to box	*faire de la boxe*
to go horseback riding	*faire de l'équitation*
to go mountain climbing	*faire de l'alpinisme*
to play basketball	*jouer au basket*
to play cards	*jouer aux cartes*
to play drums	*jouer de la batterie*
to play football	*jouer au foot*
to play tennis	*jouer au tennis*
to play the guitar	*jouer de la guitare*
to play the piano	*jouer du piano*
to play the violin	*jouer du violon*
to play volleyball	*jouer au volley*
to ski	*faire du ski*
to swim	*faire de la natation*

Baked goods

an apple turnover	*un chausson aux pommes*
a baguette	*une baguette*
a cake	*un gâteau*
a chocolate bread	*un pain au chocolat*
a chocolate cake	*un gâteau au chocolat*
a croissant	*un croissant*
a lemon pie	*une tarte au citron*
a pie	*une tarte*
a sandwich loaf	*un pain de mie*
a strawberry pie	*une tarte aux fraises*

a whole-wheat bread   *un pain complet*

Fruits, vegetables and meat

a carrot	*une carotte*
a peach	*une pêche*
a pear	*une poire*
a potato	*une pomme de terre*
a tomato	*une tomate*
an apple	*une pomme*
an apricot	*un abricot*
an eggplant	*une aubergine*
an orange	*une orange*
a banana	*une banane*
beef	*du boeuf*
a broccoli	*un brocoli*
a cabbage	*un chou*
cherries	*des cerises (f.)*
chicken	*du poulet*
duck	*du canard*
garlic	*de l'ail*
grapes	*du raisin*
green beans	*des haricots verts (m.)*
lamb	*de l'agneau*
lemon	*un citron*
lettuce	*une salade*
meat	*de la viande*
mussels	*des moules (f.)*
an onion	*un oignon*
a pineapple	*un ananas*
pork	*du porc*
salmon	*du saumon*
seafood	*des fruits de mer*
a steak	*un steak*
a strawberry	*une fraise*

tuna	*du thon*
turkey	*de la dinde*

Weather

fall	*l'automne*
hail	*la grêle*
a lightning	*un éclair*
the moon	*la lune*
rain	*la pluie*
a rainbow	*un arc-en-ciel*
snow	*la neige*
spring	*le printemps*
a star	*une étoile*
a storm	*une tempête*
summer	*l'été (m.)*
the sun	*le soleil*
a thermometer	*un thermomètre*
thunder	*le tonnerre*
winter	*l'hiver*

Days and months

a day	*un jour*
a week	*une semaine*
a month	*un mois*
Monday	*lundi*
Tuesday	*mardi*
Wednesday	*mercredi*
Thursday	*jeudi*
Friday	*vendredi*
Saturday	*samedi*
Sunday	*dimanche*
January	*janvier*
February	*février*
March	*mars*

April	*avril*
May	*mai*
June	*juin*
July	*juillet*
August	*août*
September	*septembre*
October	*octobre*
November	*novembre*
December	*décembre*

Daily activities

to drink coffee	*boire du café*
to eat	*manger*
to eat breakfast	*prendre le petit-déjeuner*
to eat dinner	*dîner*
to eat lunch	*déjeuner*
to fall asleep	*s'endormir*
to get dressed	*s'habiller*
to get ready	*se préparer*
to get up	*se lever*
to go home	*rentrer*
to go to bed	*se coucher*
to go to school	*aller à l'école*
to go to the university	*aller à l'université*
to go to the university	*aller à la fac (slang)*
to go to work	*aller au travail*
to put makeup on	*se maquiller*
to read the newspaper	*lire le journal*
to rest	*se reposer*
to shave oneself	*se raser*
to take a shower	*se doucher*
to undress	*se déshabiller*
to wake up	*se réveiller*
to watch TV	*regarder la télé*

Time

afternoon	*l'après-midi*
always	*toujours*
early	*tôt*
evening	*le soir*
every Monday	*tous les lundis*
every month	*tous les mois*
every week	*toutes les semaines*
everyday	*tous les jours*
frequently, often	*fréquemment*
from time to time	*de temps en temps*
generally	*en général, généralement*
late	*tard*
later	*plus tard*
morning	*le matin*
once a week	*une fois par semaine*
rarely, seldom	*rarement*
right now	*maintenant*
sometimes	*parfois*
today	*aujourd'hui*
tomorrow	*demain*
twice a week	*deux fois par semaine*
usually	*d'habitude*
yesterday	*hier*

Chores

to clean up, to organize	*ranger*
to do laundry	*faire la lessive*
to do the dishes	*faire la vaisselle*
to go grocery shopping	*faire les courses*
to take out the garbage	*sortir la poubelle*
to vacuum	*passer l'aspirateur*

Social activities

a bar, a pub	*un bar*
a club	*une boîte de nuit*
a housewarming party	*une pendaison de crémaillère*
a party	*une fête*
an outing	*une sortie*
to attend a party	*assister à une fête*
to go clubbing	*aller en boîte*
to go to a restaurant	*aller au restaurant*
to have a drink	*prendre un verre*
to attend a concert	*assister à un concert*
to see a play	*voir une pièce de théâtre*
to dine	*dîner*
to go out	*sortir*
to visit a museum	*visiter un musée*
to watch a football match	*assister à un match de foot*
to watch a movie	*voir un film*

Dining

a carafe, a jug	*une carafe*
a dish	*un plat*
a drink	*une boisson*
a main dish	*un plat principal*
a set meal	*une formule*
a special, a set meal	*un menu*
appetizer	*une entrée*
the check, bill	*l'addition (f.)*
a dessert	*un dessert*
the dish of the day	*le plat du jour*
the menu	*la carte*
to choose	*choisir*
to order	*commander*
to pay	*payer*
to reserve	*réserver*

water	*l'eau (f.)*

Directions

after	*après*
at the end of (the street)	*au bout de (la rue)*
at the intersection	*au carrefour*
at the stoplight	*au feu*
before	*avant*
on the avenue	*sur l'avenue*
on the boulevard	*sur le boulevard*
in the street	*dans la rue*
to be located at	*se trouver*
to cross	*traverser*
to go down	*descender*
to go to	*aller à*
to go until	*aller jusqu'à*
to go up	*monter*
to return	*revenir, retourner*
to take	*prendre*
to turn (left or right)	*tourner, prendre (à gauche ou à droite)*
to your left	*sur votre/ta gauche*
to your right	*sur votre/ta droite*

Hotel reservation

a double bed	*un lit double*
a double bedroom	*une chambre double*
a map	*un plan*
a single bed	*un lit simple*
a single bedroom	*une chambre simple*
the room number	*le numéro de la chambre*
the elevator	*l'ascenseur (m.)*
the key	*la clé*
the reception	*la réception*
towels	*des serviettes (f.)*

twin bedroom	*une chambre à deux lits*
wifi connection	*connexion wifi*
with view of	*avec vue sur*

Tourism

a brochure	*un dépliant*
a brochure	*une brochure*
a cruise	*une croisière*
a flight	*un vol*
a map	*un plan*
a map	*une carte*
a monument	*un monument*
a tour guide	*un guide touristique*
a travel agency	*une agence de voyages*
an accommodation	*un logement*
an itinerary	*un itinéraire*
a car rental	*une location de voiture*
to go for a walk, take a walk	*se promener*
to go on vacation	*partir en vacances*
to go shopping	*faire du shopping*
to go sightseeing	*faire du tourisme*
to go swimming	*se baigner*
to visit a museum	*visiter un musée*
to visit downtown	*visiter le centre-ville*
to walk	*marcher*

Celebrations

a bouquet of flowers	*un bouquet de fleurs*
a Christmas tree	*un sapin de Noël*
a gift	*un cadeau*
a greeting card	*une carte de vœux*
a party, a celebration	*une fête*
fireworks	*des feux d'artifice (m.)*
Happy new year!	*Bonne année !*

Merry Christmas ! Joyeux Noël !
to celebrate fêter

Verb Conjugations

	Present	Composed past	Imperfect	Simple future
Être (to be)	je suis	J'ai été	J'étais	je serai
	tu es	tu as été	tu étais	tu seras
	il/elle est	il/elle a été	il/elle était	il/elle sera
	nous sommes	nous avons été	nous étions	nous serons
	vous êtes	vous avez été	vous étiez	vous serez
	ils/elles sont	ils/elles ont été	ils/elles étaient	ils/elles seront
Avoir (to have)	j'ai	j'ai eu	j'avais	j'aurai
	tu as	tu as eu	tu avais	tu auras
	il/elle a	il/elle a eu	il/elle avait	il/elle aura
	nous avons	nous avons eu	nous avions	nous aurons
	vous avez	vous avez eu	vous aviez	vous aurez
	ils/elles ont	ils/elles ont eu	ils/elles avaient	ils/elles auront
Aller (to go)	je vais	je suis allé(e)	j'allais	j'irai
	tu vas	tu es allé(e)	tu allais	tu iras
	il/elle va	il/elle est allé(e)	il/elle allait	il/elle ira
	nous allons	nous sommes allé(e)s	nous allions	nous irons
	vous allez	vous êtes allé(e)s	vous alliez	vous irez
	ils/elles vont	ils/elles sont allé(e)s	ils/elles allaient	ils/elles iront
Chanter (to sing)	je chante	j'ai chanté	je chantais	je chanterai
	tu chantes	tu as chanté	tu chantais	tu chanteras
	il/elle chante	il/elle a chanté	il/elle chantait	il/elle chantera
	nous chantons	nous avons chanté	nous chantions	nous chanterons
	vous chantez	vous avez chanté	vous chantiez	vous chanterez
	ils/elles chantent	ils/elles ont chanté	ils/elles chantaient	ils/elles chanteront
Choisir (to choose)	je choisis	j'ai choisi	je choisissais	je choisirai
	tu choisis	tu as choisi	tu choisissais	tu choisiras

	il/elle choisit	il/elle a choisi	il/elle choisissait	il/elle choisira
	nous choisissons	nous avons choisi	nous choisissions	nous choisirons
	vous choisissez	vous avez choisi	vous choisissiez	vous choisirez
	ils/elles choisissent	ils/elles ont choisi	ils/elles choisissaient	ils/elles choisiront
Connaître (to know)	je connais	j'ai connu	je connaissais	je connaîtrai
	tu connais	tu as connu	tu connaissais	tu connaîtras
	il/elle connait	il/elle a connu	il/elle connaissait	il/elle connaîtra
	nous connaissons	nous avons connu	nous connaissions	nous connaîtrons
	vous connaissez	vous avez connu	vous connaissiez	vous connaîtrez
	ils/elles connaissent	ils/elles ont connu	ils/elles connaissaient	ils/elles connaîtront
Descendre (to go down)	je descends	je suis descendu(e)	je descendais	je descendrai
	tu descends	tu es descendu(e)	tu descendais	tu descendras
	il/elle descend	il/elle est descendu(e)	il/elle descendait	il/elle descendra
	nous descendons	nous sommes descendu(e)s	nous descendions	nous descendrons
	vous descendez	vous êtes descendu(e)s	vous descendiez	vous descendrez
	ils/elles descendent	ils/elles sont descendu(e)s	ils/elles descendaient	ils/elles descendront
Devoir (to have to)	je dois	j'ai dû	Je devais	Je devrai
	tu dois	tu as dû	tu devais	tu devras
	il/elle doit	il/elle a dû	il/elle devait	il/elle devra
	nous devons	nous avons dû	nous devions	nous devrons
	vous devez	vous avez dû	vous deviez	vous devrez
	ils/elles doivent	ils/elles ont dû	ils/elles devaient	ils/elles devront
Écrire (to write)	j'écris	j'ai écrit	j'écrivais	j'écrirai
	tu écris	tu as écrit	tu écrivais	tu écriras
	il/elle écrit	il/elle a écrit	il/elle écrivait	il/elle écrira
	nous écrivons	nous avons écrit	nous écrivions	nous écrirons
	vous écrivez	vous avez écrit	vous écriviez	vous écrirez
	ils/elles écrivent	lis/elles ont écrit	ils/elles écrivaient	ils/elles écriront
	je fais	j'ai fait	je faisais	je ferai

Faire (to do)	tu fais	tu as fait	tu faisais	tu feras
	il/elle fait	il/elle a fait	il/elle faisait	il/elle fera
	nous faisons	nous avons fait	nous faisions	nous ferons
	vous faites	vous avez fait	vous faisiez	vous ferez
	ils/elles font	Ils/elles ont fait	ils/elles faisaient	ils/elles feront
Partir (to leave)	je pars	je suis parti(e)	je partais	je partirai
	tu pars	tu es parti(e)	tu partais	tu partiras
	il/elle part	il/elle est parti (e)	il/elle partait	il/elle partira
	nous partons	nous sommes parti(e)s	nous partions	nous partirons
	vous partez	vous êtes parti(e)s	vous partiez	vous partirez
	ils/elles partent	ils/elles sont parti(e)s	ils/elles partaient	ils/elles partiront
Pouvoir (to be able to)	je peux	j'ai pu	je pouvais	je pourrai
	tu peux	tu as pu	tu pouvais	tu pourras
	il/elle peut	il/elle a pu	il/elle pouvait	il/elle pourra
	nous pouvons	nous avons pu	nous pouvions	nous pourrons
	vous pouvez	vous avez pu	vous pouviez	vous pourrez
	ils/elles peuvent	ils/elles ont pu	ils/elles pouvaient	ils/elles pourront
Prendre (to take)	je prends	j'ai pris	je prenais	je prendrai
	tu prends	tu as pris	tu prenais	tu prendras
	il/elle prend	il/elle a pris	il/elle prenait	il/elle prendra
	nous prenons	nous avons pris	nous prenions	nous prendrons
	vous prenez	vous avez pris	vous preniez	vous prendrez
	ils/elles prennent	ils/elles ont pris	ils/elles prenaient	ils/elles prendront
Savoir (to know)	je sais	j'ai su	je savais	je saurai
	tu sais	tu as su	tu savais	tu sauras
	il/elle sait	il/elle a su	il/elle savait	ii/elle saura
	nous savons	nous avons su	nous savions	nous saurons
	vous savez	vous avez su	vous saviez	vous saurez
	ils/elles savent	ils/elles ont su	ils/elles savaient	ils/elles sauront

Venir (to come)	je viens	je suis venu(e)	je venais	je viendrai
	tu viens	tu es venu(e)	tu venais	tu viendras
	il/elle vient	il/elle est venu(e)	il/elle venait	il/elle viendra
	nous venons	nous sommes venu(e)s	nous venions	nous viendrons
	vous venez	vous êtes venu(e)s	vous veniez	vous viendrez
	ils/elles viennent	ils/elles sont venu(e)s	ils/elles venaient	ils/elles viendront
Voir (to see)	je vois	j'ai vu	je voyais	je verrai
	tu vois	tu as vu	tu voyais	tu verras
	il/elle voit	il/elle a vu	il/elle voyait	il/elle verra
	nous voyons	nous avons vu	nous voyions	nous verrons
	vous voyez	vous avez vu	vous voyiez	vous verrez
	ils/elles voient	ils/elles ont vu	ils/elles voyaient	Ils/elles verront
Vouloir (to want)	je veux	j'ai voulu	je voulais	je voudrai
	tu veux	tu as voulu	tu voulais	tu voudras
	il/elle veut	il/elle a voulu	il/elle voulait	il/elle voudra
	nous voulons	nous avons voulu	nous voulions	nous voudrons
	vous voulez	vous avez voulu	vous vouliez	vous voudrez
	ils/elles veulent	ils/elles ont voulu	ils/elles voulaient	ils/elles voudront

Grammar Topic Index

A

adjectives, 53
adverbs, 113
aller, 112

C

c'est, ce sont, 50
closed questions, 122
combien, 58
composed past tense, 149
composed past vs. imperfect, 151

D

definite, indefinite articles, 51
demonstrative pronouns, 144
devoir, 121

E

en, pronoun, 129
-ER verbs, 44
être, 32

F

faire, 83

G

greetings, 17

H

hypothesis, 157

I

il y a, il n'y a pas de, 72
imperative mood, 136
imperfect tense, 150
-IR verbs, 104

N

nationalities and gender, 40
near future, 156
negation, 80
noun-adjective agreement for professions, 34

O

on, 119
open questions, 123

P

possessive adjectives, 66
possessive pronoun your, 59
pouvoir, 121
predictions, 157
preposition with countries, 45
prepositions of place, 73
present as future, 157
pronominal verbs, 111

Q

quantity, 90
quel, 58
questions, 122

R

-RE verbs, 135

S

s'appeler, 22

T

tonic pronouns, 81

V

vouloir, 118

Y

y, pronoun, 143

BOOK 2

Learn French Handbook for Adult Beginners

Essential French Words And Phrases You Must Know!

Explore to Win

Book 2 Description

Handle everyday situations in French, expand your vocabulary, and speak with natives with ease.

Everyone tells you that learning French takes more than a week. And let's face it. Your trip is coming up, and you don't have time to get a grasp of French.

What if you don't need to be fluent in French to get by in everyday life? Imagine easily communicating your needs in French, even if you are just a beginner, without ever needing to consult a dictionary or grammar book because you have everything in one place.

There's a simple solution: Introducing **"Learn French Handbook for Adult Beginners"** to help you learn context-based French.

It means having ready-made phrases for every situation in French, so you can find them easily whenever you need it.

In this book, you'll get 15 everyday topics every traveler needs to know. Not only that, but you'll also learn how to pronounce French and the basics of French grammar.

In **"Learn French Handbook for Adult Beginners"**, you'll discover:

- **15 topics**, focusing on everyday situations, such as greeting and civilites, meeting people, accommodation, transportation, food and drink, money, telephone and internet, health and wellness, shopping, business, time, weather, sightseeing, culture and entertainment, emergencies.
- **IPA Pronunciation Guide** to help you read the French transcription.
- A detailed **Pronunciation Guide** to pronounce vowels, consonants and learn accents in the French language (including their combinations).
- **Basic French Grammar Guide** to help you get familiar with the most frequent French words, such as pronouns, articles, adjectives or verbs.
- **Over 3,000 common phrases in French**, with an accurate translation in English.
- **Transcription** of each and every word in the phrases, included after every translation.
- **Social Etiquette Tips**

"Learn French Handbook for Adult Beginners" is for anyone who wants to handle everyday situations in French in no time and understand the basics of pronunciation and grammar. The first three chapters are created with common beginner's troubles in mind, such as understanding pronunciation, learning elementary grammar, and basic vocabulary. Whether you are traveling to France, without ever speaking French, or you are a student who wants to renew French because it's been years since you last spoke, this book allows you to start speaking French right away and participate in daily conversations.

Being exposed to all kinds of everyday sentences and vocabulary helps you become sensitive to French language patterns and be able to create sentences of your own, which is the end goal of every language learner.

Introduction

It's not just about enjoying the incredible French architecture or tasting the local food when visiting France, connecting with people is what makes each trip memorable.

Nevertheless, learning French can seem like a daunting task that requires more time than you usually have. This is particularly important since the average understanding of English in France isn't as high as it is in other countries.

You might be surprised to learn that you don't need to know too many French words or complete grammar to connect with locals. Most people use just a limited number of words and expressions in a single situation, and many of those are quite repetitive. For example, you will probably not discuss politics, if you are ordering coffee and croissants at a cafe. To help you get by in most everyday situations with the least amount of effort, this book is designed based on a context-based approach.

The book is structured into logical sequences that correspond to actual contextual situations. We carefully covered all possible situations you may encounter as a foreigner traveling around France, assembling the most important words and phrases in a logical, no-frills format. Our carefully chosen phrases are sure to make you feel confident in any given situation. The different sections of the book cover topics such as accommodation, transportation, eating and drinking, shopping, sightseeing, business, visiting a doctor, talking about hobbies and much more.

Additionally, there are sections that explain how to deal with some common problems, such as losing a passport, exchanging an item you bought, or getting lost in a city. Having traveled to foreign countries, as well as you, we understand all the crazy situations one may face.

As language lovers and learners, we have tried many different approaches and have found that internalizing situations works best. What does this mean? Imagine being in a cafe, queuing at the doctor's office or asking for directions. Creating mental images while learning is a method that enhances your memory. Because of the way our brains work, visualizing makes it easier to remember. Images by their nature are quickly recalled. The more vivid the image, the more likely we are to remember it. Our brain is automatically triggered when we see a similar scene, making it easier to recall the dialogues or useful phrases we once learned.

The purpose of this book is not to serve as a complete field guide, but rather as a reference, study, and review resource. At the beginning of the book, you'll get a basic understanding of French pronunciations and accents. You'll also learn one of the most powerful tools when learning any language – the IPA transcription system. IPA transcription is a standardized way to write speech sounds in any language, whether you can read or not. After learning the IPA elements, you'll be able to read French transcription without a single mistake.

At the beginning, you'll also be introduced to basic French grammar just enough for you to understand the most frequent words, such as pronouns, possessive pronouns, verbs and adjectives. You will note that certain structures, such as "I am", and "where is" appear frequently throughout the book. The thing is that the more you practice the essential structures included here, the easier it will be for you to recall the statements once you need them, and even create a phrase of your own.

Additionally, your experience will be enriched by a basic understanding of French etiquette. French are big on politeness, and learning a couple of politeness can take you a long way. Knowing how to address people in France can sometimes be more helpful than correctly asking for help.

In this book you'll get:

- → **IPA Pronunciation Guide** to help you read the French transcription.
- → A detailed **Pronunciation Guide** to pronounce vowels, consonants and learn accents in the French language (including their combinations).
- → **Basic French Grammar Guide** to help you get familiar with the most frequent French words, such as pronouns, articles, adjectives or verbs.
- → **Over 3 000 common phrases in French**, with an accurate translation in English.
- → **Transcription** of each and every word in the phrases, included after every translation.
- → **Social Etiquette Tips**.

Language learners often complain about not having enough material that can help them with everyday conversations. So, even if you are taking French courses, you'll find tons of useful examples and a good companion to your French classes in this book.

Besides being linguists and language enthusiasts, the authors speak French natively, so they know exactly how to apply the language in real life. Additionally, they will also be able to teach you how to speak and sound like a true native, and avoid some bookish expressions no one really uses.

Even if you don't have much time to study, simply carrying the book around will enable you to quickly find the needed French words. Having this book at your fingertips will make it easy for you to connect on a deeper level with French people and culture, and make some really good memories.

Your days founding the right word or response in French are finally over. It's time to picture yourself in France.

How to read IPA transcription

Every aspiring French learner should learn to read the *International Phonetic Alphabet* (IPA) because it's a powerful tool when learning any language. Because most languages are not spelled phonetically, we need help reading the language. IPA stands for International Phonetic Alphabet, which is a standardized alphabet for phonetic notation. Each symbol of the IPA has a unique pronunciation, no matter what language you're learning. You should know there's no one–letter–to–one–symbol correspondence between an IPA transcription and its normal spelling.

For example, the French word *"house"* is written *"maison"* but pronounced [mɛzɔ̃], according to IPA standards.

Let's see some more examples:

French spelling / IPA transcription

famille – [famij]

aussi – [osi]

enfin – [ɑ̃fɛ̃]

beaucoup – [boku]

Now that you are studying French, you should become familiar with the French sounds. Pay attention that French sounds could be different from French letters. We'll discuss this in the next chapter. The Standard French contains the following sounds:

Consonants – /b/ /d/ /f/ /k/ /l/ /m/ /n/ /p/ /s/ /t/ /v/ /z/ /g/ /ŋ/ /ʁ/ /ʃ/ /ʒ/ / dʒ / / tʃ/

Vowels – /a/ /e/ /ɛ/ /ə/ /i/ /ɔ/ /o/ /œ/ /ø/ /u/ /y/

Semi-vowels – /j/ /w/ /ɥ/

Immediately, you'll see a few sounds that aren't similar to your native language, like /ç/, /œ/ /ø/, so you'll need to take extra care to get them right.

Vowels

IPA / French vowels	French words	English Approximation
a	patte, là, femme	tr**a**p
ɑ	pâte, glas	br**a**
e	clé, les, chez, aller, pied, journée, et	l**a**ce
ɛ	baie, faite, mettre, renne, crème, peine, violet	b**e**st
ɛ : (longer)	fête, maître, reine	f**ai**ry
ə (known as e silent)	reposer, monsieur	**a**gain
i	si, île, régie, pays, fils	b**ea**t
œ	sœur, jeune, club	b**ir**d
ø	ceux, jeûner, queue	b**ur**n
o	saut, haut, chose, bureau	st**o**ry
u	coup, roue	sh**oo**t
y	tu, sûr, rue	the sound is non existent in English

Semivowels / Semiconsonants

IPA / French Semivowels	French words	English Approximation
j	payer, fille, travail, hier	**y**oga
w	oui, loi, web	**w**et
ɥ	huit	Hu**ey**

Nasal Vowels

Unlike French, English does not have nasal vowels, so the English approximation here is only a rough guide.

IPA / Nasal vowels	French words	English Approximation
ã	sans, champ, temps, vent, Jean, taon	roughly like s**ong**, but more nasalized
ɛ̃	vin, pain, plein, bien, impair, Reims, synthèse, sympathique	roughly like h**ang**, but more nasalized
œ̃	un, parfum	roughly like b**urn**, but more nasalized
ɔ̃	son, nom	roughly like dr**awn**, but more nasalized

Consonants

IPA / French consonants	French words	English Approximation
b	bon	a**b**out
d	deux, grande	to**d**ay
f	faire, vif	**f**estival
g	garçon, longue	a**g**ain
k	corps, avec	s**k**y

l	laver, seul	**l**evel
m	mère	**m**other
n	nous, bonne	**n**o
ɲ	gagner, champagne	ca**ny**on
p	père, groupe	s**p**y
ʁ	regarder, nôtre	Guttural R, non existent in English
s	sans, ça, assez	**s**ir
ʃ	chance	**sh**oe
t	thé, tout	s**t**y
v	vous, wagon, neuf heures, vous	**v**ein
z	zéro, raison, chose	**z**ero
ʒ	jamais, visage	mea**s**ure

Chapter 1: French Pronunciation and Alphabet

Avoir une autre langue, c'est posséder une deuxième âme.

Charlemagne

French uses the same 26 letters as the English alphabet. However, as you might expect, it has a different pronunciation.

These are (*a, b, c, d, e, f, g, h, i, j, k, l, m, n, o, p, q, r, s, t, u, v, w, x, y, z*).

Even though some French letters look like English letters, don't assume they are pronounced the same. It is the case with letters "j" and "g", which are proving to be a stumbling block for many French students.

While the French language has 26 letters of the alphabet, it also contains 36 sounds (phonemes), much more than the letters.

Sounds are grouped into three categories:

- vowels
- semivowels
- consonants

In some cases (well, in many cases), the pronunciation depends on the sounds surrounding it. In the following chapter, you'll be explained how vowels, semivowels, nasal vowels and consonants sound in French, and how their pronunciation changes when combined with different letters.

Vowels

There are six vowels in the French language (a, e, i, o, u, y). Sometimes, they can be written with accents. It is important to note that they do not always sound the same as in English. Combined with other vowels or consonants, they can create a completely different sound.

Vowel – A

"A" is usually pronounced like the "a" in the English word "flat", but it requires widening the corners of the mouth. In other cases, it can be pronounced like "ah" in the word "father", especially if it contains the circumflex or the grave accent.

Don't worry if you see variants of "a" with a diacritical mark (**A, À, Â**), because in all these cases the "a" is pronounced similarly.

Vowel – E

"E" can be pronounced in many ways, depending on the accent. When it is found at the end of the word, it remains silent. Like in these examples:

- petite (small) /pətitə/
- lourde (heavy) /luʀd/

The sound "e" has a variety of different spellings.

- **Without an accent**, it is often called silent "e", and it is pronounced like "oo" in the English word "look", denoted by "uh".

  - petite (small) /pətitə/

- **É** (with an acute accent)

Position your tongue like you're about to say "ay", but once you start making noise, don't move your tongue or lips. Keep them steady for the entire duration of the sound.

- été (summer) /ete/
- café (coffee) /kafe/

- **È, Ê, and Ë** (with a grave, circumflex or diaeresis mark)

It's pronounced like the "e" in the English word error, only flatter.

- très (very) /tʀe/
- rêve (dream) /ʀɛve/
- père (father) /pɛʀe/

Vowel – I

It's pronounced similarly to "ee" in the English word "meet". Orthographically, it can be written in several ways, always using one letter (**i, î, y**), except for some words that are borrowed from English. In this case, a digraph (two letters) is used to express the sound "i".

It happens with the letters **–ea** and **–ee**, like in English borrowed words such as *jean, leader, cheeseburger, feeling, meeting*.

- rire (to laugh) /ʀiʀə/
- corriger (to correct) /kɔʀiʒe/

Vowel – O

It's pronounced like the "o" in the English word "cold". However, the sound "o" has a variety of possible spellings (o, ô, au, eau).

- **O**

- abricot (apricot) /abʀiko/
- dos (back) /do/

- **Ô**

- poser (to put down) /poze/

- diplôme (diploma certificate) /diplomə/
- **AU**
- épaule (shoulder) /epolə/
- jaune (yellow) /ʒon/
- **EAU**
- bateau (boat) /bato/
- château (castle) /ʃɑto/

Vowel – U

The closest sound to "u" in English is the word "soup" or "boot". All variants of the sound "u" are pronounced the same way (*ou, où, oû, aoû*).
- oublier (to forget) /ublije/
- coûter (to cost) /kute/

Vowel – Y

It may be challenging to pronounce "Y" because the sound does not exist in English. A similar sound is "oo" as in "food," but in French, the lips are much more rounded. When producing the French "Y" sound, lips should make a small hole, while the tongue takes the same position as when pronouncing "i", with the tongue slightly bent down touching the lower teeth.

The pronunciation of "y" is unaffected by accents. So, whether it's spelled "u" or "û", the pronunciation remains the same.
- sucre (sugar) /sykʀə/
- tu (you) /ty/
- bûche (log) /byʃə/

Semi vowels / Semi consonants

In French, there are 3 semivowels, which are also called transitive sounds. All three (**u, y, i**) are formed when they come into contact with another vowel.

U + vowel / **w**

Y + vowel / **ɥ**

I + vowel / **j**

[w]

The [w] sounds like the letter "w" in English. A relaxed "wuh" followed by a quick "ah" sound. It sound similar to the beginning of the word *watch* /watʃ/ in English.

oi + vowel

louer (to rent) /lwe/

oe + vowel

foi (faith) /fwa/

ou + vowel

moelle (marrow) /mwal/

[ɥ]

It uses about the same lip position as the [w] semivowel. However, instead of keeping your tongue relaxed, your tongue should be tight against your hard palate.

u + i

cuire (to cook) /kɥiʀə/

u + some other vowel

juin (june) /ʒɥɛ̃/

[j]

Known as the "yod" in French, due to the "yuh" sound, it's often spelled with a "y." A "yuh" sound in the initial position, followed by various vowels. The initial sound is similar to that of yoga, yellow, and yes in English.

i + vowel

bien (well, good) /bjɛ̃/

y + vowel

yaourt (yogurt) /jauʀt/

–ill

abeille (bee) /abɛjə/

–ail

détail (detail) /detaj/

–eil

appareil (device) /apaʀɛj/

–ouil

soleil (sun) /sɔlɛj/

–euil

deuil (mourning, grief) /dœj/

Nasal Vowels

The French language is known for its nasal sounds that do not have any equivalent in English. There are two types of vowels in French: oral vowels (pronounced by passing air through the mouth) and nasal vowels (pronounced by passing air through the nose and the mouth, instead of just through the mouth).

Nasal sounds are vowels followed by an "n" or an "m". There are three nasal vowels used in French (nasal a, nasal i, and nasal o).

- **ã – nasal a** (pronounced like a nasalized "aun" in the word "laundry").

- ɛ̃ – **nasal i** (pronounced like a nasalized "an" in the word "angle").
- ɔ̃ – **nasal o** (pronounced like a nasalized "on" in the words "balloon" or "shadow").

Here's a table where you can find what the spelling looks like for each of the nasal vowels.

ɑ̃ – nasal a	ɛ̃ – nasal i	ɔ̃ – nasal o
Spelling **AN, AM, EM, EN**	Spelling **IN, IM, AIN, AIM, EIN, EIM, UN, UM, EN, EM final EN**	Spelling **ON, OM**
– grand (tall) /gʁɑ̃/ – blanc (white) /blɑ̃/ – ambiance (atmosphere) /ɑ̃bjɑ̃s/ – temps (weather) /tɑ̃/ – enfant (child) /ɑ̃fɑ̃/	– intéresser (to interest) /ɛ̃teʁəse/ – pain (bread) /pɛ̃/ – faim (hunger) /fɛ̃/ – imposer (to impose) /ɛ̃poze/ – Reims (city in France) /ʁɛ̃s/ – chien (dog) /ʃjɛ̃/ – thym (thym) /tɛ̃/	– bon (good) /bɔ̃/ – ombre (shadow) /ɔ̃bʁ/

However, it doesn't mean that all vowels followed by "n" or "m" make a nasal sound. French students often have trouble distinguishing between the two cases, even though the rule is simple. There are two situations in which nasal vowels aren't pronounced nasally. When the diphthong or triphthong is followed by another vowel or, when the consonant is doubled. Let's see some examples where the nasal sound isn't pronounced.

1. Followed by a vowel

aimer (to love) /eme/

vanille (vanilla) /vanij/

omettre (to left out) /ɔmɛtʁ/

2. Double Consonant

immeuble (building) /imœbl/

homme (man) /ɔm/

Consonants

In French, the most challenging part is the vowels. Having mastered those, consonants become pretty straightforward, because most consonants are pronounced like in English. Except for a few of them.

Consonants that remain the same as in English are: **b, c, d, f, g, k, l, m, n, p, s, t, v, w, x, y** and **z**.

Let's take a look at the ones that are different.

French consonants	Pronunciation	Examples
h	Always silent.	heureux (happy) /ørø/ homme (man) /ɔm/
j	Sounds like –s in the English word "television".	jupe (skirt) /ʒyp/ jaune (yellow) /ʒon/
q/que	Sounds like the letter –c, and –k in the English words "cat" and "kettle".	cinq (five) /sɛ̃k/ quatre (four) /katʀ/
r, rr	Nonexistent in the English language. It sounds like a gargling sound.	rose (pink) /ʀoz/ radis (radish) /ʀadi/

In French, when followed by certain vowels, some consonants make different sounds to English.

Consonants followed by vowels	Pronunciation	Examples
c + e, i, y	–s	cinéma (cinema) /sinema/ glace (ice) /glas/ garçon (boy) /gaʀsɔ̃/
g + e, i, y	Makes a sound like "s" in "television".	girafe (girafe) /ʒiʀaf/ singe (monkey) /sɛ̃ʒ/
s between vowels	–z	rose (rose) /roz/ maison (house) /mɛzɔ̃/ chemise (shirt) /ʃ(ə)miz/

Double consonants

When placed next to another consonant, some consonants make a different sound to English.

Double Consonants	Pronunciation	Examples
ch	–sh	chat (cat) /ˈtʃæt/ cheval (horse) /ʃ(ə)val/
th	–t	thé (tea) /te/

gn	–n, followed by "y" like in the English word "onion".	mignon (cute) /miɲɔ̃/
i + ll	English "y" sound.	famille (family) /famij/

In the case the same consonant is doubled, its pronunciation is not altered.

Silent consonants

The majority of consonants at the end of the words are not pronounced in French. These letters are referred to as silent letters. Letters *d, p, s, t, x, z* are silent at the end of a word, like in these examples:
- Beaucoup (a lot) /boku/
- Heureux (happy) /øʀø/
- Hommes (men) /ɔm/
- Pot (jar) /po/

However, the letters *c, r* and *f* can sometimes be pronounced. These letters require extra attention.
- Sac (bag) /sak/
- Neuf (new) /nœf/
- Jour (day) /ʒuʀ/

Liaisons

The French language can sound incomprehensible at times, because of a particular French characteristic that is called *"liaison"*. *"Liaison"* means that two words or even an entire sentence can sound like one word. This happens when the end of one word is linked to the next word by sounding the silent letter. The letters *d, n, s, t, x* and *z* that are normally silent, can be sounded when the next word starts with a vowel or a *h* and this is what we call *"liaison"*.

Pay attention that sounds **S** and **X** will sound like **Z** when they are followed by a vowel.

Let's see some examples:
- C'est un ami. (liaison in T between "est" and "un", and liaison in N between "un" and "ami").
- Nous avons. (liaison in Z between "nous" and "avons).
- Deux heures. (liaison in Z between "deux" and "heures").

Stress

Tonic accents in French are quite different from those in English. There is one stressed syllable in every English word, meaning that one syllable is pronounced more emphatically than the others.

In French, however, each syllable of a word is pronounced the same way, except for the final syllable of each rhythmic group (sentence).

Take a look at the place of stressed syllables in French and English. While the stress in English often changes place, it is fixed in French.

English – French

- pho**to**graphy – photograph**ie**
- edu**ca**tion – éduca**tion**
- **re**giment – régi**ment**

Whenever there is a whole sentence in French, the stress is transferred to the last syllable. Pay attention to how the stress moves with each word added.

- Je visite la cathé**drale**.
- Je visite la cathédrale Notre **Dame.**
- Je visite la cathédrale Notre Dame à Pa**ris**.

Accent

There are five different kinds of accent marks used in written French. They are:

acute accent (*accent aigu*)	grave accent (*accent grave*)	circumflex (*accent circonflexe*)	diaeresis (*tréma*)	cedilla (*cédille*)
é only	è, à, ù	â, ê, î, ô, û	ë, ï, ü, ÿ	ç only

Chapter 2: Basic French Grammar

Une langue différente est une vision différente de la vie.

Federico Fellini

Articles

The French language is one of the languages where nouns have two genders: masculine and feminine. Although there are some rules for determining whether a noun is masculine or feminine, the truth is that most of the time, you have to learn it by heart.

Articles help you determine the gender of the noun, as they stand in front of each of them. All nouns in French are either **masculine, feminine** and **singular** or **plural**.

The French language distinguishes between definite and indefinite articles.

Indefinite Articles

An indefinite article indicates an unspecified or unidentified noun. French has three types of indefinite articles, equivalent to the English "a/an" and "some".

Masculine Singular	Feminine Singular	Plural (masculine and feminine)
UN (un homme, un chien)	UNE (une femme, une maison)	DES (des maisons, des hommes, des femmes)

It is sometimes possible to choose (some, any) or even leave out a word when translating articles from French to English.

J'ai des amis formidables. – I have (some) great friends.

You don't need an article if you are talking about a person's profession, religion or in negative sentences.

Je suis étudiant en français. – I am a French student.

Je ne veux pas de chien. – I don't want a dog.

*Note that the French word **un** is both a number and an indefinite article for masculine nouns.

Definite Articles

It is also common in French to use the definite article to refer to general concepts. There is only one definite article in English: **the**. As opposed to French which has four of them (*le, la, l', les*).

Sometimes, English speakers find it challenging to add a word that is not needed in English. Try adding "generally" to the end of your sentence, and if it works, use the definite article.

Masculine Singular	Feminine Singular	Plural (masculine and feminine)
LE (l') (l'homme, le chien)	**LA (l')** (la femme, la maison)	**LES** (les maisons, les hommes, les femmes)

Nouns

Plural Nouns

To create the plural form of a noun, you have to:
- change the article to *les/des*.
- make a plural noun, according to the rules.

In general, a plural noun is formed by adding **–s**, and that –s is almost never spoken.

Singular – le billet / Plural – les billets

Singular – un billet / Plural – des billets

Apart from the general rule, in almost all other cases (when a noun ends in –eau, –au, –eu, –ou, –al, –ail) you should add **–x.**

un château – des châteaux

un cheveu – des cheveux

un genou – des genoux

un journal – des journaux

un vitrail – des vitraux

Feminine Form

As you learned, French differentiates masculine and feminine genres. This is how to form a feminine genre out of masculine.

Forming feminine form	Examples
Add **–e** to the masculine form.	*un ami => une amie (a friend)*
Change the ending **–er** to **–ère**.	*l'écolier => l'écolière (the student)*

Change the ending –**eur** to –**euse**.	*un voleur => une voleuse (a thief)*
Change the ending –**teur** to –**trice**.	*un directeur => une directrice (a director)*

Pronouns

One of the most frequent words you'll see in this guide are pronouns. They replace people, places, and things which have already been mentioned. They also reflect grammatical gender, person, and number.

Depending on its role in a sentence, a pronoun can be either the subject or the object of the sentence. In French, for each function in a sentence (subject, direct object, indirect object), the pronouns have different forms, as you can see in this table.

Personal Pronouns

Personal Pronouns (Subject Pronouns in weak form)	Subject Pronoun/ (strong form – used only without a verb)	Direct Object Pronouns	Indirect Object Pronouns
Je/J' – I	**Moi** – I	**Me/m'** – me	**Me/m'** – Me
Tu – you	**Toi** – You	**Te/t'** – you	**Te/t'** – You
Il – he **Elle** – she	**Lui** – He **Elle** – She	**Le/l'** – him, it **La/l'** – her, it	**Lui** – Him (it) **Lui** – Her (it)
Nous – We	**Nous** – We	**Nous** – Us	**Nous** – Us
Vous – You	**Vous** – You	**Vous** – You	**Vous** – You
Ils – They **Elles** – They	**Eux** – They **Elles** – They	**Les** – Them	**Leur** – Them

You choose the correct pronoun according to the noun you want to replace. Keep in mind whether the noun is masculine, feminine, singular or plural, and its grammatical value (is it subject, direct object, indirect object).

*J'ai une copine. **Elle** est très gentille et je **l**'aime beaucoup.* – I have a friend. She is very kind and I like her a lot.

(**J'** – subject pronoun, **elle** – subject pronoun, **l'** – direct object pronoun).

For example, "elle" is used to replace a feminine singular noun, serving as the subject, while "l'" refers to "copine" too, but serves as a direct object.

Subject pronouns refer to who/what is performing the action.

<u>J'</u>ai une copine. <u>**Elle**</u> est très gentille. – I have a friend. She is very kind. (weak subject form used always with the verb).

Qui chante des chansons ? – **Moi**. – Who sings songs? – Me. (strong subject form, used without a verb, and to emphasize).

Lui, il est trop gentil. / He, he is so kind. (strong subject form).

Object Pronouns refers to who/what is the direct receiver of the action. There are two types of object pronouns, according to the attachment type with the verb.

→ **Direct object pronoun** replaces a noun that comes directly after a verb without a preposition. "*Acheter un livre*" is a direct relation between a verb and an object.

J'ai acheté le livre. Je l'ai acheté. – I bought the book. I bought it.

(Je – personal pronoun, l' (it) – direct object pronoun, referring to "the book").

→ **Indirect object pronoun** replaces a noun as well as the preposition *à/de*, which introduces the indirect object. "*Chanter à*" is an example of indirect object relation.

J'ai chanté des chansons à ma copine. Je <u>lui</u> ai chanté des chansons. – I sang songs to my friend. I sang songs to her.

Adjectives

Descriptive Adjectives

The French adjectives present a bit more difficulty than the English ones. The reason is that French adjectives need to agree with the word they describe, in gender (masculine and feminine) and number (singular and plural). In fact, in French, all words in a sentence must agree with each other: verbs agree with the subject, adjectives agree with the noun or pronoun and so on.

Take the basic form of an adjective (which is always masculine) and add –**e** to create a feminine form. It's important to note that adding this –**e** causes the formerly silent consonant to be pronounced.

Singular m. – un **grand** *garçon* Singular f. – une ***grande*** *fille*

Plural m. – *des **grands** garçons* Singular f. – *des **grandes** filles*

As you may noticed, one English word "tall" has 4 different variants in French to express:

- **Singular masculin**
- **Singular feminine** / add –**e**
- **Plural masculin** / add –**s**
- **Plural feminine**/ add –**es**

Be careful when you spot masculine adjectives ending in –**e** (add –e), –**eux** (change to –**euse**), –**f** (change to –**ve**), –**er** (change to –**ère**), ending in consonants (double the final consonant).

âgé – âgée / dangereux – dangereuse / neuf – neuve / cher – chère / bon – bonne

Possessive Adjectives

Possessive adjectives are used to express ownership. Compared to English, French has a few differences, so let's take a look.

my book – **mon** livre

my house – **ma** maison

my books – **mes** livres

As you can notice, the English possessive adjective "my" has three variations in French (masculine, feminine and plural). That's why French has 18 possessive adjectives, while English has only 7.

Depending on the noun they describe, **French possessive adjectives** take different forms. In other words, if the noun is masculine and singular, the possessive adjective should be too.

The **masculine singular possessive adjectives** are: *mon, ton, son, notre, votre, leur*.

The **feminine singular possessive adjectives** are: *ma, ta, sa, notre, votre, leur*.

The **plural possessive adjectives** are the same for both genders: *mes, tes, ses, nos, vos, leurs*.

Personal Pronouns	Masculine Singular	Feminine Singular	Masculine/Feminine Plural (plural owners and plural possessions)
Je	**Mon** – my	**Ma** – my	**Mes** – my
Tu	**Ton** – your	**Ta** – your	**Tes** – yours
Il/Elle/On	**Son** – his/her	**Sa** – his/her	**Ses** – his/her
Nous	**Notre** – our	**Notre** – our	**Nos** – our
Vous	**Votre** – your	**Votre** – your	**Vos** – your
Ils/Elles	**Leur** – their	**Leur** – their	**Leurs** – their

While in English the gender of an owner is obvious, in French it's impossible to determine whether the owner is masculine or feminine. Instead, we are considering the genre of a thing owned, which is not the case in English. **"Son chapeau"** shows that the word *"chapeau"* is masculine. In English, it can be translated as either "**his** hat" or "**her** hat".

Verbs and Tenses

French has 10 indicative tenses, but not all of them are used in everyday language. For day to day conversations, you'll need the basic ones such as:

- → *le présent* (the present)
- → *le passé composé* (the simple past)
- → *l'imparfait* (the imperfect)
- → *le futur proche* (the near future)
- → *le futur simple* (the future simple)

French Conjugation

The French conjugation system is quite complex. All French verbs must be conjugated in person and number, which ends in having six different forms of each verb. Learning French conjugations involves learning which verbs are regular and which aren't. To distinguish regular from irregular verbs, French has classified all verbs into three categories known as groups in French. There are 3 groups and you'll easily recognize which verbs fall into which category by looking at their endings.

- **I group** – regular verbs whose infinitive ends in –**ER**.
- **II group** – regular verbs with an infinitive ending in –**IR**.
- **III group** – irregular verbs.

Present Tense

It is easier to use French present tense than English present tense for one reason. We have four forms of the present tense in English: the Present Simple, the Present Perfect, the Present Continuous, and the Present Perfect Continuous, while there's only one in French. French Present is used to express momentary action as well as progressive action.

The present tense in French (*le présent*) is used to talk about:

- facts that are always true.
- current situations.
- habits and repeated actions.
- scheduled future actions.

To express *Present Progressive and Present Perfect*, French uses expressions.

- → **Expressing Present Progressive in French** – use the expression "*être en train de*" or literally, "to be in the process of."

Je suis en train de lire. – I am reading.

Elle est en train de finir la course. – She's finishing the race.

- → Expressing Present Perfect – use depuis + présent de l'indicatif, which means since, for actions that began in the past and continue into the present.

J'habite à Paris depuis un an. – I've lived in Paris for a year.

J'étudie le français depuis deux ans. – I've studied French for two years (and still do).

Regular Verbs

Regular –**ER** and –**IR** verbs are conjugated the same way in all tenses and moods.

I GROUP ER – Remove the infinitive ending –**ER** and then add one of the following verb endings: –**e**, –**es**, –**e**, –**ons**, –**ez**, –**ent**.

II Group IR – Remove the infinitive ending –**IR**, and add different endings: –**is**, –**is**, –**it**, –**issons**, –**issez**, –**issent**.

Personal Pronouns	I GROUP / –RE endings	*Parler* (–RE verb)	II GROUP / –IR endings	*Finir* (–IR verb)
Je	–**e**	Parl**e** – I speak	–**is**	Fin**is** – I finish
Tu	–**es**	Parl**es** – You speak	–**is**	Fin**is** – You finish
Il/Elle/On	–**e**	Parl**e** – He/she speaks	–**it**	Fin**it** – He/She finishes
Nous	–**ons**	Parl**ons** – We speak	–**issons**	Fin**issons** – We finish
Vous	–**ez**	Parl**ez** – You speak	–**issez**	Fin**issez** – You finish
Ils/Elles	–**ent**	Parl**ent** – They speak	–**issent**	Fin**issent** – They finish

*Not every verb ending in –**er** is regular. You should always be aware of exceptions. For instance, the most common verb ***aller*** (to go) is irregular.

Irregular Verbs

Here are the most common irregular verbs in French.

	Être – to be	*Avoir* – to have	*Faire* – to do	*Aller* – to go	*Boire* – to drink	*Savoir* – to know
Je	suis	ai	fais	vais	bois	sais
Tu	es	as	fais	vas	bois	sais
Il/Elle/On	est	a	fait	va	boit	sait
Nous	sommes	avons	faisons	allons	buvons	savons

Vous	êtes	avez	faites	allez	buvez	savez
Ils/Elles	sont	ont	font	vont	boivent	savent

	Prendre – to take	*Comprendre* – to understand	*Attendre* – to wait	*Pouvoir* – can	*Venir* – to come
Je	prend**s**	comprend**s**	attend**s**	peux	viens
Tu	prend**s**	comprend**s**	attend**s**	peux	viens
Il/Elle/On	prend	comprend	attend	peut	vient
Nous	pren**ons**	compren**ons**	attend**ons**	pouvons	venons
Vous	pren**ez**	compren**ez**	attend**ez**	pouvez	venez
Ils/Elles	prenn**ent**	comprenn**ent**	attend**ent**	peuvent	viennent

Future Tenses

Future Simple

In English, the simple future is analogous to the "will" form.

The future simple is used in the following cases:

- **when talking about future intentions.**

Demain j'étudierai la grammaire. – Tomorrow I will study grammar.

- **when making suppositions or predictions about the future.**

Tu n'arriveras jamais à l'heure. – You will never arrive on time.

- **in conditional sentences.**

Si on attend les soldes, on paiera moins. – If we wait for the sales, we will pay less.

Regular Verbs

To form the future simple with regular verbs, just take the infinitive form and add the future endings: **–ai, –as, –a, –ons, –ez** and **–ont**. Take the infinitive form for **–ER** and **–IR** verbs, but remove final –E for regular **–RE** verbs, before adding endings.

Personal Pronouns	I Group – ER	II Group – IR	III Group –RE drop the –e + add endings
Je	aimer+**ai**	finir+**ai**	Prendr**e** / prendr +**ai**
Tu	aimer+**as**	finir+**as**	prendr+**as**
Il/Elle	aimer+**a**	finir+**a**	prendr+**a**
Nous	aimer+**ons**	finir+**ons**	prendr+**ons**
Vous	aimer+**ez**	finir+**ez**	prendr+**ez**
Ils/Elles	aimer+**ont**	finir+**ont**	prendr+**ont**

Irregular Verbs

Most frequent verbs are actually irregular in the future.

- aller → **ir** → j'**irai** / *I will go*
- avoir → **aur** → j'**aurai** / *I will have*
- être → **ser** → je **serai** / *I will be*
- faire → **fer** → je **ferai** / *I will do*
- pouvoir → **pourr** → je **pourrai** / *l will be able*
- devoir → **devr** → je **devrai** / *I will need*
- savoir → **saur** → je **saurai** / *I will know*
- venir → **viendr** → je **viendrai** / *I will come*
- voir → **verr** → je **verrai** / *I will see*
- vouloir → **voudr** → je **voudrai** / *I will want*
- envoyer → **enverr** → j'**enverrai** / *I will send*

Futur Proche

"*Futur proche*" refers to near future actions. This is equivalent to the English structure ***going to*** + **infinitive**, implying an intent behind the action. The *Futur proche* is used when an action shortly takes place or for planned actions in the future.

Christine va partir dans deux secondes. – Christina is leaving in two seconds.

Il va aller au supermarché. – He is going to the supermarket.

To conjugate the *futur proche*, we use the present tense of the verb ***aller*** + **verb in infinitive**.

Je	Je **vais** + **infinitive** (finir, porter, lire)
Tu	Tu **vas** + **infinitive** (finir, porter, lire)
Il/Elle	Il/Elle **va** + **infinitive** (finir, porter, lire)
Nous	Nous **allons** + **infinitive** (finir, porter, lire)
Vous	Vous **allez** + **infinitive** (finir, porter, lire)
Ils/Elles	Ils/Elles **vont** + **infinitive** (finir, porter, lire)

Past Tense

In French "*le passé composé*" corresponds to two different English past tenses: the Past Simple Tense and the Present Perfect. It's used to talk about completed actions in the past, and also to emphasize the results or consequences in the present.

We form the *passé composé* using the auxiliary verbs "*avoir*" or "*être*" followed by the past participle *(le participe passé)* of the verb. Auxiliaries are helping verbs, like "to be" and "to do" in English.

passé composé = auxiliary (avoir or être) + past participle.

Elle a fait un gâteau. – She made a cake.

The past participle usually needs to be learnt by heart. It corresponds to English verbs ending in –ed or –en. The French past participle usually ends in –*é*, –*i*, or –*u*.

Auxiliary Verbs

Some verbs go with "*avoir*" and others with "*être*". Most of them construct the *passé composé* with *avoir,* except for movement, state and pronominal verbs.

Verbs that require the auxiliary "*être*":

→ **Verbs of movement**

aller, entrer, sortir, partir, arriver, monter, descendre, tomber, passer (to go, to go in, to go out, to leave, to arrive, to go up, to go down, to fall down, to spend).

→ **Verbs of state**

naître, mourir, devenir (to be born, to die, to become).

→ **Pronominal Verbs**

Verbs accompanied by a reflexive pronoun.

se laver, se lever, se baigner, se peigner, se souvenir (to wash, to get up, to swim, to comb, to remember).

Conjugation with auxiliary "*être*"

- *Je suis entré* (*entrée* – feminine singular) – I entered.

- *Tu es entré* (*entrée* – feminine singular) – You entered.
- *Il est entré. / Elle est entrée.* (*entrée* – feminine singular) – He/She entered.
- *Nous sommes entrés* (*entrées* – feminine plural) – We entered.
- *Vous êtes entrés* (*entrées* – feminine plural) – You entered.
- *Ils sont entrés. / Elles sont entrées.* – They entered.

Conjugation with auxiliary "*avoir*"
- *J'ai fini.* – I finished.
- *Tu as fini.* – You finished.
- *Il a fini / Elle a fini.* – He/She finished.
- *Nous avons fini.* – We finished.
- *Vous avez fini.* – You finished.
- *Ils ont fini / Elles ont fini.* – They finished.

Negative Sentence

In French, a negative sentence is created by writing "*ne* + verb + *pas*". In front of verbs that start with a vowel, use "*n'*".

Je parle français. – Je ne parle pas français.

J'aime le thé. – Je n'aime pas le thé.

In spoken French, the "ne" tends to glide or even disappear. Sometimes, only the "pas" will be pronounced. So train your brain to catch it.

Qui veut de la soupe ? Pas moi ! – Who wants the soup? Not me!

Pas vraiment. – Not really.

Pas si vite. – Not so fast.

Prepositions

Prepositions of Time

→ **Avant** – before

→ **Après** – after

Je te retrouve après/avant le dîner. – I'll meet up with you after/before diner.

→ **Vers** – towards

Je vais vers la gare. – I am going towards the train station.

→ **Depuis** – since

Il habite à Paris depuis 2020. – He's been living in Paris since 2020.

→ **Pendant** – for, during

J'ai étudié le français pendant trois ans. – I studied French for 3 years.

- → **Pour** – for, in order to

C'est un cadeau pour toi. – It's a present for you.

Prepositions of Place and Movement

- → **À** – to (at, in, to)

Aller à la campagne – To go to the countryside.

Ce livre est à Marie. – This book is Marie's.

L'homme aux yeux bleus – The man with blue eyes.

Visites de 11 heures à 13 heures – Visits from 11 to 13 o'clock.

- → **Chez** – at, among

Je te verrai plus tard chez moi, non ? – I'll see you later at my place, right?

- → **Dans** – in, on

Il est dans sa chambre. – He's in his bedroom.

Dans 2 mois – in 2 months.

- → **De** – from

Le toit de la maison – the roof of the house

La voiture de Paul – Paul's car

De Londres à Paris – from London to Paris

Il vient de Londres. – He comes from London.

- → **Derrière** – behind

La porte de derrière – the back door

- → **Devant** – in front of

Il était assis devant moi. – He was sitting in front of me.

- → **En** – in, to, made

J'habite en France. – I live in France.

La mariée est en blanc. – The bride is in white.

Je le verrai en mai. – I'll see him in May.

C'est en verre. – It's made of glass.

- → **En face de** – in front of

Le bus s'arrête en face de chez moi. – The bus stops in front of my house.

- → **Loin de** – far from

La gare n'est pas très loin d'ici. – The station isn't very far from here.

- → **Parmi** – among

Ils étaient parmi les meilleurs de la classe. – They were among the best in the class.

- **Sous** – under

Sous la pluie – Under the rain

- **Sur** – on

Pose-le sur la table. – Put it down on the table.

Vous verrez la boulangerie sur votre droite. – You'll see the bakery on your right.

Chapter 3: Basic Vocabulary

Investir dans les voyages, c'est investir en soi–même.
Matthew Karsten

English and French Cognates

If reading most of these words feels like "*déjà vu*", it only indicates that your English is quite good, if not native. Words like *(location, adresse, profession, téléphone, entrepreneur, calendaire, dentiste, restaurant, pharmacie, page, fête, histoire, menu, omelette, fruit, orange, intelligent)* are called cognates.

You may feel surprised but approximately 1,500 English words derived from French are cognates – exactly the same in both languages. Words ending in **–ion, –al, able, –ible, –ance, –ence, –ent, –ct** often have the same meaning in French and English. Be aware, however, that French pronunciation is almost always different.

- **action** /aksjɔ̃/
- **ambition** /ãbisjɔ̃/
- **attention** /atãsjɔ̃/
- **célébration** /selebʀasjɔ̃/
- **communication** /kɔmynikasjɔ̃/
- **génération** /ʒeneʀasjɔ̃/
- **animal** /animal/
- **capable** /kapabl/
- **ambulance** /ãbylãs/
- **inaccessible** /inaksesibl/
- **objet** /ɔbʒɛ/
- **insecte** /ɛ̃sɛkt/
- **silence** /silãs/
- **indépendance** /ɪndɪˈpɛndəns/
- **correct** /kəˈrɛkt/
- **parfait** /paʀfɛ/

In English, many words ending in **–ical** have French equivalents ending in **–ique**:

- analytical – **analytique** /analitik/
- critical – **critique** /kʀitik/
- logical – **logique** /lɔʒik/

Many adverbs that end in **–ly** in English have an equivalent in French ending in **–ment**:

- absolutely – **absolument** /apsɔlymã/
- correctly – **correctement** /kɔʀɛktəmã/
- directly – **directement** /diʀɛktəmã/

especially – **spécialement** /spesjalmã/

Many words ending in **–ary** in English have their French equivalent as **–aire**:

- dictionary – **dictionnaire** /diksjɔnɛʀ/
- anniversary – **anniversaire** /anivɛʀsɛʀ/
- necessary – **néccessaire** /nesesɛʀ/
- contrary – **contraire** /kɔ̃tʀɛʀ/
- vocabulary – **vocabulaire** /vɔkabylɛʀ/

Qualities

proche /pʀɔʃ/ – close	**lointain** /lwɛ̃tɛ̃/ – far
jeune /ʒœn/ – young	**vieux** /vjø/ – old
vrai /vʀɛ/ – true	**faux** /fo/ – false
fort /fɔʀ/ – strong	**faible** /fɛbl/ – weak
doux /du/ – soft	**dur** /dyʀ/ – hard
grand /gʀɑ̃/ – big	**petit** /p(ə)ti/ – small
haut /o/ – high	**bas** /bɑ/ – low
puissant /pɥisɑ̃/ – strong, powerful	**faible** /fɛbl/ – weak
chaud /ʃo/ – warm	**froid** /fʀwa/ – cold
joyeux /ʒwajø/ – joyful	**triste** /tʀist/ – sad
vrai /vʀɛ/ – true	**faux** /fo/ – fake, untrue
rapide /ʀapid/ – fast	**lent** /lɑ̃/ – slow
tôt /to/ – early	**tard** /taʀ/ – late

Colors

As colors are adjectives, they must match the noun in gender and number. However, some colors come with only masculine forms such as *rouge, orange* or *jaune*, while others have both masculine and feminine.

rouge /ʀuʒ/ – red

orange /ɔʀɑ̃ʒ/ – orange

jaune /ʒon/ – yellow

vert (m.) /vɛʀ/, verte /vɛʀt/ (f.) – green

bleu (m.) /blø/, bleue (f.) /blø/ – blue

violet (m.) /vjɔlɛ/, violette (f.) /vjɔlɛt/ – purple

Blanc (m.) /blɑ̃/, blanche (f.) /blɑ̃ʃ/ – white

noir (m.) /nwar/, noire (f.) /nwar/ – black

gris (m.) /gʀi/, grise (f.) /gʀiz/ – gray

marron /maʀɔ̃/ – brown

rose /ʀoz/ – pink

bleu clair /blø klɛʀ/ – light blue

Example:

C'est un chapeau vert. /sɛtan ʃapo vɛʀ/ – It's a green hat.

C'est une robe blanche. /sɛt yn ʀɔb blɑ̃ʃ/ – It's a white dress.

Cardinal Numbers

It is very important to master the numbers 1–20 because you will see these numbers repeatedly. The number one, actually has two variants (masculine and feminine) while representing an undefined article at the same time.

0 – **zéro** /zero/

1 – **un** /ɛ̃/ or **une** /yn/

2 – **deux** /dø/

3 – **trois** /trwa/

4 – **quatre** /katr/

5 – **cinq** /sɛ̃k/

6 – **six** /sis/

7 – **sept** /sɛt/

8 – **huit** /ɥi(t)/

9 – **neuf** /nœf/

10 – **dix** /dis/

11 – **onze** /ɔ̃z/

12 – **douze** /duz/

13 – **treize** /tʀɛz/

14 – **quatorze** /katɔʀz/

15 – **quinze** /kɛ̃z/

16 – **seize** /sɛz/

17 – **dix–sept** /di(s)sɛt/

18 – **dix–huit** /dizɥit/

19 – **dix–neuf** /diznœf/

20 – **vingt** /vɛ̃/

It's easy to see that the numbers 17, 18, and 19 are simple math problems:

17 = 10 + 7, dix–sept

18 = 10 + 8, dix–huit

19 = 10 + 9, dix–neuf

All the numbers between 21 and 69 follow a similar pattern. In French, the numbers 21, 31, 41, 51, and 61 are joined with the conjunction "*and*" or "*et*", as in *vingt–et–un*. As in English, the rest of the numbers are separated by hyphens.

21 – **vingt–et–un** /vɛ̃t e ɛ̃/

22 – **vingt–deux** /vɛ̃ dø/

23 – **vingt–trois** /vɛ̃ trwa/

24 – **vingt–quatre** /vɛ̃ katr/

25 – **vingt–cinq** /vɛ̃ sɛ̃k/

26 – **vingt–six** /vɛ̃ sis/

27 – **vingt–sept** /vɛ̃ sɛt/

28 – **vingt–huit** /vɛ̃ ɥi(t)/

29 – **vingt–neuf** /vɛ☐ nœf/

There's no language that uses the same number system as French. Until 60, everything looks pretty standard, but then math takes over.

70 represents the addition of 60 and 10. And the moment you think you've got this pattern, it suddenly changes with the next number. 80 instead of addition relies on multiplication (4x20), while 90 represents the higher math problem 4x20+10.

30 – **trente** /tʀɑ̃t/

40 – **quarante** /kaʀɑ̃t/

50 – **cinquante** /sɛ̃kɑ̃t/

60 – **soixante** /swasɑ̃t/

70 – **soixante–dix** /swasɑ̃tdis/ actually 60 + 10

80 – **quatre–vingt** /katʀəvẽ/

90 – **quatre–vingt–dix** /katʀəvẽdis/

100 – **cent** /sɛnt/

1000 – ***mille*** /mil/

From 100 – 199

Use *cent* followed by the remaining number.

105 = cent–cinq /sɛnt sẽk/

144 = cent–quarante–quatre /sɛnt kaʀãt katr/

181 = cent–quatre–vingt–un /sɛnt katr/

From 200 – 999

This part is relatively simple as it follows the same pattern.

200 – deux–cents /dø sɛnt/

300 – trois–cents /trwa sɛnt/

400 – quatre–cents /katr sɛnt/

500 – cinq–cents etc. /sẽk sɛnt/

Ordinal Numbers

A noun's ordinal number indicates its position in a sequence (e.g. the first car on your left, the second house on the right). Most ordinal numbers go with both masculine and feminine words.

The important exception is "first" where we use two forms, "*première*" for feminine nouns and "*premier*" for masculine nouns.

la cinquième maison /la sẽkjɛm mɛzɔ̃/ – the fifth house

la première chanteuse /la pʀəmjer ʃa☐tœz/ – the first singer

first – **premier/première** /pʀəmje – pʀəmjer/

second – **deuxième** /døzjɛm/

third – **troisième** /tʀwazjɛm/

fourth – **quatrième** /katʀijɛm/

fifth – **cinquième** /sẽkjɛm/

sixth – **sixième** /sizjɛm/

seventh – **septième** /sɛtjɛm/

eighth – **huitième** /ɥitjɛm/

ninth – **neuvième** /nœvjɛm/

tenth – **dixième** /dizjɛm/

eleventh – **onzième** /ɔ̃zjɛm/

twelfth – **douzième** /duzjɛm/

thirteenth – **treizième** /tʀɛzjɛm/
fourteenth – **quatorzième** /katɔʀzjɛm/
fifteenth – **quinzième** /kɛ̃zjɛm/
sixteenth – **seizième** /sɛzjɛm/
seventeenth – **dix-septième** /di(s)sɛtjɛm/
eighteenth – **dix-huitième** /dizɥitjɛm/
nineteenth – **dix-neuvième** /diznœvjɛm/
twentieth – **vingtième** /vɛ̃tjɛm/

Chapter 4: Greetings and Civilities

Il nous faut accepter de dire au revoir à la vie que nous avions imaginée, pour laisser place à celle qui nous attend.

E.M.Foster

Every encounter with a French person has its own social etiquette. Depending on the context, formal or informal setting, you may opt for a firm handshake or a kiss if you are meeting French people.

A typical French greeting is a kiss (*la bise*). *La bise* can include one, two, or even three small kisses on the cheek, depending on the region. When in doubt, let the other person initiate kisses, and remember that kisses generally begin on the right side.

However, in a formal or business environment, you would not do this, and instead you would use a firm handshake. Men are also more likely to greet with a handshake than a *bise*. As a woman, you are permitted to kiss both male and female friends, acquaintances, and family members, even with people you are still not familiar with. As a guy, you can have a *bise* with female friends, associates, and family members. For two adult males, however, it is not usual to faire *la bise*, but it does happen from time to time.

Hugging French is a tricky area. In fact, hugging in France is not common between friends or even family members. It's interesting that French don't even have a word for hug, at least not in the same sense. The closest translation would be to simply "*take someone in your arms*" or "*prendre dans les bras*" or "*faire un câlin*" but both refer to a romantic gesture. It's more like a tender hug between a couple. Contrary to American greetings, hugging is reserved for children or significant others only.

Greetings

The most common French greeting is "*bonjour*" (hello). You can use *bonjour* to say "good morning" or "hello", when you meet someone for the first time of the day.

Bonjour /bɔ̃ʒuʀ/ – Hello! (also good morning)

Bonsoir /bɔ̃swaʀ/ – Good evening!

Salut /saly/ – Hi! or Goodbye! (informal) also appropriate when you see someone again later in the day.

Coucou /kuku/ – Hey there! (close friends use this casual salutation)

Âllo /alo/ – Hello (when answering the phone)

Au revoir ! /ʀəvwaʀ/ – Goodbye!

Bonne journée ! /bɔ̃ ʒuʀne/ – Good day!

Bon après–midi ! /bɔ̃ apʀɛmidi/ – Good afternoon! (After 12:00 pm)

Bonne soirée ! /bɔ̃ swaʀe/ – Good evening!

Bonne nuit ! /bɔ̃ nɥi/ – Good night !

À plus tard ! /a ply taʀ/ – See you later!

À toute à l'heure ! /atu ta lœʀ/ – See you soon!

À bientôt ! /a bjɛ̃to/ – See you soon!

À demain ! /a də.mɛ̃/ – See you tomorrow!

How are you?

After greeting someone, you should always ask "*How are you?*" as it is considered rude to skip this question. There are a lot of phrases for checking in with someone, and you'll notice that contrary to English, all questions contain the verb "*aller*" (to go) instead of "*être*" (to be).

When asked how you are, the most common responses are "*Ça va bien*" ("It's going well") or "*Tout va bien*" ("Everything's going well"). Similarly to English, it is uncommon to respond, "ça va mal" even if you aren't at your best.

You can address people formally (using *Vous*) or informally (using *Tu*).

Comment ça va ? /kɔmã sa va/ – How are you? (neutral)

Ça va ? /sa va/ – How are you doing? (condensed version of the question "Comment ça va ?")

Comment allez-vous ? /kɔmã ale vu/ – How are you? (formal)

Tu vas bien ? /ty va bjɛ̃/ – Are you doing well? (polite way to ask someone when you're expecting a positive reply).

Quoi de neuf ? /kwa də nœf/ – What's up? (very casual option to say hello in French, used only with close friends).

Et toi ? /etwa/ – And you ? (informal)

Et vous? /evu/ – And you ? (formal)

Here are the ways you can answer the above mentioned questions.

    Bien, merci ! /bjɛ̃ mɛʀsi/ – Good, thanks!

    Très bien, merci. /tʀɛ bjɛ̃ mɛʀsi / – Very well, thanks.

    Ça va. /sa va/ – I'm good.

    Ça roule. /sa ʀule/ – It's going well.

    Comme–ci, comme–ça. /kɔm si kɔm sa/ – So, so.

    Pas mal. /pa mal/ – Not bad.

    Pas pire que d'habitude. /pas piʀ ke dabityd/ – No worse than usual.

    Comme d'habitude. /kɔm dabityd/ – Same as always.

    Assez bien. /ase bjɛ̃/ – Quite well.

    Ça va bien. /sa va bjɛ̃/ – It's going well.

Tout va bien. /tu va bjɛ̃/ – Everything's going well.

Leaving

Je suis désolé(e), mais je dois y aller. /ʒə sɥi dezɔle, mɛ ʒə dwa i ale/ – I'm sorry, but I have to go.

Désolé(e), mais je dois filer ! /dezɔle mɛ ʒə dwa file/ – Sorry, but I gotta run! (informal)

Je n'ai pas le temps. /ʒə nɛ pa lə tã/ – I don't have time.

Excuse moi, je suis pressé(e). /ɛkskyze mwa ʒə sɥi prese/ – Excuse me, I am in a rush.

On se voit demain à... /ɔ̃ sə vwa d(ə)mɛ̃ a/ – See you tomorrow at...

Je t'appelle. /ʒə tap(ə)le/ – I'll call you.

Dites-leur bonjour de ma part. /dit lœʀ bɔ̃ʒuʀ d ma paʀ/ – Say hello to them for me.

Basic Courtesy

People in France are actually some of the most polite and courteous people in the world. In France, being polite is incredibly important, and everyone adheres to it. The simplest of *bonjour*, followed by *Madame/Monsieur* could open doors for you.

Whenever you enter a shop, say *bonjour* to the shopkeeper; when you board a bus, say *bonjour* to the driver; when you arrive at work, say *bonjour* to your colleagues. You can also use basic words such as "*merci*" and "*s'il vous plaît*" liberally.

Thanking

Merci. /mɛʀsi/ – Thank you.

Non merci. /nɔ̃ mɛʀsi/ – No, thank you.

Merci beaucoup. /mɛʀsi boku/ – Thank you very much.

Merci bien. /mɛʀsi bjɛ̃/ – Thank you very much.

Mille fois merci. /mil fwa mɛʀsi/ – Thank you so much. (Literally means "a thousand times thank you")

Je l'apprecie. /ʒə lapresi/ – I appreciate it.

Merci de votre aide. /mɛʀsi də votr ɛd/ – Thank you for your help.

De rien. /də ʀjɛ̃/ – You are welcome.

Pas de quoi. /pa də kwa/ – Don't mention it.

Je vous en prie. /ʒə vuz ã pri/ – It was my pleasure. (formal)

Je t'en prie. /ʒə tã pri/ – My pleasure. (informal)

S'il vous plaît. /sil vu plɛ/ – Please. (formal)

S'il te plaît. /sil tə plɛ/ – Please. (informal)

Vous êtes très gentil(le). /vuzet tʀɛ ʒãti/ – You are very kind.

Apologies, Misunderstandings and Regrets

Excusez–moi. /ɛkskyze mwa/ – Excuse me.

Excusez–moi de vous déranger. /ɛkskyze mwa də vu deʁɑ̃ʒe/ – I am sorry to disturb you.

Pardon. /paʁdɔ̃/ – I beg your pardon. (on the street)

Pardonnez–moi. /paʁdɔne mwa/ – Forgive me.

Je suis desolé(é). /ʒə sɥi dezɔle/ – I am sorry. (used to say sorry for something you have done)

Excusez–moi un instant. /ɛkskyze mwa œ̃ ɛ̃stɑ̃/ – Excuse me for a moment.

Excusez–mon retard. /ɛkskyze mɔ̃ ʁ(ə)taʁ/ – Forgive me for being late.

Excusez–moi, j'ai besoin de... /ɛkskyze mwa ʒɛ bəzwɛ̃ d/ – Excuse me, I need...

Excusez–moi, je n'ai pas bien compris. /ɛkskyze mwa ʒ nɛ pa bjɛ̃ kɔ̃pʁi/ – Excuse me, I didn't quite understand.

Ne vous inquiétez pas. /n vuz ɛ̃kjete pa/ – Do not worry.

Je n'ai pas voulu vous offenser. /ʒə nɛ pa volu vuz ɔfɑ̃se/ – I didn't mean to offend you.

Ça doit être une erreur. /sa dwa ɛtʁ yn ɛʁœʁ/ – It has to be a mistake.

J'ai fait une erreur. Je me suis trompé(e). /ʒɛ fɛ yn ɛʁœʁ/ /ʒɛ mə sɥi tʁɔ̃pe/ – I made a mistake.

Malheureusement oui/non. /malørøzmɑ̃ wi/no/ – Unfortunately yes/no.

Requests, Orders and Suggestions

Pouvez-vous m'aider ? /puve vu mede/ – Can you help me?

Pourrais-je (avoir)... ? – /puʁe ʒɛ avwaʁ/ – Can l have... ?

Pourriez–vous me dire ? /puʁje vu mə diʁ/ – Could you tell me?

J'aimerais vous demander ... /ʒɛmʁɛ vu demɑ̃de/ – I would like to ask you...

J'aimerais / Je voudrais.. /ʒɛmʁɛ / ʒɛ vudʁɛ/ – I would like....

Pourriez vous me donner un conseil ? – /puʁje vu mə dɔne œ̃ kɔ̃sɛj/ – Could you give me an advice?

Serait-il possible de... ? /sɛʁɛt il pɔsibl də/ – Would it be possible to... ?

Je voudrais parler à/avec... /ʒɛ vudʁɛ paʁle a/avɛk/ – I would like to talk with...

Je voudrais prendre un rendez–vous. /ʒɛ vudʁɛ pʁɑ̃dʁ œ̃ ʁɑ̃devu/ – I would like to take an appointment.

Pouvez-vous attendre un moment ? /puve vu atɛ̃dʁ œ̃ mɔmɑ̃/ – Could you wait for a moment?

Je pourrais l'emprunter ? /ʒɛ puʁɛ lɑ̃pʁœ̃te/ – Could I borrow it?

Je peux me joindre à vous ? /ʒɛ p vu ʒwɛ̃dʁ/ – Could I join you?

Vous viendrez me chercher ? /vu vjɛ̃dʁe m ʃɛʁʃe/ – Will you pick me up?

Pouvez-vous me passer ? /puve vu m pase/ – Could you pass me?

Je voudrais savoir si... /ʒə vudʁɛ savwaʁ si/ – I would like to know if...

Vous pouvez vous renseigner là-dessus ? /vu puve vu ʁɑ̃seɲe la dəsy/ – Can you find out about it?

Excusez–moi, j'ai besoin de... /εkskuze mwa ʒɛ bəzwɛ̃ də/ – Excuse me, I need to...

Je peux vous aider ? /ʒə pœ vuzede/ – Can I help you ?

Je cherche... /ʒə ʃɛrʃ/ – I am looking for...

Pouvez-vous m'y conduire ? /puve vu mi kɔ̃dɥiʀ/ – Can you drive me there?

Voulez–vous ? /vule vu/ – Do you want to?

Voulez–vous vous joindre à nous ? /vule vu nu ʒwɛ̃dʀ/ – Do you want to join us?

Ça vous gêne si... ? /sa vu ʒen si/ – Does it bother you if... ?

Si ça ne vous gêne pas. /si sa n vu ʒen pa/ – If you don't mind.

Vous êtes d'accord ? /vuzɛt dakɔʀ/ – Do you agree?

Vous en êtes sûr(e) ? /vuz ã ɛt syr/ – Are you sure?

Pourquoi pas ? /puʀkwa pa/ – Why not?

Attendez un moment, s'il vous plaît. /atɑ̃de œ̃ mɔmɑ̃ sil vu plɛ/ – Wait a moment, please.

Vous pouvez entrer. /vu puve ɑ̃tʀe/ – You can come in.

Entrez, s'il vous plaît. /ɑ̃tʀe sil vu plɛ/ – Please come in.

Débarrassez–vous. /debaʀase vu/ – Take your coat/jacket off.

Asseyez-vous ! /aseje vu/ – Sit down!

Mettez–vous à l'aise ! /mete vu alɛz/ – Make yourself comfortable.

Qu'est–ce que je vous sers ? /kɛsk ʒ vu ser/ – What can I get you?

Servez–vous. /sɛʀve vu/ – Help yourself.

Ressers–toi. /ʀ(ə)sɛʀ twa/ – Help yourself to more food.

Agreement and Disagreement

Agreement

Oui. /wi/ – Yes.

Bien sûr. Naturellement. /bjɛ̃ syr natyʀɛlmɑ̃/ – Of course. Naturally.

Bien entendu. Evidemment. /bjɛ̃ ɑ̃tɑ̃dy evidamɑ̃/ – Of course. Obviously.

Sans doute. Bien sûr. /sɑ̃ dut bjɛ̃ syr/ – No doubt. Of course.

Avec plaisir. /avɛk pleziʀ/ – With pleasure.

D'accord. /dakɔʀ/ – All right.

Pourquoi pas ? /puʀkwa pa/ – Why not?

Je crois que oui. /ʒə kʀwa k wi/ – I think so.

Vous avez raison. /vuzave ʀɛzɔ̃/ – You are right.

C'est vrai. /sɛ vrɛ/ – It's true.

Bonne idée. /bon ide/ – Good idea.

Pas de problème. /pas də pʀɔblɛm/ – No problem.

Sans problème. /sã pʀɔblɛm/ – No problem.

Peut–être. /pøtɛtʀ/ – Maybe.

Ça a l'air bien. /sa a lɛʀ bjɛ̃/ – It sounds good.

Disagreement

Non. /nɔ̃/ – No.

Non, merci. /nɔ̃ mɛʀsi/ – No, thank you.

Certainement pas. /sɛʀtɛnmã pa/ – Certainly not.

Pas moi. /pa mwa/ – Not me.

Pas pour moi. /pa puʀ mwa/ – Not for me.

Je ne suis pas d'accord avec vous. /ʒə nə sɥi pa dakɔʀ avɛk vu/ – I don't agree with you.

Ce n'est pas vrai. /sə nɛ pa vʀɛ/ – That's not true.

Pas du tout. /pa dy tu/ – Not at all.

En aucun cas. /a☐ okœ☐ ka/ – Under no circumstances.

Jamais. /ʒamɛ/ – Never.

Absolument pas. /apsɔlymã pa/ – Absolutely not.

Ça doit être une erreur. /sa dwat ɛtʀ yn ɛʀœʀ/ – It must be a mistake.

Malheureusement, je ne peux pas. /maløʀøzmã ʒə nə pø pa/ – Unfortunately, I can't.

Je dois refuser. /ʒə dwa ʀefyze/ – I have to refuse.

Je ne peux pas accepter. /ʒə nə pø pa aksɛpte/ – I can not accept.

Peut-être la prochaine fois. /pøtɛtʀ la pʀɔʃɛ̃ fwa/ – Maybe next time.

Wishes and Holiday Greetings

Santé ! /sãte/ – Cheers!

Félicitations ! /felisitasjɔ̃/ – Congratulations!

Bonne chance ! /bɔ̃ ʃãs/ – Good luck!

Bon voyage ! /bɔn vwajaʒ/ – Have a nice trip!

Bon anniversaire ! /bɔn anivɛʀsɛʀ/ – Happy birthday!

Amusez-vous bien ! /amyze vu bjɛ̃/ – Have a good time!

Rentrez bien ! /ʀãtʀe bjɛ̃/ – Safe travel!

Joyeuses fêtes ! /ʒwa.jøz fɛt/ – Happy holidays!

Bonnes Fêtes ! /bɔn fɛt/ – Happy Holidays!

Meilleurs Vœux ! /mɛjœʀ vø/ – Best Wishes!

Je vous souhaite de joyeuses fêtes ! /ʒə vu swɛt də ʒwajøz fɛt/ – I wish you happy holidays!

Bonne Année ! /bɔn ane/ – Happy New Year!

Meilleurs vœux pour la nouvelle année ! /mɛjœʀ vø puʀ la nuvɛl ane/ – Best wishes for the New Year!

Joyeux Noël ! /ʒwajø nɔɛl/ – Merry Christmas!

Joyeux Noël à toi et à tes proches ! /ʒwajø nɔɛl a twa e te pʀɔʃ/ – Merry Christmas to you and your loved ones!

Joyeuses Pâques ! /ʒwajøz pak/ – Happy Easter!

Chapter 5: Meeting People

Tomber amoureux, c'est facile. Faire l'amour encore plus. Mais rencontrer quelqu'un qui t'allume l'âme, ça, c'est exceptionnel.

Adelaire Landay

You'll easily meet French people in a group of friends, by simply asking their name or introducing yourself first. While waiting for a bus or queuing, it may be possible to meet someone randomly, but French people prefer silence and don't like to disturb others, so starting a deep conversation in such places may be considered rude, especially if that person isn't willing to proceed with the communication. Unlike Americans, who immediately present their name, where they are from, their job, the French consider those things quite personal. Be careful not to reveal too much about yourself too soon because it may scare some of them. In France, conversations grow as you become more familiar with each other. If you're new to France and want to meet French people, language exchange events are a good place to start as they usually lead to exchanging numbers and hanging out afterward.

What is Your Name?

Comment vous appelez vous ? /kɒmɛnt vuzap(ə)levu/ – What is your name? (formal)

Comment t'appelles tu ? /kɒmɛnt tap(ə)le ty/ – What's your name? (informal)

Quel est votre prénom ? /kɛl e tõ pʀenõ/ – What's your name? (formal)

Quel est votre nom ? /kɛl e vɔtʀ nõ/ – What's your last name? (formal)

Quel est ton prénom ? /kɛl e tõ pʀenõ/ – What's your name? (informal)

Quel est ton nom ? /kɛl e tõ nõ/ – What's your last name? (informal)

Introducing Yourself

Je m'appelle, _ . /ʒə mapɛl/ – My name is _ .

Je suis _ . /ʒə sɥi/ – I am _ .

Mon nom est _ . /mõ nõ ɛ/ – My name is _

Mon prénom est _ . /mõ pʀenõ ɛ/ – My first name is _

Moi, c'est _ . /mwa sɛ/ – By the way, I'm _ . (informal) (used when the other person's name is said first).

Je m'appelle _ , mais je me fais appeler _ . /ʒə mapɛl _ mɛ ʒə mə fɛ apəle _/ – My name is (name), but I prefer to be called (nickname).

Je me présente. Je m'appelle/Je suis _ . /ʒə m pʀezɑ̃te. ʒə mapɛl _ . or ʒə sɥi _ / – Allow me to introduce myself. My name is/I'm _ . (very formal)

Introducing Others

Comment s'appelle _ ? /kɒmɛnt sapəle/ – What's . . . name?

Example:

Comment s'appelle ta fille ? /kɒmɛnt sapəle ta fij/ – What's your daughter's name?

→ **Formal**

Je vous présente (name). /ʒə vu pʀezɑ̃te/ – Allow me to introduce (name).

Je te présente (name). /ʒə tə pʀezɑ̃te/ – Allow me to introduce (name).

Example:

Je vous présente Marie. Marie est actrice. /ʒə vu pʀezɑ̃te Mari. Mari ɛ aktʀis/ – Allow me to introduce Marie. Marie is an actress. (This is often followed by a brief explanation of who the person is).

→ **Informal**

The word "*voici*" can be used to introduce a person that's located near us, or to introduce a new person.

Voici (name). /vwasi _ /– This is (name).

Example:

Voici Marie. /vwasi Mari/– This is Marie.

When we introduce someone who is not physically near us, we have two common options.

Ça, c'est (name). /sa sɛ _/ – That person there is (name). Note that this phrase can be followed with additional information.

Example:

Ça, c'est Marie. Elle est française. – That person there is Marie. She's French.

Voilà _. /vwala/ – That's (name).

Example:

Voilà Jean. – That's Jean.

Note * we use **Voilà/Voici** to introduce things too.

Pleasure to Meet You

→ Informally you can just say:

Enchanté(e) /ɑ̃ʃɑ̃te/ – Pleasure.

→ Formally:

C'est un plaisir de vous rencontrer. /sɛt an plezir də vu ʀɑ̃kɔ̃tʀe/ – It's a pleasure to meet you. (formal version)

Enchanté(e) de faire votre connaissance. /ɑ̃ʃɑ̃te də fɛʀ vɔtʀ kɔnɛsɑ̃s/ – Pleased to meet you.

C'est un plaisir de faire votre connaissance. /sɛt an plezir də fɛʀ vɔtʀ kɔnɛsɑ̃s/ – It is a pleasure to meet you.

Personal Data – Filling in Forms

Many places require you to fill out forms and provide personal information, such as applying for a job, opening a bank account, getting insurance, and going to the hospital. Below is the most common data you'll need to enter.

les données personnelles /le dɔne pɛʀsɔnɛl/ – personal data

le prénom et nom /pʀenɔ̃ / nɔ̃/ – name and last name

la date de naissance /la dat d nɛsɑ̃s/ – the birth date

le lieu de naissance /lə ljø d nɛsɑ̃s/ – the birth place

l'état de santé /leta d sɑ̃te/ – health status

la situation familiale /la sityasjɔ̃ d famij/ – family status

    célibataire /selibatɛʀ/ – single

    marié(e) /maʀje/ – married

    divorcé(e) /divɔʀse/ – divorced

l'adresse /ladʀɛs/ – adresse

    permanente /pɛʀmanɑ̃t/ – permanent

    provisoire/actuelle /pʀɔvizwar /aktyɛl/ – current

le numéro de téléphone /lə numero d telefɔn/ – telephone number

l'adresse électronique /ladʀɛs elɛktʀɔnik/ – the email address

la formation /la fɔʀmasjɔ̃/ – education

le parcours professionnel /lə parkur pʀɔfesjɔnɛl/ – professional background

l'expérience professionnelle /lɛkspeʀjɑ̃s pʀɔfesjɔnɛl/ – professional experience

le permis de conduire /lə pɛʀmi də kɔ̃dyiʀ/ – the driving license

la date de disponibilité /la dat də dispɔnibilite/ – availability date

Do You Understand?

The French word for understand is *"comprendre"*. To say you *don't understand*, you have to use the negative *ne + pas* formation.

Est-ce que vous comprenez ? /ɛskə vu kɔ̃pʀɑ̃ne/ – Do you understand? (formal)

Est–ce que tu comprends ? /ɛskə ty kɔ̃pʀɑ̃n/ – Do you understand? (informal)

    Oui, je comprend. /wi ʒə kɔ̃pʀɑ̃n/ – Yes, I understand.

    Excusez–moi, je ne comprends pas. /ɛkskyze mwa ʒə nə kɔ̃pʀɑ̃n pa/ – Sorry, I don't understand.

Pouvez-vous répéter, s'il vous plaît ? /puvevu repete sil vu plɛ/ – Can you repeat, please? (formal)

Peux-tu répéter, s'il te plaît? /pœ ty repete sil tə plɛ/ – Can you repeat, please? (informal)

Comment dit–on ... en français ? /kɔmɑ̃ dit ɔ̃n ... ɑ̃ fʀɑ̃sɛ/– How do you say ... in French?

You could also change the word order slightly and say:

Ça se dit comment en français ? /sa sə di kɔmã ã fʀɑ̃sɛ/ – How do you say that in French?

Pouvez-vous parler plus lentement, s'il vous plaît ? /puvevu parle ply lɑ̃tmã sil vu plɛ/ – Can you speak more slowly, please?

You could replace "parler" with "répéter" – to repeat.

Pouvez-vous répéter plus lentement, s'il vous plaît ? /puvevu repete ply lɑ̃tmã sil vu plɛ/ – Can you say that again more slowly, please?

You can also ask someone to repeat themselves in less formal ways:

Qu'est–ce que t'as dit ? /kɛskə ta di/ – What did you say?

Comment ? /kɔmã/ – What was that?

Quoi ? /kwa/ – What?

How Old Are You?

In French, expressing your age differs in one word from English. French uses the verb "to have" instead of the verb "to be".

Quel âge as–tu ? /kɛl aʒ a ty/ – How old are you? (informal)

Quel âge avez-vous ? /kɛl aʒ ave vu/ – How old are you? (formal)

> **J'ai** (number of years) **ans.** /ʒe (...) ã/ – I am (number of years). Literally translated, it means "I have + age").
>
> Example:

J'ai vingt-deux ans. /ʒe vɛ̃døzã/ – I am 22 years old.

Where Do You Live?

Où habites–tu ? /u abit ty/ – Where do you live? (informal)

Où habitez-vous ? /u abite vu/ – Where do you live? (formal)

> **J'habite à Paris.** /ʒəabite a Pari/ – I live in Paris.
>
> **J'habite en France.** /ʒəabite ã fʀɑ̃s/ – I live in France.

D'où venez-vous ? /du vəne vu/ – Where do you come from? (formal)

D'où viens–tu ? /du vjɛ̃ ty/ – Where do you come from? (informal)

> **Je viens de Paris.** /ʒə vjɛ̃ də Pari/ – I come from Paris.

Je viens de France. /ʒə vjɛ̃ də fʀɑ̃s/ – I come from France.

Note that we use different prepositions according to genre and number of a country.

- For cities/towns/villages, use *à*:

J'habite à Rome. – I live in Rome.

- For feminine countries (countries ending with the letter –e), use *en*:

J'étudie en France. – I study in France.

- For masculine countries (i.e. not ending with –e or –s), use *au*:

Je travaille au Brésil. – I work in Brazil.

- For plural countries (i.e. ending with –s), use *aux* (the –x is silent):

Je suis né(e) aux Pays-Bas. – I was born in the Netherlands.

Continents

l'Afrique /lafʀik/ – Africa
l'Europe /løʀɔp/ – Europe
l'Asie /lazi/ – Asia
l'Océanie /lɔseani/ – Oceania
l'Amérique /lameʀik/ – America
l'Australie /ostʀali/ – Australia
l'Antarctique /lɑ̃taʀktik/ – Antarctica

Countries, Languages and Nationalities

	Country	**Language**	**Nationality**
Algeria	**l'Algérie** (f.) /alʒeʀi/	l'arabe /laʀab/	*Algérien(ne)* /alʒeʀjɛ̃/
Austria	**l'Autriche** /otʀiʃ/	l'allemand /lalmɑ̃/	Autrichien(ne) /otʀiʃjɛ̃/
Germany	**l'Allemagne** (f.) /almaɲ/	l'allemand	Allemande /lalmɑ̃/
Belgium	**la Belgique** /bɛlʒik/	le belge /bɛlʒ/	Belge /bɛlʒ/
Brazil	**le Brésil** /bʀezil/	*le portugais* /pɔʀtygɛ/	Brésilienne(ne) /bʀeziljɛ̃/

Canada	**le Canada** /kanada/	le français /fʀɑ̃sɛ/	*Canadien(ne)* /kanadjɛ̃/
China	**la Chine** /la ʃin/	le chinois /ʃinwa/	Chinois(e) /ʃinwa/
Denmark	**le Danemark** /danmaʀk/	le danois /danwa/	Danois(e) /danwa/
United States	**les États–Unis** (m.) /etazyni/	l'anglais /ɑ̃glɛ/	Américain(e) /ameʀikɛ̃/
Egypt	**l'Égypte** (f.) /eʒipt/	l'arabe /laʀab/	*Égyptien(ne)* /eʒipsjɛ̃/
Spain	**l'Espagne** /ɛspaɲ/	l'espagnol /ɛspaɲɔl/	Espagnol(e) /ɛspaɲɔl/
England	**l'Angleterre** (f.) /ɑ̃glətɛʀ/	l'anglais	Anglais(e)
France	**la France** /fʀɑ̃s/	le français /fʀɑ̃sɛ/	Français(e) /fʀɑ̃sɛ/
Greece	**la Grèce** /'griːs/	le grec /gʀɛk/	Grec(que) /gʀɛk/
Hungary	**La Hongrie** /ɔ̃gʀi/	le hongrois /ɔ̃gʀwa/	hongrois(e) /ɔ̃gʀwa/
India	**l'Inde** (f.) /ɛ̃d/	<u>l'hindi</u> /lɪndi/	Indien(ne) /ɛ̃djɛ̃/
Israel	**l'Israël** (m.) /isʀaɛl/	l'hébreu /lebʀø/	Israélien(ne) /Isʀaeljɛ̃/
Italy	**l'Italie** (f.) /itali/	l'italien /Italjɛ̃/	Italien(ne) /Italjɛ̃/

Ireland	**l'Irlande** (f.) /iʀlɑ̃d/	l'irlandais /Iʀlɑ̃dɛ/	Irlandais(e) /Iʀlɑ̃dɛ/
Iran	**l'Iran** (m.) /iʀɑ̃/	le perse /lə pɛrsə/	Iranien(ne) /iʀanjɛ̃/
Japan	**le Japon** /ʒapɔ̃/	e japonais /ʒapɔnɛ/	Japonais(e) /ʒapɔnɛ/
Mexico	**le Mexique** /mɛksik/	l'espagnol /ɛspaɲɔl/	Mexicain(e) /mɛksikɛ̃/
Netherlands	**les Pays–Bas** /peiba/	le néerlandais /neɛʀlɑ̃dɛ/	Néerlandais(e) /neɛʀlɑ̃dɛ/
New Zealand	**la Nouvelle–Zélande** /nuvɛlzelɑ̃d/	l'anglais	Néo–zélandais(e) /neo-zelɑ̃de/
Sweden	**la Suède** /sɥɛd/	le suédois /sɥedwa/	Suédois(e) /sɥedwa/
Portugal	**le Portugal** /pɔʀtygal/	le portugais /pɔʀtygɛ/	Portugais(e) /pɔʀtygɛ/
United Kingdom	**le Royaume–Uni** /ʀwajomyni/	l'anglais	anglais(e)
Russia	**la Russie** /ʀysi/	le russe /ʀys/	Russe /ʀys/
Turkey	**la Turquie** /tyʀki/	le turc /tyʀk/	Turque /tyʀk/
Tunisia	**la Tunisie** /tynizi/	L'arabe /aʀab/	Tunisien(ne) /tynizjɛ̃/
United Arab Emirates	**les Émirats arabes unis** /lezemiʀaaʀab yni/	l'arabe	Arabe

Nationalities

Quelle est ta nationalité ? /kɛl ɛ ta nasjɔnalite/ – What's your nationality?

> *Je suis français.* /ʒə sɥi fʀɑ̃sɛ/ – I am French. (if you are a man)
>
> *Je suis française.* /ʒə sɥi fʀɑ̃sez/ – I am French. (if you are a woman)
>
> *Je ne suis pas française.* /ʒə nə sɥi pa fʀɑ̃sɛ/ – I am not French.

As you can see, the pronunciation differs slightly if you are a woman or a man. That's because the additional –e you add to all feminine forms turns the silent consonant into a pronounced one. It happens with the letters "t" and "n".

Languages

When you are making French friends, they may also be curious about your abilities to learn new languages and how many languages you know. So it can be part of the introduction.

Quelles langues parles–tu ? /kɛl lɑ̃g parl ty/ – What languages do you speak?

Quelles langues parlez–vous ? /kɛl lɑ̃g parle vu/ – What languages do you speak?

> *Je parle français et anglais.* /ʒə parl fʀɑ̃sɛ e ɑ̃glɛ/ – I speak French and English.
>
> *J'étudie l'allemand.* /ʒə etydje almɑ̃ / – I am studying German.
>
> *J'apprends le Français depuis 3 mois.* /ʒə apʀɑ̃d lə fʀɑ̃sɛ dəpɥi tʀwa mwa/ – I have been learning French for 3 months.

Parlez–vous français ? /paʀle vu fʀɑ̃sɛ/ – Do you speak French?

> *Oui, je parle français.* /wi ʒə parl fʀɑ̃sɛ/ – Yes, I speak French.
>
> *Non, je ne parle pas français.* /no ʒə nə parl pa fʀɑ̃sɛ/ – No, I don't speak French.

Est-ce qu'il y a quelqu'un qui parle anglais ? /ɛskilja kɛlkœ̃ ki parl ɑ̃glɛ/ – Is there anyone who speaks English?

Oui, moi je parle français. /wi mwa ʒə parl fʀɑ̃sɛ/ – Yes, I speak French.

Personne ne parle français ici. /pɛʀsɔn nə parl fʀɑ̃sɛ isi/ – No one speaks French here.

Chapter 6: Time

Au lieu de regarder le temps qui passe, il vaut mieux l'utiliser.
Nouredine Meftah

There is also a cultural aspect to arriving on time or being late. For Americans, it is proper etiquette to arrive on time for a dinner. While that is the custom in America, in France, arriving on time to a dinner party is considered rude. It is likely that the host will still be preparing for the dinner party if you arrive early or on time. Arriving 15 minutes late to a party is proper etiquette.

You may be surprised to learn that shops and markets do not operate on Sundays, or if they do, they have shortened hours. Also, there are few shops with 24-hour shifts. Make sure you plan your grocery shopping accordingly.

Days, Weeks

aujourd'hui /oʒuʀdɥi/ – today

hier /jɛʀ/ – yesterday

demain /dəmɛ̃/ – tomorrow

le lendemain /lɑ̃dmɛ̃/ – the day after, the next day

avant-hier /avɑ̃tjɛʀ/ – the day before yesterday

après-demain /apʀɛdəmɛ̃/ – the day after tomorrow

maintenant /mɛ̃tənɑ̃/ – now

dans la journée /dɑ̃ la ʒuʀne/ – during the day

une fois par jour /yn fwa par ʒuʀ/ – once a day

dans trois jours /dɑ̃ trwa ʒuʀ/ – in three days

tous les jours /tu le ʒuʀ/ – everyday

tous les matins /tu le matɛ̃/ – every morning

à midi /a midi/ – at noon

ce soir /sə swaʀ/ – tonight

hier soir /jɛʀ swaʀ/ – yesterday evening

à/après minuit /a/apʀɛ minɥi/ – at/after midnight

la semaine passée/dernière /la s(ə)mɛn pase/dɛʀnje/ – last week

la semaine prochaine /la s(ə)mɛn pʀɔʃɛ̃/ – next week

une fois /yn fwa/ – once

une fois par semaine /yn fwa paʀ səmɛn/ – once a week

deux fois par semaine /dø fwa paʀ səmɛn/ – twice a week

un jour férié /ʒuʀ feʀje/ – a holiday

une journée de travail /ʒuʀne də tʀavaj/ – a working day

le crépuscule /lə kʀepyskyl/ – dusk

l'aube /lob/ – dawn

Parts of the Day

If you get confused when you see, "*journée*" and "*jour*", "*soirée*" and "*soir*", "*matinée*" and "*matin*", "*année*" and "*an*", know that the second word refers to what we mean by regular day/morning in English, while the first word (journée, soirée, matinée and année) explains the passing of time more subjectively.

un jour /ʒuʀ/ – a day

une journée /ʒuʀne/ – the day, duration of time

matin /matɛ̃/ – morning

la matinée /matine/ – morning (focusing on the duration of time)

le matin /lə matɛ̃/ – in the morning

le midi /midi/ – noon

l'après–midi /apʀɛmidi/ – afternoon

soir /swaʀ/ – evening

la soirée /swaʀe/ – evening (duration of time)

le soir /swaʀ/ – in the evening

la nuit /nɥi/ – night

minuit /minɥi/ – midnight

Days of the Week

Semaine /səmɛn/ – week

Lundi /lœ̃di/ – Monday

Mardi /maʀdi/ – Tuesday

Mercredi /mɛʀkʀədi/ – Wednesday

Jeudi /ʒødi/ – Thursday

Vendredi /vɑ̃dʀədi/ – Friday

Samedi /samdi/ – Saturday

Dimanche /dimɑ̃ʃ/ – Sunday

Date

When it comes to telling the date, there are several ways to do it.

- **C'est + le + number + month.**

C'est le quatorze juillet. /sɛ lə katɔʀz ʒɥijɛ/ – It's July 14th.

It applies to all days of the month except the first. To say the first of the month, say "*premier*".

C'est le premier janvier. /sɛ lə pʀəmje ʒãvje/ – It's January 1st.

- **Nous sommes + le + number + month.** – We are on + date.

Nous sommes le 2 avril. /nu som lə second avril/ – We are April 2nd.

- **On est + le + number + month.** – We are on + date. (impersonal)
- On est le 10 november. /ɔ̃ e lə dis nɔvãbʀ/ – It is November 10th.

Asking About Date

Quelle date sommes–nous aujourd'hui ? /kɛl dat som nu oʒuʀdɥi/ – What's the date today?

On est le sept juin. – It is June 7th.

Quel jour sommes–nous ?

    Aujourd'hui c'est lundi. /oʒuʀdɥi sɛ lœ̃di/ – Today, it's Monday.

    Aujourd'hui on est lundi. /oʒuʀdɥi ɔ̃ ɛ lœ̃di/ – Today is Monday.

En quel mois sommes–nous ?

    Nous sommes en janvier. /nu som ã ʒãvje/ – It's January.

Quelle est la date du concert ?

    C'est le 15 novembre. /sɛ lə kɛ̃z nɔvãbʀ/ – It's on November 15th.

    C'est demain. /sɛ d(ə)mɛ̃/ – It's tomorrow.

Hier, c'était dimanche. /jɛʀ setɛ dimãʃ/ – Yesterday was Sunday.

Demain, c'est mardi. /d(ə)mɛ̃ sɛ mardi/ – Tomorrow is Tuesday.

Years, Months, Seasons

le mois /lə mwa/ – month

l'an /l'année /lã – lane/ – year

cette année /sɛt ane/ – this year

l'année dernière /lane dɛʀnjɛʀ/ – last year

Il y a un ans. /ilya œ̃ ã/ – one year ago

Il y a deux ans /ilya døz ã/ – two years ago

l'année prochaine /lane pʀɔʃɛ̃/ – next year

dans deux ans /dã dø ã/ – in two years

l'année prochaine /lane pʁɔʃɛ̃/ – next year

l'année dernière /lane dɛʁnje/ – last year

toute l'année /tut lane/ – all year long

chaque année /ʃak ane/ – every year

la décennie /la deseni/ – decade

le siècle /lə sjɛkl/ – century

Seasons

le printemps /pʁɛ̃tã/ – spring

l'été (m.) /ete/ – summer

l'automne (m.) /ɔtɔn/ ––fall

l'hiver (m.) /ivɛʁ/ – winter

Months

janvier /ʒɑ̃vje/ – January

février /fevʁije/ – February

mars /maʁs/ – March

avril /avʁil/ – April

mai /mɛ/ – May

juin /ʒɥɛ̃/ – June

juillet /ʒɥijɛ/ – July

août /u(t)/ – August

septembre /sɛpˈtɛmbəʁ/ – September

octobre /ɔktɔbʁ/ – October

novembre /nɔvɑ̃bʁ/ – November

décembre /desɑ̃bʁ/ – December

Common Phrases

en juillet /ɑ̃ ʒɥijɛ/ – in july

jusqu'en février /ʒyskɑ̃ fevʁije/ – until february

à partir de novembre /a paʁtiʁ d nɔvɑ̃bʁ/ – from November

il y a un mois /ilja œ̃ mwa/ – a month ago

dans un mois /dɑ̃ œ̃ mwa/ – in a month

ce mois-ci /sə mwa si/ – this month

le mois prochain /lə mwa pʁɔʃɛ̃/ – next month

233

What Time is it ?

la seconde /la s(ə)gõd/ – second

l'heure /lœʀ/ – hour

la minute /minyt/ – minute

There are three French translations for "time," each with a different meaning but with very distinct nuances and uses.

Heure – refers to clock time.

Quelle heure est–il ? – What time is it?

Temps – means either time or weather.

Ils ont le temps de faire la fête. – They have time to celebrate.

Fois – used to refer to one or several instances of an event.

J'ai appelé Pierre quatre fois aujourd'hui ! – I called Pierre 4 times today!

Quelle heure est–il ? – What time is it?

In French, the time is expressed that way: first you tell the round hour, and then the half hour, quarter or number of minutes until 30. For the time between half an hour and the full hour, you express the number of minutes remaining until the full hour.

1h00 – Il est une heure. /il ɛ yn œʀ/ – It's 1AM.

2h00 – Il est deux heures. /il ɛ døz œʀ/ – It's 2AM.

3h15 – Il est trois heures et quart. /il ɛ tʀwaz œʀ e kaʀ/ – It's 3:15AM.

4h30 – Il est quatre heures et demie. /il ɛ katʀ œʀ e demi/ – It's 4:30AM.

4h45 – Il est cinq heures moins le quart. /il ɛ sɛ☐k œʀ mwẽ lə kaʀ/ – It's 4:45AM.

or Il est quatre heures quarante–cinq. /il ɛ katʀ œʀ kaʀãt sẽk/

5h20 – Il est cinq heures vingt. /il ɛ sɛ☐k œʀ vẽ/ – It's 5:20AM.

8h40 – Il est neuf heures moins vingt. /il ɛ nœv œʀ mwẽ vẽ/ – It's 8:40AM.

Useful Sentences

Je suis parti ce matin. /ʒə sɥi paʀti sə matẽ/ – I left this morning.

Je travaille toute la journée. /ʒə tʀavaje tut la ʒuʀne/ – I work all day.

Il y a une réunion ce soir. /ilja yn ʀeynjõ sə swaʀ/ – There's a meeting this evening.

J'ai un rendez–vous demain. /ʒɛ œ☐ ʀãdevu d(ə)mẽ/ – I have a meeting tomorrow.

Il y a trois ans que j'ai voyagé en France. /ilja tʀwazã kə ʒɛ vwajaʒ ã fʀãs/ – It has been 3 years that I traveled to France.

Je serai absent à partir du seize décembre. /ʒɛ absen a paʀtiʀ dy sɛz desãbʀ/ – I will be absent starting December 16th.

On arrive le cinq septembre. /õ aʀiv lə sẽk sɛptãbʀ/ – We arrive on September 5th.

Nous parlons depuis une heure. /nu paʀlon dəpɥi yn œʀ/ – We've been talking for an hour.

Il va parler pendant une heure. /il va paʀle pãda☐ yn œʀ/ – He's going to speak for an hour.

Nous mangerons dans 10 minutes. /nu mɑ̃ʒeron dɑ̃ diminyt/ – We'll eat in 10 minutes.

Retrouvons–nous à 10 heures. /ʀətʀuvon nu a diz œʀ/ – Let's meet at 10 o'clock.

Le bus part à 7 heures. /lə bys paʀ a setœʀ/ – The bus leaves at 7 o'clock.

Chapter 7: Weather

L'important c'est d'avoir le soleil à l'intérieur. Les nuages sont toujours passagers de toute façon.

Arisko D'Amour

The French are rumored to hate small talk. This isn't entirely true, since small talk is fine with strangers or vague acquaintances. You may meet a neighbor occasionally on the staircase whose name you don't know and it's completely okay if you begin talking about the weather. In general, older generations tend to be more accepting of small talk than younger generations who may find it shallow or fake.

There's one verb you need if you want to talk about the weather in French. It is *"faire"* or more specifically, the impersonal *"il fait"*. The French will ask **"Quel temps fait–il ?"** or "What's the weather like?". Remember that you can't use the verb *"être"* (to be), you need either *"faire"* or a specific verb like *"pleuvoir"* (to rain).

Vocabulary

la pluie /la plɥi/ – rain

le soleil /lə sɔlɛj/ – sun

le tonnerre /lə tɔnɛʀ/ – thunder

l'orage /lɔʀaʒ/ – thunderstorm

l'ouragan /luʀagɑ̃/ – hurricane

la tempête /tɑ̃pɛt/ – storm

l'éclair /eklɛʀ/ – lightning

la température /tɑ̃peʀatyʀ/ – temperature

le nuage /nɥaʒ/ – cloud

la glace /glas/ – ice

l'arc–en–ciel /laʀkɑ̃sjɛl/ – rainbow

le tremblement de terre /lə tʀɑ̃bləmɑ̃ də tɛʀ/ – earthquake

l'inondation /linɔ̃dasjɔ̃/ – flood

What's the weather like?

Let's take a look at different ways to respond or simply talk about the weather.

Il fait + adjective /il fɛ/ – It's (used to describe the most basic weather states)

Il fait beau. /il fɛ bo/ – It's nice.

Il fait chaud. /il fɛ ʃo/ – It's hot.

Il fait froid. /il fɛ fʀwa/ – It's cold.

Il fait frais. /il fɛ frɛ/ – It's fresh.

Il fait humide. /il fɛ hjuːmɪd/ – It's humide.

Il fait lourd. /il fɛ luʀ/ – It's heavy.

Il fait nuageux. /il fɛ nɥaʒø/ – It's cloudy.

Il fait orageux. /il fɛ ɔʀaʒø/ – It's stormy.

Il fait mauvais. /il fɛ mɔvɛ/ – bad weather

or **C'est + adjective** (nuageux/orageux/ pluvieux) – It's cloudy/stormy/rainy.

Il y a + noun /il ja/ – There is

Il y a du soleil /dy sɔlɛj/ – It's sunny.

Il y a du vent /dy vã/ – It's windy.

Il y a du brouillard /dy bʀujaʀ/ – It's foggy.

Il y a de l'orage. – There's a storm.

Il y a de la tempête. – There's a storm.

Il + verb – It's (used mostly when the sky is pouring something on you)

Il pleut. /il plø/ – It's raining.

Il pleut à verse. /il plø a vers/ – It's pouring rain.

Il neige. /il nɛʒ/ – It's snowing.

Il gèle. /il ʒɛl/ – It's freezing.

If you wish to put more intensity and say that the weather is very cold, humid or hot, you can always place the adverbs "*très*" or "*beaucoup*" in front of a noun.

Beaucoup /boku/ – a lot, much

Très /tʀɛ/ – very

Il fait très beau. /il fɛ trɛ bo/ – The weather is very nice.

Il y a beaucoup de vent. /ilja boku də vã/ – It's very windy.

Quel temps fait–il ? /kɛl tã fɛtil/ – What's the weather like?

    Il pleut. /il plø/ – It's raining.

Quel temps est prévu pour aujourd'hui ? /kɛl tã ɛ prevy puʀ oʒuʀdɥi/ – What's the weather forecast for today?

Quel temps est prévu pour cette semaine ? /kɛl tã ɛ prevy puʀ sɛt s(ə)mɛn/ – What's the weather forecast for this week?

    Il fera orageux cette semaine. /il fera ɔʀaʒø sɛt s(ə)mɛn /– It's going to be stormy this week.

    À partir de vendredi, le beau temps revient. /a paʀtiʀ də vãdʀədi lə bo tã ʀ(ə)vjɛ̃/ – From Friday, the good weather returns.

Il fera quel temps demain ? /il fera kɛl tã d(ə)mɛ̃/ – What will be the weather like tomorrow?

    Il fera froid demain. /il fera frwa d(ə)mɛ̃/ – It's going to be cold tomorrow.

    Demain, il va pleuvoir. /d(ə)mɛ̃ il va pløvwaʀ/ – It's going to rain tomorrow.

Il fait quelle température ? /il fɛ kɛl tãpeʀatyʀ/ – What is the temperature?

    Il fait 25 degrés. /il fɛ vẽ sɛ̃k degre/ – It's 25 degrees.

    Il fait moins deux degrés. /il fɛ mwa dø degre/ – It's minus two.

Va-t-il neiger ? /vatil neʒe/ – Is it going to snow?

Fait-il nuageux ? /fɛtil nɥaʒø/ – Is it cloudy?

Common Phrases

Le brouillard se lève. /lə bʀujaʀ sə lɛv/ – The fog is lifting.

Il y a eu du soleil toute la journée ! /il y a y dy sɔlɛj tut la ʒuʀne/ – It was sunny all day long!

Il fait un temps magnifique. /il fɛt œ̃ tã maɲifik/ – It's a gorgeous day.

Le temps s'ameliore. /lə tã sameljɔʀ/ – The weather is getting better.

Le temps se dégrade. /lə tã sə degʀad/ – The weather is getting worse.

Il y a un soleil radieux. /ilya œ̃ sɔlɛj ʀadjø/ – The sun is very bright.

Quel beau lever de soleil ! /kɛl bo ləve də sɔlɛj/ – What a beautiful sunrise!

Quel beau coucher de soleil ! /kɛl bo kuʃe də sɔlɛj/ – What a beautiful sunset!

Il pleut des cordes. /il plø de kɔʀd/ – It's raining cats and dogs.

Il est tombé quelques gouttes. /il e tɔ̃be kɛlk gut/ – We got a few drops of rain.

Il fait un temps affreux. /il fɛt œ̃ tã afʀø/ – The weather is awful.

Le ciel est couvert. /lə sjɛl e kuvɛʀ/ – The sky is overcast.

C'est la canicule. /sɛ la kanikyl/ – It's a heat wave.

D'après la météo, il fera beau. /dapʀɛ la meteo il fera bo/ – According to the weather forecast, the weather will be nice.

Il pleut toujours beaucoup en mai. /il plø tuʒuʀ boku ã mɛ/ – It always rains a lot in May.

Chapter 8: Traveling

Rester, c'est exister. Voyager, c'est vivre.
Gustave Nadaud

There's one French word you should know as a tourist: the word "*visiter*". Although similar to the English word, it means "to take" or "to go on a tour". You'll see it's everywhere you look.

In a City

le plan de la ville /lə plæn de la vil/ – city map

le centre /lə sãtʀ/ – city center

la banlieue /la bɑ̃ljø/ – suburbs

la rue /la ʀy/ – street

l'avenue (f.) /lə av(ə)ny/ – avenue

le pont /lə pɔ̃/ – bridge

la place /la plas/ – square

le jardin public /lə ʒaʀdɛ̃ pyblik/ – public garden

le stade /lə stad/ – stadium

le marché /lə maʀʃe/ – market

le marché aux puces /lə maʀʃe opys/ – flea market

la foire /la fwaʀ/ – fair

l'usine (f.) /lyzin/ – factory

le cinéma /lə sinema/ – movies

le théâtre /lə teatʀ/ – theatre

la poste /la pɔst/ – post office

l'agence de voyages (f.) /laʒɑ̃s də vwajaʒ/ – travel agency

la police /la pɔlis/ – police

le parc /lə park/ – parc

l'hôtel de la ville (m.) /lɔtɛl də la vil/ – city hall

la mairie /la meʀi/ – town hall

le palais /lə palɛ/ – palace

le château /lə ʃato/ – castle

la cathédrale /la katedʀal/ – cathedral
l'église /legliz/ – church
la tour /la tuʀ/ – tower
le monument /lə mɔnymã/ – monument
l'exposition (f.) /lɛkspozisjɔ̃/ – exhibition
le cimetière /lə simtjɛʀ/ – cemetery
les ruines (f.) /le ʀyin/ – ruin
le musée /lə myze/ – museum
la bibliotheque /la biblijɔtɛk/ – library
le port /lə pɔʀ/ – harbor
le jardin /lə ʒaʀdɛ̃/ – garden
le monastère /lə mɔnastɛʀ/ – monastery
la salle de concert /la sal d kɔ̃sɛʀ/ – concert hall

Sightseeing

le tourisme /lə tuʀism/ – sightseeing
l'attraction touristique (f.) /latʀaksjɔ̃ tuʀistik/ – tourist attraction
faire la visite /fɛʀ la vizit/ – to do the tour
le touriste /lə tuʀist/ – tourist
le guide /lə gid/ – guide book AND tour guide
la visite guidée /la vizit gide/ – guided tour
l'itinéraire (m.) /litineʀɛʀ/ – itinerary
acheter un souvenir /aʃ(ə)te œ̃ suvəniʀ/ – to buy a souvenir
les attractions (f.) /lezatʀaksjɔ̃/ – attractions
le prix d'entrée /lə pʀi ãtʀe/ – entrance fee/price
ouvert /uvɛʀ/ – open
fermé /fɛʀme/ – closed

Common Phrases

Qu'y a-t-il à voir dans cette ville ? /kjatil a vwaʀ dã sɛt vil/ – What is there to see in this city?

Vous recommandez quels monuments locaux ? /vu ʀəkɔmãde kɛl mɔnymã loko/ – What local monuments do you recommend visiting?

Où est-ce qu'on peut avoir des informations sur la ville ? /u ɛsk ɔ̃ pø avwaʀ dezɛ̃fɔʀmasjɔ̃ syʀ la vil/ – Where can we get information about the city?

C'est combien le plan de la ville ? /sɛ kɔ̃bjɛ̃ lə plã də la vil/ – How much is the city map ?

Vous avez aussi un guide en anglais ? /vuzave osi œ̃ gid ɑ̃ ɑ̃glɛ/ – Do you also have an English guide?

On aimerait visiter la ville. /ɔ̃ emrɛ vizite la vil/ – We would like to visit the city.

On aimerait réserver une visite guidée. /ɔ̃ emrɛ rezerve yn vizit gide/ – We would like to book a guided tour.

On aimerait réserver un circuit. /ɔ̃ emrɛ rezerve œ̃ sirkɥi/ – We would like to book a tour.

Combien de temps dure la visite ? /kɔ̃bjɛ̃ də tɑ̃ dyr la vizit/ – How long is the visit?

Il y a un parc près d'ici ? /ilja œ̃ park prɛ disi/ – Is there a park nearby?

Vous pouvez nous faire visiter la ville ? /vu puve nu promene dɑ̃ la vil/ – Can you take us around the city?

C'est quoi ce bâtiment/monument ? /sɛ kwa sə batimɑ̃/mɔnymɑ̃/ – What is this building/monument?

Quand est-ce que cette cathédrale a été bâtie ? /kɑ̃ ɛsk sɛt katedral a ete bati/ – When was this cathedral built?

Qui est l'architecte ? /ki ɛ larʃitɛkt/ – Who's the architect?

Quel est cet édifice ? /kɛl e sɛt edifis/ – What is this building?

On peut aller voir à l'intérieur ? /ɔ̃ pø ale vwar al ɛ̃terjœr/ – Can we go inside?

Je peux prendre des photos ici ? /ʒə pø prɑ̃dr de fɔto isi/ – Can I take pictures here?

Il y a des toilettes publiques par ici ? /ilja de twalɛt pyblik par isi/ – Are there public toilets around here?

Est-ce que je peux acheter des cartes postales / souvenirs ici ? /ɛsk ʒə pø aʃəte de kart postal isi / suvenir/ – Can I buy postcards / souvenirs here?

Purchasing Tickets

Où est-ce qu'on achète les billets ? /u esk ɔ̃ aʃət le bijɛ/ – Where do we buy the tickets?

L'entrée est payante ? /lɑ̃tre e pejɑ̃/ – Is there an entrance fee?

Combien coûte le billet d'entrée ? /kɔ̃bjɛ̃ kute lə bijɛ dɑ̃tre/ – How much does the entrance ticket cost?

Quand le musée est-il ouvert ? /kɑ̃ lə myze etil uvɛr/ – When is the museum open?

    Ouvert toute la journée. /uvɛr tut la ʒurne/ – Open all day.

À quelle heure l'église ferme-t-elle ? /a kɛl œr legliz fɛrm tel/ – What time does the church close?

In Nature

l'arbre (m.) /larbr/ – tree

la fleur /la flœr/ – flower

l'herbe (m.) /lɛrb/ – grass

le ciel /lə sjɛl/ – sky

le vent /lə vã/ – wind

le nuage /lə nɥaʒ/ – cloud

la campagne /la kãpaɲ/ – countryside

le paysage /peizaʒ/ – landscape/scenery

la forêt /la fɔʁɛ/ – forest

la terre /la tɛʁ/ – ground/earth

la colline /la kɔlin/ – hill

la montagne /la mɔ̃taɲ/ – mountain

la falaise /la falɛz/ – cliff

la vallée /la vale/ – valley

la plage /la plaʒ/ – beach

le désert /lə dezɛʁ/ – desert

la prairie /la pʁeʁi/ – meadow

la jungle /la ʒœ̃gl/ – jungle

le chemin /lə ʃəmɛ̃/ – path

la côte, le littoral /la kɔt/ /lə litɔʁal/ – coast

l'île (f.) /lil/ – island

Bodies of Water

le lac /lə lak/ – lake

la mare or le bassin /la maʁ/ /lə basɛ̃/ – pond

la source thermale /la suʁs tɛʁmal/ – thermal source

la chute d'eau /la ʃyt do/ – waterfall

le fleuve or la rivière /lə flœv/ /la ʁivjɛʁ/ – river

la mer /la mɛʁ/ – sea

l'ocean (m.) /lɔseã/ – ocean

Hiking and Mountain Climbing

la balade / la promenade /la balad/ /la pʁɔmənad/ – leisure walk

la randonnée /la ʁɑ̃dɔne/ – hike

le randonneur, la randonneuse /la ʁɑ̃dɔnœʁ/ /lə ʁɑ̃dɔnœz/ – hiker

randonner /ʁɑ̃dɔne/ – to hike

l'itinéraire (m.) /litineʁɛʁ/ – route

le panneau /lə pano/ – sign

l'ascension (f.) /asɑ̃sjɔ̃/ – ascent

le point de départ /lə pwɛ̃ də depaʀ/ – starting point

l'aller-retour (m.) /lale ʀətuʀ/ – round trip

la cabane /la kaban/ – wooden house

le refuge /lə ʀəfyʒ/ – shelter

le pique-nique /lə piknik/ – picnic

le belvédère /lə bɛlvedɛʀ/ – viewpoint

la carte /la kaʀt/ – map

Equipment

le sac à dos /lə sak ado/ – backpack

des chaussures de randonnée (f.) /de ʃosyʀ də ʀɑ̃dɔne/ – hiking shoes

la combinaison de ski /la kɔ̃binɛzɔ̃ də ski/ – ski suit

l'anorak (m.) /lanɔrak/ – ski jacket

Common Phrases

Vous organisez des excursions ? /vuzɔʀganize dezɛkskyʀsjɔ̃/ – Do you organize excursions?

On aimerait réserver une promenade. /ɔ̃ ɛmʀɛ ʀezɛʀve yn pʀɔmənad/ – We'd like to book a ride.

On voudrait faire une excursion dans les environs. /ɔ̃ vudʀɛ fɛʀ yn ɛkskyʀsjɔ̃ dɑ̃ lez ɑ̃viʀɔ̃/ – We would like to make an excursion in the surroundings.

Combien de temps prend la randonnée ? /kɔ̃bjɛ̃ də tɑ̃ pʀɑ̃d la ʀɑ̃dɔne/ – How long does the hike take?

Combien coûte une telle excursion ? /kɔ̃bjɛ̃ kut yn tɛl ɛkskyʀsjɔ̃/ – How much does such an excursion cost?

Je voudrais commander une excursion d'une journée pour quatre personnes.
/ʒə vudʀɛ kɔmɑ̃de yn ɛkskyʀsjɔ̃ dynə ʒuʀne puʀ katʀ pɛʀsɔn/ – I would like to order an all day tour for four people.

On aimerait faire une randonnée d'une journée ? / ɔ̃ ɛmʀɛ fɛʀ yn ʀɑ̃dɔne dynə ʒuʀne / – We would like to go on an all-day hike ?

On aimerait aller voir les chutes d'eau. /ɔ̃ ɛmʀɛ ale vwaʀ le ʃyt do/ – We would like to see the waterfalls.

Il y a un endroit avec une belle vue ? /ilja œ̃ ɑ̃dʀwa avɛk yn bɛl vy/ – Is there a place with a nice view?

Quel est le nom de cette montagne-là ? /kɛl e lə nɔ̃ də sɛt mɔ̃taɲ la/ – What is the name of that mountain?

Ça prend combien de temps pour y aller à pied ? /sa pʀɑ̃d kɔ̃bjɛ̃ də tɑ̃ puʀ iale apje/ – How long does it take to walk there?

C'est combien de kilomètres ? /sɛ kɔ̃bjɛ̃ də kilɔmɛtʀ/ – How many kilometers is it?

Qu'est ce qu'il faut prendre ? /kɛskil fo pʀɑ̃d/ – What should we take?

Quel est le chemin le plus court pour monter cette colline-là ? /kɛl e lə ʃəmɛ̃ lə ply kur pur monte sɛt kolin la/ – What is the shortest way to climb that hill?

On pourrait essayer de monter sur cette colline ? /ɔ̃ purɛ eseje də monte syr sɛt kolin/ – Could we try to climb this hill?

C'est accessible en voiture ? /sɛ aksesibl ɑ̃ vwatyʀ/ – Is it accessible by car?

Je suis assez fatigué. /ʒə sɥi ase fatige/ – I am quite tired.

On peut se baigner dans le lac ? /ɔ̃ pø sə beɲe dɑ̃ lə lak/ – Can we swim in the lake?

Est-ce que l'eau est potable ? /ɛsk lo e potabl/ – Is the water drinkable?

On pourrait se reposer un peu ? /ɔ☐ purɛ sə ʀəpoze œ☐ pø/ – Could we rest a bit?

Est-ce que c'est raide ? /ɛsk sɛ ʀɛdə/ – Is it steep?

Je rentre. /ʒə ʀɑ̃tʀ/ – I go home.

Camping

le terrain de camping /lə tɛʀɛ☐ də ka☐piŋ/ – camping site

la batterie /la batʀi/ – battery

la lampe de poche /la lamp də pɔʃ/ – flashlight

le matelas pneumatique /lə matəla pnømatik/ – air mattress

le réfrigérateur /lə ʀefʀiʒeʀatœʀ/ – refrigerator

la poubelle /la pubɛl/ – garbage can

la pelle /la pɛl/ – shovel

le déchet /lə deʃɛ/ – waste

l'eau potable /lo potabl/ – drinking water

le réchaud à gaz / à alcool /lə ʀeʃo a gaz / alkɔl/ – gas/alcohol stove

les allumettes (f.) /lezalymɛt/ – match

la bouteille isolante /la butɛj izolant/ – insulating bottle

l'eau chaude /lo ʃod/ – warm water

la douche /la duʃ/ – shower

Common Phrases

Est-ce que vous avez encore de la place ? /ɛsk vuzave ɑ̃kɔʀ də la plas/ – Do you still have room?

Nous restons trois jours. /nu ʀɛsto tʀwa ʒuʀ/ – We are staying for 3 days.

Combien ça coûte ? /kɔ̃bjɛ̃ pɛjt ɔ̃/ – How much is it?

    Par jour et par personne /par ʒuʀ e par pɛʀsɔn/ – per day and per person

    Pour la tente /pur la tɑ̃t/ – for the tent

    Pour la voiture /pur la vwatyʀ/ – for the car

Est-ce que vous louez des caravanes ? /ɛsk vu lwe de kaʀavan/ – Do you rent caravans?

J'ai besoin de la connexion électrique. /ʒɛ bəzwɛ̃ də la kɔnɛksjɔ̃ elɛktʀik/ – I need the electrical connection.

Où puis-je changer/remplir/prendre en location la bouteille de gaz ? /u pɥi ʒə ʃãʒe/ʀãpliʀ/pʀãdʀ ã lɔkasjɔ̃ la butɛj d gaz/ – Where can I change/fill/rent the gas bottle?

On the Beach

la piscine /la pisin/ – swimming pool
le sable /lə sabl/ – sand
la plage /la plaʒ/ – beach
le bain de soleil /bɛ̃ də sɔlɛj/ – sunbathing
la crème solaire /la crem sɔlɛʀ/ – sunscreen
la douche /la duʃ/ – shower
le maillot de bain /le majo d bɛ̃/ – swimming suit
la méduse /la medyz/ – jellyfish
l'oursin (m.) /uʀsɛ̃/ – sea urchin
l'insolation (f.) /ɛ̃sɔlasjɔ̃/ – sunstroke

Common Phrases

Baignade interdite ! /bɛɲad ɛ̃tɛʀdi/ – Swimming is forbidden!
L'eau ici est-elle profonde ? – Is the water here deep?
Peut-on prendre un bain ici ? – Can we take a bath here?
Je desire louer – I want to rent
Une cabane /yn kaban/ – shed
Un parasol /paʀasɔl/ – umbrella
Une chaise–longue /yn ʃɛz lɔ̃g/ – deckchair
Des skis nautiques /de ski notik/ – water skis

Chapter 9: Accomodation

Le monde est un livre et ceux qui ne voyagent pas n'en lisent qu'une page.

Saint Augustin

As a tourist, you can choose between hotels, hostels, airbnb, or even camping sites. If you are coming as a student, finding student housing can be much cheaper. We recommend you search for student residences first, like CROUS, because they are significantly cheaper than private housing. You can expect fierce competition, especially in larger cities like Paris, Bordeaux, or Lyon.

la réception / la ʀesɛpsjɔ̃ / – reception

la cuisine / la kɥizin / – kitchen

l'ascenseur (m.) / lasɑ☐sœʀ / – lift

hors saison / ɔʀ sɛzɔ̃ / – off season

la saison d'été / la sɛzɔ̃ dete / – summer season

la saison d'hiver / la sɛzɔ̃ diver / – winter season

la taxe de séjour / la taks d seʒuʀ / – tourist tax

le propriétaire / pʀɔpʀijetɛʀ / – owner

le garçon / l ɡaʀsɔ̃ / – waiter

la serveuse / la sɛʀv / – waitress

le cuisinier / kɥizine / – cook

le concierge / kɔ̃sjɛʀʒ / – concierge

le porteur / pɔʀtœʀ / – carrier

la femme de chambre / fam də ʃɑ̃bʀ / – maid

Making a Reservation

J'ai réservé une chambre au nom de (). /ʒɛ ʀezɛʀve yn ʃɑ̃bʀ o nɔ̃ də/ – I booked a room under the name of ().

Avez-vous des chambres libres pour (la date) ? /ave vu de ʃɑ̃bʀ libʀ puʀ/ – Do you have free rooms for (date)?

Quel type de chambre souhaitez-vous ? /kɛl tip d ʃɑ̃bʀ swetevu/ – What kind of room do you want?

> **Je voudrais réserver une chambre () pour (number of days)** /ʒə vudʀɛ ʀezɛʀve yn ʃɑ̃bʀ puʀ ()/ – I would like to book a () room for (number of days).
>
> > **une chambre individuelle** /yn ʃɑ̃bʀ ɛ̃dividɥɛl/ – a single room

une chambre double / *yn ʃɑ̃bʀ* dubl/ – a double room
avec salle de bains /avɛk sal d bɛ̃/ – with bathroom
avec balcon /avɛk balkɔ̃/ – with balcony
avec petit déjeuner /avɛk pəti deʒœne/ – with breakfast

Je voudrais /ʒə vudrɛ/ – I would like

une pension complète /yn pɑ̃sjɔ̃ kɔ̃plɛ/ – full board (breakfast, lunch and diner)
demi–pension /yn *demi pɑ̃sjɔ̃*/ – half board (breakfast and diner)

Combien de temps comptez–vous rester ? /kɔ̃bjɛ̃ də tɑ̃ kɔ̃te vu ʀɛste/ – How long do you intend to stay?

Je resterai /ʒə ʀɛsteʀɛ/ – I'll stay

- **une nuit** /yn nɥi/ – one night
- **(X) jours** / ʒuʀ / – days
- **deux semaines** /dø səmɛn/ – two weeks

Pricing

C'est combien une chambre double pour une nuit ? /sɛ kɔ̃bjɛ̃ yn ʃɑ̃bʀ dubl puʀ yn nɥi/ – How much is a double room for one night?

On paie d'avance ou au départ ? /ɔ̃ pɛj davɑ̃s u o depaʀ/ – Do we pay in advance or on departure?

Je veux annuler la réservation au nom de (name). /ʒə vø anyle la ʀezɛʀvasjɔ̃ o nɔ̃ de/ – I want to cancel the reservation under the name of ().

Vous facturez des frais d'annulation ? /vu faktyʀe de fʀɛ danylasjɔ̃/ – Do you charge cancellation fees?

Combien de temps à l'avance est-ce que je peux annuler la réservation sans frais ? /kɔ̃bjɛ̃ də tɑ̃ alavɑ̃s esk ʒə pø anyle la ʀezɛʀvasjɔ̃ sɑ̃ fʀɛ/ – How far in advance can I cancel the reservation free of charge?

La caution sera remboursée ? /la kosjɔ̃ seʀa ʀɑ̃buʀse/ – Will the deposit be refunded?

Ce montant est-il remboursable ? /sə mɔ̃tɑ̃ etil ʀɑ̃buʀsabl/ – Is this amount refundable?

Le petit déjeuner est–il inclus ? /lə deʒœne etil ɛ☐kly/ – Is breakfast included?

Arrival

Quel est le numéro de ma chambre ? /kɛl ɛ lə numeʀo də ma ʃɑ̃bʀ/ – What is my room number?

Pourriez-vous me montrer ma chambre ? /puʀije vu mə mɔ̃tʀe ma ʃɑ̃bʀ/ – Could you show me my room?

Complaints

Cette chambre ne me convient pas. /sɛt ʃɑ̃bʀ nə mə kɔ̃vnjɑ̃ pa/ – This room does not suit me.

La chambre est trop petite. /la ʃɑ̃bʀ ɛ tro pəti/ – This room is too small.

Il n'y a pas d'eau chaude. /ilnija pa do ʃo/ – There is no hot water.

Le chauffage ne marche pas. /lə ʃofaʒ n maʀʃ pa/ – The heating does not work.

Je voudrais une autre chambre. /ʒə vudrɛ yn otr ʃɑ̃bʀ/ – I would like another room.

J'ai perdu la clé de ma chambre. /ʒɛ perdy la kle də ma ʃɑ̃bʀ/ – I've lost my room key.

In a hotel

On peut garer la voiture ici ? /ɔ̃ pø gare la vwatyʀ isi/ – Can we park the car here?

On peut avoir des serviettes propres, s'il vous plaît ? /ɔ̃ pø avwar de sɛʀvjɛt propr sil vu plɛ/ – Can we have clean towels, please?

On sert le petit déjeuner/dîner à quelle heure ? /ɔ̃ ser lə pəti deʒœne/ dine a kɛl œʀ/ – What time is breakfast/dinner served?

Donnez–moi la clef de ma chambre, s'il vous plaît. /done mwa la kle də ma ʃɑ̃bʀ sil vu plɛ/ – Give me my room key, please.

Je voudrais avoir /ʒə vudrɛ avwaʀ/ – I would like to get.

    Un oreiller /œ̃ ɔʀeje/ – a pillow

Une couverture /yn kuvɛʀtyʀ/ – cover

Departure

Il faut libérer la chambre avant quelle heure ? /il fo libere la ʃɑ̃bʀ avɑ̃ kɛl œʀ/ – What time the room should be vacated ?

Je pars demain matin à huit heures. /ʒə par dəmɛ̃ matɛ̃ a ɥi(t) œʀ/ – I am leaving tomorrow morning at eight o'clock.

Appelez–moi un taxi, s'il vous plaît. /apəle mwa œ̃ taksi sil vu plɛ/ – Call me a taxi, please.

Je veux régler la note. /ʒə vø regle la not/ – I want to pay the bill.

Chapter 10: Culture and Entertainment

Toute culture naît du mélange, de la rencontre, des chocs.
A l'inverse, c'est de l'isolement que meurent les civilisations.

Octavio Paz

French culture is reflected in every building, palace, monument or even street, but the finest examples of French culture can be found in museums. A visit to France would not be complete without visiting one of its museums. However, prepare for long queuing in front of the most famous museums like the *Louvre* or *Orsay*. There are 1218 museums in France, so you're sure to find one you'll enjoy without having to wait in line. All museums are free to enter on the first Sunday of every month throughout France. There's also a discount price *"tarif reduit"* for students and seniors.

Cinema, Theater, Concert

le prix d'entrée /lə pri dɑ̃tʀe/ – entrance fee

le prix adulte /lə pri adylt/ – adult price

le tarif réduit /lə taʀif ʀedɥi/ – reduced rate

le tarif /lə tarif/ – price

    étudiant /etydjɑ̃/ – student

    enfant /ɑ̃fɑ̃/ – child

    de groupe /də gʀup/ – group rate

complet /kɔ̃plɛ/ – full

l'entrée libre /lɑ̃tʀe libʀ/ – free entrance

le concert /lə kɔnser/ – concert

le chanteur /lə ʃɑ̃tœʀ/ – singer (m.)

la chanteuse /la ʃɑ̃tœz/ – singer, (f.)

le groupe de musique /lə gʀup də muzik/ – music group

le théâtre /lə teatʀ/ – theatre

le théâtre de marionnettes /lə teatʀ də maʀjɔnɛt/ – puppet theater

le spectacle, la pièce de théâtre /lə spɛktakl/ /la pjɛs də teatʀ/ – drama, play

le thétre contemporain /lə teatʀ kɔ̃tɑ̃pɔʀɛ̃/ – modern theater

    la comédie /la kɔmedi/ – comedy

    la tragédie /la tʀaʒedi/ – tragedy

> **l'opéra (m.)** /lopera/ – opera
>
> **le ballet** /lə balɛ/ – ballet

le cinéma /le kɔmedi/ – movie theater

> **le film d'action** /lə film daksjɔ̃/ – action movie
>
> **le film policier** /lə film pɔlisje/ – police movie
>
> **le thriller / le film à suspense** /lə thriller/ /lə film a syspɑ̃s/ – thriller
>
> **le film d'horreur** /lə film ɔʀœʀ/ – horror movie
>
> **le film de guerre** /lə film də gɛʀ/ – war movie
>
> **le documentaire** /lə dɔkymɑ̃tɛʀ/ – documentary
>
> **la parodie** /la paʀɔdi/ – parody
>
> **le film romantique** /lə film ʀɔmɑ̃tik/ – romantic movie
>
> **le dessin animé** /lə desɛ̃ anime/ – cartoon

le film pour enfants /lə film puʀ ɑ̃fɑ̃/ – children's movie

Common Phrases

Est–ce que tu veux aller au cinéma ? /esk ty vø ale o sinema/ – Would you like to go to the cinema?

> **au théâtre** /o teatʀ/ – to the theatre
>
> **au concert** /o kɔ̃sɛʀ/ – to the concert
>
> **au musée** /o myze/ – to the museum

Où est-ce que je peux acheter des billets ? /u esk ʒə pœ aʃəte de bijɛ/ – Where can I buy the tickets?

Je voudrais /ʒə vudʀɛ/ – I would like...

> **un billet pour le spectacle ce samedi.** /œ̃ bijɛ puʀ lə spɛktakl sə samdi/ – one ticket for the show this Saturday.

Je voudrais réserver /ʒə vudʀɛ ʀezɛʀve/ – I would like to reserve...

> **deux places.** /dø plas/ – two seats
>
> **une place au premier rang.** /yn plas o pʀəmje ʀɑ̃/ – a seat in the first row

C'est complet. /sɛ kɔ̃plɛ/ – All tickets are sold out.

Est–ce que l'entrée est libre ? /esk lɑ̃tʀe e libʀ/ – Is entrance free?

Quel est le prix d'entrée ? /kɛl e lə pri dɑ̃tʀe/ – How much is admission?

Est-ce que vous avez un tarif réduit ? /ɛskə vuzave œ̃ tarif redɥi/ – Do you have a discount price?

Ça commence à quelle heure ? /sa kɔmɑ̃se a kɛl œʀ/ – When does it start?

Où sont nos places ? /u sɔ̃ no plas/ – Where are our seats?

Excusez–moi, ces places–ci sont à nous ? /ɛkskuze mwa se plas si son a nu/ – Excuse me, are these seats ours?

Ça vous a plu ? / sa vuza ply / – Did you like it?

    J'ai beaucoup aimé. /ʒɛ boku ɛme/ – I liked it a lot.

    Je n'ai pas trop aimé. / ʒə nɛ pa tro ɛme / – I didn't like it very much.

C'était assez intéressant. /sɛte ase ɛ̃teʀesã/ – It was quite interesting.

Sport

French uses either "*jouer*" or "*faire de*", just as English uses the verbs "*to do*" or "*to play*" with certain kinds of sports.

jouer /ʒwe/ – to play

faire de /fɛʀ də/ – to do

le football /lə futbol/ – football

le volley–ball /lə vɔlɛbol/ – volleyball

le basket /lə baskɛt/ – basketball

le tennis /lə tenis/ – tennis

les arts martiaux /lézar maʀsjo/ – martial arts

la lutte /la lyt/ – wrestling

les sports de combat /le spor d comba/ – combat sports

la natation /la natasjɔ̃/ – swimming

la plongée /la plɔ̃ʒe/ – diving

la pêche /la peʃe/ – fishing

la voile /la vwa/ – sailing

le surf /lə sœʀf/ – surfing

le ski nautique /lə ski notik/ – water skiing

la luge /la lyʒ/ – sledging

le parachutisme /lə paʀaʃytism/ – parachuting

le patinage artistique /lə patinaʒ aʀtistik/ – figure skating

l'alpinisme /lalpinism/ – mountaineering

l'équitation /ekitasjɔ̃/ – horseback riding

la dance /la dans/ – dancing

la marche /la maʀʃ/ – walking

la musculation /la myskylasjɔ̃/ – bodybuilding

la randonnée /la ʀãdɔne/ – hiking, backpacking

le cyclisme /lə siklism/ – cycling

le vélo /lə velo/ – biking

le jogging /lə dʒɔgiŋ/ – jogging

l'escrime /lɛskʀim/ – fencing

le yoga /lə jɔga/ – yoga

Equipement and Sport Terms

le terrain de sport /lə teʀɛ̃ də spor/ – sport field

le filet /lə filɛ/ – net

la raquette de tennis /la ʀakɛt d tenis/ – tennis racket

le public /lə pyblik/ – the crowd

le vainqueur /lə vɛ☐kœʀ/ – winner

les spectateurs /le spɛktatœʀ/ – spectators

la salle de sport /la sal də spor/ – gym

l'entraîneur /la☐tʀɛnœʀ/ – coach

Common Phrases

Il y un terrain de sport par ici ? /ilja œ☐ teʀɛ☐ də spɔʀ par isi/ – Is there a sport court here?

Je voudrais louer la cour pour une heure ? /ʒə vudʀɛ lwe lə kuʀ puʀ yn œʀ / – I would like to rent the court for an hour?

Quand est-ce que la cour sera libre? /kɑ̃ ɛsk lə kuʀ sera libr/ – When will the court be free?

Combien on paye pour une heure / un mois ? /kɔ☐bjɛ☐ ɔ☐ pɛj puʀ yn œʀ / œ☐ mwa/ – How much do we pay for an hour?

Je pourrais jouer avec vous ? /ʒə puʀɛ ʒwe avɛk vu/ – Could I play with you?

J'aime faire du yoga. /ʒɛm fɛʀ dy yoga/ – I like to do yoga.

Y a-t-il une salle de sport à proximité ? /jatil yn sal də spor a pʀɔksimite/ – Is there a gym nearby?

Chapter 11: Transportation

Le plus beau voyage, c'est celui qu'on a pas encore fait.

Laick Peyron

France is a very well connected country and you'll easily find transportation from one point to another. The best way to travel between bigger cities is by train, **TER** (French Regional Train) or **TGV** (high-speed train). So far, **TGV** trains only operate in the Hauts-de-France region, or Paris-Lille-Calais. The **TER** allows you to travel within a given region of France at really low prices, starting at just 2 euros, depending on the distance. There are buses that travel between cities as an alternative to trains, but they are less frequent.

Buses are common in smaller cities. The subway is the best way to get around Paris and the tram is convenient in Bordeaux. There are bicycle counters everywhere in France, so you can get around the city and enjoy the views on a bike. You can even download an app that tells you where the nearest bike rental is.

Asking for Directions

To start a conversation with a person in the street or in a store, the first thing to say is **"Excusez-moi"** which means **"Excuse me"**, followed by *"Monsieur or Madame"*. This is a polite way to grab someone's attention and signal to them that you'd like to engage with them in a conversation. In French: **"Savez-vous où se trouve** la cathédrale Notre-Dame ?"

The word **"est"** is the present tense of the verb **"être"** conjugated in the third person singular. The same verb in the third person plural is **"sont"** and it must be used with plural words. For instance, the word *restrooms* is always used in its plural form in French **"les toilettes"** and therefore you should say: **"Où sont** les toilettes publiques ?"

Let's see different ways to ask for directions:

Où est-ce ? or C'est où ? /u es/ or /se u/ — Where is it?

Comment je fais pour y aller ? /kɔmɛnt ʒə fɛ puʀ i ale/ — How do I get there?

    J'ai besoin d'aller à (). /ʒɛ bəzwɛ̃ dale a/ — I have to go to ().

Excusez-moi, où est ( ) le plus proche ? /ekskyze mwa u e lə ply pʀɔf/ — Excuse me, where is the nearest ().

C'est à quelle distance d'ici ? /se a kɛl distɑ̃s disi/ — How far is it from here?

Vous pouvez me montrer la route pour aller à () ? /vu puve mə mɔ̃tʀe la ʀut puʀ ale a/ — Can you show me the way to go to ()?

Il y a un autre chemin pour y aller ? /ilja œ□ ʃəmɛ□ puʀ i ale/ — Is there another way to get there?

Est-ce que je peux y aller à pied ? /ɛsk ʒə pø i ale a pje/ — Can I walk there?

253

Il faut combien de temps pour y aller ? /il fo kɔ̃bjɛ̃ də tɑ̃ pur i ale/ – How long does it take to get there?

Combien de temps est-ce que ça prend à pied ? /kɔ̃bjɛ̃ də tɑ̃ esk sa pʀɑ̃dʀ a pje/ – How long does it take on foot?

This will help you confirm you are taking the right route:

C'est la bonne direction pour aller à ()? /sɛ la bon diʀɛksjɔ̃ pur ale a/ – Is this the right direction to go to ()?

C'est loin d'ici () ? /sɛ lwɛ̃ disi/ – It is far from here?

If you ask someone for directions, you may hear something like this:

à côté de /a kɔte də/ – next to

en face de /ɑ̃ fas də/ – in front of

à droite de /a dʀwat də/ – on the right of

à gauche de /a goʃ də/ – on the left of

tout droit /tu dʀwa/ – straight ahead

tourner /tuʀne/ – to turn

derrière /dɛʀjɛʀ/ – behind

devant /dəvɑ̃/ – in front of

centre–ville /sɑ̃tʀ vil/ – city center

au coin de /o kwɛ̃ də/ – at the corner of

au bout de /o bu də/ – at the end of

la prochaine rue /la pʀɔʃɛ̃ ry/ – next street

la rue suivante /la ry suivant/ – next street

première à droite /pʀəmje a dʀwat/ – first to the right

deuxième à gauche /døzjɛm a goʃ/ – the second to the left

Vous devez prendre /vu deve pʀɑ̃dʀ/ – You should take

    la rue suivante /la ry sɥivɑ̃/ – next street

    la seconde à droite /la səgɔ̃d a dʀwat/ – second on the right

    la première à gauche /la pʀəmje a goʃ/ – first on the left

Le musée est au coin de (). /lə myze e o kwɛ̃ də/ – The museum is on the corner of ().

La banque est au bout de cette rue. /la bank e o bu de la ry/ – The bank is at the end of this street.

Passport Control

la frontière nationale /la frʌntɪəʳ nasjonal/ – national border

le contrôle des passeports /lə kɔ̃tʀol de paspɔʀ/ – passport control

le contrôle douanier /lə kɔ̃tʀol dwanje/ – border control

soumis à la douane /sumi a la dwan/ – subject to customs

le visa d'entrée /lə viza dɑ̃tʀe/ – entry visa

Votre passeport, s'il vous plaît. /votr paspɔʀ sil vu plɛ/ – Your passport please.

    Voici mon passeport. /vwasi mɔ̃ paspɔʀ/ – Here's my passport.

Nous serons à la frontière quand ? /nu seron ala fʀɔ̃tjɛʀ kɑ̃/ – When will we reach the border?

Avez-vous quelque chose à déclarer ? /ave vu kɛlkʃoz a deklare/ – Do you have anything to declare?

    Je n'ai rien à déclarer. /ʒə nɛ ʀjɛ̃ a deklare/ – I don't have anything to declare.

    J'ai quelque chose à déclarer. /ʒɛ kɛlk ʃoz a deklare/ – I have something to declare.

Combien de cigarettes avez-vous ? /kɔ̃bjɛ̃ də sigaʀɛt ave vu/ – How many cigarets do you have?

    Je n'ai que … paquets de cigarettes. /ʒə nɛ k.. pakɛ d sigaʀɛt/ – I only have (number) of cigarettes.

Vous pouvez ouvrir vos bagages, s'il vous plaît ? /vu puve ouvrir vo bagaʒ sil vu plɛ/ – Can you open your luggage, please?

Vous devez payer des droits de douane. /vu deve peje de drwa de dwan/ – You have to pay customs duties.

D'où venez-vous ? /du vene vu/ – Where do you come from?

Où allez-vous? /u ale vu/ – Where are you going?

    Je suis ici de passage. /ʒə sɥi isi də pasaʒ/ – I am here passing through.

    Je suis ici pour le travail. /ʒə sɥi isi pur lə tʀavaj/ – I am here for work.

    Je suis ici pour les vacances. /ʒə sɥi isi pur le vakans/ – I am here on holiday.

    Je suis ici pour deux semaines. /ʒə sɥi isi pur dø səmɛn/ – I am here for two weeks.

    Je compte loger chez … /ʒə kɔ̃t lɔʒe ʃe/ – I plan to stay at…

Je voyage /ʒə vwajaʒ/ – I travel …

    comme touriste /kɔm tuʀist/ – as a tourist

    pour mes affaires /pur mez afɛr/ – for my business

    pour rendre une visite /pur ʀɑ̃dʀ yn vizit/ – to pay a visit

Je voyage seul. /ʒə vwajaʒ sœl/ – I am traveling alone.

Nous voyageons ensemble. /nu vwajaʒ ɑ̃sɑ̃bl/ – We are traveling together.

Public transportation

la voiture /la vwatyʀ/ – car

le tram /lə tram/ – tram

le bus /lə bys/ – bus

le métro /lə metro/ – subway

l'arrêt (m.) /laʀɛ/ – station

le chauffeur, le conducteur /lə ʃofœʀ / lə kɔ̃dyktœʀ/ – driver

le ticket /lə tikɛt/ – ticket

    tarif réduit /le tarif ʀedɥi/ – reduced price

    journée /ʒuʀne/ – daily reduced price

    groupes /grup/ – reduced price for a group

le composteur /kɔ̃pɔstœʀ/ – person who validates tickets

valider/composter le ticket /valide – kɔ̃pɔste lə tikɛ/ – to validate the ticket

Making Inquiries

Où est la gare la plus proche ? /ue la gar la ply pʀɔʃ / – Where is the closest station?

Où se trouve la station de métro ? /u sə truv la stasjɔ̃ də metʀo/ – Where is the metro station?

Où est-ce que je peux acheter des billets ? /u esk ʒə pœ aʃəte de bijɛ/ – Where can I buy tickets?

Y a-t-il un arrêt près d'ici ? /jatil œ̃ aʀɛ pʀɛdisi/ – Is there a stop near here?

Quel tram/bus/train va au centre ? /kɛl tʀam/bys/tʀɛ̃ va o sɑ̃tʀ/ – Which tram/bus/train goes to the center?

Est-ce qu'il y a une station de métro près d'ici ? /eskilja yn stasjon də metro pre disi/ – Is there a subway station nearby?

Quel bus va à () ? /kɛl bys va a ( )/ – Which bus goes to ( )?

Est-ce que je peux acheter des tickets auprès du conducteur / à bord ? /eskə ʒə pœ aʃəte de tikɛ opʀɛ dy kɔ̃dyktœʀ / a bor/ – Can I buy tickets from the driver / on board?

Où est-ce que je peux valider/composter mon ticket ? /u esk ʒə pœ valide/kɔ̃pɔste mɔ̃ tikɛ/ – Where can I validate/compost my ticket?

Purchasing Tickets

Combien coûte un billet simple/aller-retour pour ( ) ? /kɔ̃bjɛ̃ kut œ̃ a bijɛ sɛ̃pl/ale retur pur / – How much is a single/return ticket to ()?

Je voudrais acheter un billet pour ( ), s'il vous plaît. /ʒə vudrɛ aʃəte œ̃ a bijɛ pur ( ) sil vu plɛ/ – I would like to buy a ticket to ..., please.

Deux billets simples pour... /dø bijɛ sɛ̃pl pur/ – Two tickets single for...

Un billet de deuxième/première classe. /œ̃ bijɛ də døzjɛm / prəmje klas/ – A second/first class ticket.

Est-ce qu'il y a des tarifs réduits pour les étudiants/enfants ? /eskilja de tarif ʀedɥi pur lezetydjɑ̃/ ɑ̃fɑ̃/ – Are there reduced rates for students/children?

Quand part le prochain train/bus pour ( ) ? /kɑ̃ paʀ lə pʀɔʃɛ̃ tʀɛ̃/bys pur ( ) / – When does the next train for ( ) leave?

Il faut combien de temps pour y aller ( ) ? /il fo kɔ̃bjɛ̃ d tɑ̃ puri ale ( )/ – How long does it take to get there?

Je voudrais réserver une place. /ʒə vudʀɛ ʀezɛʀve yn plas/ – I would like to reserve a place.

Quelle est la correspondance la plus rapide / la moins chère pour ( ) ? /kɛl e la kɔʀɛspɔ̃dɑ̃s la ply rapid / la mwɛ̃ ʃɛʀ pur/ – What is the fastest/cheapest connection for ( )?

Compartiment non-fumeurs, s'il vous plaît ? /kɔ̃paʀtimɑ̃ nɔ̃ fymœʀ sil vu plɛ/ – Non-smoking compartment, please?

Est–ce que le train s'arrête à ( ) ? /ɛsk lə tʀɛ̃ saʀet a / – Does the train stop at ( )?

De quel quai part le train pour ( ) ? /də kɛl ke par lə tʀɛ̃ pur ( )/ – From which platform does the train for ( ) leave?

Train

Quel est le nom de l'arrêt où je dois descendre ? /kɛl e le nɔ̃ delaʀɛ u ʒə dwa desɑ̃dʀ/ – What is the name of the stop where I have to get off?

Quel est le nom de cet arrêt / cette station ? /kɛl e le nɔ̃ də sɛt aʀɛ / sɛt stasjɔ̃/ – What's the name of this stop/station?

Pouvez-vous me dire quand/où je dois descendre ? /puve vu mə dir quand/u ʒə dwa desɑ̃dʀ/ – Can you tell me when/where I should get off?

    Vous passez quatre arrêts. /vu pase qatr aʀɛ / – You pass four stations.

Il reste combien d'arrêts ? /il rest kɔ̃bjɛ̃ daʀɛ/ – How many stops are left?

C'est bien le train pour … ? /sɛ bjɛ̃ lə tʀɛ̃ pur/ – Is this the train for…?

Je cherche le contrôleur. /ʒə ʃɛʀʃe lə kɔ̃tʀolœʀ/ – I'm looking for the controller.

Est–ce que cette place est occupée ? /ɛsk sɛt plas e ɔkype/ – Is this seat occupied?

Excusez–moi, c'est ma place. /ɛskuze mwa sɛ ma plas/ – Excuse me, this is my place.

Quelle est la destination de ce train ? /kɛl e la dɛstinasjɔ̃ də sə tʀɛ̃/ – What is the destination of this train?

Quel est le prochain arrêt ? /kɛl e lə pʀɔʃɛ̃ aʀɛ/ – What is the next station?

Où est le wagon–restaurant ? /u e lə vagɔ̃ ʀɛstɔʀɑ̃/ – Where is the dining car?

Voulez–vous qu'on échange les places ? /vule vu kɔ̃ eʃɑ̃ʒ le plas/ – Would you like to swap places?

Quand est-ce qu'on arrive à ( ) ? /kɑ̃ ɛskɔ̃ ariv a ( )/ – When do we get to ( )?

Où sommes–nous ? C'est quelle station ? /u sɔm nu / sɛ kɛl stasjon/ – Where are we? Which station is it?

J'ai raté ma station. /ʒɛ rate ma stasjon/ – I missed my station.

C'est le terminus. /sɛ lə tɛʀminys/ – This is the terminus.

Le train a du retard. /lə tʀɛ̃ a dy ʀətaʀ/ – The train is late.

Taxi

Y a-t-il une station de taxis près d'ici ? /jatil yn stasjɔ̃ də taksi pʀe disi/ – Is there a taxi station near here?

Taxi ! Êtes-vous libre ? /taksi ete vu libʀ/ – Taxi! Are you available?

Conduisez–moi à cette adresse, s'il vous plaît. /kɔ̃duize mwa a sɛt adʀɛs sil vu plɛ/ – Take me to this address, please.

À l'aéroport, s'il vous plaît. /a laeʀopɔʀ sil vu plɛ/ – To the airport, please.

Pouvez–vous m'appeler un taxi, s'il vous plaît. /puve vu mapele œ̃ taksi sil vu plɛ/ – Could you please call me a cab.

Déposez-moi ici. /depoze mwa isi/ – Leave me here.

Pourriez-vous faire un petit tour de la ville ? /puʀje vu fɛʀ œ̃ pəti tuʀ də la vil/ – Could you take a little tour of the city?

Pouvez-vous m'aider à mettre les bagages ? /puve vu mɛde a mɛtʀ le bagaʒ/ – Can you help me put the luggage?

Uber Drive

Où allez-vous ? /u ale vu/ – Where are you going?

Choisir un véhicule ! /ʃwaziʀ yn veikyl/ – Choose a vehicle type!

Confirmer /kɔ̃fiʀme/ – to confirm

Confirmez votre lieu de prise en charge. /kɔ̃fiʀme votʀ ljø də pʀiz ã ʃaʀʒ/ – Confirm your pickup location.

Attendez qu'un chauffeur accepte votre demande. /atã de kœ̃ ʃofœʀ aksɛpte votʀ dəmãd/ – Wait for a driver to accept your request.

Le chauffeur va arriver dans 20 minutes. /lə ʃofœʀ va aʀive dã vɛ̃ minut/ – The driver will get in 20 minutes.

Une notification vous sera envoyée lorsque le chauffeur sera à proximité de votre lieu de prise en charge. /yn nɔtifikasjɔ̃ vu sera ãvwaje lɔʀsk lə ʃofœʀ sera a pʀɔksimite də votʀ ljø dpʀiz ã ʃaʀʒ/ – You'll get a notification when the driver is near your pick-up location.

Airplane

Booking a Ticket

Je voudrais acheter un billet d'avion pour ( ), s'il vous plaît. /ʒə vudʀɛ aʃəte œ̃ a bijɛ davjon puʀ ( ) sil vu plɛ/ – I would like to buy a ticket to ( ), please./

Combien coûte un billet d'avion en première classe / classe économique ? /kɔ̃bjɛ̃ kut œ̃ bijɛ davjon ɑ̃ pʀəmje klas / klas ekɔnɔmikə/ – How much does a first class/economy class plane ticket cost?

C'est un vol direct ? /sɛt œ̃ vol diʀɛkt/ – Is it a direct flight?

C'est un vol avec escale ? /sɛt œ̃ vol avɛk ɛskal/ – Is it a flight with a stopover?

Le vol est retardé (d'une heure) /le vol e retarde (dyn œʀ)/ – The flight is late (one hour).

Votre vol est annulé ? /vɔtʀ vol etanyle/ – Is your flight canceled?

À quelle heure est le prochain vol pour ( ) ? /a kɛl œʀ e pʀɔʃɛ̃ vɔl pur ( )/ – What time is the next flight for ( )?

Je peux annuler mon billet / ma réservation ? /ʒə pø anyle mɔ̃ bijɛ/ ma ʀezɛʀvasjɔ̃/ – Can I cancel my ticket / my reservation?

Combien font les frais d'annulation ? /kɔ̃bjɛ̃ fon le fʀɛ danulasjon/ – How much are the cancellation fees?

In Airplane

On atterrit à quelle heure ? /ɔ̃ ateri a kɛl œʀ/ – What time do we land?

Je n'arrive pas à attacher ma ceinture. /ʒə naʀive pa a ataʃe ma sɛ̃tyʀ/ – I can't fasten my seat belt.

Ma liseuse ne marche pas. /ma lizøz nə maʀʃ pa/ – My reading light is not working.

Je dois aller aux toilettes. /ʒə dwa ale o twalɛt/ – I have to go to the toilets.

Les boissons sont comprises ? /le bwasɔ̃ sɔ̃ kompriz/ – Are drinks included?

Lost baggage

Où signaler la perte de bagages ? /u siɲale la pɛʀt də bagaʒ/ – Where to report lost luggage?

J'étais dans le vol numéro ( ). /ʒete dɑ̃ lə vol numero ( )/ – I was in the flight number ( ).

J'avais deux bagages. /ʒavɛ dø bagaʒ/ – I had two luggages.

C'était une valise rouge. /sɛte yn valiz ʀuʒ/ – It was a red suitcase.

Contactez-moi à ce numéro là, s'il vous plaît. /kɔ̃takte mwa a sə numero la sil vu plɛ/ – Contact me at this number, please.

J'ai vraiment besoin de mes bagages. /ʒɛ vʀɛmɑ̃ bəzwɛ̃ də me bagaʒ/ – I really need my luggages.

J'ai mon adresse dessus. /ʒɛ mɔ̃ adʀɛs dəsy/ – I have my address on it.

Combien de temps ça vous prendra de les trouver ? /kɔ̃bjɛ̃ də tɑ̃ sa vu pʀɑ̃dʀa də le tʀuve/ – How long will it take you to find them?

Où demander l'indemnisation pour bagages perdus ? /u demande lɛ̃dɛmnsjon puʀ bagaʒ peʀdy/ – Where can I claim compensation for lost luggage?

Boat and Cruise

guichet d'embarquement /giʃɛ dɑ̃baʀkəmɑ̃/ – boarding counter

passerelle d'embarquement /pasʀɛl dɑ̃baʀkəmɑ̃/ – boarding bridge

Comment peut–on arriver au port des ferries ? /kɒmɛn pøt ɔ̃ arive o poʀ de feri/ – How can we get to the ferry boat?

À quelle heure part le prochain ferry ? /a kɛl œʀ paʀ lə pʀɔʃɛ̃ feri/ – What time DOES the next feRry leave?

Quelle est la durée du voyage ? /kɛl e la dyʀe dy vwajaʒ/ – How long is the trip?

Le voyage dure environ une heure. /lə vwajaʒ dyʀ a☐viʀɔ☐ yn œʀ/ – The trip takes about an hour.

Quel est le prix pour une voiture et deux personnes ? /kɛl e lə pʀi puʀ yn vwatyʀ e dø pɛʀsɔn/ – What's the price for a car and two people?

Car

le permis de conduire /lə pɛʀmi d kɔ̃dɥiʀ/ – driving licence

le certificat d'immatriculation (carte grise) /lə sɛʀtifika imatʀikylasjɔ̃ (kaʀt gʀiz)/ – registration certificate

l'assurance traffic (carte verte) / lasyʀɑ̃s tʀæfik (kaʀt vɛʀt)/ – traffic insurance

Où est-ce que je peux louer une voiture ? /u ɛskə ʒə pø lwe yn vwatyʀ/ – Where can I rent a car?

Je voudrais louer une petite voiture économique ? /ʒə vudʀɛ lwe yn pəti vwatyʀ ekɔnɔmik/ – I would like to rent a small economy car ?

Combien consomme cette voiture ? /kɔ̃bjɛ̃ kɔ̃sɔme sɛt vwatyʀ/ – How much does this car consume?

Il y a la clim ? /ilja la klim/ – Is there air conditioning?

Combien coûte la location par jour ? /kɔ̃bjɛ̃ kut la lɔkasjɔ̃ paʀ ʒuʀ/ – How much is the rental per day?

Est–ce que l'essence est comprise ? /ɛskə lesɑ̃s e kɔ̃pʀiz/ – Is gasoline included?

Je peux quitter le pays avec cette voiture ? /ʒə pø kite le pei avɛk sɛt vwatyʀ/ – Can I leave the country with this car?

Combien de kilomètres sont inclus dans le prix ? /kɔ̃bjɛ̃ də kilɔmɛtʀ sɔ̃ ɛ̃kly dɑ̃ lə pʀi/ – How many kilometres are included in the price?

Jusqu'à quand faut-il rendre la voiture ? /ʒyska kɑ̃ fotil ʀɑ̃dʀ la vwatyʀ/ – Until when do l have to return the car?

Quel numéro appeler en cas d'accident/de panne/de vol ? /kɛl nymeʀo apəle ɑ̃ ka daksidɑ̃ /pan/vɔl/ – What number to call in case of accident/breakdown/theft?

Il me faut aussi un porte-bagages / un porte-vélos ? /il mə fo osi œ☐ poʀt bagaʒ / œ☐ poʀt velo/ – Do I also need a luggage/bike rack?

Il n'y a pas de roue de rechange. /il ni pa də ʀu d ʀəʃɑ̃ʒ/ – There is no spare wheel.

Le pneu avant/arrière droit est usé. /lə pnø avɑ̃/aʀjeʀe dʀwa e yze/ – The right front/rear tire is worn.

C'est accessible en voiture ? /sɛ aksesibl ɑ̃ vwatyʀ/ – Is it accessible by car?

Bike

Louer un vélo /lwe œ□ velo/ – rent a bike

Le point de location vélo /lə pwɛ̃ də lɔkasjɔ̃/ – bike rental point

Je voudrais me renseigner sur la location de vélos. /ʒə vudʀɛ ʀɑ̃seɲe syr la lokasjon də velo/ – I would like to inquire about bike rental.

Ce serait pour une location de deux vélos adultes avec une remorque pour enfants. /sə səʀe pur yn lokasjon də dø velo adylt avɛk yn ʀəmɔʀk pur ɑ̃fɑ̃/ – This would be for a rental of two adult bikes with a child trailer.

Je voudrais louer pour la journée. /ʒə vudʀɛ lwe pur la ʒuʀne/ – I would like to rent for a day.

Je paie maintenant ou au retour ? /ʒə pɛj mɛ̃tənɑ̃ u o ʀətuʀ/ – Should I pay now or after we come back?

Chapter 12: Food and Drink

La gastronomie est l'art d'utiliser la nourriture pour créer du bonheur.

Théodore Zeldin

There is no doubt that French cuisine has a long history. However, cooking as an art form dates back to the 14th century and culminated during Louis XIV's reign. It's not just the refined taste that makes French cuisine unique but its elegant appearance as well. French people like to enjoy simple flavors, like having only cheese and wine for dinner. Eating is almost a sacred ritual in their culture. During lunch break, the park is often full of employees and students having picnics and enjoying the sunlight.

Some of the best traditional French meals are *Boeuf Bourguignon, Escargot, Cassoulet, Quiche Lorraine, Ratatouille, Pot-au-feu,* followed by desserts such as *Tarte Tatin, Macarons, Tarte au Citron, Brioche, Madelaine* and *Palmier*.

Ordering in a Restaurant

To address a waiter, you can use **garçon** (for a waiter), or simply **Monsieur** (for a waiter). To address a waitress, you'll say **mademoiselle**.

The waiter will ask you:

Vous désirez ? /vu deziʀe/ – What would you like?

Que voulez-vous boire? / kə vule vu bwaʀ / – What would you like to drink?

Désirez-vous encore quelque chose ? /dezire ãkɔʀ kɛlk ʃoz/ – Would you like anything else?

You may ask:

Vous avez une table libre ? /vuzave yn tabl libʀ/ – Do you have a free table?

On peut se mettre ici ? /ɔ̃ pø sə mɛtʀ isi / – Can we sit here?

Non, c'est pris. /no se pri/ – No, it is taken.

Je voudrais une table pour deux. /ʒə vudʀɛ yn tabl puʀ dø/ – I would like a table for two.

Garçon, s'il vous plaît. /gaʀsɔ̃ sil vu plɛ/ – Waiter, please. (when calling a waiter)

On voudrait commander. /ɔ̃ vudʀɛ kɔmãde/ – We would like to order.

Je voudrais commander à la carte. /ʒə vudʀɛ kɔmãde a la kaʀt/ – I would like to order what's on the menu.

La carte, s'il vous plaît. /la kaʀt sil vu plɛ/ – Menu, please.

La carte des vins /la kaʀt de vɛ̃/ – wine menu

Qu'est-ce que vous recommandez ? /kɛsk vu ʀəkɔmãde/ – What do you recommend?

On a déjà commandé. /ɔ̃ a deʒa kɔmɑ̃de/ – We already ordered.

Comme entrée, je prends… /kɔm ɑ̃tʁe ʒə pʁɑ̃d/ – For starter, I take…

    une soupe / yn sup / – a soup

Quelle est votre spécialité ? /kɛl ɛ votr spesjalite/ – What's the speciality of the house?

Je voudrais quelque chose sans viande. /ʒə vudʁɛ kɛlk ʃoz sɑ̃ vjɑ̃d/ – I would like something without meat.

Un autre café, s'il vous plaît. /yn otʁ kafe sil vu plɛ/ – Another coffee, please.

On peut avoir un autre couvert ? /ɔ̃ pø avwaʁ œ̃ kuvɛʁ/ – Could we have another set of cutlery?

Il nous manque une fourchette / un couteau / une cuillère / une assiette /il nu mɑ̃k yn fuʁʃɛt / œ̃ kuto / yn kɥijɛʁ / yn asjɛt/ – We are missing a fork/knife/spoon/plate/.

Bon appétit. /bɔ̃ apeti/ – Enjoy your meal.

Vous pouvez l'enlever. /vu puve lɑ̃ləve/ – You can take the plates.

Complaints

Ce n'est pas ce qu'on a commandé. /sə nɛ pa skɔ̃ a kɔmɑ̃de/ – That's not what we have ordered.

Ce plat n'est pas bon. /sə pla nɛ pa bɔ̃/ – This dish isn't good.

Il y a trop de sel. /il ja tro də sel/ – It's too salty.

C'est cramé. /se krame/ – It's burned.

Paying

Ca fait combien ? /sa fɛ kɔ̃bjɛ̃/ – How much is that?

On paye séparément/ensemble. /ɔ̃ pɛ separemɑ̃/ɑ̃sɑ̃bl/ – We pay separately/together.

Je peux payer par carte ? /ʒə pø peje par kart/ – Can I pay by card?

Désolé, il me semble que vous nous faites payer trop cher ? /dezɔle il m sɑ̃ble kə vu nu fɛt peje tro ʃɛʁ/ – Excuse me, it looks like we have been overcharged.

On n'a pas eu ça. /ɔ̃ na pa y sa/ – We didn't get that.

C'est bon. Gardez la monnaie. /sɛ bɔ̃ garde la mɔnɛ/ – It's ok. Keep the change.

Menu

la portion /la pɔʁsjɔ̃/ – portion

    demi portion /demi pɔʁsjɔ̃/ – half portion

    portion enfant /pɔʁsjɔ̃ ɑ̃fɑ̃/ – child portion

le petit-déjeuner /lə pəti deʒœne/ – breakfast

le déjeuner /lə deʒœne/ – lunch

le dîner /lə dine/ – dinner
le hors d'oeuvre /lə ɔʀdœvʀ/ – starter
le plat principal /lə pla pʀɛ̃sipal/ – main course
le repas froid /le repa frwa/ – cold dish
le plats chaud /lə pla ʃo/ – warm dish
la grillade /la gʀijad/ – grilled meat
le repas sans viande /lə repa sã vjãd/ – meal without meat
le dessert /lə desɛʀ/ – dessert
la boisson /la bwasɔ̃/ – drink

Breakfast

le beurre /lə bœʀ/ – butter
la confiture /la kɔ̃fityʀ/ – jam
le miel /lə mjɛl/ – honey
les oeufs (m.) /le œ/ – eggs
    sur le plat /syr lə pla/ – fried eggs
    l'omelette /lɔmlɛt/ – omelet
    les oeufs brouillés /le œ bʀuje/ – scrambled eggs
    à la coque /le œ a la kɔk/ – boiled eggs
le jambon /lə ʒãbɔ̃/ – ham
    fumé /fyme/ – smoked
    cuit /kɥi/ – cooked
la saucisses /le sosis/ – sausage
le pain
    blanc /bla/ – white
    bis /biz/ – brown
    de seigle /də sɛgl/ – rye
    au lait /o le/ – with milk
le baguette /lə bagɛt/ – baguette
le croissant /lə kʀwasã/ – croissant

Lunch/Diner

Starter
la salade / la salad / – lettuce, salad

la salade de fruits / *la salad də fʀɥi* / – fruit salad
la pâte de foie / *la pat də fwa* / – liver paste
la soupe / *la sup* / – soupe
    de volaille / *də vɔlɑj* / – chicken
    de poisson / *də pwasɔ̃* / – fish
bouillon / *bujɔ̃* / – broth
le potage / *lə pɔtaʒ* / – pottage

Meat
le boeuf / *lə bœf* / – beef
le canard / *lə kanar* / – duck
le veau / *lə vo* / – veal
le porc / *lə pɔʀ* / – pork
l'agneau (m.) / *laɲo* / – lamb
le lapin / *lə lapɛ̃* / – rabbit
le sanglier / *lə sɑ̃glije* / – boar
l'oie (f.) / *lwa* / – goose
la dinde / *lə dɛ̃d* / – turkey
le poulet / *lə pulɛ* / – chicken

Fish
l'huitre / *lɥitʀ* / – oyster
le homard / *lɔmaʀ* / – lobster
les moules / *le mul* / – mussel
la truite / *la tʀɥit* / – trout
le silure / *lə silyʀ* / – catfish

Preparation
l'escalope (f.) / *lɛskalɔp* / – escalope, cutlet
de canard / *de canard* / – duck
rôti / *roti* / – roasted meat
de porc / *də pɔʀ* / – pig
d'agneau / *daɲo* / – lamb
de veau / *d vo* / – veal
grillé / *grije* / – grilled
bouilli, cuit / *buji* / / *kɥi* / – cooked

frit / fri / – fried
cru / kry / – raw
à la broche / a la bʀɔʃ / – on the spit

Spices

le poivre / lə pwavʀ / – pepper
le sel / lə sɛl / – salt
la cannelle / la kanɛl / – cinnamon
l'ail / laj / – garlic
l'oignon / lɔɲɔ̃ / – onion
le piment / lə pimã / – red chilli

Vegetables

les légumes (m.) / le legym / – vegetables
le broccoli / lə bʀɔkɔli / – broccoli
le célery / lə sɛlɑri / – celery
les champignons (m.) / le ʃampiɲɔ̃ / – mushroom
le chou-fleur / lə ʃu flœʀ / – cauliflower
le chou / lə ʃu / – cabbage
le chou de Bruxelles / lə ʃu d bʀysɛl / – Brussels sprout
les haricots / lezariko / – beans
le petits pois / lə pti pwa / – pea
le concombre / lə kɔ̃kɔ̃bʀ / – cucumber
le persil / lə pɛʀsi / – parsley
le radis / lə radi / – radish
l'asperge / laspɛʀʒ / – asparagus
la courgette / la kuʀʒet / – zucchini
la laitue / la lɛty / – lettuce
la lentille / la lãtij / – lens
les haricots verts / lezariko vɛʀ / – green beans
la carotte / la kaʀɔt / – carrot
le piment / lə pimã / – red chilli
le poireau / le pwaʀo / – leek
le poivron / lə pwavʀɔ̃ / – pepper
la tomate / la tɔmat / – tomato

l'épinard / *lepinaʀ* / – spinach

l'asperge / *laspɛʀʒ* / – asparagus

les pommes de terre / *le pɔm d tɛʀ* / – potatoes

l'artichaut / *laʀtiʃo* / – artichoke

Fruits

l'ananas (m.) / *lanana* / – ananas

l'avocat (m.) / *lavɔka* / – avocado

la banana / *la banan* / – banana

la pamplemousse / *la pãpləmus* / – grapefruit

le kiwi / *lə kivi* / – kiwi

le noix de coco / *lə nwa d koko* / – coconut

la mandarine / *la mãdaʀin* / – mandarine

la mangue / *la mãg* / – mango

la grenade / *la gʀənad* / – pomegranate

le raisin / *lə ʀɛzɛ̃* / – grape

      sec / *sɛk* / – dry grape

la pêche / *la pɛʃ* / – peach

le melon / *lə melon* / – melon

le raisin / *lə ʀɛzɛ̃* / – grape

la pomme / *la pɔm* / – apple

la fraise / *la fʀɛz* / – strawberry

l'abricot / *labʀiko* / – apricot

la poire / *la pwaʀ* / – pear

la mûre sauvage / *la myʀ sovaʒ* / – wild blackberry

le citron / *lə sitʀɔ̃* / – lemon

la pastèque / *la pastɛk* / – watermelon

la framboise / *la fʀãbwaz* / – raspberry

l'orange (f.) / *lɔʀãʒ* / – orange

la groseille / *la gʀozɛj* / – redcurrant

la figue / *la fig* / – fig

la prune / *la pʀyn* / – plum

la cerise / *la səʀiz* / – cherry

Nuts

l'amande (f.) / *lamãd* / – almond
la noisette / *la nwazɛt* / – hazelnut
la noix / *la nwa* / – walnut
    du Brésil / *dy brezil* / – Brazilian nut
    de cajou / *də kaju* / – cashew nuts
la cacahuète / *la kakaɥɛt* / – peanut

Dessert

le gâteau / *lə gato* / – cake
la tarte / *la tart* / – pie
    aux fraises / *o fʀɛz* / – strawberry pie
    aux noix / *o nwa* / – walnut pie
    aux pommes / *o pom* / – apple pie
la crêpe / *la kʀepe* / – pancake
le soufflé au riz / *le sufl o ri* / – rice souffle
la gelée de citron / *la ʒəle d sitʀɔ̃* / – lemon jelly
la glace / *la glas* / – ice cream
    au citron / *o sitʀɔ̃* / – lemon
    à la vanille / *a la vanij* / – vanila
    au chocolat / *o ʃɔkɔla* / – chocolat
aux noisettes / *o nwazɛt* / – hazelnut

Drinks

Non–Alcoholic Drinks

le café / *lə kafe* / – coffee
    au lait / *o lɛ* / – with milk
    noir / *nwar* / – black coffee
    turc / *turk* / – turkish coffee
    glacé / *glase* / – ice coffee
    avec de la crème / *avek də la krem* / – with cream
le cacao / *lə kakao* / – cocoa
le chocolat / *lə ʃɔkɔla* / – chocolate
le thé / *lə te* / – tea
au citron / *o sitʀɔ̃* / – with lemon

Alcoholic Drinks

l'alcool / *lalkɔl* / – alcohol
le vin / *lə vẽ* / – wine
    de table / *də tabl* / – table wine
    vieux / *vjø* / – old
    doux / *du* / – sweet
    sec / *sek* / – dry
    léger / *leʒe* / – light
    fort / *for* / – strong
    blanc / *blan* / – white
    rouge / *ʀuʒ* / – red
    de dessert / *də desɛʀ* / – desert
    mousseux / *musø* / – sparkling
le champagne / *lə ʃãpaɲ* / – champagne
le vin en bouteille / *lə vẽ ã butɛj* / – wine in a bottle
le cidre / *lə sidʀ* / – cider
le vermouth / *lə vermut* / – vermouth
la bière / *la bjɛʀ* / – beer
    ambre / *ambre* / – amber
    à la pression / *a la pʀesjɔ̃* / – draft beer
    blonde / *blond* / – blonde
    brune / *bryn* / – dark beer
    sans alcool / *sãzalkol* / – without alcohol
l'eau de vie / *lo d vi* / – brandy
Whisky / *lə viski* / – whisky
le cognac / *lə kɔɲak* / – cognac
le rhum / *lə ʀɔm* / – rum
la liqueur / *la likœʀ* / – liqueur

Chapter 13: Shopping

L'élégance est une question de personnalité, plus que de vêtements.

Jean Paul Sartre

It's hard to imagine a day without shopping. If you're traveling or living in France, you'll need this chapter almost every day. There are two words associated with shopping: *"vendre* (to sell) and *"acheter"* (to purchase).

vendre / *vãdʀ* / – to sell

acheter / *aʃəte* / – to buy

le magasin / *lə magazẽ* / – store

la boutique / *la butik* / – shop, boutique

le marchand / *lə maʀʃã* / – shopkeeper

la vendeuse / *la va☐dœz* / – shop assistant, female

le vendeur / *lə va☐dœʀ* / – shop assistant, male

l'échantillon / *leʃãtijɔ̃* / – sample

le client / *l klijã* / – client

les soldes / *le sɔld* / – sale

payer en espèces / *peje ã ɛspɛsə* / – to pay with cash

    par carte / *paʀ kart* / – with credit card

la cabine d'essayage / *la kabin desɛjaʒ* / – fitting room

le prix / *lə pri* / – price

    fixe / *fiks* / – fixed

    reduit / *ʀedyi* / – reduced

la note / *la not* / – bill

Basic Phrases

Upon entering a local shop, you may hear:

Bonjour Monsieur/Madame ! Que désirez-vous ? / *bɔ̃ʒuʀ məsjø/madam / kə dezire vu* / – Good day Mr/Madam! What would you like?

    Je désire / J'ai besoin ( ). / *ʒə deziʀ / ʒe bəzwẽ* / – I would like / I need ().

    Avez-vous ( ) ? / *ave vu ( )* / – Do you have ( )?

Je voudrais aller faire les magasins. / *ʒə vudʀɛ ale fɛʀ le magazẽ* / – I would like to go shopping.

Où est-ce que je peux acheter/trouver ( ) ? / u esk ʒə pø aʃəte / truve / – Where can I buy/find ( )?

Où est l'hypermarché le plus proche ? / u e lipɛʀmaʀʃe lə ply pʀɔʃ / – Where is the nearest hypermarket?

Vous avez ( ) ? /vuzave …/ – Do you have ( )?

Je peux voir ( ) ? / ʒə pø vwar / – Can I see ( )?

Y a-t-il des soldes ? / jatil de sold / – Are there sales?

C'est soldé aussi ? / sɛ solde osi / – Is it on sale too?

Veuillez me montrer ( ). / vøje mə montre ( ) / – Please show me ( ).

Vous me recommandez lequel ? / vu m ʀəkɔmɑ̃de lə kɛl / – Which one do you recommend me?

Je le/la/les prends. / ʒə lə/la/le pʀɑ̃d / – I'll take it.

Il y avait un prix réduit sur l'étiquette ? / iljave œ̃ pri ʀedyi syr letikɛt / – Was there a reduced price on the label?

Je peux avoir un sac ? / ʒə pø avwar œ̃ sak / – Can I have a bag?

Vous pouvez l'emballer ? / vu puve mɑ̃bale / – Can you wrap it?

Warranty

Vous offrez une garantie de remboursement ? / vuzɔfre yn gaʀɑ̃ti də ʀɑ̃buʀsəmɑ̃ / – Do you offer a money back guarantee?

Quelle est la durée de la garantie ? / kɛl e la dyre de la gaʀɑ̃ti / – How long is the warranty?

Est-ce que la garantie couvre aussi ( ) ? / ɛsk la gaʀɑ̃ti kuvʀ osi / – Does the waranty also cover ( )?

Comment faire pour obtenir la garantie ? / kɔmɑ̃ fɛʀ puʀ ɔptənir la gaʀɑ̃ti / – How do I get the warranty?

Reclamation

Je veux faire une réclamation sur ce produit. / ʒə vø fɛʀ yn ʀeklamasjɔ̃ syr s pʀɔdyi / – I want to make a reclamation for this product.

Ça ne marche plus. / sa n maʀʃ ply / – It does not work anymore.

J'ai suivi le mode d'emploi. / ʒɛ suivi lə mod dɑ̃plwa / – I followed the manual.

Voici le ticket de caisse. / vwasi lə tike də kɛs / – Here is the receipt.

Vous pouvez me l'échanger ? / vu puve mə leʃɑ̃ʒe / – Can you exchange it for me?

Je veux être remboursé. / ʒə vø ɛtʀ ʀɑ̃buʀse / – I would like to be reimbursed.

Pouvez-vous me prévenir par mail ? / vu puve mə pʀevənir par mɛl / – Could you notify me by email?

Votre réclamation a été rejetée ? / vɔtʀ ʀeklamasjɔ̃ a ete ʀəʒəte / – Has your claim been rejected?

Pourquoi ma réclamation a été rejetée ? / *puRkwa ma Reklamasjɔ̃ a ete Rəʒəte* / – Why was my claim rejected?

Paying

Ca coûte combien ? / *sa kut kɔ̃bjẽ* / – How much is it?

C'est trop cher. / *sɛ tro ʃɛR* / – It's too expensive.

Ce n'est pas cher. / *sə nɛ pa ʃɛR* /– It is cheap.

Je n'ai pas assez d'argent. / *ʒə nɛ pa ase daRʒã* / – I do not have enough money.

Je paye où ? / *ʒə pɛj u*/ Where do I pay?

Où est la caisse ? / *u ɛ la kɛs* / – Where is the check out?

Je peux payer en liquide ? / *ʒə pø pɛje ã likid* / – Could I pay in cash?

Je n'ai pas de monnaie. / *ʒə nɛ pa də mɔnɛ* / – I don't have change.

Vous acceptez ces chèques ? / *vuzaksɛpte se ʃɛk* / – Do you accept these checks?

Je vais payer par carte. / *ʒə vɛ pɛje par kart* / – I'll pay by card.

Je ne trouve pas mon portefeuille. / *ʒə nə pø pa truve mɔ̃ pɔRtəfœj* /– I can't find my wallet.

Vous pouvez me prêter quelques euros ? / *vu puve mə prete kɛlkzøRo* / – Can you lend me a few euros?

Comment je fais pour obtenir le remboursement de la T.V.A ? / *kɔmã ʒə fɛ pur ɔptəniR lə RãbuRsəmã də la tva* / – How do I get VAT refund?

Shops

la bouquinerie / *la bukineri* / – bookstore

la librairie / *la libReri* / – library

la pharmacie / *la faRmasi* / – pharmacy

la boucherie / *la buʃRi* / – butcher

la parfumerie / *la paRfymRi* / – perfumery

la boulangerie / *la bulãʒRi* / – bakery

la poissonnerie / *la pwasɔnRi* / – fish shop

le grand-magasin / *lə gRã magazẽ*/ – department store

la pêtisserie / *la patisRi* / – cake shop, confectionery

le bureau de tabac / *lə byRo də taba* / – tobacco store

Supermarket

Ingredients

la farine / *la farin* / – flour
le pain / *lə pɛ̃* / – bread
l'oeuf (m.) / *lœf* / – egg
le yaourt / *lə jauʀt* / – yoghurt
le lait fermentée / *lə lɛ fɛʀmɑ̃te* / fermented milk
les petits pains / *le pti pɛ̃* / – buns
la levure / *la levyr* / – yeast
le miel / *lə mjɛl* / – honey
le fromage / *lə fʀɔmaʒ* / – cheese
le lait / *lə lɛ* / – milk
le muesli / *lə myysli* / – muesli
la pâte à tartiner / *la pat a tartine* / – spread
le beurre / *lə bœʀ* / – butter
le moutarde / *lə mutaʀd* / – mustard
le saucisson / *lə sosisɔ̃* / – salami
le vinaigre / *lə vinɛgʀ* / – vinegar
le bacon / *le bekɔn* / – bacon
le sucre / *lə sykʀ* / – sugar
le sel / *lə sɛl* / – salt
le jambon / *lə ʒɑ̃bɔ̃* / – ham
le fromage / *lə fʀɔmaʒ* / – cheese
- **emmental** / *emɛ̃tal* / – emmental
- **de brebis** / *də bʀəbi* / – sheep
- **en tranches** / *ɑ̃ tʀɑ̃ʃ* / – in slices
- **bleu** / *blø* / – blue
- **fondu** / *fɔ̃dy* / – melted

Clothes

les vêtements (m.) / *le vɛtmɑ̃* / – clothes
le tee-shirt / *lə tiʃœʀt* / – T-shirt
    à manches courtes / *a mɑ̃ʃ kur* / – short sleeves
    à manches longues / *a mɑ̃ʃ long* / – long sleeves

polo / polo / – polo
la chemise / *la ʃəmiz* / – shirt
le sweat–shirt / *lə switʃœʀt* / – sweatshirt
le pull / *lə pyl* / – sweater
le blouson / *lə bluzɔ̃* / – jacket
L'anorak (m.) / *lanɔʀak* / – anorak
le manteau / *lə mɑ̃to* / – coat
le costume / *lə kɔstym* / – suit
la veste / *la vɛst* / – jacket
le gilet / *lə ʒilɛ* / – waistcoat
la robe / *la rob* / – dress
le pantalon / *lə pɑ̃talɔ̃* / – pantalon
le jean / *lə dʒin* / – jeans
le short / *lə ʃɔʀt* / – shorts
la jupe / *la ʒyp* / – skirt
le pyjama / *lə piʒama* / – pajama
le sous–vêtement / *lə suvɛtmɑ̃* / – underwear
  - **la culotte** / *la kylɔt* / – knickers
  - **le soutien-gorge** / *lə sutjẽgɔʀʒ* / – bra
  - **le slip** / *lə slip* / – knickers slip
les chaussettes / *lə ʃosɛt* / – socks
l'imperméable (m.) / *lẽpɛʀmeabl* / – raincoat
la jambe / *la ʒɑ̃b* / – trouser leg
la manche / *la mɑ̃ʃ* / – sleeve
le col / *lə kɔl* / – collar
la taille / *la taj* / – size
la longueur / *la lɔ☐gœʀ* / – length
à boutons / *a butɔ̃* / – with buttons
à fermeture éclair / *a fɛʀmətyʀ eklɛʀ* / – with zipper
Accessoires
la ceinture / *la sẽtyʀ* / – belt
les boutons (m.) / *le butɔ̃* / – buttons
le bracelet / *lə bʀaslɛ* / – bracelet
la chaîne / *la ʃɛn* / – chain

la boucle d'oreille / lə bukl dɔrɛj / – earring
le sac à main / lə sak a mɛ̃ / – handbag
le parapluie / lə paraplɥi / – rain
le bonnet / lə bɔnɛ / – a wolly hat
le chapeau / lə ʃapo / – hat
l'écharpe (f.) / leʃarp / – scarf
le foulard / lə fular / – a silk scarf
les gants (m.) / le gɑ̃ / – gloves
les lunettes de soleil / le lynet d sɔlɛj / – sunglasses

Shoes

les chaussures sans talons / le ʃosyr sɑ̃ talɔ̃ / – shoes without heels
les chaussures à talons hauts / le ʃosyr a talɔ̃ ho / – high-heeled shoes
les soulier bas / le sulje ba / – flat shoes
les mocassins (m.) / le mɔkasɛ̃ / – mocassins
les chaussures de sport / le ʃosyr d spor / – sneakers
les tennis / le tenis / – tennis
les chaussures de marche/montagne / le ʃosyr d marʃ/ mɔ̃taɲ / – hiking shoes
les sandales (f.) / le sɑ̃dal / – sandals
les bottes (f.) / les bot / – boots
les pantoufles (f.) / le pɑ̃tufl / – slippers

Common Phrases

J'ai vu en vitrine. / ʒə vy un vitrin / – I saw in the window display.
Il me faudrait la taille ( ) . / il m fodre la taj / – I would need the size ( ).
Puis-je l'essayer ? / pɥi ʒə eseje / – Could I try it on?
C'est trop / sɛ tro / – It is too
    grand / grɑ̃ / – big
    petit / pti / – small
    large / larʒ / – wide
    étroit / etrwa / – tight
    foncé / fɔ̃se / – dark
    clair / klɛr / – light

La qualité (couleur) ne me plaît pas. / la kalite / kulœr / nə mə plɛ pa / / – I don't like the quality (color).
La couleur est-elle permanente ? / la kulœr ɛtel pɛrmanɑ̃tə / – Is the color permanent?

Avez-vous quelque chose de moins cher ? / *ave vu kɛlk ʃoz də mwɛ̃ ʃɛr* / – Do you have something cheaper?

Combien coûte une pièce/paire de ( )? / *kɔ̃bjɛ̃ kut yn pjɛs/pɛrə də ( )* / – How much does an item/pair of ( ) cost?

Cela ne me va pas. / *səla nə mə va pa* / – It doesn't suit me.

Puis-je échanger cela ? / *pɥi ʒə eʃɑ̃ʒe səla* / – Could I exchange that?

Chapter 14: Bank / Exchange Office / Post Office

Les défis sont ce qui rend la vie intéressante et les surmonter est ce qui donne sens à la vie.

Joshua J. Marine

In France, banks are generally open Monday through Friday from 08:30-17:30, although most of them close between 12 p.m. and 14 p.m. for lunch. In some cases, banks may be open on Saturday mornings but closed on Mondays, so be sure to check before heading out.

le compte bancaire / lə kɔ̃t bɑ̃kɛʁ / – bank account

    compte courant / kɔ̃t kuʁɑ̃ / – current account

    compte en devises / kɔ̃t ɑ̃ dəviz / – currency account

l'ordre de virement (bancaire) (m.) / lɔʁdʁ viʁmɑ̃ / – bank transfer

la pièce de monnaie / la pjɛs d mɔnɛ / – change

le billet de banque / lə bijɛ d bɑ̃k / – banknote

le guichet / lə giʃɛ / – counter

le solde du compte / lə sɔld dy kɔ̃t / – account balance

le distributeur de billets / lə distʁibytœʁ d bijɛ / – cash machine

Exchanging money / ATM

Je veux changer de l'argent. / ʒə vø ʃɑ̃ʒe də laʁʒɑ̃ / – I would like to exchange money.

Il y a une commission ? / ilja yn kɔmisjɔ̃ / – Is there a commission?

Combien d'argent faut-il changer ? / kɔ̃bjẽ daʁʒɑ̃ fotil ʃɑ̃ʒe / – How much money should I exchange?

Vous pouvez m'échanger un billet de cinquante euros ? / vu puve meʃɑ̃ʒe œ̃ bijɛ d sɛ̃kɑ̃t øʁo / Could you exchange me a fifty euro banknote?

Je cherche un bureau de change. / ʒə ʃɛʁʃe œ̃ byʁo də ʃɑ̃ʒ / I am looking for a currency exchange office.

Je voudrais retirer de l'argent. / ʒə vudʁɛ retire də laʁʒɑ̃ / I would like to withdraw money.

Le distributeur a avalé ma carte. / lə distʁibytœʁ a avale ma kart / – The ATM swallowed my card.

Le distributeur refuse ma carte. / lə distʁibytœʁ refuz ma kart / – The ATM refuses my card. /

Bank

J'aimerais ouvrir un compte chez vous. / ʒemre ouvrir œ☐ kɔ☐t ʃe vu / – I would like to open an account here.

Il me faudra quels documents ? / il me fodʀa kɛl dɔkymã / – What documents will I need?

Quel est votre numéro de compte ? / kɛl e votr nymeʀo dkɔ̃t / – What is your account number?

Je veux retirer de l'argent de mon compte. / ʒə vø ʀətire de laʀʒã də mɔ̃ kɔ̃t / – I would like to withdraw money from my account.

Quel est le montant de retrait minimal/maximal possible ? / kɛl e lə mɔ̃tã de ʀətʀɛ minimal/maksimal / – What is the minimum/maximum possible withdrawal amount ?

Quel est le solde de mon compte ? / kɛl e lə sɔld d mɔ̃ kɔ̃t / – What is my account balance?

Je voudrais payer par virement bancaire. / ʒə vudʀɛ peje par viʀmã bãkɛʀ / – I would like to pay by bank transfer.

Le virement va prendre combien de temps ? / lə viʀmã va pʀãdʀ kɔ̃bjẽ də tã / – How long will the transfer take?

Il faut aller à quel guichet ? / il fo ale a kɛl giʃɛ / – Which counter should I go to?

Apple Pay

Connecting on Apple Pay

Connectez-vous à l'Apple Store. / kɔnɛkte vu a lApple Store / – Log in to the Apple Store.

Créer votre identifiant. / kʀee votr idãtifjã / – Create your ID.

Vous avez déjà un identifiant Apple ? Retrouvez-le ici. / vuzave deʒa œ☐ ida☐tifjã☐ (apple) ʀətʀuve lə isi / – Already have an Apple ID? Find it here.

Saisissez les informations ci-dessous pour retrouver votre identifiant Apple. / sezise lez ẽfɔʀmasjɔ̃ si desu pur retʀuve votr idãtifjã (apple) / – Enter the information below to find your Apple ID.

Saisissez les caractères / sezise le kaʀaktɛʀ / – Enter the characters.

Mot de passe oublié / mo d pas ublije / – Forgoten password.

Valider à l'aide d'un sms / appel téléphonique / valide a lɛd dœ☐ esemes / apəle telefɔnik / – Validate with an sms / phone call.

Cette adresse sera votre nouvel identifiant. / sɛt adres sera votr nuvel idãtifjã / – This address will be your new username.

Le nouveau code / lə nuvo kod / The new code.

Shopping on Apple Pay

Poursuivre vos achats / puʀsɥivʀ voz aʃa / – Continue shopping.

Votre panier est vide / votr panje e vid / – Your basket is empty.

Votre sélection / votr selɛksjɔ̃ / – Your selection.

Commandes / kɔmãd / – Orders.

Compte / kɔ̃ / – Account

Connectez-vous pour régler vos achats plus rapidement. / kɔnɛkte vu pur regle voz aʃa ply ʀapidmɑ̃ / Log in to pay for your purchases faster.

Besoin d'une aide supplémentaire ? / bəzwɛ̃ dyn ɛd syplemɑ̃tɛʀ / – Do you need additional help?

Post Office

Post offices are marked in blue with the inscription *"la poste"* or *"PTT"*. The main post office is open on weekdays from 8–17 pm and on Saturdays till 12 PM. Stamps can be bought at post offices or at tabac stores.

la poste / *la post* / – poste

la lettre / *la letr* / – letter

la carte postale / *la kart postal* / – postcard

le collis / *lə koli* / – paquet

le timbre / *lə tɛ̃bʀ* / – stamp

l'enveloppe (f.) / *lɑ̃vəlɔp* / – envelope

la rue / *la ry* / – street

la ville / *la vil* / – city

le code postal / *lə kod postal* / postal code

en recommandée / *ɑ̃ ʀəkɔmɑ̃de* / registered

par avion / *par avjɔ̃* / – by airplane

express / *ɛkspʀɛ* / express

J'aimerais envoyer une lettre recommandée. / ʒəmre ɑ̃vwaje yn letr ʀəkɔmɑ̃de / – I would like to send a registered letter.

Tarif lent, s'il vous plaît. / tarif lɑ̃ sil vu plɛ / – Regular fare, please.

Une enveloppe / un timbre s'il vous plaît. /yn ɑ̃vəlɔp/ œ̃ tɛ̃bʀ / sil vu plɛ / – An enveloppe / a stamp please.

Il me faut quel timbre pour ( ) ? / il m fo kɛl tɛ̃bʀ pur / – What stamp do I need for ( )?

Combien coûte d'envoyer un colis de 1 kilo ? / kɔ̃bjɛ̃ kut dɑ̃vwaje un koli d œ̃ kilo / – What is the cost of sending a package weighing 1 kilo?

C'est quel guichet pour envoyer une lettre ? / sɛ kɛl giʃɛ pur ɑ̃vwaje yn letʀ / – Which counter is it to send a letter?

Chapter 15: Business

La seule limite à notre épanouissement de demain sera nos doutes d'aujourd'hui.

Franklin D. Roosevelt

Learning some basic French phrases is highly recommended if you intend to settle business in France or if you are looking to work there. They will praise you if you are struggling and return to English. The value of patience will be appreciated in business communication, whereas the value of pressure will be negatively viewed. The same goes for aggressive selling techniques, it won't generate a positive response. You should instead focus on discussion and information exchange. Also, avoid discussing personal matters during business negotiations.

L'emploi (m.) / lãplwa / – employment

le travail / le boulot / lə tʀavaj / lə bulo / – job

    le petit boulot d'étudiant / lə pəti bulo detydjã / – student job

    le travail d'été / lə tʀavaj dete / – summer job

le travailleur temporaire / lə tʀavajœʀ tã pɔʀɛʀ / – temporary worker

le stage / lə staʒ / – internship

embaucher, employer / ãboʃe/ ãplwaje / – to hire

le contrat de travail / lə kɔ̃tʀa d tʀavaj / – employment contract

le contrat à durée / lə kɔ̃tʀa a dyʀe / – term contract

    determinée (CDD) / detɛʀmine / – definite time

    indeterminée (CDI) / ɛ̃detɛʀmine / – indefinite time

le congé / lə kɔ̃ʒe / – annual leave

la démission / la demisjɔ̃ / – resignation

le délais de préavis / lə delɛ d pʀeavi / – notice period

le salaire / lə salɛʀ / – the salary

le salaire horaire / lə salɛʀ ɔʀɛʀ / – the hourly wage

le salaire mensuel / lə salɛʀ mãsɥɛl / – the monthly salary

le revenu brut / lə ʀ(ə)v(ə)ny bʀyt / – the gross income

le revenu net / lə ʀ(ə)v(ə)ny nɛt / – the net income

le chèque de paie / lə ʃɛk d pɛ / – the paycheck

l'augmentation du salaire / lɔgmãtasjɔ̃ dy salɛʀ / – the salary increase

L'équipe (f.) / lekip / – team

l'équipe du matin / *lekip dy matɛ̃* / – morning team

l'équipe de l'après-midi / *lekip de lapʀɛ midi* / – afternoon team

l'équipe de nuit / *lekip de nɥi* / – night team

les heures supplémentaires / *lezœʀ syplema☐tɛʀ* / – overtime work

rémunération des heures supplémentaires / *ʀemyneʀasjɔ̃ dezœʀ syplema☐tɛʀ* / – overtime work payment

la prestation maladie / *la pʀɛstasjɔ̃ maladi* / – sickness benefit

les avantages annexes/sociaux / *lezavɑ̃taʒ anɛks / sɔsjal* / – additional benefits

le congé / les vacances / *lə kɔ̃ʒe / le vakɑ̃s* / – vacation

le tickets/chèques restaurant / *lə tikɛ / lə ʃɛk ʀɛstɔʀɑ̃* / – restaurant vouchers

la voiture de fonction / *la vwatyʀ d fɔ̃ksjɔ̃* / – company car

le travail à plein temps / *lə tʀavaj a plɛ̃ tɑ̃* / – a full-time job

le travail à temps partiel / *lə mi-temps a tɑ̃ paʀsjɛl* / – part-time work

la journée de travail / *la ʒuʀne d tʀavaj* / – working day

durée/temps/heures de travail / *dyʀe / ta☐ / œʀ də tʀavaj* / – duration/time/hours of work.

About my Job

Où travaillez-vous? / *u tʀavaje vu* / – Where do you work?

Quelle est votre profession ? / *kɛl e votʀ pʀɔfesjɔ̃* / – What is your profession?

Je suis ( ). / *ʒə sɥi* / – I am ( ).

Je travaille comme ( ). / *ʒə tʀavaje kom* / – I work as ( ).

Depuis combien de temps vous travaillez là-bas ? / *dəpɥi kɔ̃bjɛ̃ d tɑ̃ vu tʀavaje la ba* / – How long have you been working there?

Ça fait plus de cinq ans que je travaille ici. / *sa fɛ ply d sɛ̃k ɑ̃ ʒə tʀavaj isi* / – I have worked here for more than five years.

Je travaille à temps partiel/plein temps. / *ʒə tʀavaj a tɑ̃ paʀsjɛl/plɛ̃ tɑ̃* / – I work part-time/ full-time.

Je fais des heures supplémentaires. / *ʒə fɛ dezœʀ syplema☐tɛʀ* / – I work overtime.

J'ai deux emplois. / *ʒɛ dø ɑ̃plwa* / – I have two jobs.

Je suis au chômage. / *ʒə sɥi o ʃomaʒ* / – I am unemployed.

J'ai pris ma retraite. / *ʒɛ pri ma ʀətʀɛt* / – I am retired.

At work

À quelle heure tu commences à travailler ? / a kɛl œʀ ty kɔmɑ☐se a travaje / – What time do you start working?

    Je travaille de neuf à six heures. / ʒə travaj də nœf a siz œʀ / – I work from nine to six.

J'ai un horaire flexible. / ʒɛ œ☐ ɔʀɛʀ flɛksibl / – I have a flexible schedule.

Vous travaillez par relais ? / vu travaje par ʀəlɛ / – Do you work in shifts?

Est-ce que les heures supplémentaires de travail sont payées ? / ɛsk lezœʀ syplemɑ☐tɛʀ d travaj son pɛje / – Is working extra hours payed ?

J'ai droit à combien de jours de congé ? / ʒɛ drwa a kɔ̃bjɛ̃ də ʒuʀ də kɔ̃ʒe / – How many days off am I entitled to ?

Je vais prendre un congé lundi prochain. / ʒɛ ve pʀɑ̃dʀ œ☐ kɔ☐ʒe lœ☐di pʀɔʃɛ☐ / – I am going to take a day off next Monday.

Est-ce que je peux prendre un congé non payé ? / ɛsk ʒə pø pʀɑ☐dʀ œ☐ kɔ☐ʒe nɔ☐ peje / – Can I take unpaid leave ?

Je vais en voyage d'affaires en Allemagne. / ʒə ve ɑ☐ vwajaʒ dafɛʀ œ☐ almaɲ / – I am going on a business trip to Germany.

Il faut que je parte plus tôt aujourd'hui. / il fɛ k ʒə paʀt ply to oʒuʀdɥi / – I have to leave earlier today.

Je suis en congé maladie. / ʒə sɥi ɑ̃ kɔ̃ʒe maladi / – I am on sick leave.

Applying for a Job

l'agence nationale pour l'emploi / laʒɑ̃s nasjɔnal puʀ lɑ̃plwa / – national employment agency

l'agence/bureau de placement / laʒɑ̃s/byʀo d plasmɑ̃ / – placement agency/office

l'offre d'emploi / lɔfʀ dɑ̃plwa / – job offer

les petites annonces / le ptit anɔ̃s / – ads

l'entretien d'embauche / ɑ̃tʀətjɛ̃ dɑ̃boʃ / – job interview

CV / seve / – resume

Je cherche un boulot pour les vacances. / ʒə ʃɛʀʃe œ☐ bulo puʀ le vakɑ̃s / – I am looking for a job for the holidays.

Je cherche un boulot d'étudiant. / ʒə ʃɛʀʃe œ☐ bulo detydjɑ☐ / – I am looking for a student job.

Je veux trouver un petit boulot à l'étranger. / ʒə vø tʀuve œ☐ pti bulo al etʀɑ☐ʒe / – I want to find a little job abroad.

Je voudrais travailler / ʒə vudʀɛ travaje / – I would like to work

    à mi-temps / a mi tɑ̃ / – part-time

    à plein temps / a plɛ̃ tɑ̃ / – full time

En quoi consisterait le travail exactement ? / ɑ̃ kwa kɔ̃siste l tʀavaj ɛgzaktəmɑ̃ / What would the job entail?

Quand je pourrais commencer à travailler? / *kã ʒə puʀɛ kɔmãse a tʀavaje* / – When can I start working?

Est-ce que quelqu'un pourrait me montrer quoi faire ? / *ɛsk kɛlkœ☐ puʀɛ mə mɔ☐tʀe kwa fɛʀ* / – Could someone show me what to do?

Chapter 16: Health and Wellbeing

J'ai décidé d'être heureux parce que c'est bon pour la santé.

Voltaire

It happens often in France that you can't recognize the doctor from a nurse, as they rarely wear the traditional white doctor robes you're used to seeing in your country. Usually, the doctor will greet you in the waiting room instead of having a nurse calling your name while you wait. There is no need for you to arrive early most of the time, and you are perfectly fine if you are a few minutes late. When you enter a waiting room, don't ignore the other people. It's considered rude to simply sit down without saying a *bonjour*.

Body

les reins (m.) /le ʀɛ̃/ – kidneys

l'intestin (m.) /lɛ̃tɛstɛ̃/ – the intestine

la tête /la tɛt/ – the head

la gorge /la gɔʀʒ/ – the throat

le sein /lə sɛ̃/ – the breast

le foie /lə fwa/ – liver

la langue /la lɑ̃g/ – tongue

le dos /lə do/ – the back

les cheveux /le ʃevo/ – hair

l'os (m.) /lɔs/ – bone

la peau /la po/ – the skin

le sang /lə sɑ̃/ – the blood

le muscle /lə myskl/ – the muscle

le cerveau /lə sɛʀvo/ – the brain

la jambe / la ʒɑ̃b / – the leg

le nez / lə ne / – the nose

le poumon / lə pumɔ̃ / – the lung

la poitrine / la pwatʀin / – the chest

le doigt / lə dwa / – the finger

le bras / lə bra / – the arm

les organes génitaux / *lezorgan ʒenito* / – genitals

le coeur / *lə kœʀ* / – the heart

le cou / *lə ku* / – the neck

la dent / *la dã* / – the tooth

l'estomac (m.) / *lɛstɔma* / – stomach

la veine / *la vɛn* / – vein

le nerf / *lə nɛʀ* / – nerve

la glande / *la glãd* / – glande

la bile / *la bil* / – bile

At the Doctor

To make an appointment with a doctor in France, you call the "***cabinet medical***" and you say "***je voudrais prendre rendez-vous s'il vous plaît***" – "I'd like to make an appointment please" and a secretary will arrange the appointment.

le medécin / *lə medəsɛ̃* / – doctor

le spécialiste / *lə spesjalist* / – specialist

l'infirmière / *lɛ̃fiʀmje* / – the nurse

la maladie / *la maladi* / – the disease

    bénigne / *benɛ̃* / – mild

    grave / *grav* / – severe

la feuille de maladie / *la fœj d maladi* / sickness sheet

la plaie / *la plɛ* / – the wound

le régime alimentaire / *lə reʒim alimãtɛʀə* / – the diet

la grossesse / *la grosɛs* / – the pregnancy

l'accouchement (m.) / *lakuʃmã* / – childbirth

On a besoin d'un médecin. / *ɔ̃ a bəzwɛ̃ dœ̃ med(ə)sɛ̃* / – We need a doctor.

Envoyer une ambulance à ( ) / *ãvwaje yn ãbylãs* / – Send ambulance to ( ).

Quelles sont les heures de consultation ? / *kɛl sɔ̃ lezœʀ dkɔ̃syltasjɔ̃* / – What are the consultation hours?

The doctor may ask you questions like these:

- **De quoi vous plaignez-vous ?** / *də kwa plɛɲe vu* / – What are you complaining about?
- **Où avez-vous mal ?** / *u ave vu mal* / – Where does it hurt?

    J'ai mal / *ʒɛ mal* / – I have pain

        - **à la tête** / *a la tɛt* / – in head

- **à la gorge** / *a la gɔʀʒ* / – in throat
- **à l'estomac** / *a lɛstɔma* / – in stomac
- **à l'oreille** / *a lɔʀɛj* / – in ear

J'ai de la fièvre. / *ʒɛ də la fjɛvʀ* / – I have a fever.

Je souffre d'insomnie. / *ʒə sufr dɛ̃sɔmni* / I suffer from insomnia.

Je me suis évanoui. / *ʒə m sɥi evanoui* / – I fainted.

Je tousse beaucoup. / *ʒə tus boku* / – I cough a lot.

Je suis très fatigué. / *ʒə sɥi tre fatige* / – I am very tired.

J'ai du mal à respirer. / – *ʒɛ dy mal a respirer* / – I have trouble breathing.

J'ai pris froid. / *ʒɛ pri frwa* / – I caught a cold.

J'ai froid/chaud. / *ʒɛ frwa/ ʃo* / I am cold/hot.

J'ai des vomissements. / *ʒɛ de vɔmismã* / – I vomit.

J'ai de la constipation. / *ʒɛ d la kɔ̃stipasjɔ̃* / I have constipation.

J'ai des palpitations. / *ʒɛ de palpitasjɔ̃* / I have palpitations.

Je suis allergique à / *ʒə sɥi alɛʀʒik a* / – I am allergic to...

J'ai une éruption de boutons. / *ʒɛ yn eʀypsjɔ̃ d butɔ̃* / – I have a rash.

Ça démange terriblement. / *sa demãʒe teʀibləmã* / – It itches terribly.

Je me suis fait piquer par un insecte. / *ʒə mə sɥi fɛ pike par œ̃ ɛ̃sɛkt* / I got stung by an insect.

La tête me tourne. / *la tet mə tuʀn* / – I feel dizzy.

J'ai un problème avec / *ʒɛ œ̃ pʀɔblɛm avɛk* / – I have a problem with

    la jambe / *la ʒãb* / – leg

    le bras / *lə bra* / – arm

Je ne peux pas bouger le bras. / *ʒə n pø pɑ buʒe lə bra* / – I can't move my arm.

Je me sens trés mal. / *ʒə m sã tʀɛ mal* / – I feel very bad.

- **Depuis quand souffrez–vous ?** / *dəpɥi kã sufre vu* / – How long have you been in pain?

  Depuis hier soir. / *dəpɥi jɛʀ swar* / – Since yesterday evening.

  Ça dure trois jours. / *sa dyr trwa ʒuʀ* / – It has been three days.

- **Est-ce que vous digérez bien?** / *esk vu diʒeʀe bjɛ̃* / – Are you digesting well?

  Je digère mal. / *ʒə diʒɛʀ mal* / – I digest badly.

- **Avez-vous de l'appétit ?** / *ave vu d lapeti* / – Do you have appetite?

  Je n'ai goût à rien. / *ʒə nɛ gu a ʀjɛ̃* / – I don't have the sense of taste.

- **Allez-vous à la selle regulièrement ?** / *ave vu a sel ʀegyljɛʀmã* / – Do you go to the bathroom regularly?

- **Est-ce que je vous fais mal ici ?** / *esk ʒə vu fɛ mal isi* / – Does it hurt when I press here?

The doctor may also ask you to do something-

- **Déshabillez-vous jusqu'à la ceinture.** / *dezabije vu ʒyska la sẽtyʀ* / – Undress to the waist.
- **Faites voir votre langue.** / *fɛt vwar votr lãg* / – Show me your tongue.
- **Ouvrez la bouche.** / *uvʀe la buʃ* / – Open your mouth.
- **Inspirez profondément !** / *ɛ̃spiʀe pʀɔfɔ̃demã* / – Take a deep breath !
  - **par la bouche** / *par la buʃ* / – through the mouth
  - **par le nez** / *par lə ne* / – through the nose
- **Ne respirez pas !** / *nə ʀɛspiʀe pa* / – Don't breathe !

You may additionally ask questions like these:

C'est contagieux ? / *sɛ kɔ̃taʒjø* / – Is it contagious?

C'est grave ? / *sɛ grav* / – Is it serious?

Je dois prendre le médicament pendant combien de temps ? / *ʒə dwa pʀãdʀ lə medikamã pãdã kɔ̃bjɛ̃ də tã* / – For how long should I take the medicine?

Quels examens il me faudra passer ? / *kɛl ɛgzamɛ̃ il m fodʀa pase* / – What examinations will I need to pass?

J'ai besoin de mon médicament. / *ʒɛ bəzwɛ̃ də mon medikamã* / – I need my medicine.

J'ai une assurance maladie. / *ʒɛ yn asyʀãs maladi* / – I have a health insurance.

At the Dentist

J'ai / *ʒɛ* / – I have

    mal de dents / *mal də dã* / – toothache

    les dents sensibles / *le dã sãsibl* / – sensitive teeth

    les gencives douloureuses / *le ʒãsiv duluʀøz* / – sore gums

    mauvaise haleine / *mɔvɛz alɛn* / – bad breath

    une carie / *yn kari* / – caries

    une gingivite / *yn ʒɛ̃ʒivit* / – a gingivitis

    de la plaque / *də la plak* / – plaque

    une dent cassée / *yn dã kase* / – a broken teeth

    une infection / *lɛ̃fɛksjɔ̃* / – an infection

Puis-je prendre rendez-vous chez le dentiste ? / *pɥi ʒə pʀãdʀ ʀãdevu ʃe lə dãtist* / – Can I book an appointment at the dentist?

Je dois décaler mon rendez-vous chez le dentiste. / *ʒə dwa dekale mɔ̃ ʀãdevu ʃe lə dãtist* / – I have to reschedule my dentist appointment.

Un de mes plombages est parti. / *œ̃ də me plɔ̃baʒ e parti* / – One of my fillings is gone.

J'ai eu des douleurs aux gencives récemment. / ʒɛ y de dulœʀ o ʒa☐siv ʀesama☐ / – I have had gum pain recently.

S'il vous plaît, inclinez-vous et ouvrez la bouche. / sil vu plɛ ɛ̃kline vu e uvre la buʃ / – Please, bow down and open your mouth.

Tenez, enfilez ce tablier de protection. / tene ɑ̃file s tablije də pʀɔtɛksjɔ̃ / – Here, put on this protective apron.

Vous avez une inflammation des gencives. / vuzave yn ɛ̃flamasjɔ̃ de ʒɑ̃siv / – You have some inflammation of the gums.

Il faut faire une nouvelle série de radiographies. / il fo fɛʀ yn nuvɛl seri də radiografi / – A new series of x–rays should be done.

Il semble que vous ayez quelques caries. / il sɛmbl k vuzave kɛlk kari / – It looks like you have caries.

At the Pharmacy

le sparadrap / lə spaʀadʀa / – the medical plaster

la gaze / la gaz / – the gauze

les gouttes (f.) / le gut / – the drops

la médicament / le remède / la medikamɑ̃ / lə ʀəmɛd / – the medecine / the remedy

la serviette hygiénique / la sɛʀvjɛt iʒjenik / – the pad

la pilule / la pilyl / – contraceptive pill

la poudre / la pudʀ / – powder

le préservatif / lə pʀezɛʀvatif / – condom

le talc / lə talk / – talc

le comprimé / lə kɔ̃pʀime / – the tablet

Je voudrais quelque chose. / ʒə vudʀɛ kɛlk ʃoz / – I would like something.

 contre la toux / kɔ̃tʀ la tu / – against coughing

 contre la grippe / kɔ̃tʀ la gʀip / – against the flu

Ce remède n'est délivré que sur ordonnance. / sə ʀəmɛd ne delivʀe k syʀ ɔʀdɔnɑ̃s / This remedy is only available on prescription.

J'ai besoin de ce médicament. / ʒɛ bəzwɛ̃ də sə medikamɑ̃ / – I need this medicine.

Ça se prend comment ? / sa s pʀɑ̃d kɔmɑ̃ / – How is it taken?

C'est couvert par l'assurance ? / sɛ kuvɛʀ paʀ lasyʀɑ̃s / – Is it covered by insurance?

Quand dois-je prendre les comprimés? / kɑ̃ dwa ʒə pʀɑ̃dʀ le kɔ̃pʀime / – When should I take the tablets ?

 Deux fois par jour. / dø fwa paʀ ʒuʀ / – Two times a day.

 Avant (après) les repas. / avɑ̃ / apʀɛ le ʀəpa / – Before (after) meals.

Pour usage externe. / *puʀ yzaʒ ɛkstɛʀn* / – For external use.

Il faut agiter avant de s'en servir. / *il fo aʒite avã d sã sɛʀviʀ* / – You have to shake before using it.

Expressing Emotions

To express your feelings in French, you can use two verbs, either "*être*" or "*se sentir*", both followed by an adjective. Be aware that feminine adjectives acquire an -e, which changes how the last consonant is pronounced.

Comment te sens-tu ? / *kɔmã t sã ty* / – How do you feel?

Je suis / Je me sens / *ʒə sɥi / ʒə m sã* / – I am / I feel

    fâché(e) / *faʃe* / – angry

    ennuyé(e) / *enɥje* / – bored

    honteux, honteuse / *ɔ̃tø / ɔ̃tøz* / – ashamed

    tranquille / *tʀãkil* / – calm

    gai(e) / *ge* / cheerful

    assuré(e) / *asyʀe* / – insured

    désorienté(e) / *dezɔʀjãte* / – disoriented

    ravi(e) / *ravi* / – delighted

    déprimé(e) / *depʀime* / – depressed

    épuisé(e) / *epɥize* / – exhausted

    frustré(e) / *fʀustʀe* / – frustrated

    heureux, heureuse / *øʀø / øʀøz* / – happy

    horrifié(e) / *ɔʀifje* / – horrified

    excité(e) / *ɛksite* / – excited

    agacé(e) / *agase* / – annoyed

    pressé(e) / *pʀɛse* / – in a hurry

    triste / *tʀist* / – sad

    effrayé(e) / *efʀeje* / – scared

    content(e) / *kɔ̃tã* / – satisfied

    nerveux, nerveuse / *nɛʀvø / nɛʀvøz* /– nervous

    surpris(e) / *surprise* / – surprised

    fatigué(e) / *fatige* / – tired

    malheureux, malheureuse / *maløʀø / maløʀøz* / – unhappy

inquiet, inquiète / *ɛ̃kjɛ / ɛ̃kjɛt* / – worried

At the Spa

la piscine / *la pisin* / – pool

la sauna / *la sona* / – sauna

le vestiaire / *lə vɛstjɛʀ* / – locker area

le gymnase / *lə ʒimnaz* / – fitness centre

le salon de beauté / *lə salon də bote* / – beauty salon

zone d'exercices / *zon dɛgzɛʀsis* / – exercice area

la piscine d'eau salée / *la pisin do sale* / – saltwater pool

le banc de sauna / *lə bã də sona* / – sauna bench

le peignoir / *lə pɛɲwaʀ* / – bathrobe

le bain chaud / *lə bɛ̃ ʃo* / – hot tub

les pantoufles / *le pãtufl* / – slippers

la serviette / *la sɛʀvjɛt* / – towel

le traitement / *lə tʀɛtmã* / – treatment

    de beauté / *də bote* / – beauty treatment

    pour la peau / *puʀ la po* / – skin treatment

    corporel / *kɔʀpɔʀel* / – body treatment

le soin / *lə swɛ̃* / – care, treatment

    - **du visage** / *dy vizaʒ* / – facial treatment

    - **des mains** / *de mɛ̃* / – hand treatment

    - **des pieds** / *de pje* / – foot treatment

la manicure / *la manikyʀ* / – manicure

la pédicure / *la pedikyʀ* / – pedicure

le soin des ongles / *lə swɛ̃* / – nail care

l'aromathérapie / *laʀɔmateʀapi* / – aromatherapy

épilation / *lepilasjɔ̃* / – waxing, depilation

le contour des sourcils / *kɔ̃tuʀ de suʀsi* / – eyebrow threading

le bain turc / *lə bɛ̃ tyʀk* / – steam bath

le massage suédois / *lə masaʒ syedwa* / – Swedish massage

le massage sportif / *lə masaʒ spɔʀtif* / – sport massage

le massage aux pierres chaudes / *lə masaʒ o pjɛʀə ʃod* / – hot stone massage

Pouvez-vous me dire où est le jacuzzi ? / *puve vu mə diʀ u e lə ʒakyzi* / – Can you tell me where the jacuzzi is?

La piscine est-elle chauffée ? / *la pisin et el ʃofe* / – Is the swimming pool heated?

Y a-t-il un endroit pour s'allonger ? / *jatil œ☐ a☐dʀwa pur salɔ☐ʒe* / – Is there somewhere to lie down?

Proposez-vous des soins pour le corps ? / *propoze vu de swɛ̃ pur lə kor* / – Do you offer body treatments?

Est-ce que la piscine extérieure est ouverte pendant le printemps ? / *esk la pisin ɛksteʀjœʀ et uvɛʀt pãdã lə pʀɛ̃tã* / – Is the outdoor pool open in the spring?

Proposez-vous / *propoze vu* / – Do you offer

    des soins à la pierre chaude ? / *de swɛ̃ a la pjɛʀ ʃod* / – hot stone treatments?

    épilation ? / epilasjɔ̃ / – waxing

Peut-on faire un massage à deux ? / *pø ɔ☐ fɛʀ œ☐ masaʒ a dø* / – Is it possible to have a massage for two?

Où sont les vestiaires pour femmes/hommes ? / *u son le vɛstjɛʀ pur fam/ɔm ?* / – Where can I find dressing rooms for women/men?

Chapter 17: Telephone and Internet

La chose la plus importante en communication, c'est d'entendre ce qui n'est pas dit.

Peter Drucker

During a stay in France, you can benefit from the WiFi of the hotel in which you are staying, and certain public places (such as train stations and cafes). However, many tourists choose to buy a French SIM card to have internet access at all times.

The main French operators **Orange** or **SFR** offer a prepaid card without any strings attached. The package is adapted for tourists, offering 2 hours of calls in France and Europe, unlimited SMS/MMS, and a certain amount of internet in France and Europe for 14 days.

You can find the SIM card at Orange shops, tobacco stores, petrol stations, supermarkets, and at the airport. There are five languages in the accompanying booklet, so you can use it as a guide to install the card.

Telephone

le portable / *lə portabl* / – the mobile phone

la carte prépayée / *la kart prepeje* / – the prepaid card

la batterie de portable / *la batri də portabl* / – the mobile battery

le chargeur de batterie / *ʃaʀʒœʀ də batri* / – the battery charger

la ligne fixe / *la liɲ fiks* / – the fixed line

Est-ce que je peux utiliser votre téléphone ? / *ɛsk ʒə pø utilize votr telefon* / – Can I use your phone?

Allô. Oui /*alo*/ *wi* / – – Hello. Yes.

On vous appellera au téléphone ! / *ɔ̃ vuzapəlera o telefon* / – We'll call you on the phone !

Pouvez-vous répéter s'il vous plaît. / *puve vu repete sil vu plɛ* / – Could you repeat please?

Excusez-moi, j'ai dû me tromper de numéro. / *ekskuze mwa ʒɛ dy mə trompe də numero* / – Sorry, I must have gotten the number wrong.

Je vous entends mal. / *ʒə vuzɑ̃tɑ̃d mal* / – I can barely hear you.

Vous pouvez me le/la passer ? / *vu puve m lə / la pase* / – Can you pass me (person's name)?

À qui voulez-vous parler ? / *a ki vule vu parle* / – Who would you like to speak to?

J'aimerais parler avec ( ) / *ʒemrɛ parle avɛk* / – I would like to speak with ( ).

La ligne est toujours occupée. / *la liɲ e tuʒur ɔkype* / – The line is always busy.

Est-ce que je peux laisser un message ? / *ɛsk ʒə pø lese œ̃ mesaʒ* / – Can I leave a message?

Essayez de téléphoner dans une heure ? / *eseje də telefɔne da☐ yn œʀ* / – Try to call in an hour?

La batterie est presque déchargée. / *la batri e presk deʃaʀʒe* / – The battery is almost empty.

Il me faut recharger le crédit. / *il m fo ʀəʃaʀʒe lə kredi* / – I need to top up the credit.

Quel est le numéro pour appeler la police / une ambulance ? / *kɛl e lə numero puʀ apple la polis/ yn ɑ̃bylɑ̃s* / – What is the number to call the police / an ambulance?

Getting a Mobile Card

la carte sim / *la kart sim* / – to buy a sim card

    prépayée / *prepeje* / – prepaid

une recharge mobile / *yn ʀəʃaʀʒ mobil* / – a mobile recharge

le bureau de tabac / *lə buro də taba* / – the tobacco shop

les boutiques des opérateurs / *le butik dezɔpeʀatœʀ* / – operators shops

le forfait / *lə fɔʀfɛ* / – the package

    sans abonnement/engagement / *sɑ̃zabɔnmɑ̃* / *ɑ̃gaʒmɑ̃* / without subscription

Où puis-je acheter une carte SIM ? / *u pɥi ʒə aʃəte yn kart sim* / – Where can I buy a SIM card?

Je voudrais acheter une carte SIM pour 14 jours. / *ʒə vudre aʃəte yn kart sim puʀ katɔʀz ʒuʀ* / – I would like to buy a Sim card for 14 days.

Quel est le prix d'une carte SIM pour une durée d'un mois ? / *kɛl e lə pri dyn kart sim puʀ yn dyre dœ☐ mwa* / – What is the price of a monthly SIM card?

Est-ce qu'il est possible d'acheter une carte Sim en ligne ? / *ɛskil e posibl daʃəte yn kart sim ɑ̃ liɲ* / – Is it possible to buy a sim card online?

Qu'est-ce qui est inclus dans le forfait ? / *kɛskil e ɛ̃kly dɑ̃ lə fɔʀfɛ* / – What is included in the package?

Est-ce qu'on reçoit des appels illimités ? / *ɛskɔ̃ ʀəswa dezapɛl ilimite* / – Do we receive unlimited calls?

Est-ce que je peux acheter la carte sans abonnement ? / *ɛsk ʒə pø aʃəte la kart sɑ̃nz abɔnmɑ̃* / – Is it possible to buy the sim card without subscription?

Combien d'appels on obtient avec cette carte SIM ? / *kɔ̃bjɛ̃ dapɛl ɔ̃ ɔptjɛ̃ avɛk sɛt kart sim* / – How many calls do we get with this SIM card?

Les appels vers l'étranger sont-ils inclus dans le prix ? / *lezapɛl vɛʀ letʀɑ̃ʒe sɔ̃til ɛ̃kly dɑ̃ lə pri* / – Are calls abroad included in the price?

Combien d'internet est inclus dans le prix ? / *kɔ̃bjɛ̃ dɛ̃tɛʀnɛt e ɛ̃kly dɑ̃ lə pri* / – How much internet is included in the price?

Qu'est ce qui se passe si je dépasse cette limite ? / *kɛski sə pas si ʒə depas sɛt limit* / – What happens if I exceed this limit?

Comment je peux recharger le crédit ? / *kɔmɑ̃ ʒə pø ʀəʃaʀʒe lə kredi* / – How do I top up the credit?

Quel est le prix des recharges pour une durée de 6 jours ? / *kɛl e lə pri de ʀəʃaʀʒ puʀ yn dyre də si ʒuʀ* / – How much is the price for a 6 day top up?

Internet

se connecter sur Internet / se brancher sur le Net / s kɔnɛkte syr ɛ̃tɛʀnɛt/ s bʀɑ̃ʃe syr lə net / – to connect to the internet

la connexion / la kɔnɛksjɔ̃ / – the connection

 lente / lɑ̃t /– slow

 rapide / ʀapid / – fast

le réseau / lə ʀezo / – the network

le mot de passe / lə mot de pas / – password

afficher le mot de passe / afiʃe lə mo d pas / – to show the password

se connecter au réseau Wi-Fi / s kɔnɛkte o ʀezo wifi /– to connect to the Wi-Fi network

acceder à internet / aksede a ɛ̃tɛʀnɛt / – to access the internet

@ arobase / aʀobaz / – at sign

– tiret / tiʀe / – hyphen

le lien / lə ljɛ̃ / – the link

le site Web / lə sit vɛb / – the website

le courrier électronique / lə kuʀje elɛktʀɔnik / – e-mail

répondre à ses mails / ʀepondʀ a se mɛl / – answer his emails

joindre un fichier / ʒwɛ̃dʀ œ̃ fiʃje / – to attach a file

enregistrer / ɑ̃ʀəʒistʀe / – to save, to record

les réseaux sociaux / le ʀezo sɔsjo / – social media

Avez-vous une connexion Internet ? / ave vu yn kɔnɛksjɔ̃ ɛ̃tɛʀnɛt / – Do you have internet access?

Y-a-t-il une connexion Internet gratuite à proximité ? / jatil yn kɔnɛksjɔ̃ gʀatɥit a pʀɔksimite /– Is there free internet nearby?

Qu'est-ce qu'un mot de passe Internet ? / kɛsk œ̃ mo də pas ɛ̃tɛʀnɛt / – What is the internet password?

Je n'arrive pas à me connecter à l'internet. / ʒə naʀiv pa a mə kɔnɛkte alɛ̃tɛʀnɛt / – I can't connect to the internet.

Pourriez-vous partager votre internet ? / puʀje vu paʀtaʒe votʀ ɛ̃tɛʀnɛt / – Could you share your internet?

Computer

l'écran / lekʀɑ̃ /– screen

le clavier / lə klavje / – keyboard

la touche / la tuʃ / – key

 appuyer sur une touche / apɥije syʀ yn tuʃ / – to press a key

allumer l'ordinateur / *alyme lɔʀdinatœʀ* / – to start the computer

éteindre l'ordinateur / *etɛ̃dʀ lɔʀdinatœʀ* / – to shut down the computer

cliquer sur / *klikɛ syr* / – to click on

doublecliquer sur / *dubl klikɛ syr* / – to double-click on

copiercoller / *kopije kole* / – to copy and paste

Documents and emails

ouvrir / *uvʀiʀ* / – to open

    le fichier / *lə fiʃje* / – the file

    le document / *lə dɔkymã* / – the document

    le programme / *lə pʀɔgʀam* / – the program

créer un fichier / *kʀee œ̃ fiʃje* / – to create a document

fermer un fichier / *fɛʀme œ̃ fiʃje* / – to close a document

sélectionner un fichier / *selɛksjɔne œ̃ fiʃje* / – to select a document

télécharger un fichier / *teleʃaʀʒe œ̃ fiʃje* / – to download a file

sauvegarder un document / *sovgaʀde dɔkymã* / – to save a document

effacer un document / *efase dɔkymã* / – to erase a document

imprimer un document / *ɛ̃pʀime dɔkymã* / – to print a document

    l'imprimante / *lɛ̃pʀimãt* / – printer

Quelle est ton adresse e-mail ? / *kɛl e ton adʀes imel* / – What is your email adress?

Je vous envoie ci-joint le fichier. / *ʒə vuzãvwa si ʒwɛ̃ lə fiʃje* / – I am sending you a file attached.

Je dois chercher quelque chose sur internet. / *ʒə dwa ʃɛʀʃe kɛlkʃoz syr ɛ̃tɛʀnɛt* / – I have to look something up on the internet.

Je clique sur l'icône mais le document ne s'affiche pas. / *ʒə klik syr likon mɛ lə dɔkymã nə safiʃ pa* / – I click on the icon but the document doesn't appear.

Est-ce que vous pouvez imprimer en deux exemplaires ? / *ɛsk vu puve ɛ̃pʀime ã dø ɛgzãplɛʀ* / – Can you print two copies?

Mon ordinateur ne démarre pas. / *mo ɔʀdinatœʀ nə demaʀe pa* / – My computer is not starting.

Où puis-je faire réparer mon ordinateur portable ? / *u pɥi ʒə fɛʀ repare mɔ̃ ɔʀdinatœʀ portabl* / – Where can I get my laptop fixed?

Chapter 18: Emergencies

La simplification de la vie est l'une des étapes de la paix intérieure.
Milred Norman

Travelers to France, or to any country, should know their emergency numbers in case of an emergency. For French Emergency Medical Assistance, you'll need to call 15. For emergency police number, call 17, for fire brigade call 18. There's also a general Emergency number that's valid for the whole of Europe **112**.

Urgences

Au secours ! / *o səkuʀ* / – Help!

Au feu ! / *o fø* / – Fire !

Au voleur ! / *o vɔlœʀ* / – Thief !

Attention ! / *atɑ̃sjɔ̃* / – Attention !

Pouvez-vous m'aider / nous aider. / *puve vu mede / nuzede* / – Can you help me/us.

C'est très urgent. / *sɛ trezyʀʒɑ̃* / – This is very urgent.

Où est l'hôpital le plus proche ? / *u e lɔpital lə ply pʀɔʃ* / – Where is the nearest hospital?

Appelez la police / une ambulance. / *apele la polis / yn ɑ̃bylɑ̃s* / – Call the police / an ambulance.

Notre chambre a été cambriolée. / *notʀ ʃɑ̃bʀ a ete kɑ̃bʀijɔle* / – Our room was broken into.

Je n'ai pas d'argent. / *ʒə nɛ pa daʀʒɑ̃* / – I don't have money.

J'ai eu un accident. / *ʒɛ y œ̃ aksidɑ̃* / – I had an accident.

Quelqu'un a volé mon passeport. / *kɛlkœ̃ a vole mo paspɔʀ* / – Someone stole my passport.

Ma valise est perdue. / *ma valiz e perdy* / – My suitcase is lost.

J'ai besoin de prendre mes médicaments. / *ʒɛ bəzwɛ̃ də pʀɑ̃dʀ me medikamɑ̃* / I need to take my medication.

Jai mal. / *ʒɛ mal* / – I am in pain.

Je n'ai pas d'assurance voyage. / *ʒ nɛ pa dasyʀɑ̃s vwajaʒ* / – I don't have travel insurance.

Mon portable est déchargé. / *mɔ̃ portabl e deʃaʀʒe* / – My phone is dead.

Je peux passer un coup de fil chez vous ? / *ʒə pø pase œ̃ ku d fil ʃe vu* / – Can I make a phone call from your house?

Où sont les toilettes ? / *u sɔ̃ le twalɛt* / – Where is the toilet?

J'ai perdu les clés (de la voiture) . / *ʒɛ perdy le kle* / – I've lost the keys (from the car)

J'ai besoin de passer un coup de fil. / ʒɛ bəzwɛ̃ d pase œ̃ ku də fil / – I need to make a phone call.

Je me suis perdu. / ʒə m sɥi pɛrdy / – I got lost.

Je ne sais pas comment ça marche. / ʒə n sɛ pa kɔmã sa marʃ / – I don't know how it works.

Vous pouvez me le prêter ? / vu puve m lə prɛte / – Could you lend it to me?

On peut passer la nuit ici ? / ɔ̃ pø pase la nɥi isi / – Can we spend the night here?

Je m'adresse à qui ? / ʒə m adrɛs a ki / – Who am I talking to?

Je ne vous comprends pas. / ʒə n vu kɔ̃prãd pa / – I don't understand you.

Je veux un interprète. / ʒə vø œ̃ ɛ̃tɛrprɛt / – I want an interpreter.

Police

Où est le poste de police le plus proche ? / u e lə post d polis lə ply prɔʃ / – Where is the nearest police station?

Je voudrais signaler le vol / la perte / une attaque / un enlèvement. / ʒə vudrɛ siɲale lə vol / la pɛrt / yn atak / œ̃ ãlɛvmã / – I would like to report the theft / the loss / an attack / a kidnapping.

Je n'ai pas de pièce d'identité sur moi. / ʒə nɛ pa də pjɛs didãtite syr mwa / – I don't have any ID on me.

J'ai été attaqué. / ʒete atake / – I was attacked.

Ils étaient armés d'un pistolet/couteau. / ilzetɛ arme dœ̃ pistɔlɛ / kuto / – They were armed with a gun/knife.

J'ai été violé. / ʒɛ ete vjɔle / – I've been raped.

Un homme me harcèle. / œ̃ ɔm mə arsɛl / – A man is harassing me.

J'ai besoin d'aide. / ʒɛ bəzwɛ̃ dɛd / – I need help.

J'ai été témoin d'un accident. / ʒɛ ete temwɛ̃ dœ̃ aksidã / I witnessed an accident.

Je veux déposer une plainte. / ʒə vø depozer yn plɛ̃t / – I want to file a complaint.

Je voudrais parler à mon avocat. / ʒə vudrɛ parle a mɔ̃ avɔka / – I would like to speak to my lawyer.

Pourquoi je suis arrêté ? / purkwa ʒə sɥi arete / – Why am I arrested?

Pourquoi vous m'accusez ? / purkwa vu makyze / – Why are you accusing me?

Je ne connais pas cette personne. / ʒə n kɔnɛ pa sɛt pɛrson / – I don't know this person.

Je n'ai pas consommé d'alcool. / ʒə nɛ pa kɔ̃sɔme de lalkol / – I did not consume alcohol.

J'ai droit à un appel téléphonique. / ʒɛ drwa a œ̃ apɛl telefɔnik / I have the right to a phone call.

Je vais déposer une plainte. / ʒə vɛ depoze yn plɛ̃t / I am going to file a complaint.

Car Issues

Vous pouvez appeler quelqu'un pour me remorquer ? / vu puve apele kɛlkœ̃ pur m rəmɔrke / – Can you call someone to tow me?

Quel est le numéro du service de dépannage ? / *kɛl e lə numero dy servis də depanaʒ* / – What is the breakdown service number?

Je suis sur la route ( ), environ à ( ) kilomètres de la ville. / *ʒə sɥi syr la rut, ãvirõ a kilɔmɛtʀ də la vil* / – I am on route ( ), about ( ) km from town.

Où est le garage le plus proche ? / *u e lə gaʀaʒ lə ply pʀɔʃ* / – Where is the nearest garage?

Vous pouvez me remorquer à la ville la plus proche / au garage le plus proche ? / *vu puve m ʀəmɔʀke a la vil la ply pʀɔʃ / o gaʀaʒ lə ply pʀɔʃ* / Can you tow me to the nearest town / nearest garage?

Ça va couter combien ? / *sa va kute kõbjẽ* / – How much will it cost?

Vous pouvez m'emmener en ville ? / *vu puve mãməne ã vil* / – Can you take me to town?

Est-ce que je peux louer une autre voiture près d'ici ? / *esk ʒə pø lwe yn otr vwatyʀ predisi* / – Can I rent another car near here ?

Ma voiture a été enlevée. / *ma vwatyʀ a ete ãləve* / – My car has been taken away.

On a eu un accident. / *õ a y œ̃ aksidã* / – We had an accident.

Nous avons un blessé ici. / *nuzavon œ̃ blese isi* / – We have an injured here.

Ma voiture est sortie de la route. / *ma vwatyʀ e sorti də la rut* / – My car went off the road.

La priorité était à moi. / *la pʀijɔʀite ete a mwa* / – The priority was mine.

J'ai fermé la voiture avec les clés dedans. / *ʒɛ ferme la vwatyr avɛk le kle dədã* / – I locked the car with the keys inside.

On est resté bloqué dans un embouteillage. / *õ e reste blɔke dã œ̃ ãbutɛjaʒ* / – We got stuck in a traffic jam.

J'ai crevé. / *ʒɛ kreve* / – I got a flat tire.

Mes freins ont lâché. / *me fʀɛ̃ õ laʃe* / – My brakes gave out.

Le conducteur qui a causé l'accident s'est enfui. / *lə kõdyktœʀ ki a koze laksidã se ãfɥiʀ* / – The driver who caused the accident escaped.

J'ai un problème avec ma voiture. / *ʒɛ œ̃ pʀɔblɛm avɛk ma vwatyʀ* / – I have a problem with my car.

Je suis en panne d'essence. / *ʒə sɥi ã pan desãs* / – I am out of gas.

Conclusion

Everyone tells you that speaking a language is not a one-day task, and above all that it requires discipline, consistency and hard work. They assure you there's no way to be a fluent French speaker in a short period of time. Well, maybe you don't have to be fluent to deal with everyday situations in French.

Having a handbook at your fingertips is not only a great shortcut to handling all possible situations when traveling to France, but also a great starting point for anyone looking to learn French. Being exposed to all kinds of everyday sentences and vocabulary helps you become sensitive to French language patterns and be able to create sentences of your own, which is the end goal of every language learner.

Our goal was to create a book that would cover all possible situations that may arise when traveling to France. The book is structured into logical sequences that correspond to actual contextual situations. We carefully covered all possible situations you may encounter as a foreigner traveling around France, assembling the most important words and phrases in logical format. 15 topics cover the 15 most frequent everyday situations, from traveling, transportation, ordering at the restaurant, grocery shopping, going to nature, sightseeing, weather, visiting a doctor, and much more, allowing you to build your vocabulary in different areas.

However, this book does more than just prepare you to get by in all possible situations. It is designed for students who want to learn elementary grammar and see how nouns, articles, adjectives, and verbs behave in French. The first three chapters are created with common beginner's troubles in mind, such as understanding pronunciation, learning elementary grammar, and basic vocabulary. You already noted that certain structures, such as "I am", and "where is" appeared frequently throughout the book. After practicing the essential structures included here, you can recall the statements easier and even create your phrases.

We begin by focusing on greetings and civilities, then move on to meeting people and expressing time, followed by weather conditions. Having learned how to keep small talk like a French person in Paris, you head off to learn more about traveling and sightseeing in the upcoming chapter, where you get useful directions about traveling in both urban and rural areas. As you read chapter nine, you find yourself looking for a hotel room, going through the steps of booking, arriving, paying, expressing your complaints, etc. Chapter ten is about attending cultural events and entertainment. Section eleven on transportation is particularly important, since moving around is unavoidable when you are traveling.

The twelfth chapter helps you order food in a restaurant or go grocery shopping. Next, you learn about money, such as paying, going to the bank or exchanging money, even using Apple pay to process payment. Following chapters help you handle situations such as job search, going to the doctor, dentist, or pharmacy. Next, you'll get useful information about purchasing a tourist sim card with the internet, followed by essential phrases related to telephone, internet, computer or documents. At the end, the final chapter helps you solve emergency situations and potential issues.

It may surprise you to learn that you don't need to know a lot of French or complete grammar to interact with locals. Typically, people use a limited number of words and expressions in a single situation. The goal was to create a book that would reconcile your need to learn grammar with the need to cope with everyday situations in French in an easy and practical way. By accompanying the context–based vocabulary and sentences with grammar notes, we aimed to get the maximum benefit from this book.

With 15 different topics under your belt and a solid foundation in French grammar, you are well prepared to speak French, even with natives.

It gives you the freedom to get through all the most common situations, such as ordering at a restaurant, going through passport control, finding accommodation, purchasing tickets, printing documents, exchanging money, going to the doctor's office, solving computer or internet issues, and much more.

Now you just need to be brave and apply what you've learned.

~~$39~~ FREE BONUSES

Learn French Fundamentals Audiobook

+ Printable "French Verb Conjugations" Practice Worksheets Download

Scan QR code above to claim your free bonuses

—— OR ——

exploretowin.com/frenchaudio10

Ready To Start Speaking French?

Inside this **Learn French Fundamentals Audiobook** + printable practice worksheets combo you'll discover:

✓ **Pronunciation guides:** English to French pronunciation translations so you can sound right the first time which means you'll sound like a natural easily.

✓ **How to avoid awkward fumbling:** explore core French grammar principles to avoid situations where you're left blank, not knowing what to say.

✓ **Improved recall:** Confidently express yourself in French by learning high-frequency verbs conjugations - taught through fun practice sheets!

Scan QR code above to claim your free bonuses

—— OR ——

exploretowin.com/frenchaudio10

BOOK 3

Learn French with Short Stories for Adult Beginners

Engaging Stories To Shortcut Your French Fluency!
(Fun & Easy Reads)

Explore to Win

Book 3 description

Discover French grammar naturally as you read stories, expand your vocabulary, and grow fluent fast.

Have you ever noticed how hard it can be to remember grammar rules? You're not alone!

No matter how much you study, you seem unable to apply French grammar rules! Do you often struggle to stay motivated? Do you believe reading a story in French is impossible?

If so, there's a simple solution: Introducing **Learn French with Short Stories for Adult Beginners** to help you learn grammar in context.

Imagine easily understanding the story in French, even if you are just a beginner, without ever needing to consult a dictionary or grammar book, because you have everything in one place. Imagine reading a story in French that revolves around one or two grammar units, so you can focus on one point at a time and comprehend how the French grammar works.

You'll get 11 adapted French stories followed by the summary in French and English, unfamiliar vocabulary from the story, comprehension questions and grammar notes regarding the key grammar points from the story. You'll also learn the grammar rules applied in context, along with many more examples to get a grasp of them.

In **Learn French with Short Stories for Adult Beginners**, you'll discover:

- **11 stories adapted for French beginners**, focusing on one or two grammar points at a time, so you can take your time to absorb the structure and rules at your pace.
- **16 most common grammar points** needed to succeed in most conversations in French (Présents Simple, Passé Composé, Imparfait, Future proche, Future Simple, Adjectifs, Pronoms Possessifs et Adjectifs Possessifs, Articles Partitifs, Il y a, Il fait, Il est, Il + verbe, Expression d'opinion, Pronoms d'objet direct et indirect, Pronoms relatifs, Préposition de, à).
- Stories revolving around **most common everyday topics** (family, traveling, weather, house, renovation, describing people, food and cooking, job, shopping) aimed at covering most of the topics found in everyday conversations.
- **Summary of stories** in French and English, in case you need help understanding them.
- **Unfamiliar words and expressions** sorted in the chronological order they appear in the story.
- **Series of questions** to test your comprehension of the narrative, with answers included at the end.
- **Grammar notes** explaining the main grammar points used in a story in detail.

When we read stories, we keep our brains engaged in the story's development while soaking up the vocabulary, structure, and grammar.

Learn French with Short Stories for Adult Beginners is for anyone who struggles to apply grammar rules in real-life conversations. Whether you are a student who wants to renew French because it's been years since you last spoke French or a novice learner who's struggling to apply grammar and expand vocabulary, the stories in this book can set the stage for fluent conversations in French.

Introduction

Do you know what is one of the most natural ways of learning languages?

For thousands of years, stories have been a way to transfer knowledge and give sense to the world around us. The human mind has a natural ability to remember stories. If you are wondering why, it's because human creatures seek meaning more than anything else. And it's the same way when learning languages. We seek meaning, not the vocabulary to retain. Through reading stories, we help our brain understand the context and meaning beyond words. We begin to understand the relationship between words and phrases, and start seeing the big picture.

Beginners believe reading stories in French is way beyond their capabilities, and keep avoiding this effective method that gives more results than vocabulary drilling. However, finding adequate reading material adapted to a beginner's level that provides a positive feeling of accomplishment can be a challenge. Frustration is inevitable if the material exceeds your level.

Short stories in French for beginners is a collection of eleven short stories, crafted especially for high-level beginner to low-intermediate students to improve their French skills. Each story is written with common beginner's troubles in mind. Eleven stories cover eleven most frequent everyday situations, from traveling, to meeting your family, talking about habits, food, shopping, weather, house renovation, etc., allowing you to build your vocabulary in different areas.

Apart from the vocabulary, each story is focused on a different grammar point, helping you master isolated grammar points, from adjectives to basic tenses, pronouns, present, future, and past tenses. It also focuses on some common beginner's mistakes, like the difference between "possessive pronouns" and "possessive adjectives", or between "imparfait" and "passé composé".

To support you on your reading journey, as a beginner, in each chapter you'll find:

- → **Story synopsis in French and English** to give you an overview of the story.
- → **Vocabulary and expressions** from the story, bolded in the story and later placed and translated separately in the order they appear in the story.
- → **Comprehension questions** to test your understanding with answers key at the end of the book.
- → **Grammar notes** that explain the main grammar point in that particular story.
- → **Key takeaways** from the chapter.

Besides being linguists and knowing French to a T, the authors are also native speakers of French, which means that they know exactly how to use the language in real life. Additionally, they will also be able to teach you how to speak and sound like a true native.

This book is made for real beginners and low-intermediate students. Stories are crafted using high-frequency words as well as basic grammar, without subjunctives, or other complex syntax. It's made so that every beginner has a sense of accomplishment.

If you are just a beginner, or if you have been studying French some time ago, but you'd like to refresh your knowledge of French, *Short Stories for Adult Beginners*, will give you the support you need.

Guide to reading as a beginner in French

The biggest challenge when reading in a foreign language is to overcome our unrealistic expectations from reading in our mother tongue. We skip the fact that reading is a complex skill that requires a variety of micro-skills, such as scanning the page to find the needed information or reading the keywords and immediately understanding the context.

If we want to read effectively in French, we have to take a step back and remember how it was like to read in the first grade at school. Because, in terms of language, that's exactly who we are in French. Children.

Probably the most important thing to accept when reading in another language is that you won't understand everything. Making peace with ambiguity is essential to making progress. Perhaps, some learners will find this counter-intuitive, but it's actually what keeps you motivated in the long run. Imagine how little progress you'll be making if you feel the urge to understand each word from the text. Instead of moving forward, your perfectionism will keep you stuck in one place. While deep comprehension can be very important when it comes to language learning, if you cover a wider range of different structures and vocabulary, you'll be able to deal with more language complexities. Language is not about knowing a couple of words perfectly, but understanding different speaking situations.

Reading stories is a great way to help you progress in French, because it puts you in a position where understanding the story in general is more important than comprehending the isolated words. This kind of reading is called extensive reading. There are two methods of reading: intensive and extensive reading.

Intensive reading is what you have encountered in your language courses. It means that you are trying to understand each word from the textbook, focus on retaining grammar structures, and then complete certain tasks. On the other hand, extensive reading is pleasure oriented, so it helps you become comfortable with the natural language in use.

To get the most from reading stories from the book, here are a few suggestions to keep in mind.

Step 1. Get acquainted with the main topic

Read the chapter title and get acquainted with the main topic of the story. The introductory part will give you some clues about the main focus in terms of syntax, grammar, and vocabulary. You'll already be well prepared before you start.

Step 2. First-time reading

Read the story once, and don't pay much attention if you are not understanding everything. You are already making progress, even though you are not aware of it. If you really need to check some words, you can always refer to the dictionary after the story where you'll find all bolded words translated in English. However, try to keep in mind that it's okay not to understand everything.

Step 3. Read the Synopsis

When you finish the story, read the short summary, first in French, followed by English. This will give you a clear picture of how much you really understand.

Step 4. Comprehension Check

You never know how much you understood, until you check. Each story is followed with a short multiple-questions quiz.

Step 5. Second-time Reading

This time, you are allowed to focus on more details. Pay attention to the bolded vocabulary and expressions, then try to get back and see how the words behave in a context. It's even better if the word is repeated several times. Keeping your own notes is always a good idea, even though you already have vocabulary listed.

Step 6. Grammar Notes

Check out grammar notes to renew some basic grammar rules that have been repeated in the story. For instance, the first story *"Mes habitudes quotidiennes"* is written in Present Tense, and is filled with regular, irregular and reflexive verbs. The goal is to be prepared to talk about your habits after you finish the story.

Step 7. Key takeaways

Key takeaways are the summary of all the most important grammar points. Refer often to this section to retain the important information, even when you are done with the chapter.

And lastly, you shouldn't forget the sense of enjoyment and fulfillment while reading the stories. After all, it's the pleasure that gives us motivation to move forward.

These suggestions are to help you read French stories independently and without any help. Our stories help you improve your comprehension in a natural way. There should be no obstacles in your way to reading and understanding French stories. Just remember, one step at a time. Pick up your copy of ***Learn French with Short Stories for Adult Beginners*** and start improving your French right now!

Chapter 1: Habits and Present Tense

« Nous sommes ce que nous répétons chaque jour, l'excellence n'est alors plus un acte mais une habitude. »

- Aristote

We start the first chapter with a short story about what is inevitably part of everyone's lives. From the very first thing we do in the morning to the last thing before we go to bed, we are creatures of habits. That's the main reason our habits take up a large portion of our everyday conversations.

When it comes to habits in French, we use the "***Présent de l'indicatif***" which we assume you are more than familiar with. You'll find that this story has plenty of reflexive verbs that come as an essential equipment when talking about your daily routines. Feel free to move on to the grammar notes part at any time and renew French regular, irregular and reflexive verbs. You'll also learn how to express the Present Progressive and the Present Perfect in French. The beauty of this book is that it has everything in one place.

Mes habitudes quotidiennes

Chaque jour, je suis programmée pour **me lever** à la même heure. **Peu importe** si je **me couche tard**, ou très **tôt** le soir. Quand **le réveil sonne** à 7h, **je suis debout. Comme d'habitude**, la première chose à faire est de **me laver** et **me brosser les dents**. Je ne réfléchis pas. Je le **fais** et **refais** chaque matin.

Bien **rafraîchie**, je **me dirige** vers ma chambre et je **fais du yoga** pendant 15 minutes. Je **rêve** de faire du jogging, mais ça arrive rarement. Quand il fait beau, j'aime bien **faire des promenades. Ça me fait du bien** de **bouger** mon corps très tôt le matin. **Quelquefois**, si je me lève tard et que je n'ai pas le temps de faire du yoga, je **me sens mal à l'aise.**

Puis, je **me prépare** un café noir et je prends le petit-déjeuner. Le matin, je **bois souvent** du café. Mon petit ami préfère le thé. J'aime les deux, **ça dépend des jours**. Parfois, je prends du yaourt avec des fruits, d'autres fois **des tartines beurrées**. Ça dépend de si je suis **au régime** ou non. J'adore le petit déjeuner et je trouve que c'est **un rituel** intime pour moi. Je bois le café doucement et d'habitude je **prends un livre** ou j'écris mon **journal intime**. Je sais que **le cerveau** est très **réceptif** juste après **le réveil**. Alors, je **profite de ce moment** pour faire la visualisation ou justement **organiser le jour à venir**.

Le matin, je préfère **le silence**. Mais, mon petit ami **fait le contraire**. Le weekend, **dès qu'**il entre dans la cuisine, il **allume la radio** pour **écouter les informations**. Je lui **conseille** toujours d'**arrêter** cette habitude. Il dit oui, puis, il prend le journal.

Je **travaille** depuis chez moi, alors je ne me **dépêche** pas d'aller au travail. Je **prends mon temps**. Mon petit ami de l'autre côté, il est toujours **pressé**. Il se lève avant moi. Il se brosse les dents, **se rase**, et puis **fait de la musculation**. Quand il **finit** son **entraînement**, il **se douche** et puis prépare un thé.

Nous habitons à Mulhouse. Nous habitons en **banlieue** et il doit partir tôt le matin. Notre ville est très petite, et il **arrive au travail à vélo** en 15 minutes. Le weekend, il prend ses **clefs** et il **quitte** la maison pour **faire du jogging**. Eh bien moi, je **m'installe** dans le **fauteuil**, je prends ma **tasse de café** et je **rêve**.

Quelquefois, je dois **faire les courses**. Je **m'habille**, je me **coiffe et** je **me maquille**. Un petit peu de **maquillage**, ça fait du bien. Je **prends la voiture** et je mets 5 minutes pour aller au magasin. J'**achète de la nourriture** pour **préparer le dîner** et je rentre chez moi.

J'aime essayer de nouveaux **plats** et je **passe des heures** à **chercher des recettes** sur Instagram. J'y **trouve** plein de bonnes idées. Le soir, mon petit ami **rentre** et on **se détend** un peu jusqu'à l'heure du dîner. Puis nous préparons le dîner **ensemble**. À 20h30, nous dînons et ensuite nous regardons la télévision avant d'aller **nous coucher**.

Nos **vies** sont faites de petites habitudes. Il faut justement bien choisir les habitudes qui te **font plaisir**.

Résumé de l'histoire

Ce récit est raconté à la première personne. Le narrateur est une femme qui habite avec son petit ami. Elle parle de ses habitudes quotidiennes. Comme elle et son petit ami ont des métiers différents, ils ont aussi des habitudes différentes. La femme travaille de chez elle et son petit ami part au travail chaque jour.

Synopsis of the story

The story is told in the first person. The narrator is a woman who lives with her boyfriend. She talks about her daily habits. Because they have different jobs, they also have different habits. While she works from home, her boyfriend commutes to another part of the city every day for his job.

Vocabulary and Expressions

se lever - to get up

se coucher - to go to bed

un réveil - an alarm

peu importe - no matter

tard - late

tôt - early

sonner - to ring

être debout - to be up

comme d'habitude - as usual

rafraîchi / rafraîchie - refreshed
se brosser les dents - to brush one's teeth
réfléchir - to think, to reflect
faire - to do
refaire - to do again
se diriger - to head to
faire du yoga - to do yoga
faire du jogging - to jog, to go jogging
faire des promenades - to go for walks
rêver - to dream
ça me fait du bien - it makes me feel good
bouger - to move
quelquefois, parfois - sometimes
se sentir mal à l'aise - to feel uncomfortable
se préparer - to get ready
prendre le petit-déjeuner - to have breakfast
boire - to drink
souvent - often
ça dépend des jours - it depends on the days
des tartines beurrées - buttered toasts
être au régime - to be on a diet
un rituel - a ritual
prendre - to take
un journal intime - a diary
un cerveau - a brain
faire le contraire - to do the opposite
dès que - as soon as
réceptif / réceptive - receptive
se réveiller - to wake up
profiter d'un moment - to take advantage of a moment
organiser le jour à venir - to organize the upcoming day
un silence - a silence
allumer la radio - to turn on the radio
écouter les informations - to listen to the news
conseiller - to advise

arrêter - to stop
travailler - to work
se dépêcher - to hurry up
aller - to go
prendre son temps - to take one's time
être pressé - to be in a hurry
se raser - to shave
faire de la musculation - to work out
un entraînement - a workout
se doucher - to take a shower
une banlieue - a suburb
à vélo - by bicycle
arriver - to arrive
une cléf - a key
s'installer - to sit down
un fauteuil - an armchair
une tasse de café - a cup of coffee
faire les courses - to go grocery shopping
s'habiller - to get dressed
se coiffer - to do one's hair
se maquiller - to put on makeup
le maquillage - make up
la voiture - the car
acheter - to buy
de la nourriture - food
essayer - to try
un plat - a meal
passer des heures - to spend hours
chercher - to look for
une recette - a recipe
trouver - to find
rentrer - to return
se détendre - to relax
ensemble - together
se coucher - to go to bed

une vie - a life

faire plaisir - to please

Comprehension Questions

Sélectionnez une seule réponse pour chaque question.

1. Qui raconte l'histoire ?
    A. La femme
    B. L'homme
    C. Les deux

2. Ils habitent ....
    A. au centre-ville
    B. en banlieue
    C. au centre d'une petite ville
    D. à la campagne

3. Est-ce que la femme va au travail chaque jour ?
    A. Oui, elle prend la voiture chaque jour.
    B. Non, elle y va une fois par semaine.
    C. Non, elle travaille de chez elle.
    D. Oui, elle prend le bus pour aller au travail.

4. Le matin, l'homme préfère ....:
    A. le silence
    B. écouter les informations à la radio
    C. écrire un journal intime
    D. faire du yoga

5. Chaque jour le matin, l'homme ?
    A. Se rase, se lave, se brosse les dents, fait de la musculation.
    B. Se lave, prend le thé, fait du yoga.
    C. Se brosse les dents, se lave, prend le thé.
    D. Prends du café, se lave, se rase, se brosse les dents.

Grammar Notes

Le présent de l'indicatif

The present tense is the pillar of all conversations, no matter the language. If you master the present tense, you are already covering 70% of possible conversations in French. Learning languages is all about keeping the conversational odds in your favor.

There is one reason why French present tense is easier than English present tense. You know how English has even four forms of the present tense (*Present Simple, Present Perfect, Present Continuous, Present Perfect Continuous*). Well, in French, there's only one. "*Le présent de l'indicatif*" is used to express momentary action as well as progressive action.

But here comes the challenge too. If there is only one form for what English speakers perceive as four different situations, how can you express the different present meanings in French?

Want to hear a secret? French do not need a tense to express the *Present Progressive* and the *Present Perfect*. Here's how.

How to express the *Present Progressive*

Instead of using another tense, in French, you can simply use the expression "*être en train de*" or literally, "to be in the process of."

Je suis en train de lire. - I am reading.

Elle est en train de finir la course. - She's finishing the race.

How to Express the Present Perfect

Don't think the *Present Perfect* is a non-existent concept in the French universe. They simply use "**depuis + *présent de l'indicatif***", which means since, for actions that began in the past and continue into the present. Likewise, the English language uses **since + Present Perfect**. However, the French say "*Why bother with another tense if you can do it all with just one?*" And we couldn't agree more.

J'habite à Paris depuis un an. - I've lived in Paris for a year.

J'étudie le français depuis deux ans. – I've studied French for two years (and still do).

When to use the "Présent de l'indicatif"

The present tense in French (*le présent*) is used to talk about:

- **facts that are always true**

Le Soleil tourne autour de la Terre. - The sun turns around the Earth.

Mon chat s'appelle Felix. - My cat's name is Felix.

- **current situations**

Je travaille à Paris. - I work in Paris.

J'habite à Lyon. - I live in Lyon.

- **habits and repeated actions in the present**

Le matin, je bois souvent du café. - In the morning, I often drink coffee.
Chaque jour, il fait de la musculation. - Every day, he works out.

- **scheduled future actions**

Mardi prochain, son équipe a un match important. - Next Tuesday, his team has an important match.

Mon avion part à 14 heures. - My airplane leaves at 14 h.

How to form the "Présent de l'indicatif"

The fact there's only one present tense in French is the reason we consider French to be easier than English. Keep your belts tight. We are now moving on to part II "What makes French present tense more difficult than English?"

First of all, the French conjugation is quite complex. The French verbs must be conjugated in person and number, which ends in having six different forms. Another reason is that French verbs are both regular and irregular.

The way we all learn French conjugations is by learning which verbs are regular and which aren't. To distinguish regular from irregular verbs, French has classified all verbs into three categories known as 'groups' in French. There are 3 groups and you'll easily recognize which verbs fall into which category by looking at their endings.

- **I group** - regular verbs whose infinitive ends in -ER.
- **II group** - regular verbs with an infinitive ending in -IR.
- **III group** - verbs in -RE and irregular verbs.

I Group - Regular -ER verbs

Regular -ER verbs are conjugated the same way in all tenses and moods. After all, they aren't called regular for nothing.

To conjugate in Present Tense, remove the infinitive ending (**-er**) and then add one of the following verb endings (**-e, -es, -e, -ons, -ez, -ent**).

Let's take the verb "*parler*". After we remove the ending -er, we get "*parl*", and then we just add the present endings.

Pay close attention to the conjugations below.

Pronouns	Endings	**Parler**	**Aimer**	**Visiter**
Je	**-e**	parl**e**	aim**e**	visit**e**
Tu	**-es**	parl**es**	aim**es**	visit**es**
Il/Elle/On	**-e**	parl**e**	aim**e**	visit**e**
Nous	**-ons**	parl**ons**	aim**ons**	visit**ons**
Vous	**-ez**	parl**ez**	aim**ez**	visit**ez**

| Ils/Elles | **-ent** | parl**ent** | aim**ent** | visit**ent** |

Not every verb ending in -er is regular. You should always be aware of exceptions. For instance, the most common verb (**aller**) is irregular. You can find its conjugation on the following page.

II Group - Regular -IR verbs

French verbs ending in **-IR** are the second largest category, with around 300 verbs. Here, the rule of forming the Present is the same, except that this time, you are removing -ir, and adding different endings (**-is, -is, -it, -issons, -issez, -issent**).

Pronouns	Endings	**Finir**	**Choisir**
Je	**-is**	fin**is**	chois**is**
Tu	**-is**	fin**is**	chois**is**
Il/Elle/On	**-it**	fin**it**	chois**it**
Nous	**-issons**	fin**issons**	chois**issons**
Vous	**-issez**	fin**issez**	chois**issez**
Ils/Elles	**-issent**	fin**issent**	chois**issent**

III Group - Regular -RE verbs

Some French grammarians believe there isn't such a thing as regular -RE verbs. In their view, verbs ending in -re fall into the category of irregular French verbs. We have separated -re verbs as regular, because many verbs follow this pattern, such as:

- attendre: to wait
- défendre: to defend
- descendre: to go down
- entendre: to hear
- perdre: to lose
- répondre: to answer
- vendre: to sell

To conjugate them, remove the infinitive ending -RE and then add one of the following verb endings.

Pronouns	Endings	**Prendre**	**Comprendre**	**Attendre**
Je	**-s**	prend**s**	comprend**s**	attend**s**
Tu	**-s**	prend**s**	comprend**s**	attend**s**
Il/Elle/On	/	prend	comprend	attend
Nous	**-ons**	pren**ons**	compren**ons**	attend**ons**
Vous	**-ez**	pren**ez**	compren**ez**	attend**ez**
Ils/Elles	**-ent**	prenn**ent**	comprenn**ent**	attend**ent**

IV Group - Irregular Verbs

Irregular verbs follow no specific rules for verb conjugation, so you must memorize each one of them. Here is the list of some common irregular verbs you had the chance to encounter in the first story.

	Faire	**Aller**	**Boire**	**Savoir**
Je	fais	vais	bois	sais
Tu	fais	vas	bois	sais
Il/Elle/On	fait	va	boit	sait
Nous	faisons	allons	buvons	savons
Vous	faites	allez	buvez	savez
Ils/Elles	font	vont	boivent	savent

Reflexive verbs

Reflexive verbs are action verbs that you do on yourself. Usually, these are things you repeat every day. That's why we needed plenty of reflexive verbs in our story about habits. Reflexive verbs usually involve some sort of change (going to bed, going to sleep, sitting down). It's good to know that French uses reflexive verbs to a larger extent than English. Many reflexive verbs are regular -ER verbs with a reflexive pronoun "*se*".

You'll recognize reflexive verbs as "*se*" + **infinitive** ("*se*" means *oneself*). When translating reflexive verbs in English, the pronoun "*se*" is rarely translated as himself, itself and so on. Reflexive pronoun "*se*" changes to "*s'*" in front of a word starting with a vowel, most words starting with **h**, and the French pronoun **y**.

Here's how pronouns change in person and number.

Pronouns	Reflexive Pronoun se	**se lever**	**se reveiller**	**s'habiller**
Je	**me (m')**	Je me lèv**e**	Je me réveill**e**	Je m'habill**e**
Tu	**te (t')**	Tu te lèv**es**	Tu te réveill**es**	Tu t'habill**es**
Il/Elle/On	**se (s')**	Il / Elle/ On se lèv**e**	Il/Elle/On se réveill**e**	Il/Elle/ On s'habill**e**
Nous	**nous**	Nous nous lev**ons**	Nous nous réveill**ons**	Nous nous habill**ons**
Vous	**vous**	Vous vous lev**ez**	Vous vous réveill**ez**	Vous vous habill**ez**
Ils/Elles	**se (s')**	Ils/Elles se lèv**ent**	Ils/Elles se réveill**ent**	Ils/Elles s'habill**ent**

Je me lave avant le dîner. - I wash myself before dinner.

Nous nous lavons chaque jour. - We wash ourselves every day.

On se détendra dimanche. - We will relax on Sunday.

Je me lève. - I get up.

Key takeaways

- French has only one present tense (***Présent de l'indicatif***) as opposed to English that has four different tenses to express progressive and momentary actions.
- The French present is used to talk about facts, habits, current situations, and scheduled future events.
- Use "***depuis + présent de l'indicatif***", to express the Present Perfect.
- Use "***être en train de***" to express the Present Progressive.
- Reflexive verbs are action verbs with the reflexive pronoun "*se*".
- Reflexive pronoun "*se*" changes in person and number and has these forms (***me, te, se, nous, vous, se***).

Our next chapter will teach you how to use conjunctions to connect ideas into one sentence, how to describe people, and use superlatives to describe the world around you.

Chapter 2: Describing people

« *Parfois, on connaît les gens puis on se rend compte, qu'en vérité, ils sont loin d'être comme on le pensait.* »

- Auteur inconnu

While the first chapter was about our daily habits, the second one is all about describing people. Talking about ourselves and others is our favorite topic. It would be difficult to imagine a daily conversation without using adjectives to describe the world around us. Because of that, we've come up with a story filled with French adjectives to help you understand the complexity of French adjectives.

As French adjectives differ from English adjectives, feel free to move on to the grammar notes part at any time and review French adjectives and conjunctions first.

La pire combinaison astro

Ce soir, j'ai mon premier **rendez-vous à l'aveugle** et j'ai passé toute **la journée** à **nettoyer** mon appartement. Non. Le rendez-vous ne se passe pas chez moi, c'est seulement que quand je suis **nerveuse**, je nettoie. À la fin, mon appartement ressemble plutôt à une **pharmacie**, et moi, je me sens plus **calme**. **Pour être honnête**, les rendez-vous à l'aveugle **me semblent** très tristes, et **d'habitude** je refuse toutes les **offres**. Mais ma **voisine**, Marthe, qui habite dans un appartement à côté de chez moi, à chaque fois qu'on se rencontre, elle n'**arrête** pas de me montrer des photos de son cousin. Elle sait très bien que je suis **célibataire**. Une femme **sage**, mais **ennuyante** quand même. Elle me voit aux **escaliers** et immédiatement commence à parler de son cousin. Un **mec** apparemment **grand**, pour être plus **précis**, 1 m 90 cm.

À **goût**, trop grand. **Charmant, bien situé**, un appartement dans le 14ème **arrondissement**, un travail **stable** de **programmeur**. Je dois **admettre** que son cousin n'est pas **moche** du tout. Il est vraiment un **beau** mec. Et puis, je suis **terrible** à dire non. J'ai fini par accepter son offre et me voilà avec un appartement tellement **propre** qu'on peut même **lécher le sol**.

Si tout ce que Marthe **raconte à propos** de lui est vrai, c'est alors un jackpot. Mais, j'en **doute**, car personne ne croit aux **louanges** de sa famille. **Ou** aux louanges de ses amis **proches**. **Ni les uns, ni les autres** ne donnent une image réelle.

Encore cinq heures. Trois heures. Et si je prétendais être malade ? Maintenant, je commence à me sentir vraiment **mal**. De quoi on peut parler ? Je ne sais rien de lui. Martha ne m'a parlé que de son **apparence physique** et de son **salaire**. Elle n'a rien dit de ses centres d'**intérêts**. Et s'il **se révèle ennuyeux** comme un jour de pluie.

Tout à coup, je **me souviens** d'une chose. Sa date de naissance. Si je veux avoir une image réelle de sa personnalité, il faut demander l'aide de l'astrologie. C'est logique. Il y a des gens qui dès le premier rendez-vous demandent « *T'es quel **signe** ?* » et puis il y a les autres. Moi, je suis dans le premier groupe.

Voilà, je trouve sur internet qu'il est **Capricorne**. Ok, ça aurait pu être pire.

Voyons. Le signe du Capricorne est le plus **raisonnable**, le plus calme, mais avec une tendance à **fuir** les **disputes**. Il est **dévoué** aux autres et on peut **compter sur** lui. Il est **sincère, honnête et fiable**. Cependant, il déteste **la tromperie** et ne pardonne jamais. Parfois, il peut aussi être **avare**. Il peut paraître **dur** et **froid** car il ne parle pas de ses problèmes.

Il déteste les **imprévus** car il est lié à l'organisation. Sur le plan émotionnel et physique, il est assez **fragile** et parfois **dépressif. Perfectionniste, introverti,** ce qui peut **poser des problèmes** en amour. Il rencontre des difficultés à trouver **l'âme sœur**, mais une fois en couple, il est fidèle et stable. **Le poids** est également son principal problème, car il ne fait pas attention à son **alimentation**.

Donc, un mec fidèle avec des difficultés à trouver son âme sœur. C'est justement ce que je cherche. Voyons maintenant quels sont les signes **compatibles**, puisque certaines combinaisons ne **marchent** pas. Les meilleurs signes compatibles avec un Capricorne sont le **Poisson, le Taureau, le Scorpion** ou **la Vierge**.

D'accord, je ne suis ni Poisson, ni Taureau, ni Scorpion, ni Vierge. Je continue à lire. Mais pourtant, la pire combinaison de l'horoscope est Sagittaire et Capricorne. Voulez-vous deviner mon signe ? Sagittaire, bien sûr. **La chance** que j'ai. C'est décidé. J'**annule** le rendez-vous.

Résumé de l'histoire

Une jeune fille célibataire qui déteste les rendez-vous à l'aveugle, finit par accepter un tel rendez-vous. Tout est à cause de sa voisine, Marthe, qui habite au même étage. Marthe lui montre chaque jour des photos de son cousin qui est aussi célibataire. La jeune fille ne sait pas refuser et accepte finalement de rencontrer son cousin. Mais, avant de se rencontrer avec le jeune homme, elle commence à être nerveuse et se rend compte qu'elle ne sait rien de lui, sauf sa date de naissance. Alors, elle décide de trouver son signe astrologique et de voir s'ils sont compatibles.

Synopsis of the story

A young single girl who hates blind dates ends up agreeing to one. It all happens because of her neighbor, Marthe, who lives on the same floor. Marthe wants to match her cousin, a good-looking young man, with someone. Ultimately, the young girl does not know how to refuse and agrees to meet Marthe's cousin. As she gets closer to meeting the young man, she begins to get nervous and realizes that she doesn't know anything about him except for his date of birth. She decides to look up his horoscope sign and to find out if they are compatible.

Vocabulary and Expressions

un rendez-vous à l'aveugle - a blind date
une journée - a day
nettoyer - to clean
nerveux / nerveuse - nervous
une pharmacie - a pharmacy
calme - calm
d'être honnête - to be honest
sembler - to seem
d'habitude - usually
une offre - an offer
un voisin / une voisine - neighbour
arreter - to stop
célibataire - single, a bachelor
sage - wise
ennuyant / ennuyante - annoying
un mec - a guy
grand / grande - tall
précis - accurate, specific
un goût - a taste, a flavor
charmant / charmante - charming
être situé - situated
un arrondissement - a district
stable - steady, firm, stable
un programmeur - a programmer
admettre - to admit
moche - ugly
terrible - terrible
propre - clean
lécher - to lick
le sol - the floor
raconter - to tell about, to narrate
à propos - about, related to
une doute - a doubt
une louange - a praise

proche - close, nearby

ni les uns, ni les autres - neither one nor the other

mal - wrong, bad

une apparence physique - a physical appearance

un salaire - a salary

un centre d'intérêt - interest

se révéler - to turn out

ennuyeux / ennuyeuse - boring, annoying, dull

tout à coup - suddenly, all of a sudden

se souvenir - to remember, to recall

une signe - a sign

raisonnable - reasonable, sensible

fuir - to run away

disputer - to argue

dévouer - to devote

compter sur quelqu'un - to count on someone

sincère - genuine, sincere

honnête - honest

fiable - reliable

une tromperie - a deception

avare - stingy

dur / dure - hard

froid / froide - cold

imprévu - unexpected

fragile - delicate

dépressif / dépressive - depressed

perfectionniste - perfectionist

introverti / introvertie - introverted

poser des problèmes - to cause issues

une alimentation - a diet

une âme soeur - a soulmate

un poids - a weight

compatible - compatible

marcher - to walk

un Poisson - a Pisces

un Taureau - a Taurus

un Scorpion - a Scorpio

une Vierge - a Virgo

la chance - luck

annuler - to cancel

Comprehension Questions

Sélectionnez une seule réponse pour chaque question.

1. Qu'est-ce que la jeune fille pense des rendez-vous à l'aveugle ?
    A. Elle préfère les rendez-vous à l'aveugle.
    B. Elle pense que les rendez-vous à l'aveugle sont tristes.
    C. Elle n'a jamais eu de rendez-vous à l'aveugle.
    D. Elle pense que les rendez-vous à l'aveugle sont la meilleure possibilité de se marier.

2. Pourquoi la jeune fille nettoie-t-elle son appartement ?
    A. Parce qu'elle a célébré son anniversaire.
    B. Parce qu'elle adore nettoyer pendant son temps libre.
    C. Parce qu'elle va avoir le rendez-vous dans son appartement.
    D. Parce qu'elle est nerveuse.

3. Que veut dire la métaphore « *comme un jour de pluie* » ?
    A. Ennuyant
    B. Divertissant.
    C. Froid.
    D. Que l'automne est arrivé.

4. Quelles sont les caractéristiques d'un Capricorne ?
    A. Fragile, sincère, fiable et adore les imprévus.
    B. Sincère, parfois dépressif, introverti et fiable.
    C. Perfectionniste, dévoué aux autres, rarement fiable.
    D. Aventurier, fiable, sincère, introverti.

5. Quelle est la pire combinaison de signes ?
    A. Sagittaire et Capricorne
    B. Taureau et Capricorne
    C. Vierge et Sagittaire
    D. Capricorne et Lion

Grammar Notes

Adjectives

Whenever you are describing something, a place, or a thing, you need **an adjective.** The French adjectives present a bit more difficulty than the English ones. The reason is that French adjectives need to agree with the word they describe, in gender (masculine and feminine) and number (singular and plural). In fact, in French, all words in a sentence must agree with each other: verbs agree with the subject, adjectives agree with the noun or pronoun and so on.

Let's see some examples.

Singular masculin - *un grand garçon.* Singular feminine - *une grande fille.*

Plural masculin - *des grands garçons.* Singular feminine - *des grandes filles.*

As you may notice, what's one word "tall" in English, it's 4 different variants in French to express:

- Singular masculin
- Singular feminine / add **-e**
- Plural masculin / add **-s**
- Plural feminine/ add **-es**

Now, let's learn more about the rules we need to form a feminine adjective in French. You learned by far that there's always a regular and irregular side of the story. We'll treat them separately in the chapters to come. Let's get started.

Regular Adjectives - Forming the feminine adjective

Luckily, the general rule is simple. Take the basic form of an adjective (which is always masculine) and add **-e**, to create a feminine form.

Grand + e / *grande*

Petit + e / *petite*

It's important to note that adding this **-e** causes the formerly silent consonant to be pronounced. However, if -e is added to a vowel, the pronunciation remains unchanged.

Be careful when you spot masculine adjectives ending in **-e, -eux, -f,** and **-er**, because for those, you do not simply add **-e**. Here's a useful table to help you form feminine form easily.

Masculine adjective endings	Feminine endings	Examples Masculine to Feminine
é	add **-e**	âgé - âgée situé - située devoué - devouée
eux	change to **-euse**	ambitieux - ambitieuse dangereux - dangereuse

		curieux - curieuse
		sérieux - sérieuse
f	change to **-ve**	neuf - neuve
		naïf - naïve
		actif - active
er	change to **-ère**	cher - chère
		fier - fière
		étranger - étrangère
ending in consonants	**double the final consonant** before -e ending	ancien - ancienne
		bon - bonne
		cruel - cruelle
		gentil - gentille
		bas - basse

Irregular Adjectives - Forming the feminine adjective

If you are wondering what makes adjectives irregular, let us tell you. The term irregular adjective is used when an adjective changes completely in the feminine form for no logical reason. The most common example is "*beau*" which becomes "*belle*" in the feminine form. The sad truth about irregular adjectives is that they must be learned by heart.

Masculine	Feminine
beau	belle
blanc	blanche
doux	douce
faux	fausse
frais	fraîche
inquiet	inquiéte
long	longue
nouveau	nouvelle
public	publique
vieux / vieil	vieille
secret	secrète

Same form for feminine and masculine adjectives

Singular adjectives that end in silent -e, stay the same in feminine form. The spelling and pronunciation remain the same. That's the case with adjectives like: *"aimable"*, *"célèbre"*, *"faible"*, *"malade"*, *"propre"*, *"triste"*, *"sincère"*, etc.

Regular Plural Adjectives

We know it's been tough accepting that you have to learn not only adjectives, but also learn to form the feminine forms. We have to inform you that it's not the end. There's a whole new set of rules to create plural forms for both masculine and feminine adjectives.

Luckily again, most adjectives will take a simple rule of adding **-s** to the adjective. It's actually the same rule as when forming a plural noun.

Un grand lac - Deux grands lacs

Une belle fille - Cinq belles filles

Do not add -s if the adjective ends in -s or -x.

Singular - *français*. Plural - *français*.

Singular - *dangereux*. Plural - *dangereux*.

Il est surpris. Ils sont surpris. Elle est surprise. Elles sont surprises.

Masculine adjectives finishing in **-eau** and **- al** change to **-eaux or -aux.**

Singular Adjective -eau, -al	Plural masculine - **eaux / aux**	Plural feminine
loy**al**	loy**aux**	loyales
b**eau**	b**eaux**	belles
nouv**eau**	nouv**eaux**	nouvelles

You'll notice that the same rules apply when forming plural nouns. Take a look at our example.

un beau chapeau - des beaux chapeaux.

Irregular Plural Adjectives

In French, three very common adjectives have special forms in front of masculine nouns that begin with a vowel or a vowel sound.

- **nouveau** - new
- **beau** - beautiful
- **vieux** - old

Adjective	In front of a masculine noun starting with a vowel	In front of a feminine noun starting with a vowel
nouveau C'est un nouveau système.	**nouvel** C'est un nouvel hôtel.	**nouvelle** C'est une nouvelle avenue.
Beau C'est un beau plat.	**bel** C'est un bel homme.	**belle** C'est une belle femme.
Vieux C'est un vieux métier.	**vieil** C'est un vieil homme.	**vieille** C'est une vieille femme.

Be aware that the adjectives "nouvel", "bel" and "vieil" take this form only when placed in front of a noun starting with a vowel or vowel sound.

Superlatives

When comparing, the superlative is used to express the extremes. You could use superlatives to talk about someone or something that is, the best, the worst, the tallest, the shortest etc. Superlatives are always used when comparing three or more things or people.

Take a look at superlative examples in both gender and number.

*Elle est la fille **la plus intelligente**. - She is the most intelligent girl.*

*Elle est la fille **la moins intelligente**. - She is the least intelligent girl.*

*Il est le garçon **le plus intelligent**. - He is the most intelligent boy.*

*Il est le garçon **le moins intelligent**. - He is the least intelligent boy.*

*Elles sont les filles **les plus intelligentes**. - They are the most intelligent girls.*

*Ils sont les garçons **les plus intelligents**. - They are the most intelligent boys.*

To create superlative, you'll need:

le/la/les + plus/moins + adjective

Le - masculine singular noun

La - feminine singular noun

Les - masculine and feminine plural nouns

The best and the worst

People often see the world in polarities, black-white, the best-the worst. It's no wonder the most used adjectives in superlatives are adjectives "**bon**" (good) and "**mauvais**" (bad).

C'est la meilleure glace du monde. - This is the best ice cream in the world.

The adjective "**bon**" (good) in comparative and superlative:

Masculine singular - **bon** (good) -> **meilleur** (better) -> **le meilleur** (the best)

Feminine singular - **bonne** (good) -> **meilleure** (better) -> **la meilleure** (the best)

Masculine plural - **bons** (good) -> **meilleurs** (better) -> **les meilleurs** (the best)

Feminine plural - **bonnes** -> **meilleures** (better) -> **les meilleures** (the best)

The adjective **mauvais** (bad) in comparative and superlative:

Masculine singular - **mauvais** (bad) -> **plus mauvais** (worse) -> **le pire** or **le plus mauvais** (the worst)

Feminine singular - **mauvaise** (bad) -> **plus mauvaise** (worse) -> **la pire** or **la plus mauvaise** (the worst)

Masculine plural - **mauvais** (bad) -> **plus mauvais** (worse) -> **les pires** or **les plus mauvais** (the worst)

Feminine plural - **mauvaises** (bad) -> **plus mauvaises** (worse) -> **les pires** or **les plus mauvaises** (the worst)

- *le plus mauvais or le pire (masculine singular)*
- *la plus mauvaise or la pire (feminine singular)*
- *les plus mauvais or les pires (masculine plural)*
- *les plus mauvaises or les pires (feminine plural)*

Conjunctions

Conjunctions are there to help us connect two separate ideas together in a meaningful sentence. With conjunctions, we can connect two words, phrases or sentences. Alternatively, think of them as the glue that holds your sentences together.

There are two types of French conjunctions: **coordinating and subordinating** (more on these to come).

First, we'll take a look at seven coordinating conjunctions, or linking words, in French.

- **et** (and) - *Elle me voit aux escaliers **et** immédiatement commence à parler de son cousin.*
- **ou** (or) - ***Ou** aux louanges de ses amis proches.*
- **mais** (but) - *Une femme sage **mais** ennuyante quand même.*
- **donc** (so, therefore) - ***Donc**, un mec fidèle avec des difficultés à trouver son âme sœur.*
- **ni** (neither...nor) - *D'accord, je ne suis **ni** poisson, ni taureau, ni scorpion, ni vierge.*
- **or** (now, yet) - *Les meilleurs signes compatibles avec un Capricorne sont le Poisson, le Taureau, le Scorpion **ou** la Vierge.*
- **car** (because) - ***Car** personne ne croit aux louanges de sa famille.*

If it's difficult to memorize all these words at once, there's a cute mnemonic that helps children remember the seven coordinating conjunctions: "***Mais où est donc Ornicar?***" *(mais ou et donc or ni car).*

Nevertheless, make sure you don't confuse the adverb '*où*' (where) with '*ou*' (or).

Key takeaways

- French adjectives differ from English because they agree with nouns or pronouns they describe in both gender and number.
- Each French adjective comes in four different forms (masculine singular, feminine singular, masculine plural, feminine plural).
- The general rule to create feminine adjectives is by adding **-e** to a masculine adjective.
- Masculine adjectives ending in **-e, -eux, -f,** and **-er**, do not follow the general rule of adding -e to form the feminine form. To form the feminine form, masculine adjectives ending in **-e**, add *é, ending in **-eux** change to **-euse**, ending in **-f** change to **-ve, ending in consonant - double the consonant** before adding **-e**.
- Some adjectives have the same form for masculine and feminine (*aimable, célèbre, faible, malade, propre, triste, sincère etc.*).
- Irregular masculine adjective "**beau**" turns into "**belle**" in feminine form.
- To create a plural form, the general rule is to add **-s**, except if the adjective already ends in -s, or -x. In the case an adjective finishes in -s or -x, nothing is added.
- Masculine adjectives finishing in *-eau and - al* change to *-eaux or -aux*.
- Masculine adjectives "**beau**", "**nouveau**", and "**vieux**" have one more masculine form ("**bel**", "**nouvel**", "**vieil**") that is used in front of masculine nouns beginning with a vowel or a vowel sound.
- Linking words or conjunctions help us connect two ideas into one sentence. These are '**et**' (and), '**ou**' (or), '**mais**' (but), '**donc**' (so, therefore), '**ni**' (neither...nor), '**or**' (now, yet) and '**car**' (because).

After learning how to describe the world around us and how to easily connect your ideas, in the next chapter you'll learn to express quantities and talk about food.

Chapter 3: Expressing Quantity and Cooking

« Les rêves sont la nourriture des dieux. »
- Paul Ohl

After discussing daily habits and meeting people in the previous chapters, we now focus on one thing humans can't live without. It's divinity - the food.

Imagine you fly to Paris and you are unable to ask for a baguette or order coffee. A horrific situation. In this chapter, we follow a day in the life of a food blogger. You will learn how to express quantity, bargain on the market, and buy everything from your list. However, even though we mention bargaining in the story, you should never bargain in France, since it is considered extremely rude.

L'art de manger

La nourriture, c'est des émotions. **L'odeur, la texture** et **le goût** de notre gâteau préféré peuvent nous rappeler les **souvenirs** de l'enfance. On ne **jouit** pas seulement de l'arôme et de **l'odeur**, mais aussi du moment qui nous **rappelle le bonheur**. Tel est le pouvoir **des madeleines** de ma grand-mère. Tous les dimanches, elle prépare des madeleines avec amour. Elle se lève très tôt le matin pour avoir les madeleines prêtes pour **le petit déjeuner**. Toute la famille **autour de la table** prend les petits gâteaux **avec plaisir**. Les adultes les prennent avec du café, les enfants avec du chocolat chaud. À table on commence à **faire des projets** pour la journée. Quelques fois on va faire un pique-nique, ou aller à la piscine, se promener dans la forêt, **faire voler un cerf-volant**, dessiner. J'adore me rappeler de ces jours divins.

Ma grand-mère m'a donné envie de **cuisiner** moi-même. Passionnée par la cuisine et l'art culinaire, j'ai décidé de **transmettre** mon **savoir-faire** et ma passion au travers d'articles de blog. Le premier plat à **publier** sur mon blog est « Délice Céleste », **la recette** pour les madeleines de ma grand-mère. En 2021, je deviens l'une des dix plus importantes influenceuses cuisine au monde. Ma grand-mère, Marthe, est tellement **fière** de moi. Elle m'aide **régulièrement** avec ses recettes et **conseils** de cuisine. Je propose à mes visiteurs des recettes **faciles** et rapides à faire, et **j'essaie** toujours d'impressionner mes amis et **d'épater** mes invités. Et il y en a pour tous les goûts ! Je suis plus particulièrement spécialisée dans les recettes françaises, italiennes et marocaines.

Aujourd'hui c'est **l'anniversaire** de ma grand-mère et je prépare **une fête surprise.** Bien sûr, étant blogueuse, je filme chaque pas, du moment où je vais à **l'épicerie** jusqu'à la préparation des plats.

Je vais avec ma meilleure amie, Charlotte, qui est aussi photographe. C'est notre rituel de partir très tôt le matin et de prendre le petit déjeuner au café **en face du** marché. Je prends du café et des croissants et puis je bois de **l'orangeade**. Elle prend du yaourt, du fromage et du jambon.

Le petit déjeuner fini, nous allons au marché pour acheter **des ingrédients frais**. J'achète. Je parle avec les vendeurs, je **négocie** le prix. Elle **filme**.

Tout d'abord, je sors ma **liste de courses**. Elle est longue. J'achète toujours beaucoup de fruits et peu de légumes. Heureusement, c'est l'été. Je vois une dame avec **des pastèques énormes**. Je **m'approche**.

« Bonjour madame ! **Combien coûte** un kilo de pastèque ?

– **Ça fait** 1 euro le kilo.

– Donnez-moi une grande pastèque ! Celle-ci **a l'air bien**.

– 9 kilos.

– Parfait.

– Je voudrais aussi un kilo de citron, trois oranges, deux kilos de pêche, **un paquet** d'olives, deux bananes, et encore... »

J'entends mon amie dire :

« C'est trop de fruits. Nous n'avons pas besoin d'autant, merci. Tu es **folle** ! Quelqu'un doit porter tout ça !

– Ah, oui. Tu as raison. J'**oublie** que je n'ai pas pris la voiture aujourd'hui.

– **Combien dois-je payer ?**

– 25 euros, s'il vous plaît.

– Voilà madame. »

Mon amie, déjà **énervée**, crie :

« Je vois pourquoi tu m'appelles à chaque fois que tu **fais des courses** ! Je suis une artiste moi. Je ne suis pas ici pour porter des pastèques. » dit-elle en prenant notre lourde pastèque.

Je **rigole**. Elle rigole aussi. Pour un moment, je me sens **confuse**. J'ai complètement oublié ce qu'il faut acheter.

Mon amie me regarde et crie « les madeleines ! » – « Ah oui. C'est vrai. »

Alors, les ingrédients nécessaires pour préparer le gâteau d'anniversaire. Je prends ma liste. Il me faut **3 œufs**, **du sucre**, **de la farine**, **de l'huile**, **du lait**, **du beurre** et puis aussi **du café** et **du chocolat**. J'arrive dans un magasin.

« Bonjour madame.

– Bonjour.

– Je voudrais **une bouteille d'huile**, **un sachet de sucre**, **un sac de farine**, **un paquet de chocolat** et du café.

– C'est tout ?

– Non, je veux aussi du **miel** et du beurre.

– Voici le miel et le beurre.

– **Vous désirez autre chose ?**

– Oui, je prendrais aussi deux bouteilles de vin blanc. Ça fait combien ?

– 26 euros.

– Voilà, merci beaucoup madame. Au revoir. »

Maintenant, j'ai **beaucoup de** fruits, **assez de** vin, un **peu de** café et tous les ingrédients nécessaires pour faire un gâteau d'anniversaire.

Je dis à mon amie qu'on doit aussi passer chez **le fleuriste** pour acheter un bouquet de roses jaunes pour **décorer la table**. Avec la caméra dans une main et la pastèque dans l'autre, elle me **regarde de travers** et on continue.

À la fin des courses, nous sommes **épuisées**. Je prends un moment pour me reposer et je commence à faire le gâteau. Mon amie n'arrête pas de filmer. Je casse des œufs, j'ajoute du lait et du beurre fondu, je mélange et mets le gâteau **au four**. Mon amie m'aide à **mettre la table** pour dix personnes et on entend quelqu'un **sonner à la porte**. Les invités viennent d'arriver. Ma grand-mère arrive la dernière et quelle surprise.

Résumé de l'histoire

Inspirée par les connaissances culinaires de sa grand-mère, une jeune fille lance son blog pour partager ses recettes culinaires. Elle devient l'une des dix premières influenceuses culinaires au monde. Avec l'aide de sa meilleure amie, elle documente chaque recette. Elle décide un jour d'organiser une fête surprise pour sa grand-mère et demande à son amie de faire les courses avec elle.

Synopsis of the story

Inspired by the culinary knowledge of her grandmother, a young girl starts to write about cooking on her own blog. She becomes one of the top ten food influencers in the world. With the help of her best friend, she documents each recipe. She decides to throw a surprise party for her grandmother one day and asks her friend to go grocery shopping with her.

Vocabulary and Expressions

de la nourriture - food

une odeur - a smell

une texture - a texture

un goût - a taste

se souvenir - to remember

jouir - to enjoy

le bonheur - happiness

rappeler - to remember

une madeleine - French cake, madelaine

un petit-déjeuner - a breakfast

autour de la table - around the table

avec plaisir - with pleasure

faire des projets - to make plans

faire voler un cerf-volant - to fly a kite
cuisiner - to cook
transmettre - to transmit, to convey
savoir-faire - know-how
un influencer / une influenceuse - an influencer
publier - to publish
fier / fière - to be proud of
régulièrement - regularly
un conseil - an advice
facile - easy
essayer - to try
épater - to impress someone
un anniversaire - an anniversary
une fête surprise - a surprise party
une épicerie - a grocery store
en face de - in front of
un ingrédient - an ingredient
une orangeade - an orange juice
negocier - to negotiate
filmer - to film
une liste de courses - a shopping list
une pastèque - a watermelon
énorme - large, enormous
s'approcher - to approach
combien coûte ... ? - How much costs ...?
ça fait - It is/ It costs
avoir l'air bien - to look good
un paquet de - a package of
fou / folle - crazy
oublier - to forget
combien dois-je payer ? - How much should l pay?
s'enerver - to get upset
faire les courses - to go shopping
rigoler - to laugh
confus / confuse - confused

du sucre - sugar

de la farine - flour

de l'huile - oil

du lait - milk

du beurre – butter

du café - coffee

du chocolat - chocolate

une bouteille de - a bottle of

un sachet de - a little bag

un sac de - a bag of

un paquet de - a package of

un miel - honey

vous désirez autre chose? - Do you want something else ?

beaucoup de - a lot of

assez de - enough of

un peu de - a little bit of

tant de - so many

un fleuriste - a florist

décorer la table - to decorate the table

regarder de travers - to look at someone with hostility, or dissatisfied

s'épuiser - to run out, to feel exhausted

casser - to break

au four - in the oven

mettre la table - to set the table

sonner à la porte - to ring the doorbell

Comprehension Questions

1. Quel est le métier du personnage qui raconte l'histoire ?
    A. Elle est photographe.
    B. Elle est chef dans un restaurant.
    C. Elle est blogueuse.
    D. Elle est la meilleure influenceuse du monde.
2. Quels ingrédients achètent-elles pour préparer le gâteau d'anniversaire ?
    A. Trois œufs, du sucre, de la farine, de l'huile, du lait, du beurre
    B. Du café, du lait, du sucre, trois œufs, du beurre, du lait, de l'huile.

C. Trois œufs, du sucre, de la farine, de l'huile, du lait.

D. Trois œufs, du sucre, de la farine, du lait, du café, du beurre.

3. Pourquoi Charlotte dit-elle « *Je suis une artiste, moi* » ?

    A. Parce qu'elle est l'une des dix meilleures photographes du monde.

    B. Elle est fâchée de devoir porter des sacs lourds chaque fois qu'elles vont au marché.

    C. Elle est photographe et là pour filmer, et pas pour porter des sacs lourds.

    D. Elle a une exposition de photos ce mois-ci.

4. Pourquoi Charlotte est-elle énervée ?

    A. Elle doit porter une pastèque de 9 kilos.

    B. Elle doit filmer toute la journée.

    C. Elle a une exposition importante.

    D. Elle pense que sa meilleure amie profite d'elle.

5. Pourquoi vont-elles au marché ?

    A. Pour filmer et avoir le matériel pour sa prochaine publication.

    B. Pour acheter des ingrédients pour la fête surprise.

    C. Pour trouver les ingrédients les moins chers.

    D. Pour préparer le déjeuner.

Grammar Notes

Expressing quantity

A quantitative word is a word that provides information on quantity, degree or importance. Quantity can be expressed with adverbs (**beaucoup, pas mal de, assez, très, trop**), adjectives (**plusieurs, quelques, etc**.) and numbers.

When we use adverbs to express quantity, then the form remains unchanged, while in the case of adjectives, the form is variable in gender and number.

It's important to make the difference between adjective and adverb, so you could be sure early on whether there's agreement or not.

Beaucoup d'enfants recevront des bourses. (beaucoup - adverbe)

Plusieurs enfants recevront des bourses. (plusieurs - adjective)

In French, the idea of quantity differs depending on whether the noun is countable or uncountable.

If you want to express quantity for countable nouns, there are multiple ways to do it.

- **adverbs:** *beaucoup, peu, assez, trop* (always followed by the preposition *de/d'*).
- **numbers:** *100 gr de chocolat, 50 gr de beurre, six œufs.*
- **nouns:** *un litre de, un kilo de, un paquet de, un verre de, un pot de, une brique de, une tasse de.*

Partitive articles

Sometimes, the quantity is not expressed. When that happens, we need partitive articles.

1. J'ai pris du café et des croissants.
2. Tu veux de la glace à la vanille ?
3. Au déjeuner, papa a mangé de la soupe, de la viande et des frites.

In the above examples, we see that the amount of what we drink, eat or buy is not determined. In the third example, it's stated that the father ate soup for lunch (but we did not specify whether he ate a plate of soup or...), meat (we don't know how much) and french fries (the amount is not specified either).

Partitive articles (*l'article partitif*) are used when the amount of what we drink, eat, buy, etc. is undefined. They correspond to masculine and feminine articles in singular and plural, and as any article they agree with the noun in gender and number.

Take a look at the following table.

Singular	Plural
Masculin - **du/de l'/de** Feminine - **de la / de l'/ de**	Masculin and Feminin - **des / de**

The partitive articles are used in French very often when we talk about food, drink, shopping, restaurant visits, cooking and similar situations, and when the amount of what we drink, eat, buy, own, order, add to food is not determined.

Let's make sure you comprehend articles in the context.

Du - in front of masculine, singular nouns.

Je prends du cafe.

Je bois du lait.

Je mange du poulet.

De la - in front of feminine, singular nouns.

Tu prends de la salade.

Tu achètes de la viande.

Tu manges de la confiture.

De l' - in front of feminine and masculine nouns that begin with a vowel or h.

Il prends de l'eau minérale

Nous buvons de l'orangeade.

J'achète de l'huile d'olive.

Des - in front of masculine and feminine nouns in plural.

Vous prenez des frites.

Je mange des pommes.

Tu achètes des tomates.

Partitive de

When the amount of what we take, drink, eat, order, buy, etc. is certain, we use the "***de partitif***". Adverbs like *peu, beaucoup, assez, trop* mean that the quantity of food is specified. Partitive ***de*** remains unchanged.

Take a look at our examples.

*J'ai pris **peu de** frites. - I took a few fries.*

*J'ai pris **beaucoup de** frites. - I took a lot of fries.*

*J'ai pris **assez de** frites. - I took enough fries.*

*J'ai pris **trop de** frites. - I took too many fries.*

Asking about quantities

To ask about quantities, you can use:

- **Combien + nom :** *Combien d'étudiants il y a dans la classe ? - How many students are there in the class?*

- **Combien + verbe :** *Combien coûte un kilo de viande ? Combien dois-je payer ? - How much does a kilo of meat cost? How much should I pay?*

Key takeaways

- Quantity can be expressed with adverbs (***beaucoup, pas mal de, assez, très, trop***), adjectives (***plusieurs, quelques***, etc.) and numbers.
- When we use adverbs to express quantity, there's no agreement with the noun, while in the case of adjectives, the adjective has to agree on gender and number.
- Partitive articles (*les articles partitifs*) are used when the amount of what we drink, eat, buy, etc. is undefined.
- Partitive articles agree with the noun on gender and number, and the forms are: ***de la, du, de l', des***.
- When the amount of what we take, drink, eat, order, buy, etc. is defined, we use *le partitif **de***. *Le partitif de* does not change.
- To ask about quantities, use ***Combien + nom**,* or ***Combien + verbe***.

So far, all our stories have been in the present tense. The next chapter will introduce you to the most commonly used past tense (*Passé Composé*), as well as possessive adjectives.

Chapter 4: My family

« Voyager, c'est partir à la découverte de l'autre. Et le premier inconnu à découvrir, c'est vous. »
- Olivier Föllmi

Communication involves a lot of storytelling. When we say storytelling, we mean not only fairy tales. Our past events are also stories. As you assume, this chapter will revolve around the most common French tense *"Le Passé Composé"*. And, as the name suggests, this is a complex tense. In this story, you'll find plenty of examples with both auxiliary verbs *avoir* and *être*, that are used to build this complex tense.

The following story is about a family that decides to live a nomadic life. Family is usually one of the most common topics in our lives. There are plenty of possessive adjectives used to talk about your family members. This story will surely inspire you to talk about your family, and perhaps to head off on a similar adventure around the world. Who knows?

Ma famille nomade

Bonjour les esprits libres !

Je m'appelle Léa et je voyage dans le monde avec ma famille. Il y a dix ans, notre vie s'est **transformée**. Nous avons choisi de **devenir** nomades. **Voyager dans le monde**, c'est l'idée de mon mari. **Pour être honnête**, au début, moi j'étais contre cette idée. Nos deux enfants ont à peine commencé l'école et puis, moi, j'aimais ma petite ville. Mais mon mari est une **tête de mule**. Il n'a pas arrêté d'essayer de me **convaincre** chaque jour, et moi, j'ai fini par **accepter**.

Mon mari est **photographe** et toujours **à la recherche** de nouveaux **endroits** à capturer avec son **appareil photo**. Il adore regarder ses photos et les **ranger** dans un album. Moi, je suis **écrivaine**, alors déjà nos métiers ne sont pas des travaux classiques. On n'est jamais allés dans un **bureau**. Si tu veux devenir nomade, c'est important d'avoir une telle **liberté**. Un jour, nous avons fait nos **sacs à dos** et nous nous sommes **dirigés** vers notre première destination. Comme ça, nous sommes devenus une famille nomade.

Avec deux enfants, nous sommes partis **explorer le monde** sur nos vélos. Bien sûr, notre famille a dit que c'était une **folie**. Ma mère, mon père, mes sœurs et mon frère étaient tous contre. **Même aujourd'hui**, 10 ans après, ils me **conseillent** de laisser ma vie d'**aventurière** pour avoir finalement **un domicile fixe**. Une sécurité, quoi. Mais, mon mari et moi, on voyage chaque jour et on ne **regrette** pas notre décision.

Pour nous, chaque jour est une **page blanche** à écrire, un **commencement**. Chaque soir nous dormons en **tente**. Parfois il fait froid, il pleut, il fait même -40 degrés Celsius, mais on aime notre petit **cocon**. Ne pas savoir ce qui nous attend demain pour nous est un **don**.

Bien sûr, avant de **se lancer** dans une telle **aventure**, il faut se préparer **à l'avance**. Aujourd'hui heureusement il y a plein de possibilités pour trouver un **travail en ligne** et comme ça on est devenu des **nomades digitaux**. Ensemble, nous avons commencé un blog pour partager nos écrits et photographies, nos **expériences** et réflexions pour inspirer les gens à **s'ouvrir** aux possibilités infinies.

Originaires de France, nous avons **parcouru** plus de 80 000 km sur 4 continents. Cette exploration est finalement une **incroyable** aventure intérieure.

Ma fille, Layla, a parcouru le monde sur plus de 25 000 km. Elle a **traversé** tant de **paysages** différents, de l'Asie jusqu'aux États-Unis. Elle adore rencontrer de nouveaux amis et parle six langues couramment. Layla écrit de nombreuses lettres à ses amies en plusieurs langues.

Mon fils Luca a déjà exploré les régions les plus **reculées** du monde. Il a **fait connaissance** avec des grizzlys et des loups, a **traversé la taïga** sibérienne, **le désert** et a **affronté** les -30°C sur sa petite bicyclette. Il aime dire que vivre **en pleine nature** lui fait se sentir comme un loup. **Fasciné** par les animaux sauvages, il adore les dessiner. On a tellement de desseins qu'on doit les envoyer à mes parents en France chaque mois.

Je pense que passer beaucoup de temps dans la nature aide l'enfant à se développer. Nos enfants respectent la nature et les autres cultures et ils sont toujours **prêts** à apprendre de nouvelles choses. Aujourd'hui nous traversons les Alpes. **Au sommet** d'une montagne, nous **plantons la tente**, buvons un thé camomille et regardons les Alpes.

Mes amies me demandent souvent **conseil** pour se lancer dans la même aventure. Le vrai **point commun** entre tous les nomades digitaux est d'avoir un job en ligne qui vous permet de travailler tout en voyageant. Avoir un job en ligne permet de découvrir de **merveilleux** endroits, tout en **exerçant** son activité. Nous aimons rester plus longtemps dans la même ville ou le même pays. Un mois, voire trois pour vraiment découvrir l'endroit et s'habituer un petit peu. Pour nous, **s'expatrier** a été la meilleure décision de notre vie. Imagine de **plonger** dans **l'inconnu** total.

Résumé de l'histoire

Une famille décide un jour de quitter sa zone de confort et de parcourir le monde à vélo. Pour mener une vie durable, ils devaient devenir nomades numériques. L'histoire est racontée du point de vue de la mère. Comme toutes les mères, Léa était d'abord contre l'idée, mais son mari a réussi à la convaincre. Ils avaient déjà tous les deux des emplois à distance, il n'a donc pas été difficile pour eux de devenir nomades. Léa est écrivaine, tandis que son mari travaille comme photographe. Ensemble, ils ont créé un blog pour partager leurs récits de voyage et leurs photos avec les autres. Leurs deux enfants, Layla et Luca aiment aussi voyager.

Synopsis of the story

One day, a family decides to leave their comfort zone and travel the world on a bike. To live a sustainable lifestyle, they needed to become digital nomads. The story is told from the mother's perspective. Like every mother, Lea was first against the idea, but her husband managed to convince her. They both already had remote jobs, so it wasn't difficult for them to become nomads. Lea is a writer, while her husband works as a photographer. Together they created a blog to share their travel stories and photos with others. Their two children, Layla and Luca also love traveling.

Vocabulary and Expressions

se transformer - to transform

devenir - to become

voyager dans le monde - to travel the world

être honnête - to be honest

être une tête de mule - to be a stubborn person

convaincre - to convince

accepter - to accept

(un, une) photographe - a photographer

être à la recherche de - to be in search of

un endroit - a place

capturer - to capture

un appareil photo - a camera

ranger - to store

un écrivain / une écrivaine - a writer

un bureau - an office

une liberté - freedom

un sac a dos - a backpack

se diriger - to head for

explorer le monde - to explore the world

une folie - a madness, craziness

même aujourd'hui - even today

conseiller - to advise

une vie d'aventurière - an adventurous life

un domicile fixe - a permanent place of residence

regretter - to regret

une page blanche - a blank page

un commencement - a beginning

un travail en-ligne - an online / remote job

un nomad digital - a digital nomad

une tente - a tent

un cocon - a cocoon

un don - a gift

se lancer - to embark on

une aventure - an adventure

à l'avance - in advance

une expérience - an experience

s'ouvrir - to open oneself to something

être originaire de - to come from, to be native to

parcourir - to travel around

incroyable - unbelievable

traverser - to cross, to go through

un paysage - a landscape

couramment - fluently

reculé - remote

faire la connaissance de quelqu'un - to get to know someone

la taïga - the taiga

un désert - a desert

affronter - to confront, to face

fasciner - to fascinate

être prêt - to be ready

au sommet - at the top

planter la tente - to set up / to pitch the tent

un conseil - an advice

un point commun - a thing in common

merveilleux / merveilleuse - marvelous

exercer - to practice

s'expatrier - to leave one's country

plonger - to dive

un inconnu - unknown (noun), a stranger (noun), unfamiliar (adjective)

Comprehension Questions

Sélectionnez une seule réponse pour chaque question.

1. Qui a eu l'idée de devenir une famille nomade ?

    A. Léa.

    B. Le mari de Léa.

2. Est-ce que leur famille était d'accord avec eux à propos de leur idée ?

    A. Oui.

    B. Non.

3. D'après Léa, qu'est-ce qui est nécessaire pour devenir un nomade numérique ?

    A. L'argent.

    B. Le projet.

    C. Le travail en ligne.

    D. Le vélo.

4. Quels sont les métiers de Léa et son mari?

    A. Léa est photographe et son mari est entrepreneur.

    B. Le mari de Léa est photographe et Léa est écrivaine.

    C. Léa ne travaille pas et son mari est photographe.

    D. Ils ont l'aide de sa famille.

5. Comment parcourent-ils le monde ?

    A. En minibus.

    B. En train.

    C. À vélo.

    D. À pied.

6. Que signifie l'expression « les régions les plus reculées du monde » ?

    A.   Les régions les plus éloignées.

    B.   Les régions les moins éloignées.

    C.   Les régions les plus dangereuses.

    D.   Les régions les plus cachées.

Grammar Notes

Passé Composé

Le passé composé is the most important past tense in French. It corresponds to two different English past tenses, the English simple past and in some contexts even with the present perfect. The *passé composé is used to talk* about completed actions in the past and also to emphasize the results or consequences in the present.

We form the *passé composé* using the auxiliary verbs *"avoir"* or *"être"* followed by the past participle *(le participe passé)* of the verb. A little reminder that auxiliaries are helping verbs, necessary when creating a compound tense. In French, there are only two auxiliary verbs: ***"avoir"*** and ***"être"***.

How to form the *Passé Composé*?

Le Passé Composé is called this way because it is composed of two verb forms:

1. Auxiliaries "to have" or "to be" in the present indicative.
2. Past participle of the conjugated verb.

The tense finally looks like this:

Passé composé = auxiliary + past participle

Elle a fait un gâteau. - She made a cake.

As you can see, the conjugated verb *"avoir"* is followed by the verb *"faire"* in the past participle. If you are confused with the past participle at this moment, don't worry. Past participles have to be learned by heart, and it's okay if you don't know them already.

The reason we need two auxiliaries is that some verbs require *"avoir"*, and others *"être"*. Keep on reading to discover which verbs go with auxiliary *"**être**"* and which ones with *"**avoir**"*.

Verbs that go with auxiliary *"être"*

Verbs that go along with auxiliary *"être"* are specific, because they have to agree with the noun in gender and number.

When using the verb *"**être**"* as an auxiliary, the verb must agree with the subject in both gender and number.

- If the subject is singular feminine, add (-e)
- If the subject is plural masculine, add (-s)
- If the subject is plural feminine, add (-es)

Let's see how the verb *"entrer"* changes in Passé Composé.

- *Je suis entré* (entré**e** - feminine singular)
- *Tu es entré* (entré**e** - feminine singular)
- *Il est entré / Elle est entrée* (entré**e** - feminine singular)
- *Nous sommes entrés* (entré**es**- feminine plural)
- *Vous êtes entrés* (entré**es** - feminine plural)
- *Ils sont entrés / Elles sont entrées* (entrées - feminine plural)

There are 3 types of verbs that conjugate with *"être"*.

- Verbs of movement (leave, go out, go down, come, fall down, arrive)

aller, entrer, sortir, partir, arriver, monter, descendre, tomber, passer

- Verbs of state

naître, mourir, devenir

- Pronominal Verbs

Verbs that are accompanied by a reflexive pronoun: se laver, se lever, se baigner, se peigner, se souvenir, etc.

Verbs that go with auxiliary "*avoir*"

Most verbs construct the *passé composé* with "*avoir*", except for movement, state and pronominal verbs that go along with the auxiliary "*être*".

Let's take a look at how the verb "*finir*" changes in past tense.

- *J'ai fini*
- *Tu as fini*
- *Il a fini / Elle a fini*
- *Nous avons fini*
- *Vous avez fini*
- *Ils ont fini / Elles ont fini*

Possessive Adjectives

When you see an adjective, know that its purpose is to describe or determine something. In most cases, it's determining a noun more precisely. Possessive adjectives, also known as possessive determiners, belong to the same group as adjectives. The difference is possessive determiners are used to express ownership.

Specifically, French possessive adjectives tell us to whom or what the noun in questions belongs.

- *C'est votre valise.* - That's your suitcase.
- *Il est leur fils.* - He is their son.
- *Ce sont nos chiens.* - They are our dogs.

Today, we'll dive deeper into possessive adjectives and learn how possessive adjectives in French are different from the same category in English. You may be surprised.

18 French Possessive Adjectives

That's right. You heard well. There are 18 possessive adjectives in French. No wonder you are struggling with it. The expression of possession and belonging in French may not be as straightforward as in English, so let's find out why.

my book - **mon** livre

my house - **ma** maison

my books - **mes** livres

The main reason French has 18 possessive adjectives, while English has only 7, is that French nouns have masculine and feminine gender. It is only natural that the number of possessive adjectives triples given that adjectives agree with nouns in both gender and number.

Depending on the noun they describe, **French possessive adjectives** take different forms. In other words, if the noun is masculine and singular, the possessive adjective should be too. Let's kick things off by looking at all the possessive adjectives in their different variations.

The **masculine singular possessive adjectives** are: *mon, ton, son, notre, votre, leur*.

The **feminine singular possessive adjectives** are: *ma, ta, sa, notre, votre, leur*.

The **plural possessive adjectives** are the same for both genders: *mes, tes, ses, nos, vos, leurs.*

Note that the plural possessive adjectives are used to indicate the owners are more than 1, as well as the things owned.

Person	Masculine Singular	Feminine Singular	Masculine/ Feminine Plural
Je	**mon**	**ma**	**mes**
Tu	**ton**	**ta**	**tes**
Il/Elle/On	**son**	**sa**	**ses**
Nous	**notre**	**notre**	**nos**
Vous	**votre**	**votre**	**vos**
Ils/Elles	**leur**	**leur**	**leurs**

Exceptions

Without exceptions, wouldn't life be boring?

Well, it wouldn't. At least in French. But what can we do? Life can be hard when you want to be fluent in French.

The general rule is to always use (ma, ta, sa) in front of feminine nouns. However, if the word starts with a vowel or h, then you should use a possessive adjective that goes with masculine nouns (mon, ton, son).

That way we are going to say:

- *"**mon idée**"*, instead of saying *"ma idée"*.
- *"**ton histoire**"*, instead of *"ta histoire"*.
- *"**son auto**"* instead of *"sa auto"*, etc.

Differences between French and English possessive adjectives

Let's begin with a riddle. Can you determine whether the French owner is masculine or feminine?

***Son** chapeau.*

How about in English? **his** hat or **her** hat?

In English it's obvious, but not in French. That's because, in French, the gender of an owner is not relevant and it's impossible to determine whether the owner is masculine or feminine.

Instead, in French, we are considering the genre of a thing owned. In this case, *"son chapeau"* shows that the word chapeau is masculine.

Ready to take on another riddle?

his book - **his** books

son livre - **ses** livres

You'll notice that in English, the plural and singular forms of a noun do not affect the adjective in front of *"his book"* or *"his books"*. Whilst in French, the number affects the possessive adjectives.

Key takeaways

- The *passé composé* is used to talk about completed actions in the past and also to emphasize the results or consequences in the present.
- We form the *passé composé* using the auxiliary verbs "*avoir*" or "*être*" followed by the past participle *(le participe passé)* of the verb. ***passé composé = auxiliary + past participle.***
- Most verbs construct the *passé composé* with "*avoir*", except for movement, state and pronominal verbs that go along with the auxiliary "*être*".
- When using the verb "**être**" as an auxiliary, the verb must agree with the subject in both gender and number. It is not needed if you use "*avoir*" as an auxiliary.
- French possessive adjectives must agree in number and gender with the noun or pronoun they stand with, and that's the reason why there are **18 possessive adjectives** in French.
- The masculine singular possessive adjectives are: ***mon, ton, son, notre, votre, leur***.
- The feminine singular possessive adjectives are: ***ma, ta, sa, notre, votre, leur***.
- The plural possessive adjectives are the same for both genders: ***mes, tes, ses, nos, vos, leurs***.
- If the feminine noun starts with a vowel or h, then you should use a possessive adjective that typically goes with masculine nouns (mon, ton, son).
- In French, the gender of an owner is not relevant as it is in English. That's why it's impossible to determine whether the owner is masculine or feminine.

We want to congratulate you on successfully completing this chapter. It was quite a challenge. In the next chapter, you will learn how to talk about the weather and how to use prepositions *de* and *à*.

Chapter 5: Traveling and Weather

« L'espace est un corps imaginaire, comme le temps un mouvement fictif. »
- Paul Valéry

Paris has a reputation for being a rainy place, and everyone seems to be worried about the weather. Parisians constantly talk about the weather, hoping it won't rain again. After learning how to talk about the weather, you'll become the king of the small talk, once you set foot in Paris.

During the following story, you will encounter a meteorologist and learn several terms associated with the weather, as well as how to use the most common prepositions in French: *à* and *de*.

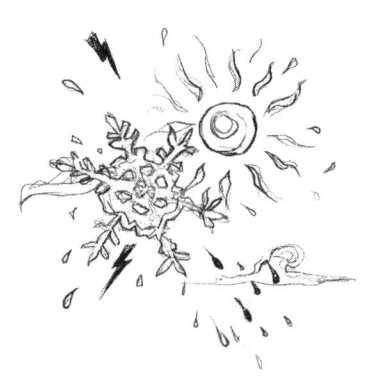

Autour du monde avec un météorologue

Le travail d'un jeune garçon qui s'appelle Lazarus, **d'origine** espagnole, est de visiter les destinations touristiques les plus **tendances**. Il est **météorologue**, mais comme il aime voyager, il a **décidé** de rendre visite aux météorologues **autour du monde**. Il **rend visite à** ses **collègues** météorologues pour savoir quelle est la meilleure **saison** pour visiter leurs pays. Il a rendu visite à ses collègues en Chine, aux États-Unis, en Italie, au Portugal, en Irak et aux Maldives. Il habite à Nice, mais il est originaire de Séville.

Comme il est nomade, il a déjà visité les plus grandes villes du monde. Il a visité Bordeaux, Rome, Moscou, Beijing, Barcelone et New York. Il a même visité la Colombie deux fois.

Et, **pendant** l'un de ses voyages, il a eu l'idée d'écrire **des reportages** sur le climat. Il a choisi le pire moment pour aller en Inde, pendant **la mousson** d'hiver. Il a passé les dix jours à l'hôtel. Puis, il a rencontré d'autres touristes qui **se sont trompés**. Quelques touristes sont venus de France, du Sénégal, des États-Unis. Et ils ont tous dû **passer** leurs vacances **enfermés**.

Depuis ce voyage, chaque année, Lazarus visite les destinations les plus tendances. Grâce à ses reportages, les touristes connaissent la meilleure saison pour visiter chaque pays.

Sa première destination est l'Islande. L'Islande est devenue **la destination à la mode**. Lazarus est arrivé à **la gare** et attend son collègue qui vient d'Espagne.

En Islande, **il y a du soleil** mais **il fait très froid. Le vent souffle** où il veut.

« J'espère que vous avez apporté **des vêtements chauds** ? Il entend **une voix** derrière son **dos**.

– Bonjour Santiago.

– Bonjour Lazarus. Bienvenue en Islande. Ici, **il fait plus froid qu'**en Espagne.

– Oui, je vois. **Il gèle.**

– Allons vous installer dans un hôtel et on va prendre un café. »

Un rayon de soleil caresse le visage de Lazarus et **une goutte d'eau** tombe sur sa main. **Le soleil brille** et **il pleut** en même temps. C'est bizarre.

« **Quel temps fait-il ?**

– Aujourd'hui **il fait chaud. Il fait moins 5 degrés**.

– Chaud, vous dites !

– **Quel est le climat en Islande ?** demande Lazarus.

– L'Islande a **un climat océanique**, un peu plus **tempéré**. Grâce au **Gulf Stream** les températures ne sont pas tellement froides. En hiver, il fait froid, un vent est souvent présent, avec de fortes **tempêtes de neige**.

– Et quelle est **la température moyenne** ?

– **Environ** 0°C, mais toujours **négative** dans **l'intérieur de l'île**.

– Alors, vous ne **conseillez** pas de venir en hiver ? répond Lazarus.

– Si, pour les gens qui viennent voir les **aurores boréales, ajoute** le météorologue.

– Quand est-ce que le climat est le plus **agréable** ?

– Pendant l'été, le climat est vraiment agréable. La température moyenne est d'environ 15°C. Mais le ciel n'est jamais complètement **ensoleillé. Les précipitations** sont fréquentes. Pour profiter le plus, je dirais que l'été est **la saison idéale**.

– Est-ce qu'il y a du vent en hiver ?

– Les vents dominants sont des **vents d'ouest**. Les vents d'est sont très rares.

– Et **les orages** ?

– Les orages sont extrêmement **rares** en Islande.

– **Au moins ça.**

– Finalement, vous conseillez de visiter l'Islande aux **mois** de mai, juin, juillet et août pour **admirer ses paysages**.

– Oui, certainement. Quelle est votre dernière destination ?

– Le mois dernier, je suis allé à Bali.

– Racontez-moi cette histoire de Bali.

– Bali est **une île** d'Indonésie, **située à l'est** de Java. Le paysage de Bali est **particulier**, fait de **montagnes**, de **volcans**, de **forêts**, de **plages**. Sur l'île, on **profite** d'**une chaleur** constante, toute l'année. Le climat de Bali représente un vrai contraste entre les journées de pluie et les journées de soleil.

Bali connaît deux saisons, l'hiver et l'été. **La saison sèche s'étend** d'avril à octobre. De décembre à février, **il pleut constamment**. Des précipitations **atteignant** 300 mm d'eau. Pendant la saison des pluies, le soleil brille quelques heures par jour, et il pleut environ trois heures le matin et trois heures le soir.

Durant les mois de mars, avril, octobre et novembre, les pluies sont moins **nombreuses**, et les températures plus **élevées.** Pendant cette période-là, **les averses** sont normales. Puis, de juin à septembre, les précipitations sont rares. En même temps, ces mois sont les plus chauds, parce qu'il manque d'**humidité**.

La période la moins **prisée par les touristes** est durant les mois d'octobre et novembre. Je recommande ces mois pour les gens qui cherchent **des vacances calmes**.

– Ça a l'air bien. Le climat de Bali est beaucoup plus agréable qu'en Islande. Et quelle est votre prochaine destination ?

– Tout d'abord je dois aller rendre visite à ma famille en Espagne et puis je pars à Dakar, au Sénégal. Je reste là-bas deux semaines, et après je vais aux Pays-Bas.

– Ah, vous vivez **la vie de rêve**. »

Résumé de l'histoire

C'est l'histoire d'un jeune garçon qui s'appelle Lazarus, d'origine espagnole. Il est météorologue, mais comme il aime voyager, il a décidé de rendre visite aux météorologues autour du monde. Il rend visite à ses collègues pour savoir quelle est la meilleure saison pour visiter leurs pays et écrire des reportages. Lazarus a la chance de visiter les destinations touristiques les plus tendances. Tout d'abord, il part en Islande pour rencontrer Santiago, son collègue d'Espagne. Santiago lui décrit le climat islandais. À la fin, Lazarus parle de Bali, sa dernière destination et ses futurs projets.

Synopsis of the story

It is the story of a young boy named Lazarus, of Spanish origin. He is a meteorologist, but since he likes to travel, he decided to visit meteorologists around the world. He visits his colleagues to find out what is the best season to visit these countries and writes articles about it. Lazarus has the chance to visit the trendiest tourist destinations. First of all, he goes to Iceland to meet Santiago, his colleague from Spain. Santiago tells him about the weather in Iceland. Finally, Lazarus talks about Bali, his last destination and upcoming trips.

Vocabulary and Expressions

une origine - an origin, root

une tendance - a trend

un, une météorologue - a meteorologist

décider - to decide

autour du monde - around the world

rendre visite à - to visit someone

un, une collègue - a colleague

pendant - while

un reportage - a report

une mousson - a monsoon

se tromper - to mislead, to make a mistake

passer - to pass
être enfermé - to be locked up
une destination - a destination
à la mode - to follow the latest fashion
une gare - a station
Il y a du soleil. - It's sunny.
Il fait très froid. - It's very cold.
Le vent souffle. - It's windy.
les vêtements chauds - warm clothes
une voix - a voice
un dos - a back
il fait plus froid que - It's colder than
Il gèle. - It's freezing.
un rayon de soleil - a sun ray
caresser - to caress
un visage - a face
une goutte d'eau - a water drop
briller - to shine
Il pleut. - It's raining.
Quel temps fait-il ? - What's the weather like?
Il fait chaud. - It's hot.
Il fait moins 5 degrés. - It's minus 5 degrees.
un climat océanique - an oceanic climate
tempéré - temperate
le Gulf Stream - the Gulf Stream
une tempêtes de neige - a snowstorm
une température moyenne - an average temperature
environ - about
négatif / négative - negative
l'intérieur de l'île - inside of the island
conseiller - to advise
une aurores boréale - an aurora borealis, northern lights
ajouter - to add
agréable - pleasant
ensolleillé - sunny

des précipitations - rainfalls
une saison idéale - an ideal season
des vents d'ouest - west winds
un orage - a storm
au moins - at least
un mois - a month
admirer les paysages - to admire the landscapes
une île - an island
située à l'est - located in the east
particulier - particular, specific
une montagne - a mountain
un volcan - a volcano
une forêt - a forest
une plage - a beach
profiter de - to thrive, to enjoy
une chaleur - a heat
une saison sèche - a dry season
s'etendre - to extend, to unroll
Il pleut. - It's raining.
constamment - constantly
atteindre - to reach, to get to
nombreux / nombreuse - many, numerous
élever - to raise
une humidité - a humidity
prisé par les touristes - popular with tourists
des vacances - holidays
une vie de rêve - a dream life

Comprehension Questions

Sélectionnez une seule réponse pour chaque question.

1. Quelle est la profession actuelle de Lazarus ?

    A. Météorologue.

    B. Journaliste.

    C. Voyageur.

2. Pourquoi Lazarus voyage autour du monde ?

A. Pour visiter les pays les plus tendances.
   B. Pour écrire sur le changement climatique.
   C. Pour écrire des reportages sur le climat des pays tendances.
   D. Pour rencontrer ses collègues météorologues.
3. Qu'est-ce que ça veut dire visiter les destinations les plus tendances ?
   A. Visiter les destinations les plus cachées du monde.
   B. Visiter les destinations à la mode.
   C. Visiter les destinations avec le meilleur climat.
   D. Visiter les pays en développement.
4. Quels sont les meilleurs mois pour visiter l'Islande ?
   A. Mai, juin, juillet et août.
   B. En hiver.
   C. D'avril à octobre.
5. À Bali, pendant la période des pluies...
   A. Il pleut toute la journée.
   B. Il pleut deux heures le matin.
   C. Il pleut trois heures le matin et trois heures le soir.
   D. Il ne pleut pas.

Grammar Notes

Talking about the Weather

Talking about the weather in French poses a couple of common issues for all beginners. Many English speakers get confused since the verb they use to explain *"It's raining"* is the verb *"être"*, while French use the verb *"make"* or *"faire"*. More specifically, the weather in French is explained with the impersonal expression *"il fait"*. *"Il fait"* refers to "it's" or " the weather is".

There are 3 ways to ask about the weather in French:

- ***Quel temps fait-il ?*** - *What's the weather like?*
- ***Combien fait-il ?*** - *What temperature is it?*
- ***Quelle température fait-il ?*** - *What temperature is it?*

The most common way to ask about the weather is the question *"Quel temps fait-il ?"*

Let's take a look at 3 ways to respond or simply talk about the weather:

- **Il y a**
- **Il fait**
- **Il + verbe**

Il y a...

Il y a du soleil. - There's sun.

Il y a du vent. - There's wind.

Il y a de la pluie. - There's rain.

Or

Il fait....

You can use the expression *"il fait"* to answer the question "***Combien fait-il ? Quelle température fait-il ?***"

Il fait 25 degrés. - It's 25 degrees.

Il fait moins dix. - It's minus ten.

Il fait chaud. - It's hot.

Il fait froid. - It's cold.

Il + verb (pleuvoir, neiger, venter)

Il pleut. - It's raining.

Il pleut à verse. - It's pouring rain.

Il neige. - It's snowing.

Il vente. - It's windy.

***C'est* + adjective**

C'est pluvieux. - It's rainy.

C'est humide. - It is wet.

C'est orageux. - It's stormy.

C'est nuageux. - It's cloudy.

C'est ensoleillé. - It's sunny.

C'est couvert. - It is overcast.

Adding "***très***" in front of the adjective adds more intensity to any French adjective.

*Il fait **très** chaud. It's boiling.*

*Il fait **très** froid. It's freezing.*

Prepositions of Place

Time and space are fundamental to how humans perceive the world. To locate someone or something in space, we locate things in comparison with other things. Prepositions help us to describe the direction of a place and orient ourselves.

In this lesson, we'll learn the French equivalent of English prepositions (*in, on, at, to, with, after*). French prepositions are invariable, which means they have a unique form that never changes and doesn't agree with the noun in gender or number.

Preposition *À* vs *De*

There are two French prepositions that cause constant problems for French beginners. It's no wonder when they both have a variety of meanings. To make things worse, they are the most common French prepositions.

- *À* - shows the point of departure and destination, cause and consequence, means and outcome.
- *De* - indicates origin, point of departure, consequence, and belonging, as well as separation.

When translated to English, it sounds like this.

à - to, at, in

de - of, from

By comparing them, you'll be able to make a better distinction.

Je parle à mon petit ami. - I am speaking to my boyfriend.

Je parle de mon petit ami. - I am speaking of my boyfriend.

Or

Je viens de Rome. - I am coming from Rome.

Je vais à Rome. - I am going to Rome.

We mentioned that prepositions do not change in French, except for these two French prepositions (à, de). These prepositions tend to contract with articles (**le, la, l', les**). Here, we'll examine the preposition *à* that contracts.

If you want to express 'to the' or 'at the' in French, use:

à + article le/la/l'/les

- **au** before a masculine word (à + le)

Je vais au supermarché - I'm going to the supermarket.

- **à la** before a feminine word (à + la)

Elle est restée à la maison. - She stayed at home.

- **à l'** before a singular word beginning with a vowel or silent -h (à + l')

Tu as parlé à l'ami de Julien ? - Did you speak to Julien's friend?

- **aux** before a word in the plural form (à + les)

Vous allez aux États-Unis ? - Are you going to the USA?

English	Masculine	Feminine	Vowel or - h	Plural
To the / at the	à + le = au	à + la = à la	à + l' = à l'	à + les = aux

If you want to express 'from' in French, use:

de + article le/la/l'/les

- **du** before a masculine word (de + le)

Je viens du supermarché - I'm coming from the supermarket.

- **de la** before a feminine word (de + la)

Je viens de la piscine. I am coming from the swimming pool.

- **de l'** before a singular word beginning with a vowel or silent -h (de + l')

Je viens de l'auberge de jeunesse. - I am coming from the youth hostel.

- **des** before a word in the plural form (de + les)

Je viens des Pays-Bas. - I am coming from the Netherlands.

English	Masculine	Feminine	Vowel or - h	Plural
from	de + le = du	de + la = de la	de + l' = de l'	de + les = des

Prepositions of place (Cities, Towns, Countries)

If you are wondering why sometimes you say *"Je vais en France."* and sometimes *"Je vais au Portugal."* stay to unravel the mystery together.

You already know that all inanimate objects in French have gender (masculine or feminine). Well, continents, countries and regions follow the same concept. They are either masculine or feminine. To remember the gender, one must learn it by heart.

Take a look at the prepositions we use in front of the cities, towns, villages and countries, according to their gender and number.

- À - for cities/towns/villages

J'habite à Paris. I live in Paris.

- En - for feminine countries (countries ending with the letter -e)

J'étudie en France. I study in France.

- Au - for masculine countries

Je travaille au Brésil. I work in Brazil.

- Aux - for plural countries

Je suis né aux Pays-Bas. I was born in the Netherlands.

Exceptions are masculine countries beginning with a vowel, which take *en* to mean "to" or "in" and *d'* to mean "from."

Exceptional rules

We know that when you learn a new rule, you tend to use it everywhere. But, the preposition isn't always required. If the city or the country is subject or direct object, you do not need a preposition.

J'ai déjà visité Lyon.

Cannes est connue pour son festival.

If you are talking about a country, precede it with an article.

J'ai visité l'Italie trois fois.

Le Vietnam est un pays d'Asie.

Key takeaways

- There are 3 ways to ask about the weather in French (**Quel temps fait-il ? /Combien fait-il ?/ Quelle température fait-il ?**).
- There are 3 ways to talk about the weather in French (**Il y a / Il fait / Il + verbe**).
- Names of cities, towns or countries are either feminine or masculine, and their gender has to be learned by heart.
- Prepositions do not change in French, except for (**à, de**). These prepositions tend to contract with articles (***le, la, l', les***).
- Contracted articles with de/ **du, de la, de l', des.**
- Contracted articles with à / **au, à la, à l', aux.**
- Use the preposition **à** in front of cities, towns or villages. Use **au** in front of the masculine countries, **en** in front of the feminine countries and **aux** in front of the plural countries. Exceptions are masculine countries beginning with a vowel, which take ***en*** to mean "to" or "in" and ***d'*** to mean "from."
- If the city or the country is subject or direct object, there is no need for a preposition.

In the next chapter, you will be covering one of the most frequent mistakes French students make as beginners. You'll finally conquer the difference between the possessive pronouns and possessive adjectives.

Chapter 6: Shopping

« La vie ce n'est pas avoir et obtenir, mais être et devenir. »
- Mirna Loy

The desire for ownership is widespread, and unlike other creatures, people like to own. That's why possessive adjectives and pronouns are one of the most important aspects when learning French.

In this story, you'll meet Charlotte, a young girl who solves all her problems by shopping. You'll be exposed to many possessive words, from possessive adjectives to possessive pronouns. But, be aware that possessive adjectives and pronouns tend to cause confusion in French. By comparing possessive pronouns and possessive adjectives in one place, you will be able to see what the difference is. Skip to the grammar notes, if you become confused at any point.

La shopping thérapie

En cas de problème, certaines personnes consultent **un psychothérapeute**, mais d'autres préfèrent **un traitement** plus **coûteux**: le shopping. Beaucoup disent que c'est simplement **pour échapper aux problèmes,** mais Charlotte dit que c'est sa manière de **se détendre.** Comme beaucoup de filles de New York, Charlotte adore faire du shopping. Le problème est qu'elle fait tellement de shopping qu'elle finit **endettée.** Charlotte **rêve** de travailler pour le plus grand journal de mode, mais elle n'a pas le courage de le faire. A chaque fois qu'elle pense à **quitter** son travail et trouver un travail qu'elle aime, elle **ressent de la crainte.** Elle a peur de **quitter sa zone de confort.** Et pour **se sentir mieux**, elle fait du shopping. **En ligne, au centre commercial,** au supermarché, peu importe. Elle achète des **vêtements, dépense de l'argent**, endettée et oublie son rêve.

Un jour, Charlotte **s'est fait virer.** Tout d'abord elle a été **contente**, parce qu'elle **détestait** son travail. Elle a vu **un poste de travail** vacant à la Grande Maison Journaliste. Elle **a postulé** et été certaine de **réussir**.

Quand elle a rendez-vous avec un client important, Charlotte n'**hésite** pas à **s'habiller à la mode.** Elle se sent plus **à l'aise** avec **une tenue classique.** Pour aller à **l'entretien**, Charlotte porte toujours **un chemisier, une jupe** et une belle **écharpe rouge**. Sa mère pense qu'elle est très élégante avec son **bracelet en or** et ses **chaussures** noires.

Malgré toutes **les attentes,** après son premier entretien, sa candidature a été **rejetée.** Elle a **pleuré** pendant des jours, mais finalement a décidé d'arrêter de **se plaindre** et faire quelque chose. Elle a décidé de faire du shopping pour **renouveler sa garde-robe.** La sienne était un peu **démodée**, et peut-être que c'était la raison de **son échec.** Charlotte a pris son **porte-monnaie**, a appelé sa meilleure copine et a oublié ses dettes.

« Salut Marie. Je suis un peu **déprimée**. Tu veux **faire les magasins** aujourd'hui ?

– Certainement. J'ai besoin d'un nouveau **pull-over** et **de sandales**. On y va comment ?

– On va prendre ta voiture parce que la mienne est chez **le mécanicien.**

– Allons-y alors. Je **te récupère** dans une demi-heure.

– Parfait. **À tout à l'heure.** »

Charlotte cherche son **chapeau**, mais **au lieu de** trouver le sien, trouve le chapeau de son père, et le chapeau de sa mère dans **le placard**. Les leurs sont peut-être des années 80, mais les années 80 sont de nouveau à la mode, elle pense. Elle n'a pas le temps de chercher le sien, et finalement elle met le chapeau de son père. Puis, il faut trouver des chaussures, mais les siennes ne sont pas **confortables**. Elle se demande si sa mère a des **chaussures à talons hauts**. Et oui, elle a de la chance. Chapeau de son père, chaussures de sa mère. Leur style est toujours **impeccable**, elle pense. Elle est maintenant prête à quitter la maison pour rencontrer sa meilleure copine.

« Salut Marie. Où est notre voiture ? Celle-ci, c'est la nôtre ?

– Non, c'est la même couleur, mais la nôtre est là-bas **au fond**.

– Ah, j'ai oublié que tu as changé de voiture. »

Les deux filles arrivent au centre commercial.

« Regarde ce pull-over vert dans **la vitrine** ! Il est très joli ! dit Marie.

– Tu veux dire que tu as **l'intention** de l'acheter ? Il est **affreux**! répond Charlotte.

– Tu as raison, et **de toute façon** le mien est plus beau.

– Le tien est de **haute qualité** et tu peux le porter pour **plusieurs occasions.**

– C'est vrai.

– J'aime bien tes sandales. Je trouve que les miennes ne sont pas aussi jolies. dit Marie.

– Qu'est-ce que tu racontes ? J'adore les tiennes. Elles me semblent très confortables.

– Oui, elles sont confortables. Charlotte regarde cette **robe**. Qu'est-ce que tu en penses ? Elle est belle, n'est pas ?

– Est-ce que tu penses qu'elle est plus belle que la mienne ?

– La tienne ? Tu as une dizaine de robes. Tu penses à laquelle ?

– Je pense à ma robe courte, élégante. Tu te rappelles, ma robe noire ? Je l'ai portée pour ton anniversaire, il y a un mois . La mienne est plutôt pour le soir peut-être.

– Ah, oui, je me rappelle. Oui, c'est vrai. La tienne est plus élégante, mais celle-ci est plutôt pour un entretien ?

– Tu as raison. Je vais l'**essayer**.

– Vas-y. Je t'attends ici et peut-être que je vais trouver quelques idées sur internet.

– Charlotte, regarde ce que j'ai trouvé sur internet. **La tenue** de Cate Blanchett. Cette robe n'est pas haute couture. La sienne c'est vraiment **prêt-à-porter**, en plus c'est une combinaison idéale pour un entretien. Regarde ses chaussures noires. Je pense que j'ai les mêmes comme les siennes.

– C'est une combinaison classique. Précisément, **le pantalon, le blouson, un manteau** et des chaussures. Peut-être que c'est une bonne idée pour un rendez-vous professionnel.

– Tu pourrais aller chercher **une vendeuse** pour t'aider à trouver le pantalon ?

– Oui. Bonne idée. »

Les copines entrent dans un magasin.

« Bonjour madame, puis-je vous conseiller ? dit la vendeuse.

– Oui, je cherche un pantalon classique pour un entretien.

– Suivez-moi, nos modèles se trouvent par ici.

– Celui-ci est très joli, l'avez-vous en blanc ?

– Oui, vous pouvez l'essayer dans **une cabine** au fond du magasin.

– Il me va très bien, c'est décidé, je l'achète.

– Quarante euros s'il vous plaît madame.

– Je n'ai pas de **monnaie**, acceptez-vous **les cartes bancaires** ?

– Oui, et je vous donne **un bon de réduction** à valoir sur notre nouvelle collection.

– Merci, je **reviendrai** vous voir à l'automne prochain.

– Excusez-moi madame, mais votre carte est **rejetée**.

– Impossible. **Réessayez,** s'il vous plaît.

– Non, ça ne marche pas.

– Désolée, je vais devoir **rendre** le pantalon. »

Charlotte se rend à la banque pour vérifier **le solde de son compte** et voit qu'elle a beaucoup de dettes. Sa carte est **bloquée**. Elle ne peut plus rien acheter. Son amie lui dit :

« Faire des courses, c'est une thérapie coûteuse. Je pense que tu as besoin d'aide.

– Je pense aussi. »

Résumé de l'histoire

Charlotte adore faire du shopping et c'est sa manière de se détendre. Quand elle se sent déprimée, elle appelle sa meilleure copine Marie et va faire du shopping. Elle a un travail qu'elle déteste et elle rêve de travailler comme journaliste de mode. Mais elle ressent de la crainte chaque fois qu'elle pense à quitter son travail. Un jour, Charlotte est renvoyée et maintenant libre de trouver le travail de ses rêves. Mais, est-ce qu'elle va réussir à surpasser sa peur.

Synopsis of the story

Charlotte loves shopping and it's her way to relax. When she feels down, she calls her best friend Marie and goes shopping. She has a job she hates and dreams of working as a fashion journalist. But every time she thinks about quitting her job, she feels fear. Charlotte gets fired one day and is now free to find the job of her dreams. But, will she be able to overcome her fear?

Vocabulary and Expressions

un psychothérapeute - a psychotherapist

un traitement - a treatment

coûteux / coûteuse - expensive

échapper aux problèmes - to escape problems

se détendre - to relax

faire du shopping - to go shopping

être endetté - to be indebted

rêver - to dream

quitter - to leave

ressentir - to feel, to experience

une crainte - a fear

une zone de confort - a comfort zone

se sentir mieux - to feel better

en ligne - online

un centre commercial - a shopping mall

un vêtement - a clothe

dépenser de l'argent - to spend money

se faire virer - to get fired

Content / contente - satisfied, content

détester - to hate

un poste de travail - a job position

postuler pour un emploi - to apply for a job

réussir - to succeed

hésiter - to hesitate

s'habiller à la mode - to dress fashionably

se sentir / être à l'aise - to feel comfortable

une tenue classique - a classic outfit

un entretien - an interview

un chemisier - a blouse

une jupe - a skirt

une écharpe - a scarf

un bracelet en or - a gold bracelet

des chaussures - shoes

une attente - an expectation

rejeter - to reject
pleurer - to cry
se plaindre - to complain
renouveler - to renew, to replace
une garde-robe - a wardrobe
démodé - old fashioned
un échec - a failure
un porte-monnaie - a wallet
déprimer - to depress
faire les magasins - to shop
un pull-over - a jumper, pull-over
des sandales - sandals
un mécanicien - a mechanic
récupérer quelqu'un - to pick up someone
à **tout à l'heure** - see you soon
un chapeau - a hat
a**u lieu de** - instead of
un placard - a locker, placard
des chaussures à talons hauts - high heeled shoes
impeccable - flawless
a**u fond** - at button, in the end
une vitrine - a showcase, shop window
une intention - an intention
affreux / affreuse - awful
de tout façon - anyway
haute qualité - high quality
pour **plusieurs occasions** - on several occasions
une robe - a dress
essayer - to try
une tenue - an outfit
prêt-à-porter - ready to wear
précisément - exactly
rendre - to return
un pantalon - pants
un blouson - a jacket

un manteau - a coat

une vendeuse - a saleswoman

une cabine - a fitting room

une carte bancaire - a bank card

un bon de réduction - a discount coupon

revenir - to come back

réessayer - to try again

un solde du compte - an account balance

bloquer - to block

Comprehension Questions

Sélectionnez une seule réponse pour chaque question.

1. Pourquoi Charlotte a pris le chapeau de son père ?

    A. Elle n'a pas réussi à trouver le sien.

    B. Elle adore porter des vêtements masculins.

    C. Elle préfère la mode des années 80.

    D. Son père a un style impeccable.

2. Pourquoi Charlotte ressent-elle de la crainte ?

    A. Elle est endettée.

    B. Elle a dépensé beaucoup d'argent.

    C. Elle a peur de réaliser son rêve.

    D. Elle a peur de quitter sa zone de confort

3. Pourquoi Charlotte toujours « fini endettée » ?

    A. Elle emprunte de l'argent à ses parents.

    B. Elle donne de l'argent à une association caritative.

    C. Elle a un petit salaire.

    D. Elle fait beaucoup de shopping.

4. Que porte Charlotte pour son interview ?

    A. Elle porte un chemisier, une jupe et une belle écharpe rouge.

    B. Elle porte un pantalon, une écharpe et un blouson.

    C. Elle porte une robe et des chaussures à talons hauts.

5. À qui appartiennent les sandales confortables ?

    A. Charlotte.

    B. Son amie.

    C. Sa mère.

D. Son père.

Grammar notes

3 ways to express possession

There are 3 ways to express possession in French:

- **être à** + **noun** (or accentuated pronoun) or **appartenir à** + **noun** (or accentuated pronoun).

*Ce livre est **à moi** ! - That book is mine!*

*Cette maison appartient **à toi** ! - This house is yours!*

- **Possessive adjectives**

*J'ai perdu **mes** clés. - I have lost my keys.*

*Prends **tes** valises. - Take your suitcases.*

- **Possessive pronouns**

Possessive pronouns are used to replace the noun and the possessive adjective at the same time. You'll learn more about them in the next grammar note.

*J'aime bien notre voiture, mais j'envie **la leur** ! - I like our car, but, I am jealous of theirs!*

Possessive pronouns

Many French students have wondered the same question. What exactly is a possessive pronoun in French? Is it like the word "*mon*" in "*mon chat*", or like "*mien*" in "*C'est le mien*". Most of the learners feel confused at first. In fact, "*mon*" is a possessive adjective, while "*mien*" is a possessive pronoun.

Possessive pronouns replace the noun and the word (usually adjective) that indicates belonging. Instead of repeating "*my dog*" all day long, occasionally we can replace it with "mine" instead. "Mine" incorporates both words, the possessive adjective and the noun (mon + chien).

C'est mon chien. C'est le mien.

C'est ma chatte. C'est la mienne.

French possessive pronouns are equivalent to English pronouns (mine, ours, yours, his, hers, its, and theirs). However, the agreement issue is what makes a significant difference between French and English. French possessive pronouns need to match the noun in number and gender, as well as to have the appropriate definite article in front.

Personal pronouns	English possessive pronouns	The possessed object is masculine, singular	The possessed object is feminine, singular	The possessed object is masculine, plural	The possessed object is feminine, plural
Je	Mine	Le mien	La mienne	Les miens	Les miennes
Tu	Yours	Le tien	La tienne	Les tiens	Les tiennes

Il/Elle	His/her/its	Le sien	La sienne	Les siens	Les siennes
Nous	Ours	Le nôtre	La nôtre	Les nôtres	Les nôtres
Vous	Yours	Le vôtre	La vôtre	Les vôtres	Les vôtres
Ils/Elles	Theirs	Le leur	La leur	Les leurs	Les leurs

Another difference that puzzles most French beginners, is that French possessive pronouns don't care about the gender of the *owner*. They agree with what they describe, not with the person who owns that thing. It can take up time to comprehend since English possessive pronouns take the gender of the owner into consideration.

For example, *"le sien"* refers to *his* or *hers*, but is only used to replace masculine singular nouns. *"La sienne"* will be used to replace feminine singular nouns. *"Les siens"* replace masculine, plural nouns and *"les siennes"* feminine plural nouns. In English, whether the noun is singular or plural the form remains the same.

Let's see some examples.

The object possessed is masculine, singular (le vélo). You see from the examples that whether the owner is masculine or feminine, it doesn't have an impact on the possessive pronoun form.

C'est le vélo de Marie ? – 'Oui, c'est le sien.' 'Is that Marie's bike?' – 'Yes, it's hers.'

C'est le vélo de Lucas ? – 'Oui, c'est le sien.' 'Is that Lucas's bike?' – 'Yes, it's his.'

The form changes, only if the possessed object is feminine, or plural.

C'est la maison d'Isabelle ? - Oui, c'est la sienne. Is that Isabelle's house? - Yes, it's hers.

C'est la maison de Lucas ? - Oui, c'est la sienne. Is that Lucas's bike? - Yes, it's his.

Possessive Adjectives vs Possessive Pronouns

In the previous chapter, you had the chance to learn about possessive adjectives. Now you are all set to compare them with possessive pronouns. So, what's the difference?

Possessive adjectives

- describes the noun.
- stands in front of the noun.

Possessive pronouns

- replaces the noun.
- stands alone.

A possessive pronoun actually gathers the meanings of both words, *a noun + adjective*, and replaces both of them.

For each possessive adjective there's an equivalent possessive pronoun. We can say that the possessive adjective *"ma"* corresponds to the possessive pronoun *"la mienne"*.

- Ma - possessive adjective (fem., singular) - la mienne - possessive pronoun (fem., singular) - mine.
- Mon - possessive adjective (masc., singular) - le mien - possessive pronoun (masc. singular).
- Ta - possessive adjective (masc. singular) - la tienne - possessive pronoun (masc., singular) - yours.
- ton possessive adjective (masc. singular) - le tien - possessive pronoun (masc., singular) - yours.

C'est ma valise. C'est la mienne. - That's my suitcase. It's mine.

C'est ton chien. C'est le tien. - That's your dog. It's yours.

Key takeaways

- **There are 3 ways to express possession in French: être à + noun** (or accentuated pronoun) or appartenir à + noun (or accentuated pronoun), **possessive adjectives** and **possessive pronouns**.
- Possessive pronouns replace the noun and the adjective that indicate belonging.
- The difference between the possessive adjective and pronoun is that adjectives describe the noun and stand in front of the noun, while pronouns replace the noun and stand alone.
- French possessive pronouns need to match the noun in number and gender, as well as to have the appropriate definite article in front.
- **La mienne, le mien, les miennes, les miens** correspond to the English possessive pronoun "mine".
- **La tienne, le tien, les tiennes, les tiens** correspond to English possessive pronoun "yours".
- **La sienne, le sien, les siennes, les siens** correspond to English possessive pronoun "his/her/its".
- **La nôtre, le nôtre, les nôtres** correspond to English possessive pronoun "ours".
- **La vôtre, le vôtre, les vôtres** correspond to English possessive pronoun "yours".
- **La leur, le leur, les leurs** correspond to English possessive pronoun "theirs".

Bravo! You are progressing quickly. So far, you covered the main grammar points in French. In the next chapter, you'll learn how to tell stories from what happened on the subway to your own life story.

Chapter 7: Telling someone about a dream

« Rien n'est plus vivant qu'un souvenir. »
- Federico Garcia Lorka

All fairytales begin the same way, but each of them finishes differently. Okay, this didn't turn out to be like Tolstoy's most famous sentence *"All happy families are alike, but every unhappy family is unhappy in its way"*. Essentially, we were trying to point out that all French stories begin the same way with *"Il était une fois"*, but each of them hopefully finishes differently. At least the good ones.

Telling stories is a social skill. From what happened at work, to a little episode from the subway or last night's dream. Telling a story is an everyday daunting task. People like good storytellers, so pay attention to this chapter.

If you want to be a good storyteller in French, you need to master past tenses and relative pronouns. Past tenses - because all stories happen in the past, and relative pronouns - because they help you connect ideas.

In French, telling a story requires two past tenses, *Passé Composé and Imperfect*. In the following chapter, you'll learn the imperfect, which is used to describe repeated actions, states or serves to describe a background process. If you are new to imperfect, skip to the grammar notes part before you read the story.

Un étranger dans le rêve

Il était une fois une jeune femme. Elle habitait dans un pays très loin de sa famille. Chaque nuit elle **rêvait** d'un étranger qui l'**amenait** dans son **enfance**. Il venait **habillé** en blanc, et **d'une voix douce** lui demandait de le suivre. Elle avait une confiance énorme. Ils **marchaient** dans le ciel, comme si c'était **une rue piétonne**, pour **traverser** les années de **souvenir.** L'étranger lui montrait **le village** où elle a **grandi**, la maison où elle a fait ses **premiers pas**, la première **plage** où elle a appris à nager. La première fois, elle regardait et ne **reconnaissait** rien. L'étranger lui demanda **doucement** : « Qu'est-ce que tu vois ? »

Tout à coup, elle **s'est rappelée**. C'était le village où elle passait ses **vacances d'été.**

« Je veux y aller, la femme a crié.

– Tout est possible. Nous sommes **près de** ta maison, répond l'étranger. Est-ce que tu **reconnais** ta maison ?

– Pas encore. Je cherche une maison dont la porte est rouge, répond la femme.

– Je vois les maisons dont les portes sont bleues, mais aucune à la porte rouge. Tu te souviens d'autre chose?

– La maison que mes grands-parents ont achetée est **énorme**. Et aussi, elle se trouve **à côté d'**une grande **forêt**.

– Il y a plusieurs maisons à côté de la forêt. C'est laquelle ?

– Voilà, je la vois. C'est celle-là. Allons-y. »

Toute ma famille était dans **le jardin**. Moi aussi, j'étais là. Justement, j'étais petite.

« Qui est cette femme-là ? me demande l'étranger.

– C'est ma mère. La femme qui aime raconter des histoires. »

L'étranger voit trois hommes dans le jardin. Il me demande « Lequel et ton père ? »

– C'est l'homme qui **joue de la guitare**. Mon père **adorait** jouer de la musique et chanter. Ensemble, mes parents avaient le pouvoir de **donner vie à** chaque **conte de fées**.

– Et la petite fille qui danse ? »

La femme rigole.

« C'est moi la petite fille qui danse. J'avais 4 ans là. Ici, j'ai mangé tous les gâteaux que maman a faits. Il n'y avait plus rien pour mon frère.

– Tu as un frère ?

– Le garçon qui est entré, c'est mon frère. Ici, il a vu **une araignée** dont il a eu peur. Il va commencer à crier dans quelques minutes. Il n'a jamais **cessé** d'avoir peur.

– Et qui sont les gens **âgés** ?

– Ce sont mes grands-parents. Ici, mon grand-père a mangé **les poires** que ma grand-mère avait achetées **au marché**. Elle est **fâchée**, parce que maintenant elle ne peut pas faire la tarte aux poires. Ils **se disputaient** souvent, mais toujours avec amour.

– **C'est l'heure de** partir. »

Elle était triste de quitter sa famille. Puisqu'elle savait que c'était la dernière fois qu'elle voyait cette période de son enfance. Ils marchaient de nouveau dans le ciel. Cette fois, elle a finalement vu **la mer, les vagues, la plage**. Sur la plage, deux personnes, elle et son père. C'était le jour où la jeune femme a appris à **nager**. « On y va. » dit son père.

Mais, elle reste sur la plage et hésite à entrer dans l'eau. Le problème c'est que la semaine précédente, elle a **failli se noyer**. C'est la raison pour laquelle son père était déterminé à lui **apprendre** à nager. Son père savait très bien que c'est important de **se confronter à ses peurs**. Maintenant elle le sait. Mais ce jour-là, elle **détestait** son père. Deux heures après, elle nageait. Il fallait que son père la sorte de force. C'était le jour où la jeune fille a surpassé **ses peurs**. Depuis ce jour, elle adorait nager. À tel point qu'elle est devenue **championne nationale de natation**.

Le matin elle **avait l'impression** d'être un enfant de 5 ans qui était encore avec sa famille. C'étaient des jours **sans souci**.

Résumé de l'histoire

La famille d'une jeune femme lui manquait parce qu'elle habitait très loin. Chaque nuit, elle rêvait d'un étranger qui l'amenait à son enfance. L'étranger lui a montré le village où elle a grandi, la maison où elle a fait ses premiers pas, la première plage où elle a appris à nager.

Dans le rêve, elle se rend dans son ancienne maison où elle voit sa famille, ses parents, son frère et ses grands-parents. Dans son rêve, elle visite le jour où elle a appris à nager avec son père. Elle avait très peur d'aller dans l'eau, parce qu'elle pouvait se noyer. Son père l'a aidée à surmonter sa peur. Ce jour, elle a appris à nager et puis elle est devenue championne nationale de natation.

Synopsis of the story

A young woman missed her family because she lived so far away. Every night she dreamed of a stranger who took her back to her childhood. The stranger showed her the village where she grew up, the house where she took her first steps, the first beach where she learned to swim.

In the dream, she goes to her old house where she sees her family, her parents, her brother and her grandparents. In her dream, she visits the day she learned to swim with her father. She was very afraid to go into the water, because she could drown. His father helped her overcome her fear. That day, she learned to swim and then she became a national swimming champion.

Vocabulary and Expressions

rêver - to dream

amener - to bring

une enfance - childhood

habillé - dressed

une voix - a voice

doux / douce - sweet, soft

marcher - to walk

une rue piétonne - a pedestrian street

traverser - to go through

un souvenir - a memory

un village - a village

grandir - to grow up

un pas - a step

une plage - a beach

reconnaître - to recognize

tout à coup - all of a sudden

se rappeler - to remember

les vacances d'été - summer vacation

être près de - to be near
enorme - enormous
un foret - a forest
un jardin - a garden
jouer de la guitare - to play the guitar
adorer - to adore
donner vie à - to give life to
une conte de fées - a fairytale
rigoler - to laugh
une araignée - a spider
cesser - to stop
âgé / âgée - old
une poire - a pear
au marché - at the market
fâché / fâchée - angry
se disputer - to argue
C'est l'heure de - It's time
la mer - the sea
une vague - a wave
faillir se noyer - almost drown
confronter ses peurs - to confront one's fears
détester - to hate
surmonter ses peurs - to overcome one's fears
championne nationale de natation - national swimming champion
avoir l'impression de - to have the impression of
sans souci - carefree

Comprehension Questions

Sélectionnez une seule réponse pour chaque question.

1) Où le personnage principal a-t-il voyagé dans le rêve ?
    A. À la plage, au village, à la maison de son enfance.
    B. À la maison de son enfance, à la plage.
    C. À la maison de ses grands-parents, au village, à la plage.
2) Qui a mangé toutes les poires ?
    A. Son frère.

B. Grande-mère.

C. Grand-père.

D. Personne.

3) Pourquoi son père est-il déterminé à lui apprendre à nager ?

  A. Elle avait peur d'entrer dans l'eau.

  B. Il voulait qu'elle devienne une championne de natation.

  C. Parce qu'elle a failli se noyer la semaine précédente.

  D. Parce qu'il voulait qu'elle surmonte ses peurs.

4) Qui était dans le jardin de son ancienne maison ?

  A. Ses grands-parents, sa mère, son père et son frère.

  B. Ses parents et ses grands-parents.

  C. Ses parents, ses grands-parents, son frère et elle à l'âge de cinq ans.

  D. Son grand-père, son frère et ses parents.

5) Que signifie « revivre un conte de fées » ?

  A. Vivre comme dans un conte de fées.

  B. Raconter une histoire de façon vivante.

  C. Lire souvent des histoires.

  D. Écrire une histoire.

Grammar notes

L'imparfait

The French imperfect (*l'imparfait*) is a descriptive past tense that describes ongoing actions or repeated states. Just think about how all stories start in French (*Il était une fois*). You'll notice that they all use the imperfect. It's because all stories are filled with descriptions of past states or some repeated situations.

The imperfect corresponds to more English structures such as "used to" and "would", the past progressive, and past simple occasionally.

Je marchais dans la rue. - I was walking down the street.

We use French imperfect to:

- **to express habits, repeated actions or states.**
- *Tous les jours, elle lisait un livre. - Every day, she was reading a book.*
- **to describe (time, weather, age, feelings).**

    Il faisait beau pendant mes vacances. - The weather was nice during my holiday.

    Quand il avait 5 ans, il n'arrêtait pas de parler. - When he was 5, he couldn't stop talking.

- **to emphasize the duration.**

J'espérais le voir avant son départ. - I was hoping to see him before he leaves.

- **to describe a background process,** with the *passé composé*.

    J'étais à la plage quand l'avion est passé. - I was at the beach when the airplane passed by.

How to conjugate the imperfect tense in French

French Imperfect tense is quite easily formed, as both regular and irregular verbs are formed the same way.

To form the imperfect tense, take the 1st person plural form in the present tense, drop the -ons, and add the following endings. The only irregular verb in imperfect is *"être"* ("to be") as in the present tense *"nous sommes"* there's no -*ons* to drop.

In the table below, you'll see imperfect endings, imperfect conjugation of the verb "dormir" and the irregular verb "être".

Pronouns	Imperfect Endings	Dormir	Irregular verb être
Je	- ais	- dormais	- étais
Tu	- ais	- dormais	- étais
Il/Elle	- ait	- dormait	- était
Nous	- ions	- dormions	- étions
Vous	- iez	- dormiez	- étiez
Ils/Elles	- aient	- dormaient	- étaient

Relative Pronouns

If you want to join two sentences in French, you are in desperate need of relative pronouns.

A French relative pronoun can be translated into who, what, that, which, whose, where, and when. But, while in English relative pronouns are optional, in French they are obligatory.

J'ai acheté un appartement. Cet appartement a deux pièces. - I bought an apartment. This apartment has two rooms.

When you join the sentences, the second sentence's subject can be replaced with a relative pronoun:

J'ai acheté un appartement qui a deux pièces. - I bought an apartment which has two rooms.

French relative pronouns are **qui, que, où, dont.** We'll examine them separately.

Qui

"Qui" is both:

- a relative pronoun.

- a question word (who).

When used as a relative pronoun, it can mean *who* or *what*. The most important thing to remember about *"qui"*, is that it replaces a subject in a sentence.

C'est une fille. Cette fille danse très bien. - It's a girl. That girl dances very well.

Here we have two independent clauses listed. The word that repeats in both sentences is *"fille"*. If we want to avoid repeating the word *"fille"*, we can use the relative pronoun *"**qui**"* and get a complex sentence like this.

C'est une fille qui danse très bien. - It's a girl who dances very well.

Let's see more examples.

C'est Marie qui a fait ça.- It's Marie who did it.

La chanteuse qui chante très bien en chinois, c'est Isabelle. - The singer who sings very well in Chinese is Isabelle.

Que

"Que" is used when the noun replaced is a direct object, whether it's a person or thing.

C'est le cahier. J'ai acheté le cahier hier.

In the above example we have two sentences. The repeated word is *"cahier"*, so if we want to avoid repeating that word, we can make one sentence out of those two, by using the direct object *"que"*.

C'est le cahier que j'ai acheté hier. - It's the notebook I bought yesterday.

"Que" contracts to *"**qu'**"* before a vowel sound.

J'ai vu la maison qu'il va acheter.

*Note that **"qui"** does not contract before a vowel sound, unlike que.

Où

The relative pronoun *"**où**"* indicates a place and is translated as "where". It can also indicate a place in time.

Où - where

La fromagerie où j'ai acheté le brie est à la campagne. - The cheese shop where I bought the brie is in the countryside.

Où - when

Il pleuvait le jour où elles sont arrivées. -It was raining the day they arrived.

Dont

French students find *"dont"* to be the most challenging relative pronoun in French. "Dont" is used to replace people or objects coming after the preposition *"de"*.

Here is an example of a person preceded by *"de"*:

Tu vois cet homme ? - Do you see that man?

*Je t'ai parlé **de** cet homme. - I spoke to you about that man.*

*C'est l'homme **dont** je t'ai parlé. - That's the man I talked to you about.*

J'ai besoin d'une fourchette. - I need a fork.

La fourchette est sur la table. - The fork is on the table.

La fourchette dont j'ai besoin est sur la table. - The fork that I need is on the table.

Understanding the rules for using "*dont*" is not as difficult as knowing which verbs and expressions are followed by "*de*".

Interrogatives (Lequel, Laquelle, Lesquels, Lesquelles)

Lequel, means "which one" and can be:

- an interrogative pronoun.
- A relative pronoun.

As an interrogative pronoun, it is equivalent to the interrogative adjective "*quel*". Just like possessive pronouns replace both the noun and the adjective, "*lequel*" replaces replaces

quel + noun.

The same way as "*quel*", "*lequel*" has four different forms depending on the gender and number of the noun it replaces.

Singular, masculine	Singular, feminine	Plural, masculine	Plural, feminine
lequel	laquelle	lesquels	lesquelles

Take a look at these examples to see how "*lequel*" replaces "*quel* + noun".

Quel crayon veux-tu ? Lequel veux-tu ? > Which crayon do you want? Which one do you want?

Je veux la banane là-bas. Laquelle ? > I want the banana over there. Which one?

As a relative pronoun, "lequel" substitutes an inanimate object of a preposition. When the preposition is applied to a person, use "qui".

Take a look at the following examples.

Le cahier dans lequel j'ai écrit... > The book in which I wrote...

La ville à laquelle je rêve... > The town about which I'm dreaming...

Key takeaways

- The French imperfect (*l'imparfait*) is a descriptive past tense that describes ongoing actions or repeated states. It's often used to represent the background process in contrast to another action in Past Tense.
- The imperfect corresponds to English structures such as "used to" and "would", and the past progressive.
- To form the imperfect tense, take the 1st person plural form in the present tense, drop the **-ons**, and add the following endings **(ais, ais, ait, ions, iez, aient)**. The only irregular verb in imperfect is "être" (**étais, étais, était, étions, étiez, étaient**).
- Use relative pronouns (**qui, que, dont, où**) to join two sentences in French.
- "***Qui***" is both a relative pronoun and a question word (who). When used as a relative pronoun, it can mean "who" or "what". The most important thing to remember about "qui" is that it replaces a subject in a sentence. "Qui" never contracts in front of the vowel sound.
- "***Que***" is used when the noun replaced is a direct object, whether it's a person or a thing. "Que" contracts to "qu' " before a vowel sound.
- "Que" is a direct object (person or thing), while "qui" is a subject (person or thing).
- The relative pronoun "**où**" indicates places or places in time. It can be translated as "where" or "when".
- "***Dont***" is used to replace people or objects coming after the preposition "de".
- "***Lequel***", "***laquelle***", "***lesquels***", "***lesquelles***" all mean "which one" and can be used as interrogative pronouns or relative pronouns.

In the following chapter, you will learn a wide range of vocabulary related to your profession, education, and career.

Chapter 8: Finding a job

« Faire ce que tu aimes, c'est la liberté. Aimer ce que tu fais, c'est le bonheur. »
- Raphaëlle Giordano

Ever since we were children, everyone has been asking us the same question *"What do you want to be when you grow up?"* We pretended to be artists, doctors, and cashiers to find a profession that suited us. Just think how much time and energy we spend on searching for a job, discussing our education or our profession. That's why this topic made its place in our book.

The following story introduces words that describe the whole area of job search. Once again, you'll open up more possibilities for conversations in French and you'll also learn how to use indirect object pronouns.

Un travail de rêve

Luca est un jeune homme qui a changé trois fois d'**emploi** en un an. Il était **bénévole**, il a travaillé comme **gestionnaire**, comme **enseignant de langues étrangères**, et finalement il a **quitté son emploi** et est devenu **chômeur**. Luca est **diplômé** de la faculté de **gestion**. Immédiatement après ses études, il a commencé à chercher un emploi. Il n'a pas pu en trouver un facilement. Il avait un **CV**, une **lettre de recommandation** et a **postulé** pour une **dizaine** d'emplois. Cependant, il était un étudiant **diplômé** sans expérience et personne ne voulait **l'embaucher**. Puis, Luca **s'est inscrit à pôle emploi**. C'est l'endroit où on va pour chercher un emploi en France. Là, il l'a trouvé. Il a travaillé pour une entreprise qui vend des **matelas** pendant 6 mois. Il les vendait chaque jour. En tant que **bénévole,** il voulait beaucoup apprendre.

Son stage professionnel s'est terminé après 6 mois. Maintenant Luca **avait l'espoir de** pouvoir trouver un emploi **convenable**. Il cherchait mais il n'y avait pas beaucoup d'emplois **sur le marché du travail. Au fil du temps**, il a trouvé. Il a trouvé le poste de gestionnaire des ventes dans une entreprise qui **exporte** du fromage. Il n'aimait pas trop cet emploi.

Son parcours professionnel l'a aidé à avoir un entretien. Après avoir envoyé son CV et sa lettre de motivation, deux semaines **se sont écoulées.** Luca a commencé à **s'inquiéter**. Cependant, ce jour-là, il était invité à un entretien, et on lui a posé de nombreuses questions. Luca a répondu à toutes les questions **avec confiance**. Ils lui ont **offert** deux options, **un travail à temps plein ou à mi-temps**.

Il avait son **bureau** où il travaillait avec **les clients**. Et en plus, il avait pour **tâche** de **superviser la production**. Il a reçu **un salaire moyen**. Son chef lui avait **promis une promotion**. Il **bénéficiait** d'un mois **de congés payés** et **d'une allocation sociale.** Au début, Luca avait beaucoup d'enthousiasme et faisait souvent **des heures supplémentaires** pour terminer le travail.

Cependant, après 5 mois, Luca n'a pas reçu la promotion promise. Il était déjà **épuisé** et a décidé de prendre deux semaines de **repos**. Il est **allé voir** son chef, mais le chef a refusé.

Découragé, Luca a continué à travailler, **venait toujours à l'heure** mais ne faisait plus **d'heures supplémentaires**. Son patron l'a **remarqué**. Un jour, il lui a dit qu'il **avait l'impression** que Luca travaillait moins **dur**. Luca **croyait** à nouveau **obtenir** une promotion. Alors il a continué à travailler de plus longues heures chaque jour. Mais, le mois suivant, il n'a pas reçu son salaire. L'entreprise était temporairement **en difficulté financière** et aucun des **travailleurs** n'a reçu son salaire. Luca était complètement **déçu**. Le lendemain, il a **démissionné**.

Puis il a trouvé **un travail en ligne** pour enseigner le français. Il pouvait **travailler à domicile**, il avait **des horaires de travail flexibles**. Le salaire était bas, mais il voulait essayer. Cependant, Luca n'aimait pas être enseignant. Il se rappelait de son enfance, où il rêvait d'être **pompier, opticien, avocat** ou **boulanger**. Cependant, il aimait le plus devenir boulanger. Quand il avait du temps, il **confectionnait** diverses **pâtisseries** et **gâteaux**. Sa famille les adorait. Les jours passaient et Luca rêvait de faire des pâtisseries. Il rentrait à la maison motivé pour essayer une nouvelle recette. Tous les soirs, il faisait de **la pâte**.

Son meilleur ami lui a **conseillé** d'ouvrir une boulangerie. Luca était **sceptique**. Il n'avait pas d'argent pour l'ouvrir. Avoir une boulangerie **coûte cher**. Son ami était **persévérant**. Il a trouvé **une fondation** qui aide **les entreprises en démarrage**. Chaque année, elle **accordait** de l'argent à des jeunes **entrepreneurs** pour créer une entreprise. Luca était maintenant convaincu.

Il a **rempli les formulaires**, les a **envoyés** et a attendu. Il était **impatient**. Un jour, il a reçu **un e-mail de confirmation**. Son idée a été **sélectionnée**. Il a reçu un financement de l'État pour ouvrir une petite boulangerie à Paris. Il l'a ouvert et a ressenti une vraie joie pour la première fois. Enfin, il a le travail qu'il aime.

Résumé de l'histoire

Luca est un jeune homme qui a fini son université et a commencé à chercher un emploi. Tout d'abord, il était stagiaire dans une entreprise qui vend des matelas. Son second emploi était dans une entreprise qui exporte du fromage. Quand son entreprise finit endettée, il démissionne. À la fin, il travaillait comme enseignant de langues. Il commence à se souvenir de son enfance et des métiers qu'il aimait. Il se rend compte qu'il voulait devenir boulanger. Cependant, avoir une boulangerie est cher. Son ami l'a aidé à trouver un moyen d'ouvrir sa boulangerie sans investir son propre argent.

Synopsis of the story

Luca is a young man who just finished university and started looking for a job. First, he was an intern in a company that sells mattresses. His second job was in a company that exports cheese. He quit his job when the company went into debt and was unable to pay salaries. After that, he became a language teacher. He begins to reminisce about his childhood and the jobs he loved. He realizes that he wanted to become a baker. However, owning a bakery is expensive. With the help of a friend, he finds a way to open his bakery without investing his own money.

Vocabulary and Expressions

un emploi - a job

un / une bénévole - a volunteer

un gestionnaire - a manager

professeur de langues étrangères - professor of foreign languages

quitter son travail - to quit a job

chômeur - unemployed person

diplômé de - graduated from

une lettre de recommandation - a recommendation letter

postuler pour un emploi - to apply for a job

embaucher - to hire

pôle emploi - job center

s'inscrire - to register

un matelas - a mattress

un stage professionnel - a professional internship

avoir l'espoir de - to have hope

convenable - suitable

sur le marché du travail - on the job market

au fil du temps - over time

exporter - to export

un parcours professionnel - a career path

s'écouler - to run out

s'inquiéter - to worry

avec confiance - with confidence

offrir - to offer

un travail à temps plein - a full-time job

un travail à mi-temps - a part-time job

un bureau - an office

un client / une cliente - a client

une tâche - a task

superviser la production - to monitor the production

reçevoir - to receive

un salaire moyen - an average salary

promettre une promotion - to promise a promotion

bénéficier - to benefit

des congés payés - paid vacation
une allocation sociale - a social allowance
repos - rest
aller voir - to go and see, to visit
venir à l'heure - to come on time
des heures supplémentaires - overtime
remarquer - to notice
avoir l'impression - to have the impression that
dur - difficult
croire - to believe
obtenir - to obtain
en difficulté financière - in financial difficulty
un travailleur / une travailleuse - a worker, en employee
déçu / déçue - disappointed
demissionner - to resign, to quit
un travail en ligne - an online job
travailler à domicile - to work from home
des horaires flexibles - flexible hours
un pompier - a firefighter
un opticien - an optician
un avocat - a lawyer
un boulanger - a baker
confectionner - to make
une pâtisserie - a pastry
un gâteau - a cake
une pâte - a dough
conseiller - to advise
sceptique - sceptical
coûter cher - to be costly
persévérant - persevering
une fondation - a foundation
une entreprise en démarrage - start-up business
accorder - to grant
un entrepreneur / une entrepreneure - an entrepreneur
remplir les formulaires - to fill the forms

envoyer - to send
impatient - impatient, anxious, hasty
un email de confirmation - a confirmation email
sélectionner - to select

Comprehension Questions

Sélectionnez une seule réponse pour chaque question.

1. Quels emplois Luca a-t-il exercés ?
    A. Bénévole, gestionnaire et boulanger.
    B. Gestionnaire, enseignant de français et chômeur.
    C. Bénévole, gestionnaire, enseignant de langues étrangères et chômeur.
    D. Gestionnaire, gestionnaire des ventes et enseignant de langues étrangères.

2. Pourquoi personne ne voulait embaucher Luca au début ?
    A. Luca n'avait pas de diplôme.
    B. Luca n'avait pas d'expérience.
    C. Luca était chômeur.
    D. Luca n'avait pas de bonnes notes à l'université.

3. Pourquoi Luca a-t-il fait des heures supplémentaires à la fromagerie ?
    A. Parce qu'il aimait manger du fromage.
    B. Pour recevoir une promotion.
    C. Parce qu'il n'avait rien d'autre à faire.
    D. Pour prendre des vacances de deux semaines.

4. Y avait-il beaucoup d'opportunités sur le marché du travail ?
    A. Oui.
    B. Non.

5. Luca a des horaires de travail flexibles pour quel travail ?
    A. Gestionnaire à l'entreprise des fromages.
    B. Bénévole à l'entreprise qui produit des matelas.
    C. Enseignant de langues étrangères.
    D. Boulanger.

6. Pourquoi Luca était-il sceptique lorsque son ami lui a proposé d'ouvrir une boulangerie ?
    A. Il n'avait pas d'argent.
    B. Il ne voulait pas trouver un nouvel emploi.
    C. Il ne voulait pas être boulanger.

D. Il a décidé de rester au même lieu de travail.

Grammar notes

Object Pronouns

As you know, pronouns are words which replace nouns. Now, object pronouns are words which replace object nouns in a sentence. Let's begin with an English example.

I eat pizza. -> I eat it.

I look at the man. -> I look at him.

In French, there are two kinds of object pronouns:

- direct object (used for verbs without prepositions)

Je mange la pizza. Je la mange.

- indirect object (used with verbs with the preposition à)

J'écris à mes amis. Je leur écris.

Direct Object Pronouns

Direct object pronouns are used for verbs without prepositions in French. Direct means there is no preposition following the verb and preceding the noun. Language defines a direct object as a noun that receives action from a verb.

For example:

Je vois la fille. - I see the girl.

Je la vois. - I see her.

Take a look at the table and see which French direct object pronouns correspond to English.

Personal pronouns	Direct object pronouns	English pronouns
Je	**me / m'**	me
Tu	**te/ t'**	you
Il	**le**	him
Elle	**la**	her
Nous	**nous**	us
Vous	**vous**	you
Ils/Elles	**les**	them

Notice how *"me"* and *"te"* change to *m'* and *t'*, in front of a vowel or mute H.

As you notice in the following examples, the object (le film, Anne and Pierre) are replaced by the direct object pronouns (le, la, le).

Je regarde le film. Je le regarde. - *I watch the movie. I watch it.*

Je connais Anne. Je la connais. - *I know Anne. I know her.*

Je connais Pierre. Je le connais. I know Pierre. l know him.

Typical verbs requiring direct object

Following are examples of verbs that take a direct object without the preposition *à*.

- **aimer** - to like, to love
- **acheter** - to buy
- **écouter** - to listen
- **attendre** - to wait
- **inviter** - to invite
- **comprendre** - to understand
- **prende** - to take
- **connaître** - to know

Indirect Object Pronouns

So, first, let's solve this doubt.

What is the indirect object and why do we need them at all?

Indirect objects determine the recipients, or what is affected, by the action of the verb. In other words, it's to or for whom the action occurs.

Je parle à Lucas. - *I'm talking to Lucas.*

To whom am I talking? To Lucas.

Indirect object pronouns, on the other hand, replace the names of people and nouns, placed after the preposition *à* (to). You'll be able to spot them easily.

Je l'ai donné à Mathieu. Je le lui ai donné. - *I gave it to Mathieu. I gave it to him.*

As you notice, "à Mathieu" is replaced by the indirect object "*lui*".

In the following table, you'll be able to see all the indirect object pronouns.

Personal pronouns	Indirect object pronouns	English pronouns
Je	**me / m'**	me
Tu	**te/ t'**	you
Il/Elle	**lui**	him, her

Nous	**nous**	us
Vous	**vous**	you
Ils/Elles	**leur**	them

Notice how *"me"* and *"te"* change to *m'* and *t'*, in front of a vowel or mute H.

The French word *"lui"* functions as two different types of pronouns.

Lui replaces masculine and feminine nouns in the singular form:
- *Je parle à Paul. I'm talking to Paul. → Je lui parle. I'm talking to him.*
- *Je parle à Marie. I'm talking to Marie.→ Je lui parle. I'm talking to her.*

Leur replaces masculine or feminine nouns in the plural form.
- *J'écris à mes amis. I'm writing to my friends. → Je leur écris. I'm writing to them.*

Typical verbs requiring the preposition à

Parler à - to talk to someone

Demander à - to ask someone

Dire à - to say to someone

Écrire à - to write to someone

Téléphoner à - to call someone

Offrir à - to offer to someone

Key takeaways
- In French, there are two kinds of object pronouns: direct object (used for verbs without prepositions) and indirect object (used with verbs with the preposition *à*).
- **French direct objects** are: **me, te, le, la, nous, vous, les**.
- An indirect object determines the recipients, or what is affected, by the action of the verb. In other words, it's to or for whom/what the action occurs.
- **French indirect objects** are: **me, te, lui, nous, vous, leur**.
- *Me* and *te* change to *m'* and *t'*, in front of a vowel or mute h.

Finally, in the next chapter, you get to learn all about the future simple tense. Prepare to tell your French friends what you're planning for the future. It's time to dream big.

Chapter 9: Traveling

« Le plaisir est toujours passé ou futur, jamais présent. »
- Giacomo Leopardi

If you want to talk about your plans, predictions, future actions, and dreams, you need to master the future tense. In French, you can express the Future with the "Futur Proche" and the "Futur Simple". There is also the "Futur Antérieur", but you'll discover it in more advanced lessons.

In this chapter, you'll learn the future tense in its true form - Future Simple. For those who are unfamiliar with this tense, the verbs may seem strange at first. The Future Simple tense in French is fairly easy to form with regular verbs, but they also contain a few irregular ones. Make sure you read the grammar notes after or even before you read the story, as the majority of the story is told in the future tense.

Un voyage imaginaire

Maria vit dans une petite ville du **nord** de la Suède. Elle vit **seule** avec sa fille Lara, mais la voit **seulement** le soir. Elle travaille **dur du matin jusqu'au soir**. Elle **voudra** passer plus de temps avec sa fille. Le soir, les deux aiment parler de voyages. Sa fille aime **la neige**, mais **rêve d'**aller à la mer. Elle n'y est jamais allée. En effet, elle n'a jamais quitté sa petite ville. Lara **ouvre l'atlas** et trouve leur **prochaine** destination. **De telle manière**, elles ont déjà parcouru **la moitié du monde**. Maman lui dit qu'un jour elles partiront **vraiment**. Lara la croit.

Un soir, **avant** d'aller se coucher, maman lui dit: « Chère Lara, tu **feras tes valises** ce soir. Parce que dans une semaine, nous **irons** à la mer. »

Lara : Vraiment ? Lara était **ravie**. Et où allons-nous, maman ?

Maman : Nous déciderons ce soir. **Apporte**-moi l'atlas et nous découvrirons **un endroit** idéal.

Lara a immédiatement trouvé le pays.

Lara : Nous irons à Cuba.

Maman : Un excellent choix. Nous **devrons** d'abord acheter des billets. Nous **aurons besoin** de deux **billets aller-retour** pour **la semaine** prochaine.

Lara : Qu'est-ce qu'on **fera là-bas** ?

Maman: On **restera dans un hôtel** quatre **étoiles** et nous mangerons dans des **restaurants locaux**. Tous les matins, tu **te réveilleras** à sept heures. Je resterai un peu **au lit** et je **me lèverai** à sept heures et **demie**. Je prendrai ma douche et je m'habillerai. Ensuite, nous prendrons notre petit-déjeuner. Pendant notre petit-déjeuner, je lirai un peu et j'écouterai la radio. Ensuite, nous nous préparerons pour partir à la plage. Je me brosserai les dents, toi aussi, je me maquillerai, toi non. Nous **mettrons nos maillots de bain** et nous partirons. Tu **nageras,** moi je lirai un livre et je te regarderai. Tu resteras **pendant des heures** dans l'eau. Tu aimeras nager. Tu **joueras** avec **les enfants** cubains. À **midi**, nous irons déjeuner. Après le déjeuner, nous irons **faire la sieste** à l'hôtel. **Quelquefois**, tu me **convaincras** d'aller à la plage. Chaque jour, tu mangeras de **la pastèque, de la noix de coco et des mangues.** Le soir, nous **flânerons le long de la plage.**

Lara avait beaucoup de questions. Elle voulait tout savoir.

Lara : Combien de **valises** allons-nous **apporter** ?

Maman : Nous apporterons deux valises et je porterai **un sac à dos.**

Lara : Combien **coûteront** les billets ?

Maman : Je ne sais toujours pas, mais ne t'**inquiète** pas, ce ne sera pas très cher.

Lara : Comment allons-nous **nous rendre à l'aéroport** ?

Maman : Nous irons **d'abord** en ville **en train**. Là, nous **prendrons un taxi** pour l'aéroport **à la gare**.

Lara : Est-ce que nous nous **assoirons près de la fenêtre** ?

Maman : Nous prendrons **des sièges côté fenêtre** si tu le **souhaites**.

Lara : À quelle heure **sera le vol** ?

Maman : Il **aura lieu à** 11h.

Lara : Combien de temps prendra le vol ?

Maman : De la Suède à Cuba, il **faudra** 10 heures.

Lara : Qu'est-ce qu'on fera dans l'avion ?

Maman : Nous regarderons des films, lirons **des contes de fées** et dormirons.

Lara : Moi, je ne pourrai pas dormir. À quelle heure arriverons-nous ?

Maman : Nous arrivons à 9h du soir.

Lara : Que ferons-nous à l'aéroport ?

Maman : Nous **passerons** d'abord **le contrôle des passeports**, prendrons nos **bagages** et trouverons un taxi jusqu'à notre hôtel.

Lara : Et puis nous nous coucherons ?

Maman : Oui, ma **chérie.**

Lara : Quel temps fera-t-il à Cuba ?

Maman : Il fera beau tous les jours.

Lara : Trouverons-nous des amis ?

Maman : Nous y **aurons** beaucoup d'amis.

Lara : **Verrons**-nous des animaux ?

Maman : Bien sûr. Les plus vieilles **tortues** du monde y vivent. Tu **pourras** nager avec les tortues. Nous visiterons le zoo et nous verrons des lions, des girafes et des éléphants.

Lara : Est-ce que tu travailleras là-bas maman ?

Maman : Non, ma chérie. J'**aurai** beaucoup **de temps libre** et nous serons heureuses tous les jours. Nous jouerons à tous les **jeux** que tu aimes.

Lara : Combien de temps allons-nous rester à Cuba ?

Maman: Nous resterons un **mois** et si tu veux, **l'éternité.**

Lara : Maman, ce sera le plus beau des voyages.

Résumé de l'histoire

Maria vit seule avec sa fille Lara, au nord de la Suède. Elle travaille dur et ne passe pas beaucoup de temps avec sa fille. Chaque soir, maman et fille parlent de voyages. Sa fille n'a jamais vu la mer, et rêve d'y aller. Un soir, avant d'aller se coucher, maman lui dit de faire ses valises, parce qu'elles partent à la mer. Maria dit à sa fille de choisir la destination. La petite fille prend l'atlas et choisit Cuba. Avant de partir, la fille a plein de questions et sa mère lui répond patiemment.

Synopsis of the story

Maria lives alone with her daughter Lara, in the north of Sweden. She works hard and doesn't spend much time with her daughter. Every evening, mom and daughter talk about traveling. Her daughter has never seen the sea and dreams of going. One evening, before going to bed, mum told her to pack her bags because they are going to the sea. Maria tells her daughter to choose the destination. The little girl takes the atlas and chooses Cuba. Before leaving, the girl has lots of questions. Her mother is there to patiently answer all of them.

Vocabulary and Expressions

le nord - north

seul / seule - alone, single

seulement - only

travailler dur - to work hard

du matin jusqu'au soir - from the morning till the evening

voudra (vouloir) - future of the verb "vouloir"/ to want

la neige - the snow

rêver de faire qqch. - to dream to do something

ouvrir - to open

un atlas - an atlas

prochain / prochaine - next, upcoming

de telle manière - like, in such a way that

la moitié du monde - half of the world

avant - before

feras tes valises (faire ses valises) - future of the verb "faire", to pack one's suitcase

irons (aller) - future of the verb "aller" / to go

ravi / ravie - delighted, thrilled, pleased

apporter - to bring

un endroit - a place

devrons (devoir) - future of the verb "devoir" / have to, must

aurons besoin (avoir besoin) - future of the verb "avoir" / to need, to require

un billet aller-retour - a round-trip ticket

une semaine - a week

ferra (faire) - future of the verb "faire" / to do

là-bas - there

rester dans un hôtel - to stay in a hotel

une étoile - a star

locaux (local) - plural of the adjective local

se réveiller - to wake up

au lit - in bed

se lever - to get up

demi / demie - half

mettrons (mettre) - future of the verb "mettre" / to put

un maillot de bain - a swimming suit

nager - to swim

pendant des heures - for hours

jouer - to play

un enfant - a child

à midi - at noon

faire la sieste - to take a nap

quelquefois - sometimes, from time to time

convaincre - to convince

une pastèque - a watermelon

une noix de coco - a coconut

une mangue - a mango

flâner - to stroll

au long de la plage - along the beach

une valise - a suitcase

apporter - to bring

un sac à dos - a backpack

coûter - to cost

s'inquiéter - to worry

se rendre à l'aéroport - to get to the airport

d'abord - first of all, at first

en train - by train

prendre un taxi - to take a cab

une gare - a station

s'asseoir - to sit

près de - next to

une fenêtre - a window

un sièges - a seat

côté fenêtre - next to the window

souhaiter - to wish

sera (être) - future of the verb "être" / to be

un vol - a flight

avoir lieu - to take place

faudra (falloir) - future of the verbe "falloir" / need to, have to, must

un conte de fée - a fairytale

passer le contrôle des passeports - to go through the passport control

un bagage - a baggage

chéri / chérie - dear

aurons (avoir) - future of the verb "avoir" / to have

verrons (voir) - future of the verb "voir" / to see

une tortue - a turtle

pourras (pouvoir) - future of the verb "pouvoir" / can, may

aurai (avoir) - future of the verb "avoir" / to have

avoir du temps libre - to have free time

un jeu - a game

un mois - a month

une éternité - an eternity, a lifetime

Comprehension Questions

Sélectionnez une seule réponse pour chaque question.

1. La fille a-t-elle déjà voyagé ?
    A. Elle a parcouru la moitié du monde.
    B. Non, elle n'a jamais quitté son pays.
    C. Elle n'a jamais vu la mer.

2. Comment ont-elles choisi la destination ?
    A. Lara a pris l'atlas et choisit le pays.
    B. Maria a acheté des billets aller-retour.
    C. Elles ont tout planifié en avance.
    D. Elles ont gagné des billets.

3. La mère et la fille passent-elles beaucoup de temps ensemble ?
    A. Oui, elles passent chaque soir ensemble.
    B. Non, elles ne passent que les soirs ensemble.

4. Que feront maman et sa fille avant d'aller à la plage ?
    A. Elles se doucheront, s'habilleront, prendront leur petit-déjeuner, se brosseront les dents, se maquilleront et mettrons leurs maillots de bain.
    B. Elles se doucheront, s'habilleront, prendront leur petit-déjeuner, se brosseront les dents, et elles mettront leurs maillots de bain.
    C. Elles se doucheront, s'habilleront, prendront leur petit-déjeuner, se brosseront les dents, maman se maquillera et elles mettront leurs maillots de bain.
    D. Elles se doucheront, s'habilleront, se brosseront les dents, maman se maquillera et elles mettront leurs maillots de bain.

5. Quels animaux verront-elles à Cuba ?
    A. Des tortues, des lions, des girafes, des éléphants.
    B. Elles ne verront pas un seul animal.
    C. Des tortues.
    D. Des lions, des girafes, des éléphants.

Grammar notes

Future Simple

The Future simple tense is typically used to talk about future plans, intentions, or about making predictions about what may happen. In English, the simple future is analogous to the will form.

It makes sense that the future simple is named simple. The reason is that it's a one-verb tense, or in other words, it lacks auxiliary verbs.

The futur simple is used in the following cases:

- **when talking about future intentions**

Demain j'étudierai la grammaire.

- **when making suppositions or predictions about the future.**

Tu n'arriveras jamais à l'heure.

- **in conditional (if sentences) sentences**

Si on attend les soldes, on payera moins.

Regular Verbs

The formation of the future is actually quite easy with regular verbs. You just take the infinitive form and add the future endings (*-ai, -as, -a, -ons, -ez* and *-ont*).

Take the infinitive form for **-er**, and **-ir** verbs, but remove final -e for regular **-re** verbs, before adding the endings.

Let's see one example for each verb group.

Pronouns	**I Group**	**II Group**	**III Group** drop the -e
Je	aimer+**ai**	finir+**ai**	Prendr<u>e</u> / prendr +**ai**
Tu	aimer+**as**	finir+**as**	prendr+**as**
Il/Elle	aimer+**a**	finir+**a**	prendr+**a**
Nous	aimer+**ons**	finir+**ons**	prendr+**ons**
Vous	aimer+**ez**	finir+**ez**	prendr+**ez**
Ils/Elles	aimer+**ont**	finir+**ont**	prendr+**ont**

Irregular Verbs

Since there's no auxiliary, the Future Simple is supposed to be simple, but in reality it's more of an exception chart with a lot of irregular verbs.

Exceptions to the conjugation rules:

- All verbs with a short *e* in the stem change to *(accent grave)* in the *futur simple*.

peser - je p<u>è</u>serai

- Some verbs **double their consonants**.

jeter - je je<u>tt</u>erai

- Some verbs ending in **-rir**, have *i* omitted before the future ending.

courir - je courrai

    mourir - je mourrai

- Verbs ending in **-yer**, have y transformed to i in the *futur simple*.

employer - j'emploierai, tu emploieras, il emploiera, nous emploierons, vous emploierez, ils emploieront

Note that verbs ending in *-ayer*, have two possibilities: y and i are permitted. *payer - je payerai/paierai*

Frequent Irregular Verbs in Future
- aller → **ir** → j'**irai**
- avoir → **aur** → j'**aurai**
- être → **ser** → je **serai**
- faire → **fer** → je **ferai**
- pouvoir → **pourr** → je **pourrai**
- devoir → **devr** → je **devrai**
- savoir → **saur** → je **saurai**
- venir → **viendr** → je **viendrai**
- voir → **verr** → je **verrai**
- vouloir → **voudr** → je **voudrai**
- envoyer → **enverr** → j'**enverrai**

Be aware that the conditional and the future simple take the same stem to create the tense. You can distinguish them by simply looking at their endings.

Key takeaways

- The Future Simple is used when talking about future intentions, making predictions about the future, or in conditional sentences.
- In English, the simple future is analogous to the **will form**.
- To form the future simple, you just take the infinitive form and add the future endings (**-ai, -as, -a, -ons, -ez** and **-ont**), for verbs finishing in **-er**, and **-ir**. For verbs finishing in **-re**, first we drop -e, and then add the endings.
- Be aware that the conditional and the future simple take the same stem. The only way to distinguish these is to look at the endings.

Now that you have covered all the essential tenses in present, past, and future, it's time to take your French conversations to the next level. In the next chapter, you will find out how to express your opinion loud and clear.

Chapter 10: Expressing opinions

« La lumière est dans le livre. Ouvrez le livre tout grand. Laissez-le rayonner. Laissez-le faire. »
- Victor Hugo

People love to share their opinions no matter how knowledgeable or uninformed they are about a subject. And we are all the same in this matter. You must be ready for a heated debate if you are out with French, since French love arguing long hours. In this chapter, we give you the basic equipment you need to share your thoughts and defend your opinion. This story is also great for exploring the *l'imparfait* and *passé composé,* both of which are combined in this narrative.

Un bibliophile

Éric adore les livres. Chaque dimanche, il fréquente des **bouquinistes**, pour trouver un nouveau **trésor**. Il a visité toutes les **librairies** à Bordeaux, où il habite. Il connaît **personnellement** tous les bouquinistes à Bordeaux.

Un jour, il était en train de décider entre deux livres, entre *L'Insoutenable Légèreté de l'Être* et *La Peste*. **Alors qu'**il réfléchissait à quel livre prendre, une fille a pris son livre. Éric voulait dire « C'est mon livre », mais il est resté **stupéfait** par la beauté de la fille. Il a perdu **sa voix.**

La fille de la librairie est devenue pour lui la Dulcinée de Cervantes, la Béatrice de Pétrarque. Il la comparait aux plus belles **héroïnes** de la littérature. Il voulait savoir où elle habitait, et où il pouvait la rencontrer. Il venait à la librairie à la même heure tous les jours. Elle n'était pas là. Les semaines ont passé et il a oublié la fille.

Un samedi, Éric est allé à **un club littéraire**. Ce soir-là, ils ont parlé du livre L'Insoutenable Légèreté de l'Être, le livre préféré d'Éric.

Tout d'abord, le professeur de littérature a **dit quelques mots** sur le livre.

L'Insoutenable Légèreté de l'Être est le cinquième roman de Milan Kundera, écrit en 1982 et publié en 1984, en France. **L'intrigue,** qui **se situe** à Prague en 1968, **s'articule autour de** la vie des artistes et des intellectuels **au cours de** la période communiste.

Éric voulait partager son opinion.

Éric : Le livre **traite** de plusieurs thèmes et les personnages **incarnent** de grandes idées. Je pense que Milan Kundera est un des **principaux écrivains contemporains**. **La plupart** de ses romans sont philosophiques. **À mon avis,** pour Kundera la vie c'est **saisir les opportunités**. C'est l'idéal de son **personnage** principal Tomas.

À ce moment, une fille répond à Éric.

Fille : Je **ne suis pas d'accord** avec vous. **Selon moi**, Tomas cherche de **la légèreté**. Il ne cherche pas à saisir les opportunités.

Éric : **Je trouve que** c'est la même chose. Mais, **peut-être avez-vous raison**. Il ne cherche pas à saisir les opportunités, mais il prend **ce qui** est facile.

Fille : **Il semble que** Tomas ne veut pas avoir des **relations étroites**. Il aime les situations faciles. Mais pour **approfondir** la relation, il faut **parfois traverser** des situations difficiles.

Éric : **Je suis d'accord** avec vous. C'est là que **réside** la beauté du livre de Kundera. Kundera **aborde l'idée** de Parménide, un philosophe **grec**. Il voit **le monde divisé en paires opposées** : **lumière-obscurité, entité** positive **d'un côté** et négative **de l'autre**. Selon Parménide, la légèreté est **positive, le poids** est **négatif**.

Fille : **Cependant**, la vie n'est jamais en noir et blanc.

Éric : Oui, mais la littérature **peut l'être**.

Fille : Je **suis sûre que** Tomas a peur de s'ouvrir et d'être honnête.

Éric : Je trouve que chaque personne a peur de **s'ouvrir**. C'est un sentiment universel.

À la fin du **débat**, Éric **s'est approché** de la fille.

Éric : Bonsoir mademoiselle. Vous avez fait de bons commentaires.

Fille: Merci. Vous aussi.

Éric : C'est quoi votre livre préféré ?

Fille : Mon livre préféré ? C'est une question difficile !

Éric : Pourquoi ? On a tous un livre préféré !

Fille : Moi non. J'aime lire mais je n'ai pas de livre préféré. **Ça dépend** toujours de mon **état actuel**. Parfois, j'aime les livres philosophiques, parfois les **romans d'amour** ou historiques, parfois **les livres policiers**. Je lis tous **les genres littéraires**. Et ton livre préféré ?

Éric : L'un de mes livres préférés est *L'Insoutenable Légèreté de l'Être*. Mais, comme toi, j'adore les différents genres littéraires. Je rêve d'avoir une librairie un jour.

Fille : Vraiment ? C'est mon rêve aussi.

À ce moment, Éric se rend compte qu'elle est la fille qu'il a cherché depuis trois semaines.

Résumé de l'histoire

Éric adore les livres et a visité presque toutes les librairies à Bordeaux. Chaque dimanche, il fréquente des bouquinistes, pour trouver un nouveau livre. Un jour il réfléchissait entre deux livres, mais pendant ce temps-là, une fille prend son livre. Éric est tombé amoureux de cette fille. Au cours des semaines suivantes, Éric va tous les jours à la librairie pour voir la fille. Mais sans succès. Un jour, Éric va à une rencontre littéraire. Éric commence à discuter avec une fille à propos du livre. Il se rend compte que c'est la fille qu'il cherchait.

Synopsis of the story

Eric loves books and has visited almost all the bookstores in his city. Every Sunday, he goes to booksellers to find a new book. One day, while deciding between two books, a girl takes one of Eric's books. Eric falls in love with this girl. Over the next few weeks, he goes to the bookstore every day to see the girl, but without success. One day, Eric goes to a literary club. Eric starts debating with one girl about the book and realizes this is the girl he was looking for.

Vocabulary and Expressions

un bouquiniste - a bookseller

une librairie - a library

un trésor - a treasure

personnellement - personally

un jour - one day

L'insoutenable Légèreté de l'Être - The Unbearable Lightness of Being

La Peste - The Plague

alors que - whereas, while

stupéfait / stupéfaite - stunned

une voix - a voice

une héroïne - a heroine

un club littéraire - a book club

dire quelques mots - to say a few words

une intrigue - a plot

se situer - to be situated

s'articuler autour de - to revolve around

au cours de - during

traiter - to deal with

incarner - to embody

principal / principale - major, main, primary

écrivain / écrivaine - a writer

contemporain / contemporaine - contemporary

la plupart - most

à mon avis - in my opinion

saisir l'opportunité - to take the chance

un personnage - a character

à ce moment - at this moment

depuis - from, since, for

je ne suis pas d'accord - I do not agree
selon moi - in my opinion
une légèreté - a lightness
je trouve que - I think that
peut être - perhaps, maybe
avoir raison - to be right
ce qui - what
il semble que - it seems like
une relation - a relationship
étroit / étroite - narrow, tight
approfondir - to deepen
parfois - sometimes
traverser - to cross, to pass through
je suis d'accord - I agree
résider - to reside
aborder l'idée - to bring up the idea
grec / grecque - Greek
un monde - a world
divisé - divided
une paire - a pair
opposé - opposed
une lumière - a light
obscurité - darkness
entité - entity
d'un côté, de l'autre - On the one hand, on the other hand
positif / positive - positive
négatif / négative - negative
un poids - a weight
peut l'être - it can be
je suis sûre que - I am sure that
s'ouvrir - to open up
un débat - a debate
s'approcher - to approach
ça dépend - it depends
un état - a state

actuel / actuelle - current, actual

parfois - sometimes

un roman d'amour - a love novel

un livre policier - a detective book

un genre littéraire - a literary genre

Comprehension Questions

Sélectionnez une seule réponse pour chaque question.

1. Pourquoi Eric allait-il à la librairie à la même heure tous les jours ?

    A. Pour acheter des livres.

    B. Parce qu'il est bibliophile.

    C. Parce qu'il veut avoir une librairie.

    D. Parce qu'il voulait rencontrer la fille.

2. Qui pense ainsi « *la vie c'est saisir les opportunités* » ?

    A. Kundera.

    B. Kundera et Tomas.

    C. Eric.

    D. Tomas.

3. Qui est Tomas ?

    A. C'est un personnage du livre.

    B. C'est le personnage favori de Kundera.

    C. C'est le personnage favori d'Éric.

    D. C'est le bouquiniste.

4. Selon la fille, pourquoi Tomas cherche-t-il la légèreté ?

    A. Il est paresseux.

    B. Il aime les situations difficiles.

    C. Il a peur de s'ouvrir et d'être honnête.

    D. Il veut avoir des relations étroites.

5. La fille a-t-elle un livre préféré ?

    A. Non, elle lit tous les genres littéraires.

    B. Oui, son livre préféré est *L'Insoutenable Légèreté de l'Être*.

Grammar notes

Expressing your opinion

Expressing your thoughts and feelings in any language is crucial. If you want to engage in a discussion in French or if you want to state your beliefs, you must be familiar with key vocabulary and expressions. Most students believe that expressing their opinion is difficult, when in fact it is quite the opposite. Building up your vocabulary with a variety of phrases is the best way to achieve it. The best place to start is with verbs like "*aimer*".

- *J'aime / Je n'aime pas* - I like / I don't like
- *J'adore* - I love / I adore
- *J'apprécie / Je n'apprécie pas* - I appreciate / I don't appreciate
- *Je déteste* - I hate

In the story you just read, we introduced plenty of expressions and opinion phrases. To express your opinion, you can either use an opinion verb or an opinion expression. We'll examine what are the most popular verbs and expressions in the next section.

Verbes

These verbs are followed by the indicative in the affirmative form. Start the sentence with one of them when you want to express yourself.

- **Penser que** - to think

Je pense que c'est normal. - *I think it's normal.*

- **Croire que** - to believe

Je crois que les films étrangers sont trop difficiles à comprendre. - *I believe that foreign films are too difficult to understand.*

- **Trouver que** - to find

Je trouve que les enseignants nous donnent trop de devoirs à faire. - *I think teachers give us too much homework.*

- **Être persuadé(e) que** - to be persuaded, convinced

Je suis persuadé que tu vas réussir ton examen. - *I am convinced you'll pass your exam.*

- **Être sûr(e) que** - to be certain, sure

Je suis sûre que tu peux le faire. - *I am sure you can do it.*

- **Sembler que** - to seem

Il semble qu'il va pleuvoir. - *It looks like it's going to rain.*

- **Douter que**

Je doute que nous aurions pu avancer à ce point. - *I doubt that we could have advanced to this point.*

- **Être certain(e) que**

Je suis certain que nous arriverons à l'heure. - *I am sure we'll arrive on time.*

Les expressions

- **Selon moi** - in my view

Selon moi, Victor Hugo est un bon écrivain. - In my view, Victor Hugo is a good writer.

- **À mon avis** - in my opinion

À mon avis, il va pleuvoir demain. - In my opinion, it will rain tomorrow.

- **Personnellement** - personally

J'ai personnellement plus de plaisir à comprendre les hommes qu'à les juger. - I personally enjoy understanding men more than judging them.

Key takeaways

- Use these verbs to state your opinion: **penser que, croire que, trouver que, être persuadé(e) que, être sûr(e) que, sembler que, douter que, être certain(e) que**.
- Expressions that you can use to state your opinion are: **selon moi, à mon avis, personnellement.**

In the next chapter, you'll learn an easy future tense that sometimes can replace the simple future tense and that's often used in everyday situations.

Chapter 11: Apartment Renovation

« Rien de tel que de rester à la maison pour un vrai confort. »
- Jane Austin

Here we are at another common topic people love to discuss: their home. In this story, vocabulary revolves around the renovation and decoration of an apartment. You'll be exposed to many specific terms, and you'll spend a lot of time checking the vocabulary section. Don't be discouraged. After this lesson, you'll be prepared in case you inherit an apartment in Paris and have to do all the renovation by yourself.

While you get a long list of vocabulary, you'll be exposed to a fairly simple grammar topic - the *Futur Proche*, which is a near future tense, very commonly used in everyday conversations.

Appartement en rénovation

Pierre vit à Paris dans un petit **appartement**. Il vient d'**hériter** d'un grand appartement dans le quatrième **arrondissement**. Un jour, il a **reçu** une lettre. Son oncle lui a laissé un appartement près de Notre-Dame. Son **avocat** l'avertit qu'il faut **engager quelqu'un pour faire** certains **travaux**. L'appartement est vieux et en très mauvais état.

Jusque-là, Pierre vivait en **banlieue** parisienne. Il allait au travail en métro et chaque jour il lui **fallait une heure** pour y arriver. Quand il a obtenu les clés de l'appartement et quand il y est entré **pour la première fois**, il a compris que **la rénovation** allait être chère. Il va **investir** au moins 10 000 euros dans la rénovation. Cependant, Pierre n'a jamais **été doué** pour **le bricolage**. Il va donc **engager une agence**. Il a appelé l'agence pour **se renseigner** sur les prix et les conditions.

« Bonjour madame. J'ai un vieil appartement à rénover.

– Je comprends. **À l'époque de** la construction de votre ancien appartement, **les modes de vie** étaient différents. Pour s'adapter à nos **styles de vie actuels**, une **réorganisation de l'espace** est conseillée.

– Oui, certainement. Quel est le prix pour rénover un appartement ?

– Tout **dépend des travaux**. Nous offrons trois possibilités : **rénovation partielle, rénovation complète ou rénovation lourde**. Je vous explique la différence. La rénovation partielle comprend **la réfection de la cuisine** et la rénovation de la **salle de bains**. Dans **ce cas, l'architecte** n'est pas nécessaire. La rénovation complète comprend la rénovation de la cuisine et de la salle de bains, la rénovation de **l'électricité**, la rénovation de **la plomberie** et des **réseaux d'eau** et le **remplacement des fenêtres**. Dans ce cas, l'architecte est recommandé. Enfin, la rénovation lourde comprend la rénovation complète et toute autre **modification structurelle** de l'appartement. Dans ce cas, l'architecte est obligatoire. Quelles interventions désirez-vous monsieur ?

– Il faut faire **la vitrification du sol, la réfection des peintures, des murs et des plafonds**, puis la rénovation de la salle de bains et la rénovation de la cuisine. **Quel est le prix ?**

– Il y d'**autres critères** qui **affectent le prix**. Comme **la superficie** de l'appartement à **rénover** et le **nombre de pièces**.

– La superficie est de 85m2 et l'appartement a deux **salles de bains**, trois **chambres à coucher**, **une cuisine, un salon, un couloir, un séjour** et **une terrasse**.

– Je vais vous dire **le coût** de chaque intervention dans un moment monsieur. Selon vos besoins, il vous convient la rénovation partielle. Quel est votre budget pour **refaire un appartement** ?

– Entre 10.000 et 15.000$.

– Très bien monsieur.

– **Le projet peut démarrer** en septembre. Est-ce que ça vous convient ?

– Oui, c'est parfait. »

Les menuisiers ont travaillé pendant deux mois. Fin novembre, les travaux étaient terminés. Maintenant c'est le moment pour la décoration. Le nouveau **propriétaire** veut **donner une identité au lieu**. Pierre veut **réaliser son séjour sur mesure**. Il veut **une pièce à vivre conviviale** et charmante. Mais, il a déjà dépensé beaucoup d'argent dans la rénovation. Alors, il ne va pas engager **un décorateur d'intérieur**. Il va décorer son appartement seul. Pour s'inspirer, il fait un tour sur le web. Il faut penser aux couleurs et à **l'éclairage**. **Les tons clairs** vont **agrandir l'espace**. Alors il va acheter d**es meubles** en tons clairs comme blanc et jaune. Pour accentuer, il va mettre des **coussins, des vases, des rideaux dans ce style**. Il va mettre d**es plantes** dans toutes les pièces, du salon à la salle de bains ! Les plantes ne coûtent pas trop cher. Il va acheter **une commode**, six **chaises**, une **grande table à manger**, **un grand lit** pour **la chambre à coucher**, un **fauteuil**, **un canapé** et **une étagère à livres**. Mais comme Pierre n'a pas beaucoup de budget, il va acheter **des meubles d'occasion**. Pour trouver de la décoration authentique, il va aller au **marché aux puces**. Comme son appartement est **spacieux**, **l'éclairage** est important. Pierre va acheter beaucoup de lampes. Dans la salle de bains, il va poser un grand **miroir doré**. Pierre espère que la décoration de l'appartement va être finie fin décembre. Il veut **faire une grande fête de Nouvel An** avec sa famille.

Résumé de l'histoire

Pierre vit en banlieue de Paris, dans un petit appartement. Un jour, il hérite d'un grand appartement près du centre-ville. Mais, c'est un appartement ancien et en très mauvais état, et il faut le moderniser. Cependant, Pierre n'a jamais été doué pour le bricolage. Il va donc engager une agence pour faire les travaux. Il faut faire la vitrification du sol, la réfection des peintures, des murs et des plafonds, puis la rénovation de la salle de bains et la rénovation de la cuisine. Il a déjà dépensé beaucoup d'argent dans la rénovation, alors il va décorer son appartement seul. Il va acheter des meubles d'occasion et la décoration sur le marché aux puces. Il veut finir la décoration pour célébrer le nouvel an avec sa famille.

Synopsis of the story

Pierre lives in the suburbs of Paris, in a small apartment. One day he inherites a big apartment near the city center. But, it is an old apartment and in very bad condition, so it must be modernized. However, Pierre has never been good at DIY. He will hire an agency to do the work. It is necessary to do the vitrification of the floor, to paint the walls and ceilings, then to renovate the bathroom and the kitchen. He wants to decorate his apartment alone, since he spent so much money on the renovation. He goes to buy second-hand furniture and decorations at the flea market. He wants to finish the decoration to celebrate the new year with his family.

Vocabulary and Expressions

un appartement - an apartment

hériter - to inherit

un arrondissement - a district

recevoir - to receive

un avocat - a lawyer

avertir - to warn

engager quelqu'un - to hire someone

une banlieue - a suburb

il fallait une heure - it took an hour

pour la première fois - for the first time

une rénovation - a renovation

investir - to invest

être doué(e) - to be gifted, to have talent

le **bricolage** - do-it-yourself, DIY

engager une agence - to hire an agency

se renseigner - to ask about

à l'époque de - at the time of

un mode de vie - a way of life

un style de vie - a lifestyle

une réorganisation de l'espace - a reorganization of the space

dépendre - to depend

une rénovation partielle - a partial renovation

une rénovation complète - a complete renovation

une rénovation lourde - a heavy renovation

une réfection de la cuisine - a kitchen renovation

une salle de bains - bathroom

dans ce cas - in this case

un architecte - an architect

l'électricité - the electricity

la plomberie - the plumbing

des réseaux d'eau - water networks

un remplacement des fenêtres - a replacement of windows

une modification structurelle - a structural modification

une vitrification de sol - a floor vitrification

une réfection des peintures - a painting repair

un mur - a wall

un plafond - a ceiling

autres - others

un critère - a criterion

affecter le prix - to affect the price

une superficie - a surface, size

une pièce - a room

une salle de bains - a bathroom

une chambre à coucher - a bedroom

une cuisine - a kitchen

un salon - a living room

une couleur - a color

un séjour - a living room

une terrasse - a terrace

refaire un appartement - to redo an apartment

le projet peut démarrer - the project can start

un menuisier - a carpenter

un propriétaire - an owner

donner une identité au lieu - to give the place an identity

réaliser le séjour sur mesure - to create a custom-made living room

une pièce à vivre - a living space

un décorateur d'intérieur - an interior designer

un éclairage - a lighting

les tons clairs - light tones

agrandir l'espace - to make the space bigger

les meubles - the furniture

un coussin - a cushion

un vase - a vase

un rideau - a curtain

dans ce style- in this style

des plantes - plants
une commode - a commode
une chaise - a chair
une table à manger - a dinner table
un lit - a bed
un fauteuil - an armchair
un canapé - a couch
une étagère à livres - a bookshelf
un meuble d'occasion - a second-hand furniture
un marché aux puces - a flea market
spacieux / spacieuse - spacious
un miroir - a mirror
doré - golden
faire une fête - to have a party
Nouvel An - New Year

Comprehension Questions

Sélectionnez une seule réponse pour chaque question.

1. Qu'est-ce que ça veut dire que Pierre n'est pas doué pour le bricolage ?
    A. Il est bon en bricolage.
    B. Il est mauvais en bricolage.
    C. Il va engager une agence.

2. Pourquoi est-il conseillé de réorganiser l'espace dans un appartement ancien ?
    A. La plupart des gens aiment avoir un style américain.
    B. Pour s'adapter au nouveau style de vie.
    C. Parce que les modes de vie étaient différents.

3. Qu'est-ce que comprend la rénovation partielle ?
    A. La rénovation de la cuisine et de la salle de bains, la rénovation de l'électricité, la rénovation de la plomberie et des réseaux d'eau et le remplacement des fenêtres.
    B. La réfection de la cuisine et la rénovation de la salle de bains.
    C. La rénovation complète et toute autre modification structurelle de l'appartement.

4. Dans quel cas l'architecte est recommandé ?
    A. Dans le cas de la rénovation lourde.
    B. Dans le cas de la rénovation complète.
    C. Dans le cas de la rénovation partielle.

5. Quels critères affectent le prix de la rénovation ?
    A. Le nombre de pièces et l'état de la salle de bains.
    B. Le nombre de pièces et l'étage auquel se trouve l'appartement.
    C. La surface et la location de l'appartement.
    D. La surface et le nombre de pièces.
6. Qu'est que Pierre va faire pour dépenser moins sur la décoration ?
    A. Pierre va acheter des meubles d'occasion.
    B. Pierre va acheter des meubles au marché aux puces.
    C. Pierre va faire ses propres meubles.
    D. Pierre va utiliser ses vieux meubles.

Grammar notes

Futur Proche

Le *Futur Proche*, also called le *futur composé*, refers to near future actions. This is equivalent to the English structure *going to* plus infinitive, implying an intent behind the action.

When to use the *futur proche*

Le *futur proche* is used in the following situations:

- When an action shortly takes place.
- *Christine va partir dans deux secondes. - Christina is leaving in two seconds.*
- For a planned action in the near future.
- *Il va aller au supermarché. - He is going to the supermarket.*

How to conjugate the *futur proche* in French

To conjugate the *futur proche*, we use the present tense of the verb *aller* + verb in infinitive.

Je	Je vais + infinitive (finir, porter, lire)
Tu	Tu vas + infinitive (finir, porter, lire)
Il/Elle	Il/Elle va + infinitive (finir, porter, lire)
Nous	Nous allons + + infinitive (finir, porter, lire)
Vous	Vous allez + + infinitive (finir, porter, lire)
Ils/Elles	Ils/Elles vont + infinitive (finir, porter, lire)

Key takeaways

- The *futur proche* is used for actions that will shortly happen or for planned actions in the near future.
- The *futur proche* is equivalent to the English structure **going to** + infinitive.
- To create the *futur proche*, we need to conjugate the verb **aller** **in the present tense** + **verb in infinitive.**

Answers

Chapter 1

    1. Who tells the story?

A

    2. They live ....

B

    3. Does the wife go to work every day?

C

    4. In the morning, the man prefers ....:

B

    5. Every day in the morning, the man likes to?

A

Chapter 2

    1. What does the girl think of blind dates?

B

    2. Why is the girl cleaning the apartment?

D

    3. What does the metaphor "comme un jour de pluie" mean?

A

    4. What are the characteristics of a Capricorn?

B

    5. What is the worst combination of signs?

A

Chapter 3

    1. What is the job of the character telling the story?

C

    2. What ingredients do they buy to prepare the birthday cake?

A

    3. Why Charlotte says "Je suis une artiste, moi"?

C

    4. Why is Charlotte upset?

A

    5. Why are they going to the market?

B

Chapter 4

1. Who had the idea of becoming a nomadic family?

B

2. Did their family agree with them about their idea?

B

3. According to Lea, what is needed to become a digital nomad?

C

4. What is the job of Lea and her husband?

B

5. How do they travel the world?

C

6. What does it mean "les régions les plus **reculées** du monde"?

A

Chapter 5

1. What is Lazarus' profession?

A

2. Why does Lazarus travel around the world?

C

3. What does it mean to visit the trendiest destinations?

B

4. What are the best months to visit Iceland?

A

5. In Bali during the rainy season....

C

Chapter 6

1. Why did Charlotte take her father's hat?

A

2. Why does Charlotte feel fear?

D

3. Why does Charlotte always "end up in debt"?

D

4. What does Charlotte wear for her interview?

A

5. Who owns comfortable sandals?

406

B

Chapter 7

1. Where has the main character traveled to?

A

2. Who ate all the pears?

C

3. Why is her father determined to teach her to swim?

C

4. Who was in the garden of her old house?

C

5. What does "revivre un conte de fées" means?

B

- **Chapter 8**

1. What jobs did Luca have?

C

2. Why did no one want to hire Luca at first?

B

3. Why did Luca work extra hours at the cheese company?

B

4. Was there a lot of opportunity on the market?

B

5. Luca has flexible working hours for which job?

C

6. Why was Luca skeptical when his friend suggested opening a bakery?

A

Chapter 9

1. Has the girl traveled?

B

2. How did they choose the destination?

A

3. Do mother and daughter spend a lot of time together?

B

4. What will mom and daughter do before going to the beach?

C

5. What animals will they see in Cuba?

A

Chapter 10

1. Why did Eric go to the bookstore at the same time every day?

D

2. Who thinks like this "*la vie c'est saisir les opportunités*"?

A

3. Who's Tomas?

A

4. According to the girl, why is Tomas looking for lightness?

C

5. Does the girl have a favorite book?

A

Chapter 11

1. What does it mean that "Pierre n'est pas doué pour le bricolage"?

B

2. Why is it advisable to rearrange the space in an old apartment?

B

3. What does partial renovation include?

B

4. When is the architect recommended?

B

5. What criteria affect the price of renovation?

D

6. What is Pierre going to do to spend less on decoration?

A

Conclusion

First of all, let us congratulate you on your achievements. Learning a language is not a one-day task, and above all requires discipline, consistency, and moving forward despite the frustration.

For a beginner in French, reading stories may seem insurmountable. Ordinary stories are often too complex, filled with advanced grammar and an overly eloquent narrative, preventing French beginners from even getting started. As language learners, we realized there's the traditional grammar-focused method on the one side, and on the other side, there's the story learning method. The two approaches seem at odds with each other. Yet, they complement one another. For that reason, we wanted to create a book that reconciles the need to understand grammar with the need to get a natural and motivational way to learn French. By accompanying the story with grammar notes, we aimed to get the maximum benefit from the story learning.

Our goal was to create a book that would allow you to focus on one grammar point at a time. The best way to learn grammar in French is to observe how it naturally appears within stories, rather than relying on a "rules first" methodology. Taking this approach allows you to see how grammar functions in the context, and even if you don't yet know the rules, you will still be able to understand a lot!

Through eleven stories you build your grammar skills with each story read. As each story is written with common beginner's troubles in mind, you progress gradually, starting with beginner lessons (Present Tense, Adjectives, Partitive articles) and progressing up to more advanced ones (Basic Past Tenses, Relative Pronouns, Expressing your Opinion, Direct and Indirect Object). The stories invite the reader to explore further the language curiosities and examine the story back and forth with the new grammar tools.

Most of the topics in this book are related to our everyday lives. Eleven stories cover the eleven most frequent everyday situations, from traveling to meeting your family, talking about habits, food, shopping, and weather, allowing you to build your vocabulary in different areas.

We begin by focusing on daily habits, then move on to describing people in the next chapter. The third story is all about grocery shopping and cooking, while the next one touches on your family members. In the fifth chapter, you are already on the road and discussing the weather. Having learned how to keep small talks like a French in Paris, you head off to learn more shopping vocabulary in the upcoming chapter. In chapter seven, you are finally able to tell a story of your own, as you get introduced to another past tense - the imperfect. Next, you cover the career area, then you get to travel again. In the tenth chapter, you get the basic equipment you need to share your thoughts and defend your opinion. Finally, you finish with another frequent topic, discussing your home and renovation. Topics that cover all aspects of your daily life are ideal for beginners.

Story learning prevents you from becoming infatuated with rules by encouraging you to focus on understanding and purely enjoying the story first and foremost. Through this approach, you end up learning so many global aspects of the language including sentence structure, narrative, and sequencing events.

With eleven stories under your belt and a solid foundation in French grammar, you are well prepared to speak French, even with natives. You now have the freedom to talk about your family, career, shopping, cooking, travel, weather, house renovations, and even express your opinions in a variety of ways in French. All that's left is to apply what you've learned.

BOOK 4

Learn Intermediate French for Adults Workbook:

Go from French Beginner to Intermediate in 30 Days!

Explore to Win

Book 4 description

Have you hit a wall in your French language learning journey? Do you find it difficult to retain more vocabulary, improve your pronunciation and understand more complex grammar rules? Have you reached a point where you no longer progress as fast as you wished? Does it seem like your goal of speaking French like a native has become even more out of reach?

If you answered yes to any one of the questions above, then this book is for you. Say goodbye to your frustrations and hello to the solution you have been waiting for: ***Learn Intermediate French for Adults Workbook: Go from French Beginner to Intermediate in 30 Days!***

Yes, this is not a dream. With this book, you will be able to move to an Intermediate level of fluency in French within 30 days. Written by French linguists who have helped many learners go beyond that exasperating plateau, this book was designed to fast-track your Intermediate language learning in a fun and efficient way. If you have acquired our first book, you know we're serious when it comes to the theory behind language acquisition. This book follows a spiral structure, so you will progress at a sustained speed without being bogged down by an overload of new information. The lessons are also based on a communicative framework: we don't teach vocabulary or grammar out of context. Inside, you will find dialogues and a ton of example sentences to help you make sense of the French language!

With ***Learn Intermediate French for Adults Workbook: Go from French Beginner to Intermediate in 30 Days!***, you'll discover:

- sample dialogues and texts to see the language-at-work at an Intermediate level.
- vocabulary related to more abstract and technical topics.
- clear grammar explanations to help you produce more elaborate and nuanced sentences.
- a pronunciation guide, a vocabulary list by theme, verb conjugation references, exercises with answer key after each chapter.
- and overall: the secrets to acquiring an Intermediate level of French fluency.

At some point in their journey, all learners will feel like they've hit a dead-end. This has nothing to do with their talent in acquiring languages or their skills. Reaching a plateau is, simply put, quite normal. This is why you shouldn't let discouragement dictate what you do. Don't beat yourself up. Instead, beat the plateau. This book will help you do precisely that and bring you closer to your goal of becoming a fluent French speaker.

Introduction

You need to step out of your comfort zone, and you need to do it now. Time is of the essence in language learning. If you are reading this, we take it you've acquired a beginner's level in French (perhaps through our *Learn French for Adult Beginners Workbook*). You are now capable of talking about basic topics related to you and your immediate surroundings. You can now order at a restaurant, talk about the future, and even handle holidays in a francophone country. But if you wish to achieve native fluency, you have to keep yourself from getting too comfortable at this level. You need to move to your growth zone while the momentum lasts.

Intermediate language learners often confront similar problems. The first is what specialists call a "plateau", or in layman's terms: a slump. As you finish a level, you find yourself hitting a dead-end. You're improving, yes, but not as fast as you had hoped. And then, to add to this, is your staggering motivation. You feel like you will never be able to master French vocabulary or grammar. Everything is just too frustrating: the interminable list of rules and exceptions, the number of tenses to memorize, the exasperating phonetics of the language. You will find yourself wanting to just stop at elementary fluency, telling yourself it's good enough to just know the basics. But giving up now would be a pity, *quel dommage !* as the French would say. If you look at the big picture, you are halfway there. Just a little push and you can speak like a French native, do you really want to just call it a day?

How do you then proceed from here? The key is moving from your comfort zone to the growth zone. First, remember why you decided to learn French. Commit your goal to memory. Next, build a learning habit that works for you. Devote yourself to it. Finally, find the right material — a book that builds on what you already know while providing you with new challenges... But wait, you just did!

About this book

Learn Intermediate French for Adults Workbook: Go from French Beginner to Intermediate in 30 Days! is designed to help you achieve an intermediate level of French. This means that by the end of this 30-day course, you will be able to:

- understand and discuss a wide range of topics, concrete or abstract.
- communicate in more specific commercial situations and work-related scenarios.
- express point of view on subjects related to current issues in the society.
- express hesitation, doubt, regret, certainty, agreement and disagreement.
- summarize events and structure speech through logical connectors.

The goal of this book is to have you speak intermediate French within 30 days. We will help you move to the growth zone and sustain that momentum! You'll find that the lessons in this book have just the right amount of new, essential words and grammar topics. You will learn more advanced and more nuanced subjects, but you won't drown or be overwhelmed in the process (this is the magic of spiral learning, as we will talk about in a bit). With this book, you will go beyond the comfort of basic fluency and reach the next level of your learning within just a month.

Each chapter features the **Lesson proper** which revolves around a specific communicative function and discusses related grammatical concepts and vocabulary. We've also added short texts and dialogues to some lessons so you can see the language at-work.

At the end of each chapter, you will find a **Key Takeaways** section that summarizes the main points learned, as well as **Exercises** with **Answer Keys** so you can confirm your understanding of the lesson. You'll also find **Culture Tips** that provide useful facts about French etiquette, customs, and language.

As always, we also included in the final pages of the book **Vocabulary Lists by Theme**, **Verb Conjugations** and a **Grammar Topic Index**, for your reviewing purposes.

Our approach to learning

This book was prepared by French linguists who have made it their life's mission to make language learning fun, accessible and efficient. They've helped many learners achieve an intermediate level of fluency in the language. They know about their tribulations, their frustrations, their hopes, and they've discovered the best strategies in helping them.

Just like our first book in this series, **Learn Intermediate French for Adults Workbook** is founded on a communicative approach and a spiral lesson structure. The communicative approach prioritizes getting the learner to speak and actually use the language. This is why everything is taught in context. A spiral lesson structure means you expand your knowledge by building on what you already know. Revisiting vocabulary or grammar elements is important here, for it allows you to retain them in your long-term memory bank.

How to use this book

This book can be used as a **stand-alone resource for self-study**. It is no secret that studying a language on your own can be tough. We recommend keeping it simple and using a single resource. You would be tempted to know everything you can, the fastest way you can. And you might think this entails hoarding many materials. In this book, we pooled everything you need to know to become an intermediate French speaker. More importantly, we paced it in a way that promotes and improves learning. Let us lead, we will get you there.

While this book stays true to a specific structure, remember that you have control over your learning. You can take the time to revisit a chapter if you need to. You can use learning strategies that are effective for you. Write down new vocabularies, or draw them! Chat with a native speaker. Start a journal in French. Listen to the audio supplement of this book in repeat. Studying this book, as you will soon realize, opens up many possibilities and occasions of learning.

You can also use this book as **a complement to a French beginners' course** you are taking. If you need more explanations about a grammar concept or if you wish to expand your French vocabulary, look no further. The index of this book is particularly helpful for searching for a specific topic you want to focus on.

Some final tips

- **Engage with the lessons.** Don't just read the lessons, engage with them. Repeat aloud the phrases and words you will encounter. If presented with a dialogue, enact it. Take notes while reading the book. The goal is for you to get used to these sounds and structures. And the only way to do that is by using the language.

- **Speak up.** Now is the time to speak up. Find a language learning partner, or a native speaker to practice with. Don't let fear or lack of confidence get in the way of your learning. As you go through this book, you will gain most of the tools needed for any intermediate-level conversation. Make the most out of these tools.
- **Immerse yourself in everything French.** If you haven't done it before, start your language immersion. Even at home! Watch a very long French series, listen to French songs, learn more about French history. Surround yourself with the language.
- **Enjoy the ride.** We've said it before, and we'll say it again: language learning is a road trip. The destination is important of course. But so is the journey. Celebrate your achievements. There is no such thing as "small wins". Each step matters, because however small you think it may be, it still brings you closer to your goal of native fluency.

Are you ready to level up? Let's get this road on the show! For your first lesson, we head to the stars...

Abbreviations

lit.	literal translation
for.	formal
inf.	informal
m.	masculine
f.	feminine
sing.	singular
plur.	plural
n.	noun
v.	verb
adj.	adjective
adv.	adverb
prep.	preposition

Pronunciation Guide

Consonants

Letters	Examples	Pronunciation Guide
b	**b**lanc	Pronounced the same as in English.
d	**d**eux	
f	**f**ilm	
k	**k**ilo	
l	**l**it	
m	**m**ain	
n	**n**on	
p	**p**ère	
s	**s**ol	
t	**t**erre	
v	**v**oix	
z	**z**ut	
c	**c**arte /kart/	C is pronounced as /k/ before A, O, and U.
	côte /koht/	
		C is pronounced as /s/ Before E, I and Y.
	cette /seht/	
	i**c**i /ee-see/	Ç with cedilla is pronounced like an /s/ as well.
ç	le**ç**on /leu-sohñ/	
ch	**ch**apeau /shah-po/	CH is pronounced like /sh/ as though you are producing a shushing sound.
q	**q**uiz /kweez/	QU and Q as final letters are both pronounced as /k/.
	cin**q** /sank/	
g	**g**olf /golf/	Before the vowels A, O, and U, the letter G is pronounced like the English G in *great*.
		GU before the vowels E, I and Y are pronounced the same way.
	guitare /gee-tar/	

	manger /mahn-zheh/	G is pronounced as /zh/ before the letters E, I and Y. This sound is the same as the *s* in the word *leisure*.
gn	magnifique /mah-nyee-feek/	GN is pronounced as /ny/, like the *ni* in the word *opinion*.
h	hôpital /oh-pee-tahl/	H is generally mute in French.
j	jouer /zhoo-weh/	J is pronounced like /zh/, again like the *s* in the English word *leisure*.
r	rue /rew/	To pronounce the French *R*, place the tip of your tongue at the bottom of your mouth, against your front teeth.
s	sol /sohl/ maison /meh-zohñ/	S is pronounced the same as in English unless it is sandwiched by two vowels. In this case, it is pronounced like a /z/.
th	thon /ton/	TH is pronounced like an English /t/.
x	excellent /ekseh-lahñ/	X is pronounced as /ks/ when followed by a consonant.
	exemples /egzohm-pleuh/	When followed by a vowel, it is pronounced as /gs/.
	six /sees/	Pronounce X as /s/ when it is the final letter.

Vowels

Letters	Examples	Pronunciation Guide
a	m**a**l /mahl/	Pronounced as /ah/
à	voil**à** /vwa-lah/	
â	p**â**te /paht/	
ai	m**ai** /meh/	Pronounced as /eh/
au	f**au**x /fo/	Pronounced as /o/
eau	p**eau** /po/	
e	l**e** /leu/ pr**e**mier /preu-myeh/	E is pronounced as /eu/ in one syllable words, or when followed by a consonant in long words.

é	th**é** /tay/	Pronounced as /ay/
ez	n**ez** /nay/	
è	m**è**re /mehr/	Pronounced as /eh/
ê	t**ê**te /teht/	
et	m**et**s /meh/	
ei	s**ei**ze /sehz/	
i	l**i**vre /leev-reu/	Pronounced as /ee/
î	**î**le /eel/	
o	o**c**éan /o-seh-yahñ/	Pronounced as /o/
ô	h**ô**te /ot/	
ou	p**ou**r /poohr/	Pronounced as /ooh/
u	t**u** /tchew/	Pronounced as /ew/

Semi-vowels

Letters	Examples	Pronunciation Guide
y	**y**aourt /yah-oort/	Pronounced as /yuh/
yer	pa**yer** /peh-yeh/	
ille	f**ille** /fiy/	
ouill	m**ouill**é /mou-yeh/	
eil	bout**eil**le /boo-tey/	
ail	**ail** /ahy/	
euille	f**euille** /feuy/	
ui	l**ui** /loo-wee/	Pronounced as /wuh/
ué(e)	r**uée** /rew-weh/	
uin	j**uin** /zhoo-wañ/	
ueu	s**ueu**r /sew-weur/	
oi	m**oi** /mwah/	Pronounced as /wah/
oy	empl**oy**é /ahm̃-plwah-yeh/	
oui	L**oui**s /loo-weeh/	Pronounced as /weeh/
oue	**oue**st /ou-west/	

Nasal vowels

Nasal sounds are produced by letting air pass through the nose. In this book, we use the tilde symbol (~) to indicate a nasal sound.

Letters	Examples	Pronunciation Guide
an	enfant /ahñ-fahñt/	Pronounced as /ahñ/ or /ahm̃/, like the preposition *on* in English, but without stressing the letter *n*.
am	chambre /shahm̃b-reu/	
en	en /ahñ/	
em	embarras /ahm̃-bah-rah/	
in	matin /mah-tañ/	Pronounced as /añ/ or /am̃/, like the article *an* in English, but without stressing the letter *n*.
im	impoli /am̃-po-lee/	
ain	pain /pañ/	
aim	faim /fam̃/	
ien	bien /byañ/	Pronounced as /yañ/
on	son /sohñ/	Pronounced as /ohñ/ or /ohm̃/
om	nom /nohm̃/	
un	un /uhñ/	Pronounced as /uhñ/

Pronunciation and spelling tips

- The French language has five letter accents: the acute (é); the grave (à, è, ù); the circumflex which resembles a roof (â, ê, î, ô, û); the cedilla (ç) and the dieresis (ë, ï).
- The final consonant of a word is generally not pronounced, except for the letters C, R, F and L. For example, in the word *bas* /bah/ (below), the –s is mute. But in the word *truc* /trewk/ (thing), the final –c is pronounced. The exception is for verbs, where the final R is not pronounced. For example, *manger* (to eat) is pronounced as /mahñ-zheh/.
- If you wish to sound native, one of the most important things to learn is the *liaison*. Liaison means pronouncing the final consonant of a word with the first vowel of the next word. For example, in the sentence:

Vous êtes français.

We link the final -s of the word *vous*, with the ê- of *êtes*. We thus pronounce it as such: /Voo zeht frahN-seh/.

Chapter 1: Lights, Camera, Action!

La gloire est un effort constant.

Fame is a constant effort.

- Jules Renard

The difference between learning at the beginner's level and at the intermediate level has to do with the range of topics you can communicate about. At the start of your language journey, you spent your time learning how to talk about you and things related to you. As we move onto the next level, we redirect our focus, enlarge it to include the people around you, subjects not of immediate relevance to you, more abstract concepts, and so on. Succinctly put, the intermediate level is all about expanding the world of your language knowledge.

In this lesson, we will take you to the stars, the industry of fame. You will learn how to describe someone's physical attributes, including vocabularies related to cinema. In terms of grammar, relative pronouns *qui* and *que* take the center stage. "Camera, lights, action" or as they say in French, *Moteur, ça tourne, action !*

Describing someone's physical appearance

Georges describes a famous actress to her friend Chloe. Look closely at the highlighted phrases:

> **Georges :** *Tu as vu le dernier film d'action « Indéniable » ? C'est excellent !*
> **Chloé :** *Euh… je ne connais pas. C'est quel genre ?*
> **Georges :** *C'est un film d'action avec l'actrice Natasha Bertrand.*
> **Chloé :** *Je ne connais pas non plus l'actrice.* <u>**Tu peux la décrire ?**</u>
> **Georges :** *Mais elle est très célèbre !* <u>**Elle a les yeux bleus, les cheveux courts, bouclés et blonds…**</u>
> **Chloé :** *Ça ne me dit rien.*
> **Georges :** <u>**Elle est mince et très grande. Elle a la peau bronzée.**</u> *Elle était mannequin avant de devenir actrice. C'est l'actrice qui a joué Sophie dans la série « Rappelle-moi ».*
> **Chloé :** *Ah oui ! Je la connais. C'est l'actrice que ma mère adore !*
>
> **Georges:** Did you see the latest action film "Indéniable"? It's superb!
> **Chloé:** Um… I don't know it. What genre of film is it?
> **Georges:** It's an action film with the actress Natasha Bertrand.
> **Chloé:** I don't know the actress either.
> **Georges:** But she's so famous! She has blue eyes, short, curly blond hair…
> **Chloé:** Doesn't ring a bell.
> **Georges:** She's very tall. She has a tan. She was a model before she became an actress. It's the actress who played Sophie in the series "Remind me".
> **Chloé:** Ah yes! I know her. It's the actress my mother likes!

To ask how someone looks like, we can follow Chloé and ask:

Tu peux le/la décrire ? or ***Vous pouvez le/la décrire ?***
Can you describe him/her?

You can also use these expressions:

De quoi il/elle a l'air ? or ***Il/Elle a l'air de quoi ?***
À quoi il/elle ressemble ? or ***Il/Elle ressemble à quoi ?***

These both mean, "What does he/she look like?"

General descriptions

To describe *l'apparence physique* (m.) or the physical appearance of someone, one can simply say:

Il est beau. / Elle est belle.
He is handsome. / She is beautiful.

Or alternatively (but we discourage being rude!):

Il est laid. / Elle est laide.
Il est moche. / Elle est moche. (inf.)
He is ugly. / She is ugly.

You can also refer to the age of the person you are describing:

Il/Elle est jeune.
He/She is young.
Il est âgé. Elle est âgée.
Il est vieux. Elle est vieille.
He is old. She is old.

Now's a good time to review the adverb *assez* (rather, quite) and *très* (very):

- ***La femme est très belle.*** The woman is very beautiful.
- ***Mathis est assez jeune.*** Mathis is quite young.
- ***Il n'est pas très vieux.*** He is not that old.

Hair and face

Now, if you want to get into the specifics of describing one's appearance, you would need to know how to say the different parts of *le visage* (m.) or a face.

	Translation
le visage	face
la tête	head
les cheveux (m. plur.)	hair

l'oeil (m.)	eye
les yeux (m. plur.)	eyes
le sourcil	eyebrow
le nez	nose
les lèvres (f. plur.)	lips
les joues (f. plur.)	cheeks
le menton	chin
une moustache	mustache
une barbe	beard

Let us begin with describing someone's hair. Notice that we use the structure *avoir* + definite article. For example:

Elle a les cheveux longs.
She has long hair.

Il a les cheveux blonds.
He has blond hair.

In French, *les cheveux* is always plural. A quick grammar refresher: the adjective agrees in gender and number with the noun. Since *les cheveux* is masculine and plural, we use the corresponding adjective forms *longs* and *blonds*. In general, adjectives are placed after the noun they are describing.
You can refer to the color or the style by saying *les cheveux*...

- ***frisés/bouclés*** curly
- ***raides*** straight
- ***courts*** short
- ***mi-longs*** mid-length
- ***longs*** long
- ***blonds*** blond
- ***bruns*** brown
- ***châtains*** light-brown
- ***gris*** gray
- ***blancs*** white
- ***roux*** red

Certain words indicate hairstyles or color without specifying the noun *les cheveux*. For example:

- ***Il/Elle est chauve.*** He/She is bald.
- *Il est brun. / Elle est brune.* He is brunette. / She is brunette.
- *Il est blond. / Elle est blonde.* He is blond. / She is blond.
- *Il est roux / Elle est rousse.* He is red-headed. / She is red-headed.

Moving on to the window to the soul, the eyes or *les yeux*. You might have noticed above that the words for "eye" and "eyes" are different. If referring to a single eye alone, we say *l'oeil* (m.) and for both eyes, we say *les yeux*.

To describe someone's eyes, we use *avoir* with the definite article as well:

Noé a les yeux verts.
Noé has green eyes.

Monique a les yeux marrons.
Monique has brown eyes.

You can refer to the color of the eyes by using these words, *les yeux*…

- **bleus** blue
- **verts** green
- **marrons** brown

You can also describe someone's features using the vocabulary of the parts of the face above. Let's look at some examples:

- **Il a une barbe courte/longue.** He has a short/long beard.
- **Il a une moustache.** He has a mustache.
- **Elle a un petit nez.** She has a small nose.
- **Elle a le visage rond.** She has a round face.

Look at yourself in the mirror. Can you try describing yourself aloud using what we learned? Imagine a family member's face. Try describing his or her physical appearance.

Physique

Let's now focus on the physique, starting with essential words:

	Translation
le corps	the body
grand(e)	tall
petit(e)	short
mince	thin, slender
gros(se)	fat
rond(e)	plump
la peau	skin
la peau bronzée	tanned skin
la peau pâle	pale skin

Study the following examples:

Mon frère, Lucas, est très grand.
My brother, Lucas, is very tall.

Le mannequin est mince.
The model is slender.

Louise a la peau bronzée.

Louise has tanned skin.

L'acteur a la peau pâle.
The actor has pale skin.

Height and weight

When describing someone, it probably won't get as specific as indicating one's height or weight. Still, it is essential to know how to do so!

If you wish to specify the height or *la taille* of someone, you can use the verb *mesurer*, as in:

Nathalie mesure 2 mètres.
Nathalie is 2 meters tall.

Jacques mesure 1 mètre 80.
Jacques is 1 meter and 80 centimeters tall.

Note that the French measure height in meters, and not in feet.

As for weight or *le poids*, we use either the verb *faire* or *peser*.

Je fais 60 kg.
I weigh 60 kg.

Mon mari pèse 75 kg.
My husband weighs 75 kg.

GRAMMAR TIP

Relative pronouns qui and que

What are relative pronouns? Like any pronoun, relative pronouns replace nouns that are previously mentioned in order to avoid repetitions in a conversation. They are called "relative" because they introduce relative clauses. A relative clause introduces new information in a sentence about a noun. To simplify, let's study these two examples from the dialogue above:

C'est l'actrice <u>qui</u> a joué Sophie dans la série « Rappelle-moi ».
It's the actress who played Sophie in the series "Remind me".

C'est l'actrice <u>que</u> ma mère adore !
It's the actress that my mother loves!

The relative pronouns here are *qui* and *que*. Focus on the first sentence. The relative pronoun *qui* here introduces the clause "played Sophie in the series…". Instead of having to repeat the word "actress" like this:

C'est **l'actrice**. **L'actrice** a joué Sophie dans la série « Rappelle-moi ».

It's the actress. The actress played Sophie in the series "Remind me".

We use *qui* to replace the noun and avoid repetition.

In English, we have the relative pronouns "who" and "that" and their use depends on the kind of noun, whether it is a person or a thing. In French, *qui* and *que* have nothing to do with the kind of noun but the grammatical identity of it.

We use *qui* for the subject of the sentence. As such, it is always followed by a verb. We use *que* for the object of the sentence. As such, it is always followed by a noun or pronoun. Let's look at other examples:

C'est **l'acteur qui** a remporté l'Oscar.

It's the actor who won the Oscar.

Qui here refers to the "actor" (*l'acteur*), the subject of the sentence and the doer of the action. Next example:

C'est **l'acteur que** tout le monde aime.

It's the actor that everyone loves.

Que here refers to the "actor" too, but this time it's the object of the sentence, the receiver of the action. The subject in this sentence is *tout le monde* (everyone).

Remember that *qui* and *que* are not equivalent to "who" and "that". For instance, *qui* can be used to refer to a thing:

*C'est **le livre qui** a changé ma vie !*

This is the book that changed my life!

While in English, it is grammatically correct to sometimes omit the relative pronoun, this is not the case in French. For instance, one might say "It's the film I love", without the pronoun "that". But in French, the relative pronoun *que* cannot be omitted: *C'est le film **que** j'aime.*

Cinema vocabulary

	Translation
le cinéma	cinema, movie theater
un film	movie
une scène	a scene
un documentaire	a documentary
une série	a (TV) series
un film d'action	action movie
un film d'aventures	adventure movie
un film d'animation	animated movie
un film d'horreur	horror movie
un film policier	detective movie
un film de science-fiction	science-fiction movie
une comédie	comedy
le premier rôle	leading actor
le premier rôle féminin	leading actress
tourner	*to shoot (a movie or scene)*
un réalisateur	a director
une réalisatrice (f.)	a director

CULTURE TIP

Movie night!

Sharing one's thoughts about a movie is all part of the fun. To describe a movie in French, there is an abundance of adjectives we can use. One can talk about the story itself, *l'histoire*, which could be *originale* (original), *médiocre* (second-rate) or *géniale* (brilliant). You can also talk about the acting: perhaps it is *surjoué* (exaggerated)? Most beginners will overuse the adjective *intéressant* to describe everything: *C'est un film intéressant !* But how about trying these other adjectives instead?

C'est un film...

- ***amusant*** entertaining
- ***drôle*** funny

- ***émouvant*** moving, touching
- ***effrayant*** scary
- ***ennuyeux*** boring
- ***exceptionnel*** exceptional, remarkable
- ***impressionnant*** impressive
- ***sublime*** sublime, magnificent
- ***triste*** sad

Key Takeaways

- To ask how someone looks like, we use the following expressions:

Ask how someone looks like
Tu peux le/la décrire ? or *Vous pouvez le/la décrire ?*
De quoi il/elle a l'air ? or *Il/Elle a l'air de quoi ?*
À quoi il/elle ressemble or *Il/Elle ressemble à quoi ?*

- To describe someone, we can say:

General descriptions	
être beau/belle	*être laid(e)*
	être moche (inf.)
être jeune	*être âgé(e)*
	être vieux/vieille

Hair and face
avoir les cheveux frisés/bouclés/raides/courts/mi-longs/longs/blonds/bruns/châtains/gris/blancs/roux
être chauve
être brun(e)
être blond(e)
être roux/rousse
avoir les yeux bleus/verts/marrons

Physique
être grand(e)/petit(e)/mince/gros(se)/rond(e)
avoir la peau bronzée/pâle

Height and weight
mesurer.... mètres.
faire... kg / peser... kg

- The relative pronouns are used to avoid repetition and to introduce a relative clause.
- We use the relative pronoun *qui* to refer to the subject of the sentence. As such, it is always followed by a verb.
- We use *que* to refer to the object of the sentence. As such, it is always followed by a noun or pronoun.

In the next chapter, we will continue studying how to describe someone. This time, we will focus on one's qualities and weaknesses. We will also review adjective placement and learn how to compare.

Exercises

1-3. Complete the following sentences with the missing word:

1. - Vous _____ la décrire ?
   - Oui. Elle est grande. Elle a les cheveux roux et les yeux marrons.

2. - À _____ il ressemble ?
   - Il est chauve et assez jeune.

3. Ton amie a l'air de quoi ?
   - Elle a les _____ bouclés. Elle a les yeux verts.

4-6. In each list, find the word that does not belong.

4. blond – roux – châtain – mi-long
5. jeune – laid – âgé – vieux
6. brun – mince – rond – petit

7-10. *Qui* or *que* ? Complete the sentences with the correct relative pronoun.

7. C'est la chanson _____ Nathalie aime beaucoup.
8. Brad Pitt est un acteur américain _____ est très célèbre.
9. Tu as vu le voleur _____ a pris mon sac ?
10. C'est un film _____ nous avons regardé il y a longtemps.

Answer Key

1. pouvez
2. quoi
3. cheveux
4. mi-long (it's the only one referring to length)
5. laid (it's the only one that has nothing to do with age)
6. brun (it's the only one referring to hair color)
7. que
8. qui
9. qui
10. que

Chapter 2: All manner of people

On voit les qualités de loin et les défauts de près.

One sees the qualities from afar and the flaws up close.

- Victor Hugo

They say beauty is only skin deep, and that what's inside is more important than what can be seen by the naked eye. When we think of someone we know, we might conjure up a visual image of that person in our mind. But we will also most likely think about what this person is like. Shy? Outgoing? Talkative? Perhaps a bit eccentric?

In this lesson, you will learn how to describe someone's traits, be it positive or negative. You will also study how to compare. Finally, we will look more closely at the feminine and plural forms of adjectives.

Describing someone's personality

A person has both *des qualités* (f.), the positive things about him or her, and *des défauts* (m.), the negative stuff we often don't talk about! To ask about someone's personality, we can say:

Comment il/elle est ?
Il/Elle est comment ?
What is he/she like?

Qualities and flaws

Let's look at this short text describing two sisters:

> *Léa et sa sœur Sophie sont très différentes. Léa est plutôt timide. Elle n'aime pas sortir. Elle est introvertie. Elle est aussi gentille, honnête et sérieuse. Par contre, elle est un peu pessimiste. Sophie est extravertie. Elle est très bavarde ! Elle a beaucoup d'amis, c'est une fille vraiment sociable. Mais contrairement à Léa, elle est parfois menteuse et méchante.*

Can you find within this text, pairs of adjectives that are antonyms of each other?

Here are the antonym pairs in this text: *timide-sociable ; introverti-extraverti ; gentil-méchant ; honnête-menteur*. Did you get them all right?

To describe someone's quality or flaws, we use the verb *être* like in the text above. Adverbs like *parfois* (sometimes), *un peu* (a little), *très* (very), *plutôt* (rather), and *vraiment* (really) may be used to nuance these descriptions.

Below is a list of words related to qualities and flaws. Pro tip: memorizing the following as antonym pairs will help you retain them easier.

	Translation		Translation
calme	calm	*inquiet(-ète)*	anxious
confiant(e)	confident		
courageux(-euse)	courageous	*peureux(-euse)*	fearful
dynamique	energetic		
fort(e)	strong	*faible*	weak
généreux(-euse)	generous	*égoïste*	selfish
gentil(le)	kind	*méchant(e)*	mean
honnête	honest	*menteur(-euse)*	liar
humble	humble	*arrogant(e)*	arrogant
introverti(e)	introverted	*extraverti(e)*	extrovert
		sociable	sociable
optimiste	optimistic	*pessimiste*	pessimistic
patient(e)	patient	*impatient(e)*	impatient
poli(e)	polite	*impoli(e)*	impolite
réservé(e)	reserved, quiet	*bavard(e)*	talkative
responsable	responsible	*irresponsable*	irresponsible
sensible	sensitive	*insensible*	insensitive
sérieux(-euse)	hardworking	*paresseux(-euse)*	lazy

When describing someone, we can also use the expressions *quelqu'un de* + adjective or *avoir l'air* + adjective:

C'est quelqu'un de gentil.
He's a kind person.

Il a l'air gentil.
He seems kind.

GRAMMAR TIP

Adjectives: feminine and plural forms

At the beginner's level, you were taught the general rule to form the feminine of adjectives: by adding an -e at the end of the word. While there are exceptions to this rule, the good news is that they can also be grouped into categories:

Endings	Feminine form	Examples
-el	→ -elle	*naturel* → *naturelle*
-en	→ -enne	*ancien* → *ancienne*
-on	→ -onne	*bon* → *bonne*
-er	→ -ère	*léger* → *légère*
-eux	→ -euse	*heureux* → *heureuse*
-et	→ -ète	*inquiet* → *inquiète*
-f	→ -ve	*neuf* → *neuve*

To form the plural, the general rule is to add -s. Here are a few exceptions:

Endings	Plural form	Examples
-eau	→ -eaux	*nouveau* → *nouveaux*
-al	→ -aux	*national* → *nationaux*

Comparing

Let's look at another text. This time, Michel is describing himself while comparing his personality to his wife Anne.

> *Je suis quelqu'un de très calme. Ma femme, Anne, est plutôt dynamique. Elle est <u>plus sociable que</u> moi. Elle aime bien sortir avec ses amis, visiter des musées... Elle n'est pas timide du tout et elle est très confiante. Je l'admire vraiment. C'est <u>la personne la plus souriante que</u> je connais ! Moi, je suis <u>moins optimiste qu'</u>elle. Je suis d'un naturel inquiet.*

> I am a very calm person. My wife, Anne, is quite dynamic. She's more social than me. She likes going out with her friends, going to museums... She's not shy at all and she's very confident. I really admire her. She is always smiling. I am less optimistic than her. I'm a natural worrier!

In English, we use "more" or add -er to form the comparative. To compare in French, we simply use the expressions *plus*, *moins* and *aussi* with *que*. The structure is as follows:

PLUS / AUSSI / MOINS + ADJECTIVE + QUE or QU'

Plus is the equivalent of "more", *aussi* of "as", and *moins* of "less". Let's look at some examples.

> *Il est **plus grand que** moi.*
> He is taller than me.

*Léo est **aussi courageux que** son frère.*
Léo is as brave as his brother.

*La voiture est **moins rapide que** le train.*
The car is slower than the train.

Note that before a vowel, *que* contracts to *qu'*:

*Mathis est plus pessimiste **qu'elle**.*
Mathis is more pessimistic than her.

*Sophie est aussi heureuse **qu'Anne**.*
Sophie is as happy as Anne.

To form the superlative in English, we use "most" or add -est. In French, we follow this structure:

NOUN + DEFINITE ARTICLE (*LA, LE, LES*) + *PLUS / MOINS* + ADJECTIVE

Study these examples:

*Cette montagne est **la plus haute** du monde.*
This mountain is the highest in the world.

*C'est l'étudiant **le moins sérieux** dans cette classe.*
He's the least hardworking student in this class.

*Maria et Lucile sont les actrices **les plus célèbres** dans ce pays.*
Maria and Lucile are the most famous actresses in this country.

Note that the definite article changes according to the gender and number of the noun referred to. The same goes for the adjective.

If you look at the first example above, the adjective *haute* is in feminine form because it refers to the noun *la montagne,* which is feminine. In the third example, we use *célèbres* in plural form, for it refers to the plural noun *les actrices*.

CULTURE TIP

Who has long teeth?

There are many idiomatic expressions you can also use to describe someone's traits. We list here some of them:

- ***être mal dans sa peau*** to feel bad about oneself
- ***avoir les dents longues*** to be ambitious (lit. to have long teeth)
- ***avoir les pieds sur terre*** to be down-to-earth
- ***avoir la main verte*** to have a green thumb (lit. to have a green hand)

- ***avoir les chevilles qui enflent*** to be full of oneself (lit. to have ankles that swell)

Key Takeaways

- To ask or describe how someone is like, we say:

Ask about someone's personality
Comment il/elle est ?
Il/Elle est comment ?
Describe someone's personality
être + adjective
être quelqu'un de + adjective
avoir l'air de + adjective

- To form the comparative, we use the expressions *plus, aussi* and *moins* + adjective + *que* or *qu'*.
- To form the superlative, we use the following structure: noun + *le/la/les* + *plus/moins* + adjective.
- In general, we add an -e to form the feminine of adjectives. There are exceptions, in which case we replace the endings as such: -el → -elle ; -en → -enne ; -on → -onne ; -er → -ère ; -eux → -euse ; -et → -ète ; -f → -ve.
- To form the plural, we add an -s. However, for nouns ending in -eau and -al, we add an -x.

In the next chapter, we will learn how to shop for clothes. We will learn vocabulary related to clothing and accessories. As for the grammar, we will focus on direct object pronouns and adverbs of intensity.

Exercises

1-5. Translate the following sentences. Remember that the adjectives must agree with the gender and number of the noun being described.

1. David is very generous.
2. Monique and Fabienne are polite.
3. She is more energetic than her friend.
4. Are you an introvert or an extrovert?
5. My wife is the kindest person in the world!

6-8. Transform the adjective in parentheses into the superlative form, following the examples. The symbol + represents the most, and − represents the least. Don't forget to change the adjectives in feminine or plural form if needed. Let the example below guide you.

ex. *Le SCMaglev est le train (+ rapide) _____ du monde.*
[Answer: Le SCMaglev est le train le plus rapide du monde.]

6. Le Burj Khalifa à Dubai est le bâtiment (+ haut) _____ du monde.
7. Sophie est la personne (+ intelligent) _____ que je connaisse !
8. Cette ville est (- peuplé) _____ du monde.

9-10. Complete the idiomatic expressions with the missing word.

9. Mon collègue a les _____ longues, il va tout faire pour devenir chef !
10. Vivienne est très douée pour le jardinage, elle a la main _____.

Answer Key

1. David est très généreux.
2. Monique et Fabienne sont polies.
3. Elle est plus dynamique que son ami(e).
4. Es-tu introverti(e) ou extraverti(e) ? OR Êtes-vous introverti(e) ou extraverti(e) ?
5. Ma femme est la personne la plus gentille du monde !
6. le plus haut
7. la plus intelligente
8. la moins peuplée
9. dents
10. verte

Chapter 3: Fits like a glove

S'habiller est un mode de vie.

Dressing is a way of life.

- Yves Saint Laurent

Shopping! Who doesn't love shopping? Well, probably a lot of people. Still, it's one of those things we do quite a lot. On a regular basis, we go to the stores to buy necessities. Sometimes, we treat ourselves to a well-deserved reward, a new pair of shoes, a new bag, or perhaps a new tie. On special occasions, we also take our time to buy gifts for our loved ones. But while shopping can seem like a solo experience, much of it is spent communicating with salesclerks. Knowing how to ask more about a product or specify a size is thus primordial!

In this lesson, you will learn how to shop for clothes. We will study words related to clothing. We will also look at direct object pronouns and adverbs of intensity.

Shopping for clothes

At the clothes' shop, you might get asked:

Je peux vous aider ?
May I help you?

Vous cherchez quelque chose en particulier ?
Are you looking for something in particular?

For those who love to do the shopping on their own, a quick reply would be:

Non, merci, je regarde.
No thank you, I'm just looking around.

Trying clothes on

Let's look at this quick dialogue. Sophie is at the mall hoping to buy a new blouse.

> ***Vendeur :*** *Bonjour Madame, je peux vous aider ?*
> ***Sophie :*** *Oui, j'aime bien ce chemisier. Est-ce que je peux l'essayer ?*
> ***Vendeur :*** *Bien sûr.*
> ***Sophie :*** *Où sont les cabines, s'il vous plaît ?*
> ***Vendeur :*** *Juste au fond, Madame.*
> *[Un peu plus tard...]*
> ***Sophie :*** *Je pense que c'est trop grand... Normalement, je fais du 36.*
> ***Vendeur :*** *Je peux vous apporter un 38.*

Sophie : *D'accord, merci.*
Salesclerk: Good day Madam, may I help you?
Sophie: Yes, I like this blouse. Can I try it?
Salesclerk: Of course.
Sophie: Where are the changing rooms, please?
Salesclerk: Just at the back, Madam.
[A little bit later...]
Sophie: I think it's too big. I'm normally a size 36.
Salesclerk: I can bring you a size 38.
Sophie: Okay, thank you.

To ask if you can try on clothing, you can use the following expressions. At the beginner's level, we learned that we use *est-ce que* to formulate slightly formal questions:

Est-ce que je peux essayer ce chemisier ?
Je peux essayer ce chemisier ?
Can I try this blouse?

Où sont les cabines (d'essayage) ?
Where are the changing rooms?

Indicating size

To ask someone's size, you'll usually hear:

Quelle taille portez-vous ?
Vous portez quelle taille ?
What size do you wear?

To indicate one's size, we use the verb *faire* with the article *du*:

Sophie fait du 36.
Sophie is a size 36.

Je fais du 40.
I'm a size 40.

It is also useful to remember the terms for clothing sizes: *petite taille* (small), *taille moyenne* (medium) and *grande taille* (large). If you wish to ask for a different size, you might say:

Avez-vous une plus grande taille ? / Vous avez une plus grande taille ?
Do you have a larger size?

Avez-vous une plus petite taille ? / Vous avez une plus petite taille ?
Do you have a smaller size?

To indicate how a clothing fits (or does not fit) you, you can also use these phrases:
- ***Ça me va.*** It fits me.
- ***La couleur ne me va pas.*** The color doesn't fit me.

- ***C'est trop court.*** It's too short.
- ***C'est trop petit/grand.*** It's too small/big.
- ***C'est trop serré.*** It's too tight.

Notice that we use the verb *aller* figuratively, to mean "to fit". As for the last three examples, you can see the use of the adverb *trop* (too). *Trop* is placed before the adjective unlike most adverbs.

Clothing vocabulary

	Translation
des chaussettes (f.)	socks
des sous-vêtements (m.)	underwear
un caleçon	boxer shorts
un chemisier	a blouse
un costume	a suit
un imperméable	a raincoat
un jean	jeans
un manteau	a coat
un pantalon	pants
un polo	a polo shirt
un pull	a sweater
un short	shorts
un slip	briefs
un soutien-gorge	a bra
un t-shirt	a t-shirt
une chemise	a long-sleeved or short-sleeved shirt (usually men's)
une culotte	panties
une jupe	a skirt
une robe	a dress
une veste	a jacket

GRAMMAR TIP

Adverbs of intensity: trop and assez

Adverbs are words or phrases used to qualify a verb, an adjective or another adverb. There are adverbs that express intensity that you are most likely familiar with by now: *très* (very), *beaucoup* (a lot) and *un peu* (a little). Let us review these adverbs by studying some examples:

- ***J'aime beaucoup le café.*** I like coffee a lot.
- ***Michel a travaillé un peu ce matin.*** Michel worked a little this morning.
- ***Il fait très chaud aujourd'hui.*** It's very hot today.

Now, let's learn some new adverbs of intensity: *trop* and *assez*.

The adverb *trop* translates to "too" or "too much". Because it is an adverb, it can be used to qualify an adjective, another adverb or a verb:

- ***C'est trop cher.*** It's too expensive.
- ***Il marche trop lentement.*** He walks too slowly.
- ***Tu parles trop !*** You talk too much.

Note that *trop* is placed before an adjective or an adverb, but <u>after</u> a verb.

Trop can also be used with a noun, but it should be combined with the preposition *de*. In this case, it means "too many of" or "too much of". For example:

- ***J'ai trop de travail !*** I have too much work!
- ***Ma fille a trop de vêtements.*** My daughter has too many clothes.

The preposition *de* is invariable, meaning it does not change according to gender or number. However, it contracts to *d'* before a vowel.

The adverb *assez*, on the other hand, may mean "quite" or "enough". For example:

- ***L'appartement est assez grand pour un couple.*** The apartment is big enough for a couple.
- ***Mon enseignant est assez jeune.*** My teacher is quite young.
- ***Je bois assez d'eau.*** I drink enough water.

Bargaining

As a beginner, you know that we can use the expression **Combien ça coûte ?** to ask for a price. If you are hoping to find something within your budget range at a store, there are other phrases you need to know. Imagine that you are buying jewelry, the salesclerk might ask your budget by saying:

Vous voulez mettre combien ?
What is your budget? (lit. How much do you want to put in?)

Quel est votre budget ?

What is your budget?

To this you can say, for example: *300 euros au maximum*. To ask for products within the same price range, you can say:

Est-ce que vous avez quelque chose d'autre dans ces prix-là ?
Est-ce que vous avez quelque chose d'autre dans le même ordre de prix ?
Do you have something else in the same price range?

In certain places, like in *un marché aux puces* (a flea market), you might have the chance to bargain. Here are some other useful phrases you need to know:

Je vous le vends/fais à 20 euros.
I can sell it to you for 20 euros.

Je vous le prends à 30 euros.
I will take it for 30 euros.

Notice that the verb *faire* is used in the first example, to mean "to sell".

GRAMMAR TIP

Direct object pronouns

In the earlier dialogue we saw this sentence: *Est-ce que je peux l'essayer ?*. Likewise, in the example above: *Je vous le vends*. *L'* and *le* here are what we call direct object pronouns.

As the name suggests, object pronouns are pronouns that replace the direct object of the sentence. A direct object is the receiver of the action. It follows a verb which answers the question "what" or "whom". For example, let's look at this sentence in English:

I eat an apple.

"I" is the subject, "eat" is the verb. Now the receiver of the action is the apple, so it is the object. If we ask, "I eat what?" The answer is apple. In its French equivalence, we find the same structure:

Je mange <u>une pomme</u>.

Mange quoi ? (Eat what?) *Une pomme. Une pomme* is thus the direct object of the sentence.

Now in English, we would replace the direct object with "it", as in: "I eat it". In French, it would be *Je la mange*. Here are the direct object pronouns in French:

Direct object pronouns	Translation
me/m'	me
te/t'	you (inf.)
le/l'	him / it (masc.)
la/l'	her / it (fem.)
nous	us
vous	you (for.)
les	them

Notice that before a vowel, most of these pronouns contract. Let's look at some examples for clarity. Study how the nouns are replaced by the direct object pronouns below:
- ***Je vends <u>l'ordinateur</u>. Je <u>le</u> vends.*** I sell the computer. I sell it.
- ***J'adore <u>le livre</u>. Je <u>l'</u>adore.*** I love the book. I love it.
- ***Il achète <u>les vêtements</u>. Il <u>les</u> achète.*** He buys the clothes. He buys them.
- ***Je vois <u>ta sœur</u>. Je <u>la</u> vois.*** I see your sister. I see her.

Look at these other examples:
- ***Tu me vois ?*** Do you see me?
- ***Je t'aime.*** I love you.
- ***Elle nous regarde.*** She's watching us.

Accessories vocabulary

	Translation
(en) argent	silver
(en) or	gold
des bijoux (m.)	jewelry
des boucles d'oreille (f.)	earrings
des gants (m.)	gloves
un bonnet	a winter hat
un bracelet	a bracelet
un chapeau	a hat
un collier	a necklace
un foulard	a light scarf, a head scarf
un sac à main	a handbag
une bague	a ring
une casquette	a cap
une ceinture	a belt
une cravate	a tie
une écharpe	a scarf

CULTURE TIP

Les soldes

A sale is called *les soldes* (m. plur.) in French. During this period, products are *en promotion* (in promotion) or *à prix réduit* (in reduced price). In France, the sale seasons are regulated and set by the government:

- ***les soldes d'hiver*** (winter sales) from January onwards.
- ***les soldes d'été*** (summer sales) from June onwards.

Each sale season lasts 5 weeks. The goal is to clear their inventory, so shops would sell even at a loss. You can only imagine how much discount you can get!

Key Takeaways

- To communicate while shopping, we use the following expressions:

Je peux vous aider ?	*Non, merci, je regarde.*
Vous cherchez quelque chose en particulier ?	
Trying clothes on	
Est-ce que je peux essayer ce chemisier ?	
Je peux essayer ce chemisier ?	
Où sont les cabines (d'essayage) ?	
Indicating size	
Quelle taille portez-vous ?	
Vous portez quelle taille ?	
faire du + size	
Avez-vous une plus grande taille ? / Vous avez une plus grande taille ?	
Avez-vous une plus petite taille ? / Vous avez une plus petite taille ?	
Bargaining	
Vous voulez mettre combien ?	
Quel est votre budget ?	
Est-ce que vous avez quelque chose d'autre dans ces prix-là ?	
Est-ce que vous avez quelque chose d'autre dans le même ordre de prix ?	
Je vous le vends/fais à 20 euros.	
Je vous le prends à 30 euros.	

- The adverb *trop* (too, too much) is placed before an adjective and an adverb, and after a verb.

- The expression *trop de* is invariable and followed by a noun.
- The adverb *assez* (quite, enough) is placed before an adjective and an adverb, and after a verb.
- The direct object pronouns are *me/m', te/t', le/l', la/l', nous, vous* and *les*.

In the next chapter, you will learn how to talk about your health and consult a doctor. We will also study temporal markers, logical connectors and the pluperfect tense. To expand your vocabulary, we will also look at the parts of the body and words related to health and illness.

Exercises

1-3. Complete the following sentences with the missing word:

1. - Vous portez quelle taille ?
 - Je _____ du 38.
2. - Est-ce que vous avez quelque chose d'autre dans le _____ ordre de prix ?
 - Nous avons cette bague à 120 euros.
3. - Cette chemise est trop grande. Avez-vous une plus petite _____ ?
 - Oui, je vous l'apporte tout de suite.

4-6. Replace the underlined noun with the correct object pronoun. Rewrite the entire sentence to place the pronoun correctly.

4. Vous voulez essayer cette <u>jupe</u> ?
5. Je vais donner les <u>livres</u> à ma sœur.
6. Mathis achète une <u>cravate</u> et un <u>sac</u>.

7-10. *Trop* or *trop de*? Add the correct phrase to the following sentences.

7. Sophie a fait _____ erreurs dans son essai.
8. Tu conduis _____ rapidement !
9. Mes enfants mangent _____.
10. Les chaussettes sont _____ grandes pour moi.

Answer Key

1. fais
2. même
3. taille
4. Vous voulez l'essayer ?
5. Je vais les donner à ma sœur.
6. Mathis les achète.
7. trop d'
8. trop
9. trop
10. trop

Chapter 4: Feeling under the weather

J'ai décidé d'être heureux parce que c'est bon pour la santé.

I decided to be happy because it's good for the health.

- Voltaire

Being fit and healthy is one of the most important things in our daily life. It is however inevitable that on some days, we don't feel at our best. If in a foreign country, going to the doctor and asking for help can be both challenging and daunting.

In this lesson, you will learn how to communicate at the doctor's office, how to explain your symptoms or relate your medical history. We will also study the temporal markers and logical connectors to structure your speech. Finally, we will have a look at the pluperfect tense.

Explaining symptoms

The expression *avoir mal à* is useful when explaining symptoms. It roughly translates to "to have pain in". Note that the preposition *à* changes according to the gender and number of the noun that follows:

- ***J'ai mal à la tête.*** I have a headache. (lit. I have pain in the head.)
- ***J'ai mal à la gorge.*** I have a sore throat.
- ***J'ai mal au ventre.*** I have a stomach ache.
- ***J'ai vraiment mal au dos.*** I have a bad backache.

You can also say *ça fait (vraiment) mal* to say "it hurts" or "I'm in pain". To explain your symptoms, you can also use the following expressions:

- ***J'ai la grippe.*** I have the flu.
- ***J'ai un rhume.*** I have a cold.
- ***J'ai de la fièvre.*** I have fever.
- ***J'ai vomi.*** I vomited.
- ***Je tousse.*** I cough.
- ***J'éternue.*** I sneeze.
- ***J'ai tout le temps des problèmes de dos.*** I always have back problems.
- ***Je souffre de douleurs articulaires.*** I suffer from joint pain.

Now the doctor will most likely *examiner le/la patient(e)* (examine the patient), *prescrire des médicaments* (prescribe medication) or order for some other tests like *une IRM* (MRI), *un scanner* (scan), *une radio* (x-ray), or *une analyse de sang* (blood test).

CULTURE TIP

Is the doctor in?

To see the doctor in France, you'd have to call their office and ask for an appointment. If it's your first time seeing that doctor, getting an appointment won't be easy. In fact, you might have to wait for a few days!

Patients usually seek out *des médecins généralistes* (general practitioners), who would then redirect them to the *spécalistes* (specialized practitioners) if necessary. If living in France, it is a good idea to register with *un médecin traitant* (primary care doctor), who will act as your main doctor. While it is not required by the government, it makes setting up appointments much easier, and it also means you get a higher reimbursement for the medical costs.

Anatomy vocabulary

	Translation
la tête	head
le cou	neck
la gorge	throat
les épaules (f.)	shoulders
le bras	arm
la poitrine	chest
le ventre	stomach
la main	hand
les doigts (m.)	fingers
les ongles (m.)	nails
le pouce	thumb
la jambe	leg
le genou	knee
les pieds	feet
les fesses	butt
le coeur	heart
les os (m.)	bones
le cerveau	brain
les poumons	lungs
l'estomac (m.)	stomach
le sang	blood

Relating medical history

Let's study this dialogue. Georges is at the doctor's because he hasn't been feeling well for months.

> ***Le médecin :*** *Bonjour Monsieur. Qu'est-ce qui vous amène ?*
> ***Georges :*** *Bonjour docteur. Je suis venu vous voir parce que je souffre de problèmes de dos depuis maintenant un mois. Il y a trois mois, je suis tombé dans les escaliers. J'avais déjà fait des séances de kiné mais la douleur ne s'en va pas…*
> ***Le médecin :*** *Vous avez déjà eu des maux de dos avant l'accident ?*
> ***Georges :*** *Oui, j'avais des problèmes de sciatiques il y a deux ans. Je passe beaucoup de temps assis devant l'ordinateur.*
> ***Le médecin :*** *Bon, vous allez d'abord faire un scanner puis on va se revoir après.*
> **The doctor:** Hello Sir. What brings you here?
> **Georges:** Hello Doctor. I came to see you because I've been suffering from back problems for a month now. Three months ago, I fell down the stairs. I have already done some physio sessions but the pain is not going away.
> **The doctor:** Did you already have backaches before the accident?
> **Georges:** Yes, I had sciatica problems two years ago. I spend a lot of time sitting down in front of the computer.
> **The doctor:** Alright, you are going to take a scan first then we'll see each other again after.

When relating medical history, you can use temporal markers to refer to a period of time. *Il y a* means "ago". Notice how in French this expression comes before the noun referring to the time, and not after. And so, Georges says *il y a trois mois* (three months ago) and *il y a deux ans* (two years ago).

Other temporal markers include *dans* (in), *pendant* (during, for) and *depuis* (since). Look at how they are used below:

- ***Les résultats seront prêts dans deux heures.*** The results will be ready in two hours.
- ***J'avais mal à la tête pendant quatre heures !*** I had a headache for four hours!
- ***Je fais des séances de kinésithérapie depuis un mois.*** I've been taking physical therapy sessions for one month.

Remember that *dans* is used when referring to a future period of time. The preposition *depuis* is used to refer to an action that has started in the past, and is still ongoing. So, in the last example, it is implied that the subject is still taking these physical therapy sessions.

In the dialogue above, we also saw some basic logical connectors. Remember these:

- ***mais*** but
- ***car*** because
- ***parce que*** because

They are used the same way as in English. Note that *car* and *parce que* are synonymous, but *car* is most often used in written French.

GRAMMAR TIP
Pluperfect tense

The pluperfect tense is used to refer to something that had happened in the past. For example, the simple past tense of the verb "watch" in English would be "watched", and the pluperfect would be "have/had watched".

Like in English, the pluperfect in French also has two parts: the imperfect tense of the verb *avoir* or *être* and the past participle. To make things simpler, it's as if you're taking the composed past tense and changing the auxiliary *avoir* or *être* to imperfect tense. We have studied the composed past and the imperfect tenses at the beginner's level. If you need to review them, check out our first book or the verb conjugations list in the annex of this one.

Let's look at some examples, the verb *manger* and the verb *partir*. We know that to form the composed past of *manger*, we use *avoir mangé*, and for *partir*, *être parti(e)*. Instead of conjugating *avoir* and *être* in the present, we change them to the imperfect tense to form the pluperfect:

manger	*partir*
J'avais mangé	J'étais parti(e)
Tu avais mangé	Tu étais parti(e)
Il/Elle/On avait mangé	Il/Elle/On était parti(e)
Nous avions mangé	Nous étions parti(e)s
Vous aviez mangé	Vous étiez parti(e)s
Ils/Elles avaient mangé	Ils/Elles étaient parti(e)s

Like with the composed past, the past participle changes according to the gender and number of the subject when the auxiliary is *être*. Now, let's look at this verb tense at-work:

- ***Nous avions déjà mangé quand il est arrivé.*** We had already eaten when he arrived.
- ***J'étais déjà allé à la pharmacie avant de voir le médecin.*** I had already gone to the pharmacy before seeing the doctor.

Key Takeaways

- To explain one's symptoms, we can use the following expressions:

Explain symptoms
avoir mal à...
souffrir de...
avoir des problèmes de...
avoir la grippe
avoir un rhume
avoir de la fièvre
vomir
tousser
éternuer

- The basic logical connectors include *mais*, *car* and *parce que*. *Car* is mostly used in written French.

- To relate medical history, we use temporal markers such as *il y a*, *dans*, *pendant*, and *depuis*.

- The pluperfect tense is formed by combining *avoir* or *être* in the imperfect tense with the past participle of the verb. It is used to refer to events or actions that had happened in the past.

In the next chapter, we will learn how to relate news using the recent past tense and the present progressive tense. This time, we will have a look at vocabulary related to life milestones.

Exercises

1-5. Conjugate the verbs in parentheses in the pluperfect tense.

1. Je (regarder) _____ ce film.
2. Mathis (répondre) _____ au message de son père.
3. Annie (aller) _____ au cinéma.
4. Ils (jouer) _____ au foot avant de rentrer.
5. Léo (acheter) _____ une voiture.

6-8. *Dans*, *depuis*, or *il y a*? Complete the sentences with the correct preposition.

6. Je vais partir pour le Japon _____ deux semaines.
7. Ma mère est allée à l'hôpital _____ trois jours.
8. Éric a des douleurs _____ une semaine.

9-10. Complete the following sentences with the missing word.

9. J'ai _____ à la gorge et j'ai toussé toute la nuit.
10. Suite à un accident, j'ai mal _____ épaules.

Answer Key

1. J'avais regardé
2. avait répondu
3. était allée
4. avaient joué
5. avait acheté
6. dans
7. il y a
8. depuis
9. mal
10. aux

Chapter 5: Bearer of news

L'amitié ne connaît ni feinte ni déguisement, tout y est sincère, tout part du cœur.

Friendship knows neither pretense nor disguise, everything is sincere, everything comes from the heart.

- French proverb

Thanks to social media, we are now constantly updated with our family and friends' lives. Friend one got a new cat, friend two finally got his dream job, and friend three is now in a complicated relationship (sometimes we even know too much about other peoples' lives!). Still, much of our in-person conversations revolve around knowing what they are up to or how they've been doing.

In this lesson, you will learn how to ask for and share news related to one's life. We will be tackling two verb tenses, namely the recent past tense and the present progressive tense.

Asking for news

Chloé bumps into an old friend from college, Marine. She asks how their other classmates are doing. Let's look at their conversation:

>**Chloé :** *Marine ! Ça fait un bail ! Comment ça va ?*
>**Marine :** *Oui, ça fait vraiment longtemps ! Je vais bien. Je viens de déménager ici il y a un mois. Et toi ?*
>**Chloé :** *Ça va, je travaille dans une boîte de cosmétiques depuis deux ans. Tu as des nouvelles de Gabriel ?*
>**Marine :** *Je ne suis pas vraiment au courant… mais la dernière fois que je l'ai vu, il faisait son master en informatique.*
>**Chloé :** *Et Jade ? Qu'est-elle devenue ?*
>**Marine :** *Jade s'est mariée avec Léo. Elle vient de donner naissance à un garçon.*
>
>**Chloé:** Marine! It's been ages! How are you?
>**Marine:** Yes, it's been a long time! I'm doing well. I just moved here a month ago. And you?
>**Chloé:** I'm doing well, I've been working for a cosmetics company for two years now. Do you have any news about Gabriel?
>**Marine:** I'm not really up-to-date… but the last time I saw him, he was taking his Masters in IT.
>**Chloé:** And Jade? What has become of her?
>**Marine:** Jade married Leo. She just gave birth to a boy.

To ask updates about a friend, we might use the following expressions:

- ***Tu as des nouvelles de Gabriel ?*** Do you have news about Gabriel?
- ***Que devient Gabriel ?*** What becomes of Gabriel?

- *Qu'est-il devenu ?* What has become of him?
- *Qu'est-elle devenue ?* What has become of her?

Now, to these questions, one might reply:

- *Je n'ai pas de nouvelles.* I don't have news.
- *Je ne suis pas au courant.* I'm not up-to-date. / I'm not informed.

GRAMMAR TIP

Recent past tense

The recent past tense is used to denote an action or event that had just happened. In English, it is the equivalent of the structure "just" + past participle.

In French, the recent past is composed of three elements. It's quite simple though:

VENIR in present tense + *DE/D'* + **unconjugated verb.**

The preposition *de* is contracted before a vowel. Let's look at the verb *regarder* and *sortir* in recent past tense:

regarder	*sortir*
Je viens de regarder	Je viens de sortir
Tu viens de regarder	Tu viens de sortir
Il/Elle/On vient de regarder	Il/Elle/On vient de sortir
Nous venons de regarder	Nous venons de sortir
Vous venez de regarder	Vous venez de sortir
Ils/Elles viennent de regarder	Ils/Elles viennent de sortir

Now, let's look at this verb tense at-work:

- *Je viens de rentrer.* I just came home.
- *Mathis et Chloé viennent de dîner dans un restaurant.* Mathis and Chloé just dined at a restaurant.
- *Tu viens de sortir de l'école à l'instant ?* You just got out of school right now?

Sharing news

To share rumored news about someone, we can use the expression *Il paraît que* (It seems that) or *J'ai entendu dire que* (lit. I heard one say that):

- *Il paraît qu'il a quitté son travail.* It seems he left his job.

- ***J'ai entendu dire qu'elle a déménagé en Chine.*** I heard she moved to China.

You can also use verb tenses like the recent past to share news about someone:

- ***Elle vient de donner naissance à une fille.*** She just gave birth to a girl.
- ***Adrien vient de créer sa propre entreprise.*** Adrien just started his own company.

CULTURE TIP

12C4

Like in other cultures, the French use texting abbreviations to be able to type and send out SMS much quicker. One of these is *12c4* (un-deux-c-quatre), which when read out loud sounds like the expression *un de ces quatre* (one of these days). And so, you might text for instance:

On se revoit 12c4 ?

Let's meet up one of these days?

Here are other useful texting abbreviations. Remember that these are <u>very</u> informal and are only used in SMS:

- **A+** *(à plus)* see you later
- **a2m1** *(à demain)* see you tomorrow
- **b1sur** *(bien sûr)* of course
- **biz** *(bisous)* kisses
- **mr6** *(merci)* thanks
- **tjs** *(toujours)* always

Life milestones vocabulary

	Translation
la naissance	birth
le mariage	marriage
la séparation	separation
déménager	to move (to a new place, home, etc.)
se marier (avec quelqu'un)	to get married (with somebody)
épouser (quelqu'un)	to marry (somebody)
avoir des enfants	to have kids
donner naissance	to give birth
divorcer	to divorce
démissionner	to resign (from a job)
être licencié(e)	to get fired

se reconvertir	to change careers
créer une entreprise	to start a business
lancer une entreprise	

GRAMMAR TIP

Present progressive tense

In French, the present tense is commonly used as both present and present progressive tense. For instance, *Je mange* can both be translated to "I eat" or "I am eating."

However, if you want to emphasize that an action is currently being done, you can use the following structure:

ÊTRE + EN TRAIN DE / D' + unconjugated verb

And so, you might say:

Je suis en train de manger.

I am in the process of eating.

The preposition *de* is contracted before a vowel:

Noémie est en train d'étudier.

Noémie is in the process of studying.

When sharing news about someone, it would be common to use the present tense to indicate an ongoing action or event. For example, you might hear:

Elle fait le tour du monde.

She is traveling around the world.

The verb *faire* here is in present tense, although it is technically an ongoing action.

Key Takeaways

- To ask or share news, we can use the following expressions:

Ask news
Tu as des nouvelles de...
Que devient...

Qu'est-il/elle devenu(e) ?
Share news
Je n'ai pas de nouvelles.
Je ne suis pas au courant.
Il paraît que...
J'ai entendu dire que...
Il/Elle vient de...

- The recent past tense is formed by combining the verb *venir* in present tense with the preposition *de* or *d'* and the unconjugated form of the main verb.

- The present progressive tense is formed by combining the verb *être* in the present tense with the phrase *en train de* or *d'* and the unconjugated form of the main verb.

In the next chapter, we will move to the topic of career. You will learn how to understand a job advertisement and communicate during a job interview. We will also discuss chronological connectors and indirect object pronouns.

Exercises

1-3. Complete the sentences with the missing words.

1. J'ai entendu _____ que Mathis a déménagé au Japon.
2. Il _____ que Léo s'est marié avec une amie d'enfance.
3. Qu'_____ -elle devenue ?

4-7. Conjugate the verbs in parentheses in the recent past tense.

4. Marine et Éric (démissionner) _____.
5. Mon frère (divorcer) _____.
6. Vous (déménager) _____ à Paris ?
7. Nous (lancer) _____ une entreprise de nettoyage.

8-10. Conjugate the verbs in parentheses in the present progressive tense.

8. Les enfants (jouer) _____ dans le parc.
9. Je (réparer) _____ ma voiture.
10. Ma mère (cuisiner) _____ mon plat préféré.

Answer Key

1. dire
2. paraît
3. est
4. viennent de démissionner
5. vient de divorcer
6. venez de déménager
7. venons de lancer
8. sont en train de jouer
9. suis en train de réparer
10. est en train de cuisiner

Chapter 6: You're hired

Le travail a des racines amères mais des fruits sucrés.

Work has bitter roots but sweet fruits.

- French proverb

If you've decided to settle in a francophone country, having a source of income is primordial. This means finding a stable job, which then entails responding to a job advertisement or acing an interview. Job hunting can be a tough task. Interviews, no matter the language of communication, also pose quite a challenge. Knowing key words and phrases will be helpful to best present yourself and your talents.

In this lesson, you will learn how to understand a job ad and communicate during a job interview. We will learn ways to structure your speech using expressions of time and chronological connectors. We will also tackle indirect object pronouns and vocabularies related to school and career.

Understanding a job advertisement

Let's begin by studying this excerpt of a job ad:

CONSEILLER DE VENTE H/F

Nous recrutons un conseiller de vente H/F pour notre magasin LA MODE BIO à Paris (12ᵉ arrondissement)

Qui sommes-nous ?
Créée en 2004, LA MODE BIO propose une large gamme de produits prêt-à-porter et compte actuellement 100 magasins en France. Nous privilégions des matières éco-responsables ainsi que des processus de fabrication éthiques. Rejoignez-nous pour faire partie d'une entreprise qui s'engage pour changer le monde et protéger l'environnement !

At the heading of an ad, you'll usually find *le poste* or the job position being advertised. *Le poste* in masculine is not to be confused with *la poste* which is the post office! In the ad above, *le poste* is *conseiller de vente* (sales advisor) open to both men and women, *homme/femme* or *H/F*.

The first part of the ad will usually include a simple introduction to the company, with its date of creation, main products, and so on. Study the translation of the excerpt above here:

SALES ADVISOR M/F

We are recruiting a M/F sales consultant for our LA MODE BIO store in Paris (12th arrondissement).

Who are we?

Founded in 2004, LA MODE BIO offers a wide range of ready-to-wear products and currently has 100 stores in France. We favor eco-responsible materials as well as ethical manufacturing processes. Join us to be part of a company that is committed to changing the world and protecting the environment!

Let us keep reading the rest of this job ad:

Vos missions :
- *accueillir et conseiller les clients.*
- *proposer des produits.*
- *réaliser des ventes pour atteindre les objectifs mensuels.*

Votre profil :
Vous avez une formation commerciale et une première expérience réussie dans les ventes. Vous êtes assidu(e) et ponctuel(le). Vous aimez le travail en équipe. Vous êtes passionné(e) par la mode.

Vous souhaitez postuler pour cette offre d'emploi ? Envoyez-nous votre CV et une lettre de motivation !

Type d'emploi : *Temps plein, CDI*
Nombre d'heures : *35 heures par semaine*
Salaire : *1 400€ à 1 700€ par mois*

Your duties:

• receive and advise customers.
• offer products.
• make sales to reach the monthly turnover.

Your profile:
You have commercial training and a first successful experience in sales. You are diligent and punctual. You like teamwork. You are passionate about fashion.

Do you want to apply for this job offer? Send us your CV and a cover letter!

Type of employment: Full time, permanent contract
Number of hours: 35 hours per week
Salary: €1,400 to €1,700 per month

One of the most important parts of the job ad is your duties, called les *missions* (f.). And then, *le profil*, which lists the requirements for the job. For instance, you might be required to have a degree related to fashion, *une formation en mode* (schooling in fashion), or *une première expérience*, a first experience, in the field.

Finally, you'd want to look at the details of the job. Is it a *CDD - Contrat à Durée Déterminée* (temporary contract) or a *CDI - Contrat à Durée Indéterminée* (permanent contract). Of course, most would want *un CDI*! You'll also see in the ad *le salaire* (salary) proposed. Note that in France, full-time work usually means 35 hours per week.

Job search vocabulary

	Translation
une candidature	an application
poser sa candidature	to send an application
une offre d'emploi	a job offer
un contrat de travail	a work contract
un salaire	a salary
un/une salarié(e)	an employee
un/une employé(e)	
un employeur	an employer
un CDD	temporary contract *(Contrat à Durée Déterminée)*
un CDI	permanent contract *(Contrat à Durée Indéterminée)*
à plein temps	full-time
à mi-temps	part-time (50%)
à temps partiel	part-time (around 70 – 80%)
le SMIC	minimum wage *(Salaire Minimum Interprofessionnel de Croissance)*
le salaire brut	gross salary
le salaire net	net salary
les études	studies or schooling
la formation	
un stage	an internship
un demandeur d'emploi	a job seeker
un/une chômeur(-euse)	an unemployed person
un CV	CV or curriculum vitae
une lettre de motivation	cover letter
un entretien	an interview

GRAMMAR TIP
Indirect object pronouns

As the name suggests, indirect object pronouns replace the indirect object of the sentence.

In Chapter 3, we studied direct object pronouns, which in sum replace the direct object or the receiver of the action. Now, an indirect object is different, for it is the person who receives the action indirectly. Let's look at this sentence:

Je donne la lettre à Marie.
I give the letter to Marie.

Can you tell which is the direct object and indirect object in the sentence?

The direct object is *la lettre*, while the indirect object is Marie. If the direct object answers the question "what" or "whom", the indirect object answers "to whom" or "for whom". And so: I give what? the letter (direct object). I give to whom? Marie (indirect object).

Here are the indirect object pronouns in French:

Indirect object pronouns	Translation
me/m'	me
te/t'	you (inf.)
lui	him/her
nous	us
vous	you (for.)
leur	them

If we were to replace Marie in the sentence above, it would thus be: *Je lui donne la lettre.* Notice that it is placed before the verb, like the direct object pronouns.

Let's look at more examples:
- *Mathis offre un cadeau à sa mère. Mathis lui offre un cadeau.* Mathis offers a gift to his mother. Mathis offers her a gift.
- *J'envoie le colis à Chloé et Lucas. Je leur envoie le colis.* I send a package to Chloé and Lucas. I send them a package.
- *Elle achète des livres pour Anne et moi. Elle nous achète des livres.* She buys books for Anne and me. She buys us books.

Communicating in a job interview

Introductions

At the beginning of the interview, it is common to be asked about your *parcours* (m.) (studies or career) or your *formation* (f.). If an interviewer asks you: *Quel est votre parcours scolaire ?* or *Pouvez-vous me parler de votre parcours ?*, you are expected to talk about your degree or training in the relevant field. Let's look at some sample answers:

- ***J'ai passé un bac pro de vente et j'ai suivi un stage de 3 mois dans une boutique de mode.*** I received my highschool diploma in sales and I did a 3-month internship in a fashion store.
- ***J'ai fait un Master en sociologie.*** I got my Master's degree in Sociology.
- ***Après mes études en marketing, j'ai obtenu mon diplôme en 2020.*** After studying Marketing, I received my diploma in 2020.

Keep in mind the frequent verb-noun combinations when talking about your studies:

- *passer/avoir/obtenir son bac*
- *faire/obtenir un master*
- *faire/obtenir une licence*
- *obtenir son diplôme*

If you are currently studying, you can use the verb *préparer*, as in:

- ***préparer le bac*** working on one's highschool diploma
- ***préparer un master / une licence*** working on a Master's degree / on a bachelor's degree

---

CULTURE TIP

A for effort!

The French education system might seem a bit complicated at first glance, but we'll help clear things up!

The education system is composed of 3 parts: the primary, secondary and higher levels. Primary education consists of the *école maternelle* (ages 3 up) and the *école élémentaire* (ages 6 to 11). Once completed, students then move to secondary education which is *collège* for 4 years, then *lycée* for 3 years. And then they'd have to take a national exam called *le bac* or *le baccalauréat*. This is the equivalent of a high school diploma.

After *lycée*, students have many different paths they can take. For example, they can go to a university and get *une licence* (a bachelor's degree), then *un master* (a master's degree) and *un doctorat* (a PhD). Otherwise, they can obtain vocational diplomas such as *DUT* or *Diplôme Universitaire de Technologie* or *BTS* or *Brevet de Technicien Supérieur*.

Qualifications and experiences

An interviewer might then ask you to talk about your professional experiences, as in *Parlez-moi de votre expérience professionnelle.*

You are expected to talk about your previous work, while highlighting your skills.

Let's look at an example:

> ***Après mes études, j'ai travaillé comme commercial au sein d'une agence de voyages pendant 4 ans. Ça a été une expérience très enrichissante. Ensuite, j'ai eu l'occasion de voyager à Londres et de travailler comme chargé de communication dans un centre touristique. Grâce à ce séjour, je maîtrise parfaitement l'anglais.***

> After my studies, I worked as a sales representative in a travel agency for 4 years. It was a very enriching experience. Then I had the opportunity to travel to London and work as a communications officer in a tourist center. Thanks to my stay there, I have a perfect command of English.

To talk about a previous position, you can use the expressions *J'ai travaillé comme* or *J'ai été* in composed past.

When relating more than one experience, it'd be a wise idea to structure your speech using chronological connectors such as:

- ***d'abord/premièrement*** first
- ***ensuite/puis*** then
- ***après*** after
- ***avant*** before
- ***enfin/finalement*** finally, lastly

GRAMMAR TIP

Expressions of time

Here are other expressions of time that you can use to structure your speech:

Use	Expressions	Examples
Anteriority	**dès que** as soon as	***Dès que*** *j'ai vu l'annonce, j'ai postulé pour l'offre.* As soon as I saw the advertisement, I applied for the offer.
	après que after	***Après que*** *j'ai obtenu une licence, j'ai déménagé en ville.* After I got a bachelor's degree, I moved to town.

	maintenant que	*Maintenant que je suis à Paris, je cherche un travail à plein temps.*
	now that	Now that I'm in Paris, I'm looking for a full-time job.
Simultaneity	*quand*	*Quand je suis arrivée, il était déjà parti.*
	when	When I arrived, he had already left.
	lorsque	*Lorsqu'il m'a vu, il m'a salué.*
	when	When he saw me, he greeted me.
	pendant que	*Pendant que je faisais mon Master, j'ai eu quelques offres d'emploi en freelance.*
	while	While I was doing my Masters, I had a few freelance job offers.

Note that *quand* and *lorsque* both mean "when", but *lorsque* is more formal.

Key Takeaways

- A job advertisement generally includes the following parts: *qui sommes-nous, vos missions, votre profil, le type d'emploi, le nombre d'heures* and le *salaire*.
- The indirect object pronouns are *me/m', te/t', lui, nous, vous* and *leur*.
- To communicate in an interview, we can use the following expressions:

Talk about one's studies
passer/avoir/obtenir son bac
faire/obtenir un master / une licence
obtenir son diplôme
préparer le bac / un master / une licence
Talk about one's experiences
J'ai travaillé comme...
J'ai été...

- The main chronological connectors are: *d'abord/premièrement, ensuite/puis, après, avant,* and *enfin/finalement*.
- To express anteriority, we can use the expressions *dès que, après que* and *maintenant que*.
- To express simultaneity, we can use the expressions *quand, lorsque* and *pendant que*.

In the next chapter, we will stay in the world of careers! This time, we will focus on talking about obligations and giving advice. We will also have a look at the subjunctive mood.

Exercises

1-3. Complete the sentences with the missing words.

    1. J'ai _____ mon bac en 2006.
    2. À Montréal, j'ai travaillé _____ comptable pendant 2 ans.
    3. Actuellement, je _____ un Master en informatique.

4-7. Rewrite the sentences by replacing the underlined nouns with the correct indirect object pronoun.

    4. Les enfants envoient une carte postale <u>à leurs parents</u>.
    5. Je demande <u>à Michel</u> de me rappeler.
    6. Tu téléphones <u>à Cécile</u> ?
    7. Nous parlons <u>à toi</u>.

8-10. Connect the two sentences using the expressions of time in parentheses.

    8. (dès que) J'ai obtenu mon diplôme. J'ai trouvé un travail.
    9. (pendant que) Il dort. Je travaille.
    10. (quand) Tu es prêt. Tu peux m'appeler ?

Answer Key

1. passé OR eu OR obtenu
2. comme
3. fais OR prépare
4. Les enfants <u>leur</u> envoient une carte.
5. Je <u>lui</u> demande de me rappeler.
6. Tu <u>lui</u> téléphones ?
7. Nous <u>te</u> parlons.
8. <u>Dès que</u> j'ai obtenu mon diplôme, j'ai trouvé un travail.
9. <u>Pendant qu'</u>il dort, je travaille.
10. <u>Quand</u> tu es prêt, tu peux m'appeler ?

Chapter 7: Go above and beyond

La responsabilité est le prix de la liberté.

Responsibility is the price of freedom.

- Cyrille Guimard

Obligation, such a heavy word. Most of our days are replete with them — do the groceries, send an email, walk the dog... At work, the stakes are even higher. We have to complete a list of tasks, take instructions or give them. Still, at the end of the day, being able to do even one or two of our most important responsibilities gives us a sense of fulfillment.

In this lesson, you will learn how to talk about obligations and give advice and commands. We will study the subjunctive mood as well as irregular imperative conjugations.

Talking about obligations

At the beginner's level, we learned how to indicate obligations using the verb *devoir* (to have to). Here, we will study how to do the same with the verb *falloir*.

Expressions with falloir

The verb *falloir* is an impersonal verb used to express an obligation or a need. It is impersonal, meaning it only has one conjugation, the third person *il*. This way, it is similar to the impersonal expression *Il fait*, used when talking about the weather.

To conjugate *falloir*: in the present, *il faut*, in the imperfect tense, *il faudrait*, and in the future, *il va falloir* or *il faudra*.

Il faut can be roughly translated to "need to" or "it's necessary". There are a few ways we can use this expression. For example, followed by a verb:

STRUCTURE 1 : *IL FAUT* + INFINITIVE OF THE VERB

STRUCTURE 2 : *IL FAUT QUE* + VERB IN SUBJUNCTIVE MODE

- ***Il faut travailler.*** It's necessary to work.
- ***Il faut savoir parler anglais.*** It's necessary to know how to speak English.
- ***Il faut que tu organises une réunion.*** You have to set up a meeting.
- ***Il faut que je parte.*** I have to go.

Note that in structure 1, the obligation is general and does not pertain to a specific person. For example, if one says *Il faut travailler*, it could mean the person speaking, or spoken to, or someone else entirely, has to work. In structure 2 however, the person who needs to do the action is specified. In a while, we will learn how to conjugate verbs in the subjunctive mode.

STRUCTURE 3 : *IL FAUT* + NOUN

STRUCTURE 4 : *IL* + INDIRECT OBJECT PRONOUN + *FAUT* + NOUN

Examples:

- ***Il faut une clé.*** A key is needed. / It's necessary to have a key.
- ***Il faut un manteau.*** It's necessary to have a coat
- ***Il me faut une clé.*** I need a key.
- ***Il vous faut un manteau.*** You need a coat.

GRAMMAR TIP

Subjunctive mood

The subjunctive mood has quite a bad rep in the French language learning world. Learners specifically have trouble figuring out when it should or should not be used. In this book, we will learn the subjunctive mood progressively.

For now, keep in mind that after the expression *il faut que*, the verb is conjugated in the subjunctive.

To conjugate in this mood, take the present tense conjugation of the verb in *ils*, and replace *-ent* with the following endings: *-e, -es, -e, -ions, -iez, -ent*.

adorer → (ils) ador~~ent~~ → *ador-*		
Je	+e	adore
Tu	+es	adores
Il/Elle/On	+e	adore
Nous	+ions	adorions
Vous	+iez	adoriez
Ils/Elles	+ent	adorent

This is the conjugation we follow for all regular verbs, no matter the ending. Let's look at two other verbs in the subjunctive mood:

partir → (ils) part~~ent~~ → *part-*	
Je	parte
Tu	partes
Il/Elle/On	parte

vendre → (ils) vend~~ent~~ → *vend-*	
Je	vende
Tu	vendes
Il/Elle/On	vende

Nous	partions		**Nous**	vendions
Vous	partiez		**Vous**	vendiez
Ils/Elles	partent		**Ils/Elles**	vendent

Work tasks vocabulary

	Translation
organiser (une réunion)	set up a meeting
assister (à une réunion)	to attend (a meeting)
imprimer (un document)	to print (a document)
signer (un document)	to sign a document
photocopier	to photocopy
une imprimante	a printer
une photocopieuse	a copy machine
faire du réseau	to do networking
réserver une salle	to reserve a room
recruter (quelqu'un)	to recrute (somebody)
embaucher (quelqu'un)	to hire (somebody)
déléguer (les responsabilités)	to delegate (tasks/responsibilities)
rédiger une lettre	to write a letter
échanger (sur un projet)	to talk about a project

Giving advice

In our previous book, you learned about the imperative mood, used mainly to give commands, advice or warnings. Recall that to form the imperative, we use the present tense conjugation of the verbs *tu*, *vous* and *nous*. For -ER verbs, however, we remove the -s when forming the imperative mood in the second person *tu*.

We will now learn about irregular conjugations in the imperative mood, in particular for the verbs *avoir*, *être* and pronominal verbs. Imagine that you are about to have a job interview in French, you look up some tips online and come across a list of advice:

- ***Soyez à l'heure.*** Be on time.
- ***Renseignez-vous sur l'entreprise.*** Look into / Do some research on the company.
- ***Ayez une tenue propre et correcte.*** Wear clean and appropriate clothing (lit. Have a clean and appropriate outfit).
- ***Entraînez-vous à répondre aux questions.*** Practice answering questions.

Imperative mood: avoir and être

The verbs *avoir* and *être* follow an irregular conjugation in the imperative mood.

avoir
(tu) aie
(nous) ayons
(vous) ayez

être
(tu) sois
(nous) soyons
(vous) soyez

Imperative mood: pronominal verbs

For pronominal verbs, we follow the general rule to conjugate them, but we invert the position of the pronoun and the verb and add a hyphen, like in *renseignez-vous* or *entraînez-vous*. Let's look at some more examples.

- **Lève-toi.** Get up.
- **Préparons-nous pour le départ.** Let's get ready to leave.
- **Asseyez-vous.** Sit down.

This is the rule for affirmative commands. When negated, we do not invert the pronoun and verb:

- **Ne te lève pas.** Don't get up.
- **Ne vous asseyez pas.** Don't sit down.

CULTURE TIP

From 9 to 5

The French have a 35-hour work week. The start of the work day in France is usually at 8:30 a.m., but this varies according to one's job. Employees would often take a break to have coffee, what is known as *une pause-café* (a coffee break), in the morning and in the afternoon. Lunch, *la pause-déjeuner*, is around 12 noon to 2 p.m. Before 2021, employees in France were not allowed, according to the French labor law, to eat lunch at their desks! But this has now been legalized by the government. Incidentally, the labor law is also quite strict when it comes to working on Sundays. This is why most shops are closed during this day.

Key Takeaways

- To talk about obligations and necessities, we can use the verb *falloir*. There are four structures to follow:

Expressions with *falloir*
Il faut + infinitive of the verb
Il faut que + verb in subjunctive mood
Il faut + noun
Il + indirect object pronoun + *faut* + noun

- To conjugate *falloir*: in the present, *il faut*, in the imperfect tense, *il faudrait*, and in the future, *il va falloir* or *il faudra*.
- To form the subjunctive mood, we take the present tense conjugation of the verb in *ils*, and replace *-ent* with the following endings: *-e, -es, -e, -ions, -iez, -ent*.
- To conjugate the verb *avoir* in the imperative: (tu) *aies*, (nous) *ayons* and (vous) *ayez*.
- To conjugate the verb *être* in the imperative: (tu) *sois*, (nous) *soyons* and (vous) *soyez*.
- To form the imperative with pronominal verbs, we conjugate the verb in the imperative mood, and then invert the pronoun and verb, combined with a hyphen.
- Negated pronominal verbs in the imperative mood do not undergo the same inversion.

In the next chapter, we will take some calls! You will learn how to communicate by phone using the most commonly used expressions. We will also study double pronouns.

Exercises

1-5. Subjunctive or infinitive? Conjugate the following verbs in the subjunctive or retain the infinitive (unconjugated) form if necessary.

    1. (porter) Il faut que vous _____ une tenue correcte.
    2. (boire) Il faut_____ au moins 1,5 litres d'eau par jour.
    3. (partir) Il faut que Hugo _____ une heure en avance.
    4. (signer) Il faut que nous _____ ce contrat aujourd'hui.
    5. (choisir) Il faut _____ le meilleur candidat.

6-10. Transform the following sentences into commands with the imperative mood.

    6. Tu ne dois pas être en retard.
    7. Il faut que vous ayez une bonne posture.
    8. Vous devez vous préparer pour l'entretien.
    9. Il ne faut pas se lever.
    10. Vous devez vous entraîner.

Answer Key

1. portiez
2. boire
3. parte
4. signions
5. choisir
6. Ne sois pas en retard.
7. Ayez une bonne posture.
8. Préparez-vous pour l'entretien.
9. Ne te lève pas. OR Ne vous levez pas.
10. Entraînez-vous.

Chapter 8: Call me back

La communication est une science difficile.

Communication is a difficult science.
- Jean-Luc Lagardère

Texting, chatting or emailing might be a preferred way of communication for some. But when we want to get a message across urgently, or when things have reached a point when there are just too many texts or emails, we pick up the phone. Most language learners have difficulty understanding French in the context of a phone call. It's not surprising, given that the audio quality can be poor. To top it all off, there are no visual cues to help contextualize what is being said. The key to getting past this particular challenge is knowing what phrases and words to expect. When you know them, even if you just hear the last two syllables of what the caller says, you'd have a better chance figuring out the appropriate response.

In this lesson, you will learn how to make formal and informal calls, including in dreaded situations of technical difficulties. We will also study here what we call double pronouns.

Formal calls

Making and taking a call

Let's begin with a dialogue. Lucas is hoping to talk to an employee of the PLM company.

> ***Le réceptionniste :*** *Société PLM, je vous écoute.*
> ***Lucas :*** *Bonjour, je voudrais parler à Madame Houdard, s'il vous plaît.*
> ***Le réceptionniste :*** *C'est de la part de qui ?*
> ***Lucas :*** *Lucas Dupont.*
> ***Le réceptionniste :*** *Ne quittez pas.*
> *(un peu plus tard...)*
> ***Le réceptionniste :*** *Je suis désolé mais elle est actuellement indisponible. Vous voulez laissez un message ?*
> ***Lucas :*** *Oui, pourriez-vous lui dire de me rappeler s'il vous plaît ?*
> ***Le réceptionniste :*** *Bien sûr. Quel est votre numéro de téléphone ?*
> ***Lucas :*** *C'est le 06 40 89 22 19.*
> ***Le réceptionniste :*** *C'est noté.*
> **Receptionist:** PLM Company, I'm listening.
> **Lucas:** Hello, I would like to speak to Madame Houdard, please.
> **Receptionist:** Who's on the line?
> **Lucas:** Lucas Dupont.
> **Receptionist:** Please stay on the line.

(a bit later...)
Receptionist: I'm sorry but she is currently unavailable. Do you want to leave a message?
Lucas: Yes, could you tell her to call me back please?
Receptionist: Of course. What is your phone number?
Lucas: It's 06 40 89 22 19.
Receptionist: Noted.

Companies usually introduce the name of their business first, and ask how they might help using the expressions *Comment puis-je vous aider ?* (How may I help you?) or *Je vous écoute* (lit. I'm listening).

Here are other common phone expressions you will hear in a formal call:

- *C'est de la part de qui ?* Who's calling?
- *Un instant.* Just one moment.
- *Ne quittez pas.* Stay on the line (lit. Don't leave.)
- *Il/Elle est actuellement indisponible.* He/She is currently unavailable.
- *Il/Elle est actuellement occupé(e).* He/She is currently busy.
- *Il/Elle est en ligne.* He/She is on the phone.
- *La ligne est occupée.* The line is busy.
- *Vous voulez laisser un message ?* Would you like to leave a message?

Transferring a call

When calling a big company, it is common to be transferred to the correct phone line. To ask to be transferred to a department, you can say:

Est-ce que vous pouvez me passer le/la [name of department] ?
Can you transfer me to the [name of department]?

To indicate you are transferring a call, you can use the expression:

Je vous le/la passe.
I am transferring the call to him/her.

Je vous passe mon collègue.
I am transferring the call to my colleague.

GRAMMAR TIP

Double pronouns

In the example above, *Je vous le passe,* there are two pronouns: *vous* and *le*. These are what you call double pronouns. In English, we can also have double pronouns in sentences. For example:

I will give the gift to Sophie. I will give **it** to **her**.

Here, we have two pronouns: *it* and *her*. In French, this sentence would be:

*Je vais donner le cadeau à Sophie. Je vais **le lui** donner.*

You will observe however that the position of these pronouns in French differ from English. From our previous lessons (Chapters 3 and 6), you know that the pronoun *le* here is the direct object pronoun and that *lui* is the indirect object pronoun. In this grammar tip, we will learn how to combine pronouns and where to place them. Here is the structure you need to commit to memory:

		me		**le/l'**		**lui**		
Subject	+	**tes**	+	**la/l'**	+	**leur**	+	**verb**
		nous		**les**				
		vous						

There can only be a maximum of two pronouns per sentence. The structure above will help you know how to place the two specific pronouns you intend to use. Let's look at some examples:

- *Lucas montre le tableau à nous. Lucas **nous le** montre.*
  Lucas shows the painting to us. Lucas shows it to us.

- *J'ai envoyé une lettre à papa. Je **la lui** ai envoyée.*
  I sent a letter to dad. I sent it to him.

- *Je partage les nouvelles à mes amis. Je **les leur** partage.*
  I share the news to my friends. I share it to them.

Informal calls

When answering an informal phone call, you can use the expression *Allô ?*, like the "Hello?" phone greeting in English. Let's look at another dialogue. This time, Lucas is calling the home of his friends.

Chloé : Allô ?
Lucas : Chloé ? C'est Lucas. Est-ce que Mathis est là ? Tu peux me le passer ?
Chloé : Salut Lucas. Mathis est au travail. Il rentre vers 19h.
Lucas : Ah, d'accord. Tu pourras lui dire de me rappeler s'il te plaît ? Je n'arrive pas à le joindre sur son portable.
Chloé : Bien sûr. Pas de souci.

Chloé: Hello?
Lucas: Chloé? It's Lucas. Is Mathis there? Can you put him on?
Chloé: Hey Lucas. Mathis is at work. He comes home at around 7 pm.
Lucas: Oh, okay. Can you tell him to call me back please? I can't reach him on his mobile.
Chloé: Sure. No worries.

We also use the expression *passer à quelqu'un* (transfer the call to somebody, put on somebody) in informal calls. Take note of the various verbs related to calling:

- ***appeler quelqu'un*** to call somebody
- ***téléphoner à quelqu'un*** to call somebody
- ***rappeler quelqu'un*** to call back somebody
- ***joindre quelqu'un*** to reach somebody

Both *appeler* and *téléphoner* mean "to call somebody". *Appeler*, however, can also signify calling out to somebody in person. *Téléphoner*, as the name suggests, makes use of a phone. One common mistake of French learners is confusing the use of the preposition *à* with these two verbs. Remember that *appeler* is always followed by the direct object, while *téléphoner* is always followed by the preposition *à* and then the indirect object.

- J'**appelle** mon ami.
- Je **téléphone à** mon ami.

This is very important especially when using object pronouns. Say, we replace the nouns in the sentences above, this is what it would look like:

- J'appelle mon ami. Je **l'**appelle.
- Je téléphone à mon ami. Je **lui** téléphone.

Since the verb *téléphoner* is always followed by the preposition *à*, the object is replaced with an indirect object pronoun, in this case *lui*. Saying *je le téléphone* is thus incorrect.

Technical problems

Here are some expressions you can use in informal phone calls, in case of technical difficulties:

- ***Je ne t'entends pas.*** I don't hear you.
- ***Ça coupe.*** You're breaking up.
- ***Je ne capte pas très bien.*** I don't hear you well. (lit. I don't receive you well.)

In formal calls, you can say:

- ***Nous avons été coupés***. It was disconnected.
- ***Je ne vous entends pas très bien***. I don't hear you very well.

CULTURE TIP

***Dring, dring!* Leave a message.**

Dring, dring is the word for the sound a phone makes in French. It is the equivalent of "kring, kring" in English. In this tip, we'll teach you how to make your own voicemail message in French. A typical formula that won't go wrong sounds like this:

> ***Bonjour, vous êtes bien sur le portable de Lucas Dupont. Je ne suis pas disponible pour l'instant. Laissez-moi un message et je vous rappellerai dès que possible.***
>
> Hello, you have reached Lucas Dupont's mobile phone. I'm not available at the moment. Leave me a message and I will call you back as soon as possible.

Here's another example:

> ***Bonjour, vous êtes bien sur le répondeur de Lucas Dupont. Laissez-moi un message et je vous rappellerai.***
>
> Hello, you have reached Lucas Dupont's answering machine. Leave me a message and I'll call you back.

How about recording yours right now?

Key Takeaways

- To communicate during phone calls, use the following expressions:

Formal calls	
Je voudrais parler à...	*Comment puis-je vous aider ?*
	Je vous écoute.
	C'est de la part de qui ?
	Un instant.
	Ne quittez pas.
	Il/Elle est actuellement indisponible.
	Il/Elle est actuellement occupé(e).
	Il/Elle est en ligne.
	La ligne est occupée.
	Vous voulez laisser un message ?
Est-ce que vous pouvez me passer le/la [name of department] ?	*Je vous le/la passe.*
	Je vous passe mon collègue.

Informal calls
Allô ?
Est-ce que... est là ?
Tu peux me le/la passer ?

Technical problems

> *Je ne t'entends pas.*
>
> *Ça coupe.*
>
> *Je ne capte pas très bien.*
>
> *Nous avons été coupés.*
>
> *Je ne vous entends pas très bien.*

- In using double pronouns in a sentence, we follow this order: subject + *me/tes/nous/vous* + *le/la/l'/ les* + *lui/leur* + verb.
- Verbs related to communication include *appeler, téléphoner à, rappeler* and *joindre*.

In the next chapter, we will delve into a different method of communication: emails. You will learn how to write informal and formal emails. We will also look at the relative pronoun *dont*.

Exercises

1-5. Complete the dialogue with the correct missing words.

- Société Quick, comment puis-je vous 1._____ ?
- Bonjour, je voudrais 2._____ à Monsieur Bernard s'il vous plaît.
- C'est de la part de 3._____ ?
- Amélie Martin.
- Ne quittez pas. [...] La ligne est actuellement 4._____. Vous voulez laisser un 5._____ ?
- Non merci, je rappellerai plus tard.

6-10. Replace the two underlined nouns with double pronouns. Rewrite the entire sentences and remember to follow the correct order.

6. Je donne le cadeau à Sophie.

7. Les enfants montrent leurs dessins aux enseignants.

8. Tu envoies la lettre au client au plus vite ?

9. Mathis dit la vérité à nous.

10. Elle explique la situation aux policiers.

Answer Key

1. aider
2. parler
3. qui
4. occupée
5. message
6. Je le lui donne.
7. Les enfants les leur montrent.
8. Tu la lui envoies.
9. Mathis nous la dit.
10. Elle la leur explique.

Chapter 9: To whom it may concern

J'ai écrit parce que c'était la seule façon de parler en se taisant.

I wrote because it was the only way to speak silently.

- Pascal Quignard

Many businesses rely on emailing, as it is one of the most efficient and convenient ways of contacting colleagues and clients. That said, it is also a much-needed means of communication outside the workplace. When dealing with administrative tasks, inquiring about products or services, or even filing a complaint, we sometimes need to take recourse to emailing as it is a proof of documentation that cannot be erased or altered.

In this lesson, you will learn how to write both formal and informal emails. We will not go into the specifics of different types of letters, but discuss instead how to form its basic structure. Much like in face-to-face conversations, polite expressions are important in writing emails in French. We will also take the time to look at vocabulary related to emails, as well as the relative pronoun *dont*.

Formal emails

Greetings

A good formal email begins with the appropriate greeting. The standard greeting involves addressing the person directly as in:

__Monsieur Lucas Dupont,__

or:

__Madame Marie Dupont,__

If you do not know who will read the message, you can simply say *Bonjour* or address it anonymously:

__Monsieur, Madame,__

This greeting is similar to the English "Dear Sir/Madam". Of course, the best practice is to find out the full name of the person you are writing to, and address them accordingly.

Introductions

After greeting the receiver of the message, one would normally state the reason for writing. You may use the following expressions to do so:

__Je vous écris concernant...__
I am writing to you about...

> ***Je vous écris pour demander si / pour savoir si...***
> I am writing to you to ask if / to know if...

> ***Je m'adresse à vous pour demander si / pour savoir si...***
> I am addressing you to ask if / to know if...

> ***Je voudrais des renseignements concernant...***
> I would like some information regarding...

Attachments

If you wish to indicate attached documents, you can write:

- ***Veuillez trouver ci-joint le/la/les...*** Please see attached the...
- ***Je joins le/la/les...*** I am attaching the...
- ***Je vous mets ci-joint le/la/les...*** I am attaching the...

The first expression is the most formal one out of the three. While the *veuillez* is a conjugated form of the verb *vouloir* (to want), its most accurate translation when used is "Please" or "Kindly" in English.

Conclusions

To end a formal letter, you can write:

> ***Je vous remercie et vous souhaite une bonne journée.***
> I thank you and wish you a good day.

> ***En vous remerciant et en vous souhaitant une bonne journée.***
> Thanking you and wishing you a good day.

Or you can leave your contact details if needed:

> ***Je reste à votre disposition au [phone number].***
> I remain at your disposition at [phone number].

> ***Vous pouvez me joindre au [phone number].***
> You can reach me at [phone number].

Remember to end your message with the expression *Cordialement*, which is similar to the English "Sincerely". A less formal concluding expression is *Bien à vous* (Best regards).

GRAMMAR TIP

Relative pronoun dont

In the previous chapters, we learned about the relative pronouns *qui* and *que*. The relative pronoun *dont* replace relative clauses preceded by the preposition *de*. Let's look at an example:

La ville est splendide. Je parle <u>de cette ville</u>.

The city is splendid. I speak <u>of this city</u>.

To avoid repetition, we will replace *de cette ville* with the preposition *dont*, and combine the two sentences. And so, it becomes:

La ville <u>dont</u> je parle est splendide.

The city which I speak of is splendid.

It is important to remember that *dont* only replaces a person or a thing preceded by the preposition *de*. It can also be used to indicate possession:

Je connais un homme. La femme <u>de cet homme</u> est enseignante.

I know a man. This man's wife is a teacher.

Je connais un homme <u>dont</u> la femme est enseignante.

I know a man whose wife is a teacher.

Just like in our previous example, the noun being replaced here is preceded by the preposition *de*. It acts however as a possessive in this case. Study these other examples:

- *C'est un bon achat. Je suis très satisfait <u>de l'achat</u>.* → **C'est un bon achat <u>dont</u> je suis très satisfait.**
- *C'est un livre intéressant. Le titre <u>du livre</u> est Le Petit Prince.* → **C'est un livre intéressant <u>dont</u> le titre est Le Petit Prince.**

Email vocabulary

	Translation
un email	an email
une adresse email	an email address
l'objet	the subject
envoyer	to send
enregistrer	to save
répondre	to reply

transférer	to forward
supprimer	to delete
la boîte de réception	the inbox
la boîte d'envoi	the outbox
un destinataire	a recipient
un expéditeur(-trice)	a sender

Informal emails

Greetings & introductions

To greet a recipient in informal emails, you use the expression *Cher* (m.) or *Chère* (f.), which translates to "Dear" in English. For instance, you can write *Cher Lucas* or *Chère Marie*. Alternatively, you can also use the expression *Salut*, or directly address him or her by name.

Depending on the content of your message, a great way to start an informal one is by asking how the recipient is, with *Comment ça va ?* or *Tu vas bien ?*

Conclusions

You can end your email with *Bisous* (kisses) if you are close to the recipient. Otherwise, you can simply write *Bonne journée*.

CULTURE TIP

@...com

In many instances, as in dealing with paperwork, you will be asked to dictate your contact details and thus, your email address. Let's look at an example:

lucasdupont@mail.com.fr

To read this address, one would say: *lucas, dupont, arrobase, mail, point, com, point, /ef/, /er/*.

The @ symbol is read as *arrobase* /ah-roh-baz/. The dot is read as point /pwahñ/ and "com" as /kohm/. Letters are pronounced the way you would when reading the alphabet.

If you haven't yet, study how to pronounce the French letters! You'll find that every once in a while, you will be asked to spell out your email address or even your name when traveling to francophone countries.

Key Takeaways

- To write emails, we use the following expressions:

Formal emails
Monsieur..., / Madame...,
Monsieur, Madame,
Je vous écris concernant...
Je vous écris pour demander si / pour savoir si...
Je m'adresse à vous pour demander si / pour savoir si...
Je voudrais des renseignements concernant...
Veuillez trouver ci-joint le/la/les...
Je joins le/la/les...
Je vous mets ci-joint le/la/les...
Je vous remercie et vous souhaite une bonne journée.
En vous remerciant et en vous souhaitant une bonne journée.
Je reste à votre disposition au...
Vous pouvez me joindre au...
Cordialement,
Bien à vous,
Informal emails
Cher..., / Chère...,
Salut...,
Comment ça va ? / Tu vas bien ?
Bisous
Bonne journée

- The relative pronoun *dont* is used to replace relative clauses preceded by the preposition *de*. It can also indicate possession.

In the next chapter, you will learn how to rent an apartment or buy a property in French. As for the grammar, we will tackle the passive voice and the expression of restriction *ne...que*. We will also study vocabulary related to housing and real estate.

Exercises

1-5. Complete the following formal email with the appropriate words.

Madame, Monsieur,

Je vous écris pour savoir 1. _____ l'entrée à la bibliothèque est gratuite pour les étudiants. Je fais actuellement mon Master à l'Université de Paris. Veuillez trouver 2._____ mon certificat de scolarité. Je voudrais également des renseignements 3. _____ l'inscription. Dois-je apporter avec moi d'autres justificatifs ?

En vous remerciant et en vous 4. _____ une bonne journée.
5. _____

Lucas Dupont

6-10. Replace the underlined noun with the relative pronoun *dont* and combine the two sentences into one.

6. Mathis adore le film. Je parle <u>de ce film</u>.
7. Je connais une femme. Le prénom <u>de cette femme</u> est Jeanne.
8. Sophie a une amie. Le mari <u>de cette amie</u> est un acteur célèbre.
9. C'est un produit très efficace. Les clients sont satisfaits <u>de ce produit</u>.
10. La famille vit dans une petite maison. La porte <u>de la maison</u> est verte.

Answer Key

1. si
2. ci-joint
3. concernant
4. souhaitant
5. Cordialement, OR Bien à vous,
6. Mathis adore le film <u>dont</u> je parle.
7. Je connais une femme <u>dont</u> le prénom est Jeanne.
8. Sophie a une amie <u>dont</u> le mari est un acteur célèbre.
9. C'est un produit très efficace <u>dont</u> les clients sont satisfaits.
10. La famille vit dans une petite maison <u>dont</u> la porte est verte.

Chapter 10: Welcome home

Un bûcheron est maître dans sa maison.

A woodcutter is master in his house.

- Quebecois proverb

You have decided to make a francophone country your new home, except you still have to *find* a home. Renting an apartment or buying a property can be tricky for many reasons. The search for a lodging that fits your needs, requirements, and budget can be tough. And if on top of all this, you struggle to communicate with your real estate agent, you might end up with an apartment or house that does not feel like your dream home.

Not to fret, for in this lesson we will study precisely how to rent an apartment and how to buy a property. We will look at vocabulary related to real estate, so you have all the tools you need to find the right home. Finally, we will look at two grammar topics: the passive voice and the expression of restriction *ne...que*.

Renting an apartment

Calling the real estate agency

At the beginner's level, you learned how to understand a rental ad, as well as vocabulary for the parts of the home. Let us now study how to communicate with a real estate agent when searching for an apartment.

Oscar had just moved to Paris. He saw a rental ad online for an apartment that looks exactly like what he is searching for. He has decided to call the real estate agency in charge to ask for more information and to schedule a visit:

> **Oscar :** *Bonjour. Je vous appelle concernant un appartement à louer, un T2 dans le 5ᵉ. Est-il toujours disponible ?*
> **L'agent immobilier :** *Bonjour Monsieur. Malheureusement, cet appartement n'est plus disponible.*
> **Oscar :** *Ah, d'accord. Est-ce que vous avez d'autres appartements dans le coin ?*
> **L'agent immobilier :** *Vous êtes à la recherche d'un appartement vide ou meublé ?*
> **Oscar :** *Meublé si possible.*
> **L'agent immobilier :** *Avec deux pièces, c'est ça ?*
> **Oscar :** *Tout à fait.*
> **L'agent immobilier :** *Alors... je regarde... On n'a qu'un trois pièces, vide, avec un petit balcon. Il fait 40m2.*
> **Oscar :** *Et le loyer est de combien ?*

L'agent immobilier : *1300 euros, toutes charges comprises. Vous voudriez le visiter ? Il y a une visite prévue demain à 13h.*
Oscar : *Parfait, je serai là. Quelle est l'adresse s'il vous plaît ?*

Oscar: Hello. I am calling you regarding the apartment for rent, a 2-room flat in the 5th (arrondissement). Is it still available?
Real estate agent: Hello Sir. Unfortunately, this apartment is no longer available.
Oscar: Oh okay. Do you have any other apartments in the area?
Real estate agent: Are you looking for an unfurnished or a furnished apartment?
Oscar: Furnished if possible.
Real estate agent: With two rooms, right?
Oscar: That's right.
Real estate agent: So... Let me see... We only have a three-room apartment, unfurnished, with a small balcony. It is 40m2.
Oscar: And how much is the rent?
Real estate agent: 1300 euros, charges included. Would you like to visit it? There's a visit scheduled tomorrow at 1:00 p.m.
Oscar: Perfect, I'll be there. What is the address please?

To indicate you are searching for an apartment, you can say, like in the dialogue, *Je vous appelle concernant un appartement à louer*. Alternatively, you can also say *Je suis à la recherche d'un appartement à louer* (I am looking for an apartment to rent.) Note that a real estate agency is called *une agence immobilière* and a real estate agent, *un agent immobilier*.

There are some specific questions you can ask about the apartment:

- ***Est-il vide ou meublé ?*** Is it unfurnished or furnished?
- ***Le loyer est de combien ?*** How much is the rent?
- ***Il fait quelle surface ?*** What is the surface area?
- ***Les charges sont-elles comprises ?*** Are the utility fees included (in the rent)?
- ***Le chauffage est-il individuel ou collectif ?*** Is the heating individual or collective?

In France, there are different types of apartments. There is *un studio* (a studio), also called *un T1*, the number 1 referring to the number of rooms. *T* refers to the *pièces* (f.) or the rooms. A studio has only 1 room which serves as the bedroom, kitchen and living room. *Un T2* has two rooms or *deux pièces*. This means it has 1 bedroom and 1 other room (for example a kitchen or a living room). *Un T3* has 2 bedrooms and 1 other room, *un T4* has 3 bedrooms and 1 other room, and so on.

When searching for an apartment, you might also want to ask the agent to specify if it is *en bon état* (in good condition), perhaps it was *refait à neuf* (renovated). You can also ask for an apartment with a view for example, of the courtyard: *un appartement avec vue sur la cour* or *un appartement qui donne sur la cour* (an apartment that overlooks the courtyard).

GRAMMAR TIP

Restriction with ne...que

The expression *ne...que* roughly translates to the adverb "only" in English. In the dialogue above, the agent said:

On n'a qu'un trois pièces.

We only have a three-bedroom (apartment).

Notice how the *ne* and *que* "sandwiches" the verb *avoir*, much like the expression *ne...pas*. We can also observe in this example that *ne* contracts to *n'* before a vowel. *Que* also contracts to *qu'* before a vowel. Study these other examples:

- *Nous ne proposons qu'un studio.* We are only offering a studio.
- *Cet hôtel n'a que deux étoiles.* This hotel only has two stars.
- *Il n'y a que deux personnes dans la chambre.* There are only two people in the room.
- *L'appartement ne fait que 17m2.* The apartment is only 17m2.

Real estate vocabulary

	Translation
un immeuble	a building
un logement social	a social lodging
un loyer	rent (price)
la location	renting, rental
une colocation	house-share, apartment-share
un propriétaire	owner
un locataire	tenant
emménager	to move in
déménager	to move out
une superficie	surface area
le chauffage	heating, heater
un bien	a property
les honoraires (f. pl.)	agency fees
la vente	sales
la caution	guarantee

CULTURE TIP

An apartment for rent

Many ads for apartments or houses for rent in France can be found online. Rental prices vary according to the city of choice. In Paris, for instance, the most expensive city in the country, prices can go up to 1,000 euros for a small studio.

To rent an apartment, you would need to prepare *un dossier* (a file) which compiles all the documents required by the landlord. Most of these documents serve as proof that you are financially capable of renting the apartment. Generally, a *dossier* would have:

- ***une pièce d'identité*** identification card
- ***un justificatif de domicile*** proof of address
- ***un contrat de travail*** employment contract (for employees)
- ***un certificat de scolarité*** certificate of attendance (for students)
- ***des bulletins de salaire*** (m.) payslips

Buying a home

This time, let's examine an ad for a house for sale:

Maison d'architecte à vendre, 4 pièces, 83m2

L'agence immobilière CHEZ MOI vous propose une maison d'architecte à Bordeaux avec un vaste terrain clos et sans vis à vis. Idéalement située dans le centre-ville, la maison est proche de l'école, des commerces et des transports publics. Cette maison originale et créative a été conçue par l'architecte Hugo Lavigne, propriétaire actuel du bien. Elle comprend une entrée, un grand salon avec une cheminée, une salle à manger, une cuisine entièrement rénovée, une chambre et une suite parentale qui se partagent une salle de bain.

Votre nouvelle maison vous attend. Contactez-nous pour une visite.

Prix du bien : 450 000 euros
Honoraires TTC : 5% soit 22 500
Date de réalisation du diagnostic énergétique : 03/09/22
Référence annonce : 1248798744BBn

Architect house for sale, 4 rooms, 83m2

The real estate agency CHEZ MOI proposes an architect's house in Bordeaux with a large enclosed land and without vis-à-vis. Ideally located in the city center, the house is close to the school, shops and public transport. This original and creative house was designed by the architect Hugo Lavigne, current owner of the property. It includes an entrance, a large living room with a fireplace, a dining room, a completely renovated kitchen, a bedroom and a master suite which share a bathroom.

Your new home is waiting for you. Contact us for a visit.

Price of the property: 450,000 euros
Fees including VAT: 5% or 22,500
Date of fulfillment of energy diagnosis: 03/09/22
Ad reference: 1248798744BBn

When searching for a house, you will encounter familiar vocabulary like names of the rooms and descriptions of amenities. Agencies will usually be paid what is called *les honoraires* (fees), and they usually indicate if these include VAT using the expression *TTC* or *Toutes Charges Comprises* (all fees included).

The paperwork when buying a property is of course a tad more complicated than when renting an apartment. The sale usually begins with *une offre d'achat* (offer to buy) which makes your intent to buy official. This is not, however, the equivalent of a purchase contract. There are two types of a sales agreement contract in France, for example, *une promesse de vente* and *un compromis de vente*. This latter is more common. After signing a purchase contract, you are of course required to complete your acquisition of the property.

GRAMMAR TIP
Passive voice

In the world of grammar, the term "voice" indicates the relationship between subject and verb. There are two types of voice: active and passive. Let's look at this sentence from the ad above:

Cette maison a été conçue par l'architecte Hugo Lavigne.
This house was designed by the architect Hugo Lavigne.

This sentence is in the passive voice. Now, compare it to this one:

L'architecte Hugo Lavigne a conçu cette maison.
The architecte Hugo Lavigne designed this home.

This second sentence is in the active voice. Can you tell the difference between the two?

In the passive voice, we emphasize that an action is being done to the subject (*cette maison*). Notice how in sentence 1, our attention is on the house, but in sentence 2, it is on the architect.

To form the passive voice, we use this structure:

ÊTRE conjugated + past participle of the verb

The past participle of the verb should agree with the subject in gender and number. You can use the passive voice in any tense or mood, by conjugating the verb *être* accordingly. Let's look at some more examples:

Active voice	Passive voice
Les maçons construisent les fondations d'une maison.	*Les fondations d'une maison sont construites par les maçons.*
Émile Zola a écrit le roman L'Assommoir.	*Le roman L'Assommoir a été écrit par Émile Zola.*
Elle préparera les valises.	*Les valises seront préparées par elle.*

The agent of the action can be anonymous in the passive voice. For example, one can say *La maison a été rénovée.* (The house was renovated.), without indicating who renovated it.

Key Takeaways

- To ask about an apartment, we use the following expressions:

Rent an apartment
Est-il vide ou meublé ?
Le loyer est de combien ?
Il fait quelle surface ?
Les charges sont-elles comprises ?
Le chauffage est-il individuel ou collectif ?

- An apartment can be *un studio, un T1, un T2, un T3*, and so on, depending on the number of rooms it has.
- When buying a home, the following contracts may be signed: *une offre d'achat, une promesse de vente* or *un compromis de vente*.
- The expression *ne...que* is used to indicate restriction. *Ne* is placed before the verb and *que*, after. Both *ne* and *que* contract to *n'* and *qu'* respectively before a vowel.
- The passive voice is used to put emphasis on the subject upon which an action is enacted. It is formed by conjugating the verb *être* and adding the past participle of the verb. The past participle agrees with the subject in gender and number.
- The agent of the action in the passive voice is introduced by the preposition *par*.

In the next chapter, you will learn how to compare products using the adjectives *bon* and *mauvais*. After buying a home, household items come next in the list! To that end, we will look at vocabulary related to appliances.

Exercises

1-5. Translate the following to French.

    1. a furnished apartment
    2. What is the surface area?
    3. a tenant
    4. an offer to buy
    5. a property

6-7. Rewrite the sentences to include the expression of restriction *ne...que*.

    6. Lola et Jules mangent des légumes.
    7. Nous avons une maison de 8 pièces.

8-10. Transform the following sentences into the passive voice.

    8. Ma famille loue cet appartement.
    9. Mes frères ont rénové cette salle.
    10. Marine fera le gâteau.

Answer Key

1. un appartement meublé
2. Il fait quelle surface ? OR Quelle surface fait-il ?
3. un locataire
4. une offre d'achat
5. un bien
6. Lola et Jules <u>ne</u> mangent <u>que</u> des légumes.
7. Nous <u>n'</u>avons <u>qu'</u>une maison de 8 pièces.
8. Cet appartement est loué par ma famille.
9. Cette salle a été rénovée par mes frères.
10. Le gâteau sera fait par Marine.

Chapter 11: It's a bargain!

En commerce, l'occasion est tout.

In commerce, opportunity is everything.

- Honoré de Balzac

After finding a new home, furnishing it with new shiny things is often next in the list. At the beginner's level, it is common to be introduced to key phrases used during simple commercial transactions, as in at the bakery or at the post office. As you move onto the next level, it is necessary to look at more specific scenarios like comparing or asking for a reimbursement or an exchange.

In this lesson, you will learn how to compare using the adjectives *bon* and *mauvais*. We will also study key phrases used to ask for an exchange or a reimbursement. As for the vocabulary, we will look at words related to household appliances as well as terms for different kinds of stores.

Asking for comparisons

Let's begin with a dialogue. Jeanne has rented a new, unfurnished apartment and is now on the lookout for a good hotplate:

> **Le vendeur :** *Bonjour Madame, je peux vous aider ?*
> **Jeanne :** *Oui, quelle est la différence entre ces deux plaques de cuisson ?*
> **Le vendeur :** *Alors, celle-ci est une plaque à induction, puis celle-là est une plaque vitrocéramique. Elles ont deux systèmes de cuisson nettement différents. La cuisson par induction se fait par un champ magnétique alors que pour la cuisson vitrocéramique, les sources d'énergie sont ce qu'on appelle les halogènes.*
> **Jeanne :** *Laquelle est plus efficace ?*
> **Le vendeur :** *La cuisson par induction est plus rapide. On peut régler la température d'une façon très précise, et ce n'est pas très compliqué à utiliser.*
> **Jeanne :** *Et laquelle consomme moins d'électricité ?*
> **Le vendeur :** *La plaque à induction a une consommation d'énergie plus faible.*
> **Jeanne :** *D'accord... euh, je ne sais pas trop laquelle prendre.*
> **Le vendeur :** *Personnellement, je trouve que la plaque à induction est meilleure que la vitrocéramique... C'est un peu plus cher mais ça vaut le coup.*
> **The salesperson:** Hello Madam, can I help you?
> **Jeanne:** Yes, what is the difference between these two hotplates?
> **The salesperson:** So this one is an induction plate, then that one is a ceramic hob. They have two distinctly different cooking systems. Induction cooking is done by a magnetic field whereas for ceramic cooking, the energy sources are the so-called halogens.
> **Jeanne:** Which one is more effective?
> **The salesperson:** Induction cooking is faster. You can adjust the temperature in a very precise way, and it's not very complicated to use.

Jeanne: And which one consumes less electricity?
The salesperson: The induction plate has a lower energy consumption.
Jeanne: Alright... uh, I'm not sure which one to take.
The salesperson: Personally, I find that the induction plate is better than the ceramic hob... It's a little bit more expensive but it's worth it.

Asking for comparisons

To ask for two things to be compared, we can say the keyphrase, just like in the dialogue:

> *Quelle est la différence entre* **[noun]** *et* **[noun]** *?*
> What is the difference between [noun] and [noun]?

Alternatively, we can use the interrogative pronoun *lequel*:

> *Lequel est plus/moins* + **adjective** *?*
> *Laquelle est plus/moins* + **adjective** *?*
> Which one is more/less + adjective?
>
> *Lequel/laquelle* + **verb** *?*
> Which one + verb?

As you might have guessed, *lequel* is used for masculine nouns and *laquelle* for feminine nouns. Note that there are also plural variations to this interrogative pronoun. Let's look at more examples:

- *Lequel consomme le moins d'énergie ?* Which one (m. sing.) consumes the least energy?
- *Lesquels sont les plus chers ?* Which ones (m. plur.) are the most expensive?
- *Laquelle est plus abordable?* Which one (f. sing.) is more affordable?
- *Lesquelles sont les plus populaires ?* Which ones (f. plur.) are the most popular?

GRAMMAR TIP

Comparisons with bon and mauvais

In Chapter 2, we learned how to compare using *plus* and *moins*. The French adjective *bon* (good) has, however, irregular comparative and superlative forms. Study the table below.

	Comparative	Superlative
masculine singular	***meilleur***	***le meilleur***
feminine singular	***meilleure***	***la meilleure***
masculine plural	***meilleurs***	***les meilleurs***
feminine plural	***meilleures***	***les meilleures***

The equivalent of *meilleur* in English is "better", and *le meilleur*, "best". Let's look at some examples:

- ***Ce four est meilleur que celui-là.*** This oven is better than that one.
- ***Ce sont actuellement les meilleurs ordinateurs portables sur le marché.*** These are currently the best laptops in the market.
- ***La télévision que j'ai achetée est meilleure que la tienne.*** The television that I bought is better than yours.

The adjective *mauvais* uses both regular and irregular forms. It is thus possible to say, *plus mauvais* or *le plus mauvais*. Otherwise, the term *pire* is used.

	Comparative	Superlative
masculine singular	***pire***	***le pire***
feminine singular		***la pire***
masculine plural	***pires***	***les pires***
feminine plural		

To summarize, both *plus mauvais* and *pire* refer to the English "worse". *Le plus mauvais* and *le pire* may be translated to "the worst". Let's look at some more examples:

- ***Cet aspirateur est le pire !*** This vacuum cleaner is the worst!
- ***Cette bouilloire est pire que celle-là.*** This kettle is worse than that one.

Household appliances vocabulary

	Translation
un aspirateur	a vacuum cleaner
une cafetière	a coffee maker
un climatiseur	an air conditioner
une cuisinière	a stove
un fer à repasser	an iron
un four	an oven
un lave-vaisselle	a dishwasher
une machine à laver	a washing machine
un micro-onde	a microwave
un radiateur	a heater
un sèche-cheveux	a hair dryer
un sèche-linge	a clothes dryer
une télévision	a TV

Other services at the store

Asking for an exchange

When asking for an exchange, you would need to present *un justificatif d'achat* (a justification of sale), more specifically *un ticket de caisse* (a receipt). You can then use the following expressions to indicate your intent:

> ***Est-ce que je peux échanger ce produit ?***
> Can I exchange this product?

> ***Est-ce que je peux l'échanger ?***
> Can I exchange it?

> ***Je souhaite faire un échange.***
> ***Je voudrais faire un échange.***
> I would like to make an exchange.

Note that while some products bought in the store are *échangeable* (exchangeable) some are *non écheangeable*.

Asking for a reimbursement

To receive *un remboursement* (a reimbursement), you can say:

> ***Est-ce que je peux être remboursé(e) de...***

Can I be reimbursed of...
Je souhaite être remboursé(e).
Je voudrais être remboursé(e).
I would like to be reimbursed.

CULTURE TIP

Hello shopaholic!

An alternative way of saying to go shopping, instead of *faire du shopping*, is *faire les magasins*. In France, you can refer to shops using the term *chez*. For example, *chez le fleuriste* (the florist's) or *chez le cordonnier* (the shoemaker's). Other terms for shops include:

- ***un kiosque*** a newsstand
- ***un magasin de jouets*** a toy store
- ***un marchand de vins*** a wine shop
- ***une bijouterie*** a jewelry store
- ***une laverie automatique*** a laundromat
- ***une librairie*** a bookstore
- ***une papeterie*** a stationery shop
- ***une parfumerie*** a perfume shop
- ***une quincaillerie*** a hardware store
- ***une teinturerie*** a dry cleaner's

Key Takeaways

- For specific commercial transactions, we use the following expressions:

Comparisons
Quelle est la différence entre [noun] *et* [noun] *?*
Lequel est plus/moins + adjective *?*
Laquelle est plus/moins + adjective *?*
Ask for an exchange
Est-ce que je peux échanger ce produit ?
Est-ce que je peux l'échanger ?
Je souhaite faire un échange.
Je voudrais faire un échange.
Ask for a reimbursement
Est-ce que je peux être remboursé(e) de...
Je souhaite être remboursé(e).
Je voudrais être remboursé(e).

- The interrogative pronoun *lequel* refers to "which one". It changes according to the gender and number of the noun referred to: *lequel, lequels, laquelle, lesquelles*.
- The comparative forms of the adjective *bon* are *meilleur(s)* and *meilleure(s)*. The superlative forms are *le meilleur, la meilleure* and *les meilleur(e)s*.
- The comparative form of the adjective *mauvais* can be *plus mauvais(es)* or *pire*. The superlative forms are *le plus mauvais, la plus mauvaise, les plus mauvais(es)* or *le/la/les pire(s)*.

In the next chapter, you will learn how to relate an event and explain an accident. We will study reported speech and adverbs with *-ment*. We will also have a look at vocabulary related to automobiles and accidents.

Exercises

1-3. Translate the following to French.

    1. What is the difference between this washing machine and that one?
    2. I would like to make an exchange.
    3. Which one (m.) is more expensive?

4-5. Complete the sentences with the correct comparative form of the adjective *bon*.

    4. Ce parfum est _____ que celui-là.
    5. Sa première chanson est _____ que celles plus récentes.

6-7. Complete the sentences with the correct comparative form of the adjective *mauvais*.

    6. Ce magazine est _____ que celui-là.
    7. Tes photos sont _____ que celles que j'ai prises.

8-10. Complete the sentences with the correct superlative form of the adjectives *bon* and *mauvais*.

    8. (mauvais) – Son livre sur les dauphins est _____ !
    9. (bon) – C'est _____ cafetière.
    10. (mauvais) – Ses films sont _____ que je n'ai jamais vus.

Answer Key

1. Quelle est la différence entre cette machine à laver et celle-là ?
2. Je souhaite faire un échange. OR Je voudrais faire un échange.
3. Lequel est plus cher ?
4. meilleur
5. meilleure
6. plus mauvais OR pire
7. plus mauvaises OR pires
8. le plus mauvais OR le pire
9. la meilleure
10. les plus mauvais OR les pires

Chapter 12: Accident prone

*Il n'y a point d'accidents si malheureux
dont les habiles gens ne tirent aucun avantage.*

There are no accidents so unfortunate
from which skilful people do not draw any advantage.

- Honoré de Balzac

Accidents happen, and when they do, we find ourselves in incredibly stressful situations. In these instances, relating what happened can be difficult even in our mother tongue. In a foreign language, this difficulty is somewhat multiplied. While such mishaps cannot be prevented, it is important to know how to react or what to say, so as to prevent sinking into a deeper state of confusion.

In this lesson, you will learn how to talk about an accident, such as when reporting to the police or declaring a car accident. We will tackle reported speech as well as adverbs. Finally, we will have a look at automobile vocabulary, as well as terms related to accidents.

Reporting a crime

It is not uncommon to become a victim of theft, especially when one is traveling to an unfamiliar area. At the police station, you can report a robbery by using the expressions *porter plainte* or *faire une déclaration*.

Je voudrais porter plainte pour vol.
I would like to file a complaint for theft.

Je voudrais faire une déclaration de vol.
I would like to report a theft.

Describing the incident

You can describe what has happened, using the passive voice that we learned earlier. Alternatively, you can also use the pronoun *on*:

- ***Mon portefeuille a été volé.*** My wallet was stolen.
- ***On m'a volé mon portable.*** Someone stole my phone.
- ***Je me suis fait voler mon sac.*** My bag was stolen from me.

The last example makes use of the pronominal verb *se faire*, in the composed past form. It roughly translates to "to have something done to", and is always followed by the infinitive verb. This verbal expression transforms a sentence into the passive voice. So, for instance you can say:

Elle s'est fait voler son portefeuille.
Her bag was stolen from her.

Je me suis fait cambrioler hier.
[My place] got burglarized yesterday.

Giving details

When declaring a theft, you have to describe exactly what happened, when and where. The police officer might ask the following questions:

- *Le vol s'est passé quand et où ?* The theft happened when and where?
- *Pouvez-vous me raconter ce qui s'est passé ?* Can you tell me what happened?
- *Comment ça s'est passé ?* How did it happen?

All these questions make use of the pronominal verb *se passer*, which means "to happen".

Now, let's look at an example of a description of a theft:

> **Ça s'est passé dans la rue des Moulins, ce soir, à 10h. Un monsieur m'a bousculé, il a arraché mon portable et il s'est enfui. Tout s'est passé très rapidement. J'ai essayé de l'attraper, mais c'était trop tard.**

To describe events, you can use the action verbs above: *bousculer* (to shove), *voler* (to steal), *agresser* (to mug, to assault), *s'enfuir* (to run away) and *attraper* (to catch).

Review tip: study the verb conjugations in the excerpt above. Can you tell why most verbs use the composed past, and only one is in the imperfect tense?

After describing an incident, the police officer will then most likely ask you to describe the offender:

> ***Pouvez-vous décrire la personne / le voleur ?***
> Can you describe the person / the thief?

> ***Il/elle était comment ?***
> What does he/she look like?

GRAMMAR TIP

Adverbs in -ment

In the excerpt above, we saw the sentence:

Tout s'est passé rapidement.

Everything happened quickly.

The word *rapidement* (quickly) is an adverb. Recall that adverbs are words used to describe an adjective, a verb or another adverb. In this sentence *rapidement* is describing the verb *se passer*. Many adverbs of manner are in fact formed by adding *-ment* to a corresponding adjective. *Rapidement*, for example, is a combination of the adjective *rapide* (quick, fast) and *-ment*.

The formation of adverbs in *-ment* is based on the following rules:

Rule	Example
feminine adjectives ending in e + ment	• générale + ment = **généralement** (generally) • rapide + ment = **rapidement** (quickly)
masculine adjectives ending in i, u or é + ment	• poli + ment = **poliment** (politely) • absolu + ment = **absolument** (absolutely) • forcé + ment = **forcément** (surely)
adjectives ending in -ent and -ant → emment / amment	• violent → **violemment** (violently) • suffisant → **suffisamment** (sufficiently)

Remember that generally, adverbs of manner are placed after the verb.

Crimes vocabulary

	Translation
arrêter (quelqu'un)	to arrest (somebody)
l'extorsion (f.)	extorsion
l'incarcération	imprisonment
la fraude	fraud
les urgences	the emergency room
un agresseur	an assailant
un cambriolage	a burglary

un cambrioleur(-euse)	a burglar
un délit	a crime
un pickpocket	a pickpocket
un plaignant(e)	a plaintiff
un témoin	a witness
une victime	a victim
un vol	a theft
un voleur(-euse)	a thief
une agression	an attack, a mugging
une contravention	a fine, a parking ticket
une enquête	an investigation
une infraction	an offense

Reporting an accident

At the site of an accident

After a car accident, the involved parties would fill in what is called *un constat amiable* (accident report) at the scene for insurance purposes. You will state in this report, the names of *les conducteurs* (drivers) and *les temoins* (witnesses), details regarding *les permis de conduire* (driver's licenses), the location of the accident and *les dégâts matériels* (material damages) if there are any. Both drivers will sign the report, which should then be sent to their respective insurance companies.

At the insurance company

To report a car accident, you can say:

> ***Je souhaite déclarer un accident de voiture.***
> ***Je voudrais déclarer un accident de voiture.***
> I would like to report a car accident.

You will usually be asked to describe what happened. Study the expressions below:

- ***Un minivan a percuté ma voiture.*** A van crashed into my car.
- ***Un camion a heurté ma voiture.*** A truck hit my car.
- ***Ma voiture est endommagée.*** My car is damaged.
- ***Les phares sont cassés.*** The headlights are broken.

GRAMMAR TIP

Reported speech

When reporting a crime or an accident, knowing how to report speech indirectly will be most useful. Let us look at these two different types of speech:

(Direct speech) **Mathieu dit : « Je pars ».** Mathieu says, "I'm leaving."

(Reported speech) **Mathieu dit qu'il part.** Mathieu says that he is leaving.

To form the reported speech, we use this structure: reporting verb + *que* or *qu'*. Verbs like *dire* (to say), *demander* (to ask), *informer* (to inform) or *annoncer* (to announce) are commonly used in reported speech.

If the reported speech is in the present tense, the verb does not change, just like our example above. However, if it is in the past, it changes accordingly:

- present tense → imperfect tense
- composed past tense → pluperfect tense
- simple future → present conditional
- near future → imperfect + infinitive

Study the following examples:

- *Il a dit : « Un voleur prend son sac ».* → **Il a dit qu'un voleur prenait son sac.**
- *Il a dit : « Un voleur a pris mon sac ».* → **Il a dit qu'un voleur avait pris son sac.**
- *Il a dit : « Je porterai plainte ».* → **Il a dit qu'il porterait plainte.**
- *Il a dit : « Je vais porter plainte ».* → **Il a dit qu'il allait porter plainte.**

Note that the other conjugations — imperfect, pluperfect and conditional present — do not change, even in past reported speech.

Automobile vocabulary

	Translation
avancer	to move forward
couper (le moteur)	to turn off the engine
démarrer (le moteur)	to start the engine
doubler	to overtake
l'accélérateur	the accelerator
l'embrayage	the clutch

l'essuie-glace (m.)	the windshield wiper
le capot	the hood
le clignotant	the blinker
le coffre	the trunk (of a car)
le frein	the brake
le frein à main	the handbrake
le klaxon	the horn
le moteur	the engine
le pare-brise	the windshield
le pare-chocs	the bumper
le phare	the headlight
le pot d'échappement	the exhaust pipe
le réservoir	the gas tank
le rétroviseur	the rear-view mirror
le volant	the steering wheel
les feux	lights
reculer	to reverse
rouler	(car) to run, to drive
un véhicule	a vehicle
une bagnole	a car (slang)
une voiture	a car

CULTURE TIP

The infamous code de la route

Getting a *permis de conduire* or a driver's license in France is infamously difficult. You will have to pass a theory test and a hands-on driving test. To succeed in the theory test, you would have to study the French highway code, known as *le code de la route*.

In France, penalties are based on a specific point system. A driver generally has an initial 12 points, from which one deducts according to the gravity of an offense. If you have just received your license, you have only 6 points during the first three years of driving.

Key Takeaways

- To report a crime, we use the following expressions:

Report a crime
Je voudrais porter plainte pour vol.
Je voudrais faire une déclaration de vol.
Describe an incident
[noun] *a été volé.*
On m'a volé [noun].
Je me suis fait voler mon [noun].
Be asked for details
Le vol s'est passé quand et où ?
Pouvez-vous me raconter ce qui s'est passé ?
Comment ça s'est passé ?
Pouvez-vous décrire la personne / le voleur ?
Il/elle était comment ?

- Adverbs in *-ment* are formed based on the following rules: feminine adjectives ending in e + ment ; masculine adjectives ending in i, u or é + ment and finally, adjectives ending in -ent and -ent → emment / amment.
- To report an accident, we use the following expressions:

Report an accident
Je souhaite déclarer un accident de voiture.
Je voudrais déclarer un accident de voiture.
Describe an accident
Un minivan a percuté ma voiture.
Un camion a heurté ma voiture.
Ma voiture est endommagée.
Les phares sont cassés.

- To form the reported speech, we use this structure: reporting verb + *que* or *qu'*. In present reported speech, the conjugation of the verb does not change. In past reported speech, verb tenses are transformed as such: present tense → imperfect tense, composed past tense → pluperfect tense, simple future → present conditional and near future → imperfect + infinitive.

In the next chapter, you will learn expressions of complaint, of cause and of consequence. We will study complex negations and vocabulary related to computer technology.

Exercises

1-3. Which word does not belong?

    1. un vol – une victime – un embrayage
    2. une bagnole – une voiture – un réservoir
    3. le frein – le rétroviseur – un agresseur

4-6. Complete the sentences with the correct missing verb.

    4. Je souhaite _____ un accident de voiture.
    5. Je voudrais _____ une déclaration de vol.
    6. Je voudrais _____ plainte pour vol.

7-9. What are the equivalent adverbs of the following adjectives?

    7. méchant
    8. sûr
    9. joli

10. Transform the following to past reported speech:

    10. François a dit : « Un camion a heurté ma voiture. »

Answer Key

1. un embrayage (it's the only word pertaining to parts of a car)
2. un réservoir (it's the only word that does not mean "car")
3. un agresseur (it's the only word not related to automobile)
4. déclarer
5. faire
6. porter
7. méchamment
8. sûrement
9. joliment
10. François a dit qu'un camion avait heurté sa voiture.

Chapter 13: Blow a fuse?

La douleur est toujours moins forte que la plainte.

Pain is always less strong than complaint.

- Jean de la Fontaine

You bought something new from a store, say a gadget. You go home excited and immediately put it to use, but it refuses to turn on! You are pissed, as you should be. So you go back to the store to complain and perhaps get a brand new one. For some, complaining might come easy. But for others, especially those who avoid confrontation, speaking out against someone or something may prove to be unmanageable.

In this lesson, you will learn how to complain about something, indicate the cause and consequence of a problem. We will also tackle vocabulary related to computer technology and types of complex negations. Now, we can't promise this will make confrontations much easier, but at the very least you'll be able to get your message across without difficulty.

Complaining about a product

Let's begin with a dialogue. Lucile has just brought a brand-new phone. But when she gets home and tries it out, it doesn't seem to work! She returns to the store to complain:

> **L'employé :** *Bonjour Madame, je peux vous aider ?*
> **Lucile :** *Oui, j'ai acheté cet ordinateur portable chez vous il y a 2 heures et c'est déjà en panne !*
> **L'employé :** *En panne ? Madame, il s'agit d'un ordinateur portable tout neuf, la boîte n'a jamais été ouverte.*
> **Lucile :** *Comme je vous dis, il est en panne. Il ne s'allume pas !*
> **L'employé :** *Malheureusement, notre technicien n'est actuellement pas ici. Pourriez-vous revenir dans une semaine ?*
> **Lucile :** *Dans une semaine ? Mais ce n'est pas possible !*
> **L'employé :** *Je ne peux pas vous proposer d'autres solutions.*
> **Lucile :** *C'est inacceptable Monsieur ! Je demande un remboursement intégral.*
> **Employee:** Hello Madam, can I help you?
> **Lucile:** Yes, I bought this laptop from you 2 hours ago and it's already broken!
> **Employee:** Broken? Madam, this is a brand-new laptop, the box has never been opened.
> **Lucile:** As I'm telling you, it broke down. It does not turn on!
> **Employee:** Unfortunately, our technician is currently not here. Could you come back in a week?
> **Lucile:** In a week? But that is not possible!
> **Employee:** I can't offer you any other solutions.
> **Lucile:** This is unacceptable sir! I request a full refund.

Like in the dialogue above, there are many expressions one can use to indicate frustration when filing a complaint:

- *Ce n'est pas possible.* This is not possible.
- *C'est inacceptable.* This is unacceptable.
- *C'est inadmissible.* This is inadmissible.
- *C'est scandaleux !* This is scandalous!
- *Cela ne va pas du tout.* It's not good/working at all.

Note that these phrases indicate exasperation and can thus be offensive in certain cases.

When explaining that a product is defective, you can use the expression *en panne*, which means "out of order" or "not working". Alternatively, you can say:

- *Il ne fonctionne pas du tout.* It's not working at all.
- *Il ne marche pas du tout.* It's not working at all (slang).
- *Il ne s'allume pas.* It's not turning on.

CULTURE TIP

Computer terms in French

Many French learners change the language of their gadgets, such as phones and computers, to their target language for a worthwhile immersion. This is a great idea, though it definitely takes some time to get used to. Here are some basic computer terms in French to help you decode some unfamiliar terms:

- *un fichier* a file
- *un logiciel* a software
- *un navigateur* a browser
- *un mot de passe* a password
- *copier* to copy
- *coller* to paste

Trivia: did you know that the French keyboard is different from English ones? Unlike the QWERTY first row lineup, French ones have AZERTY!

Computer technology vocabulary

	Translation
allumer	to turn on
bugger	to be buggy
éteindre	to turn off
le Wifi	wifi
télécharger	to download

tomber en panne	to break down
un cable	a cable
un disque dur	a hard drive
une montre connectée	a smart watch
un smartphone	a smartphone
une appli(cation)	an app
une clé USB	a thumb drive
une tablette	a tablet

GRAMMAR TIP

Complex negation

By now, you already know how to use *ne...pas* for simple negations, as well as *ne...que* for expressions of restriction. Let us look at some other French negative adverbs:

Adverb		Example
ne... pas du tout	not at all	*Il ne fonctionne pas du tout.* It's not working at all.
ne... pas encore	not yet	*Je n'ai pas encore acheté de portable.* I haven't bought a phone yet.
ne... jamais	never	*Je n'ai jamais eu un problème pareil.* I never had a problem like this.
ne... plus	not anymore, no more	*Je ne veux plus utiliser cet ordinateur.* I don't want to use this computer anymore.

These negative adverbs are positioned the same way as the simple negation *ne...pas*, i.e. before and after the verb.

Expressing cause and consequence

Expressions of cause

Some of the common terms used to express cause are *parce que* (because), *puisque* (since) and *car* (because) — all of which you have learned previously. Let's look at other expressions of cause and how they are used.

The following expressions are used in this structure:

CONJUNCTION + CAUSE IN THE INDICATIVE MODE

- ***étant donné que*** given that, since
- ***vu que*** given that, since
- ***sous prétexte que*** on the pretext that

Let's look at some examples:

- ***Étant donné qu'il fait mauvais, il n'y a personne dans le parc.*** Since the weather is bad, there's no one in the park.
- ***Vu que son ordinateur ne fonctionnait pas, il n'a pas pu travailler.*** Since his computer was not working, he was not able to work.
- ***Il n'est pas allé en cours, sous prétexte qu'il était malade.*** He did not go to class, on the pretext that he was sick.

The following expressions of cause are used in this structure:

CONJUNCTION + NOUN

- ***en raison de*** because of
- ***faute de*** for lack of
- ***suite à*** following
- ***à cause de*** due to
- ***grâce à*** thanks to

Study how these expressions are used:

- ***En raison d'une maladie, il a arrêté son projet.*** Due to an illness, he stopped his project.
- ***Faute d'argent, nous ne pouvons pas voyager.*** For lack of money, we cannot travel.
- ***Suite à un accident, il a annulé son rendez-vous.*** Following an accident, he canceled his appointment.
- ***L'ordinateur portable est tombé en panne à cause d'un problème technique.*** The laptop broke down due to a technical problem.
- ***Grâce à sa prouesse, elle a réussi à traverser la rivière.*** Thanks to her prowess, she managed to cross the river.

It is important to note that the term *en raison de* is neutral, while *à cause de* often has negative connotations. *Grâce à*, like its English equivalent, has positive connotations.

Expressions of consequence

Other than *donc* and *alors*, which are both equivalent of the English "so", there are other terms one can use to indicate consequence in French.

The following expressions are used in the structure:

CONJUNCTION + CONSEQUENCE IN THE INDICATIVE MODE

- ***en conséquence*** consequently
- ***par conséquent*** consequently
- ***c'est pourquoi*** this is why
- ***au point que*** so much so that, to such an extent that

Look at the following examples:

- ***On a joué toute la nuit. En conséquence, on est tous fatigués.*** We played all night. Consequently, we are all tired.

- *Elle a perdu son sac. C'est pourquoi elle est frustrée.* She lost her bag. That's why she is frustrated.
- *Il est parti tard, au point qu'il a raté le bus.* He left late, so much so that he missed the bus.

The expressions *si... que* and *tellement... que* (so / so much... that) are used however in the following structure:

CONJUNCTION + ADJECTIVE / ADVERB + *QUE* + CONSEQUENCE IN THE INDICATIVE MODE

- *Il est arrivé au travail tellement tôt que le bureau était toujours fermé.* He arrived so early at work that the office was still closed.
- *Je suis si triste que j'ai pleuré toute la nuit.* I was so sad that I cried all night.

GRAMMAR TIP

The adverb *tout*

The adverb *tout* may be roughly translated to "very" or "entirely". It can be variable or invariable depending on its use.

When referring to an adverb or when used as part of an expression, *tout* does <u>not</u> change according to gender and number. Look at these examples:

- *La voiture roule <u>tout</u> doucement.* The car drives very slowly.
- *<u>Tout</u> à coup, l'ordinateur s'est éteint.* Suddenly, the computer shut down.

In the first example, *tout* is invariable because it refers to the adverb *doucement*. In the second, it is invariable because it is part of the fixed expression *tout à coup* (suddenly).

If acting as an adjective, *tout* changes according to gender and number:

masculine singular	*tout*
masculine plural	*tout*
feminine, singular, starting with a consonant	*toute*
feminine, singular, starting with a vowel or *h*	*tout*
feminine, plural	*toutes*

Study the following examples:

- *Il est <u>tout</u> content.* He is very happy.
- *Ils sont <u>tout</u> contents.* They (m.) are very happy.
- *Elle est <u>toute</u> contente.* She is very happy.
- *Elles sont <u>toutes</u> contentes.* They (f.) are very happy.
- *Elle est <u>toute</u> élégante.* She is very elegant.

Key Takeaways

- To complain about a product or service, we use the following expressions:

Ce n'est pas possible.
C'est inacceptable.
C'est inadmissible.
C'est scandaleux !
Cela ne va pas du tout.
Il ne fonctionne pas du tout.
Il ne marche pas du tout.
Il ne s'allume pas.

- Complex negative adverbs include *ne...pas du tout* (not at all), *ne...pas encore* (not yet), *ne...jamais* (never) and *ne...plus* (not anymore).
- Expressions of cause used with the indicative mode include: *étant donné que* (given that, since), *vu que* (given that, since) and *sous prétexte que* (on the pretext that).
- Expressions of cause used with nouns include: *en raison de* (because of), *faute de* (for lack of), *suite à* (following), *à cause de* (due to), *grâce à* (thanks to).
- Expressions of cause used with the indicative mode include: *en conséquence* (consequently), *par conséquent* (consequently), *c'est pourquoi* (this is why), *au point que* (so much so that, to such an extent that).
- The expression *si/tellement...que* (so much...that) is placed with an adjective/adverb + *que* + consequence in the indicative mode.
- The adverb *tout* is invariable when it refers to an adverb or when part of a fixed expression. It is variable however, before an adjective: *tout* (m. sing./pl.), *toute* (f. sing.), *tout* (f. sing. before a vowel) and *toutes* (f. pl.).

In the next chapter, you will learn how to explain a social issue and describe a goal. We will also have a look at expressions used to give opinions. For vocabulary, we will study terms related to the environment.

Exercises

1-3. Rewrite the sentences by adding the indicated complex negative adverb.

    1. (ne... pas du tout) Je suis content de ce produit.
    2. (ne... jamais) Le technicien est arrivé.
    3. (ne... pas encore) Éric semble prêt.

4-8. Connect the two phrases with the indicated expression of cause or consequence.

    4. (grâce à) l'aide de Mathis — elle a réussi l'examen.
    5. (sous prétexte que) il a annulé le rendez-vous — il a eu un accident.
    6. (vu que) il fait froid — Sophie veut rester chez elle.
    7. (si...que) il fait chaud — nous transpirons tous.
    8. (c'est pourquoi) il s'est couché tard — il est tout fatigué.

9-10. Complete the sentence with the correct form of *tout*.

    9. Margaux habite _____ près de nous.
    10. Cette soupe est _____ froide !

Answer Key

1. Je <u>ne</u> suis <u>pas du tout</u> content de ce produit.
2. Le technicien <u>n'</u>est <u>jamais</u> arrivé.
3. Éric <u>ne</u> semble <u>pas encore</u> prêt.
4. <u>Grâce à</u> l'aide de Mathis, elle a réussi l'examen.
5. Il a annulé le rendez-vous <u>sous prétexte qu'</u>il a eu un accident.
6. <u>Vu qu'</u>il fait froid, Sophie veut rester chez elle.
7. Il fait <u>si</u> chaud <u>que</u> nous transpirons tous.
8. Il s'est couché tard, <u>c'est pourquoi</u> il est tout fatigué.
9. tout
10. toute

Chapter 14: Time for a change

Notre maison brûle et nous regardons ailleurs.

Our house burns and we look elsewhere.

- Jacques Chirac

As you move on to the upper intermediate level of your language learning, you will discover topics more abstract, and not always related to your immediate, daily environment. Being able to talk about social issues and share your opinion are important skills to acquire at this stage.

In this lesson, you will learn how to explain a subject related to current affairs. You will also study how to indicate an objective and share your opinion. We will be focusing on problems and solutions related to the environment.

Explaining a social issue

Let's look at an excerpt of an interview. Here, an expert explains the dangers facing our planet, specifically global warming.

> **Le journaliste :** *Pourquoi, selon vous, notre planète est-elle en danger ?*
> **Le spécialiste :** *Nous sommes actuellement confrontés à un nombre important de problèmes liés à notre environnement. Prenons, par exemple, le changement climatique qui présente des risques pour l'humanité. Il y a aussi la pollution, la perte de biodiversité, ou bien, la déforestation.*
> **Le journaliste :** *Pourriez-vous élaborer un peu plus sur cette question de changement climatique ?*
> **Le spécialiste :** *Oui, le changement climatique se réfère aux modifications du climat, caractérisées par une augmentation des températures moyennes. Il s'agit d'un phénomène écologique, entraîné par ce que l'on appelle « le réchauffement climatique » — autrement dit, le réchauffement de la Terre en raison de l'accumulation de gaz à effet de serre. Il faut savoir que les humains sont en grande partie responsables de ce réchauffement.*

The journalist: Why do you think our planet is in danger?
The expert: We are currently facing a large number of problems related to our environment. Take, for example, climate change which poses risks to humanity. There is also pollution, loss of biodiversity, or deforestation.
The journalist: Could you elaborate a bit more on this issue of climate change?
The expert: Yes, climate change refers to changes in the climate, characterized by an increase in average temperatures. It is an ecological phenomenon, driven by what is called "global warming" — in other words, the warming of the Earth due to the accumulation of greenhouse gases. It should be noted that humans are largely responsible for this warming.

Giving a definition

To give a definition, we can use the verbs *désigner* (to indicate, refer to) or *se référer* (refer to). Like in the dialogue, we can also use the impersonal expression *Il s'agit de*, which roughly translates to "to be about, to be a question of" or "concerning". This expression can be followed by a noun or a verb. Study the examples below:

- ***Il s'agit d'un phénomène écologique.*** It is an ecological phenomenon.
- ***Il s'agit d'un problème grave.*** It is a serious problem.
- ***Il s'agit de prendre conscience de son rôle dans la protection de l'environnement.*** It is a matter of becoming aware of one's role in protecting the environment.

Providing examples

What better way to elaborate on a complicated topic than to give concrete examples? In French, we can use the following expressions to do so:

- ***Prenons, par exemple,*** Take, for example,
- ***Citons, par exemple,*** Let us cite, for example,
- ***On peut citer, à titre d'exemple*** One can cite, by way of example,

Let's look at these sentences:

- ***Prenons, par exemple, le cas de la France.*** Take, for example, the case of France.
- ***Citons, par exemple, la fonte des glaces.*** Let us cite, for example, glacial melting.
- ***On peut citer, à titre d'exemple, la pollution atmosphérique.*** One can cite, by way of example, air pollution.

Pointing to references

When explaining a concept, it can also be useful to refer to authorities, institutions or other texts by quoting them directly or indirectly:

- ***selon*** according to
- ***d'après*** according to
- ***comme le dit [quelqu'un]*** like [someone] says
- ***si l'on en croit*** according to (lit. if one were to believe)

Let's look at some examples:

- ***Selon les climatologues, notre planète est en danger.*** According to climatologists, our planet is in danger.
- ***D'après le journaliste, la personne interviewée est spécialiste en géologie.*** According to the journalist, the interviewee is a geology expert.
- ***Si l'on en croit Louis Pasteur, la science ne connaît pas de patrie.*** According to Louis Pasteur, science knows no country.
- ***Comme le dit Sénèque, c'est l'âme qu'il faut changer, et non le climat.*** Like Seneca says, it is the soul that must be changed, not the climate.

Rephrasing

In the dialogue above, the interviewee rephrased his own words using the expression *autrement dit* (in other words, put in another way).

[...] « le réchauffement climatique » — autrement dit, le réchauffement de la terre en raison de l'accumulation de gaz à effet de serre.
[...] "global warming" — in other words, the warming of the earth due to the accumulation of greenhouse gases.

Here are two other key terms to remember:
- ***en quelque sorte*** sort of, kind of
- ***pour ainsi dire*** so to speak

Let's look at these expressions at-work:
- ***C'est en quelque sorte un cercle vicieux.*** It is sort of a vicious circle.
- ***Il a forgé ce terme, pour ainsi dire.*** He coined this term, so to speak.

Environment vocabulary

	Translation
éviter	to avoid
l'écologie (f.)	ecology
l'environnement (m.)	the environment
la biodiversité	biodiversity
la déforestation	deforestation
la pollution	pollution
la Terre	Earth
le gaspillage	waste
le réchauffement climatique (m.)	global warming
le recyclage	recycling
les gaz à effet de serre (m.)	greenhouse gases
lutter contre	to fight against
promouvoir	to promote
protéger	to protect
un écosystème	an ecosystem
une espèce	species

Indicating an objective

This time, let's look at an excerpt of a brochure from an organization called *Un monde d'arbres* (A world of trees):

> ***Créée en 2022, l'association*** Un monde d'arbres ***a pour objectif de lutter contre le réchauffement climatique à travers la reforestation. Nous rassemblons des volontaires pour planter des arbres dans la partie nord du pays. L'association se***

donne pour mission de planter 100 000 arbres chaque année. En même temps, nous cherchons à sensibiliser les gens aux enjeux liés à notre environnement.

Created in 2022, the association *A world of trees* aims to fight against global warming through reforestation. We gather volunteers to plant trees in the northern part of the country. The association has made it a mission to plant 100,000 trees each year. At the same time, we seek to raise people's awareness of issues related to our environment.

To indicate an objective, we can use verbal phrases with the infinitive just like in the excerpt above:
- ***avoir pour objectif de*** to aim to (lit. to have as objective to)
- ***se donner pour mission de*** to make it a mission to
- ***chercher à*** to seek to
- ***viser à*** to aim to

Alternatively, we can use conjunctions and prepositions.

Expressions with conjunctions

Recall, as we learned in Chapter 7: to form the subjunctive mood, we take the present tense conjugation of the verb in *ils*, and replace *-ent* with the following endings: *-e, -es, -e, -ions, -iez, -ent*.

The following conjunctions, used to indicate an objective, are always followed by the subjunctive mood.
- ***pour que*** so that
- ***afin que*** so that
- ***de manière / façon / sorte que*** in such a way that, so that

Let's look at some examples:
- ***Nous avons créé cette association pour qu'on puisse lutter contre le changement climatique.*** We created this association so that we can fight against climate change.
- ***Nous travaillons en collaboration avec d'autres organismes de manière que nous soutenions les initiatives des uns et des autres.*** We work in collaboration with other organizations in such a way that we support each other's initiatives.

GRAMMAR TIP

Irregular verbs in the subjunctive mode

By now you know how to conjugate most verbs in the subjunctive mode. Certain verbs, however, do not follow this regular conjugation:

avoir	
J'	aie
Tu	aies
Il/Elle/On	ait
Nous	ayons
Vous	ayez
Ils/Elles	aient

être	
Je	sois
Tu	sois
Il/Elle/On	soit
Nous	soyons
Vous	soyez
Ils/Elles	soient

faire	
Je	fasse
Tu	fasses
Il/Elle/On	fasse
Nous	fassions
Vous	fassiez
Ils/Elles	fassent

pouvoir	
Je	puisse
Tu	puisses
Il/Elle/On	puisse
Nous	puissions
Vous	puissiez
Ils/Elles	puissent

savoir	
Je	sache
Tu	saches
Il/Elle/On	sache
Nous	sachions
Vous	sachiez
Ils/Elles	sachent

aller	
Je	aille
Tu	ailles
Il/Elle/On	aille
Nous	allions
Vous	alliez
Ils/Elles	aillent

Expressions with prepositions

We can also use prepositions to indicate an objective. The following are always followed by infinitive verbs:

- *pour* for, in order to
- *afin de* in order to

- ***de façon à*** so as to
- ***dans le but de*** in the objective of
- ***en vue de*** in order to, with the aim of
- ***dans l'intention de*** with the aim of

Study the following examples:

- ***Nous avons créé cette fondation <u>pour</u> protéger l'environnement.*** We created this foundation to protect the environment.
- ***Nous plantons des arbres <u>de façon à</u> diminuer la pollution.*** We plant trees so as to reduce pollution.
- ***Nous protégeons les arbres <u>en vue de</u> purifier l'air.*** We protect trees with the aim of purifying air.

CULTURE TIP

Rain or shine

A great way to flex your French language skills is showing off your repertoire of idiomatic expressions. Here are three to keep in mind, related to nature:

- *couper l'herbe sous le pied* to beat someone to it
- *faire la pluie et le beau temps* to call the shots, to run the show
- *se faire une montagne de quelque chose* to exaggerate the importance or difficulty of something.

How about some examples ?

- ***Il a créé un site web innovatif et a ainsi coupé l'herbe sous les pieds de ses concurrents.*** He created an innovative website and beat all of his competitors to it.
- ***Dans ma famille, c'est mon frère qui fait la pluie et le beau temps.*** In my family, it's my brother who calls the shots.
- ***Elle s'est fait une montagne d'un prix qu'elle a reçu, qui n'était finalement pas aussi prestigieux.*** She made a mountain out of an award she received, which turned out to be not so prestigious.

Key Takeaways

- To explain a social issue, we can use the following expressions:

Give a definition
désigner
se référer
Il s'agit de...
Provide examples
Prenons, par exemple...
Citons, par exemple...
On peut citer, à titre d'exemple...
Point to references
Selon
D'après
Comme le dit
Si l'on en croit
Rephrase
Autrement dit
En quelque sorte
Pour ainsi dire

- To indicate an objective, we can use the following expressions:

With verbal phrases	
avoir pour objectif de	
se donner pour mission de	
chercher à	
viser à	
With conjunctions	
pour que	
afin que	
de manière que	+ subjunctive mood
de façon que	
de sorte que	
With prepositions	
pour	+ infinitive

afin de	
de façon à	
dans le but de	
en vue de	
dans l'intention de	

In the next chapter, we will talk about food and nutrition. You will study how to express agreement and disagreement, and how to indicate concession. We will also be reviewing the subjunctive mood.

Exercises

1-5. Complete the sentences by choosing the correct missing word or phrase from the list below.

promouvoir — pour — de manière que — se donne — le gaspillage

« Paris sans déchet » est une association fondée en 2010 à Paris, en France. Elle a 1. _____ objectif de 2. _____ le recyclage dans la capitale. Elle 3. _____ aussi pour mission d'aider les gens à éviter 4. _____ et à favoriser des pratiques écologiques. Nous préparons actuellement un projet que l'on appelle « Fait-maison ». Nous allons rendre visite à des familles parisiennes et leur partager des pratiques écologiques 5. _____ nous leur apprenions comment réutiliser des produits non-recyclables.

6-10. Infinitive or subjunctive? Complete the sentences with the appropriate conjugation of the indicated verb.

6. On ne prend pas sa voiture pour (éviter) _____ la pollution.
7. L'association vise à (promouvoir) _____ le recyclage.
8. Elle a déménagé dans la campagne pour qu'elle (pouvoir) _____ vivre près de la nature.
9. On peut faire des gestes écologiques au quotidien de façon à (participer) _____ à la protection de l'environnement.
10. Il a écrit ce livre afin que les gens (pouvoir) _____ apprendre comment trier des déchets.

Answer Key

1. pour
2. promouvoir
3. se donne
4. le gaspillage
5. de manière que
6. éviter
7. promouvoir
8. puisse
9. participer
10. puissent

Chapter 15: Food for thought

Dis-moi ce que tu manges, je te dirai qui tu es.

Tell me what you eat, I will tell you who you are.

- Jean Anthelme Brillat-Savarin

If one were to believe Brillat-Savarin's philosophy, then we might say we can know someone by knowing what he eats. Food is not just material sustenance — though it certainly is important to ponder about the question of eating healthily — it is also a big part of our society, our culture, our lifestyle. If food says something about who we are, it can very well be said that it also makes us up, both literally and figuratively.

In this lesson, you will learn the key phrases necessary in debating about an issue, specifically those related to nutrition. We will study how to express agreement and disagreement. We will also be reviewing the subjunctive mode.

Debating about an issue

Let's look at an excerpt of an interview where a nutritionist talks about food supplements.

> **Le journaliste :** On dit que les compléments alimentaires présentent des risques pour la santé, qu'est-ce que vous en pensez ?
>
> **Le spécialiste :** Je suis tout à fait d'accord. Les compléments alimentaires doivent être pris selon les conseils des professionnels de santé. On doit éviter, par exemple, le risque de surdosage. Il y a aussi certains compléments que certains groupes de personnes — les enfants, les femmes enceintes, etc. — ne doivent pas consommer. Mais il faut aussi savoir que ces compléments peuvent avoir un effet bénéfique. À mon avis, il y a des avantages et des inconvénients. L'essentiel, c'est d'en parler avec des spécialistes.

> **The journalist:** Food supplements are said to pose health risks, what do you think?
>
> **The Expert**: I completely agree. Food supplements should be taken as advised by healthcare professionals. One must avoid, for example, the risk of overdose. There are also certain supplements that certain groups of people — children, pregnant women, etc. — must not consume. But you should also know that these supplements can have a beneficial effect. In my opinion, there are pros and cons. What's essential is to talk about it with specialists.

Asking for one's opinion

To ask one's thoughts on a matter, we use the following expressions:

Qu'est-ce que vous en pensez ?
Qu'en pensez-vous ?
What do you think?

Y croyez-vous ?
Do you believe it?

Quelle est votre opinion ?
Quel est votre avis ?
What is your opinion?

In French, the word "opinion" can be translated to *une opinion* or *un avis*. Note that the word *avis* can also mean "a public/legal notice."

Expressing agreement

To express your agreement about something, you can use these phrases:

Je partage votre/ton idée.
Je partage votre/ton point de vue.
I share your point of view.

Je suis entièrement d'accord avec vous/toi.
I entirely agree with you.

In the last example, adverbs like *totalement* (totally), *tout à fait* (entirely), *parfaitement* (perfectly) or *absolument* (absolutely) can also be used. If you are only in partial agreement with the other person, you can say: *Je suis partiellement d'accord avec vous*.

In more formal contexts, as in meetings, you might also hear the following expressions:

- **Je suis pour...**
- **Je suis en faveur de...**
- **Je me prononce pour...**

All of the above translate to "I am in favor of...". To use in a sentence, we can take as example:

<u>Je suis pour</u> l'augmentation des salaires des employés.
I am in favor of increasing the employees' salaries.

Expressing disagreement

To express disagreement, we can simply negate the expressions above:

- **Je ne partage pas votre/ton idée / point de vue.**
- **Je ne suis pas d'accord avec vous/toi.**

Otherwise, we can use these phrases:

- *Je m'oppose à...* I am not in favor of...
- *Je suis défavorable à...* I am not in favor of...
- *Je n'adhère pas à vos idées.* I do not agree with your ideas.

CULTURE TIP

Le goûter

Le goûter can be roughly translated to "snacks". Traditionally, kids enjoy a snack every day at around 4 pm. These afternoon snacks commonly include sweet treats like biscuits or bread. While kids are mostly the ones having a *goûter*, adults are welcome to do so as well!

Incidentally, the word *goûter* can also refer to the verb "to taste" or "to try". Its root word is in fact *le goût*, which refers to the sense of taste.

Expressing opinion and concession

Expressing one's opinion

Like in the dialogue at the beginning of the chapter, one can use the expression *à mon avis* (in my opinion) to indicate that one is about to share his point of view. Alternatively, we can also use phrases like *pour moi* (for me) or *selon moi* (lit. according to me.) These expressions are usually placed at the beginning of a sentence:

> *Pour moi, le véganisme est plus qu'un régime alimentaire,*
> *c'est un mode de vie.*
> For me, veganism is more than an alimentary diet,
> it's a lifestyle.

One might also use the expression *Il me semble que* (it seems to me that):

> *Il me semble que c'est une bonne solution pour réduire le gaspillage alimentaire.*
> It seems to me that this is a good solution to reduce food waste.

Finally, verbal phrases can also be used to share one's perspective:

- *croire que* to believe that
- *penser que* to think that
- *trouver que* to find that
- *imaginer que* to imagine that
- *être persuadé(e) que* to be convinced that

These verbal phrases are followed by the indicative mode, but only if they are in the affirmative. If negated, they require the subjunctive mode. Study the two sentences below:

> *Je crois qu'on <u>peut</u> trouver une solution.*
> I think we can find a solution.

Je ne crois pas qu'on <u>puisse</u> trouver une solution.
I don't think we can find a solution.

Notice how in the affirmative *Je crois que*, we use the indicative mode of the verb *pouvoir*, which is *peut*. However, when negated to *Je ne crois pas que*, we use the subjunctive mode of *pouvoir*, which is *puisse*. Let's look at one more example:

***Je suis persuadé que l'activité physique
<u>a</u> un effet positif sur la santé.***
I am convinced that physical activity
has a positive effect on one's health.

***Je ne suis pas persuadé que l'activité physique
<u>ait</u> un effet positif sur la santé.***
I am not convinced that physical activity
has a positive effect on one's health.

To summarize, here are the verbal phrases that require the subjunctive:

- ***ne pas croire que*** not to believe that
- ***ne pas penser que*** not to think that
- ***ne pas trouver que*** not to find that
- ***ne pas imaginer que*** not to imagine that
- ***ne pas être persuadé(e) que*** not to be convinced that
- ***douter que*** to doubt, to be uncertain about

Remember that *douter que*, though not negated, is always followed by the subjunctive mood.

Expressing concession

By concession, we refer to the intent to concede. Expressions of concessions include conjunctions, prepositions and linking words.

The most common conjunctions of concession are *même si* and *bien que*, which both translate to "although" or "even though". These two differ, however, in that *même si* is always followed by the indicative mode and *bien que*, by the subjunctive mode. Look at these examples:

***Même si la nourriture industrielle <u>est</u> mauvaise pour la santé,
il continue à la consommer.***
Even though processed food is bad for the health,
he continues to consume it.

***Bien que la nourriture industrielle <u>soit</u> mauvaise pour la santé,
il continue à la consommer.***
Even though processed food is bad for the health,
he continues to consume it.

The expression *même si* is thus followed here by the indicative mode of the verb *être*, which is *est*, while *bien que* is followed by the subjunctive form *soit*.

Expressions of concession can also take the form of prepositions, as in:

- ***malgré*** despite
- ***en dépit de*** despite of

These prepositions are interchangeable, and are always followed by a noun:

Les produits bio sont populaires malgré leurs prix élevés.
Organic products are popular despite their high price.

En dépit des conseils du médecin, il refuse de manger sainement.
Despite the advice of the doctor, he refuses to eat healthily.

Finally, linking words can also be used to express concession:

These include:

- **pourtant** yet
- **cependant** however
- **quand même** still, even so
- **toutefois** however, nevertheless

Study the examples below to see how these linking words are used:

- **Elle est en forme. Pourtant, elle ne fait pas d'exercices du tout !** She is in great shape. And yet, she doesn't exercise at all!
- **Manger des légumes est important. Cependant, on ne doit pas oublier qu'il faut adopter une alimentation variée.** Eating vegetables is important. However, we must not forget that we must adopt a varied diet.
- **Je ne mange pas beaucoup, mais je suis quand même en bonne santé.** I don't eat a lot, but even so, I am healthy.
- **Il déteste faire de l'exercice. Toutefois, il fait du jogging tous les matins pour brûler des calories !** He hates exercising. Nevertheless, he jogs every morning to burn some calories.

Nutrition vocabulary

	Translation
consommer	to consume
des nutriments (m.)	nutrients
l'alimentation (f.)	food, diet, nutrition
l'alimentation équilibrée	balanced diet
l'alimentation saine	healthy diet
l'alimentation variée	varied diet
l'équilibre alimentaire	food balance
la nourriture industrielle	processed food
le véganisme	veganism
le végétarisme	vegetarianism
les habitudes alimentaires (f.)	eating habits
manger équilibré	to eat a balanced diet
manger sainement	to eat healthily

produits bio (m.)	organic products
une calorie	calorie
une vitamine	vitamin

Key Takeaways

- To debate about an issue, we can use the following expressions:

Ask for opinion
Qu'est-ce que vous en pensez ?
Qu'en pensez-vous ?
Y croyez-vous ?
Quelle est votre opinion ?
Quel est votre avis ?
Express agreement
Je partage votre/ton idée.
Je partage votre/ton point de vue.
Je suis entièrement / tout à fait / parfaitement / absolument d'accord avec vous/toi.
Je suis partiellement d'accord avec vous/toi.
Je suis pour...
Je suis en faveur de...
Je me prononce pour...
Express disagreement
Je ne partage pas votre/ton idée / point de vue.
Je ne suis pas d'accord avec vous/toi.
Je m'oppose à...
Je suis défavorable à...
Je n'adhère pas à vos idées.

- To express opinion or concession, we can say:

Express opinion	
Pour moi	
Selon moi	
À mon avis	
croire que *penser que* *trouver que* *imaginer que* *être persuadé(e) que*	+ indicative mood
ne pas croire que	+ subjunctive mood

ne pas penser que *ne pas trouver que* *ne pas imaginer que* *ne pas être persuadé(e) que* *douter que*	
Express concession	
même si + indicative mode	
bien que + subjunctive mode	

malgré *en dépit de*	+ noun

pourtant   *cependant*   *quand même*   *toutefois*

In the next and final chapter of this book, we will focus our attention on media and the internet. You will learn how to explain a function and how nominalization in French grammar works. We will also study how to express fear, regret and wants using the subjunctive mode.

Exercises

1-5. Complete the sentences with the correct preposition:

    1. Qu'_____ pensez-vous ?
    2. _____croyez-vous ?
    3. Je partage votre point _____ vue.
    4. Qu'est-ce que vous _____ pensez ?
    5. Je n'adhère pas _____ vos idées.

6-10. Indicative or subjunctive? Complete the sentences with the appropriate conjugation of the indicated verb.

    6. Même si elle (manger) _____ beaucoup, elle ne gagne pas de poids.
    7. Je ne pense pas qu'il (faire) _____ du sport régulièrement.
    8. Elle est persuadée qu'un régime végétarien (être) _____ bon pour la santé.
    9. Bien que Mathis (suivre) _____ un régime restrictif, il mange équilibré.
    10. Je doute qu'ils (pouvoir) _____ réduire leur consommation d'alcool.

Answer Key

1. en
2. Y
3. de
4. en
5. à
6. mange
7. fasse
8. est
9. suive
10. puissent

Chapter 16: Making headlines

Rumeur : le plus vieux média du monde.

Rumor: the oldest media in the world.

- Jean-François Revel

A few decades ago, were we to talk about media, we'd be talking about newspapers or perhaps the radio. These days, media has come to mean many different things and has taken on various forms: social media, online newspapers, podcasts, tweets, the list goes on. Everyone is informed about everything at all times. And while the accuracy of these tidbits of information we receive cannot always be verified, we can say that we now live in one where they have gained much currency.

In this lesson, we will talk about the media and the internet. We will study how to explain a process and a function. We will also have a look at expressions of doubt, certainty and fear.

Functions and nominalization

Let's begin with an excerpt of a text, in which a blogger explains the functions of social media:

> **Les réseaux sociaux se réfèrent à l'ensemble des services disponibles en ligne qui permettent aux gens d'interagir. Ils servent donc à promouvoir les interactions sociales en temps réel et la communication malgré la distance. Ils permettent aussi aux utilisateurs de partager des photos, des vidéos, voire de vendre leurs biens !**

Social media refers to all the services available online that allow people to interact with each other. They therefore serve to promote real-time social interactions and communication despite distance. They also allow users to share photos, videos, and even sell their goods!

Explaining a function

When explaining the function of something, as in the example above, we can use the verbs *permettre* or *servir*. These two verbs make use of specific prepositions that we will discuss here.

The verb *permettre* means "to allow to", "to enable to" or "to make [something] possible to do". It is used with the prepositions *à* and *de*: *permettre à quelqu'un de faire quelque chose* (to allow someone to do something). Look at the example below, while examining the prepositions used:

> **Le moteur de recherche permet aux internautes de trouver des informations rapidement.**
> Search engines allow users to find information quickly.

The verb *permettre* can also be used with a noun:

> **Internet permet la diffusion rapide des informations.**

The Internet makes possible the quick dissemination of information.

The verb *servir*, on the other hand, is used to mean "to be used to" or "to serve to/as". Its meaning changes according to the preposition used:

- ***servir à* + verb** to be used to, to serve to
- ***servir de* + noun** to serve as
- ***se servir de* + noun** to use

Study the following examples below:

- ***Les réseaux sociaux servent à faciliter la communication.*** Social media are used to facilitate communication.
- ***Les réseaux sociaux servent de plateformes de communication.*** Social media serve as communication platforms.
- ***On se sert des réseaux sociaux pour rester connectés à ses proches.*** People use social media to stay connected to their loved ones.

Nominalization

Nominalization refers to the process of transforming verbs or adjectives into nouns. Many nouns in French undergo this transformation.

Let's look at some examples. The following verbs or adjectives are transformed into nouns through the addition of suffixes. The most common suffixes include: *-age*, *-ment*, *-tion*, *-ation* and *-ure*:

- ***stocker*** (to store) → ***le stockage*** (storage)
- ***fonctionner*** (to function) → ***le fonctionnement*** (operation, functioning)
- ***communiquer*** (to communicate) → ***la communication*** (communication)
- ***modifier*** (to modify) → ***la modification*** (modification)
- ***briser*** (to break) → ***une brisure*** (a crack)

Internet vocabulary

	Translation
chatter	to chat
en direct	live
en streaming	streaming
interagir	to interact
Internet (m.)	the Internet
les réseaux sociaux (m.)	social media
liker	to like
poster	to post
surfer sur Internet	to surf the Internet (slang)
taguer	to tag
tweeter	to tweet
un blog	a blog

un hashtag	a hashtag
un internaute	internet user, netizen
un lien	a link
un moteur de recherche	a search engine
un selfie	a selfie
un site web	a website
un tag	a tag
un tweet	a tweet
un(e) émoticôn(e)	an emoticon

Fear, regret and wants

Let's examine some example sentences where internet users share their opinion, wants and apprehensions regarding social media and computer technology:

- *Avoir un site web pour son entreprise peut être utile, à condition qu'il soit informatif et clair.*
- *Mes parents ne nous achètent pas de portables, de crainte que nous soyons moins actifs.*
- *Je crains que les relations virtuelles remplacent les interactions en personne.*
- *Je veux que les internautes aient un comportement plus respectueux et amical.*
- *J'ai peur que mes enfants soient accros à Internet. Ils passent trop de temps sur leur portable !*
- *Il est certain que l'on ne peut plus vivre sans Internet.*
- *Je regrette que les jeunes passent moins de temps à jouer à l'extérieur, et plus de temps sur les jeux vidéo.*

- Having a website for your business can be useful, provided it is informative and clear.
- My parents don't buy us cell phones for fear that we'll be less active.
- I fear that virtual relationships will replace face-to-face interactions.
- I want Internet users to behave more respectfully and friendly.
- I am afraid that my children are addicted to the Internet. They spend too much time on their phones!
- It is certain that we can no longer live without the Internet.
- I'm sorry that young people spend less time playing outside, and more time on video games.

As you can see in the examples above, many of the phrases used to express fear, regret or wants are followed by the subjunctive mood.

Expressions of fear and regret

To express fear, we can use the following expressions:

- ***de crainte que*** (for fear of)
- ***de peur que*** (for fear of)
- ***craindre que*** (to fear that)
- ***avoir peur que*** (to fear that)

+ subjunctive mood

All of these expressions are, as noted above, followed by the subjunctive.

To express regret, we can use the expression:

- ***regretter que*** (to be sorry that, to regret that) + subjunctive mood

Expressions of want

The following expressions of want are also always followed by the subjunctive mood:

- ***désirer que*** (to desire that)
- ***aimer que*** (would like)
- ***souhaiter que*** (to wish that)
- ***vouloir que*** (to want that)

+ subjunctive mood

Expressions of condition

To express condition, we can use the phrase:

- ***à condition de*** (provided that)   + infinitive
- ***à condition que*** (provided that) + subjunctive

Look at these two sentences:

- ***Ils peuvent jouer aux jeux vidéo à condition de <u>ne pas dormir</u> trop tard.*** They can play video games as long as they don't sleep too late.
- ***Ils peuvent jouer aux jeux vidéo à condition qu'ils <u>ne dorment pas</u> trop tard.*** They can play video games as long as they don't sleep too late.

Impersonal expressions

Impersonal expressions, specifically those that are followed by *que*, require the subjunctive in certain cases:

- ***Il est important que*** (It is important that)
- ***Il est dommage que*** (It is a pity that)
- ***Il est possible que*** (It is possible that)

+ subjunctive mood

Others are followed by the indicative mode:

- ***Il est évident que*** (It is evident that)
- ***Il est clair que*** (It is clear that)
- ***Il est certain que*** (It is certain that)
- ***Il est probable que*** (It is likely that)

+ indicative mood

Remember that *Il est possible que* is followed by the subjunctive, while *Il est probable que* is followed by the indicative. The reason is simple: the subjunctive mood is in fact used to indicate doubt. The word *possible* indicates that there is less than 50% chance that something happens, but *probable* indicates there is more than 50% chance it would! Thus, we use the indicative for *probable* but not for *possible* which indicates doubt.

- ***Il est possible qu'il fasse froid.*** It is possible it would be cold (-50% chance).
- ***Il est probable qu'il fera froid.*** It is likely it will be cold (+50% chance).

CULTURE TIP

Anglicisme, c'est quoi ?

Many contemporary terms related to the Internet and to computer technology have a French equivalent. Quite often, however, the English words are retained. This is especially true in informal conversations. Be careful though, for while they are *anglicismes* (English loan words), they are pronounced following the French phonetics!

- ***un hacker*** /a-keur/ a hacker
- ***un bug*** /beug/ a bug
- ***un hashtag*** /ash-tag/ a hashtag
- ***le wifi*** /wee-fee/ wi-fi

Key Takeaways

- To explain a function, we can use the following verbal phrases: *permettre à (quelqu'un) de (faire quelque chose), permettre de (faire quelque chose), servir à (faire quelque chose), servir de (quelque chose), se servir de (quelque chose).*
- Many nouns in French are formed by adding the suffixes *-age, -ment, -tion, -ation* and *-ure* to certain verbs.
- Expressions of fear, regret, wants and conditions often require the subjunctive mode:

Express fear	
de crainte que	
de peur que	+ subjunctive mood
craindre que	
avoir peur que	
Express regret	
regretter que	+ subjunctive mood
Express want	
désirer que	
aimer que	+ subjunctive mood
souhaiter que	
vouloir que	
Express condition	
à condition de + infinitive	
à condition que + subjunctive	

- Impersonal expressions require either the indicative or subjunctive mode:

Impersonal expressions	
Il est important que	
Il est dommage que	+ subjunctive mood
Il est possible que	
Il est évident que	
Il est clair que	+ indicative mood
Il est certain que	
Il est probable que	

Félicitations ! Congratulations! You have reached the final chapter of this book. Pat yourself on the back, give yourself a reward — you can now proudly say you have reached a new milestone in your French language learning journey. If you're hankering for more, don't forget to check out the vocabulary lists and verb conjugations in the annex.

What's next

You've already made it to this stage, what's there to stop you? If you wish to make it to the finish line and achieve full native fluency, you would want to check out the next book in our series: ***Learn Advanced French for Adult Students***. With this book, you will be able to build on what you learned here and achieve an advanced level of fluency in French. This book will serve as your map to becoming bilingual and to being able to talk about anything and everything, just like a true native. *À bientôt l'aventurier*, see you soon adventurer!

Exercises

1-4. Complete the sentences with the correct preposition:

1. Les souris servent _____ déplacer le curseur de l'écran.
2-3. Les réseaux sociaux permettent _____ membres des familles _____ rester connectés.
4. Je me sers _____ mon ordinateur pour travailler.

5-10. Indicative or subjunctive? Complete the sentences with the appropriate conjugation of the indicated verb.

5. Il est dommage que beaucoup de jeunes (être) _____ accros aux jeux vidéo.
6. J'ai peur que les gens (être) _____ remplacés par des robots.
7. Les enfants peuvent utiliser des gadgets, à condition que les parents les (accompagner) _____.
8. Il est probable que de nouvelles formes de technologie informatique (être) _____ populaires dans les prochaines décennies.
9. Les internautes souhaitent que leurs données personnelles (être) _____ protégées.
10. Il est possible qu'elle (poster) _____ des photos de sa nouvelle maison sur les réseaux sociaux demain.

Answer Key

1. à
2. aux
3. de
4. de
5. soient
6. soient
7. accompagnent
8. seront
9. soient
10. poste

Vocabulary Lists by Theme

Cinema

a (TV) series	*une série*
a director	*un réalisateur, une réalisatrice (f.)*
a documentary	*un documentaire*
a scene	*une scène*
action movie	*un film d'action*
adventure movie	*un film d'aventures*
animated movie	*un film d'animation*
cinema, movie theater	*le cinéma*
comedy	*une comédie*
detective movie	*un film policier*
horror movie	*un film d'horreur*
leading actor	*le premier rôle*
leading actress	*le premier rôle féminin*
movie	*un film*
science-fiction movie	*un film de science-fiction*
to shoot (a movie or scene)	*tourner*

Characteristics

anxious	*inquiet(-ète)*
arrogant	*arrogant(e)*
calm	*calme*
confident	*confiant(e)*
courageous	*courageux(-euse)*
energetic	*dynamique*
extrovert	*extraverti(e)*
fearful	*peureux(-euse)*
generous	*généreux(-euse)*
hardworking	*sérieux(-euse)*
honest	*honnête*
humble	*humble*
impatient	*impatient(e)*

impolite	*impoli(e)*
insensitive	*insensible*
introverted	*introverti(e)*
irresponsible	*irresponsable*
kind	*gentil(le)*
lazy	*paresseux(-euse)*
liar	*menteur(-euse)*
mean	*méchant(e)*
optimistic	*optimiste*
patient	*patient(e)*
pessimistic	*pessimiste*
polite	*poli(e)*
reserved, quiet	*réservé(e)*
responsible	*responsable*
selfish	*égoïste*
sensitive	*sensible*
sociable	*sociable*
strong	*fort(e)*
talkative	*bavard(e)*
weak	*faible*

Clothing

a blouse	*un chemisier*
a coat	*un manteau*
a dress	*une robe*
a long/short-sleeved shirt	*une chemise*
a polo shirt	*un polo*
a raincoat	*un imperméable*
a skirt	*une jupe*
a suit	*un costume*
a sweater	*un pull*
a t-shirt	*un t-shirt*
boxer shorts	*un caleçon*
a bra	*un soutien-gorge*
briefs	*un slip*

a jacket	*une veste*
jeans	*un jean*
panties	*une culotte*
pants	*un pantalon*
shorts	*un short*
socks	*des chaussettes (f.)*
underwear	*des sous-vêtements (m.)*

Accessories

a belt	*une ceinture*
a winter hat	*un bonnet*
a bracelet	*un bracelet*
a cap	*une casquette*
a handbag	*un sac à main*
a hat	*un chapeau*
a light scarf, a head scarf	*un foulard*
a necklace	*un collier*
a ring	*une bague*
a scarf	*une écharpe*
a tie	*une cravate*
earrings	*des boucles d'oreille* (f.)
gloves	*des gants* (m.)
gold	*(en) or*
jewelry	*des bijoux* (m.)
silver	*(en) argent*

Anatomy

arms	*le bras*
blood	*le sang*
bones	*les os* (m.)
brain	*le cerveau*
butt	*les fesses*
chest	*la poitrine*
feet	*les pieds*

fingers	*les doigts* (m.)
hand	*la main*
head	*la tête*
heart	*le coeur*
knee	*le genou*
leg	*la jambe*
lungs	*les poumons*
nails	*les ongles* (m.)
neck	*le cou*
shoulders	*les épaules* (f.)
belly	*le ventre*
stomach	*l'estomac* (m.)
throat	*la gorge*
thumb	*le pouce*

Life milestones

birth	*la naissance*
marriage	*le mariage*
separation	*la séparation*
to change careers	*se reconvertir*
to divorce	*divorcer*
to get fired	*être licencié(e)*
to get married (with somebody)	*se marier (avec quelqu'un)*
to give birth	*donner naissance*
to have kids	*avoir des enfants*
to marry (somebody)	*épouser (quelqu'un)*
to move (to a new place, home, etc.)	*déménager*
to resign (from a job)	*démissionner*
to start a business	*créer/lancer une entreprise*

Job search

a job offer	*une offre d'emploi*
a job seeker	*un demandeur d'emploi*
a salary	*un salaire*

a work contract	*un contrat de travail*
an application	*une candidature*
an employee	*un/une salarié(e), un/une employé(e)*
an employer	*un employeur*
an internship	*un stage*
an interview	*un entretien*
an unemployed person	*un/une chômeur(euse)*
cover letter	*une lettre de motivation*
CV or curriculum vitae	*un CV*
full-time	*à plein temps*
gross salary	*le salaire brut*
minimum wage	*le SMIC (Salaire Minimum Interprofessionnel de Croissance)*
net salary	*le salaire net*
part-time (50%)	*à mi-temps*
part-time (70 – 80%)	*à temps partiel*
permanent contract	*un CDI (Contrat à Durée Indéterminée)*
studies or schooling	*les études, la formation*
temporary contract	*un CDD (Contrat à Durée Déterminée)*
to send an application	*poser sa candidature*

Work tasks

a copy machine	*une photocopieuse*
a printer	*une imprimante*
to print (a document)	*imprimer (un document)*
to set up a meeting	*organiser (une réunion)*
to attend (a meeting)	*assister (à une réunion)*
to delegate (tasks/responsibilities)	*déléguer (les responsabilités)*
to do networking	*faire du réseau*
to hire (somebody)	*embaucher (quelqu'un)*
to photocopy	*photocopier*
to recrute (somebody)	*recruter (quelqu'un)*
to reserve a room	*réserver une salle*
to sign a document	*signer (un document)*
to talk about a project	*échanger (sur un projet)*
to write a letter	*rédiger une lettre*

Email vocabulary

a recipient	*un destinataire*
a sender	*un expéditeur(-trice)*
an email	*un email*
an email address	*une adresse email*
the inbox	*la boîte de réception*
the outbox	*la boîte d'envoi*
the subject	*l'objet*
to delete	*supprimer*
to forward	*transférer*
to reply	*répondre*
to save	*enregistrer*
to send	*envoyer*

Real estate

a building	*un immeuble*
a property	*un bien*
a social lodging	*un logement social*
agency fees	*les honoraires (f. pl.)*
guarantee	*la caution*
heating, heater	*le chauffage*
house-share, apartment-share	*une colocation*
an owner	*un propriétaire*
a rent (price)	*un loyer*
renting, rental	*la location*
sales	*la vente*
a surface area	*une superficie*
tenant	*un locataire*
to move in	*emménager*
to move out	*déménager*

Household appliances

a clothes dryer	*un sèche-linge*
a coffee maker	*une cafetière*
a dishwasher	*un lave-vaisselle*

a hair dryer	*un sèche-cheveux*
a heater	*un radiateur*
a microwave	*un micro-onde*
a stove	*une cuisinière*
a TV	*une télévision*
a vacuum cleaner	*un aspirateur*
a washing machine	*une machine à laver*
an air conditioner	*un climatiseur*
an iron	*un fer à repasser*
an oven	*un four*

Crimes

a burglar	*un cambrioleur(-euse)*
a burglary	*un cambriolage*
a crime	*un délit*
a fine, a parking ticket	*une contravention*
a pickpocket	*un pickpocket*
a plaintiff	*un plaignant(e)*
a thief	*un voleur(-euse)*
a victim	*une victime*
a witness	*un témoin*
an assailant	*un agresseur*
an attack, a mugging	*une agression*
an investigation	*une enquête*
an offense	*une infraction*
arrest (somebody)	*arrêter (quelqu'un)*
extorsion	*l'extorsion (f.)*
fraud	*la fraude*
imprisonment	*l'incarcération*
the emergency room	*les urgences*
a theft	*un vol*

Automobile vocabulary

(car) to run, to drive	*rouler*
a car	*une voiture*
a car (slang)	*une bagnole*
a vehicle	*un véhicule*
the accelerator	*l'accélérateur*
the blinker	*le clignotant*
the brake	*le frein*
the bumper	*le pare-chocs*
the clutch	*l'embrayage*
the engine	*le moteur*
the exhaust pipe	*le pot d'échappement*
the gas tank	*le réservoir*
the handbrake	*le frein à main*
the headlight	*le phare*
the hood	*le capot*
the horn	*le klaxon*
lights	*les feux*
the rear-view mirror	*le rétroviseur*
to start the engine	*démarrer (le moteur)*
the steering wheel	*le volant*
the trunk (of a car)	*le coffre*
to move forward	*avancer*
to overtake	*doubler*
to reverse	*reculer*
to turn off the engine	*couper (le moteur)*
the windshield	*le pare-brise*
the windshield wiper	*l'essuie-glace (m.)*

Computer technology

a cable	*un cable*
a hard drive	*un disque dur*
a smart watch	*une montre connectée*
a smartphone	*un smartphone*
a tablet	*une tablette*

a thumb drive	*une clé USB*
an app	*une appli(cation)*
to be buggy	*bugger*
to break down	*tomber en panne*
to download	*télécharger*
to turn off	*éteindre*
to turn on	*allumer*
wifi	*le Wifi*

Environment

an ecosystem	*un écosystème*
biodiversity	*la biodiversité*
deforestation	*la déforestation*
Earth	*la Terre*
ecology	*l'écologie (f.)*
global warming	*le réchauffement climatique* (m.)
greenhouse gases	*les gaz à effet de serre* (m.)
pollution	*la pollution*
recycling	*le recyclage*
species	*une espèce*
the environment	*l'environnement* (m.)
to avoid	*éviter*
to fight against	*lutter contre*
to promote	*promouvoir*
to protect	*protéger*
waste	*le gaspillage*

Nutrition

balanced diet	*l'alimentation équilibrée*
calorie	*une calorie*
eating habits	*les habitudes alimentaires (f.)*
food balance	*l'équilibre alimentaire*
food, diet, nutrition	*l'alimentation (f.)*
healthy diet	*l'alimentation saine*
nutrients	*des nutriments (m.)*

organic products	*produits bio (m.)*
processed food	*la nourriture industrielle*
to consume	*consommer*
to eat a balanced diet	*manger équilibré*
to eat healthily	*manger sainement*
varied diet	*l'alimentation variée*
veganism	*le véganisme*
vegetarianism	*le végétarisme*
vitamin	*une vitamine*

Internet

a blog	*un blog*
a hashtag	*un hashtag*
a link	*un lien*
a search engine	*un moteur de recherche*
a selfie	*un selfie*
a tag	*un tag*
a tweet	*un tweet*
a website	*un site web*
an emoticon	*un(e) émoticôn(e)*
interact	*interagir*
internet user, netizen	*un internaute*
live	*en direct*
social media	*les réseaux sociaux* (m.)
streaming	*en streaming*
the Internet	*Internet* (m.)
to chat	*chatter*
to like	*liker*
to post	*poster*
to surf the Internet	*surfer sur Internet* (slang)
to tag	*taguer*
to tweet	*tweeter*

Verb Conjugations

	Present	Composed past	Imperfect	Simple future	Subjunctive
Être (to be)	je suis	j'ai été	j'étais	je serai	que je sois
	tu es	tu as été	tu étais	tu seras	que tu sois
	il/elle est	il/elle a été	il/elle était	il/elle sera	qu'il/elle soit
	nous sommes	nous avons été	nous étions	nous serons	que nous soyons
	vous êtes	vous avez été	vous étiez	vous serez	que vous soyez
	ils/elles sont	ils/elles ont été	ils/elles étaient	ils/elles seront	qu'ils/elles soient
Avoir (to have)	j'ai	j'ai eu	j'avais	j'aurai	que j'aie
	tu as	tu as eu	tu avais	tu auras	que tu aies
	il/elle a	il/elle a eu	il/elle avait	il/elle aura	qu'il/elle ait
	nous avons	nous avons eu	nous avions	nous aurons	que nous ayons
	vous avez	vous avez eu	vous aviez	vous aurez	que vous ayez
	ils/elles ont	ils/elles ont eu	ils/elles avaient	ils/elles auront	qu'ils/elles aient
Aller (to go)	je vais	je suis allé(e)	j'allais	j'irai	que j'aille
	tu vas	tu es allé(e)	tu allais	tu iras	que tu ailles
	il/elle va	il/elle est allé(e)	il/elle allait	il/elle ira	qu'il/elle aille
	nous allons	nous sommes allé(e)s	nous allions	nous irons	que nous allions
	vous allez	vous êtes allé(e)s	vous alliez	vous irez	que vous alliez

	ils/elles vont	Ils/elles sont allé(e)s	ils/elles allaient	ils/elles iront	qu'ils/elles aillent
Chanter (to sing)	je chante	j'ai chanté	je chantais	je chanterai	que je chante
	tu chantes	tu as chanté	tu chantais	tu chanteras	que tu chantes
	il/elle chante	il/elle a chanté	il/elle chantait	il/elle chantera	qu'il/elle chante
	nous chantons	nous avons chanté	nous chantions	nous chanterons	que nous chantions
	vous chantez	vous avez chanté	vous chantiez	vous chanterez	que vous chantiez
	ils/elles chantent	ils/elles ont chanté	ils/elles chantaient	ils/elles chanteront	qu'ils/elles chantent
Choisir (to choose)	je choisis	j'ai choisi	je choisissais	je choisirai	que je choisisse
	tu choisis	tu as choisi	tu choisissais	tu choisiras	que tu choisisses
	il/elle choisit	il/elle a choisi	il/elle choisissait	il/elle choisira	qu'il/elle choisisse
	nous choisissons	nous avons choisi	nous choisissions	nous choisirons	que nous choisissions
	vous choisissez	vous avez choisi	vous choisissiez	vous choisirez	que vous choisissiez
	ils/elles choisissent	ils/elles ont choisi	ils/elles choisissaient	ils/elles choisiront	qu'ils/elles choisissent
Connaître (to know)	je connais	j'ai connu	je connaissais	je connaîtrai	que je connaisse
	tu connais	tu as connu	tu connaissais	tu connaîtras	que tu connaisses
	il/elle connait	il/elle a connu	il/elle connaissait	il/elle connaîtra	qu'il/elle connaisse
	nous connaissons	nous avons connu	nous connaissions	nous connaîtrons	que nous connaissions
	vous connaissez	vous avez connu	vous connaissiez	vous connaîtrez	que vous connaissiez

	ils/elles connaissent	ils/elles ont connu	ils/elles connaissaient	ils/elles connaîtront	qu'ils/elles connaissent
Descendre (to go down)	je descends	je suis descendu(e)	je descendais	je descendrai	que je descende
	tu descends	tu es descendu(e)	tu descendais	tu descendras	que tu descendes
	il/elle descend	il/elle descendu(e)	il/elle descendait	il/elle descendra	qu'il/elle descende
	nous descendons	nous sommes descendu(e)s	nous descendions	nous descendrons	que nous descendions
	vous descendez	vous êtes descendu(e)s	vous descendiez	vous descendrez	que vous descendiez
	ils/elles descendent	ils/elles sont descendu(e)s	ils/elles descendaient	ils/elles descendront	qu'ils/elles descendent
Devoir (to have to)	je dois	j'ai dû	je devais	je devrai	que je doive
	tu dois	tu as dû	tu devais	tu devras	que tu doives
	il/elle doit	il/elle a dû	il/elle devait	il/elle devra	qu'il/elle doive
	nous devons	nous avons dû	nous devions	nous devrons	que nous devions
	vous devez	vous avez dû	vous deviez	vous devrez	que vous deviez
	ils/elles doivent	ils/elles ont dû	ils/elles devaient	ils/elles devront	qu'ils/elles doivent
Écrire (to write)	j'écris	j'ai écrit	j'écrivais	j'écrirai	que j'écrive
	tu écris	tu as écrit	tu écrivais	tu écriras	que tu écrives
	il/elle écrit	il/elle a écrit	il/elle écrivait	il/elle écrira	qu'il/elle écrive
	nous écrivons	nous avons écrit	nous écrivions	nous écrirons	que nous écrivions
	vous écrivez	vous avez écrit	vous écriviez	vous écrirez	que vous écriviez
	ils/elles écrivent	lis/elles ont écrit	ils/elles écrivaient	ils/elles écriront	qu'ils/elles écrivent

Faire (to do)	je fais	j'ai fait	je faisais	je ferai	que je fasse
	tu fais	tu as fait	tu faisais	tu feras	que tu fasses
	il/elle fait	il/elle a fait	il/elle faisait	il/elle fera	qu'il/elle fasse
	nous faisons	nous avons fait	nous faisions	nous ferons	que nous fassions
	vous faites	vous avez fait	vous faisiez	vous ferez	que vous fassiez
	ils/elles font	Ils/elles ont fait	ils/elles faisaient	ils/elles feront	qu'ils/elles fassent
Partir (to leave)	je pars	je suis parti(e)	je partais	je partirai	que je parte
	tu pars	tu es parti(e)	tu partais	tu partiras	que tu partes
	il/elle part	il/elle est parti (e)	il/elle partait	il/elle partira	qu'il/elle parte
	nous partons	nous sommes parti(e)s	nous partions	nous partirons	que nous partions
	vous partez	vous êtes parti(e)s	vous partiez	vous partirez	que vous partiez
	ils/elles partent	ils/elles sont parti(e)s	ils/elles partaient	ils/elles partiront	qu'ils/elles partent
Pouvoir (to be able to)	je peux	j'ai pu	je pouvais	je pourrai	que je puisse
	tu peux	tu as pu	tu pouvais	tu pourras	que tu puisses
	il/elle peut	il/elle a pu	il/elle pouvait	il/elle pourra	qu'il/elle puisse
	nous pouvons	nous avons pu	nous pouvions	nous pourrons	que nous puissions
	vous pouvez	vous avez pu	vous pouviez	vous pourrez	que vous puissiez
	ils/elles peuvent	ils/elles ont pu	ils/elles pouvaient	ils/elles pourront	qu'ils/elles puissent
Prendre	je prends	j'ai pris	je prenais	je prendrai	que je prenne

(to take)	tu prends	tu as pris	tu prenais	tu prendras	que tu prennes
	il/elle prend	il/elle a pris	il/elle prenait	il/elle prendra	qu'il/elle prenne
	nous prenons	nous avons pris	nous prenions	nous prendrons	que nous prenions
	vous prenez	vous avez pris	vous preniez	vous prendrez	que vous preniez
	ils/elles prennent	ils/elles ont pris	ils/elles prenaient	ils/elles prendront	qu'ils/elles prennent
Savoir (to know)	je sais	j'ai su	je savais	je saurai	que je sache
	tu sais	tu as su	tu savais	tu sauras	que tu saches
	il/elle sait	il/elle a su	il/elle savait	ii/elle saura	qu'il/elle sache
	nous savons	nous avons su	nous savions	nous saurons	que nous sachions
	vous savez	vous avez su	vous saviez	vous saurez	que vous sachiez
	ils/elles savent	ils/elles ont su	ils/elles savaient	ils/elles sauront	qu'ils/elles sachent
Venir (to come)	je viens	je suis venu(e)	je venais	je viendrai	que je vienne
	tu viens	tu es venu(e)	tu venais	tu viendras	que tu viennes
	il/elle vient	il/elle est venu(e)	il/elle venait	il/elle viendra	qu'il/elle vienne
	nous venons	nous sommes venu(e)s	nous venions	nous viendrons	que nous venions
	vous venez	vous êtes venu(e)s	vous veniez	vous viendrez	que vous veniez
	ils/elles viennent	ils/elles sont venu(e)s	ils/elles venaient	ils/elles viendront	qu'ils/elles viennent
Voir (to see)	je vois	j'ai vu	je voyais	je verrai	que je voie
	tu vois	tu as vu	tu voyais	tu verras	que tu voies

	il/elle voit	il/elle a vu	il/elle voyait	il/elle verra	qu'il/elle voie
	nous voyons	nous avons vu	nous voyions	nous verrons	que nous voyions
	vous voyez	vous avez vu	vous voyiez	vous verrez	que vous voyiez
	ils/elles voient	ils/elles ont vu	ils/elles voyaient	Ils/elles verront	qu'ils/elles voient
Vouloir (to want)	je veux	j'ai voulu	je voulais	je voudrai	que je veuille
	tu veux	tu as voulu	tu voulais	tu voudras	que tu veuilles
	il/elle veut	il/elle a voulu	il/elle voulait	il/elle voudra	qu'il/elle veuille
	nous voulons	nous avons voulu	nous voulions	nous voudrons	que nous voulions
	vous voulez	vous avez voulu	vous vouliez	vous voudrez	que vous vouliez
	ils/elles veulent	ils/elles ont voulu	ils/elles voulaient	ils/elles voudront	qu'ils/elles veuillent

Grammar Topic Index

A

adjectives, 28
adverbs in -ment, 113
adverbs of intensity, 38
assez, 38

C

cause, expression of, 123
comparison, 29
comparison with bon and mauvais, 105
complex negation, 123
concession, expression of, 144
condition, expression of, 155
consequence, expression of, 124

D

direct object pronouns, 40
dont, 88
double pronouns, 80

E

expressions of time, 66

F

falloir, 70
fear and regret, expression of, 154

I

il faut, 70
imperative, 72
impersonal expressions, 155
indirect object pronouns, 63

N

ne...que, 96
nominalization, 153

O

objective, expression of, 133
opinion, expression of, 143

P

passive voice, 99

pluperfect tense, 48
present progressive tense, 56

Q

qui, que, 21

R

recent past tense, 54
reported speech, 115

S

subjunctive, 71
subjunctive, irregular verbs, 134

T

tout, 125
trop, 38

W

want, expression of, 155

BOOK 5

Learn French with Short Stories for Adult Intermediates

Engaging Stories To Shortcut Your French Fluency!
(Fun & Easy Reads)

Explore to Win

Book 5 description

Discover French grammar naturally as you read stories, expand your vocabulary, and grow fluent fast.

Have you ever noticed how hard it can be to remember grammar rules? You're not alone!

No matter how much you study, you seem unable to apply French grammar rules! Do you often struggle to stay motivated? Do you believe reading a story in French is impossible?

If so, there's a simple solution: Introducing *"Learn French with Short Stories for Adult Intermediates"* to help you learn grammar in context.

Imagine easily understanding the story in French, even if you are just intermediate, without ever needing to consult a dictionary or grammar book, because you have everything in one place. Imagine reading a story in French that revolves around one or two grammar units, so you can focus on one point at a time and comprehend how the French grammar works.

You'll get 11 adapted French stories followed by the summary in French and English, unfamiliar vocabulary from the story, comprehension questions and grammar notes regarding the key grammar points from the story. You'll also learn the grammar rules applied in context, along with many more examples to get a grasp of them.

In *"Learn French with Short Stories for Adult Intermediates"*, you'll discover:

- **11 stories adapted for French intermediate**, focusing on one or two grammar points at a time, so you can take your time to absorb the structure and rules at your pace.
- **12 most common grammar points** needed to succeed in most conversations in French: Indefinite Adjectives, Prepositions of place, Agreement and Different uses of Past Participle, Use of *Imparfait* and *Passé Composé*, Gerundiv, Relative Pronouns (*lequel, auquel, duquel*), Indefinite Relative Pronouns (*ce qui, ce que, ce dont*), Expressing Cause and Consequence, Expressing Duration, Conditional, Pluperfect, Subjunctive.
- Stories revolving around **most common everyday topics** (friends, city sightseeing, traveling, going to a bar, museum, flea market, doctor's office or a birthday party) aimed at covering most of the topics found in everyday conversations.
- **Summary of stories** in French and English, in case you need help understanding them.
- **Unfamiliar words and expressions** sorted in the chronological order they appear in the story.
- **Series of questions** to test your comprehension of the narrative, with answers included at the end.
- **Grammar notes** explaining the main grammar points used in a story in detail.

When we read stories, we keep our brains engaged in the story's development while soaking up the vocabulary, structure, and grammar.

"Learn French with Short Stories for Adult Intermediates" is for anyone who struggles to apply grammar rules in real-life conversations. Whether you are a student who wants to renew French because it's been years since you last spoke French or an intermediate learner who's struggling to apply

grammar and expand vocabulary, the stories in this book can set the stage for fluent conversations in French.

Introduction

Do you know what is one of the most natural ways of learning languages?

For thousands of years, stories have been a way to transfer knowledge and give sense to the world around us. The human mind has a natural ability to remember stories. If you are wondering why, it's because human creatures seek meaning more than anything else. And it's the same way when learning languages. We seek meaning, not the vocabulary to retain. Through reading stories, we help our brain understand the context and meaning beyond words. We begin to understand the relationship between words and phrases, and start seeing the big picture.

We introduced some basic grammar concepts in the first book of the series, including articles, plural nouns and adjectives, the formation of tenses such as *présent, passé composé, futur proche, futur simple*, and l'*imparfait*, as well as possessive adjectives and pronouns, simple relative pronouns (*qui, que, où, dont*), interrogative pronouns (*lequel, laquelle*), direct and indirect object pronouns, reflexive verbs, and neutral constructions "il y a" and "il fait". The second book for intermediate students is a logical continuation of the first one, in terms of vocabulary and grammar.

Short stories in French for intermediate learners is a collection of eleven short stories, crafted especially for intermediate students to improve their French skills. Each story is written with common intermediate troubles in mind. Our eleven stories again cover eleven most frequent everyday situations, from meeting new people, talking about your friends, sharing a bad experience, getting engaged, city sightseeing, celebrating an anniversary, going to a bar, to the art gallery and flea market, reading the newspaper, talking about recycling, or going to the doctor's office, allowing you to build your vocabulary in different areas of life. When it comes to vocabulary drilling, reading stories makes more sense.

Apart from the vocabulary, each story includes grammar explanations, so you can reread the story with an eye for grammar the second time. Each story is focused on a different grammar point, helping you master isolated grammar points, from past tenses to conditional, gerundive, direct and indirect objects, prepositions of place, indefinite adjectives and, indefinite and definite relative pronouns. You'll also learn how to oppose two ideas, express cause and consequences, and finally make subjunctive sentences. There is also a focus on some common intermediate mistakes, like the difference between direct and indirect object, the agreement of the past participle with "avoir", "être" and pronominal verbs, the difference between "future" and "conditionnel", between "imparfait" and "passé composé", "participe" and "gérondif" or between "depuis", "pendant", "il y a", and much more. As a result, it gets easier to recognize grammar patterns in context.

When you are an intermediate student, your vocabulary is broader, and you can sometimes comprehend the meaning without understanding each word individually. By reading stories, it will soon become evident to you how French is structured.

To support you on your reading journey, as an intermediate, in each chapter you'll find:
- → **Story synopsis in French and English** to give you an overview of the story.

- → **Vocabulary and expressions** from the story, bolded in the story and later placed and translated separately in the order they appear in the story.
- → **Comprehension questions** to test your understanding with answers key at the end of the book.
- → **Grammar notes** that explain the main grammar point in that particular story.
- → **Key takeaways** from the chapter.

This book is made for intermediate students. Stories are crafted using more advanced words as well as intermediate grammar, introducing a variety of relative sentences, helping you learn how to express hypothesis, opposition, give suggestions or advice, express wishes or demands. You'll learn how to keep your speech flowing, easily switching from one idea to another.

Besides being linguists and language enthusiasts, the authors speak French natively, so they know exactly how to apply the language in real life. Additionally, they will also be able to teach you how to speak and sound like a true native, use slang, and avoid some bookish expressions no one really uses.

If you are an intermediate student, or if you have been studying French some time ago, but you'd like to refresh your knowledge of French, *Short Stories for Adult Intermediate*, will give you the support you need.

Guide to reading as an intermediate in French

The biggest challenge when reading in a foreign language is to overcome our unrealistic expectations from reading in our mother tongue. We skip the fact that reading is a complex skill that requires a variety of micro-skills, such as scanning the page to find the needed information or reading the keywords and immediately understanding the context.

If we want to read effectively in French, we have to take a step back and remember what it was like to read in the first grade at school. Because, in terms of language, that's exactly who we are in French. Children.

Probably the most important thing to accept when reading in another language is that you won't understand everything. Making peace with ambiguity is essential to making progress. Perhaps, some learners will find this counter-intuitive, but it's actually what keeps you motivated in the long run. Imagine how little progress you'll be making if you feel the urge to understand each word from the text. Instead of moving forward, your perfectionism will keep you stuck in one place. While deep comprehension can be very important when it comes to language learning, if you cover a wider range of different structures and vocabulary, you'll be able to deal with more language complexities. Language is not about knowing a couple of words perfectly, but understanding different speaking situations.

Reading stories is a great way to help you progress in French, because it puts you in a position where understanding the story in general is more important than comprehending the isolated words. This kind of reading is called extensive reading. There are two methods of reading: intensive and extensive reading.

Intensive reading is what you have encountered in your language courses. It means that you are trying to understand each word from the textbook, focus on retaining grammar structures, and then complete certain tasks. On the other hand, extensive reading is pleasure oriented, so it helps you become comfortable with the natural language in use.

To get the most from reading stories from the book, here are a few suggestions to keep in mind.

Step 1. Get acquainted with the main topic

Read the chapter title and get acquainted with the main topic of the story. The introductory part will give you some clues about the main focus in terms of syntax, grammar, and vocabulary. You'll be already well prepared before you start.

Step 2. First-time reading

Read the story once, and don't pay much attention if you are not understanding everything. You are already making progress, even though you are not aware of it. If you really need to check some words, you can always refer to the dictionary after the story where you'll find all bolded words translated in English. However, try to keep in mind that it's okay not to understand everything.

Step 3. Read the Synopsis

When you finish the story, read the short summary, first in French, followed by English. This will give you a clear picture of how much you really understand.

Step 4. Comprehension Check

You never know how much you understood, until you check. Each story is followed with a short multiple-questions quiz.

Step 5. Second-time Reading

This time, you are allowed to focus on more details. Pay attention to the bolded vocabulary and expressions, then try to get back and see how the words behave in context. It's even better if the word repeats several times. Keeping your own notes is always a good idea, even though you already have vocabulary listed.

Step 6. Grammar Notes

Check out grammar notes to renew some basic grammar rules that have been repeated in the story. For instance, the second story *"Une guerre paisible* is written in "Imparfait" and "Passé Composé", and is filled with regular and irregular verbs. The goal is to be prepared to talk about your own stories and experiences, after you finish the story.

Step 7. Key takeaways

Key takeaways are the summary of all the most important grammar points. Refer often to this section to retain the important information, even when you are done with the chapter.

And lastly, you shouldn't forget the sense of enjoyment and fulfillment while reading the stories. After all, it's the pleasure that gives us motivation to move forward.

These suggestions are here to help you read French stories independently and without any help. Our stories help you improve your comprehension in a natural way. There should be no obstacles in your way to reading and understanding French stories. Just remember, one step at a time. Pick up your copy of ***Learn French with Short Stories for Adult Intermediate*** and start improving your French right now!

Chapter 1: City Sightseeing

Mais Paris est un véritable océan. Jetez-y la sonde, vous n'en connaîtrez jamais la profondeur.
- Honoré de Balzac

Every traveler should read a story like this. It is a story-like guide to handling most common traveling situations, such as buying tickets, storing luggage while sightseeing, asking for help when lost, etc.

The story is filled with prepositions of place, your best friends when asking for directions, like (*à côté de, à gauche de, autour de, en face de, loin de, près de, au coin de, au-dessous de, au-dessus de, à l'extérieur de, à l'intérieur de*). Many French students are able to ask for directions, but when it comes to understanding the answer, this is where the trouble begins. Getting directions is not just about knowing how to ask, but also understanding what you hear. Additionally, you'll also learn how to use indefinite adjectives (*tout, chaque, même, autre, quelque*) within context. Get ready to discover all the perks of exploring the depths of Paris.

Première visite à Paris

Pierre **est de passage** dans **la capitale** française. Il veut **saisir l'occasion** de **se plonger** dans la culture française et de visiter des **lieux magnifiques**. Il a même créé **une liste de choses à faire**.

Il va rester deux jours chez son **ami d'enfance**. Son ami Michel habite dans **la banlieue** de Paris. Comme son ami travaille pendant la journée, Pierre va découvrir la ville tout seul. Avant d'arriver, il a passé la nuit à observer la carte de la ville.

Le lendemain, il est arrivé en avion à 10 heures, et après le contrôle des passeports, il s'est dirigé vers la gare. **Cependant**, il n'a vu aucun **panneau indiquant la gare**. Il a dû **demander de l'aide**.

« Excusez-moi Monsieur, savez-vous où se trouve **le distributeur** le plus proche ? demanda Pierre.

— Oui, continuez **sur ce chemin** et vous le trouverez.

— **Merci mille fois.** »

Dans une grande salle, Pierre a vu quelques **distributeurs de billets**. Tous les distributeurs **se ressemblaient**, alors il en a choisi un au hasard. Il voulait acheter un billet, mais il n'a pas **réussi** à le faire. Il a choisi un autre distributeur. La même chose **s'est produite**. Une femme **s'est approchée** de lui et a dit que toutes les machines **étaient en panne** pour le moment. Il est possible d'acheter des billets **au guichet** ou de trouver un autre **moyen**. Pierre l'a remercié et s'est dirigé vers le guichet. Là, devant chaque guichet, il y avait une longue **file d'attente**. Quelques guichets ne **fonctionnaient** même pas. Après 30 minutes d'attente, il a finalement réussi à acheter un billet. Il est arrivé à la Gare du Nord.

Comme son ami ne rentrait du travail qu'à 18 heures, Pierre avait encore six heures avant de **s'installer**. La première chose à faire était de **se débarrasser** de **ses bagages**. Autour de la gare, il y avait plein de cafés. Il **s'est assis** dans un café pour utiliser internet et trouver l'endroit **le plus proche** pour laisser ses bagages. Il a commandé du café et des croissants et **s'est connecté à internet**. Il avait hâte de passer quelques jours à Paris. **Selon un article** trouvé sur google qui s'appelait *Que faire lors d'une première visite de la capitale ?*, la tour Eiffel était **incontournable**.

Après avoir **déposé** ses bagages, il voulait d'abord voir la tour Eiffel. Pierre se trouvait en face de la gare. Il fallait aller tout droit **le long du** boulevard de Denais pour arriver à la rue Lafayette. De là, il fallait continuer tout droit jusqu'au Louvre. Devant le Louvre, il a **pris un moment** pour admirer **le bâtiment**. Autour du Louvre, il y avait plein d'endroits à visiter : le jardin des Tuileries, le Pont Neuf, le Palais Royal. Puis il a continué jusqu'à la tour Eiffel, mais il a **remarqué** qu'une partie de la route était **en reconstruction**.

« Excusez-moi Monsieur, comment peut-on arriver jusqu'à la tour Eiffel d'ici ?

— Normalement, il faut **suivre** la rivière à droite, mais quelques rues sont en reconstruction. Alors, il faut **prendre une autre route** pour arriver à la tour Eiffel. Tout d'abord, vous devez prendre la prochaine rue à gauche. Puis traversez le pont, et ensuite **tournez à droite**. Enfin continuez tout droit et vous allez voir la tour Eiffel. C'est près du Musée d'Orsay.

— Merci beaucoup Monsieur. Et, pourriez-vous me dire, s'il vous plaît, où est-ce que je peux acheter des billets pour monter dans la tour Eiffel ?

— À l'intérieur de la tour, vous verrez un guichet.

— Un grand merci, Monsieur. »

Une heure plus tard, Pierre est finalement arrivé **au pied de** la tour Eiffel. Il **est monté dans la tour**. La vue **en haut de** la tour était **incroyable**. En bas de la tour Eiffel, les gens **ressemblaient à des fourmis**. Derrière la tour se trouvait le Champ de Mars. Pierre monta au deuxième étage. À **l'extérieur de** la tour, il faisait froid, alors il est entré **à l'intérieur**. Depuis la tour, il a vu beaucoup de gens **pique-niquer** sur **le champ de Mars**. Il avait un sandwich dans son sac à dos et voulait se reposer sur **l'herbe**. **En bas de** la tour Eiffel, il a vu trois énormes **rats** marcher librement dans la rue. Il n'avait jamais vu des rats aussi gros ! **Pierre était stupéfait** parce que personne **ne prêtait attention aux** rats. Les rats marchaient **au milieu de la rue**, mais il était le seul à les observer.

Il a décidé **d'annuler** son pique-nique et de **s'éloigner**. Il avait encore faim. Il s'est souvenu que son ami lui avait parlé d'un bon restaurant dans le Quartier latin. Alors, la prochaine destination était la cathédrale Notre-Dame et le **Quartier** latin. Le Quartier latin **se situait** sur **la rive** gauche de la Seine dans le 5ème **arrondissement**. Comme c'était loin, il a décidé de **prendre le métro**. Par contre, il ne voyait aucun **arrêt de métro** près de la tour Eiffel.

Alors, il a demandé à un homme de l'aider.

« Excusez-moi Monsieur, y a-t-il une station de métro près d'ici ?

— Oui. Vous avez une station **de l'autre côté** du pont d'Iéna. Tout d'abord, **traversez** le pont et puis tournez à droite. Vous verrez le signe du métro **au coin de** la rue.

— Est-ce que c'est loin d'ici ?

— Non, pas loin. Cela vous prendra cinq minutes.

— Merci Monsieur.

— Je vous en prie. »

Lorsqu'il a traversé le pont, il a immédiatement **repéré** la station de métro. Il est descendu, a acheté des billets et est arrivé **à l'autre bout de** Paris.

Pierre a eu un coup de foudre pour **le quartier**. Il pouvait ressentir **la joie de vivre**. C'est un quartier très **fréquenté par** les touristes, mais aussi par les étudiants. Le restaurant que son ami lui avait recommandé était loin de la cathédrale et il **avait mal aux jambes**. Il a pensé à son sandwich qui était dans son sac. En face de Notre-Dame, il y avait un petit jardin où il a décidé de se reposer. Sur le côté gauche de la cathédrale se trouvait **le marché aux fleurs** et sur le côté droit se trouvait la Seine. Il appréciait **les rayons du soleil** et la musique **des musiciens de rue.** Au moment où il s'apprêtait à prendre son sandwich, **un pigeon** l'a **volé**. D'abord un rat, maintenant un pigeon. Dans cette ville, il faut vraiment **faire attention à** son déjeuner !

Résumé de l'histoire

Pierre est de passage dans la capitale française et séjourne chez son ami. Arrivé à la gare, il a essayé d'acheter un billet au distributeur, mais aucun ne fonctionnait. Ainsi, il a dû attendre longtemps au guichet. Comme son ami travaille jusqu'à six heures du soir, il a passé toute la journée à se promener seul. Il voulait visiter la tour Eiffel, mais tout d'abord, il devait laisser ses bagages. Dans le café, il a utilisé internet pour rechercher la consigne à bagages la plus proche. Il a visité la tour Eiffel, le Louvre et le Quartier latin. Il était surpris de voir de gros rats près de la tour Eiffel, et était encore plus surpris quand un pigeon a pris son sandwich.

Synopsis of the story

Pierre is passing through the Parisian capital and staying at his friend's house. When he arrived at the station, he tried buying a ticket from the machine, but none of them worked, so he had to wait for a long time at the counter. Since his friend works until six in the evening, he spent the whole day wandering around the city by himself. He wanted to visit the Eiffel Tower, but first, he needed to find a place to leave his luggage. In the cafe, he used the internet to search for the nearest storage locker. He visited the Eiffel Tower, the Louvre, and the Latin Quarter. He was surprised to see big rats near the Eiffel Tower, and even more so when a pigeon took his sandwich.

Vocabulary and Expressions

être de passage - to be passing

la capitale - the capital

saisir l'occasion de faire quelque chose - to seize the opportunity to do something

se plonger - to get absorbed, to dive in

le lieu - the place

magnifique - magnificent, superb

une liste de choses à faire - a to do list

un ami d'enfance - a childhood friend

la banlieue - the suburbs

le lendemain - the following day

cependant - however

le panneau - the sign

indiquer - to point out

la gare - the train station

demander de l'aide - to ask for help

le distributeur de billets - the vending machine, ticket machine

le chemin - the way

Merci mille fois - thanks a lot / literal meaning: thank you a thousand times

se ressembler - to look alike

réussir - to be successful

se produire - to take place

être en panne - to have broken down

s'approcher - to approach

le guichet - the counter

un moyen - a way

une file d'attente - a waiting line

fonctionner - to work, to function, to operate

s'installer - to settle in

se débarrasser de - to get rid of

le bagage - the luggage

s'asseoir - to sit down

le plus proche - the nearest

se connecter à internet - to connect to the internet

selon l'article - according to the article

incontournable - inevitable, inescapable

déposer - to leave, to put down

le long de - along

prendre un moment - to take a moment

le bâtiment - the building

remarquer - to notice

être en reconstruction - to be under reconstruction

suivre - to follow

prendre une autre route - to take another route

tourner à droite - to turn right

monter dans la tour - to climb up the tower

au pied de - at the bottom of, at the base of

en haut de - at the top of

incroyable - incredible, unbelievable

ressembler à quelque chose - to be like something

la fourmi - the ant

en arrière de - behind

à l'extérieur de - outside

à l'intérieur de - inside

pique-niquer - to have a picnic

le champ - the field

l'herbe - the grass

en bas de - at the bottom of

un rat - a rat

stupéfait(e) - astonished, amazed

prêter attention à quelque chose - to pay attention to something

au milieu de la rue - in the middle of the street

annuler - to cancel

s'eloigner - to move away

le quartier - the neighborhood

se situer - to be situated

la rive - the bank

un arrondissement - a district

prendre le métro - to take the subway

un arrêt de métro - a subway stop

de l'autre côté de - on the other side of

traverser - to cross, to go through

au coin de - on the corner of

repèrer - to spot

à l'autre bout de - at the other end of

la joie de vivre - the joy of living

être fréquenté par - to be frequented by

avoir mal aux jambes - to have leg pain

le marché aux fleurs - the flower market

les rayons du soleil - sun rays

des musiciens de rue - street musicians

un pigeon - a pigeon

voler - to steal

faire attention à - to pay attention to

Comprehension Questions

Sélectionnez une seule réponse pour chaque question.

1. Pourquoi Pierre a-t-il fait la queue à la gare ?

    A. Tous les distributeurs de billets étaient en panne.

    B. Il ne comprenait pas la langue.

    C. Il est plus facile d'acheter des billets au guichet.

2. Pourquoi Pierre avait-il besoin d'utiliser internet ?

    A. Il voulait savoir quelles attractions parisiennes visiter.

    B. Pour trouver la consigne à bagages la plus proche.

    C. Il voulait voir le plan de la ville.

3. Pierre a-t-il mangé son sandwich ?

    A. Non, il a oublié son sandwich à la gare.

    B. Non, il a laissé tomber son sandwich en voyant le rat.

    C. Non, un pigeon a volé son sandwich.

4. Pourquoi Pierre a-t-il demandé de l'aide ?

    A. Pour se rendre à la tour Eiffel, pour trouver le distributeur de billets à la gare et la station de métro.

    B. Pour se connecter à internet, pour trouver l'arrêt de métro, le chemin vers la tour Eiffel et le distributeur de billets à la gare.

    C. Pour trouver une consigne à bagages où il pourrait déposer ses bagages, pour arriver à la tour Eiffel et pour trouver le distributeur de billets à la gare.

Grammar Notes

Indefinite Adjectives

Similar to English, an indefinite adjective refers to a type of adjective used to describe things or people in a general sense, without giving any specific details about them. This type of adjectives appear before nouns.

Most of these indefinite adjectives have different forms for masculine, feminine, and singular and plural nouns. For example, "quelques", distinguishes only masculine and feminine plural forms, while "autre", distinguishes only singular and plural forms.

The following are the most common French indefinite adjectives:

Masculine Singular	Feminine Singular	Masculine Plural	Feminine Plural	Meaning
autre	autre	autres	autres	other
chaque	chaque			every, each
même	même	mêmes	mêmes	same
/	/	quelques	quelques	some, few
tout	toute	tous	toutes	every, all

Autre

*J'ai une **autre** obligation.* (feminine, singular) - I have another engagement.

*Demain est un **autre** jour.* (masculin, plural) - Tomorrow is another day.

Chaque

***Chaque** garçon a un vélo.* (masculine, singular) - Every boy has a bicycle.

***Chaque** fille a un vélo.* (feminine, singular) - Every girl has a bike.

Même

*Ils ont le **même** âge.* (masculine, singular) - They are the same age.

*J'ai ressenti la **même** chose.* (feminine, singular) - I felt the same way.

*Je traverse les **mêmes** problèmes.* (masculine, plural) - I'm having the same problems.

*Ils partagent les **mêmes** croyances.* (feminine plural) - They share the same beliefs.

Tout

***Tout** mon corps est douloureux.* (masculine, singular) - My whole body is sore.

*Ici, il fait très froid **toute** l'année.* (feminine, singular) - Here, it's very cold all year.

***Tous** les commentaires sont les bienvenus.* (masculine, plural) - Any comments are welcome.

***Toutes** nos tentatives furent vaines.* (masculine, plural) - All our attempts were in vain.

Prepositions of Place

A preposition describes where, when or how something is, in relation to something else.

à côté de - next to, beside

à droite de - to the right of

à gauche de - to the left of

à l'extérieur de - outside of
à l'intérieur de - inside of
au coin de - in the corner of
au-dessous de - below, underneath
au-dessus de - higher than, above
autour de - around
en arrière de - behind
en bas de - below, at the bottom of
en dehors de - outside of
en dessous de - lower than, below
en face de - facing, across from
en haut de - above, at the top of
hors de - outside of
loin de - far from
près de - near to

Prepositions with de

Prepositions with "de" often need to be followed by a definite article. Pay attention that the preposition contracts in front of the masculine article "le" and the plural article "des". With masculine singular nouns, *de + le* becomes *du*. With all plural nouns *de + les* become *des*. Before a vowel or a silent h, *de* becomes d'.

La table est à côté du lit. – The table is next to the bed.

Le chat est au milieu des fleurs. – The cat is in the middle of the flowers.

Key takeaways

- Indefinite adjective refers to a type of adjective used to describe things or people in a general sense without giving any specific details about them. They are always placed before nouns. The most commonly used indefinite adjectives are: ***autre, chaque, même***, quelque, tout. As adjectives, most of them agree with the noun in number and genre.
- **Autre** - other.
- **Chaque** - every, each.
- **Même** - same.
- **Quelques** - some, few.
- Prepositions with "de" are followed by a definite article. Before masculine singular nouns, *de + le* becomes ***du***. Before plural nouns *de + les* become ***des***. Before a vowel or a silent h, *de* becomes ***d'***.

The next chapter will introduce you to two of the most important narrative tenses in French. You'll learn how to distinguish the ongoing and completed actions in the past and create a captivating story.

Chapter 2: Telling stories

Ceux qui aiment la paix, doivent apprendre à s'organiser aussi efficacement que ceux qui aiment la guerre.

- Martin Luther King

Knowing how to tell stories in French is more important than you think. The experiences we have are the stories we tell. The first chapter in the book is therefore focused on telling stories as a must have skill in everyday living. You'll learn two essential narrative tenses in French, *imparfait* and *passé composé*, the most commonly used couple in French grammar.

So far, you have been exposed to these tenses separately, but here you get to see how these tenses work together. Telling the differences between *imparfait* and *passé composé* is essential for the purpose of storytelling or reading almost any story in French.

Une guerre paisible

Le père d'Antoine, Charles, aime **raconter des histoires**. Ses histoires semblent parfois irréalistes et Antoine ne le **croit** pas. Il est souvent **en colère contre** son père. Un jour, Antoine emmène sa future **épouse**, Maria, pour **rencontrer** ses parents. Ses parents étaient heureux et ont préparé un repas. Antoine **interdit** à son père de raconter ses histoires. Il ne voulait pas que sa petite amie découvre que son père était **un menteur**. À table, ils parlaient **des choses quotidiennes**. Son père était **silencieux** tout le temps.

Alors qu'ils dînent **tranquillement**, quelqu'un a **sonné à la porte**. Ils cherchaient Antoine. Antoine était médecin et devait rentrer en ville en **urgence**. Sa petite amie est restée. Antoine n'est pas revenu pendant plusieurs jours, et **pendant ce temps**, son père et Maria parlaient **de plus en plus**. Un soir, alors qu'il pleuvait, Maria a demandé à Charles de lui raconter une histoire de famille. Il a décidé de raconter l'histoire de sa vie.

Il avait trente ans **lorsqu'il** est parti à **la guerre**. Quand il avait 20 ans, Charles a rencontré Charlotte, sa future épouse. Alors qu'ils se préparaient pour **le mariage**, Charles a reçu **une lettre de mobilisation pour la guerre**. Il ne voulait pas **quitter** sa future épouse, mais il devait partir. Charlotte l'a attendu pendant cinq longues années.

Alors que les **bombes tombaient** tous les jours, il **a réussi** à écrire une lettre tous les soirs. Il n'écrivait jamais sur **les horreurs de la guerre**. Il lui parlait de ses amis, de la nourriture qu'ils préparaient, des endroits qu'ils visitaient. Un jour, alors que les soldats préparaient le dîner, quelqu'un leur **a signalé une attaque**. Ils se sont tous levés et ont cherché leurs **armes**. Mais rien ne s'est passé.

Avant **l'aube,** ils ont entendu **du bruit**. C'étaient des **soldats ennemis**. Mais désarmés, **fatigués** et **affamés**.

Charles était prudent. Cependant, les soldats ennemis voulaient juste se reposer. Ils **erraient** dans la forêt depuis plusieurs jours, sans nourriture ni eau. Pour eux, le concept de guerre **avait perdu tout sens**. Il y avait une **trentain**e de soldats des deux **côtés**. Charles et ses amis ont décidé de préparer **un repas** pour tous. Tout le monde **s'est assis autour du feu** et il **mangeait en silence**. **Le lendemain** matin, les deux parties ont décidé de **s'unir** et de quitter **la zone de guerre**. Ils cherchaient **l'endroit** le plus **caché** du pays. Les soldats **avaient beaucoup de chance**. Ils ont traversé des forêts **denses**, mais n'ont rencontré personne.

Lorsqu'ils **ont atteint** la partie la plus **reculée** du pays, ils **ont réalisé** qu'ils n'étaient pas seuls. **Une cinquantaine** de soldats des deux côtés étaient déjà là. Des soldats qui avaient décidé de **se retirer** jusqu'à la fin de la guerre. **La communauté** des soldats avait déjà un **système développé**. Certains **préparaient** de **la nourriture**, les uns **chassaient**, d'autres **cueillaient** des fruits dans la forêt. Comme Charles et le reste des soldats étaient **désarmés**, la communauté les **a acceptés**.

L'endroit est devenu un petit **paradis sur terre**. Il y avait **un lac à proximité** où ils se **baignaient**, il y avait plein de fruits dans la forêt. Certains **fabriquaient** même des instruments pour **égayer** les soldats. Dans la communauté, il y avait des soldats qui **se sont installés** depuis le début de la guerre. Il y a un an que Charles est arrivé là.

Ils vivaient **paisiblement**, mais **dans l'isolement**. Ils n'avaient aucune **nouvelle** de la guerre et les soldats **avaient peur de** quitter **l'oasis**. Il était **interdit** de partir. Les jours **passaient**. **Pendant son séjour**, Charles ne pouvait pas écrire de lettres. Et il savait que Charlotte était **inquiète**.

Un matin, alors que tout le monde dormait, il a quitté **la zone de sécurité**. Cela faisait un an qu'ils y habitaient. Il était temps de revenir. Il est retourné **prudemment** à la civilisation, mais quand il est arrivé, il ne voyait **aucun** soldat, seulement des gens **ordinaires** dans les rues. Tout **semblait** normal. Un passant lui a dit « Il y a huit mois que la guerre s'est terminée. » Charles n'était ni heureux, ni content. Il se sentait stupide. Il savait que Charlotte l'attendait et qu'elle croyait qu'il était mort.

Il **s'est précipité** vers ses amis. Cependant, quand il est arrivé, tout le monde l'a accueilli avec **hostilité**. Ils pensaient qu'il les avait **trompés**. Heureusement, il a réussi à **s'échapper**. Il est retourné au village et puis dans son pays. Mais son fils n'a jamais cru à son histoire. Cependant, Maria sentait **la sincérité de ses paroles**. Dix ans après, son fils lisait le journal et a aperçu un titre *Un groupe de soldats, cachés de la guerre, vivaient isolés pendant 30 ans.*

Résumé de l'histoire

Le père d'Antoine, Charles, aime raconter des histoires, mais Antoine ne le croit pas. Un jour, Antoine amène sa future épouse, Maria, pour rencontrer ses parents. Antoine interdit à son père de raconter ses histoires. Il ne voulait pas que sa petite amie découvre que son père était un menteur. Antoine est docteur et il a dû rentrer en ville en urgence. Sa petite amie est restée, et son père lui a raconté l'histoire de sa vie.

Charles est parti à la guerre. Mais, avec d'autres soldats, il voulait s'échapper. Les soldats ont décidé de se retirer jusqu'à la fin de la guerre. Ils ont trouvé un endroit caché, et y sont restés pendant un an. La guerre était déjà finie, mais ils ne le savaient pas. Un jour, Charles a décidé de quitter la communauté. Il a découvert que la guerre était déjà finie. Il a annoncé la nouvelle aux autres soldats, mais ils ne le croyaient pas. Il est alors rentré dans son pays, et les soldats ont continué à vivre en communauté. Un jour, dans le journal, Antoine découvre que l'histoire de son père est vraie.

Synopsis of the story

Antoine's father, Charles, likes to tell stories, but his son doesn't believe him. One day, Antoine brings his future wife, Maria, to meet his parents. Antoine forbids his father to tell his stories. He didn't want his girlfriend to find out her father was a liar. Antoine works as a doctor and he had to go back to town urgently. His girlfriend stayed at his parent's house, and wanted to hear one of the family stories. So, Charles started telling his life story. It goes like this.

Charles went to war. He, along with other soldiers, wanted to escape. The soldiers decided to withdraw until the end of the war. After finding a hidden place, they stayed there for a year. They were unaware of the war's ending. One day, Charles decided to leave the community. As he left, he learned the war was over. The other soldiers didn't believe him when he told them the news. He then returned to his country, and the soldiers continued to live in community. After reading the newspaper one day, Antoine discovers that his father's story is true.

Vocabulary and Expressions

raconter des histoires - to tell stories

croire - to believe

être en colère contre qqn. - to be angry against someone

une épouse - a spouse

rencontrer qqn. - to meet someone

interdire à qqn. - to forbid to someone

un menteur – a liar

les choses quotidiennes - everyday things

silencieux(-euse) - quiet

tranquillement - calmly

sonner à la porte - to ring the doorbell

d'urgence - urgently

pendant ce temps - during this time

de plus en plus - more and more

lorsque - when, during

à la guerre - at war

un marriage - a marriage

une lettre de mobilisation pour la guerre - a letter of mobilization for the war

quitter - to leave

alors que - whereas

une bombe - a bomb

tomber - to fall

réussir - to succeed

les horreurs de la guerre - horrors of war
signaler une attaque - to report an attack
une arme - a weapon
l'aube - dawn
un bruit - a noise
un soldat ennemi - an enemy soldier
fatigué - tired
affamé - hungry
errer - to wander
perdre tout sens - to lose all meaning
une trentaine - around thirty
un côté - a side, quarter, share
un repas - a meal
s'asseoir - to sit down
autour du feu - around the fire
manger en silence - to eat in silence
lendemain - the following day, tomorrow
s'unir - to unite
la zone de guerre - the war zone
l'endroit - the place
caché - hidden
avoir de la chance - to be lucky
dense - dense
atteindre - to reach
reculer - to move back, to retreat
réaliser - to realize
une cinquantaine - around fifty
se retirer - to withdraw
la communauté - the community
un système développé - a developed system
préparer - to prepare
la nourriture - the food
chasser - to hunt
cueillir - to pick
désarmé(e) - disarmed

accepter - to accept

un paradis sur terre - a heaven on earth

un lac - a lake

à proximité - near, close by

se baigner - to swim

fabriquer - to manufacture

égayer - to brighten up

s'installer - to settle

paisiblement - peacefully

dans l'isolement - in isolation

une nouvelle - news

avoir peur de - to be afraid of

un oasis - an oasis

interdit(e) - forbidden

passer - to pass

pendant son séjour - during his stay

inquiète(e) - worried, anxious, restless

une zone de sécurité - a safe zone

prudemment - carefully, cautiously

aucun(e) - none, no one

ordinaire - ordinary

sembler - to seem

se précipiter - to precipitate, to hurl

une hostilité - hostility

tromper - to deceive

s'echapper - to escape

une sincérité - sincerity

une parole - a word, a speech

Comprehension Questions

Sélectionnez une seule réponse pour chaque question.

1. Pourquoi Antoine ne veut pas que son père raconte des histoires à sa petite amie ?

    A. Les histoires de son père sont ennuyantes.

    B. Il pense que son père raconte des mensonges.

    C. Il ne veut pas que son père raconte des histoires de son enfance.

2. De quoi parlait Antoine dans ses lettres à sa femme ?
    A. De la guerre et de sa communauté.
    B. De leur futur mariage.
    C. Des endroits qu'il visitait, de ses amis.
3. Pourquoi les soldats ennemis sont-ils venus au milieu de la nuit ?
    A. Les soldats ennemis voulaient les tuer.
    B. Les soldats ennemis étaient affamés et voulaient se reposer quelque part.
    C. Les soldats ennemis avaient faim et soif.
4. Pourquoi les militaires sont-ils allés vivre dans la communauté ?
    A. Pour échapper aux horreurs de la guerre.
    B. Pour former une société paisible.
    C. Parce qu'ils ne voulaient pas tuer les soldats ennemis.
5. Qu'a découvert Antoine lorsqu'il a quitté la communauté ?
    A. Qu'il a reçu plein de lettres de sa femme.
    B. Personne n'a survécu à la guerre.
    C. Que la guerre est déjà terminée.

Grammar notes

Imparfait vs Passé Composé

It is probably the most difficult thing for an English speaker to know when to use *passé composé* or *imparfait*, since you cannot translate English literally. A simple distinction of *Passé composé* and *Imparfait* can be made by deciding whether a specific event is taking place (*Passé composé*) or is an ongoing background event (*Imparfait*). However, you'll soon see it's more complicated than that.

Let's begin with English equivalents.

- **Passé composé** - English Past Simple, Present perfect.
- **Imparfait** - Past Progressive Tense (verb + ing), used to, but also it corresponds to simple past tense, and to "would" in some situations.

The problem is "I bought" or other verbs in the English perfect tense which can be translated as:

- j'achetais (*Imparfait*)
- j'ai acheté (*Passé composé*)

Context ultimately determines which tense to use, so the rest of the sentence ultimately tells you what tense you need.

This table will help you understand in which situations we use these two tenses.

Imparfait	Passé composé
Ongoing Action - indicates an ongoing state of being or feeling. J'aimais l'école. - I used to love school.	**New Action** - describes a change in feeling, a new state of being. J'ai été inspiré pour écrire un livre. - I was inspired to write a book.
Background Action - describes what was happening or how something was in the past. J'étais à Paris.	**Event** - while the passé composé interrupted with news of some occurrence. ... quand il a commencé à neiger.
Uncounted Action - actions that used to happen regularly, or happened an indefinite number of times. Je perdais constamment mes clés. - I was constantly losing my keys.	**Counted Action** - indicates what happened a specific number of times. J'ai perdu mes clés deux fois. - I lost my keys twice.
Incomplete Action - There was no indication of what was happening, when it ended or even if it had ended. J'étais à Paris.	**Complete Action** - Passé composé announces what happened, what was accomplished. Je suis arrivé tard.

Pendant, Depuis, Il y a

These three French expressions are called temporal expressions and are used to express the passage of time or to refer to a specific period of time.

The rough translation will give you the gist, but their meaning is much more than this literal translation, which you'll see in the following sections.

- Depuis - since
- Pendant - during
- Il y a - ago

Depuis

We use *depuis* to:

- Refer to an action that started in the past and is still ongoing now.

Ma sœur joue de la guitare depuis six mois. - My sister has been playing the guitar for six months.

- Since then

J'ai commencé mon régime la semaine passée. Depuis, je bois du thé tous les matins. - I started my diet last week. Since then, I have been drinking tea every morning.

- When an action has been started but interrupted by another action.

Je dormais depuis une heure quand quelqu'un a sonné. - I had been sleeping for one hour when someone rang.

Pendant

We use *pendant* to:

- describe an action with a concrete starting and ending point in the past, present or future.

J'ai joué au foot pendant trois heures aujourd'hui. - I played soccer for three hours today.

Sometimes, you can even use *pour* to talk about a future action with a concrete start and end. *Pour* is used when referring to the duration of something, and it corresponds to the English word "for". However, *pour* can only be used to refer to something that will happen in the future. *Pendant* in this case can be substituted for *pour*.

Je vais voyager à Paris pour trois semaines. - I am going to visit Paris for three weeks.

Il y a

Perhaps you are confused because so far, you have seen *il y a*, in the context of there is/are. But in the context of a temporal expression, *il y a* indicates the idea of "ago".

Use *il y a* to:

- talk about completed actions followed by a period of time.

Je me suis réveillé il y a dix minutes. - I woke up 10 minutes ago.

Key takeaways

- *Passé composé* corresponds to English Past Simple and Present perfect.
- *Imparfait* corresponds to Past Progressive Tense (verb + ing), used to, but also sometimes to simple past tense, and "would" in some situations.
- Use *imparfait* to talk about ongoing actions, background, uncounted and incomplete actions.
- Use *passé composé* to talk about new actions, events, counted actions and complete actions.
- *Depuis* roughly means "since" and refers to an action that started in the past and is still ongoing now. It's also used to describe an action that has started but is interrupted by another action. The translation can also be *"since then"*.

- **Pendant** describes an action with a concrete starting and ending point happening in the past, present or future. Most often is translated as "during".
- **Pour** corresponds to the English word "for" and can be used interchangeably with *pendant*, to talk about future actions with a concrete starting and ending point. However, *pour* only refers to future events.
- **Il y a** can be used as a temporal expression and indicates "*ago*". It's used to talk about completed actions followed by a period of time.

Next, you'll learn how to turn your bad experiences into a story, while also learning how to use the past participle. You'll go through all the cases in which the agreement is necessary, in which it isn't and when it's an exception. The next chapter will give you a better understanding of one of the most common difficulties faced by French learners.

Chapter 3: Bad Experience

Une mauvaise expérience vaut mieux qu'un bon conseil.
- Paul Valéry

Sometimes, when we travel, things don't go as planned. There are times when flights are delayed, buses are missed, passports are forgotten, and luggage is lost. Hopefully, that doesn't happen often, but when it does, it's good to know you can share your experiences with others. In the following story, a young couple goes through an unfortunate series of events on their trip.

In terms of grammar, the story emphasizes different uses of *participe passé* in French and resolves the mystery of agreement and disagreement. Identifying situations where you have to agree or disagree with the past participle is something that most students struggle with.

You'll find all you need to know about past participles in the grammar notes section, provided with many examples in the story.

Une mauvaise expérience

J'avais un plan **extrêmement** original pour **demander** ma copine **en mariage**. Ma copine, qui s'appelle Anne, voulait voyager en Orient depuis longtemps. Un soir, nous étions avec notre ami qui voyageait tout le temps. Il nous a donné les meilleures idées. Ma copine, Anne, était fascinée par ses histoires. Elle était particulièrement fascinée par le voyage au Cambodge et n'a pas **cessé** d'en parler pendant des jours. Les semaines passaient, et l'idée de visiter le Cambodge était **oubliée**. J'attendais juste une occasion d'**économiser suffisamment** d'argent pour acheter les billets pour le Cambodge. Tout cela **faisait partie du plan**. Je voulais **surprendre** ma petite amie et acheter des billets d'avion.

Quelques mois ont passé et j'ai finalement économisé **assez** d'argent. J'ai acheté les billets en décembre pour arriver au Cambodge avant notre **anniversaire**. Les billets que j'ai achetés n'étaient pas chers. Je les ai achetés deux mois **en avance**. La maison que j'ai réservée était située dans **un endroit** romantique sur la plage. Tout était parfait.

Une semaine avant notre voyage, j'ai demandé à Anne de **faire ses valises** parce que nous partions au Cambodge. Mais elle était **déçue** et **en colère**. Pourquoi est-elle fâchée ? Le problème c'est qu'Anne avait la même idée. Elle a également acheté des billets pour le Cambodge, le même jour. J'étais **surpris** et un peu **en colère contre la vie**. Nous sommes tous les deux **allés au lit** nerveux. Après avoir fait de nombreux appels téléphoniques, heureusement les billets pouvaient être **remboursés**. J'ai appris ma leçon : Ne fais pas de grandes surprises sans **consulter** l'autre partie.

Le jour du voyage est arrivé. Nous avons **imprimé** les deux billets **restants** et les avons mis dans nos **passeports**. Nous sommes allés à l'aéroport avec nos valises. Cependant, notre **malchance** a continué. **Le vol** que nous avons **pris** n'était pas direct. Nous nous sommes arrêtés aux Émirats et avons eu 10 heures **d'attente**. Fatigués, nous avons décidé de **poser nos valises à côté** de nous et de nous **reposer** un peu à l'aéroport.

Pendant que nous dormions, nous nous sommes fait **voler** notre valise. La même valise où j'ai mis **la bague de fiançailles** ! Nous avons **signalé le cas** et les policiers sont venus immédiatement nous **interroger**. Ils m'ont demandé **ce qu'il y avait dans la valise**, mais je ne pouvais pas **révéler** que je portais une bague de fiançailles. C'était mon secret, je ne l'ai pas révélé.

Les instructions que **le policier** nous a données étaient **confuses**. Nous devions continuer notre voyage et ils ont promis **de** nous **tenir informés**. Heureusement, les passeports étaient dans une autre valise. Je les ai pris et mis dans ma **poche**. **Le lendemain**, nous sommes finalement arrivés au Cambodge. Pas de valise. Pas de bague de fiançailles.

Avant d'arriver, j'ai **téléchargé la carte de la ville** et je l'ai étudiée **attentivement**. J'ai trouvé quel train **se rendait à** notre hôtel "Le Soleil", et je l'ai mémorisé. Cependant, notre train a été **annulé en raison de la reconstruction de la route**. Les billets, que nous avons achetés, ne **servaient** plus **à rien**. Ma copine **s'est rendue** à la station pour **obtenir** le **remboursement des billets**. Elle y a passé une heure **sans succès**. Nous avons dû chercher une alternative et nous l'avons trouvée.

Une femme locale voulait nous aider. Elle nous a **recommandé une autre route**. Nous avons écouté son **conseil**. Mais, nous nous sommes bien **trompés**. Elle nous a dirigés vers un autre hôtel qui s'appelait aussi "Le Soleil". **Au lieu d'**arriver à notre hôtel, nous sommes arrivés dans la partie opposée de la ville. À ce moment, nous avons décidé de prendre un taxi.

Le lendemain, **le téléphone a sonné**. Ma copine **a répondu au téléphone**. Ils nous ont appelés de l'aéroport pour dire que la valise avait été **retrouvée** et que la bague de fiançailles était **à l'intérieur**. Quelle surprise pour ma copine !

Résumé de l'histoire

C'est l'histoire d'un jeune homme qui voulait demander sa copine en mariage le jour de leur anniversaire, au Cambodge. Il décide d'économiser de l'argent et d'acheter deux billets pour l'Est Mais sa petite amie avait également acheté des billets pour la même destination. Heureusement, ils parviennent à obtenir un remboursement pour ces billets. Mais le cycle d'événements malheureux ne s'arrête pas. En attendant le vol de correspondance, ils s'endorment et leur valise se fait voler. Bien que le jeune homme signale le vol à la police de l'aéroport, il ne révèle pas l'existence d'une bague de fiançailles dans la valise. Le dernier accident survient à leur arrivée au Cambodge. Il s'avère que le train qu'ils devaient prendre ne circule plus. Une femme a proposé de les aider, mais elle leur a donné la mauvaise adresse, alors ils ont passé toute la journée à chercher leur hôtel. Le téléphone sonne le lendemain et la fille répond. Apparemment, la police a trouvé une valise et une bague de fiançailles.

Synopsis of the story

This is a story of a young man who wanted to propose to his girlfriend on their anniversary, by taking her on a trip to Cambodia. He decides to save some money and buy two tickets for the East. As he tells his girlfriend about his ticket purchase, she feels disappointed rather than surprised. The problem was, she had also purchased tickets for the same day. Somehow, they manage to return the tickets, and go on a trip, but the cycle of unfortunate events doesn't stop. While waiting for a connecting flight, they fall asleep and their suitcase gets stolen. Although the young man reports the theft to the airport police, he can't tell them that there's an engagement ring in the suitcase. The last accident occurs when they arrive in Cambodge. It turns out the train they needed to take no longer runs. One woman offered to help them, but she gave them the wrong address, so they spent the whole day searching for their house. The phone rings the next day, and the girl answers. Apparently, they have found a suitcase and a wedding ring.

Vocabulary and Expressions

extrêmement - extremely

demander qqn en mariage - to propose to someone

cesser - to stop

oublier - to forget

économiser - to save

suffisamment - enough

faire partie du plan - to be part of the plan

surprendre - to surprise

assez - enough

un anniversaire - an anniversary

en avance - in advance

un endroit - a place

faire les valises - to pack

déçu(e) - disappointed

être en colère - to be angry

surpris(e) - surprised

en colère contre la vie - angry with life

aller au lit - to go to bed

rembourser - to pay back

consulter - to consult

imprimer - to print

restant(e) - remaining

un passeport - a passport

une malchance - a bad luck

prendre le vol - to take a flight

une attente - a wait

poser les valises à côté - to put the bagages aside

reposer - to rest

voler - to steal
la bague de fiançailles - engagement ring
signaler le cas - to report the case
interroger - to question, to interrogate
ce qu'il y avait dans la valise - what was in the bagage
révéler - to reveal
une instruction - an instruction
le policier - the police officer
confus(e) - confused
de tenir informé - to keep informed
la poche - the pocket
le lendemain - the next day
télécharger - to download
la carte de la ville - city map
attentivement - carefully, attentively
se rendre à - to go somewhere
annuler - to cancel
en raison de - because of
la reconstruction de la route - the reconstruction of the road
servir à rien - to serve no purpose
se rendre à - to go to
obtenir - to get
le remboursement - the refund
un billet - a ticket
sans succès - without success
recommander une autre route - to recommend another route
le conseil - the advice
se tromper - to make a mistake
au lieu de - instead of
le téléphone - the telephone
sonner - to ring
répondre au téléphone - to answer the phone
retrouver - to find
à l'intérieur - inside

Comprehension Questions

Sélectionnez une seule réponse pour chaque question.

1. Pourquoi le jeune homme veut visiter le Cambodge ?
    A. Parce qu'il aime les pays de l'Est.
    B. Parce qu'il veut demander sa copine en mariage au Cambodge.
    C. Parce qu'il veut quitter son emploi.

2. Pourquoi la petite amie était-elle en colère quand il lui a parlé de leur voyage au Cambodge ?
    A. Parce qu'elle a aussi acheté des billets.
    B. Parce qu'elle n'aime pas le Cambodge.
    C. Parce qu'elle veut rompre avec lui.

3. Que s'est-il passé avec les billets de train ?
    A. Ils ont acheté les billets pour les mauvaises dates.
    B. Ils ont acheté des billets de bus au lieu de billets de train.
    C. Ils ont acheté les bons billets mais le parcours est en reconstruction.

4. Que s'est-il passé avec la valise à l'aéroport ?
    A. Leur valise a été volée.
    B. Le jeune homme a perdu la bague de fiançailles.
    C. Ils ont perdu leurs passeports.

5. Pourquoi le jeune homme n'a-t-il pas pu dire ce qu'il y avait dans sa valise ?
    A. Parce qu'il est illégal de transporter des bijoux dans l'avion.
    B. Parce qu'il ne voulait pas révéler qu'il allait demander sa copine en mariage.
    C. Parce qu'il cache quelque chose d'illégal.

Grammar Notes

Past Participle

Le participe passé, or past participle, is very similar in French and English. Past participles in French end in (**-é, -i,** or **-u**) while their English equivalents end in (**-ed** or **-en**) as in "walked" or "opened". We usually relate past participle with complex past tenses, like *passé composé*, however, past participle can be used in several different ways.

There are three main uses for the past participle in French. You can use past participle:

- to form compound tenses (*Steve a ouvert la porte - Steve had opened the door*).
- in the passive voice (*La porte a été ouverte par Steve - The door was opened by Steve*).
- as an adjective (*La porte ouverte - The opened door*).

We'll start by learning how to form past participles.

Forming Past Participle

As always, there is a regular and irregular way to form pretty much anything in French, and it's the same story with participles. To form the past participle of French regular verbs, use the infinitive of the verb, and add the following endings.

For **-er** verbs, you replace the **-er** at the end of the infinitive with **-é**.
- donner (to give) - **donné**
- tomber (to fall) - **tombé**

For **-ir** verbs, you replace the **-ir** at the end of the infinitive with **-i**.
- finir (to finish) - **fini**
- partir (to leave) - **parti**

For **-re** verbs, you replace the **-re** at the end of the infinitive with **-u**.
- attendre (to wait) - **attendu**
- descendre (to go down, to come down) - **descendu**

Irregular Past Participle

A second way is the unbeaten path or irregular past participles. Learning them by heart is the only way to win this game. Here are some of the most commonly used ones:
- Être (to be) - **été**
- Faire (to do) - **fait**
- Mettre (to put) - **mis**
- Pouvoir (to be able, can) - **pu**
- Prendre (to take) - **pris**
- Savoir (to know) - **su**
- Tenir (to hold) - **tenu**
- Venir (to come) - **venu**
- Voir (to see) - **vu**
- Vouloir (to want) - **voulu**

Agreement of the past participle

Given that the past participle is considered to be an adjective too, when we say it "agrees", we mean that it changes its form depending on whether it is masculine or feminine, singular or plural. Just like all French adjectives.

The endings are the same as for normal adjectives:
- If the subject is singular feminine, add **-e**.
- If the subject is plural masculine, add **-s**.
- If the subject is plural feminine, add **-es**.

The agreement happens mostly in the complex tenses like **passé composé**, **futur proche**, or **plus-que-parfait**. All complex tenses in French are formed with the auxiliary verb *avoir* or *être* followed by the past participle. Remember that the past participle agrees with *être*, but not with *avoir*.

When using the verb ***être*** as an auxiliary, you must accord the verb with the subject. It happens in both genre and number.

Let's take the verb *entrer* and see how it changes in *Passé Composé*.

- Je suis entré(e) (entrée - feminine singular).
- Tu es entré(e) (entrée - feminine singular).
- Il est entré. / Elle est entrée. (entrée - feminine singular).
- Nous sommes entré(e)s (entrées- feminine plural).
- Vous êtes entré(e)s (entrées - feminine plural).
- Ils sont entrés. / Elles sont entrées. (entrées - feminine plural).

It's easy to remember which verbs go with *être*, and which with *avoir*, as most verbs construct the *passé composé* with *avoir*, except for movement, state and pronominal verbs that go along with the auxiliary *être*.

Elles ont marché pendant deux heures. - They walked for two hours.

Despite the fact that the subject is clearly feminine and plural (*elles*), the past participle lacks any gender or number markers, because it's related to auxiliary *avoir*.

Exceptions

It's no longer a surprise that after each general rule, there's one or two exceptions waiting behind the corner. In general, the participle does not agree with the auxiliary when it is "avoir". Except in the case when a direct object precedes the past participle. That case is the only time you will have an agreement with *avoir*.

Listed below are two examples of the same sentence, where one places the direct object before and one places it after. Note that in case of a direct object following the past participle, the agreement will not happen.

Observe the differences:

- No agreement / *J'ai acheté une jupe jaune.* - I bought a yellow skirt.

Since the direct object appears after the verb, there is no agreement.

- Agreement / *La jupe que j'ai achetée est jaune.* - *The skirt that I bought is yellow.*

The direct object *jupe* is placed before the verb, so the past participle agrees with the noun *jupe*.

When it comes to reflexive verbs, the general rule is that they usually agree with their past participles. However, if the reflexive verb has an object, the past participle agrees with the object rather than the subject.

Take a look at the examples below:

- Agreement / *Elle s'est peignée ce matin.* - *She combed this morning.*

There is no object following the verb *peigner*, so the past participle agrees with the subject *elle*.

- No agreement / *Elle s'est peigné les cheveux ce matin.* - *She combed her hair this morning.*

The verb *peigner* is followed by the direct object *les cheveux*, so there is no agreement between the past participle and the subject.

No Agreement

No agreement happens in these cases:

with *avoir*

Tu as commis une erreur. - You made a mistake.

when a verb is followed by a direct object

Il a recommandé une autre route. - He recommended taking a different path.

with an indirect object

Il nous a donné les meilleures idées. - He gave us the best ideas.

with adverbial pronouns

Mathilde était à la banque, elle y a passé toute la journée. - Mathilde was in the bank, she spent all day there.

in the causative construction

La voiture que j'ai fait réparer est encore en panne. - The car I had repaired broke down again.

with verbs of perception

Les poèmes que j'ai entendu réciter. - The poems I heard recited.

In certain expressions, such as ***faire*** + infinitive, ***laisser*** + infinitive, ***se rendre compte***, and others, an infinitive holds the place of the direct object and therefore there's no agreement.

Mathilde a fait faire ces portraits de ses chiens. → Elle <u>les</u> a <u>fait</u> faire.

Mathilde had portraits of her dogs made. → She had them made.

Past Participle as Adjective

In French, the past participle can also have the function of adjective. It is possible to form the adjective by using the past participle alone or by combining it with the verb *être* (to be). It is also important that the past participle and the noun it refers to agree in gender and number.

La porte est ouverte. - The door is open.

Michel est un acteur connu de tout le monde. - Michel is an actor known by everyone.

Key takeaways

- To form a past participle / For **-er** verbs, you replace the **-er** at the end of the infinitive with **-é**. / For **-ir** verbs, you replace the **-ir** at the end of the infinitive with **-i**. / For **-re** verbs, you replace the **-re** at the end of the infinitive with **-u**.

- Past participle is considered to be an adjective too, so it agrees with the subject or object in gender and number. Add **-e** for singular feminine, add **-s** for plural masculine, add **-es** for plural feminine. The agreement happens mostly in the complex tenses like ***passé composé***, ***futur proche***, or ***plus-que-parfait***. In case of complex tenses, the past participle *always* agrees when the verb takes "être", but almost never when the verb takes "avoir". The only time we have agreement with *avoir* is when a direct object precedes the past participle.

- The general rule for reflexive verbs is that they agree with their past participles. When the reflexive verb has an object, the past participle agrees with the object rather than the subject.

- No agreement happens with the verb *avoir*, adverbial pronouns (*en*, *y*), indirect object, verbs of perception, when a verb is followed by a direct object, in the causative constructions, or in certain expressions such as ***faire*** + infinitive, ***laisser*** +infinitive, ***se rendre compte***.

- In French, the past participle can also have the function of adjective. It is possible to form the adjective by using the past participle alone or by combining it with the verb *être* (to be).

In the next chapter, you'll learn French relative pronouns that refer to people and things that have already been mentioned. This will make it easier for you to combine two ideas into a single sentence. You'll also learn the complex variants of French relative pronoun *lequel* used after prepositions such as "à" and "de".

Chapter 4: Talking with Friends

Les amies sont les compagnons de voyage qui nous aident à avancer sur le chemin d'une vie plus heureuse.

- Pythagore

We often like to talk about the good old days we once had, with our family and friends. The best storytellers are those who can vividly recall memories. If you want to remind your French friends about experiences you went on together, you can start by asking "Tu te rappelles ?" Oftentimes, people don't remember well, and you need to give specific explanations of the thing you are talking about. A relative pronoun is a way of connecting ideas and adding additional information within one sentence. You'll need relative pronouns: *lequel, laquelle, lesquels, lesquelles*, as well as complex relative pronouns: *auquel, duquel, à laquelle, de laquelle, auxquels, auxquelles, desquels, desquelles*, in order for your ideas to come across clearly.

Tu te rappelles ?

Nicole a maintenant cinquante-et-un ans. À vingt ans, elle est venue étudier à Arras, une petite ville du **Nord** de la France. C'était la plus belle année de sa vie. Pour la première fois, elle s'est sentie complètement libre d'**explorer**, de rencontrer de nouvelles personnes, de **découvrir un nouveau monde**. Là, elle a rencontré ses meilleurs amis, Jeanne, Monique, Hellène et Catherine. Elles ont toutes étudié la littérature française. Elles étaient toutes différentes, mais **complémentaires**.

Les cinq amies étaient **logées** dans la même **résidence**. Nicole et Jeanne partageaient **un mur**. Elle se souvenait de tout. De longues conversations, des **promenades** encore plus longues jusqu'à **l'épuisement**, des **rires**. **L'amitié** n'a jamais eu une plus belle forme.

Un jour devant le Beffroi, **une tour** du centre-ville, elles se sont toutes **jurées** de revenir à Arras dans 30 ans. La date de leurs **retrouvailles** était le 30 novembre. Trente ans **se sont écoulés** vite.

Jeanne pensait à Nicole depuis des jours. Un jour, le téléphone **a sonné**. Jeanne a répondu et Nicole, **sans dire rien d'autre**, a demandé :

« Tu te rappelles la date de laquelle on **s'approche** ?

— Je me rappelle. Jeanne a répondu.

— C'est le moment.

— D'accord. J'achète les billets.

— Appelle les autres. » - a dit Nicole et **a raccroché**.

La date de leurs retrouvailles est restée la même. Elles devaient se retrouver à midi sur **la place** devant le Beffroi. Comme d'habitude, Jeanne est arrivée la première. Puis Hellène et Catherine l'**ont rejoint**, ensuite Nicole. À ce moment, vient Monique avec un **énorme sac** dans lequel elle porte des photos. Les filles ne pouvaient pas croire qu'elles étaient ensemble !

Les filles **se sont installées** au café dans lequel elles allaient souvent. Monique a sorti de son sac les photos prises trente ans plus tôt.

Elle a sorti une photo.

« Les filles, vous vous rappelez ? C'est le train dans lequel nous **sommes montées** pour aller à Dunkerque.

— Mais qui a continué dans la direction **opposée**, a ajouté Hellène.

— Non, non. Le train auquel tu penses allait à Lille.

— Ah, oui. Tu as raison. **C'était marrant** quand même. Nous **avions dépensé** tout notre argent pour les nouveaux **billets**. Puis nous n'avions rien mangé de toute la journée.

— Et là, c'est la ville dans laquelle nous nous sommes **perdues**. Nous avons cherché **le centre-ville** toute la journée, et nous l'avons trouvé à la fin de notre **séjour**, une heure avant de partir.

— Et comment allez-vous les filles ? Nicole, **qu'est-ce qui t'intéresse en ce moment** ?

— **Les passe-temps** auxquels je m'intéresse sont des activités **solitaires**, a répondu Nicole.

— Alors, tu n'as pas changé. Et toi Catherine ?

— Ah, **la discipline** à laquelle elle s'intéresse est **exigeante**. C'est de trouver les meilleures destinations de vacances, a répondu Hellène.

— C'est ce que tu as toujours voulu faire.

— C'est vrai.

— Voulez-vous aller au parc Paul Doumer ? a demandé Nicole.

— Pourquoi là-bas ? a répondu Monique.

— Souvenez-vous, c'est un parc au milieu duquel il y a le meilleur gâteau au monde. Nous **avons passé des heures** là-bas. **Les chemins le long** desquels nous avons marché étaient **en terre**. Tu te demandais toujours pourquoi ce parc n'était pas **pavé**. Et tu te **plaignais** toujours à propos de **la boue**.

— Le parc auquel elle pense, c'est le parc à côté **du musée des Beaux-Arts**, a **corrigé** Jeanne.

— Ah, oui. Tu as mauvaise mémoire Nicole.

— Toujours.

— Et souvenez-vous du **supermarché** où on a découvert **le jus de banane** ? a demandé Jeanne.

— C'est le supermarché près duquel il y a **l'église**, n'est-ce pas ? a demandé Catherine.

— J'en **buvais** tous les jours. Mais un jour j'**ai vomi** et j'ai arrêté d'en boire, a expliqué Jeanne.

— Et souvenez-vous du premier jour à l'université ? a demandé Hellène.

— La classe près de laquelle nous nous sommes trouvées était très grande. Et tu m'as demandé de **prendre une photo de** toi.

— Oui, je voulais la montrer à mes parents.

— Les filles, voici **la boulangerie** où nous avons acheté le gâteau pour l'anniversaire de Nicole.

— C'est la boulangerie près de laquelle il y a l'église, n'est-ce pas ?

— Oui, c'est ça.

— J'étais tellement surprise. Tu avais même **laissé une note** sur ma porte, a dit Nicole.

— Et vous vous rappelez notre ami de Turquie ? Il nous a **apporté** des gâteaux turcs.

— Ses cousins de Turquie avec lesquels nous avons parlé dans le bus étaient très intéressants. Je me demande où ils sont maintenant.

— Moi aussi. Particulièrement notre ami d'Espagne.

— Quel ami d'Espagne ? **Tu veux dire** Gabriel ?

— Non. La personne à laquelle je pense est Aldo.

— Non, je ne me rappelle pas.

— Tu te souviens quand nous sommes allées à ce **spectacle avant-garde** ? C'était **une pièce à propos de** laquelle nous avions longuement **discuté** avec Aldo. Nous avons même eu **une dispute**, dit Catherine.

— Oh, oui. Après ça, vous n'avez pas parlé pendant trois jours, a répondu Monique.

— C'est vrai. Il me manque. J'aimerais le voir.

— Et tu te souviens de **Noël** que nous avons passé ensemble dans ma chambre ?

— Nous avons fait une grande **fête**. **Chacune** a apporté quelque chose. Nous étions comme une vraie famille.

— **Si seulement on pouvait** retourner **à cette époque**. »

Résumé de l'histoire

Un groupe de filles se réunit à l'endroit de leur première rencontre, trente ans plus tard. Elles se sont rencontrées lors d'un échange étudiant dans une petite ville au Nord de la France. L'accord était de se rencontrer 30 ans plus tard à midi, au centre-ville. Dans un café, elles commencent à regarder les photos prises cette année où elles se sont rencontrées. En regardant les photos, elles essaient de se souvenir des expériences vécues.

Summary of the story

A group of girls reunites at the place where they first met, thirty years later. They met during a student exchange in a small town in the north of France. The agreement was to meet 30 years later at noon, downtown. In a café, they begin to look at the photos taken that year. As they look at the photos, they try to recall everything they experienced.

Vocabulary and Expressions

le Nord - the north

explorer - to explore

découvrir - to discover

un nouveau monde - a new world

complémentaire - complementary

loger - to stay

la résidence - the residence

le mur - the wall

la promenade - the walk

un épuisement - an exhaustion

le rire - the laughter

une amitié - a friendship

une tour - a tower

jurer - to swear

les retrouvailles - the reunion

s'écouler - to pass

sonner - to ring

sans dire rien d'autre - without saying anything else

s'approcher - to approach

raccrocher - to hang up

la place - the square

rejoindre - to meet

énorme - huge

un sac - a bag

s'installer - to sit down

monter - to get on

opposé(e) - opposite

c'était marrant - it was funny

dépenser - to spend

le billet - the ticket

se perdre - to get lost

le centre-ville - the city center

le séjour - the stay

qu'est-ce qui t'intéresse en ce moment - what are you interested in right now

le passe-temps - the pastime
solitaire - solitary
la discipline - the discipline
exigeant(e) - demanding
passer des heures - to spend hours
le chemin - the path
le long de - along
en terre - earthen
pavé(e) - paved, cobbled
se plaindre - to complain
la boue - the mud
le musée des Beaux-Arts - the Museum of Fine Arts
corriger - to correct
le supermarché - the supermarket
le jus de banane - the banana juice
une église - a church
boire - to drink
vomir - to vomit
prendre une photo de - to take a picture of
la boulangerie - the bakery
laisser une note - to leave a note
apporter - to bring
tu veux dire - you mean
un spectacle avant-garde - an avant-garde show
une pièce - a play
à propos de - about
discuter - to talk, to debate
une dispute - an argument
le Noël - Christmas
la fête - the celebration, the party
chacune - each
si seulement on pouvait - if only we could
à cette époque - at that time

Comprehension Questions

Sélectionnez une seule réponse pour chaque question.

1. Qui a appelé Jeanne au téléphone ?
   A. Monique
   B. Catherine
   C. Nicole

2. Par erreur, elles sont montées dans le train qui allait ... ?
   A. à Dunkerque
   B. à Arras
   C. à Lille

3. L'anniversaire de qui a-t-on fêté à Arras ?
   A. de Monique
   B. de Nicole
   C. de Jeanne

4. Ont-elles passé beaucoup de temps dans le parc Paul Doumer ?
   A. Oui.
   B. Non.

5. Pourquoi Catherine s'est-elle disputée avec Aldo ?
   A. À cause du spectacle.
   B. À cause des gâteaux turcs.
   C. Parce qu'elle était amoureuse de lui.

Grammar Notes

Relative pronoun (Lequel, Laquelle, Lesquels, Lesquelles)

A relative pronoun refers to a person or thing that has been mentioned previously. French relative pronoun *lequel* (which, whom, that) is used after a preposition such as "à", "de" or "pour" to talk about things.

Lequel, means "which one" and can be:

- an interrogative pronoun.
- relative pronoun.

As an interrogative pronoun, it's equivalent to the interrogative adjective *quel*. Just like the possessive pronouns replace both the noun and the adjective, *lequel* replaces **quel** + **noun**.

The same way as *quel*, *lequel* has four different forms depending on the gender and number of the noun it replaces. It has to agree with the noun it replaces.

Singular, Masculine	Singular, Feminine	Plural, Masculine	Plural, Feminine
lequel	laquelle	lesquels	lesquelles

Take a look at these examples to see how *lequel* replaces *quel* + noun.

Quel crayon veux-tu ? Lequel veux-tu ? > Which crayon do you want? Which one do you want?

Je veux la banane là-bas. Laquelle ? > I want the banana over there. Which one?

As a relative pronoun, "lequel" substitutes an inanimate object of a preposition. When the preposition is applied to a person, use qui.

Take a look at the following examples:

Le cahier dans lequel j'ai écrit... > The book in which I wrote...

Le ville à laquelle je rêve... > The town about which I'm dreaming...

Lequel + prepositions

As you noticed, *lequel*, *laquelle* and *lesquels*, are all composed of an article (**le**, **la**, **les**) + the interrogative adjective **quel**. Remember what happens with **à** and **de** when combined with the definite article **le, la, les**? They turn into **au**, **à la**, **aux**, and **du**, **de la** and **des**.

Take a look at the table here:

Masculine, Singular	Feminine, Singular	Masculine, Plural	Feminine, Plural
auquel	à laquelle	auquels	auxquelles
duquel	de laquelle	desquels	desquelles

Take a look at these examples to see how *lequel* replaces *quel* + noun:

- **As an interrogative pronoun**

Je pense à mon oncle. – Auquel penses-tu ? À quel oncle... - I'm thinking about my uncle. Which one are you thinking about?

Il se souvient de notre voyage. – Duquel ? Celui en France ou en Italie ? - He remembers our trip. Which one? The one in France or in Italy?

- **As a relative pronoun**

La maison à laquelle je songe... - The house about which I'm dreaming...

L'examen auquel j'ai réussi a été très facile. - The exam that I passed was very easy.

La maison de laquelle je parle est vendue. - The house I'm talking about is sold.

Key takeaways

- A **relative pronoun** refers to a person or thing that has been mentioned previously and is used after prepositions such as **"à", "de" or "pour"**.
- *Lequel* means "which one" and can be an interrogative pronoun or relative pronoun. It also replaces ***Quel* + noun**.
- There are four different forms of the relative pronoun *lequel*, depending on the gender and number of the noun it replaces: **lequel, laquelle, lesquels, lesquelles**.
- As a relative pronoun, "lequel" substitutes an inanimate object of a preposition. When the preposition is applied to a person, use *qui*.
- When the preposition "à" appears in front of the relative pronoun *lequel*, it becomes *à + lequel* = ***auquel***; *à + laquelle* = ***à laquelle***; *à + lesquels* = **auxquels**; *à + lesquelles* = **auxquelles**.
- When the preposition "de" appears in front of the relative pronoun *lequel*, it becomes *de + quel* = ***duquel***; *de + quel* = ***de laquelle***; *de + quels* = **desquels**; *de + quelles* = **desquelles**.

In the next chapter, you'll learn how to describe a work of art and learn relative pronouns *ce qui*, *ce que* and *ce dont*.

Chapter 5: In the Museum

La normalité est une rue pavée : on y marche aisément mais les fleurs n'y poussent pas.
-Vincent Van Gogh

You can't visit France without going to at least one museum. And, the moment you visit one, you'll realize it's hard to stop. Luckily, there are enough cultural experiences in Paris to fill a lifetime.

This story takes you to Orsay's museum to discover impressionism, an early 1900s French movement. As you read the story, you'll find expressions related to art, techniques, and styles. Not only will you be exposed to new vocabulary, but you'll also learn a couple of historic facts. The conversation about art will no longer be challenging after that. Furthermore, the story introduced indefinite relative pronouns *ce que, ce qui* and *ce dont*.

Qu'est-ce que cela représente ?

De nombreux monuments et **musées** sont **gratuits** le premier **dimanche** du **mois** en France. Chaque mois, mes amis et moi, nous allons visiter un nouveau musée en France. Ce dimanche, nous allons découvrir le musée d'Orsay. Il a la plus riche **collection de tableaux impressionnistes et postimpressionnistes** au monde. Il s'agit notamment de **chefs-d'œuvre peints par** des artistes légendaires comme Van Gogh, Manet et Monet. Non seulement **les ouvrages** sont **remarquables**, mais l'espace l'est aussi, comme le musée est situé dans l'ancienne Gare d'Orsay.

L'œuvre que j'**avais hâte de** voir est *La Nuit étoilée*. Cette fois, nous avons organisé **une visite guidée**, ce qui nous **a permis d'**apprendre beaucoup plus que d'habitude.

Nous avons commencé par le premier **tableau** impressionniste, *Soleil levant* de Monet.

Nous avons écouté le guide parler.

« Cette œuvre est la première œuvre qui représente **le mouvement** impressionniste. Peint à **coups de pinceau** libres, il ressemble à **une toile inachevée**, ce que beaucoup pensaient **à l'époque**. **Dans cette peinture, les fumées des usines** remplacent **le paysage** naturel, ce qui montre l'entrée de **l'époque industrielle** dans l'art. Les artistes impressionnistes créent une nouvelle **esthétique**, ce qui **bouleverse** le monde de l'art. Ce dont ils **s'occupent** sont **la vie quotidienne**, **les loisirs** modernes, le paysage, le monde industriel. Leurs **toiles capturent** l'atmosphère de Paris, mais aussi la vie populaire des quartiers, ce qui a contribué à la popularité de Montmartre par exemple.

— Pourquoi les impressionnistes ont-ils commencé à **peindre** à l'extérieur ? a demandé mon ami.

— À cette époque, apparaissent **des peintures en tube**, ce qui permet aux artistes de peindre **en plein air**.

— À quelle époque l'œuvre a été réalisée ?

— Le tableau a été peint à la fin du XIXe siècle, a répondu le guide.

— Quelle **technique** ont-ils utilisée ? j'ai demandé.

— Ils utilisaient **les couleurs complémentaires l'une à côté de l'autre**, ce qui donne **l'illusion**. Cette technique, **typique** de l'impressionnisme, était **étonnante** pour l'art de l'époque. »

Puis, nous nous sommes dirigés vers la salle post-impressionniste. Van Gogh **dominait** la salle, ce qui **m'a fait très plaisir**.

Le guide a commencé son **exposé** sur Van Gogh.

« Incompris et ignoré de son vivant, Vincent van Gogh devient l'un des grands **maîtres**, mais après sa mort. **Selon la légende**, il a vendu un seul tableau **de son vivant**, ce qui confirme **à quel point** il a été **incompris, le guide a affirmé**. »

Nous nous sommes approchés du tableau *La Nuit étoilée*, dont la beauté m'a **enchantée**.

« Qu'est-ce que vous pouvez **ressentir au premier coup d'œil** ?, le guide a demandé.

— Moi, je me sens **mal à l'aise** en regardant ce tableau. Il me semble que les étoiles **tournent** follement dans un vortex » mon amie a répondu.

Le guide a continué de parler de **la biographie de l'artiste**. Ce dont elle parlait, j'avais déjà tout lu, mais je m'intéressais plutôt à ce que le tableau représentait.

« Excusez-moi, qu'est-ce que ça représente ? j'ai demandé.

— Le tableau que vous voyez représente ce que Van Gogh pouvait voir de la chambre qu'il occupait à **l'asile** de Saint Rémy. Le tableau exprime toute **la violence** de **sa psychologie troublée**. En 1889, il **souffre de dépression,** ce qui devient son état **chronique**. Il décide d'entrer à l'asile, ce qui l'aide à continuer à peindre. Van Gogh était obsédé par la représentation de la nuit et des étoiles. À votre avis, pourquoi était-il tellement obsédé par les étoiles ?

— Je pense qu'il voulait représenter **l'univers** qui respire.

— Exact. Dans son œuvre, il décrit de **véritables phénomènes d'astrophysique**. En 2019, la lumière **crépitante** a attiré l'attention de deux **chercheurs** australiens qui **perçoivent un phénomène des fluides** sur les tableaux de Van Gogh, le guide a affirmé.

— L'âme d'artiste peut vraiment expliquer la réalité d'une manière **intuitive**. »

Résumé de l'histoire

En France, chaque premier dimanche du mois, les musées sont gratuits pour tous. Un groupe d'amis a décidé d'en profiter et de visiter un nouveau musée chaque mois. Cette fois, il voulait découvrir le mouvement impressionniste. Ils réservent un guide au musée d'Orsay. Accompagnés de leur guide, ils examinent deux toiles : *Soleil Levant* et *La Nuit étoilée*. Ils apprennent aussi pourquoi le mouvement impressionniste était révolutionnaire, et ils découvrent la technique et la vie de Van Gogh, un peintre post-impressionniste.

Summary of the story

In France, museums are free for all on the first Sunday of every month. A group of friends decided to take advantage of this and to visit a different museum every month. This time, they wanted to know more about the Impressionist movement. They book a guide at the Musée d'Orsay. Together with their guide, they examine two paintings, *Rising Sun* and *The Starry Night*. They also learn why the Impressionist movement was revolutionary, and they discover the technique and life of Van Gogh, a post-impressionist painter.

Vocabulary and Expressions

le musée - the museum

gratuit(e) - free

dimanche - sunday

mois - month

la collection de tableaux impressionnistes et post-impressionnistes - the collection of impressionist and post-impressionist paintings

le chef-d'œuvre - the masterpiece

peints par - painted by

un ouvrage - a piece of work

remarquable - remarquable

une œuvre - a work of art

avoir hâte de - to look forward to

La Nuit étoilée - The Starry Night

une visite guidée - a guided visit

permettre de - to allow to

le tableau - the painting

Soleil Levant - Rising Sun

le mouvement - the movement

les coups de pinceau - brush strokes

inachevé(e) - unfinished

à l'époque - at that time

dans cette peinture - in this painting

la fumée des usines - the factory smoke

le paysage - the landscape

l'époque industrielle - the industrial era

une esthétique - aesthetic

bouleverser - to shake up

s'occuper de - to be in charge of
la vie quotidienne - everyday life
les loisirs - hobbies
la toile - the canvas
capturer - to capture
peindre - to paint
la peinture en tube - paint in tubes
en plein air - in the open air, outdoors
une technique - a technique
les couleurs complémentaires - complementary colors
l'une à côté de l'autre - one next to the other
une illusion - an illusion
typique - typical
étonnant(e) - amazing
dominer - to dominate
faire plaisir - to please
un exposé - a presentation
un maître - a master
selon la légende - according to the legend
de son vivant - in his lifetime
à quel point - how much, at what point, to what extent
incompris(e) - misunderstood
affirmer - to claim
être enchanté(e) - to be enchanted
ressentir - to feel
au premier coup d'œil - at first sight
être mal à l'aise - to be uncomfortable
tourner - to turn
la biographie de l'artiste - the artist's biography
un asile - an asylum
la violence - the violence
psychologie - psychology
troublée - disturbed
souffrir de dépression - to suffer from depression
un état chronique - a chronic condition

un univers - a universe

véritable - real, true

un phénomène d'astrophysique - an astrophysical phenomenon

crépitant(e) - sizzling

un chercheur, une chercheuse - a scientist, a researcher

percevoir - to perceive

un phénomène des fluides - a fluid phenomenon

intuitif, intuitive - intuitive

Comprehension Questions

Sélectionnez une seule réponse pour chaque question.

1. Quels nouveaux sujets ont été introduits avec le nouveau mouvement impressionniste ?

    A. Le plein air.

    B. L'atmosphère de Paris et la vie populaire des quartiers.

    C. La vie quotidienne, les loisirs modernes, le paysage, le monde industriel.

2. À l'époque, la plupart des gens pensaient que le premier tableau impressionniste ressemblait :

    A. Aux fumées d'usines.

    B. Au paysage urbain.

    C. À un tableau inachevé.

3. Pourquoi les impressionnistes ont-ils commencé à peindre en plein air ?

    A. Les artistes voulaient aborder de nouveaux sujets.

    B. Parce que des peintures en tube apparaissent.

    C. Les artistes voulaient représenter la vie quotidienne.

4. Pourquoi on a dit que : « L'âme d'artiste peut vraiment découvrir la réalité d'une manière intuitive. » ?

    A. Van Gogh a réussi à transmettre l'esprit de l'époque.

    B. Les étoiles de Van Gogh capturent le phénomène astrophysique des fluides.

    C. Les tableaux de Van Gogh expriment toute la violence de sa psychologie troublée.

5. Qu'est-ce qu'un asile ?

    A. Un hôpital psychiatrique.

    B. Une station balnéaire.

    C. Un hôtel.

Grammar Notes

Relative Pronouns

In order to understand indefinite relative pronouns, first we have to understand the relative pronouns **qui**, **que** and **dont**.

Relative pronouns are all about language economics, so by using them you can avoid repeating subjects and objects in the following sentence. You can refer to any idea you had in the first sentence without the need to repeat it. The thing or idea you are referring to is called an antecedent.

Let's see an example:

*J'ai <u>une tante</u> **qui** joue au basket.* - I have an aunt that plays basketball.

Here we have a main and a relative sentence, connected by the relative pronoun **qui**. Antecedent is "*une tante*", and it is replaced by the relative pronoun **qui**.

Let's see examples with other relative pronouns:

*La grande femme **que** je connais joue au basket.* - The tall woman I know plays basketball.

*Voici la famille **dont** je parle.* - This is the family I'm talking about.

Indefinite Relative Pronouns

We use relative pronouns when the antecedent is specific, and indefinite relative pronouns, when the antecedent (what's being talked about) is unknown.

Indefinite Relative Pronouns are **ce + relative pronoun**.

We are going to take a look at three main French indefinite relative pronouns: **ce dont**, **ce que** and **ce qui**. Confusingly, all have the same English equivalents and translate like "what".

If you are unsure which pronoun to use, the following grammatical structure determines your choice.

- **Qui** - replaces a subject.
- **Que** - replaces a direct object.
- **Dont** - replaces an object complement introduced by *de*.

Once again, if it refers to a noun (expressed before), then you will use **que/qu"**. If it refers to the whole part of the sentence, the whole idea, then it will be **ce que / ce qui**.

Characteristics of indefinite relative pronouns

1. Provides a connection between relative clauses and main clauses.
2. Impersonal and invariable.
3. Takes the role of a subject, direct object, or object with a preposition.

Let's examine each of the pronouns separately :

Ce qui - takes the place of a subject in a relative clause.

*Je comprends **ce qui** est important.* - I understand what's important.

Ce que - takes the place of a direct object in a relative clause.

*Je ne comprends pas **ce que** tu veux.* - I don't understand what you want.

Ce dont - takes the place of an indirect object introduced by the preposition *de*.

*Je ne comprends pas **ce dont** tu parles.* - I don't understand what you are saying.

It's important to note that the verb "parler" requires the preposition *de*, and therefore **ce dont** has to be used.

Key takeaways

- We use relative pronouns when the antecedent is specific, and indefinite relative pronouns when the antecedent (what's being talked about) is unknown. Three main French indefinite relative pronouns are: ***ce dont***, ***ce que*** and ***ce qui***, and all translate like "what".
- **Ce qui** - takes the place of a subject in a relative clause.
- **Ce que** - takes the place of a direct object in a relative clause.
- **Ce dont** - takes the place of the object with the preposition "de".

The next chapter will explain why you should visit the French flea markets at least once while in France. Furthermore, you will be taught indefinite pronouns, such as "each one", "another one", "others", "several", "someone", "somebody", "anyone", "nothing", "no one", "anything", "nobody" and you'll be introduced to French gerund.

Chapter 6: At the Flea Market

Car si le visage est le miroir de l'âme, les yeux en sont les interprètes.
- Cicéron

In France, flea markets are a tradition. For lovers of designer furniture, antiques and odds they feel like opening Ali Baba's caves. Strolling along the Seine, the famous booksellers offer many old and second-hand books as well as engravings, postcards and other collectors' items. The most famous flea market in Paris is *Les Puces de Saint-Ouen*, known as *Les Puces*. It is considered one of the biggest antique markets in the world, attracting approx 120,000 visitors a weekend!

In this warm story, you'll find a taste of the French flea market atmosphere. Additionally, the story is filled with indefinite pronouns like *certain, autre, plusieurs, quelqu'un, quiconque, tout le monde*, etc. You'll also be introduced to the French gerund, that's used to express simultaneous actions and is often translated as the while + -ing form.

Marché aux puces

Le marché aux puces est une tradition en France. En fréquentant les marchés aux puces avec ma famille, j'ai beaucoup appris du style, des époques, de l'histoire. Ma famille trouvait toujours de petits **trésors** au marché aux puces. En regardant les objets, on imaginait les histoires derrière. C'est pourquoi j'y vais fréquemment.

Au marché, on peut trouver des **bibelots rustiques**, du **mobilier**, des **ustensiles de cuisine**, de **la verrerie**. Bref, tout pour **aménager** son nouvel appartement. Chacun peut y trouver quelque chose ! J'ai le sens du détail et je peux trouver des objets d'**une qualité rare** et au **prix bas**. Mon appartement est **rempli de** choses achetées au marché aux puces.

Une fois, j'ai vu un miroir rustique **dans le coin**. Personne n'y prêtait attention. Il était un peu **usé**, alors **le vendeur** m'en a proposé un autre. En regardant des miroirs, je me suis souvenue d'un miroir de ma grande mère. Je me souviens que ma grand-mère avait un énorme miroir **doré** dans **le couloir**. **Quiconque** venait l'admirait. **J'avais l'impression** de devenir plus beau chaque fois que je me regardais. En me regardant, je **remarquais** que mon **dos s'était redressé**, que mes yeux étaient plus **brillants** et que j'**avais l'air** plus fort.

Dans ce miroir, personne n'avait l'air **moche**. Ma grand-mère aimait aussi se regarder dans ce miroir. Un jour, en se regardant dans le miroir, elle m'a **avoué un secret**. Elle a dit que le miroir avait un pouvoir magique - le pouvoir de donner la beauté et la confiance à quiconque le regarde. Tous dans ma famille ont **pris de la force** en se regardant. En allant à un examen, avant un grand voyage ou événement, le miroir a donné de la force à chacun.

Un jour, j'étais chez ma grand-mère et quelqu'un a sonné à la porte. Parce que ma grand-mère n'entendait pas bien, j'ai crié "Il y a quelqu'un à la porte !" Elle a ouvert la porte. C'était la police. Personne ne savait que mes grands-parents étaient **lourdement endettés**. La police est venue **récupérer** leurs **affaires**. Grand-mère, en pleurant, regardait les policiers **enlever** son miroir. C'était la dernière fois que je l'ai vu.

En pensant au miroir de ma grand-mère, je me suis éloigné du marché. J'ai passé la semaine suivante à penser au miroir du marché. Quelque chose dans ce miroir m'attirait. J'ai décidé d'y retourner la semaine suivante. **J'ai reconnu** le vendeur, mais je n'ai pas vu le miroir cette fois. J'étais tellement **déçu**. J'ai demandé au vendeur où était le miroir. Il ne s'en souvenait pas.

Il m'en a montré plusieurs. À ce moment-là, j'ai commencé à lui parler du miroir de ma grand-mère. Je parlais longtemps, me souvenant de tous les détails. En parlant, j'ai mentionné le nom de ma grand-mère. À ce moment, le vendeur s'est dirigé vers son **camion** et a apporté un grand miroir doré. Le nom de ma grand-mère était écrit **au dos du** miroir. En pleurant, j'ai serré le miroir dans mes bras. Même le vendeur a pleuré. N'importe qui pouvait l'acheter, mais le miroir m'attendait. Ma grand-mère m'a toujours dit que **rien ne survient par hasard**. Elle **avait raison**.

Résumé de l'histoire

Le personnage principal est un homme qui aime fréquenter les marchés aux puces. C'était une tradition qu'il partageait avec ses proches. Il adorait imaginer des histoires derrière les objets qu'il trouvait. Un samedi, il tombe sur un miroir doré. Le miroir lui rappelait le miroir de sa grand-mère, lequel avait un étrange pouvoir. Quiconque se regarderait dans le miroir devenait plus beau et plus confiant. Toutefois, ses grands-parents étaient endettés et la police a confisqué tout leur mobilier, y compris le miroir.

Summary of the story

The main character is a man who likes to visit flea markets. It was a tradition he shared with his family. Ever since, he loved to imagine stories behind objects he'd find. One Saturday, he comes across a golden mirror. The mirror reminded him of his grandmother's mirror, which had a strange power. Anyone who looked in the mirror became more beautiful and confident. However, her grandparents were in debt and the police confiscated all of their furniture, including the mirror.

Vocabulary and Expressions

le marché aux puces - the flea market

un trésor - a treasure

un bibelot rustique - a rustic trinket

le mobilier - furniture

des ustensiles de cuisine - cooking utensils

la verrerie - glassware

aménager - to furnish

une qualité rare - a rare quality

prix bas - low price, cheap

rempli de - full of

dans le coin - in the corner

usé(e) - worn out

le vendeur - the salesman

doré(e) - golden

le couloir - the corridor

quiconque - anybody, anyone, whoever

avoir l'impression - to be under the impression, to feel

remarquer - to notice

le dos - the back

se redresser - to straighten

brillant - shiny

avoir l'air - to look like

moche - ugly

avouer un secret - to confess a secret

prendre de la force - to gain strength

lourdement - heavily

être endetté - to be indebted

récupérer - to collect

des affaires - belongings

enlever - to remove

reconnaître - to recognize

déçu(e) - disappointed

un camion - a truck

au dos de - on the back of

rien ne survient par hasard - nothing happens by chance

avoir raison - to be right

Comprehension Questions

Sélectionnez une seule réponse pour chaque question.

1. Pourquoi le personnage principal aime-t-il visiter les marchés aux puces ?
    A. Il aime imaginer les histoires derrière les objets.
    B. Il veut apprendre du style, des époques, de l'histoire.
    C. Il aime trouver des objets à moindre coût.
2. Quel pouvoir avait le miroir de sa grand-mère ?

A. De donner la beauté et la confiance à quiconque le regarde.

   B. De donner la beauté et la confiance à sa famille.

   C. Pour faciliter la prise de décision.

3. Qu'est-il arrivé au miroir sa grand-mère ?

   A. Le miroir a été volé.

   B. Le miroir s'est cassé.

   C. La police a emporté le miroir.

4. Pourquoi le personnage principal pleurait-il ?

   A. Parce qu'il a retrouvé le miroir de sa grand-mère.

   B. Parce qu'il a finalement acheté un miroir.

   C. Parce qu'il a obtenu un rabais.

5. Que signifie « rien ne survient par hasard » ?

   A. Tout est une coïncidence.

   B. Tout arrive pour une raison.

   C. Il n'y a pas de règles dans la vie.

Grammar Notes

Indefinite Pronouns

The indefinite pronouns refer to people or things without explicitly identifying them. There is no specific person, thing, or amount associated with them, which makes them vague or "not definite." As pronouns, they stand alone. Pay attention to the difference between indefinite pronouns and adjectives. In a sentence, they take the role of the subject, the verb's object, or the preposition's object.

Il a acheté quelque chose. - He bought something.

J'ai un cadeau pour quelqu'un. - I have a gift for someone.

Characteristics of indefinite pronouns:

1. Substitutes an indefinite adjective and a noun placed together.

2. There are several indefinite pronouns that are identical to French indefinite adjectives.

3. Depending on the noun they replace, they may need to agree on gender or number.

4. They take the role of a subject, direct object, indirect object, or the preposition's object.

There are two types of indefinite pronouns:

- **Variable** (have to agree in number and gender with the noun they replace).
- **Invariable** (have one single form).

Variable Indefinite Pronouns

Un autre, certains, chacun, quelques-uns have to agree with the nouns they replace in gender, and some of them in number. All other indefinite pronouns are invariable.

Here are the most common French indefinite pronouns:

Chacun (m.) /chacune (f.) - each one

Chacun a son propre caractère. - Everyone has a character of their own.

Chacune d'elles a reçu un cadeau. - They each received a present.

Quelques-un (m.) /quelques-une (f.) - somebody, someone, anybody, anyone

*Il y a **quelqu'un** à la porte.* - There's someone at the door.

*Nous ferons escale dans **quelqu'une** de ces îles.* - We will stop in one of these islands.

Quelques-uns (m.) /quelques-unes (f.) - someone

*Pas de problème, j'en ai **quelques-unes**.* - No problem, I have some.

***Quelques-uns** l'accusent même de trahison.* - Some even accused him of treason.

Un autre (m.) / une autre (f.) - another one

*Veuillez m'en montrer **un autre**.* - Please show me another one.

*Savoir est une chose, enseigner en est **une autre**.* - To know is one thing, to teach is another.

Autres - others

Il y en a d'autres. - There are others.

Plusieurs - several

*Il y en a **plusieurs**.* There are several of them.

Invariable indefinite pronouns

Tout le monde / Tous - all, everything, anything

Tout le monde est arrivé sain et sauf. - Everyone arrived safe.

Quelque chose - something, anything

Ai-je dit quelque chose ? - Did I say something?

Quiconque - anyone

Quiconque vient est le bienvenu. - Whoever comes is welcome.

Personne - no one

Personne ne lui prêtait attention. - Nobody was paying attention to him/her.

Rien - nothing

Rien ne survient par hasard. - Nothing happens by chance.

N'importe qui - anyone

N'importe qui peut le faire. - Anyone can do it.

N'importe quoi - anything

Demande-moi n'importe quoi ! - Ask me anything!

Antecedent

Certain French indefinite pronouns need to have an antecedent. Just a reminder, antecedent is an earlier mentioned or implied noun, making their meaning obvious.

Indefinite pronouns that require antécédent are: **Autre, d'autres, certains, chacun, plusieurs,** et **quelques-uns**.

J'ai deux enfants, et chacun nettoie sa chambre. - I have two kids, and each of them cleans his own room.

Il a pris deux cafés et un autre l'attend sur la table. - He's had two coffees and another is waiting for him on the table.

Indefinite Pronouns expressing quantity

Some indefinite pronouns express quantity. When they take the role of an object in a sentence, the adverbial pronoun "en" is required, along with the indefinite pronoun (*Autre, d'autres, certains, plusieurs,* and *quelques-uns*) that replaces the noun.

J'ai oublié d'acheter des serviettes. - I forgot to buy towels.

Pas de problème, j'en ai quelques-unes. - No problem, I have some.

Gerundiv

In terms of structure, French present participles are similar to English verb+ing. Using gerundiv, French speakers can modify verbs and express simultaneity and causality.

Forming a Gerundiv

The French gerund has this structure: **en** + **the present participle** of a verb.

Here, you'll need to learn how to form the present participle. You take the verb in first person plural in present tense, and you drop its ending. Then add **-ant**.

Here are a few examples:

dormir (to sleep) → *nous dormons* (we sleep) → *en dormant* (while sleeping)

regarder (to watch) → *nous regardons* (we watch) → *en regardant* (while watching)

écouter (to listen) → *nous écoutons* (we listen) → *en écoutant* (while listening)

Let's see an example in a sentence.

Pauline étudie en écoutant de la musique. - Pauline studies while listening to music.

Meaning

French gerund can have several meanings in English.

While

A gerund indicates an action that occurs simultaneously or immediately before the main verb.

Elle pleurait en racontant ses souvenirs. - She cried while telling her memories.

Because/By

It reveals why or how the main verb happens.

En me réveillant à 6h, j'ai fini avant midi. - By waking up at 6 am, I finished before noon.

Upon

When describing the causation or the moment in which something happened, it's equivalent to the English "upon."

J'ai crié en tombant de l'échelle. - I screamed when/upon/at the moment when/because I fell off the ladder.

Who/That

The gerund can sometimes be used instead of a relative clause.

Les voyageurs venant de l'Europe. - Travelers coming from Europe.

Present participle vs Gerund

While the present participle and gerund look identical, the gerund is almost always indicated by the preposition *en*, and the meaning is different.

Present participle - is modifying the nearest noun.

Nous avons vu Pauline mangeant en ville. - We saw Pauline (as she was) eating in town.

Gerund - is modifying a verb.

Nous avons vu Pauline en mangeant en ville. - We saw Pauline (at the same time) as we were eating in town.

Key takeaways

- **Variable Indefinite Pronouns: chacun** - each one / **quelques-un** - somebody, anybody / **un autre** - another one / **plusieurs** - several.
- *Un autre, certains, chacun, quelques-uns,* have to agree with the nouns they replace in gender, and some of them in number. All other indefinite pronouns are invariable.
- **Invariable Indefinite Pronouns: Tout le monde, Tous** - all / **Quelque chose** - something, anything / **Quiconque** - anyone / **Personne** - nobody / **Rien** - nothing / **N'importe qui** - anyone / **N'importe quoi** - anything.
- Gerund = *en* + **the present participle** of a verb.
- To form the present participle, you take the verb in first person plural in present tense, and you drop the ending. Add **-ant** to that base.
- There are several meanings of the French gerund in English. It can be translated as while, because, by, upon, who, that.

- There is a difference between the present participle and gerund. Present participle is modifying the nearest noun, while gerund is modifying a verb.

In the next chapter, you'll learn how to properly express cause and consequence in French, in multiple ways. You'll finally learn the difference between the similar expressions *parce que*, *car*, and *puisque*, and go beyond by learning more than ten ways to express cause or consequence.

Chapter 7: About my Friend

La conséquence ne peut pas exister sans la cause.
- Simon Kadoche

Every action that occurs in the universe produces a reaction, no matter what. This is the law of cause and effect. The human brain is wired to think in terms of causes and consequences. It is for this reason that we have so many expressions to organize our chaotic thoughts.

This story is filled with French words like *puisque, parce que, comme, car, donc, alors, faute de, en effet, à cause de, grâce à, par conséquent, c'est pourquoi, si bien que,* to help you understand the logic behind French cause and consequence. With this lesson, you'll be able to express all the shades of cause and consequence in French.

Une autre vie

Mon meilleur ami, Lazar, il n'aime pas changer les choses. Il travaillait comme **vétérinaire** parce qu'il adorait passer du temps avec les animaux. Mais la vie en ville le **dérangeait**. Nous nous sommes rencontrés à l'université, et depuis que je le connais, il a toujours été anxieux. Pour chaque examen il **s'inquiétait**, même s'il avait étudié pendant des mois. En effet, pas seulement pour les examens, les choses les plus insignifiantes l'inquiétaient. Il **s'énervait** quand il devait **faire la queue** pendant longtemps. Il **était gêné par la circulation dense** lorsqu'il allait au travail. Il s'énervait quand ses voisins **faisaient du bruit**. Et surtout quand il se retrouvait dans une nouvelle situation. **Entretiens d'embauche**, examens, nouveaux projets, nouvel environnement. À cause de son **anxiété**, il a décidé de ne pas changer les choses. Il fréquentait les endroits qu'il connaissait. Il avait son café, son **cercle d'amis**, son travail.

Même si sa vie en ville était **stressante**, il **craignait** de **déménager**. Lazar désirait la tranquillité mais il lui manquait du courage pour **faire le premier pas**. À la recherche d'un moyen pour **se détendre**, il a découvert **la méditation**. Puisqu'il était stressé tout le temps, il essayait de méditer tous les matins. Au début **ça marchait bien**. Mais, **faute d'**espace dans sa maison, sa famille **l'interrompait** souvent. **Par conséquent**, il ne pouvait pas se concentrer. Si quelqu'un le dérange, toute la journée tourne mal. Comme il vivait avec ses parents, il n'y avait aucune chance que la situation **s'améliore**.

Un jour, un ami du Danemark lui a proposé un poste de vétérinaire, dans un village **éloigné** dans le nord du pays. Il a automatiquement **refusé** le poste, car l'idée de déménager lui faisait peur. Il s'est **posé** mille **questions**. Parviendra-t-il à apprendre la langue ? Est-ce qu'il pourra s'intégrer ? Sera-t-il capable de le faire seul ? Après un mois de réflexion, il a finalement décidé de donner une chance à cette nouvelle opportunité. Alors, il fallait apprendre une nouvelle langue en six mois. Comme il n'avait jamais étudié le danois, c'était un vrai défi pour lui. Faute d'argent, il a commencé à l'apprendre tout seul.

Il a étudié pendant un mois, mais **a progressé** très lentement. Un jour, son ami du Danemark voulait avoir une conversation en danois, pour vérifier ses **progrès**. Son ami parlait déjà **couramment** danois, car il y avait habité pendant presque cinq ans là-bas. Ils ont commencé à parler en danois, mais son ami le comprenait peu. En effet, Lazar avait une amie danoise, et il lui a demandé de l'aider à apprendre. Mais elle ne parlait pas **la langue standard**. À cause des heures passées avec son amie, il a appris **l'argot**. La manière dont il parlait n'était pas adaptée à la communication professionnelle. Son premier entretien en danois **aura lieu** dans une semaine et il devra tout oublier et recommencer. **C'est pourquoi** il a décidé de prendre des cours avec une professeure particulière.

Il était tellement motivé qu'il étudiait le danois chaque jour. Il a étudié dur à tel point qu'il oubliait de manger. Donc, il **avait maigri**. Quand je l'ai vu, j'ai été **stupéfait**. En effet, il avait tellement maigri qu'il devait acheter de nouveaux pantalons.

Le jour de l'entretien, Lazar était très nerveux. L'employeur a remarqué que Lazar était stressé, mais il le comprenait, puisque lui-même était souvent stressé dans des situations similaires. Il avait également **quitté la vie urbaine** pour vivre plus **sereinement** dans un village. Ils ont parlé en danois. Grâce à son enseignante, Lazar pouvait répondre à quelques questions liées à son expérience professionnelle. Il parlait en danois si bien que son employeur l'avait invité à commencer à travailler tout de suite.

Une semaine après, Lazar est arrivé au Danemark et **s'est installé** dans un village à côté de la forêt. C'était si calme qu'il pouvait entendre les feuilles tomber. Il n'y avait pas de bruit, de circulation, de voisins, alors il n'**était** plus **gêné** le matin. Comme il aimait les animaux, il a commencé à les **élever**. En raison des animaux, il a aussi commencé à **cultiver des plantes**. Puisqu'il habitait à dix minutes de son travail, il se rendait au travail en bicyclette. Le matin, il pouvait méditer avant le travail car c'était calme. Grâce à son nouveau travail, il a finalement trouvé la paix. Il a arrêté de stresser.

Résumé de l'histoire

Le narrateur parle de son meilleur ami, Lazar. Son ami n'aime pas quand les choses changent. Il travaille comme vétérinaire mais la vie en ville le dérange. Il a toujours été anxieux. À la recherche d'un moyen de se détendre, il a découvert la méditation. Mais, faute d'espace dans sa maison, sa famille l'interrompait souvent. Un jour, un ami du Danemark lui a proposé un poste de vétérinaire dans un village danois éloigné. Il finit par accepter, même si l'idée de déménager lui faisait peur. Pour le premier entretien il fallait apprendre un peu le danois. Comme toujours, Lazar était stressé pendant l'entretien, mais son employeur le comprenait puisque lui-même était souvent stressé dans des situations similaires. Une semaine après son entretien, Lazar a déménagé au Danemark. Grâce à son nouveau travail, il a finalement arrêté de stresser.

Summary of the story

The narrator talks about his best friend, Lazar. His friend doesn't like to change things. He works as a veterinarian but city life bothers him. He was always feeling anxious. Looking for a way to relax, he discovered meditation. But, due to lack of space in his house, his family often interrupted him. One day, a friend from Denmark offered him a job as a veterinarian in a remote village. He ended up accepting, even if the idea of moving scared him. For the first interview, he had to learn a little Danish.

As always, Lazar was stressed during the interview, but his employer understood that since he himself was often stressed in similar situations. A week later, Lazar came to Denmark. Thanks to his new job, he finally stopped stressing.

Vocabulary and Expressions

vétérinaire - veterinarian

déranger - to bother, to disturb

s'inquieter - to worry

s'énerver - to get angry, to get worked up

faire la queue - to line up, to queue up

être gêné(e) - to be annoyed

la circulation dense - the heavy traffic

faire du bruit - to make noise

un entretien d'embauche - a job interview

anxiété - anxiety

un cercle d'amis - a circle of friends

stressant(e) - stressful

craindre - to fear

déménager - to move out

faire le premier pas - to take the first step

se détendre - to relax

la méditation - meditation

ça marche bien - it works well

faute de - by lack of

interrompre - to interrupt

par conséquent - therefore

s'améliorer - to improve

éloigné(e) - remote

refuser - to refuse

se poser des questions - to ask oneself questions

progresser - to progress

des progrès - progress

couramment - fluently

la langue standard - the standard language

de l'argot - slang

avoir lieu - to take place, to occur, to happen

c'est pourquoi - that is why

maigrir - to lose weight

stupéfait(e) - stunned, amazed, astonished

quitter - to leave, to quit

la vie urbaine - city life, urban living

sereinement - serenely

s'installer - to settle down

être gêné(e) - to be bothered

élever - to raise

cultiver des plants - to cultivate plants

Comprehension Questions

Sélectionnez une seule réponse pour chaque question.

1. Pourquoi n'a-t-il pas réussi à méditer en paix dans sa maison ?
    A. À cause de sa famille qui le dérangeait.
    B. À cause des voisins qui faisaient du bruit.
    C. Faute d'espace dans sa maison.

2. Qu'est-ce qui s'est passé quand Lazar a parlé à son ami en danois ?
    A. Ils ne se comprenaient pas parce que son ami ne parlait pas le danois.
    B. Son ami ne l'a pas compris car Lazar parlait en argot.
    C. Ils ne se comprenaient pas parce qu'il parlait la langue standard.

3. Qu'est-ce qui énerve Lazar ?
    A. Faire la queue pendant longtemps, la circulation dense, les voisins qui font du bruit, se retrouver dans une nouvelle situation.
    B. Les entretiens d'embauche, les examens, les nouveaux projets
    C. Le bruit, sa famille, se retrouver dans une nouvelle situation.

4. Pourquoi Lazar n'a-t-il pas voulu apprendre la langue avec un professeur de langue étrangère ?
    A. Il avait un ami du Danemark qui l'aidait.
    B. À cause de l'argent.
    C. Il connaissait déjà les bases de la langue danoise.

5. Pourquoi son employeur le comprenait ?
    A. Parce qu'il a quitté la vie citadine comme Lazar.
    B. Parce que Lazar parlait bien le danois.
    C. Puisque lui-même était souvent stressé dans des situations similaires.

Grammar Notes

Expressing Cause and Consequence

Inevitably, our brains are wired to think in terms of causes and consequences. Cause and consequence are directly linked one to the other, where the first action influences the second one. We can use conjunctions like **parce que**, **puisque**, **car**, **à cause de**, **en effet** etc. to give reasons for an event or behavior, as well as to justify one's actions.

In French, there are four main ways to express cause using: *parce que, car, puisque, comme*. To some extent, *car, parce que,* and *puisque* are interchangeable. So you can understand the nuanced differences, let's examine them first.

Parce que - because, for

It introduces a cause, explanation, or motive explaining why something is done.

J'ai assez faim parce que je n'ai pas mangé depuis ce matin. - I'm quite hungry since I haven't eaten since this morning.

Car - because

It expresses the justification of what has just been stated or indicates a reason. It is mainly found in formal and written French.

Car je connais le chinois. - Because I can speak Chinese.

Puisque - since, as

It could replace both "parce que" and "car", but its usage implies that this fact is already well known or obvious. Instead of giving a cause, it provides an obvious explanation or justification.

Puisque vous êtes fatiguées, vous devriez vous reposer. - Since you're tired, you should rest.

Comme - as, since, as though

It highlights the link between a consequence and its result. It always appears at the beginning of the sentence.

Comme il doit économiser pour acheter la maison, il travaille dur. - Since he has to save money to buy the house, he works hard.

Other expressions include:

Faute de (by lack of)

Nous ne pouvons pas partir en vacances cet été, faute d'argent. - We can't go on vacation this summer because of a lack of money.

En effet (indeed, in fact)

It is placed at the beginning, in the middle or at the end of the sentence introducing an explanation.

En effet, il semble que ce soit une erreur. - It may, indeed, be a mistake.

Expressing positive, neutral and negative cause

Causes can be positive, negative or neutral. We have a separate expression for each of these cases.

Grâce à - the positive cause (thanks to)

Grâce à elle, j'ai réussi à résoudre le problème. - Thanks to her, I managed to solve the problem.

En raison de - the neutral cause (because of, due to)

En raison de la forte pluie, nous arrivâmes trop tard à l'école. - We were late for school because it rained heavily.

À cause de - negative cause (due to, owing to)

À cause de la pluie, il y a du trafic. - Because of the rain, there is traffic.

Because there's a preposition "de" or "à", you should be careful to make the adequate changes based on the following word, gender, number or first letter).

Expressing consequence

To express the consequence means to show the result, the consequences or the effects of an action or an event.

These are the conjunctions and turns of phrase which express the consequence in French.

Donc - so, therefore, thus

Tu as beaucoup étudié, donc tu vas réussir ton examen. - You have studied hard, so you will pass your exam.

Alors - so, then

Alors, quel est ton problème ? - So, what's your problem?

Par conséquent (therefore, accordingly)

Il n'a pas du tout étudié. Par conséquent, il n'a pas réussi l'examen. - He didn't study at all. Therefore, he did not pass the exam.

C'est pourquoi - that is why

C'est pourquoi je suis en colère après lui. - That is why I am angry with him.

Si bien que - so that

Il fait très froid, si bien que les élèves ne vont pas à l'école. - It is very cold, so that the students do not go to school.

Si/tellement + adjectif/adverbe ... que - so..that

Elle est si/tellement motivée qu'elle étudie chaque soir. - She is so motivated that she studies every night.

À tel point que ... Au point de ... / que ... - to the point that

Il y avait une grande baisse du nombre de touristes à tel point que / au point que plusieurs hôtels étaient fermés. - There was a big drop in tourist numbers to the point that several hotels were closed.

Key takeaways

- In French, there are four main ways to express cause, using **parce que, car, puisque, comme**, and they are interchangeable to some extent.
- **Parce que** (because, for) introduces a cause, or motive explaining why something is done.
- **Car** (because) expresses the justification of what has just been stated or indicates a reason. It is mainly found in formal and written French.
- **Puisque** (since, as) could replace both "parce que" and "car", but its usage implies that this fact is already well known or obvious.
- **Comme** (as, since, as though) highlights the link between a cause and its result. It always appears at the beginning of the sentence.
- **Faute de** (by lack of).
- **En effet** (indeed, in fact).
- To express a positive cause, use **grâce à** (thanks to).
- To express a neutral cause use **en raison de** (because).
- To express a negative cause use **à cause de** (due to, owing to).
- To introduce consequence, we can use **donc** (so, therefore, thus), **alors** (so, then), **par conséquent** (therefore, accordingly), **c'est pourquoi** (that's why, which is why), **c'est pour cela que** (that's why), **si bien que** or **si/tellement** + adjectif/adverbe (so that), **à tel point que / au point de** (to the point that).

In the next chapter, you'll discover how young people order drinks in a bar, about *apéro* tradition in France, and also a couple of slang words. Additionally, you'll learn how to express duration of an action in more than ten ways, using prepositions like *dans, pour, en, jusqu'a, pendant, depuis*, but also using expressions like *il y a*, or *ça fait*.

Chapter 8: In a Bar

"On ne boit pas, on donne un baiser à son verre et le vin rend une caresse.

-Montaigne

If you are invited to an *apéro* in France, here's what you should do. If you are wondering, is it a dinner or a drink, it's actually a pre-dinner drink or a light meal. If you're at a restaurant, an *apéro* is what you drink during your wait for the first course. Despite understanding aperitif very well, you might be wondering why it is such a big deal in France.

The purpose of this is not to drink; it's to socialize, to share a moment with friends, and, mainly, to get ready for dinner. Typically, *apéritif* food is finger food, especially if it's served at home. Time isn't fixed, but it usually happens after work until just before supper, lasting about an hour between 5:30 and 9 pm. In this story, you'll follow the conversation of three friends over an *apéro* hour. After this story, you'll be able to order a drink, pay for the bill and have a casual conversation in French, even learn a bit of slang. As well as this, the story includes several expressions focusing on the duration of the action, such as *depuis, il y a, pendant, pour* etc.

L'heure de l'apéro

Marie, Léa et Matteo sont amis depuis longtemps. Marie a des **nouvelles à partager** et elle appelle Léa et Matteo pour **organiser un rendez-vous**.

Marie : Tu fais quoi ce soir ?

Léa : Rien de spécial.

Marie : **Ça te dit d'**aller boire un verre ?

Léa : Pourquoi pas ? À quelle heure ?

Marie : On pourrait se rencontrer **à l'heure de l'apéro**.

Léa : **Ça marche**. Je suis chez toi en une heure.

Marie et Léa ont convenu de se rencontrer chez Marie. De là, elles sont allées au bar. Quand elles se sont assises, **le serveur** s'approcha d'elles.

Serveur : Désirez-vous un apéritif ?

Marie : Oui. Je voudrais **une pinte de blonde,** s'il vous plaît.

Léa : J'aimerais **un verre de rosé**, s'il vous plaît. Et est-ce que vous avez des petites choses à **grignoter** ?

Serveur: Oui. Je vous les apporte.

Marie : Merci bien.

Léa: J'ai beaucoup de choses à te raconter !

Marie : J'ai hâte de le savoir ! Moi aussi j'ai des nouvelles à te raconter. Quoi de neuf chez toi ?

Léa: Je partirai en Belgique dans un mois.

Marie : Ce n'est pas vrai ! Comment ?

Léa : Je vais **faire du bénévolat** pendant trois mois dans une école primaire. Ça fait trois mois que j'attendais les résultats. **J'ai postulé** il y a trois mois.

Marie : C'est génial ! Et pendant que tu feras du bénévolat, moi je travaillerai à Bordeaux.

Léa : Ce n'est pas vrai ! Combien de temps vas-tu y rester ?

Marie : Pour commencer, j'ai un contrat de trois mois et ensuite je ne sais pas. Et toi ?

Léa : Je vais rester là jusqu'en novembre. Mais attends. **Le mec** qui te plaît habite à Bordeaux, **n'est-ce pas** ?

Marie : Oui. Je reste chez lui.

Léa : Enfin ! Ça fait trois mois que tu ne l'as pas vu.

Marie : Honnêtement, moi, je pensais que notre **histoire** n'avait pas d'avenir.

Léa : Moi aussi je le pensais. Quand pars-tu ?

Marie : Je pars dans dix jours. Et toi ?

Léa : Je pars dans un mois.

Entre-temps, on leur apporte l'apéro.

Marie : **Santé !**

Léa : **À la tienne !**

À ce moment, Matteo appelle au téléphone.

Marie : Salut Matteo. On est dans un bar près de la place Vendôme.

Matteo : Je peux être au bar en quinze minutes. À bientôt.

Marie : Matteo va nous rejoindre aussi.

Léa : Super !

Marie : Ah, le voilà ! Matteo, nous sommes ici !

Matteo : Salut les filles.

Léa : Salut Matteo. Comment ça va ?

Matteo : Je vais très bien. J'ai une nouvelle à partager avec vous !

Marie : Toi aussi ? Tout le monde a des nouvelles aujourd'hui.

Serveur : **Qu'allez-vous boire ?**

Matteu : On va prendre une bouteille de champagne.

Serveur : Et pour vous Mesdames ?

Marie : Une autre bière, s'il vous plaît.

Léa : Rien pour moi, merci. Je ne veux pas être trop **bourrée**.

Léa : Nous sommes impatientes. Raconte-nous la nouvelle !

Matteo : J'ai acheté **un fourgon** et je vais voyager pendant six mois.

Marie : **C'est fou** ! Comment as-tu eu l'idée d'acheter un fourgon ?

Matteo : Je voulais le faire depuis longtemps. Et, cet été, pendant les vacances, j'ai rencontré une famille qui voyageait avec un fourgon. Ils m'ont encouragé à le faire. Pendant six mois, j'ai cherché une fourgonnette pas cher. Je l'ai cherché jusqu'à hier. Hier, quand la famille que j'ai rencontrée m'a appelé pour dire qu'ils vendaient le leur. Ils m'ont demandé si je voulais l'acheter. Ça fait six mois que j'économise de l'argent et heureusement j'avais la somme qu'ils ont demandée.

Léa: Combien de temps comptes-tu voyager ?

Matteo : Pour trois mois.

Marie : Quand pars-tu ?

Matteo : Je partirai en Italie dans trois semaines.

Marie : Alors, félicitations Matteo !

Matteo : Merci. Et quoi de neuf chez toi Marie ?

Marie : J'**ai trouvé un emploi** à Bordeaux.

Léa : Elle a trouvé **un copain** à Bordeaux !

Matteo : Vraiment ? Depuis combien de temps vous connaissez-vous ?

Marie : Ça fait huit mois qu'on s'est rencontrés. On se connaît depuis mon dernier anniversaire l'année dernière. Nous étions ensemble jusqu'en mars cette année, mais il a trouvé un emploi à Bordeaux. C'est alors que nous avons décidé de rompre.

Matteo : Avez-vous communiqué depuis ?

Marie : Nous n'avons pas parlé pendant deux mois. Une semaine à Paris, nous nous sommes rencontrés **par hasard**. Jusque-là, je n'avais pas réalisé **à quel point** il me **manquait**. Depuis juillet nous sommes à nouveau ensemble. Puis une opportunité d'emploi s'est présentée à Bordeaux et je l'ai saisie. Je pars à Bordeaux dans deux semaines.

Matteo : Félicitations Marie ! Je suis content pour toi ! On va prendre une autre bouteille de champagne !

Le gars de la table voisine s'approche et demande : « **Vous avez du feu** ? »

Léa : Non, je ne fume pas.

Matteo sort des **clopes** et **un briquet**.

Matteo : On y va ? Je **paye ma tournée**.

Marie : Allons-y.

Matteo : L'**addition** s'il vous plaît.

Serveur : Ça fait 30 euros.

Matteo : Que voulez-vous faire maintenant ?

Léa : On s'installe sur **les quais** ?

Marie : Ou on peut aller en boîte.

Matteo : Il y a **une grosse teuf** chez ma copine si vous voulez.

Marie : Pourquoi pas ? Je suis pour.

Léa : D'accord mais je ne veux pas rentrer tard.

Marie : Moi non plus.

Chez la copine de Matteo, il y avait plein de gens. Sa copine avait des amis musiciens. L'un jouait de la guitare, et l'autre du saxophone.

Léa : Je vais rentrer, amusez-vous bien !

Marie : Moi aussi, je suis fatiguée, j'y vais.

Léa : On va prendre un taxi.

Marie : Pourquoi tu ne restes pas chez moi ce soir ?

Léa : Bonne idée ! Je pourrais. Demain c'est dimanche. D'accord.

Matteo : **Rentrez-bien**, bonne soirée !

Le lendemain matin, les filles se sont réveillées.

Marie Oh là là, j'**ai la gueule de bois**.

Léa : On s'est bien amusés hier ! **À refaire** très bientôt !

Marie : À Bordeaux, ou en Belgique.

Résumé de l'histoire

Maria, Léa et Matteo sont amis depuis longtemps. Maria a des nouvelles à partager et elle appelle Léa et Matteo pour arranger un rendez-vous. Ils se rencontrent dans un bar pour prendre un apéro. Chacun a des nouvelles à partager. Marie à obtenu un nouveau poste à Bordeaux, Léa va en Belgique pour faire du bénévolat dans une école, et Matteo à acheté un fourgon. Après l'apéro ils vont chez la copine de Matteo qui organise une fête.

Summary of the story

Maria, Léa and Matteo have been friends for a long time. Maria has some news to share and she calls Léa and Matteo to arrange a meeting. They meet in a bar for an aperitif. It turns out that everyone has news to share. Marie has got a new job in Bordeaux, Lea is going to Belgium to volunteer at school, and Matteo has bought a van and intends to travel. After the aperitif they go to Matteo's girlfriend's house who is organizing a party.

Vocabulary and Expressions

des nouvelles à partager - news to share

organiser un rendez-vous - to arrange an appointment

Ça te dit de faire quelque chose ? - Would you like to do something?

À l'heure de l'apéro - At apéritif time.
Ça marche - that works
le serveur - the waiter
une pinte de blonde - a pint of lager
un verre de rosé - a glass of rosé wine
grignoter - to nibble
faire du bénévolat - to do volunteer work
postuler - to apply
le mec - the guy
n'est-ce pas - Isn't it?
une histoire - history
Entre temps - meanwhile
Santé ! - To your health! (when making a toast)
À la tienne ! - Cheers
Qu'allez-vous boire ? - What are you going to drink ?
être bourré(e) - to be drunk
un fourgon - a van
C'est fou ! - It's crazy!
trouver un emploi - to find a job
un copain - a friend or a boyfriend
par hasard - by chance, by accident
à quel point - at what point, how much
manquer - to lack, to miss
un gars - a guy
vous avez du feu ? - Do you have a lighter?
des clopes - cigarettes
un briquet - a lighter
payer sa tournée - to pay for a round of drinks
une addition - a bill
les quais - the docks
une teuf - a party
gros(se) - big
Rentrez-bien ! - Get home safe!
Avoir la gueule de bois - to be hangover
À refaire ! - To redo!

Comprehension Questions

Sélectionnez une seule réponse pour chaque question.

1. Quelles nouvelles Léa a-t-elle à partager ?
   A. Elle va faire du bénévolat dans une école primaire.
   B. Elle va partir en Italie pour six mois.
   C. Elle va travailler à Bordeaux.
2. Quelles nouvelles Marie a-t-elle à partager ?
   A. Elle va faire du bénévolat dans une école primaire.
   B. Elle va travailler à Bordeaux.
   C. Elle a trouvé un emploi à Bordeaux et déménage chez son copain.
3. Qui part dans dix jours ?
   A. Matteo.
   B. Léa.
   C. Marie.
4. Combien de temps Léa a-t-elle attendu les résultats du concours ?
   A. Deux semaines.
   B. Trois semaines.
   C. Trois mois.
5. Qui fume parmi eux ?
   A. Léa.
   B. Matteo.
   C. Marie.

Grammar Notes

Expressing Duration in French

French prepositions for time are confusing to many students. It is difficult to keep track of a variety of French temporal prepositions, and all the different meanings. Be aware that some of these propositions may be used to express the location as well. In this chapter, we'll focus only on their relation to time.

Here is a brief overview of French temporal prepositions.

Depuis - since, for

It refers to an action which started in the past and continues in the present. In English, instead of using the preposition, it is indicated by the present perfect or present perfect progressive.

- **depuis** + **durée** = for + [duration]

Depuis quand étudiez-vous les langues étrangères? - How long have you studied foreign languages?

J'étudie le français depuis trois ans. - I've studied foreign languages for three years (and still do).

- **depuis** + **date** = since + [date]

J'étudie la peinture depuis 2009. - I've been studying painting since 2009.

Pendant - during

It refers to an action that has a concrete start and ending point. It can be used to describe such actions in the present, past (with *passé composé*), or future.

Il resta silencieux pendant le repas. - He kept silent during the meal.

En - in

It introduces the time needed to do something.

Je peux être chez toi en vingt minutes. - I can be at your house in twenty minutes.

Dans - in

It indicates how long before an action will take place.

Je partirai en France dans une semaine. - I will be going to France in a week.

Pour - for

It introduces the period during which we will do something.

Je voyagerai pour cinq mois. - I will be traveling for five months.

Jusqu'à - until

It introduces the moment in which the action stops, whether it's in the past, future or present.

J'étudierais jusqu'à 8 heures. - I would study until 8 o'clock.

Il y a, ça fait ... que, voilà ... que

Il y a ... que, **ça fait ... que** and, more emphatic, **voilà ... que** expresses the duration of one action or situation that has begun in the past but continues in the present. Unlike *depuis*, they are always used at the beginning of a sentence.

Il y a deux mois que j'étudie. - I have been studying for two months.

Ça fait longtemps que tu enseignes à l'école ? - How long have you been teaching in school?

Voilà un an que j'enseigne ici. - I have been teaching here for a year.

Il y a - ago

Il y a is used to talk about completed actions followed by a length of time. Furthermore, it introduces the past moment that is separate from the present moment.

Claise s'est réveillée <u>il y a dix</u> minutes. - Claire woke up ten minutes ago.

J'ai vu Pierre il y a six mois. - I saw Pierre six months ago.

Il y a ... que

It conveys the idea of "have been doing X for...". As opposed to English, which uses the present perfect continuous, French uses the present tense after "que".

<u>Il y a trois ans que</u> je travaille ici. - I have been working here for three years.

Note that you can express the same idea in multiple ways. For instance, in the sentence "They've been waiting for 45 minutes." in French, one can use these structures:

Ça fait 45 minutes qu'ils attendent.

Ils attendent depuis 45 minutes.

Il y a 45 minutes qu'ils attendent.

Key takeaways

- **Depuis** - since, for. It is used to express an ongoing action. *depuis + durée* = for + [duration], *depuis + date* = since + [date].
- **Pendant** - during. It refers to an action that has a concrete start and ending point.
- **En** - in. It introduces the time needed to do something.
- **Dans** - in. It indicates how long before an action will take place.
- **Pour** - for. It introduces the period during which we will do something.
- **Jusqu'à** - until. It introduces the moment in which the action stops, whether it's in the past, future or present.
- **En** - in. It introduces the time needed to do something.
- **Il y a** - ago.
- **Il y a ... que**. It conveys the idea of "have been doing X for...".
- **Il y a ... que**, **ça fait ... que** and **voilà ... que** expresses the duration of one action or situation that has begun in the past but continues in the present. Unlike *depuis*, they are always used at the beginning of a sentence.

In the next chapter, you'll be introduced to a hypothetical form - the conditional mood. After the next chapter, you'll be able to talk about imagined realities that exist only under certain conditions.

Chapter 9: Our planet

La planète n'a pas besoin de gens qui réussissent. La planète a désespérément besoin de plus de faiseurs de paix, de guérisseurs, de conteurs d'histoires et passionnés de toutes sortes.

-Dalai Lama

Imagine, living in a world without thinking about all possibilities the future can bring. If you want to discuss possibilities, you will need to use the conditional. The conditional is not a tense, but a mood, and it refers to a person's mental state. When a conditional is used, the subject describes a possible situation: could, should, would? Conditionals allow us to talk about hypothetical or imagined realities that can only exist under certain conditions.

The following story will reveal the use of conditional, as well as open up a new topic about recycling and ecology. You'll read about children who are thinking about different ways to recycle and improve our planet.

Un héros de la forêt

Eliot est un homme d'une quarantaine d'années. Quand il était étudiant, il a commencé à **s'engager dans l'activisme**. Il **lutte** pour **les droits des animaux**, pour **la préservation des forêts**, et aujourd'hui il s'intéresse de plus en plus au **recyclage**. Sa fille Charlotte **est** également **fascinée** par ces sujets et veut **suivre les traces de** son père. Chaque matin, avec sa fille, Eliot lit **les actualités du monde** de l'écologie. **À la une**, l'image d'une tortue dans un sac plastique **attire l'attention** de sa fille.

Charlotte : Écoute ce que l'article dit. « Aujourd'hui, une **écrasante majorité des plastiques jetés** dans **l'environnement** sont des **emballages ménagers à usage unique.** Il ne s'agit en effet plus de simplement **consommer** moins de plastique, mais de trouver de nouvelles utilisations **aux polymères existants. L'opinion publique mondiale** découvre des photos de **mammifères marins emprisonnés** dans divers sacs plastiques, **filets de pêche, ou bouteilles d'eau.** C'est horrible. Pauvres animaux. Nous devrions faire quelque chose.

Elle a dit toute **bouleversée**.

Quelques jours plus tard, Charlotte a eu une idée.

Charlotte : Tu te souviens de la tortue du journal ? J'ai trouvé le moyen d'aider à **réduire** le plastique. Sais-tu ce qu'on pourrait faire papa ?

Eliot : Non. Mais il me semble que tu as une idée.

Charlotte : Tu pourrais devenir le héros de la forêt.

Eliot : Le héros de quoi ?

Charlotte : De la forêt ! Ils cherchent quelqu'un pour **diriger le projet** « sauver la forêt » et éduquer les jeunes gens.

Eliot : **Fais-moi voir**.

Charlotte : Voilà. C'est **sur la deuxième page**.

Eliot : Aimerais-tu le faire avec moi ?

Charlotte : Ouiiii ! Ce serait merveilleux.

Eliot : D'accord. Je pourrais **m'inscrire** alors.

Charlotte : Non ! Tu t'inscriras !

Eliot : Donc, **c'est réglé**.

Un mois après, Eliot **a animé un atelier de recyclage** pour une vingtaine d'enfants. Charlotte était à côté de lui, **en tant qu'**assistante. Eliot a montré des images d'une petite tortue piégée à l'intérieur d'un sac plastique. Il a demandé aux enfants : « J'aimerais connaître votre réaction face à ces photos que vous voyez ici ? »

Camille : C'est triste.

Manon : Je pense que la plupart des gens ne savent pas ce qui se passe avec le plastique après.

Pierre : Moi, je suis d'avis qu'ils ne veulent même pas y penser.

Eliot : **Le fait est** qu'il y a beaucoup de plastique sur la planète. Recycler et **réutiliser le plastique déjà existant**, notamment quand celui-ci est **fabriqué à partir de matières non renouvelables**, c'est **contribuer à une utilisation rationnelle des ressources terrestres**. Ainsi, il est nécessaire de **changer globalement nos modes de consommation et de production**. J'aimerais connaître votre avis sur le recyclage. Que peut-on recycler ?

Marie : On pourrait recycler **les barquettes de légumes, sacs et films plastiques**.

Pierre : Toutes les bouteilles et **flacons en plastique**, et aussi les **pots de yaourts**.

Eliot : Et comment recyclez-vous ?

Marie : Je **fais le tri** de mes **déchets** plastiques à la maison et les **dépose dans le conteneur**.

Eliot : Très bien. **La circularité**, c'est **prendre en compte** tout le cycle de vie du plastique, de sa production à sa réutilisation. Comment résoudriez-vous le problème du recyclage ?

Pierre : **Il faudrait remplacer** tous les sacs plastiques par des sacs en papier. Nous devrions également utiliser le plastique existant.

Lucas : On pourrait trouver d'autres moyens de l'utiliser.

Eliot : Devenue partie intégrante de notre société, la consommation de plastique a été multipliée par vingt depuis les cinquante dernières années. Certains pays ne recyclent pas. Que feriez-vous à leur place ?

Camille : Je pense qu'**il faudrait passer une loi** sur le recyclage obligatoire.

Manon : J'enseignerais aux gens pourquoi il est important de recycler.

Hugo : Moi, j'irais au pays où on ne fait pas le recyclage et je parlerais avec les responsables de l'environnement. Ensuite, je les aiderais à **mettre en place** le recyclage.

Camille : Je pense que nous devrions **faciliter** le recyclage.

Eliot : Comment ?

Camille : Je mettrais **des conteneurs de tri** partout. De cette manière, les déchets pourraient être triés.

Camille : Je ferais du recyclage un plaisir.

Eliot : Comment feriez-vous du recyclage un plaisir ?

Camille : J'utiliserais le plastique pour fabriquer d'autres choses.

Eliot : C'est une excellente idée. Comment utiliseriez-vous le plastique ? Donnez-moi quelques façons de recycler vos bouteilles en plastique au lieu de les mettre à **la poubelle**.

Camille : Ça pourrait devenir **une mangeoire** pour des chatons.

Pierre : Ou pour les oiseaux.

Marie : Je ferais **un sapin de Noël**.

Lucas : Moi je ferais **un porte-brosse à dents**.

Eliot : **Face à l'étendue du problème**, il est plus que jamais nécessaire pour les pays de **collaborer**. Êtes-vous d'accord avec cela ?

Camille : Je suis **à cent pour cent d'accord** avec vous. Le plastique est un problème **mondial**.

Lucas : Une action locale seule ne **résoudrait** pas **le problème**.

Eliot : Aujourd'hui nous avons des pays de différentes régions du monde qui **font équipe** pour lutter contre les déchets plastiques. Le projet aidera **les pays en développement à mettre en œuvre** les meilleures **pratiques**.

Après la réalisation de ce projet, Eliot a continué à **traiter** la question du recyclage avec sa fille. Ensemble, ils ont réussi à planter 1000 arbres. L'année dernière, Eliot a été **récompensé** pour son **engagement** et sa contribution remarquable à l'amélioration des forêts. Depuis, il a également **contribué** à améliorer l'éducation des enfants dans des **domaines variés** tel que l'écologie. Le monde a besoin de héros. La planète a besoin de héros.

Résumé de l'histoire

Eliot est un homme d'une quarantaine d'années qui s'est engagé dans l'activisme quand il était étudiant. Sa fille Charlotte est également fascinée par l'écologie. Chaque matin, avec sa fille, Éliot lit les actualités du monde de l'écologie. Une image d'une tortue piégée dans un sac plastique attire l'attention de sa fille. Charlotte a été bouleversée et a voulu trouver un moyen d'aider à réduire le plastique. Elle a vite trouvé un projet pour son père. Il s'agit du projet « sauver la forêt » qui a pour objectif d'éduquer les jeunes gens sur le recyclage. Un mois après, Eliot et sa fille animent un atelier de recyclage pour une vingtaine d'enfants. Après la réalisation de ce projet, Eliot a continué à traiter la question du recyclage avec sa fille. Ensemble, ils ont réussi à planter 1000 arbres.

Summary of the story

Eliot is a man in his forties, who has been an activist since his student days. Charlotte, his daughter, is also fascinated by ecology. Every morning, with his daughter, Eliot reads the latest ecology news. The image of the turtle trapped in a plastic bag captures his daughter's attention. Charlotte feels overwhelmed and wants to find a way to help reduce plastic. She finds the "save the forest" project that aims to raise young people's awareness of recycling, and suggests that her father takes part in it. A month later, Eliot and his daughter lead a workshop on recycling. After the completion of this project,

Eliot continued to deal with the issue of recycling with his daughter. Together they succeeded in planting 1,000 trees.

Vocabulary and Expressions

s'engager dans l'activisme - to engage in activism

lutter pour - to fight for

les droits des animaux - the animal rights

la préservation des forêts - the forest preservation

le recyclage - the recycling

être fasciné(e) par - to be fascinated by

suivre les traces - to follow in the footsteps

les actualités du monde - the world news

à la une - on the first page, on the cover page

attirer l'attention de - to draw the attention of

écrasant(e) - overwhelming, massive

majorité de - majority of

le plastique - the plastic

jeter - to throw

l'environnement - the environment

un emballage - a packing, a wrapping paper

ménagers - household, domestic

un usage unique - a disposable, single use

consommer - to consume, to use

le polymère - the polymer

existant(e) - existing

l'opinion publique mondiale - the world public opinion

un mammifère - a mammal

marin - marine

emprisonnés - trapped

un filet de pêche - a fish net

une bouteille d'eau - a water bottle

bouleverser - to shatter

réduire - to cut, to reduce

diriger un projet - to lead a project

fais-moi voir - Let me see

sur la deuxième page - on the second page

s'inscrire - to register

c'est réglé - it's done

animer un atelier de recyclage - to run a recycling workshop

en tant que - as

le fait est - the fact is

réutiliser le plastique déjà existant - to reuse existing plastic

fabriquer - to make, to produce

à partir de - from, with

des matières non renouvelables - non-renewable materials

contribuer à - to contribute to

une utilisation rationnelle des ressources terrestres - a rational use of earth resources

changer globalement - to change globally

un mode de consommation et de production - a mode of consumption and production

une barquette de légumes - a vegetable tray

un sac plastique - a plastic bag

le film plastique - the plastic film

un flacon en plastique - a plastic flask

un pot de yaourt - a yogurt pot

faire le tri - to sort

un déchet - a waste

déposer dans le conteneur - to put in the container

la circularité - the circularity

prendre en compte - to take into account

il faut remplacer - it is necessary to replace

faire passer une loi - to pass a law

mettre en place - to implement

faciliter - to facilitate

un conteneur de tri - a sorting container

une poubelle - a garbage bin

une mangeoire - an animal feeder

un sapin de Noël - a Christmas tree

un porte-brosse à dents - a toothbrush holder

face à l'étendue du problème - given the scope of the problem

collaborer - to collaborate

être à cent pour cent d'accord - to agree one hundred percent
mondial - global
résoudre le problème - to solve the problem
faire équipe - to team up
les pays en développement - developing countries
mettre en œuvre - to implement
une pratique - a practice
tratiter - to deal
récompenser - to reward
un engagement - a commitment
contribuer - to contribute
un domaine - a domain, a field
varier - to vary

Comprehension Questions

Sélectionnez une seule réponse pour chaque question.

1. Quelles idées les enfants ont-ils suggérées pour recycler les bouteilles en plastique ?
   A. Un porte-brosse à dents, une mangeoire pour chatons et un sapin de Noël.
   B. Un sapin pour chatons et oiseaux, ou un porte-brosse à dents.
   C. Une mangeoire pour chatons ou pour les oiseaux, un sapin de Noël, ou un porte-brosse à dents.

2. Pourquoi est-il nécessaire de réinventer globalement nos modes de consommation et de production ?
   A. Parce qu'il est plus que jamais nécessaire pour les pays de collaborer.
   B. Parce que cela contribuerait à une utilisation rationnelle des ressources terrestres.
   C. Parce qu'il y a beaucoup de plastique sur la planète.

3. Pourquoi Charlotte a-t-elle proposé à son père de postuler pour le projet ?
   A. Parce qu'elle a été bouleversée par l'impact du plastique dans la nature.
   B. Elle voulait devenir une activiste comme son père.
   C. Elle voulait sauver la tortue.

4. Comment Pierre résoudrait-il le problème du recyclage ?
   A. Pierre a suggéré de remplacer tous les sacs plastiques par les sacs en papier et de réutiliser le plastique existant.
   B. Pierre a suggéré de réutiliser le plastique existant et de créer des mangeoires pour chatons.
   C. Pierre a suggéré de trouver d'autres manières de l'utiliser.

5. Sur quelle page dans les journaux se trouvait l'image de la tortue ?

    A. Ce n'était pas dans le journal.

    B. Sur la première page.

    C. Sur la deuxième page.

Grammar Notes: Conditional

Conditional

It is a hypothetical form of the tense that allows us to express our wildest hopes and dreams. This tense represents the future as seen from the past. Conditionals allow us to talk about hypothetical or imagined realities that can only exist under certain conditions. The French word *conditionnel* is often translated into English as "would" or "could".

J'aimerais aller en France. - I'd like to go to France.

The conditional is used in the following situations in French:

- to express a wish, a possibility, or a hypothesis in the present or the future.

Marie aimerait être en vacances. - Mary would like to be on holiday.

- as a tense to talk about the future from a past point of view.

Marie pensait qu'elle pourrait partir en voyage. - Marie thought she could go on a trip.

- in if-clauses.

S'il partait pour l'Espagne, il pourrait voir la Sagrada Familia. - If he left for Spain, he could see the Sagrada Familia.

- to make polite requests.

Pierre, est-ce que tu pourrais m'apporter un verre d'eau ? - Pierre, could you bring me a glass of water?

Forming Conditional Present

To form the conditional present in French, you have to use:

- the infinitive of **-er** and **-ir** verbs **(aimer-, sortir-)**.
- the infinitive without the final (e) of **-re** verbs, for example, **attendr-**.

Then add the following endings to the stem: **-ais, -ais, -ait, -ions, -iez, -aient**.

Are you noticing something? Conditional endings are the same as those we add to form *imparfait*. The difference is that we add them to different stems, or the future simple form of the verb.

Irregular Verbs in Conditional

There are a few common verbs that have irregular stems in conditional.

être — ser- (elle serait)

avoir — aur- (j'aurais)

aller — ir- (nous irions)

faire — fer- (tu ferais)

vouloir — voudr- (ils voudraient)

pouvoir — pourr- (vous pourriez)

devoir — devr- (elle devrait)

falloir — faudr- (il faudrait)

Future vs Conditional

Future tense and conditional look very similar, so be careful not to mix them up.

Future	**Conditional**
J'aimerai	J'aimerais
Tu aimeras	Tu aimerais
Il/Elle aimera	Il/Elle aimerait
Nous aimerons	Nous aimerions
Vous aimerez	Vous aimeriez
Ils/Elles aimeront	Ils/Elles aimeraient

Key takeaways

- Conditional is a hypothetical form of the tense allowing us to talk about hypothetical or imagined realities that can only exist under certain conditions. It is often translated into English as "would" or "could".

- To form the conditional present in French, you have to use: the infinitive of **-er** and **-ir** verbs or the infinitive without the final (e) of **-re** verbs, and then add the following endings to the stem: **-ais, -ais, -ait, -ions, -iez, -aient**.

- The conditional is used to express a wish, a possibility, or a hypothesis in the present or the future, to talk about the future from a past point of view, in if-clauses or to make polite requests.

In the next chapter, you'll be presented with a new tense - pluperfect, which is used to express the anteriority of an action in relation to another past action. You will learn how to tell a story in a chronological or non-chronological order.

Chapter 10: Anniversary

Impossible de vous dire mon âge. Il change tout le temps.
-Allphonse Allais

When you host or attend a dinner party in France, making sure you understand the etiquette is essential. There is a tacit rule that you should arrive 15 minutes late so that your host has ample time to prepare. Don't forget to bring dessert or wine when you're invited, or simply ask your host if you should bring anything. During the mealtime, wait until everyone else is served before you begin eating. It's only after the main host sits down, and says « Bon appétit ! » that you can start eating. In the case of an unofficial dinner party, you are completely welcome to bring your own drinks.

Birthdays in France are typically celebrated with a simple homemade cake, food, and dancing. Neither do they throw large and expensive parties, nor do they buy lavish cakes. For a birthday, it's completely normal to have a tart or even a cupcake. If it's a milestone birthday, the cake might be a more sophisticated cake, but otherwise it might be a simple homemade treat. Refrain from asking questions about their age, even at birthday parties.

In this story, you'll also be introduced to pluperfect, a tense that expresses the anteriority of an action in relation to another past action. Pay attention to its form, which is very similar to *imparfait*.

Anniversaire

Hier, nous **avons fêté** le vingtième anniversaire de ma sœur Mathilde. Elle adore **célébrer** son anniversaire. Elle aime **recevoir des cadeaux**, mais elle n'aime pas **les surprises**. Il arrivait souvent qu'elle n'aimait pas du tout le cadeau. Cette année elle **avait dressé une liste** de cadeaux d'anniversaire et l'a donné à notre famille. Chacun lui avait acheté une chose de la liste. La liste comprenait **des pantoufles**, une guitare, **une couverture à manches** et un livre. Moi, j'ai choisi de lui acheter la couverture à manches. Mon frère Liam **était contre**. Il ne voulait pas acheter le cadeau que Mathilde avait proposé. Il avait une autre idée. Je savais bien qu'elle n'allait pas aimer les cadeaux surprises, mais **que faire maintenant**. Nos parents ont choisi de lui acheter une guitare. Au moins, ils étaient **raisonnables**.

Elle avait invité ses amis à venir à 20 heures mais j'étais là plus tôt pour **l'aider aux préparatifs**. **J'ai mis la table**, **posé les bougies** et **décoré** son appartement avec des ballons. J'avais fini quand quelqu'un a sonné à la porte. Un groupe d'amis est arrivé, et ils **ont apporté** un énorme cadeau. En entrant, ses amis criaient « Joyeux anniversaire ! » et « Bon anniversaire ! ». Les gens venaient **les uns après les autres**. Toute notre famille était venue aussi.

La nourriture **était** déjà **servie** sur la table quand tout le monde est arrivé. Les gens se servaient à manger, buvaient du vin, quand l'un de ses amis a commencé à jouer de la guitare. Mathilde a reçu beaucoup de **cartes d'anniversaire**, de **bouquets de fleurs** et de super cadeaux. Chaque **invité** avait écrit **une note** gentille pour elle. Tout le monde savait qu'elle avait gardé toutes les notes de ses anniversaires dans une petite **boîte**.

Vers 21 heures, l'atmosphère est devenue plus **chaleureuse**. Mathilde et moi avions préparé **un buffet** dans la cuisine. Nous avions préparé **des mini-tartelettes garnies de thon** et **de fromage aux herbes**. On a aussi préparé **un plateau de charcuteries variées (jambons, pâtés, saucissons)**, un plateau de fromage, **des quiches**, et plein d'autres choses délicieuses et **faciles à manger**. Ma mère disait toujours « Le buffet doit être original, varié, car en amitié, comme en amour, le grand ennemi, c'est la monotonie. » Chacun pouvait se servir **à sa guise**.

Dans le salon, on **avait poussé les meubles** pour pouvoir danser. Les danseurs fatigués pouvaient venir boire ou **grignoter** dans la cuisine. J'ai demandé à ma sœur : « Veux-tu que j'apporte quelque chose ? » Elle m'a demandé de sortir le vin, mais j'avais oublié de l'acheter. Je ne voulais pas lui dire que j'avais oublié car elle me l'avait rappelé cent fois. Je **suis passée inaperçue** et je suis allée au magasin pour acheter quelques bouteilles. J'avais attendu longtemps à **la caisse**.

Quand je suis rentrée, j'ai vu **des rubans** et du papier cadeau **déchirés par terre** dans **le couloir**. J'étais **étonnée** de voir ça. J'**ai suivi la trace** et j'ai découvert **les malfaiteurs** : les chats de Mathilde avaient déchiré **l'emballage** d'un petit cadeau. Pendant qu'un chat jouait avec **le nœud**, l'autre voulait manger le gâteau d'anniversaire. C'est le gâteau que Mathilde avait commandé chez **un pâtissier artisanal**. Sur le gâteau, il était écrit avec de la crème, « Joyeux anniversaire Mathilde ». J'**ai vite confisqué** le gâteau qui était déjà un peu entamé. Personne n'a découvert que j'avais sauvé le gâteau des chats. Puis j'ai remarqué que le chat avait mangé les deux lettres. Je suis rapidement allée à la cuisine pour **réparer** le gâteau. Tout le monde a commencé à crier « Le gâteau, le gâteau ! » mais je n'avais pas encore fini **la réparation**. Finalement, j'ai fini la réparation et je pouvais le sortir. J'ai mis vingt bougies dessus et je l'ai sorti.

Ma sœur a voulu **souffler les bougies** mais je l'ai arrêtée. J'ai dit « Fais un vœu. » Elle a fermé les yeux, a imaginé son souhait et a soufflé. Tout le monde a chanté « Joyeux anniversaire ! ».

Nous nous assîmes pour **déguster** le gâteau d'anniversaire. Ma sœur a remercié tout le monde d'être venu et puis elle a **trinqué**. « Tchin-tchin ! »

Après minuit, ma famille est lentement rentrée chez elle, tandis que les amis de ma sœur sont restés. En sortant, ma mère a dit « Merci pour ce délicieux repas. »

Ma sœur a passé le reste de la soirée à ouvrir des cadeaux. Sa partie préférée des anniversaires était toujours l'ouverture des cadeaux. Elle a reçu quelques livres, des billets d'opéra, des fleurs, des bougies parfumées et des pantoufles. Puis elle a ouvert les cadeaux que notre famille lui avait offerts. Elle avait aimé mon cadeau, la guitare aussi, et puis elle a ouvert le cadeau de notre frère. La boîte était énorme. Son idée géniale était de lui offrir **des pneus d'hiver** pour sa voiture. Elle ne savait pas quoi dire, car elle n'avait pas de voiture. Lian a dit « Je voulais voir ton expression quand tu ouvres le cadeau. Bien sûr, c'est **une blague**. Voilà ton livre. »

Résumé de l'histoire

C'est le vingtième anniversaire de Mathilde. Elle adore célébrer son anniversaire. Même si elle aime recevoir des cadeaux, elle n'aime pas les surprises. Cette année elle avait dressé une liste de cadeaux d'anniversaire et l'a donnée à sa famille. Mathilde a invité sa famille et ses amis à sa fête. Sa sœur est venue plus tôt pour l'aider aux préparatifs. Toute la famille a suivi la liste, mais son frère voulait jouer un tour à Mathilde, lui offrant un cadeau hors de la liste.

Summary of the story

It's Mathilde's twentieth birthday, and she loves celebrating it. Although she enjoys receiving gifts, she dislikes surprises. To avoid unpleasant surprises, she had made a list of birthday gifts and gave it to her family. Earlier in the day, Mathilde's sister came to help her with preparations. The whole family followed the list, but her brother wanted to play a trick on Mathilde, giving her a gift off the list.

Vocabulary and Expressions

fêter - to celebrate

célébrer - to celebrate

recevoir des cadeaux - to get presents

une surprise - a surprise

dresser une liste - to make a list

des pantoufles - slippers

une couverture à manches - a blanket with sleeves

être contre - to be against

que faire - what to do

raisonnable - reasonable

aider aux préparatifs - to help with preparations

mettre la table - to set the table

poser les bougies - to put the candles

décorer un appartement - to decorate an apartment

apporter - to bring

l'un après l'autre, les uns après les autres - one after another

servir - to serve

la carte d'anniversaire - the birthday cards

le bouquet de fleurs - the flower bouquet

un(e) invité(e) - a guest

une note - a note

une boîte - a box

chaleureux, chaleureuse - warm-hearted

un buffet - a buffet

des mini-tartelettes - the mini-tarts

garnies de thon - stuffed with tuna

du fromage aux herbes - herb cheese

un plateau de charcuteries variées - a platter of assorted cold meats

le jambon - ham

le pâté - pâté

le saucisson - dry sausage, salami

une quiche - a quiche

faciles à manger - easy to eat

à sa guise - as it pleases

pousser - to push, to move

les meubles - the furniture

grignoter - to nibble

passer inaperçue - to go unnoticed

la caisse - the checkout

un ruban - a ribbon

déchirer - to tear

par terre - on the ground

le couloir - the hallway

être étonné(e) - to be surprised

suivre la trace - to follow the trail

un malfaiteur - a criminal

un emballage - a wrapping paper

un nœud - a bow

un pâtissier artisanal - an artisanal pastry chef

confisquer - to confiscate

réparer - to fix

la réparation - the repair

souffler les bougies - to blow out the candles

déguster - to savor

trinquer - to make a toast

Tchin-tchin - cheers

des pneus d'hiver - winter tyres

une blague - a joke

Comprehension Questions

Sélectionnez une seule réponse pour chaque question.

1. La sœur de Mathilde voulait passer inaperçue pour faire quoi ?

    A. Acheter le cadeau.

    B. Acheter le vin qu'elle a oublié.

    C. Réparer le gâteau.

2. Que manquait-il au gâteau ?

    A. Des lettres.

    B. De la crème.

    C. Des bougies.

3. Qu'a-t-elle reçu pour son anniversaire de la part de son frère ?

    A. Une guitare.

    B. Des pneus d'hivers.

    C. Un livre.

4. Pourquoi Mathilde a-t-elle dressé une liste de cadeaux d'anniversaire ?

    A. Parce qu'elle veut faciliter la tâche à sa famille.

    B. Parce qu'elle n'aime pas recevoir de cadeaux.

    C. Parce qu'elle n'aime pas les surprises.

5. Qui a déchiré l'emballage d'un cadeau ?

    A. Les chats de Mathilde.

    B. Le frère de Mathilde.

    C. La sœur de Mathilde.

Grammar Notes

Pluperfect

Using the French *plus-que-parfait* with another tense of the past (*passé composé* ou *passé simple*) makes it possible to express the anteriority of an action in relation to another past action. When used in affirmative sentences, it is usually accompanied by the adverb *déjà* (already). In English the *plus-que-parfait* is indicated by **had + past participle**.

Except for the combination of **passé composé + imparfait** you can also combine **plus-que-parfait + imparfait**. The second combination indicates two actions, with one occurring before the other. If the events are told in chronological order, you'll use the *passé composé + imparfait*. In contrast, if the events are recounted in a different order, *plus que parfait + imparfait* are appropriate.

Quand j'avais mangé, je me sentais mieux. - When I had eaten, I felt better.

Elle m'a dit qu'il ne l'avait jamais vu. - She told me he had never seen her.

Forming the pluperfect

We form the *plus-que-parfait* with the auxiliary "be" or "have" in the imperfect followed by the past participle. The same rules that apply for all complex tenses in French, regarding the choice of auxiliaries "avoir" and "être", apply also here.

avoir/être* in imperfect + *participe passé

J'avais	aimé	J'étais	parti (Masculine, Singular)
Tu avais		Tu étais	partie (Feminine, Singular)
Il/Elle/On avait		Il/Elle/On était	partis (Masculine, Plural)
Nous avions		Nous étions	parties (Feminine, Plural)
Vous aviez		Vous étiez	
Ils/Elles avaient		Ils/Elles étaient	

Key takeaways

- Use *plus-que-parfait* with another tense of the past (*passé-composé ou passé simple*) to express the anteriority of an action in relation to another past action.
- If the events you are telling are in chronological order, use the **passé composé + imparfait.** If the events are recounted in a different order, use **plus-que-parfait + imparfait**.
- When used in affirmative sentences, *plus-que-parfait* is usually accompanied by the adverb *déjà* (already).
- In English, the *plus-que-parfait* is indicated by **had + past participle**.
- To make *plus-que-parfait*, take the ***avoir/être* in imperfect + *participe passé***.

You know you have advanced in French once you start using the subjunctive mood. As we move towards the end of the book, we will introduce you to a formal and polite way of communicating in French.

Chapter 11: At the Doctor's

Guérir c'est toucher avec amour ce qui a été précédemment touché avec la peur.
-Stephen Levine

The final chapter in this book refers to subjunctive, which is a clear sign that your French skills are moving to an advanced level. You know you have advanced in French when you begin using the Subjunctive form. While in English, subjunctive is uncommon and rather formal, in French it is very commonly used in everyday conversations. By using subjunctive, the subject expresses their feelings (wishes, hopes, fears, uncertainties...) - usually related to another person. In this story, you'll be introduced to a number of different situations that require the use of Subjunctive. Additionally, you will learn how to book a doctor's appointment and describe your symptoms to your doctor.

Chez le Médecin

Il y a quelques semaines que Gabriel a commencé à avoir des **insomnies** et à **manquer d'énergie**. Il a essayé différentes **façons** de **se sentir mieux**, mais cela n'a pas **fonctionné**. Il a commencé à boire plus d'eau, à ne pas utiliser le téléphone avant d'aller se coucher et à **réduire** sa **consommation** de sucre, mais **en vain**. Un soir, il parlait de **sa santé** avec sa femme, Juliette.

Juliette : Il faut que tu ailles chez **le médecin**.

Gabriel : Je doute que le médecin puisse m'aider.

Juliette : Je te conseille d'aller voir un médecin. Je crains que ce soit **quelque chose de grave**. J'aimerais mieux que tu y ailles.

Gabriel : Je déteste aller chez le médecin.

Juliette : Je regrette que tu doives y aller. Mais demain je vais **prendre un rendez-vous** pour toi.

Juliette a téléphoné pour prendre rendez-vous pour son mari.

Juliette : Bonjour, je vous appelle pour prendre rendez-vous chez **un médecin généraliste**.

Secrétaire : Bonjour Madame. Nous **avons des créneaux disponibles** à partir du 10 avril.

Juliette : Ça ne **m'arrange** pas trop. Est-ce que vous **avez des disponibilités** pour le mercredi 12 avril ?

Secrétaire : Oui. Vous préférez le matin ou l'après-midi ?

Juliette : Je préfère le matin.

Secrétaire : Quel est votre nom ?

Juliette : C'est pour mon mari. Il s'appelle Gabriel Dupont.

Secrétaire : Très bien, **c'est noté**.

Juliette : Oui, c'est parfait. Merci. Au revoir.

Juliette s'est tournée vers son mari.

Juliette : Tu as rendez-vous chez mon médecin à 11 heures, la semaine prochaine. Il faut que tu viennes à l'heure.

Gabriel : Ah, bon. Il vaut mieux que je fasse ce que tu dis.

Juliette : Il vaut mieux. Je suis contente que tu ailles chez le médecin.

Une semaine plus tard, Gabriel se trouve dans **le cabinet médical**.

Gabriel : Bonjour. J'ai rendez-vous à 11 heures.

Secrétaire : Asseyez-vous monsieur. Le médecin **avait une urgence** et sera un peu en retard.

Gabriel : Combien de temps le docteur sera-t-il en retard ?

Secrétaire : Maximum 40 minutes. Voulez-vous l'attendre ?

Gabriel : Je n'**ai pas d'autre choix**.

L'infirmière : Il est possible qu'il vienne plus vite.

Gabriel : Je ne pense pas qu'il vienne.

Autre patient : J'espère qu'il vient à l'heure.

Le médecin arrive dans **la salle d'attente**. **La secrétaire** informe le médecin que **le patient** l'attend.

Médecin : Je suis désolé que vous ayez dû m'attendre.

Gabriel : Vous n'êtes pas si en retard après tout.

Médecin : Alors, Monsieur Gabriel. **Qu'est-ce qui ne va pas ?**

Gabriel : Je ne sais pas docteur. Je me sens fatigué.

Médecin : Vous vous sentez fatigué. Vous dormez bien la nuit ?

Gabriel : Non, pas du tout, je dors très mal, j'ai des insomnies.

Médecin : Vous mangez bien ?

Gabriel : Non, je n'ai jamais faim, je n'ai pas envie de manger.

Médecin : Vous **avez des douleurs quelque part** ?

Gabriel : Oui Monsieur, j'**ai mal partout**.

Médecin : Vous avez mal partout. Où par exemple ?

Gabriel : J'**ai** souvent **mal à la tête**. Je **prends de l'aspirin**e mais **ça ne me fait rien**.

Médecin : Vous **suivez un traitement** ? Vous **prenez des médicaments** ?

Gabriel : Non. Je ne prends rien en ce moment.

Médecin : Êtes-vous **allergique à quelque chose** ?

Gabriel : Je ne sais pas.

Médecin : Il est nécessaire que je vous fasse des tests d'allergie. Il est possible que vous soyez allergiques au gluten.

Gabriel : D'accord.

Médecin : Vous **êtes stressé** en ce moment. Avez-vous des problèmes au travail ?

Gabriel : En ce moment, je travaille sur un projet très important. Il n'est pas sûr que je puisse terminer ce projet à l'heure. Je me sens déprimé parce qu'il y a de nombreuses choses que je dois faire. Mon chef voudrait que je finisse le projet en un mois.

Médecin : Je comprends.

Gabriel : **Qu'est-ce que j'ai** Docteur ? **C'est grave** vous pensez ?

Médecin : Non, ce n'est pas grave… **Il est clair** que vous êtes stressé. Un peu **d'anxiété** c'est tout.

Gabriel : Que devrais-je faire ?

Médecin : Je propose que vous preniez du repos quelques jours. Je conseille de faire un peu de sport chaque jour. Il faut que vous veniez chez moi la semaine prochaine pour faire **des analyses supplémentaires**.

Médecin : Bien, je vais vous **faire une ordonnance**. Je vous suggère aussi que vous essayiez **l'aromathérapie**.

Quand Gabriel est arrivé chez lui, il discutait avec sa femme.

Juliette : **C'est dommage** que tu doives prendre des médicaments mais il est important que tu prennes tes médicaments à l'heure. Je souhaite que tu ailles mieux.

Gabriel : Je pense qu'il est temps que je fasse un peu d'exercice. Je souhaite que tu viennes courir avec moi.

Juliette : Mon chéri, il vaut mieux que je vienne à l'aromathérapie avec toi.

Résumé de l'histoire

Gabriel a commencé à avoir des problèmes d'insomnie. Il a essayé différentes façons de se sentir mieux, mais cela n'a pas fonctionné. Sa femme lui prend un rendez-vous chez un médecin. Le médecin se rend compte que Gabriel a des problèmes liés au stress. Il lui suggère de prendre quelques jours de congé, de faire de l'exercice et de l'aromathérapie.

Summary of the story

Gabriel started having problems with insomnia. He tried different ways to feel better, but nothing worked. Then his wife arranges for him to see a doctor. It becomes apparent to the doctor that Gabriel has a stress problem. He suggests that he take a few days off, exercise, and go to aromatherapy.

Vocabulary and Expressions

une insomnie - an insomnia

manquer d'énergie - to lack energy, to run out of energy

une façon - a way, a manner

se sentir mieux - to feel better

fonctionner - to work, to function

réduire - to reduce, to cut, to lower

consommation - consumption

en vain - in vain

la santé - the health

aller chez le médecin - to go to the doctor

quelque chose de grave - something serious, something bad

prendre un rendez-vous - to make/book an appointment

un médecin généraliste - a general practitioner

avoir des créneaux disponibles - to have available slots

arranger - to suit

avoir des disponibilités - to have availabilities

c'est noté - it is noted

le cabinet médical - the doctor's office

avoir une urgence - to have an emergency

n'avoir d'autre choix - to have no other choice

la salle d'attente - the waiting room

la secrétaire - the secretary

le patient - the patient

qu'est-ce qui ne va pas ? - what's the matter?

avoir des douleurs quelque part - to have pain somewhere

avoir mal partout - to hurt everywhere

mal à la tête - a headache

prendre de l'aspirine - to take aspirin

ça ne me fait rien - nothing helps me

suivre un traitement - to undergo treatment

prendre des médicaments - to take medications

être allergique à quelque chose - to be allergic to something

être stressé(e) - to be stressed out

qu'est-ce que j'ai ? - what do I have?

c'est grave - it's serious

il est clair - it is clear

une anxiété - an anxiety

les analyses supplémentaires - additional analyses

faire une ordonnance - to make a prescription

une aromathérapie - an aromatherapy

c'est dommage - it is too bad

Comprehension Questions

Sélectionnez une seule réponse pour chaque question.

1. Pourquoi Gabriel va-t-il chez le médecin ?
    A. Il a des problèmes d'insomnie.
    B. Il se sent fatigué.
    C. Il est allergique au gluten.

2. Est-ce que Gabriel a suivi un traitement ?
    A. Oui.
    B. Non.
    C. Oui. Il prend l'aspirine.

3. Quels sont les symptômes de Gabriel ?
    A. Il se sent fatigué. Il a des insomnies et il a mal à la tête.
    B. Il a mal partout. Il se sent fatigué et il a des insomnies.
    C. Il se sent fatigué, il n'a pas envie de manger, il a mal à la tête et il a des insomnies.

4. Que recommande le médecin ?
    A. Le médecin propose de faire des analyses supplémentaires.
    B. Le médecin suggère de prendre quelques jours de congé, et d'aller en aromathérapie.
    C. Le médecin propose du repos, un peu d'exercices chaque jour et d'essayer l'aromathérapie.

5. Pourquoi Gabriel est-il stressé ?
    A. À cause de son travail.
    B. Il a des problèmes à la maison.
    C. Il se dispute souvent avec sa femme.

Grammar Notes

Subjunctive

You know you have advanced in French once you start learning the Subjunctive form. While in English subjunctive is uncommon and rather formal, in French it is very commonly used in everyday conversations. The subjunctive is a mood: it describes the attitude of the subject. By using subjunctive, the subject expresses their feelings (wishes, hopes, fears, uncertainties...) about a fact or an idea - usually related to another person.

In this sentence, English will use the regular present tense, but French will use the subjunctive.

*Il est important que **tu fasses** tes devoirs.* - It's important for you to do your homework.

Whenever you want to express doubt, desire, necessity, possibility, and judgment, you need the subjunctive mood. Subjunctive mood appear like Present, Past, Imperfect and Pluperfect. In this chapter, we'll focus on the present subjunctive mood.

Forming Regular Present Subjunctive

To conjugate regular verbs, we take the 3rd person plural form (*ils*) of the present indicative tense, and then remove the -ent. To that stem, for:

- verbs that end in **-er** or **-re**, we add endings: **-e, -es, -e, -ions, -iez,** and **-ent**.
- verbs that end in **-ir** we add endings: **-isse, -isses, -isse, -issions, -issiez, -issent**.

Let's take the verb "regarder", as an example.

Qu'ils regard<u>ent</u> / regard + -e, -es, -e, -ions, -iez, and -ent.

At the end, it looks like this:

Que je regarde / tu regardes / il/elle/on regarde / nous regardions / vous regardiez / ils/elles regardent.

Irregular Present Subjunctive

As in life, grammar has its unconventional, rule-breaking few, which cannot be avoided.

Here are the most common irregular verbs in the subjunctive.

	Aller - to go	**Avoir** - to have	**Être** - to be	**Devoir** - to have to, must	**Dire** - to say	**Faire** - to do
Je	aille	aie	sois	doive	dise	fasse
Tu	ailles	aies	sois	doives	dises	fasses
Il/Elle/	aille	ait	soit	doive	dise	fasse
Nous	allions	ayons	soyons	devions	disions	fassions
Vous	alliez	ayez	soyez	deviez	disiez	fassiez

| Ils/Elles | aillent | aient | soient | doivent | disent | fassent |

	Pouvoir - to be abe, can	**Vouloir -** to want to	**Prendre -** to take	**Venir -** To come	**Savoir -** to know
Je	puisse	veuille	prenne	vienne	sache
Tu	puisses	veuilles	prennes	viennes	saches
Il/Elle/On	puisse	veuille	prenne	vienne	sache
Nous	puissions	voulions	prenions	venions	sachions
Vous	puissiez	vouliez	preniez	veniez	sachiez
Ils/Elles	puissent	veuillent	prennent	viennent	sachent

When to Use Subjunctive ?

Subjunctive in French require two conditions:

→ A minimum of 2 subjects.

subject 1 wanting, wishing, ordering, or fearing and

subject 2 to take the required action.

Je veux que vous fassiez la vaisselle. - I want you to do the dishes. (me wanting you to do it)

→ An expression which is specifically followed by the subjunctive (list below).

If you have two subjects in a sentence, like *"I want him to be happy"*, in English you can use the infinitive of the verb (*to be*). On the other hand, in French, you have to use subjunctive for the second verb.

Nous voulons qu'elle soit heureuse. - We want her to be happy.

To become proficient, you will need to know by heart which expressions are followed by the subjunctive (versus which ones are followed by the indicative). While there is still logic behind its usage, don't rely solely on your understanding. Your subjunctive proficiency also depends on learning expressions by heart.

Many French students wrongly believe that subjective comes after the expressions that include *que*. Even though many expressions that require subjunctive, also contain *que*, this does not imply that the verb will be subjunctive.

The most important difference between using the subjunctive and the indicative is whether the person's standpoint shows a reality or subjective view. The difference between indicative and subjunctive is a little bit like the difference between reality and uncertainty. For instance, if you use some of these expressions like (*Il est clair que*), it means that you are obviously quite certain in your point of view, so you'll have to use indicative. Same goes for the following expressions:

- il est clair que + indicative – it's clear
- il est certain que + indicative – it's obvious
- il est sûr que + indicative – it's sure

It is sometimes difficult to spot the difference between the verbs or expressions that require subjunctive and the ones that don't. For instance, while we use subjunctive after verbs like *souhaiter* or *désirer*, but indicative for the verb *espérer*. This can only be explained by the fact that *espérer* conveys a certain level of belief, opposed to *souhaiter* or *désirer*. On the other hand, the same verb *espérer*, is followed by a subjunctive when expressing a higher level or uncertainty: in interrogative, negative, and imperative sentences.

A negative verb, or a negative inverted interrogative form, may be followed by either a subjunctive or indicative verb, depending on its degree of certainty.

J'espère que Gabriel viendra. - I hope he comes.

but

Je n'espère pas que Gabriel vienne. - I don't hope that he's coming.

Subjunctive Verbs

There are hundreds of verbs, expressions, and conjunctions that use the subjunctive, so it's helpful to divide them into themes. We classified verbs into six categories: **wish**, **likes** and **dislikes**, **fear**, **regrets**, **doubt**, **order**.

The following are the verbs that require subjunctive. These verbs express certain emotional states like:

→ **Wish**

souhaiter

vouloir

désirer

suggérer

proposer

conseiller... + que + subjunctive

→ **Likes and Dislikes**

aimer que

aimer mieux que

préférer que

détester

adorer... + que + subjunctive

→ **Fears**

avoir peur

craindre

redouter... + que + subjunctive

→ **Regrets**

regretter

être désolé... + que + subjunctive

→ **Doubts**

douter... + que

→ **Opinion**

valoir mieux que - would be better

→ **Order**

vouloir

ordonner

exiger

permettre

refuser

supplier... + que + subjunctive

Expressions and conjunctions requiring Subjunctive

The subjunctive may also appear in some expressions that begin with *il*:

- il faut que - it is necessary that
- il vaut mieux que - it is better that
- il est/c'est important que – it's important that
- il est/c'est dommage que – it's too bad that
- il est/c'est impossible – it's impossible that
- il est/c'est possible que – it's possible that

Subjunctive is required after conjunctions with *que*, such as: *avant que, jusqu'à ce que, pour que, afin que, bien que, quoique, à condition que, pourvu que, sans que.*

Key Takeaways

- The **French subjunctive** expresses some sort of subjectivity, uncertainty, or unreality in the mind of the speaker. Whenever you want to express doubt, desire, necessity, possibility, and judgment, you'll have to use the subjunctive mood.

- Verbs that require subjunctive are the ones that express **wish**, **likes** and **dislikes**, **fear**, **regrets**, **doubt**, **order**.
- Subjunctive in French require two conditions: a minimum of 2 subjects in one sentence, and an expression which is specifically followed by the subjunctive.
- To conjugate regular verbs, we take the 3rd person plural form (*ils*) of the present indicative tense, and then remove the -ent. To that stem, for verbs that end in **-er** or **-re**, we add endings: **-e, -es, -e, -ions, -iez**, and **-ent**, and for verbs that end in **-ir**, we add endings: **-isse, -isses, -isse, -issions, -issiez, -issent**.
- Subjunctive is required after conjunctions with *que*, such as: *avant que, jusqu'à ce que, pour que, afin que, bien que, quoique, à condition que, pourvu que, sans que.*
- The subjunctive may also appear in some expressions that begin with *il*: *il faut que, il vaut mieux que, il est important que, il est dommage que, il est impossible, il est possible que.*

Answer Key

Chapter 1

1. Why did Peter stand in line at the station?

A

2. What was Peter's reason for using the Internet?

B

3. Did Peter eat his sandwich?

C

4. Why did Peter ask for help?

A

Chapter 2

1. Why does Antoine not want his father to share stories with his girlfriend?

B

2. What did Antoine talk about in his letters to his wife?

C

3. What was the reason for the enemy soldiers coming so late at night?

B

4. What motivated the soldiers to move into the community?

A

5. When Antoine left the community, what did he discover?

C

Chapter 3

1. Why does the young man want to visit Cambodia?

B

2. Why was the girlfriend angry when he told her about their trip to Cambodia?

A

3. What happened with the train tickets?

C

4. What happened to their luggage at the airport?

A

5. Why couldn't the young man say what was in his suitcase?

B

Chapter 4

1. Who called Jeanne on the phone?

C

2. By mistake, they got on the train that was going…?

C

3. Whose birthday did they celebrate in Arras?

B

4. Did they spend a lot of time in Paul Doumer Park?

A

5. Why did Catherine argue with Aldo?

A

Chapter 5

1. What new subjects have been introduced with the new movement ?

C

2. At the time, most people thought the first impressionist painting looked like:

C

3. Why did the Impressionists start painting outdoors?

B

4. Why has it been said that: "L'âme d'artiste peut vraiment découvrir la réalité d'une manière intuitive"?

B

5. What is an asylum?

A

Chapter 6

1. Why does the main character like to visit flea markets?

A

2. What power did her grandmother's mirror have?

A

3. What happened to her grandmother's mirror?

C

4. Why was the main character crying?

A

5. What does « rien ne survient par hasard » mean?

B

Chapter 7

1. Why didn't he manage to meditate in peace in his house?

A

2. What happened when Lazar spoke to his friend in Danish?

B

3. What's annoying Lazar?

A

4. Why didn't Lazar want to learn the language with a foreign language teacher?

B

5. Why did his employer understand him?

C

Chapter 8

1. What news has Lea?

A

2. What news has Marie to share?

C

3. Who leaves in ten days?

C

4. How long did Léa wait for the results of the exam?

C

5. Who smokes among them?

B

Chapter 9

1. What ideas did the children come up with for recycling plastic bottles?

C

2. Why is it necessary to globally reinvent our modes of consumption and production?

B

3. Why did Charlotte ask her father to apply for the project?

A

4. How would Peter solve the recycling problem?

A

5. On which page in the newspapers was the image of the turtle?

B

Chapter 10

1. What did Mathilde's sister want to do unnoticed?

B

2. What was missing from the cake?

A

3. What did she get for her birthday from her brother?

C

4. Why did Mathilde draw up a list of birthday presents?

C

5. Who tore the wrapping of a gift?

A

Chapter 11

1. Why does Gabriel go to the doctor?

A

2. Did Gabriel follow a treatment?

B

3. What are Gabriel's symptoms?

C

4. What does the doctor recommend?

C

5. Why is Gabriel stressed?

A

Conclusion

First of all, let us congratulate you on your achievements. Learning a language is not a one-day task, and above all requires discipline, consistency, and moving forward despite the frustration.

For a French learner, reading stories may seem insurmountable. Ordinary stories are often too complex, filled with advanced grammar and an overly eloquent narrative, preventing French learners from even getting started. As language learners, we realized, there's the traditional grammar-focused method on the one side, and on the other side, there's the story learning method. The two approaches seem at odds with each other. Yet, they complement one another. For that reason, we wanted to create a book that reconciles the need to understand grammar with the need to get a natural and motivational way to learn French. By accompanying the story with grammar notes, we aimed to get the maximum benefit from the story learning.

Our goal was to create a book that would allow you to focus on one grammar point at a time. The best way to learn grammar in French is to observe how it naturally appears within stories, rather than relying on a "rules first" methodology. Taking this approach allows you to see how grammar functions in the context, and even if you don't yet know the rules, you will still be able to understand a lot!

Through eleven stories you build your grammar skills with each story read. As each story is written with common intermediate's troubles in mind, you progress gradually. We first set the ground with lessons like Indefinite Adjectives, Prepositions of place, Past Participle agreement and the difference between the Imperfect and the Past Tense, which form the basis of all stories. Then we start progressing up to more advanced grammar points such as Indefinite Relative Pronouns, Gerundiv, Expressing Duration, Cause and Consequence, Pluperfect, Conditional and Subjunctive. The stories invite the reader to explore further the language curiosities and examine the story back and forth with the new grammar tools.

Most of the topics in this book are related to our everyday lives. Eleven stories cover the eleven most frequent everyday situations, from city sightseeing to speaking with your friends, going to a bar, in the museum or at the flea market, visiting a doctor, celebrating birthdays, moving abroad, or having issues on your trip, allowing you to build your vocabulary in different areas.

Story learning prevents you from becoming infatuated with rules by encouraging you to focus on understanding and purely enjoying the story first and foremost. Through this approach, you end up learning so many global aspects of the language including sentence structure, narrative, and sequencing events.

With eleven stories under your belt and a solid foundation in French grammar, you are well prepared to speak French, even with natives. You now have the freedom to talk about your friends, attend a party, go to a museum, bar, doctor's office, flea market, even discuss some topics like ecology. All that's left is to apply what you've learned.

$39 FREE BONUSES

Learn French Fundamentals Audiobook

+ Printable "French Verb Conjugations" Practice Worksheets Download

Scan QR code above to claim your free bonuses

—— OR ——

exploretowin.com/frenchaudio10

Ready To Start Speaking French?

Inside this **Learn French Fundamentals Audiobook** + printable practice worksheets combo you'll discover:

✓ **Pronunciation guides:** English to French pronunciation translations so you can sound right the first time which means you'll sound like a natural easily.

✓ **How to avoid awkward fumbling:** explore core French grammar principles to avoid situations where you're left blank, not knowing what to say.

✓ **Improved recall:** Confidently express yourself in French by learning high-frequency verbs conjugations - taught through fun practice sheets!

Scan QR code above to claim your free bonuses

—— OR ——

exploretowin.com/frenchaudio10

Printed in Great Britain
by Amazon